D1144568

COLLECTABLES
HANDBOOK

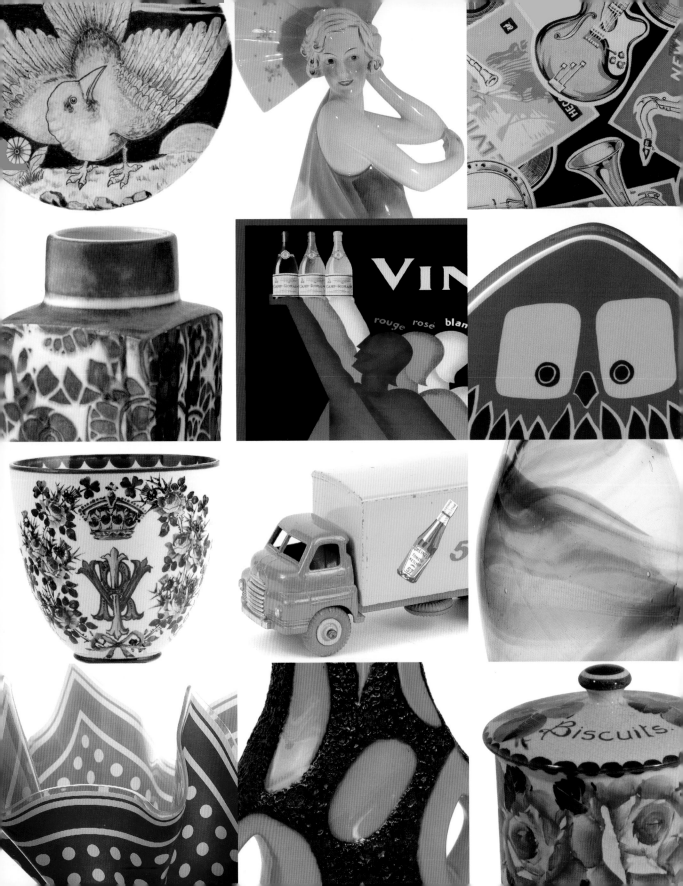

COLLECTABLES
HANDBOOK

Judith Miller
and Mark Hill

MILLER'S

Miller's Collectables Handbook
was first published as 'Miller's Collectables Handbook 2010-2011' in 2010

First published in Great Britain in 2010 by Miller's, a division of Mitchell Beazley,
imprints of Octopus Publishing Group Ltd, Endeavour House,
189 Shaftesbury Avenue, London, WC2H 8JY.
An Hachette Livre UK Company.
www.hachette.co.uk

Miller's is a registered trademark of Octopus Publishing Group Ltd.
www.millersonline.com

Copyright © Octopus Publishing Group Ltd 2010
Reprinted in 2011 and 2012
This edition in association with WHSmith

All rights reserved. No part of this work may be reproduced or utilised in any form
or by any means, electronic or mechanical, including photocopying, recording or
by any information storage and retrieval system, without the prior permission of
the publishers.

While every care has been exercised in the compilation of this guide,
neither the authors nor publishers accept any liability for any financial or
other loss incurred by reliance placed on the information contained in
Miller's Collectables Handbook.

ISBN 978 1 84533 768 1

A CIP catalogue record for this book is available from the British Library.

Set in Frutiger

Colour reproduction by United Graphics, Singapore
Printed and bound in China by Toppan Printing Company

Authors Judith Miller & Mark Hill

Publishing Manager Julie Brooke
Editors Davida Saunders, Carolyn Madden
Digital Asset Co-ordinator Katy Armstrong
Editorial Assistants Laura Hill, Danielle Shaw
Advertising Sales Christine Havers

Photography Graham Rae, Jeremy Martin, Robin Saker

Design Tim & Ali Scrivens, TJ Graphics
Indexer Diana LeCore
Production Lucy Carter
Jacket Design Pene Parker

Photographs of Judith Miller and Mark Hill by Chris Terry and Graham Rae

CONTENTS

LIST OF CONSULTANTS 7
HOW TO USE THIS BOOK 7
INTRODUCTION 8
ADVERTISING 9
AERONAUTICA 13
ART DECO FIGURES 15
AUTOMOBILIA 16
AUTOGRAPHS 22
BANKNOTES 24
BEADS 26
BOOKS 28
CAMERAS 34
CANES 38
CERAMICS
  Beswick 40
  Briglin Pottery 43
  Carlton Ware 44
  Clarice Cliff 47
  Cups & Saucers 53
  Doulton 61
  Fulper 68
  Hornsea 70
  Hull Pottery 72
  Italian Ceramics 74
  LLadro 77
  Lotus Pottery 78
  Martin Brothers 80
  Moorcroft 82
  Nursery Ware 86
  Picasso Ceramics 89
  Poole Pottery 91
  Rookwood 93
  Roseville 95
  Royal Copenhagen 99
  Royal Worcester 101
  Scandinavian Ceramics 106
  Shelley 107
  Stangl 109
  Studio Ceramics 110
  Susie Cooper 116
  Szeiler 117
  Teapots 118
  Tiles 120
  Troika Pottery 121
  Wade 124
  Wedgwood 130
  Weller 133
  Wemyss 136
  West German Ceramics 139
  Other Makers 146
CHARACTER COLLECTABLES 156
CLOCKS 161
COMMEMORATIVES
  Royal Commemoratives 162
  Political Commemoratives 165
COSTUME JEWELLERY 168
DOLLS
  Plastic Dolls 172
  Bisque Dolls 182
  Other Dolls 183
  Shallowpool Dolls 186
EYEWEAR 187
FASHION
  Costume 190
  Shoes 197
  Handbags 202
  Accessories 205
FIFTIES, SIXTIES & SEVENTIES 206
GLASS
  Caithness Glass 208
  Champagne Glasses 211
  Chance Glass 213
  Czech Glass 214

Dartington Glass 220
Gallé 222
Holmegaard 223
Lalique 230
Mdina & Isle of Wight Studio Glass 232
Murano Glass 235
Scandinavian Glass 245
Peter Layton 252
Studio Glass 254
Webb 257
Whitefriars 258
Other Makers 263
Bottles 268
INUIT ART 269
JAMES BOND COLLECTABLES 274
MARBLES 279
METALWARE 281
ORIENTAL 284
PAPERWEIGHTS 286
PENS & WRITING EQUIPMENT
Early Pencils 288
Fountain Pens 289
Other Writing Equipment 299
PLASTICS & BAKELITE 300
POSTCARDS 301
POSTERS
Film 302
Eastern European 305
Railway 306
Other travel 308
Product 310
POT LIDS 313
RADIOS 318
RAILWAYANA 322
ROCK & POP 324

SCIENTIFIC INSTRUMENTS 328
SILVER 329
SMOKING MEMORABILIA 331
SPORTING
Football 333
Baseball 340
Cricket 345
Racing 347
Golf 348
Other Sports 351
TEDDY BEARS
Teddy Bears 353
Character Bears 363
Artist Bears 364
TELEPHONES 367
TOYS & GAMES
Corgi 369
Dinky 374
Matchbox 380
Tinplate 382
Trains 392
Lead Figures 398
Schoenhut 400
Cult, TV & Film Toys 402
WATCHES 404
KEY TO ILLUSTRATIONS 408
DIRECTORY OF SPECIALISTS 411
INDEX TO ADVERTISERS 415
DIRECTORY OF MARKETS & CENTRES 416
DIRECTORY OF AUCTIONEERS 418
MAJOR FAIR & SHOW ORGANISERS 421
CLUBS & SOCIETIES 422
COLLECTING ON THE INTERNET 425
INDEX 426

LIST OF CONSULTANTS

AUTOMOBILIA
Geoffrey Weiner
carsofbrighton.co.uk

BEADS
Victor Caplin
Alfie's Antiques Market,
London

BOOKS
Roddy Newlands
Bloomsbury Auctions,
London

CERAMICS
**Beth & Beverley
Adams**
Alfie's Antiques Market,
London

Dr Graham Cooley
Private Collector

William Farmer
Fielding's Auctioneers,
Stourbridge

Kevin Graham
potteryandglass.forum
andco.com

**Patrick & Petra
Folkersma**
outernational.info

FASHION &
ACCESSORIES
Dawn Crawford
candysays.co.uk

Kerry Taylor
Kerry Taylor Auctions,
London

**Sparkle Moore &
Cad van Swankster**
thegirlcanthelpit.com

GLASS
Dr Graham Cooley
Private Collector

William Farmer
Fielding's Auctioneers,
Stourbridge

Nic Wilson
zeitgeist-i.com

INUIT ART
Duncan McLean
Waddingtons, Toronto,
Canada

PENS & WRITING
EQUIPMENT
Simon Gray
penhome.co.uk

POSTERS
Patrick Bogue
onslows.co.uk

RADIOS
Steve Harris
vintageradio.co.uk

TOYS, TEDDY BEARS
& DOLLS
Susan Brewer
britishdollshowcase.co.uk

Colin Lewis
The Magic Toybox,
Hampshire

Leanda Harwood
leandaharwood.co.uk

SPORTING
Graham Budd
Graham Budd Auctions,
London

We are also grateful to all our
friends and experts who gave us
so much help and support – Nigel
Benson of 20thcentury-glass.com,
Ian Broughton of Alfie's Antique
Market, Mark Block, Simon
Cooper of Rosebery's, David Encill,
Julie D'Arcy Evans, Jeanette
Hayhurst, Kevin Harris of
undercurrents.biz, Michael Jeffrey
of Woolley & Wallis, Mark Laino of
Mark of Time, Peter Layton, Kathy
Martin, Lesley McNamee of
retropolitan.co.uk, Marcus
Newhall of sklounion.com, Steven
Moore of Anderson & Garland,
Wesley Payne of Alfie's Antiques
Market, Thomas Plant of Special
Auction Services, Geoffrey
Robinson of Alfie's Antiques
Market, Alison Snelgrove of
thestudioglassmerchant.co.uk,
Ron & Ann Wheeler of
artiusglass.co.uk, and Nigel
Wiggin of The Old Hall Club.

HOW TO USE THIS BOOK

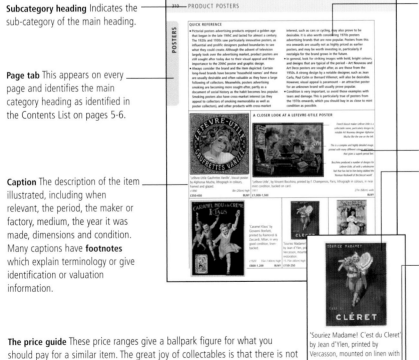

Subcategory heading Indicates the sub-category of the main heading.

Page tab This appears on every page and identifies the main category heading as identified in the Contents List on pages 5-6.

Caption The description of the item illustrated, including when relevant, the period, the maker or factory, medium, the year it was made, dimensions and condition. Many captions have **footnotes** which explain terminology or give identification or valuation information.

The price guide These price ranges give a ballpark figure for what you should pay for a similar item. The great joy of collectables is that there is not a recommended retail price. The price ranges in this book are based on actual prices, either what a dealer will take or the full auction price.

Quick reference Gives key facts about the factory, maker or style, along with stylistic identification points, value tips and advice on fakes.

Quick reference and **closer look** These are where we show identifying aspects of a factory or maker, point out rare colours or shapes, and explain why a particular piece is so desirable.

The object The collectables are shown in full colour. This is a vital aid to identification and valuation. With many objects, a slight colour variation can signify a large price differential.

Source code Every item has been specially photographed at an auction house, a dealer, an antiques market or a private collection. These are credited by code at the end of the caption, and can be checked against the Key to Illustrations on pages 408-410.

Welcome to the new edition of Miller's Collectables Handbook. As ever, you will find a selection of thousands of items from across the world, all illustrated in colour and accompanied by a descriptive caption and price guide. Additional information and insiders' tips are included in the 'Quick Reference' sections and footnotes, while our 'Closer Look' features help you to understand more. The result is the best full-colour, fully illustrated collectables price guide in the world.

This year is an important one for Miller's. As well as continuing to publish a range of exciting books, we are developing our new website at www.millersonline.com. We are delighted that many of you have already explored the site. For those of you who have not visited it yet, the site is packed with useful tips and information including what we believe is the most comprehensive fully illustrated A-Z of terms available. You can also search a catalogue containing tens of thousands of antiques and collectables, each with a description and price guide, and browse the innovative Dealers & Auctioneers listings. All of this is available at no cost. And we are not stopping there. Keep checking back, as there are plenty of exciting developments in store.

Of course, the past year has been a notable one. With the collapse of an international bank and the 'credit crunch' it's not surprising that the market for antiques and collectables has been dramatically affected. However, a couple of months after the recession began, an unexpected development occurred: rather than saving their money, many people began to buy antiques and collectables. Perhaps they saw it as a way to invest their cash in tangible goods that had the potential to hold their value. Attendance at fairs rocketed, and auctions reported strong sales, particularly for scarcer, finer pieces.

Although this has subsided, many dealers and auction houses continue to report strong sales. This follows the advice of an analyst at the firm of accountants, Deloitte, who reported that he believed the credit crunch had encouraged people 'to put their money into a range of assets' and that antiques 'generally avoid the big price swings seen in financial markets'. It's certainly true that vintage, retro and antique items hold more value than most

A Czechoslovakian Chlum u Trebone glassworks vase worth £100-150

of their contemporary counterparts. Not only that but you can cherish and enjoy them in your home – they are far more attractive than money or shares in a bank.

Another exciting development is the new initiative Antiques are Green, which aims to promote antiques as an alternative form of recycling and means of conserving natural resources. By encouraging new and existing antiques and collectables buyers to see their collections as the ultimate in recycled goods, it hopes to make a tangible difference and be part of an environmental conscience which will eventually permeate all areas of daily life.

A De La Rue 'Onoto The Pen' worth £120-180

While prices for low- and mid-range items have remained largely static, or have perhaps even fallen slightly, prices for the very best have risen. Fashion also plays an important role. Even though the 'Ikea-style' modern look is still popular, a strong trend for creating unique interiors filled with antique and vintage statement pieces is developing. If the style of an item appeals, it will be desirable. Although many traditional areas such as blue and white ceramics are still in the doldrums, it seems we are not the only ones who have noticed that low prices mean now is the time to buy, and a revival in these areas seems likely.

On more specific fronts, costume jewellery continues to be hotly soughtafter, particularly pieces by major designers and makers. Twentieth century glass, especially examples from Murano and Czechoslovakia, is also receiving the attention it deserves, at long last. As demand from an increasing number of collectors grows against a limited supply, prices have risen. Now that fountain pens dating from before WWII have become both valuable and scarce, models from the 1960-90s have risen in price. You will find comprehensive sections covering all these areas in this edition.

We have also included some new sections this year, including ceramics by Pablo Picasso, paperweights, and ceramics by Wade. You will also notice that we have included areas from other countries, such as the work of a few American potteries. This reflects the truly global nature of collecting today, and also gives you the edge over everyone else. Often ignored in this country, values can be high. We feel that our new, larger format combined with this variety and depth of information and coverage makes this edition the best yet. We hope you agree.

QUICK REFERENCE

- Vintage advertising is a good way to track changing styles, social trends and aspirations. Although 19thC advertising and packaging can be found, most items available today date from the early 20thC, when advertising began to diversify rapidly. Collectors typically focus on one subject area, such as tobacco, or one type of object (tins or signs are the most popular), or a brand. Items from popular brands, such as Kellogg's, attract the most collectors and therefore tend to fetch the highest prices. Items with cross-market interest, such as railway advertising, will appeal to a greater number of collectors.

- Tins holding biscuits, tobacco and sweets were common between 1860-1950. From the 1890s, the shapes of these became more inventive, as companies tried to outdo each other to appeal to customers. Many tins from this period were designed to be kept and used as storage containers or toys.

- Examples by major manufacturers, such as Huntley & Palmers, and those with moving parts, are often the most valuable.

- Do not ignore packaging that would have been thrown away. Even if many examples were produced, few may have survived. If both rare and desirable, the item's value can be surprisingly high. Vintage packaging in mint condition is particularly rare and consequently sought after. If the original contents are included this will not necessarily increase value, unless the package is also sealed.

- Look for visually appealing advertising in good condition, which represents the brand effectively, subject area or period. The colour, style of lettering and logo will help with dating. Art Nouveau, Art Deco and 1950s-style pieces will usually find favour with collectors, as will eye-catching, designs featuring bright colours, recognisable logos and popular characters.

A very rare W.K. Kellogg 'Drinket' tin, with dated paper label.

Kellogg's sold two soft drinks, the coffee-like 'Drinket' from 1914-21 and 'Fizz-Aide' from 1956-58. The early date makes this one of the first tins of 'Drinket' produced.

1915.   4.25in (10.5cm) high

£40-60   BH

An American 'Postmaster Smokers' printed tinplate tobacco tin.

Although dented, the graphics and bright colour are appealing, and tobacco advertising and packaging is sought after.

5.5in (13.5cm) high

£15-20   BH

A Co-operative Wholesale Society lithographed tinplate 'Crumpsall Cracker' travelling trunk biscuit tin, in good condition.

4.75in (12cm) wide

£20-30   SAS

A 1960s Huntley & Palmers 'Butlinland' biscuit tin, with printed photographic decoration, and printer's code '61/2649'.

8.75in (22cm) wide

£5-8   SAS

A Wade Bell's Scotch Whisky commemorative advertising ceramic bell-shaped bottle, with applied gilt label with wording 'A MEMENTO OF YOUR VISIT TO BELL'S HEAD OFFICE'.

6.25in (16cm) high

£15-20   DSC

A 1950s full-length male painted advertising figure, possibly for 'Aertex' underwear, modelled standing, on a plinth base.

Male and female underwear advertising figures have become sought after in recent years. The eye-appeal of the figure is important to value. Modelling, facial features and hair style that are typical of their time add to desirability. Always examine a piece closely, as many have become worn.

19.75in (50cm) high

£550-750   SAS

A CLOSER LOOK AT A STORE DISPLAY

These would have been used as dramatic store displays, or even parade figures, at a time when exotic animals such as tigers were fashionable.

Rare surivors, a pair is extremely unusual, and these are in excellent condition, and complete with their packing cases which bear amusing wording.

With their crouching poses and bared, snarling teeth, the tigers are full of drama and would make superb display pieces today.

Learbury Clothes was based in Syrcacuse, New York, and produced fine quality menswear which often bore the labels of other brands. As it was a lesser known brand, few of these expensive displays would have been produced.

A pair of crated papier mâché advertising tigers, on moulded naturalistic bases, marked 'Learbury Tiger', with original packing crates marked 'Handle With Care This Box Contains Learbury Fashion Display', in excellent condition. c1910-20

£10,000-15,000   JDJ

A 1930s possibly French male mannequin head, naturalistically painted with applied hair.

12.5in (32cm) high

£200-300   SAS

An Art Deco Harley Sport plaster male display bust, with painted features in composition plaster, the bust inscribed 'Harley Sport' in painted blue, on a rectangular plinth and square base.

23.5in (60cm) high

£400-600   SAS

An Art Deco French jewellery display bust, the cut-out bust modelled as a glamorous young woman, on a square wooden plinth, with an Art Deco green and white beadwork fringe necklace.

£300-500   SAS

A 1950s-60s French Lalique moulded glass shop display sign, with moulded and gilded lettering.

£70-100   CARS

ADVERTISING & PACKAGING

JUNKTION
Early Advertising Bought and Sold

Enamel signs, tin/card advertisements, neon signs, pictorial posters, early biscuit/ toffee/ tobacco tins, display figures. Also advertising chairs, dog bowls, etc. Vending machines.Chemist shop drawers, seedsman drawers, drapers shop shirt drawers, shop display cabinets, Fry's etc. Biscuit display racks, ornate shop tills, shop counters, bar fittings, cast iron pub tables, tradesman's hand carts, bicycles, etc.

Always a large interesting quality stock

JUNKTION ANTIQUES
The Old Railway Station, New Bolingbroke, Boston, Lincs
Tel: +44 (0)1205 480068
Mobile: 07836 345491
Email: junktionantiques@hotmail.com
Web: www.junktionantiques.co.uk
OPEN WED, THURS & SATURDAY

A 1940s 'Drink SamBo Chocolate Malted Milk' printed tin advertising sign.

£250-350   MAS

A 1950s Pepsi Cola transfer-printed tinplate shop large sign.

49in (124cm) high

£300-500   QU

Insure your collection at home and away – apply online at

www.connoisseurpolicies.com

Follow the simple instructions on the "buy online" pages on our website and you should be able to buy up to £50,000 of specialist insurance cover within a matter of minutes

Connoisseur Policies Ltd is a wholly owned subsidiary and appointed representative of Anthony Wakefield and Company Ltd, which is authorised and regulated by the Financial Services Authority

Telephone: 0870-241-0-142
information@connoisseurpolicies.com

'Connoisseur'® is a registered trademark of Connoisseur Policies Limited

A Coca Cola printed tinplate advertising tray, made by The H.D. Beech Co., of Coshocton, Ohio.

Coca Cola trays are highly sought after, particularly if made before 1930 or bearing artwork by Hamilton King. This very early example is known as 'The Exhibition Girl' as the 1909 World's Fair in Seattle can be seen behind her.

1909   13.25in (33.5cm) high

£600-900   **SOTT**

A very rare 1940s 12-sized aluminium Coca Cola bottle carrier.

This is very rare as most bottle carriers were made for 6-packs. Aluminium was a typical material used during this period as large supplies were produced for the war effort and were turned over for civilian use after the end of World War II.

16.25in (41cm) wide

£70-100   **SOTT**

A CLOSER LOOK AT AN ADVERTISING CALENDAR

This is a very early and very rare advertising calendar, but the truly superb condition makes it even rarer and more desirable.

The Daisy BB gun subject matter also contributes to the value – in the US, where this was sold, vintage guns and related memorabilia are highly collectable.

The printing is very fine, with a good level of detail and several colours – note how one of the daisies has been drawn over the inset of the boys in a skiff to add perspective.

The first Daisy BB gun was given away by the Plymouth Iron Windmill Co. as a promotion to farmers who bought a windmill. In 1895 the nearly bankrupt company changed its name to Daisy and limited itself to manufacturing guns.

A very rare Daisy Manufacturing Co. 'Model 96' air rifle calendar, lithographed in colours by Calvert Lith. Co., with illustration of two boys in a skiff with a gun, and complete with 12 date sheets and brass ring grommet, in excellent condition with only a few scuffs.

1896

£4,000-6,000   **JDJ**

A 1950s-60s Royal Alma circular Double Diamond Advertising Dish, the back with black printed mark.

5in (12.5cm) diam

£12-18   **RET**

A Hamleys 'The Finest Toy Shop In the World' catalogue, illustrated with sepia overprinted primary colours showing toys, games, activities including Meccano, FROG, Schuco and Trix products.

1938

£30-50   **SAS**

A Hires Munimaker marble, nickel, and glass syrup dispenser, the square marble base with brass Hires plaques on four sides and topped with a flared white milk glass globe.

c1900-10   35in (89cm) high

£1,500-2,500   **JDJ**

A chrome plated steel Schneider Trophy commemorative ashtray, the plane based on the Rolls Royce powered Supermarine S6B Schneider Trophy seaplane, with rotating propeller.

4.5in (11.5cm) high

£100-150   **CARS**

A De Havilland DH 106 Comet silver plated presentation model, mounted on an onyx ashtray base, with a good level of detailing.

Factors that influence values of airplane ashtrays include the model of plane, the size, materials used, and the level of detail. If the piece is connected to a famous event or aviator, the price can rise.

10in (25.5cm) wide

£200-250   **GROB**

A World War II onyx and metal airplane ashtray, with a Supermarine Spitfire mounted on top of a chome plated sphere.

8.25in (21cm) long

£80-120   **CW**

A World War II aluminium 'Trench Art' airplane ashtray with Supermarine Spitfire model with moving propellor, mounted on a machine component, possibly a cylinder head.

c1945   *6.5in (16cm) high*

£70-90   **GCHI**

A 1930s chrome plated airplane ashtray, with seaplane model, the base with with 'SP' within a shield mark.

6in (15cm) high

£60-90   **CW**

A Skyland Models showroom Concorde model, F-BVFA, with Air France livery, in excellent condition and with original display stand.

Concorde made its maiden flight in 1975, and was retired in 2003. It can now be seen at Dulles Airport, Washington DC. In 1998 it completed a round-the-world trip in 41 hours and 27 minutes.

48in (122cm) long

£400-600   **TCA**

A B&M Ceramics United States Navy 'Tactical Support Center' transfer-printed souvenir mug, with 'Tobias' transfer.

3.5in (9cm) high

£3-4   **AEM**

A rare 1920-30s South Coast Flying Club member's car badge, decorated with four colours of enamel, with some repairs, the back stamped with 'COLLINS LONDON' makers mark.

If the enamel was undamaged, the value might rise to £500.

£350-450   **CARS**

4.25in (10cm) high

An unusual Schneider Trophy commemorative vase, probably made by Bough, with panels of anthropomorphic birds in blue, between Scottish rose and foliate borders on a yellow ground, the base painted 'EJMJ Mifflin, SOUTHAMPTON SEPTEMBER 1929, Schneider Trophy won by G Brit Waghorn'.

The origins of this cup or trophy are unclear. The name Mifflin cannot be found connected with this event, which was held over the Solent some distance away from the city of Southampton. Waghorn did, however, win the event. The Art & Crafts styling is unusual for this date.

£300-400   **W&W**

10in (25.5cm) high

A Brooklands Aero Club octagonal enamelled metal member badge for 1937, numbered '255', with original cord, the back moulded 'NOT TRANSFERABLE' and with ' W.O. LEWIS B'HAM' maker's mark.

1.5in (3.5cm) high

£200-250   **CARS**

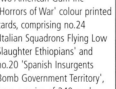

Two American Gum Inc 'Horrors of War' colour printed cards, comprising no.24 'Italian Squadrons Flying Low Slaughter Ethiopians' and no.20 'Spanish Insurgents Bomb Government Territory', from a series of 240 cards.

1936   *3.25in (8cm) wide*

£5-8 EACH   **SOTT**

A Bishops & Stonier ceramic child's bowl with a transfer-printed scene of Blériot's plane.

9.25in (23.5cm) diam.

£150-200   **PC**

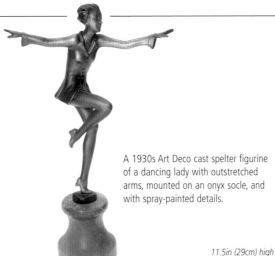

A 1930s Art Deco cast spelter figurine of a dancing lady with outstretched arms, mounted on an onyx socle, and with spray-painted details.

11.5in (29cm) high

£100-150   CARS

A CLOSER LOOK AT AN ART DECO STATUE

Inexpensive statuettes made from moulded plastic and a lightweight metal alloy called spelter were produced during the 1920s and 30s to imitate more expensive carved ivory and cast bronze statues by Ferdinand Preiss, Demêtre Chiparus and others.

Pieces can be found for around £30-150 depending on the quality, size and pose, and offer the look of more expensive figurines, without the high prices

This is one of the better examples, with a lively pose, a sense of movement to the dress, a necklace, and fashionably bobbed hair.

The detail is not as fine as the pieces it was designed to imitate, and examples are frequently damaged or stained.

A 1930s Art Deco spelter statuette of a lady leaning backwards in a dance, with spray painted details and cream moulded plastic head and hands, mounted on an onyx socle.

9in (23cm) high

£100-150   CARS

An Art Deco gilt bronze figure, modelled as a naked female dancer upon a circular green onyx socle, signed 'Renz', gilding badly damaged.

Although little is known about the designer, this figurine is gilt bronze suggesting a quality figure and the pose is desirable.

10in (25.5cm) high

£500-600   GHOU

A 1930s Art Deco spelter statuette, with draped shawl under her arms and spray painted details, the onyx base with a striker cigarette or cigar lighter, with some wear to the spray paint.

10in (25.5cm) high

£50-70   CARS

A 1930s Art Deco spelter statuette, of a standing girl, with flower-like skirt, fan, and disc-shaped hat, mounted on a marble base.

10in (25.5cm) high

£80-120   CARS

A 1930s Art Deco spelter statuette of a kneeling girl with an onyx ball, mounted on an oval onyx base.

This may have been one of a pair of bookends.

7in (17.5cm) high

£150-200   CARS

QUICK REFERENCE

- Automobilia is a diverse global collecting area, surrounding the lively vintage car market and encompassing everything from car parts to advertising to works of art. In general, appealing pieces that look good on display from the major marques are at the higher end of the market. These marques include Bentley, Rolls Royce, Jaguar, Buick, Ferrari and Chevrolet. Collectors tend to focus on one marque, or on a particular type of item.
- Apart from the cars themselves, car mascots usually fetch the largest sums of money. These were mounted on the front of the bonnet of a car, and can be found in many different shapes. Types include 'manufacturer mascots', made by the company that made the car, 'advertising mascots' made by a company such as Michelin to advertise its products, and 'accessory mascots' which include animals, figures and characters.
- Look for examples that conjure up feelings of the excitement and speed of motoring. Novelty forms can also be popular. Names to look for include Lalique, Red Ashay, Sabino and A & E Lejeune. Condition counts, and reproductions are known, so try to view and handle as many authentic examples as possible.
- Car badges, which adorned car grilles, are also popular and often more affordable. Most showed membership of an association such as an enthusiasts club. They are usually made from nickel- or chrome-plated cast brass, which may then be enamelled with a colourful design. Appealing pieces from major marques, or smaller but well-known clubs from the 1900s-30s, tend to be the most desirable.
- Many associations also produced badges for their members, and these have been rising in value recently. As before, appeal and marque are key factors to desirability and value. Also look out for lamps and advertising pieces, such as enamel signs. Items related to famous drivers, such as Stirling Moss, or events, such as Grand Prix, are also desirable due to their association.

A 1920s French A.E. Lejeune Bentley 'Flying B' chrome plated brass car mascot, stamped 'AEL' and mounted on a mottled brown Bakelite stand, made for a Pacific Open Tourer.

3.5in (9cm) high

£250-300   CARS

A large 1920s Joseph Fray chrome plated brass Bentley 'Flying B' car mascot, stamped 'JOS. FRAY B'HAM' and mounted on a Bakelite stand.

This mascot is smaller than similar examples. It may have been designed for an opening bonnet.

2.75in (7cm) high

£350-450   CARS

A 1920s Joseph Fray chrome plated brass Bentley 'Flying B' car mascot, mounted on a brown Bakelite stand, stamped 'JOS. FRAY B'HAM'.

Made for, and generally seen on, a Bentley Open Tourer. This example would have been worth more had it not been over-polished, leading to its plating being polished away and becoming 'brassed'.

Mascot 2in (5cm) high

£250-300   CARS

A late 1930s Bentley 'Flying B' car mascot, with the 'B' leaning back and stamped with registered design no. 'REG8211907' for 1937, mounted on a rectangular Bakelite plinth.

This example is quite worn, with much of the detail on the feathers having been worn away through excessive polishing. If it was crisper, the value would be around £250-300.

5.25in (13cm) long

£200-250   CARS

A CLOSER LOOK AT A BENTLEY CAR MASCOT

This is a rare prototype design that did not go into production and was never used on a car – very few examples exist.

The style reflects the Art Deco tastes of the period, but lacks the elegance and sense of speed of other designs.

It may have been designed by Frederick Gordon Crosby, who designed the logo for the first car in 1921.

It was probably made by Joseph Fray, who made most of Bentley's mascots.

A 1930s Bentley chrome plated brass 'Flying B' car mascot, with long wings, mounted on a brown Bakelite stand.

This was not used for a long period as it was deemed too large, particularly the wings. Look out for examples with only one wing behind, as these are very rare.

5.25in (13cm) long

£550-600   CARS

A rare 1930s chrome plated brass prototype Bentley 'Flying B' car mascot, possibly designed by Frederick Gordon Crosby and made by Joseph Fray, unmarked and mounted on a metal stand.

3.5in (9cm) high

£550-600   CARS

Lalique 'Chrysis' shown in frosted christal adoring & adorning the radiator of the fabulous Dusenberg, both reflecting the Art Deco period beautifully. By the French motoring artist Francois Vanaret

U N I Q U E   L A L I Q U E   C A R   M A S C O T S

www.laliquemascots.co.uk Club: www.brmmbrmm.com/lbcc.bb
Phone/Fax: 01273 622722 M: 07890 836734
E: laliquemascots@fsmail.net

The complete collection of R.Lalique car mascots using the Lalique factory catalogue numbers along with the date of introduction of each piece:

Sirene/Small Mermaid 831 introduced in 1920 as a statuette adapted and used as a car mascot from 1925
Naiade/Large Mermaid 832 ditto as above
Cinque Chevaux/Five Horses 1122 introduced on 26/8/1925
Comète Etoile Filante/Comet Shooting Star 1123 24/8/25
Faucon/Falcon 1124 5/8/25
Tireur d'Arc/Archer 1126 3/8/26
Coq Nain/Cockeral 1135 10/2/28
Tête de Bélier/Rams Head 1136 3/2/28
Tête de Coq/Cockerals Head 1137 3/2/28
Tête d'Aigle/Eagles Head 1138 14/3/28
Tête d'Épervier/Hawks Head 1139 21/1/28
Tête de Peon/Peacocks Head 1140 3/2/28
Lévrier/Greyhound 1141 14/3/28
Saint Christophe/St Christopher 1142 1/3/28
Hirondelle/Swallow 1143 10/2/28
Petite Libellule/Small Dragonfly 1144 12/4/28
Grande Libellule/Large Dragonfly 1145 23/4/28
Grenouille/Frog 1146 3/5/28
Victoire/Victory Spirit of the Wind 1147 18/4/28
Longchamp A/Horse A 1152A 12/6/29
Longchamp B/Horse B 1152B 10/9/29
Epsom/Horse 1153 5/6/29
Sanglier/Wild Boer 1157 3/10/29
Perche Poisson/Perch Fish 1158 20/4/29
Vitesse/Speed Goddess 1160 17/9/29
Coq Houdan/Proud Cock 1161 30/4/29
Pintade/Guinea Fowl 1164 28/9/29
Hibou/Owl 1181 27/1/31
Renard/Fox 1182 9/12/30
Chrysis/Nude Female 1183 21/3/31

BEAT THE CREDIT CRUNCH!... INVEST IN LALIQUE

AUTOMOBILIA

A late 1920s French Lalique 'Cinque Chevaux' (Five Horses) moulded glass car mascot, no.1122, moulded 'R.LALIQUE FRANCE' mark, mounted on a period display base.

This design was introduced on 26th August 1925, and was originally mounted on an illuminated radiator fitting made by Brèves Galleries of Knightsbridge. This example has a couple of internal air bubbles, which may deter some collectors. Without bubbles the value could increase by around £500.

5.5in (14cm) long

£6,000-6,500   **CARS**

A CLOSER LOOK AT A LALIQUE CAR MASCOT

Beaks were often damaged, as the mascot is top heavy. If the beak is not damaged the value can rise to £2,500-3,500.

This dramatic and evocative mascot was model no.1124, and was introduced on the 5th August 1925.

Very few Lalique car mascots were produced in coloured glass, with tinted glass being slightly more common.

Beware of modern fakes, where a colourless mascot has been treated with radiation to add a tint – these are usually darker: lilac examples are more purple in tone.

A late 1920s French Lalique 'Faucon' (Falcon) moulded glass car mascot, with a faint lilac tint, moulded 'R.LALIQUE' and etched 'FRANCE' marks.

6in (15cm) high

£2,000-2,500   **CARS**

A 1930s French Lalique 'Sirene' (Mermaid) opalescent moulded glass car mascot, moulded 'R.LALIQUE' mark.

This example has a chipped base, a common problem with vintage car mascots, but luckily the damage does not affect the figure itself. In perfect condition, it might fetch up to £1,500. Sirene was numbered 831 as a statuette in 1920. It was turned into a car mascot in 1925.

4in (10cm) high

£900-1,200   **CARS**

A 1950s-60s French Lalique colourless glass 'Perche Poisson' (Perch) moulded glass car mascot, no.1158, introduced on the 20th April 1929, the base with 'LALIQUE FRANCE' acid stamp.

Note that the glass on mascots from this period is slighty darker in tone than more modern examples, such as the one to the right, which are brighter and cleaner. This shape was discontinued in 2006.

3.75in (9.5cm) high

£550-650   **CARS**

A 1980s-90s French Lalique colourless glass 'Perche Poisson' (Perch) moulded glass car mascot, no.1158, introduced on the 20th April 1929, the base with diamond point engraved 'LALIQUE FRANCE' inscription and factory labels.

3.75in (9.5cm) high

£550-650   **CARS**

A 1980s-90s French Lalique clear and frosted moulded glass 'Sanglier' (Wild Boar) car mascot, no.1157 introduced on the 3rd October 1929, the base with diamond point engraved 'Lalique France' script mark.

2.75in (6.5cm) high

£350-450   **CARS**

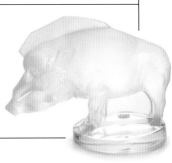

A CLOSER LOOK AT A GORDON CROSBY JAGUAR CAR MASCOT

Known as the 'mottled cat', this was designed by Gordon Crosby, who designed the famous 'Leaping Cat' mascot for Jaguar in 1937.

It was used for one year from 1935-36 only on a Jaguar car, before being relaced by the more familiar design as Jaguar founder Sir William Lyons did not like it.

It was re-used on the Panther J72 built by Jankel during the late 1970s and early 1980s, which itself was loosely based on a Jaguar SS100 from the late 1930s.

The value given is for the mascot only, the cap itself is worth around £50.

A large Panther chrome plated car mascot, for a Jaguar model J72, designed by Gordon Crosby, on a radiator cap with an applied black enamel Panther winged logo.

7.25in (8cm) high

£350-450   **CARS**

A 1950s Jaguar chrome plated brass 'Leaping Cat' car mascot, with longer tail, designed by Gordon Crosby, for an Mk6, on a cylindrical mount stamped 7/2645/0, the base of the mascot ground down.

If the base had not been ground down, the value might have been £450-550. If the shaft is missing, the value falls by around £50.

8in (20.5cm) long

£300-350   **CARS**

A 1960s Jaguar chome plated brass 'Leaping Cat' car mascot, designed by Gordon Crosby, for S-Type models, on a long mount with two fixing screws.

7.75in (19.5cm) long

£100-150   **CARS**

A Singer Gazelle chrome plated car mascot, mounted on a wooden plinth.

Mascot 6in (15cm) long

£100-150   **CHT**

A modern reproduction chrome plated flying stork car mascot, in the style of Frederick Bazin, mounted on a radiator cap.

5.5in (14cm) high

£70-100   **CHT**

A Rolls Royce nickel-plated brass large 'Spirit of Ecstasy' car mascot, for a Phantom II, stamped with copyright marks and 'Charles Sykes', mounted on a wooden base.

1919-25   *6in (15cm) high*

£900-1,200   **CARS**

AUTOMOBILIA

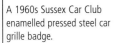

An Automobile Association type 1B nickel plated brass full member's badge, impressed 'Stenson Cooke Secretary', numbered '4410'.

6in (15cm) high

£100-150   **CHT**

A late 1950s-60s Automobile Association (AA) enamelled and chromed car grille badge, in original condition with double screw fitting for a grille, numbered '38774Z'.

3.5in (9cm) high

£25-30   **CARS**

A Royal Automobile Club (RAC) Centenary commemorative chrome plated and enamelled car grille badge.

Only available in the centenary year of 1997, members were allowed to buy two examples, at a cost of £29.95 each.

1997   *4.75in (12cm) high*

£65-75   **CARS**

A 1950s-60s Company of Veteran Motorists member's grille badge, awarded to a member of 49 years standing, the back marked 'THE PROPERTY OF C.V.M.'.

THE CVM was founded in 1932 and promoted safe driving. In 1983 it became GEM, and then GEM Motoring Assist.

3.75in (9.5cm) high

£7-10   **CARS**

An Royal Automobile Club of Italy type 3B badge, enamelled in blue, white, red and black, with some enamel losses.

4.5in (11.5cm) wide

£35-45   **CHT**

A 1960s Sussex Car Club enamelled pressed steel car grille badge.

As this was a smaller regional club, fewer badges would have been made, meaning they are harder to find today even though demand for them is limited.

4.5in (11.5cm) high

£40-50   **CARS**

A 1960s Aston Martin Owner's Club enamelled chromed brass car grille badge.

The original owner has removed his name under the enamelled area with a drill, revealing the brassy metal. If this had not been done, the value may have risen to £40-50. Also look out for more decorative vitreous enamelled examples, as these can fetch £70-100.

6in (15cm) high

£30-40   **CARS**

WANTED!

Motoring bygones, bonnet mascots, badges, instruments, early motoring coats, enamel advertising signs, garage petrol pumps, glass petrol pump globes. Michelin ashtrays, compressors etc. Early photographs, books, early toys, pedal cars. Anything old and interesting.
Try us.

JUNKTION ANTIQUES
The Old Railway Station,
New Bolingbroke, BOSTON, Lincs
OPEN WED, THURS & SAT
Tel: +44 (0)1205 480068
Mobile: 07836 345491
Email: junktionantiques@hotmail.com
Web: www.junktionantiques.co.uk

POOKS BOOKS

Britain's most exciting transport bookshop

LIBRARIES/COLLECTIONS BOUGHT

3,500 square feet stacked with Books, Brochures, Badges, Automobilia, 300+ Enamel Signs/Posters.

POSTAL SERVICE WORLDWIDE

**Fowke Street, Rothley
Leics LE7 7PJ**

(10 mins from Junction 21a on M1)

**Tel: +44 (0)116 237 6222
Fax: +44 (0)116 237 6491**

pooks.motorbooks@virgin.net

MONDAY TO FRIDAY

A Brooklands Automobile Racing Club member's enamel badge set, comprising member's badge on cord and two guest badges, each numbered '404'.

1926   *1.25in (3cm) high*

£280-320   **CHT**

A Brooklands Automobile Racing Club blue enamelled gold-metal member's badge for 1929, together with a bow-shaped guest pin, each numbered 189, the back moulded 'W.O. LEWIS B'HAM'. *Introduced in 1907, these sets have become highly sought after. A full set comprises one member's badge and two guest pins. If this set had been complete, it could have been worth up to £100 more.*

1928   *1.5in (3.5cm) high*

£200-250   **CARS**

A CLOSER LOOK AT A MEMBER'S BADGE SET

The brightly coloured geometric Art Deco style, and the design shaped like the front of a car, makes this set highly desirable.

The design was changed every year, so that current members could be quickly and easily identified.

This is a complete set. Always look for matching numbers on each piece – the original box adds up to 50% of the value of the pins.

1939 was the last year these sets of badges were made. Members' badges were produced from 1941-42, before they too were phased out.

Look out for sets of 1916 badges made in cream Bakelite as a complete set can fetch up to £2,000.

A Brooklands Automobile Racing Club member's enamel badge set, comprising member's badge on cord and two guest badges, each numbered 805, in original box, with printed membership number and rules to lid.

1939   *1.25in (3cm) high*

£500-700   **CHT**

AUTOMOBILIA

AUTOGRAPHS

A Charlie Chaplin signed manuscript letter and photograph, the letter addressed from Los Angeles, California, with stamped hand written envelope, mounted in composite frame.

£450-540   AH

A Pete Best signed photograph of the Beatles.

Best was the original drummer for the Beatles, from 1960-1962. He was replaced by Ringo Starr.

10in (25.5cm) wide

£30-40   ACOG

A Maria Teresa de Filippis signed Silverstone motor racing programme

9in (23cm) high.

£25-35   COC

A Gerald Ford signed presidential portrait.

£450-550   MAS

A Harrison Ford as Han Solo signed photograph.

The signature isn' t his best as it runs across a dark area of the photograph and appears lost.

c1980

£150-250   PC

A Stephen Fry signed postcard.

Dedications are less desirable.

6in (15cm) high

£10-15   PC

A Whoopi Goldberg signed photograph.

£35-45   ACOG

An Audrey Hepburn signature, mounted with a photograph from the film 'Breakfast at Tiffany's'.

16in (40.5cm) wide

£180-200   PC

AUTOGRAPHS

 **INTERNATIONAL AUTOGRAPH AUCTIONS LTD**

Great Britain's leading specialist autograph auctioneers.

Winston Churchill signed photograph sold for £8900

IAA Ltd. hold regular auctions of autograph letters, signed photographs and historical documents.

A wide variety of autographs are offered in each auction including signatures of the famous, and infamous, from all walks of life -
Cinema, Music, Literature, History, Art, Exploration and Science,
Military and Aviation, World War II, Royalty, Politics etc.

We offer expert valuations on all autographs, with a view to sale, from single items to collections.

If you would like to be kept informed of future auctions please provide us with your e-mail address. info@autographauctions.co.uk

Illustrated catalogues available by subscription £60 for eight issues.

Entries continually invited for future auctions.

Commission rate 17.5%

(20.56% including VAT)

Harry Houdini (above)
Signed quotation sold for £770

Charles Chaplin (left)
Signed photograph sold for £500

For further details please contact

Richard Davie, IAA Ltd., Foxhall Business Centre, Foxhall Road,
Nottingham, NG7 6LH. Telephone: 0115 845 1010 Fax: 0115 845 1009

www.autographauctions.co.uk   info@autographauctions.co.uk

BANKNOTES

A British one pound note for use by the British Military Expeditionary Forces in the Mediterranean and the Naval Expeditionary Forces in 1915, signed by John Bradbury, Secretary to the Treasury, overprinted in Arabic.

£1,800-2,400   PAMW

A Bank of England five pound note, signed by E.M.Harvey, issued in Hull.

1918

£700-800   PAMW

An British Treasury ten shilling note, signed by John Bradbury.

Treasury notes signed with Bradbury's name are known as 'Bradburys'.

£100-150   CWD

Quality British Banknotes

**Buying/Selling paper money
of the British Isles
Bank of England Treasury
Jersey Guernsey Isle of Man
Scottish Irish
Postal Orders**

Pam West British Notes
PO Box 257 Sutton
Surrey SM3 9WW
Tel: 0208 641 3224
Email: pamwestbritnotes@aol.com

www.britishnotes.co.uk

A Bank of England Britannia series ten shilling note, signed by L.K. O'Brien.

This note has a million serial number.

1955

£40-60   PAMW

A first issue Bank of England fifty pound note, A01 prefix.

1981

£100-150   CWD

A French Revolutionary assignat five livres note, year 2.

£5-10   CWD

A German fifty million mark note, from the Hyper Inflation period.

£2-3   CWD

A French one hundred new francs note, with Napoleon portrait.

£20-25   CWD

A Munster & Leinster five pound Ploughman note, signed by J.L. Gubbins, dated.

1929

£700-900   PAMW

A Japanese occupation of Malaya one thousand dollar note.

£1-2   CWD

A USA Confederate States fifty dollar note, with Lincoln portrait.

1864

£40-60   CWD

A USA five dollar Pioneer Family series note,.

1907

£100-150   CWD

BEADS

QUICK REFERENCE

- Beads were one of the earliest types of personal adornment. The very earliest beads were made from natural materials, such as shells, pebbles, bone fragments, seeds and feathers. The oldest examples known are shells dating from approximately 100,000 years ago. Many cultures attached social or cultural importance to beads, and status to those who made and wore them.
- As human societies developed, so did the forms, designs and materials used for beads. Glass beads were introduced around 30,000 years ago, with perhaps the oldest being Egyptian. Glass bead-making grew during the Phoenician and Roman periods.
- The value of a bead depends on a number of factors including its age, material, size, quality of decoration, rarity and desirability to collectors. Due to this wide variation, beads make an ideal collecting field to suit a wide range of budgets and tastes.
- A necklace does not always have to have its original stringing as most of the value is often in the beads themselves. However, if the original stringing was metal, or unique in some way, then it will be important to value.
- Examine beads for wear or damage, although a degree of wear is acceptable in older examples.
- Beads have been made in nearly every country at some point, and many are being reproduced today, so consulting a reliable dealer and buying a comprehensive reference book is highly recommended to help differentitate originals and copies.

Two early Venetian glass elongated barrel-shaped beads, with applied combed red and white striped trails on opaque dark bodies.

largest 0.75in (2cm) long

£15-25 EACH   VC

An early Venetian glass bead, with spiralling pink, white and green striped trail over a 'coiled' opaque dark body.

0.5in (1.5cm) long

£25-35   VC

Two early Venetian glass spherical beads, with applied white and multicoloured spots on opaque dark bodies.

0.5in (1cm) long

£15-25 EACH   VC

A 1930s Venetian lamp-wound 'Wedding Cake' blue spherical glass bead.

0.5in (1.5cm) long

£3-5   VC

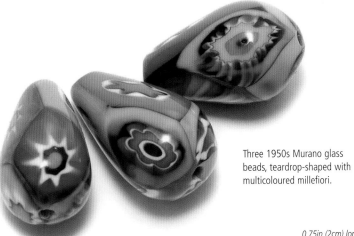

Three 1950s Murano glass beads, teardrop-shaped with multicoloured millefiori.

0.75in (2cm) long

£2-3 EACH   VC

A CLOSER LOOK AT A VENETIAN BEAD NECKLACE

The beads are complex, with more details than on other examples.

These are known as 'Wedding Cake' beads as the details are built up individually, using molten glass, much like the icing on a wedding cake.

A 1930s necklace with Venetian lamp-wound 'Wedding Cake' green spherical glass beads.

Necklace 15in (38cm) long

£50-70 VC

This necklace has more beads, and so is more valuable than an example with fewer beads.

Each bead in handmade, with flowers, curling and swirling lines and spots being typical decoration – check that there is no damage and look for signs of age as they are being reproduced.

A 1930s necklace with Venetian lamp-wound 'Wedding Cake' green spherical glass beads.

Necklace 15in (38cm) long

£70-90 VC

A 1930s necklace with Venetian lamp-wound 'Wedding Cake' green, red and blue spherical glass beads.

Necklace 15in (38cm) long

£60-80 VC

Four Parthian period shaped 'etched' carnelian beads, from Ur.

Four Parthian period shaped 'etched' carnelian spherical beads, from Ur.

c2,500 BC   largest 0.5in (1.5cm) long

£35-45 EACH VC

Despite being known as 'etched', the pattern was not carved at all, but was instead painted on using an alkaline solution. Each bead was then baked to set and fix the pattern.

c2,500 BC   largest 0.75in (2cm) long

£35-45 EACH VC

BOOKS

QUICK REFERENCE

• A true first edition will be from the first print run (impression) of the first published hardback edition. First editions can then have subsequent impressions, in which errors are corrected, but these are less desirable. A small first edition print run is likely to make a book more desirable. Consequently, although famous, iconic titles will always be prized, first edition books written at the height of an author's power may be worth less than early/less-well received books, as fewer were published. Those with an eye for the future may choose to buy (preferably) signed first editions of up-and-coming authors nominated for major prizes, such as the Man Booker, before the winner is announced.

• Learn how to recognise the different styles of numbering. This often takes the form of a '1' in the series of numbers on the inside copyright page that indicates the edition of the book. Other publishers state that a book is the first edition or use a sequence of letters. Check that the publishing date and

copyright date match, and that these match the original publishing date and publisher for the title in a reference book.

• Though there are consistently popular classic authors, such as Ian Fleming and Agatha Christie, fashion can dictate which authors are most desirable. The popular rediscovery of a classic or a successful film or TV series adaptation will usually increase value of first editions.

• The author's signature adds value, particularly if on a limited special edition. Dedications are typically less desirable, unless the recipient is famous or connected to the author. Book signings are becoming more common, so this may become less of a factor in future.

• Condition is extremely important: mint condition commands a premium. Dust jackets should be clean, un-faded and un-damaged, though many can be restored. If the jacket is missing, value can fall by over 50 per cent. You should also check that the book is complete and has not been defaced or damaged.

Edgar Rice Burroughs, 'The Eternal Lover', first American edition, published by A.C. McClurg and Co. of Chicago, with illustrations by St John, original black-stamped blue cloth boards with faded spine and dust jacket with light wear.

1925
£1,000-1,500   BLNY

Pearl S. Buck, 'The Good Earth', first American edition, first issue, with pictorial endpapers, modern full brown morocco and gilt binding by Bayntun-Riviere.

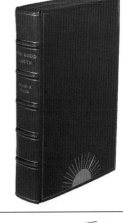

The misspelling of 'fleas' as 'flees' on p.100 identifies this as the first issue of the first edition. This novel won a Pulitzer prize in 1932, and returned to the bestseller list after being included on Oprah Winfrey's Book Club in 2004.
1931
£350-450   BLO

Edgar Rice Burroughs, 'Tarzan and the Jewels of Opar', first edition, published by A.C. McClurg and Co. of Chicago, with frontispiece and illustrations by St John, dark green gilt-stamped cloth and dust jacket with minor losses, and corners clipped.
1918
£1,000-1,500   BLNY

John Le Carré, 'The Spy Who Came in from the Cold', first edition, first impression, published by Gollancz, London, signed presentation copy, dust jacket, with small chips.
1963
£1,800-2,200   BLO

Robert Bloch, 'Psycho', first American edition, published by Simon and Schuster, New York, with original half cloth in dust jacket.
1959
£600-900   BLNY

Agatha Christie, 'Evil Under The Sun', first edition, published by Collins, London, with original orange cloth, pictorial dust wrapper, price '7s 6d.', backstrip slightly faded and with small chips to head and tail.

1941

£400-600   **L&T**

G.K. Chesterton, 'The Father Brown Stories', first edition, published by Cassell & Co., London, with inked name on front free endpaper, original cloth, dust jacket, price clipped, and with rubbed corners.

1929

£250-300   **BLO**

A CLOSER LOOK AT A BURROUGHS FIRST EDITION

Burroughs' seminal work was first published by Olympia Press in Paris in 1959, titled 'The Naked Lunch'.

The first American edition was published three years later as it had been deemed pornographic. 'The' was dropped from the title, as the author never intended it to be there.

This American edition is also different from the Olympia Press edition as it was based on an earlier manuscript from 1958 owned by Burroughs' friend, the poet Allen Ginsberg.

Time magazine included the book in its list of '100 Best English-language Novels from 1923 to 2005'. It was made into a film by David Cronenberg in 1991, reigniting interest in it.

William Burroughs, 'Naked Lunch', first American edition, third printing, published by Grove Press, with black cloth over grey boards, dust jacket with very light rubbing to top and head of spine.

1962

£150-250   **BLNY**

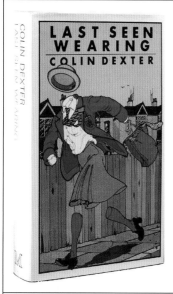

Colin Dexter, 'Last Seen Wearing', first edition, first impression publisher's sample copy, published by Macmillan, signed by the author on the title page, with publisher's stamp on front endpaper, with original boards and dust jacket.

This is Dexter's second novel in the popular Inspector Morse series. It is also the scarcest first edition in the series.

1976

£1,000-1,500   **BLO**

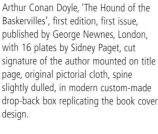

Arthur Conan Doyle, 'The Hound of the Baskervilles', first edition, first issue, published by George Newnes, London, with 16 plates by Sidney Paget, cut signature of the author mounted on title page, original pictorial cloth, spine slightly dulled, in modern custom-made drop-back box replicating the book cover design.

1902

£1,800–2,200   **BLO**

Arthur Conan Doyle, 'The Hound of the Baskervilles, Another Adventure of Sherlock Holmes', first edition, published by George Newnes, London, illustrated with frontispiece and 15 plates, one plate detached but present, endpapers foxed and page edges lightly browned, cloth with few small stains.

1902

£1,000-1,500   **BLNY**

BOOKS

Oliver La Farge, 'Laughing Boy', first American edition, published by Houghton Mifflin Company, Cambridge, with publisher's thickly woven yellow cloth, maroon lettering to spine and upper cover, in slightly rubbed dust jacket, with slightly faded spine.

This novel won a Pulitzer Prize in 1930.

1929

£300-400   **BLNY**

A CLOSER LOOK AT A T. PRATCHETT FIRST EDITION

This is the scarce first edition of the first book of the internationally popular Discworld series.

This copy was bought direct from the publisher at the time of publication – reputedly only 506 copies were printed.

This true first impression of the first edition has no price, but bears a sticker reading ' Publisher' s Price £7.95' .

Later issues had overlays, or stickers, with book reviews on the flaps, this copy does not.

Mervyn Peake, 'The Gormenghast trilogy', comprising three first editions, published by Eyre & Spottiswoode, London, comprising 'Titus Groan', 'Gormenghast', and 'Titus Alone', original red cloth, dust wrappers, some slight offsetting to endpapers.

1946-59

£900-1,200   **L&T**

Terry Pratchett, 'The Colour of Magic', first edition, first impression, published by Colin Smythe, Gerrards Cross, original boards, dust jacket, with price sticker on inside front flap, slight rubbing to fore edges and corners.

1983

£4,000-6,000   **BLO**

Terry Pratchett, 'Mort', first edition, published by Gollancz, London, with original boards and dust jacket, in excellent condition.

The fourth book of the Discworld series and many readers' favourite, ensuring a strong following.

1987

£300-500   **BLO**

Philip Pullman, 'The Subtle Knife', first edition, published by Scholastic Press, London, with full number line, original green cloth and gilt stamp of dagger, dust jacket, and bookplate of The Children's Book Award on front free endpaper.

1997

£300-500   **L&T**

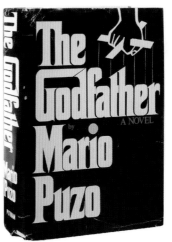

Mario Puzo, 'The Godfather', first edition, first impression, published by Putnam, New York, with red endpapers, original black and off-white cloth lettered in gilt, dust jacket, slight staining and creasing to jacket.

As the jacket is priced '$6.95' and bears the code numbering '6903', it is a first edition jacket. This copy is made more desirable as it is signed by Puzo. This was his first 'commercial' fiction book, following two moderately successful titles — it went on to outsell every other book during the 1970s.

1969

£1,200-1,800   **BLO**

QUICK REFERENCE – HARRY POTTER

J. K. Rowling's Harry Potter titles are among the most widely prized first editions on today's market. The first title in the series, 'Harry Potter and the Philosopher's Stone' has gained an almost legendary status. According to the publisher Bloomsbury, only 500 copies of the first print run of the first edition were produced, most of which were sold to British libraries or schools. This copy is one of those, and shows the level of wear and damage that can be expected from use in a school, as well as bearing the school library's stamp. Had it been in mint condition, the price could have risen to over £10,000. The true first editions have a full line of numbers on the imprint page, leading down to a '1', and do not have a dust jacket. Even the first British paperback issue of this title, also published in 1997, is sought after – copies have fetched over £1,500, as reputedly only 200 were printed.

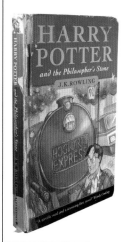

J.K. Rowling, 'Harry Potter and the Philosopher's Stone', first edition, first impression, published by Bloomsbury, London, with unusual slight browning, ex-library copy with stamp and small sticker to verso of title, new endpapers, original pictorial boards, worn at edges and corners, loss and tape repairs around spine.

1997
£1,500-2,000   BLO

J.K. Rowling, 'Harry Potter and the Chamber of Secrets', uncorrected proof copy, original blue and white printed wrappers.

A 'proof copy' is sent out by a publisher to people including major booksellers, literary editors, and reviewers. The purpose is to promote the book before the final version is printed, and to give the author and publisher the chance to make final corrections or revisions. However, by this stage, the text is usually the closest version to the final product.

1998
£800–1,200   BLO

J.K. Rowling, 'Harry Potter and the Prisoner of Azkaban', first edition, first issue, published by Bloomsbury, London, with original pictorial boards and dust jacket.

This can be identified as the first issue due to the copyright wording reading 'Joanne Rowling' rather than 'J.K. Rowling', and the dropped text on p.7.

1999
£500-700   BLO

Siegfried Sassoon, 'Memoirs of a Fox-Hunting Man', Faber & Faber, London, first English illustrated edition, published by Faber & Faber, London, no.224 from a limited edition of 300 signed by the author and illustrator, illustrations by William Nicholson, original vellum lettered in black with designs in red and black.

1929
£700-1,000   L&T

Victoria (Vita) Sackville-West, 'Challenge', first edition, second American issue, published by Doran, New York, with original titled red cloth, dust jacket with light surface marking, and spine slightly dulled, with some tears.

This book was scheduled to be published by Collins in the UK, but Sackville-West withdrew it after pressure from her mother and her husband, Harold Nicolson. Doran used Collins' sheets, insert a new title page, to produce 2,000 copies. Supposedly written with Vita's female lover Violet Trefusis, the lead character is called Julian, which was the name used by Vita when she dressed as a man while travelling with Trefusis. Due to this connection, Vita's mother banned the British version, which was not published until 1974, 12 years after Vita's death.

1923
£350-450   BLO

Mickey Spillane, 'I, the Jury', first edition, published by E. P. Dutton & Co., New York, with original black cloth and slightly creased and rubbed dust jacket, with some tape residue.

1947
£800-1,200   BLNY

L. Frank Baum, 'The New Wizard of Oz', first edition with pictorial endpapers of stills from the 1939 MGM film, published by Bobbs Merrill, illustrated by W. W. Denslow, including eight coloured plates, pictorial endpapers, spine lightly faded, bookplate on front pastedown, damp stained dust jacket, price clipped.

From the Fred. M. Meyer collection.

£300-500   **BLNY**

L. Frank Baum, 'The Road to Oz', first edition, published by Reilly & Britton Co., illustrated by John R. Neill, printed on paper of several different colours, colour stamped green cloth with some fading and rubbing, owner's signatures on ownership leaf and half-title.

This copy can be identified as a first edition as it has the publisher's name at the foot of the spine in upper and lowercase, 'Toto on' in line four of p.34 and the numeral on p.121 in perfect type and other features. From the Fred M. Meyer collection.

1909

£400-600   **BLNY**

A CLOSER LOOK AT AN OZMA OF OZ FIRST EDITION

The dust jacket, missing on this copy, is extremely rare and can double the value.

The 'O' in the word 'Ozma' on the fifth line of the Author's Note on p.11 is present, indicating this is an early example of the first issue, as it 'fell out' during the print run.

This, and ' The Patchwork Girl of Oz' (1913), were the most lavishly illustrated of all the Oz Books, with full-page and textual pictures in full colour throughout.

Pages 135-6 and 221-2 are integral to the rest of the book – during the print run, these pages smudged in many copies, so were taken out and replaced.

L. Frank Baum, 'Ozma of Oz', first edition, published by Reilly & Britton Co., Chicago, illustrated by John R. Neil, with colour stamped tan cloth, pictorial endpapers, housed in a lettered clamshell case, spine lightly faded with tips gently rubbed.

1907

£600-900   **BLNY**

L. Frank Baum, 'Rinkitink in Oz', first edition, published by Reilly & Britton Co., Chicago, illustrated by John R. Neill, 12 colour plates tipped in, stamped pictorial light blue cloth and pictorial endpapers, covers rubbed and soiled, name and address rubberstamped on ownership page.

1916

£400-600   **BLNY**

Dorothy Craigie, (Graham Greene), 'The Little Train', first edition, published by Eyre & Spottiswood, London, with cloth boards, dust jacket with losses and rubbing, and very clean interior.

A rare copy of Graham Greene's first book for children, written anonymously while working as a director for the publisher Eyre & Spottiswoode.

1946

£500-700   **L&T**

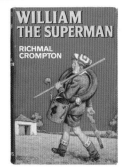

Richmal Crompton, 'William the Superman', first edition, original boards, dust jacket in very good to excellent condition.

1968

£200-300   **BLO**

Captain W.E. Johns, 'Sergeant Bigglesworth C.I.D.', first edition paperback, published by Hodder & Stoughton.

1954

£4-6   ZDB

Elinor Lyon, 'The King of Grey Corrie', first edition, published by the Brockhampton Press, signed by the author on the title page, rubbed and creased dust jacket.

1975

£150-250   BLO

John R. Neill, 'The Scalawagons of Oz', first edition, published by Reilly & Lee Co., Chicago, illustrated by the author, red cloth, pictorial label and endpapers, jacket slightly faded with a few small nicks.

1941

£300-500   BLNY

Garth Nix, 'Sabriel', first edition, published by Harper Collins.
1995

£15-25   BIB

Dr. Seuss (Theodor Seuss Geisel), 'The Cat in the Hat Comes Back', first edition, published by Random House, New York, illustrated, with original boards and slightly rubbed dust jacket, interior very clean.
1958

£400-600   L&T

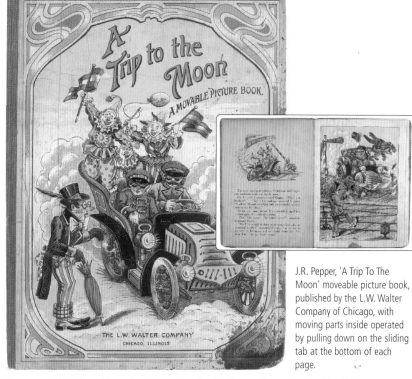

J.R. Pepper, 'A Trip To The Moon' moveable picture book, published by the L.W. Walter Company of Chicago, with moving parts inside operated by pulling down on the sliding tab at the bottom of each page.

This was possibly released in conjunction with, or inspired by, a silent animation film of the same name released in the same year. Written and directed by Vincent Whitman, all copies of the film have been lost meaning this may be the only record of the story. It may have been based on Frenchman Georges Melies' earlier film of 1902, which is widely said to be the first successful science fiction film.

1914

£200-300   PC

QUICK REFERENCE

- The first photography dates from 1839, when Louis Daguerre launched the daguerreotype: the first commercially viable photographic process. However, these early cameras were bulky, expensive and difficult to use. By the 1880s, with the ready availability of prepared 'dry' photographic plates and advances in camera design, the market was opened to many more people. A large number of these wood- and brass- bodied, dry-plate cameras survive and they are often desirable (though less than the earlier wet-plate cameras). Collectors should look for names including Sanderson, Watson and Lancaster.

- The world's most collectable camera is perhaps the Leica, made by Leitz, in Wetzlar, Germany. Developed in 1913, the Leica used 35mm film and was small, light and easy to use. It had a fixed lens until 1930, when interchangeable screw-fit lenses were introduced. This system only changed in

1954, with the bayonet lens mounts of the 'M' series. Many are still usable, or can be repaired due to Leitz's fine quality engineering

- Each Leica has a unique serial number on its top plate, which you can use to identify the model and year of manufacture. Prices range from around £100 for more common models, such as the Model IIIa, to tens of thousands. Variations and unusual engravings add value, as will accessories such as lenses. Scratches, dents, and damaged mechanisms will seriously affect value, with most Leica collectors looking to buy in mint condition.

- With other mass-produced cameras, look for fine quality construction and well known brand names, such as Nikon Voigtlander, Canon and Zeiss Ikon. Condition is important, but usually not as much as for Leicas. Variation in colour and features, such as lenses, adds value.

A Canon S-II camera, no.15326, chrome, engraved 'Seiki-Kogaku, Tokyo', with shutter speeds 20–500, slow speeds dial, with a 'Nippon Kogaku' Nikkor-Q.C. f/3.5 5cm lens no. 570999, body covering replaced.

This can be dated to 1946, as in 1947 the company name changed to 'Canon Camera Company Ltd', replacing the 'Seiki Kogaku' wording.
1946

£300-400   SK

A Franke & Heidecke Wide-Angle Rolleiflex Reflex twin lens reflex camera, no.W2490135, with Zeiss Distagon 1:4 f=55mm lens.

£600-900   ROS

A Franke & Heidecke Tele Rolleiflex twin lens reflex camera, no.S2302261, with Zeiss Sonnar 1:4 f=135mm lens.

£120-180   ROS

1953-57

£250-300   ROS

A Hasselblad 1000F camera, with a Tessar 1:2.8 f=80mm lens.

Of fine and functional quality, the 1000F, and its predecessor the 1600F, can be hard to find in working order.

A Kodak no.5 Cirkut revolving back cycle view 360 degree panoramic roll film camera, no.46969, patented by William Folmer.
c1915-1917

£200-300   ROS

CAMERAS

A Kodak 3A Panoram panoramic roll film camera.
c1926-1928

£60-80 ROS

A Leica IIIC camera, no.502557, chrome, with Leitz f3.5 Elmar lens and cap, with leather case, some faults.
1950

£150-250 TOV

A Leica MI camera, no.967287, chrome, with Leitz 50mm Elmar lens, and leather case.
1959

£200-300 TOV

A CLOSER LOOK AT A LEICA CAMERA

Leica cameras are hotly sought after by many collectors across the world. Those produced in strictly limited numbers are among the most desirable and valuable.

As well as model and age, condition is key – those in truly mint condition will always fetch more than used examples, particularly when they have their paperwork and box, as here.

This example is from a limited edition of 150 cameras, but only 30 had this lens type, commemorating the 150th anniversary of the Wetzlar Optisches Institut.

This is no ordinary M6 with a commemorative engraving – each one is platinum plated, covered with karung leather, and has a unique, special serial number relating to a year from 1849-1999.

A Leica M6 platinum 150th anniversary camera, no. 2490145, commemorative no.1994, the top-plate engraved '150 Jahre Optik 1849–1999 Summilux-M f/1.4 35 ASPH', with diced green-grey leather body covering, with a commemorative Leitz Summilux-M f/1.4 35mm lens, in silk-lined polished walnut root case, with warranty, manual, commemorative booklet, receipt, hood, caps, and strap.
1999

£3,500-5,000 SK

A Leica M4 50th anniversary camera, no.1412936, black, the front with commemorative '50 Jahre' laurel leaf motif, the back numbered '136-E', complete with manual, registration certificate and card box.

According to Leitz records, 1,730 units of this model were made, 350 each with the letters L, E, I and C, and 330 with the letter A.
1974

£2,200-2,800 SK

A Leica M4 50th anniversary

A rare Japanese chrome Muley Leica-type camera, no.102, the base plate engraved 'Made in Occupied Japan', leather-covered body, speed-housing engraved in script 'Muley' and in capitals 'G.T.S.'

A rare Japanese copy of a Lecia Standard by an unknown (and presumably small) Japanese workshop.
c1946-52

£2,000-3,000 SK

CAMERAS

A Nikon F2, with chrome body, and Nikkor 50mm F.1.4 lens.
c1971

£100-150   ROS

A Zeiss Ikon Kolibri 523/18 compact camera, with rimset Compur shutter, and Tessar f=3.5 lens.
1930-35

£50-80   ROS

A CLOSER LOOK AT A NIKON CAMERA

Like Leica, Nikon has a large following of collectors around the world, which means demand is high for rare models.

This first civilian Nikon camera is the 'holy grail' for many collectors, and only around 700 examples are thought to have been produced.

Its serial number, 609117, dates from early on in the production, dating from before some 200 additional Nikon Is were converted into Nikon Ms by changing the focal plane, top and base plates and adding a sprocket wheel.

Examples in such excellent condition are rare and this affects value.

A Nikon I camera, no.609117, chrome with leather-covered body, with back numbered internally '609117', base-plate engraved 'Made in Occupied Japan', with a Nippon Kogaku W-Nikkor C f/3.5 3.5cm lens no.9101079.
1948

£6,000-9,000   SK

A rare black Nikon S 'Life Magazine' camera, no.6101424, black with leather-covered body, the top plate engraved 'Nippon Kogaku, Tokyo', enlarged wind and rewind knobs for field use, chrome lens and tripod mounts and a Nippon Kogaku Nikkor-H.C. f/2 5cm lens no.625463.

This Nikon S was produced for 'Life' magazine photographers and is extremely rare. Only 20 examples were commissioned by the magazine after they were impressed by photographs of the Korean war taken by war photographers such as David Douglas Duncan and Carl Mydams – this is one of only two surviving cameras known.

£15,000-20,000   SK

A Zeiss Ikon, Contarex Special camera, no meter, interchangeable reflex or prism view hood, with a Planar 1:2 f=50mm lens.
c1966

£300-400   ROS

A Zeiss Ikon Contarex Super Second 35mm camera, chrome, with a Zeiss 1:4 f=35mm lens.

c1970

£180-220   ROS

A late 19thC Sanderson mahogany and brass quarter plate field folding camera, with black leather bellows, spare plates, tripod, and other accessories.

£280-320   **FLD**

A Paillard Bolex H8 Reflex cine camera, the C mount fitted with 1:1.3 f=12.5mm, 1:1.4 f=36mm and Cine-Tele-Xenar 1:2.8/75 lenses in fitted leather maker's case, with accessories and instruction leaflets.

£60-80   **ROS**

A CLOSER LOOK AT A ZEISS CAMERA

Introduced in 1935, many consider this to be one of the most technically impressive cameras ever built, but it was heavy and tricky to use.

It was the first camera to have a built-in light meter, and was extremely expensive in its day, costing £233 including a Sonnar lens in 1939.

This camera is in excellent, working condition – if it is worn through use, or the shutter or light meter do not work, the value will be reduced by over a half as it is complex to repair.

This example has its original Sonnar lens plus a Tessar lens, manual, case, and a collection of accessories, many of which can be hard to find today and add value.

A Zeiss Contaflex twin lens reflex camera, no.A46226, chrome with leather-covered body, with a Zeiss f/2.8 8cm viewing lens no.1724131 and a Zeiss Tessar f/2.8 5cm taking lens no.1514331, in maker's case, together with a Zeiss Sonnar f/2 8.5cm taking lens no.2401465 in leather pouch and maker's box, manual, leather hood and accessories.

£1,200-1,800   **SK**

A Houghton-Butcher 'Ensign Special' Reflex Tropical model camera with brass-bound teak body.

'Tropical' cameras were made using teak and the fabric bellows were treated so they repelled insects when used in tropical climes.

£200-300   **ROS**

A Paillard Bolex H-16 cine camera, the C mount fitted with a Yvar 1:2.8 f=75mm, a Trioplan 1:2.8 Foc 3in, and a Ross 1in F 1.9 cine lens.

£50-70   **ROS**

A 1960s-70s Kodak shop display over-sized model of an Instamatic camera, with attached 'flash bulb' fitting.

£60-80   **ROS**

A carved walking cane, by 'Schtockschnitzler' Simmons, with bird whistle grip.

29in (73.5cm) high

£600-900   POOK

A carved cane, by 'Schtockschnitzler' Simmons, with bird grip.

£500-800   POOK

A carved cane with bird grip, by 'Schtockschnitzler' Simmons.

£800-1,200   POOK

A Bally carver cane, with painted bird grip.

33in (84cm) high

£2,500-3,500   POOK

QUICK REFERENCE – FOLK ART CANES

'Folk Art' is the term given to unique works by untrained or self-trained, usually country-based, artisans. This varied area has become immensely popular with collectors over the past few years, after being largely ignored for decades. Although folk art is now collected all over the world, the US market is the strongest and generally sees the highest prices. Prices paid for folk art walking canes have now even exceeded those paid for gadget canes containing functional items. Although the level of detail, condition, subject and date count, the primary consideration is the artist. 'Schtockschnitzler' Simmons was an itinerant German, whose nickname means 'cane carver'. He paid for his bed and board around Pennsylvania from c1895-1910 by selling his carvings, which also included decorative trees with seated birds. This rare and desirable example (below) retains its original paint, which is also unusually bright and unworn; for a functional item this is very rare. Birds are his hallmark design and are highly sought after, and this is a particularly desirable 'bird in hand' design.

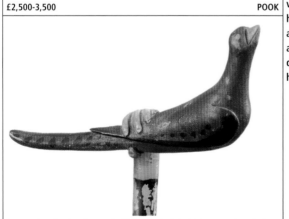

A carved and painted cane, by 'Schtockschnitzler' Simmons, the grip in the form of a hand clasping a bird.

38.25in (97cm) high

£4,000-6,000   POOK

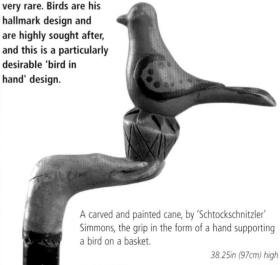

A carved and painted cane, by 'Schtockschnitzler' Simmons, the grip in the form of a hand supporting a bird on a basket.

38.25in (97cm) high

£6,000-9,000   POOK

A Bally carver cane, the handle carved as a bird and leaves.

33in (84cm) high

£400-600　　　　**POOK**

A folk art carved cane, with grip in the form of a dog with a turtle in its mouth, the stock carved with various animal heads, and silver band and tip.

c1900　　　*33.25in (84.5cm) high*

£300-400　　　　**POOK**

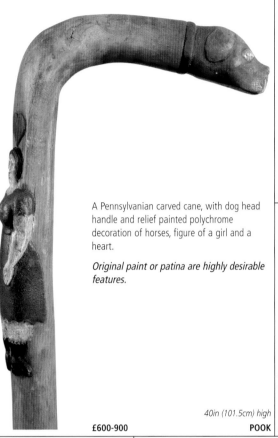

A Pennsylvanian carved cane, with dog head handle and relief painted polychrome decoration of horses, figure of a girl and a heart.

Original paint or patina are highly desirable features.

40in (101.5cm) high

£600-900　　　　**POOK**

A carved cane with hound head grip, by 'Schtockschnitzler' Simmons, above a cockerel and sawtooth band.

33in (84cm) high

£600-900　　　　**POOK**

A folk art carved cane, the handle carved as a seated dog on its haunches, wearing a long hat.

37in (94cm) high

£250-350　　　　**POOK**

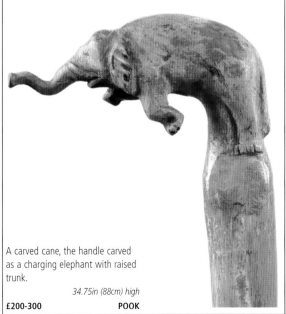

A carved cane, the handle carved as a charging elephant with raised trunk.

34.75in (88cm) high

£200-300　　　　**POOK**

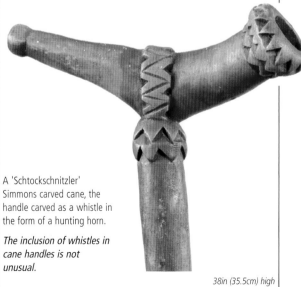

A 'Schtockschnitzler' Simmons carved cane, the handle carved as a whistle in the form of a hunting horn.

The inclusion of whistles in cane handles is not unusual.

38in (35.5cm) high

£400-500　　　　**POOK**

CERAMICS

QUICK REFERENCE

- The Beswick Pottery was founded in Loughton, Staffordshire in 1894. The animal figurines for which Beswick is now best known began to appear as early as 1900. By 1930, they had become a major part of production. The company was sold to Royal Doulton in 1969, but the Beswick name was in use until 1989, when the production of Beswick and Doulton animal figurines was merged under the Royal Doulton name. The Beswick name was used again from 1999 until the factory closed in 2002. Prices rose after the closure and remain strong.
- Collectors tend to focus on one type of animal, with cattle currently one of the most popular. Other popular figurines include the series of Beatrix Potter characters launched in

1946 and the subsequent range of Disney figurines.
- The work of Arthur Gredington, who joined in 1939, is desirable. Other notable modellers include Colin Melbourne, Graham Tongue, Albert Hallam and Alan Maslankowski.
- Look for variation in colour, glaze, form (i.e. differently positioned legs), as these will affect value. 'Roan' and 'Rocking horse grey' are typically valuable. Similarly, matt glazes can be more valuable than glossy. Early pieces are generally the most desirable, but can be hard to identify as the Beswick backstamp and shape numbers were only used from 1934. Limited editions from as late as 1990 can be valuable if the edition was small. Condition is important. Examine protruding horns, thin legs and tails for breakages.

A Beswick 'Leghorn Cockerel' figurine, model 1892, designed by Arthur Gredington, the base with impressed mark.

1963-83   *9.75in (25cm) high*
£150-200   **LOC**

A Beswick 'Green Woodpecker' bird figure, model 1218, designed by Arthur Gredington, with gloss finish, the base with impressed marks and applied paper label.

The original version, produced from 1961-67, had high relief flowers applied to the base, and can be worth up to twice the value of this example.
1967-89   *8.75in (22cm) high*
£150-200   **WW**

A Beswick 'Songthrush' bird figure, model 2308, designed by Albert Hallam, with gloss finish, the base with impressed mark.

1970-89   *5.75in (14.5cm) high*
£100-150   **WW**

A Beswick 'Grouse (pair)' figure, model 2063, designed by Albert Hallam, impressed factory marks.

1966-75   *6in (15cm) high*
£350-450   **WW**

A Beswick 'Fan-tailed Dove' figure, model 1614, designed by Arthur Gredington, the base with impressed and printed mark.
1959-69   *6in (15.5cm) high*
£180-220   **WW**

A set of three Beswick 'Mallard' graduated wall plaques, model 596, designed by Mr Watkin, with gloss finish, the backs with impressed and printed marks.

1938-73   Largest 11.75in (30cm) wide
£100-150   WW

A Beswick 'Bird' figurine, model 1415, designed by Colin Melbourne, from the CM series, the base with factory marks.

1956-1962   5.25in (13.5cm) high
£150-200   W&W

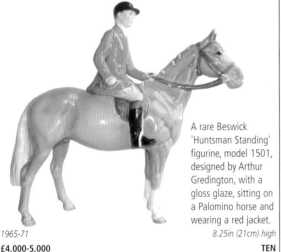

A rare Beswick 'Huntsman Standing' figurine, model 1501, designed by Arthur Gredington, with a gloss glaze, sitting on a Palomino horse and wearing a red jacket.

1965-71   8.25in (21cm) high
£4,000-5,000   TEN

A rare Beswick 'Huntsman Standing' figurine, model 1501, designed by Arthur Gredington, with a gloss glaze, on a Skewbald horse and wearing a red jacket.

The horse in this model is an exceptionally rare colour, and is not listed in any standard reference books on Beswick. Nevertheless, this very high price shows what can happen when a small number of collectors in a specialist market compete to own a rare piece.

8.25in (21cm) high
£5,000-6,000   TEN

A Beswick 'Huntswoman' figurine, model 982, designed by Arthur Gredington, with gloss finish and factory marks to base.
1942-67   10.25in (26cm) high
£200-250   LOC

A Beswick 'Huntsman on Rearing Horse', model 868, designed by Arthur Gredington, with a dark chestnut horse, red jacket and factory marks to base.

1940-52   9.5in (24cm) high
£180-220   LOC

CERAMICS

A Beswick 'King Charles Spaniel Josephine of Blagreaves' figurine, model 2107B, designed by Arthur Gredington, with gloss finish.

1967-94   *7.5in (19cm) long*

£20-30   **SAS**

A Beswick 'Elephant And Tiger' figurine, model 1720, designed by Arthur Gredington, with a gloss finish, and circular printed mark.

1960-75   *11.75in (30cm) high*

£200-300   **SWO**

A CLOSER LOOK AT A BEATRIX POTTER CHARACTER FIGURINE

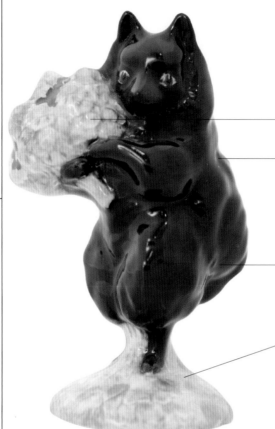

This is the rare, first model of Duchess, the second has her holding a pie rather than flowers and was produced from 1979-82.

When released, she was not popular with collectors or the buying public, so very few examples were sold at the time, making her hard to find today.

The value of this model varies widely depending on the location and demand at the time of sale – prices have ranged from £500 to over £2,000 during the past five to seven years.

The base has an oval shaped printed 'Beswick England' mark – those with circular marks are even rarer and were the earliest of this model ever produced.

A Beswick Beatrix Potter 'Duchess' figurine, model 1355, designed by Graham Orwell, with gloss finish and printed gold oval factory mark.

1955-67   *3.75in (9.5cm) high*

£1,000-1,500   **FLD**

A Beswick Beatrix Potter 'Benjamin Bunny' figurine, model 1105/3, third version with brown shoes, and ears and shoes tucked in, the base with printed factory mark.

Earlier models had arms extended with shoes held out and protruding ears, but as these parts were often broken the design was changed on later models.

c1980-2000   *4in (10cm) high*

£20-30   **SAS**

A Beswick Beatrix Potter 'Anna Maria' figurine, model 1851, designed by Albert Hallam, the base with printed brown five line mark.

1974-83

£50-70   **PC**

A Beswick Beatrix Potter 'Mr Alderman Ptolemy' figurine, model 2424, designed by Graham Tongue, with printed brown five line mark to base.

1974-1985

£25-35   **PC**

QUICK REFERENCE – BRIGLIN POTTERY

The Briglin Pottery was founded in central London in 1948 by Brigitte Appleby and Eileen Lewenstein. Each piece was potted and decorated by hand, with sgraffito and wax-resist techniques being used, often with a manganese oxide glaze. Colours tend towards earthy browns, beiges and creams, sometimes with a light blue, or greeny-blue. Patterns focus on the natural world, with stylisation being common and desirable to collectors. A white clay gave way to a more common red clay in the late 1950s. Pieces are generally marked with a 'BRIGLIN' impressed mark. Despite being highly successful in the 1960s and 70s, the pottery closed in 1990.

A 1970s Briglin cylinder vase, with wax-resist design of a seeding flower in cream and blue glazes, the base impressed 'BRIGLIN'.

7.25in (18.5cm) high

£50-70　　　　　　GC

A 1970s Briglin vase, with wax-resist and manganese oxide black flowers with incised detail, the base impressed 'BRIGLIN'.

7.75in (19.5cm) high

£30-40　　　　　　GC

A Briglin waisted cylindrical vase with wax-resist leaf design, the base with impressed 'BRIGLIN' mark.

9.75in (24.5cm) high

£60-80　　　　　　GC

A Briglin baluster vase, with design of green leaves on a cream ground, the base impressed 'BRIGLIN'.

7.75in (19.5cm) high

£40-60　　　　　　GC

A very large Briglin bowl, with wax-resist design of country flowers with a brushed brown glaze, and covered with a transparent glaze, the base inscribed 'BRIGLIN POTTERY AP'.

The 'AP' may stand for Alan Pett, a thrower at the London pottery. These bowls must have been among the largest pieces made at the pottery.

12.75in (32cm) diam

£200-250　　　　　　GC

A very large Briglin bowl, with wax-resist design of seeding country flowers, and covered with a transparent glaze, the base impressed 'BRIGLIN'.

12.75in (32cm) diam

£200-250　　　　　　GC

QUICK REFERENCE

- The Carlton Works were established in Stoke-on-Trent in 1890 by Wiltshaw & Robinson. Pieces were produced under the name 'Carlton Ware' from 1894 and this became the company's name in 1958, although most production before this is generally known as Carlton Ware.
- In the 1920s and 1930s, Carlton Ware became known for its rich Art-Deco-styled lustre pieces, created in response to Wedgwood's more expensive Fairyland Lustre range.
- The factory also introduced a completely different style of ceramic in the 1930s, which became a mainstay of Carlton Ware for nearly two decades. This pastel-coloured, moulded range used flowers, leaves and fruit either as decorative motifs or as the main shape of the piece. Certain motifs,

such as 'Cherries', and colours are rare, as are some combinations. For example, 'Buttercup' is easy to find in yellow, but relatively rare in pink and consequently more desirable. As a large number of pieces were produced, condition is very important – inspect lids, rims and bases as these are often damaged. Look for boxed gift sets, and even empty boxes, as these add value.

- Carlton Ware went bankrupt in 1989, but the name and some moulds were bought by Francis Joseph in 1997, who continues to sell ceramics under the brand. There are Carlton Ware fakes on the market, so you should examine pieces closely and ensure the back stamp is appropriate for the item and period of manufacture.

A Carlton Ware embossed yellow and pink 'Waterlily' mug, the base impressed '1787'.

4.25in (11cm) high

£60-80   BEV

A Carlton Ware embossed yellow and green 'Waterlily' mug, the base with printed factory mark and impressed '1783'.

4.25in (11cm) high

£60-80   BEV

A Carlton Ware embossed pink 'Buttercup' mug, the base with printed marks and impressed '1585'.

This is a more desirable colour.

4.25in (11cm) high

£80-100   BEV

A Carlton Ware embossed yellow cabbage leaf milk jug, with printed factory mark and impressed '1524'.

4.25in (11cm) high

£80-120   BAD

A 1930s Carlton Ware embossed green and yellow 'Lily' teapot, the base with printed factory mark and impressed '1786'.

5.25in (13.5cm) high

£80-120   BAD

A 1930s Carlton Ware large embossed yellow 'Apple Blossom' jug, the base with printed factory mark and impressed '1700/1'.

This the largest of three sizes.

14.5in (37cm) high

£200-300   **BAD**

A CLOSER LOOK AT A CARLTON WARE BISCUIT BARREL

This is one of the rarest and most desirable items from the fruit and floral embossed ranges.

The geometric, Art Deco shape is unusual within the range, and is highly desirable.

This shape was only used for this biscuit jar and a small jam pot, and in Raspberry and Blackberry only.

Always check the corners, handles and lid for damage – note how the foot and knob on the lid are modelled as a raspberries.

A 1930s Carlton Ware Art Deco pink fruit embossed Raspberry biscuit jar, the base with factory marks and impressed '1565'.

5.5in (14cm) high

£200-250   **BEV**

A Carlton Ware Salad Ware embossed pink 'Buttercup' dish, the base with printed mark and impressed '1395'.

4.5in (11.5cm) long

£35-45   **BAD**

A Carlton Ware Salad Ware yellow embossed 'Buttercup' crescent dish, the base with printed factory mark and impressed '1529/3'.

7.5in (19cm) long

£35-45   **BAD**

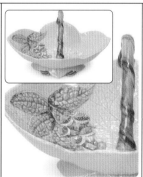

A Carlton Ware embossed green 'Foxglove' handled basket, with printed and impressed marks to base.

10.25in (26cm) long

£80-120   **BEV**

A Carlton Ware yellow embossed 'Lily' Salad Ware toast rack, the base with printed marks and impressed '1861'.

4in (10cm) long

£80-120   **BEV**

CERAMICS

A 1930s Carlton Ware 'Handcraft' plate, hand painted with a longboat, the back with printed and painted marks.

Introduced in 1928 and produced until the late 1930s, this entirely hand painted range is usually found with a matte finish. Colours tend to be bright, and the more Art Deco the pattern is, the more valuable it is likely to be.

10.5in (27cm) diam

£350-450   WW

A 1930s Carlton Ware 'Hollyhocks' bowl, pattern no.3973, printed and painted in colours and gilt on a green lustre ground, printed and painted marks.

10.75in (27cm) wide

£100-150   WW

A 1930s Carlton Ware 'Secretary Bird' twin-handled oval dish, pattern 4017, decorated on an orange lustre ground with gilded highlights.

The Japanese-inspired Secretary Bird pattern is scarce and sought after.

12in (30.5cm) wide

£200-300   GHOU

A 1930s Carlton Ware hand painted novelty 'Humpty Dumpty' toby jug.

These can also be found with musical mechanisms, but these are even rarer and can fetch up to £500-800.

7.5in (19cm) high

£300-500   BAD

A scarce 1930s Carlton Ware hand painted mushroom-shaped cruet set, with printed marks to base, lacking spoon.

Always examine all parts carefully as cracks or chips are common.

5in (12.5cm) diam

£150-200   BEV

A 1970s Carlton Ware orange owl money box, the base printed 'Carltonware made in England' and with trademark.

5in (12.5cm) high

£30-40   CANS

A 1970s Carlton Ware yellow-lime green lidded butter dish, with black printed mark to base.

5.75in (14.5cm) long

£18-22   RET

QUICK REFERENCE

- Clarice Cliff is one of the most desirable names in Art Deco ceramics. Prices can start as low as £50, but can rise into many thousands for rare and sought-after designs. Born in 1899 in Tunstall in the heart of the Staffordshire Potteries, Cliff began her career as an apprentice decorator at Linguard Webster & Co. in 1912, before joining A.J. Wilkinson in 1916.
- Her talents became obvious at Wilkinson, and the company's owner, Colley Shorter, gave Cliff her own studio in 1920 at the recently acquired Newport Pottery. There, she hand-painted defective blank wares with striking geometric or stylised floral patterns in bright colours, which covered the flaws. These developed into the now legendary 'Bizarre' series, launched in 1928.
- Neither 'Bizarre' (used until 1935) nor 'Fantasque' (used 1928-34) are range names, but are instead general titles, with patterns usually having their own names. Cliff trained a team of women, known as the 'Bizarre Girls' to produce these designs, which were applied to modern shapes.
- When evaluating desirability and value, consider the shape and size of the piece, the pattern and the colours used. Some patterns, and colourways within these patterns, are rarer than others. Orange tends to be more commonly found, while blue and purple are often rarer. Muted colours and more traditional floral designs are less sought after.
- In general, Cliff's brightly coloured, highly stylised Art Deco designs from 1928-c1934 are the most sought-after. If the shape is modern and Art Deco too, so much the better. Always look at the mark, and ensure that it is under the glaze. Beware as fakes do exist – experience of handling authentic pieces will help you to spot them.

A Clarice Cliff Bizarre 'Autumn Crocus' pattern Stamford shape milk jug and sugar bowl, with printed marks to base.

2.75in (7cm) high

£280-320   **WW**

A Clarice Cliff Bizarre 'Autumn Crocus' pattern Perth shape jug, printed mark to base and some wear to glaze.

5in (13cm) high

£80-120   **WW**

A Clarice Cliff Bizarre 'Blue Crocus' pattern ribbed beer tankard, with printed mark to base, minor scuffs to banding.

c1935   *6.25in (16cm) high*

£200-300   **FLD**

A pair of Clarice Cliff Bizarre 'Autumn Crocus' pattern square-section candlesticks, with 'Bizarre' and 'CROCUS' printed marks.

Candlesticks are comparatively scarce, and the corners are often chipped through use.

c1930   *7.75in (20cm) high*

£350-450   **FLD**

A Clarice Cliff Bizarre 'Autumn Crocus' pattern Isis shape vase, with large script printed mark.

c1929   *9.75in (25cm) high*

£750-950   **FLD**

CERAMICS

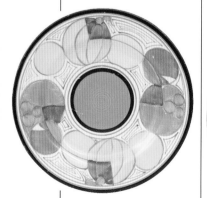

A Clarice Cliff Fantasque Bizarre 'Pastel Melon' pattern Athens shape jug, with combined printed 'FANTASQUE' and 'Bizarre' mark.

c1930   7in (18cm) high

£350-450   **FLD**

A Clarice Cliff Fantasque 'Melon' pattern vase, shape 376.

7in (18cm) high

£800-1,200   **GHOU**

A CLOSER LOOK AT A CLARICE CLIFF MELON JUG

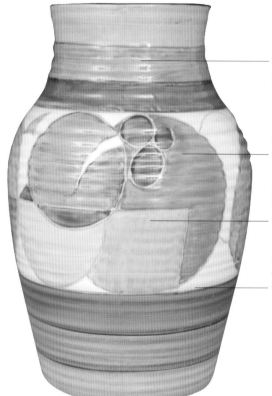

Melon was produced from 1930-32 in orange, green, red and pastel colourways – orange is the most common with pastel being rarer.

The pattern of stylised fruit may have been inspired by Cubist paintings, as well as the geometric Art Deco style of the time.

The Lotus jug (the handle is not seen here) is a very popular form and displays the pattern well. It tends to be hard to find.

Note how the shapes are outlined in yellow rather than black to give more emphasis to the coloured forms rather than the outlines.

A Clarice Cliff 'Pastel Melon' single-handled Lotus jug, with combined printed 'FANTASQUE' and 'Bizarre' mark, with a few minor paint scuffs.

c1931   11.5in (29cm) high

£800-1,200   **FLD**

A Clarice Cliff Fantasque 'Melon' pattern circular plate, with printed 'Fantasque' mark, few minor scuffs.

c1930   10in (25.5cm) diam

£120-180   **FLD**

A Clarice Cliff Fantasque 'Melon' pattern vase, shape no.358.

8in (20cm) high

£650-850   **GHOU**

A Clarice Cliff 'Green Melon' pattern octagonal plate, with printed 'Fantasque' mark and 'Lawleys' gold back stamp, with broken body and chips to rim.

Lawleys were a specialist retailer of ceramics who dealt with many leading ceramics factories.

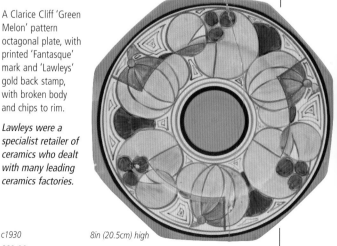

c1930   8in (20.5cm) high

£60-90   **FLD**

A Clarice Cliff Bizarre 'Rhodanthe' pattern Tyrol shape bowl, with printed 'Bizarre' mark, and a few minor scuffs to decoration.
c1934   *4in (10cm) wide*
£480-520   **FLD**

QUICK REFERENCE – RHODANTHE PATTERN

Rhodanthe was introduced in 1934 and shows stylised trees with flower-like foliage and sinuous trunks and branches. It became very popular and took over from Crocus as Cliff's best-selling pattern. As this design was still produced after World War II, it is comparatively common today. It shows a move away from the typical Bizarre style – the pattern is not banded, geometric or heavily outlined. Also, the hand-painted colours were blended into each other in a process known as 'etching'. The most common colourway is shown here, with dominant orange tones. Variations in colour have different names – the pink Viscaria and the blue Aurea. Both are less common, Viscaria particularly so.

A Clarice Cliff Bizarre 'Rhodanthe' pattern Conical sugar sifter, with printed 'Bizarre' mark, restored chips.
c1934   *4in (10cm) wide*
£480-520   **FLD**

A Clarice Cliff Bizarre 'Aurea' Mei Ping vase, shape 14, with printed 'Bizarre' mark.
c1936   *8.75in (22.5cm) high*
£450-550   **FLD**

A Clarice Cliff Bizarre 'Rhodanthe' vase, shape 212, with Delecia glazed interior, and plain 'Claire Cliff' script printed mark.
c1935-6   *5.5in (14cm) high*
£350-450   **FLD**

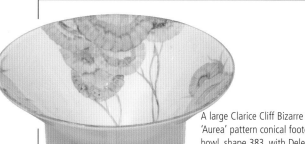

A large Clarice Cliff Bizarre 'Aurea' pattern conical footed bowl, shape 383, with Delecia streaked glazed exterior, and painted green 'Clarice Cliff' and 'Bizarre' mark, chip to foot and some scratching.
9in (23cm) wide
£180-220   **FLD**

A Clarice Cliff Bizarre 'Viscaria' pattern Leda plate, with printed mark to underside.

9in (23cm) wide
£100-150   **GORL**

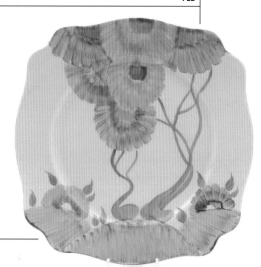

CERAMICS

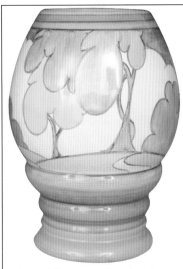

A Clarice Cliff Fantasque Bizarre 'Pastel Autumn' pattern vase, shape 362, painted with a stylized tree and cottage landscape, with printed marks and light crazing to the glaze.

c1932   8.25in (21cm) high

£1,200-1,500   **FLD**

A CLOSER LOOK AT AN ORANGE AUTUMN WALL PLAQUE

Clarice Cliff's plaques were pressed from solid clay making them one of the most easily broken pieces – few have survived compared to the number made.

Made in 10.5in (25.5cm), 13in (33cm) and 18in (46cm) sizes, they display the pattern extremely well and are popular with collectors. The footrim was drilled for hanging.

Autumn was produced in many different colourways, with Red being the earliest and first made in 1931, and Pastel being scarcer. Variations abound.

A Clarice Cliff Bizarre 'Orange Autumn' large wall plaque, with printed 'Bizarre' mark.

c1932   13in (33cm) diam

£1,800-2,200   **FLD**

A Clarice Cliff 'Pastel Autumn' small pedestal nut bowl, shape 260, with combined 'FANTASQUE' and 'Bizarre' printed marks.

c1931   2.25in (6cm) high

£350-450   **FLD**

A Clarice Cliff Fantasque Bizarre 'Blue Autumn' large cauldron, with printed 'FANTASQUE' and 'Bizarre' marks, with a few minor scuffs.

c1931   4.25in (11cm) high

£350-450   **FLD**

A Clarice Cliff Bizarre 'Green Autumn' pattern flying swan flower block, shape 423, with a brightly coloured relief moulded bird, and printed 'Bizarre' mark.

c1931   6.25in (16cm) high

£400-600   **FLD**

A Clarice Cliff Bizarre 'Broth' globe vase, shape 370, with printed 'Bizarre' mark, with a few minor scuffs and light crazing to glaze.

c1930   5.5in (14cm) high

£1,200-1,800   **FLD**

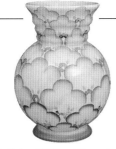

A Clarice Cliff 'Cloud Flowers' vase, shape 896, the base with relief moulded script signature mark.

The cloud-like design recalls Chinese textiles, showing the breadth of Cliff's sources of inspiration. It is also sometimes known as Nemesia and can be found in other colours.

c1935   8.75in (22.5cm) high

£350-450   **FLD**

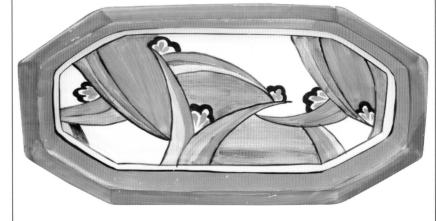

A Clarice Cliff Fantasque 'Comets' sandwich tray, shape 334, with printed 'Fantasque' mark, with minor scuffs.

This is a desirable and early abstract pattern.

c1929

£550-650   **FLD**

A Clarice Cliff Bizarre 'Delecia' range shape no.451 vase, with dripped glazes and printed marks.

8in (20.5cm) high

£180-220   **WW**

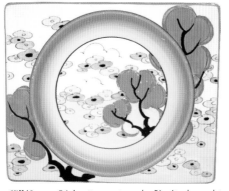

A Clarice Cliff 'Orange Erin' pattern rectangular Biarritz shape plate, with Royal Staffordshire 'Biarritz' mark, a few minor scuffs.

c1933   9in (23cm) wide

£300-400   **FLD**

A Clarice Cliff 'Green Erin' pattern circular plate, with printed 'Bizarre' mark.

c1933   9in (23cm) diam

£300-400   **FLD**

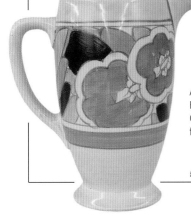

A Clarice Cliff Fantasque Bizarre 'Red Gardenia' pattern Coronet shape jug, with some fading.

7in (18cm) high

£150-200   **GHOU**

A Clarice Cliff 'Latona Dahlia' pattern fruit bowl, with 'Bizarre' and 'LATONA' printed marks.

c1931   7in (18cm) wide

£280-320   **FLD**

CERAMICS

A Clarice Cliff oval lily bowl, shape no.973, with printed marks to base.

Designed to hold flower bulbs, this shape was introduced in 1938 and produced until the late 1950s. Reputedly over 250,000 were sold.

9in (23cm) wide

£50-70   GHOU

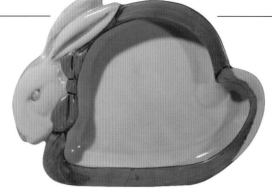

A Clarice Cliff Bizarre nursery ware bowl, the rim modelled as a rabbit, with printed factory mark and wear to blue band.

8.5in (21.5cm) wide

£250-300   WW

A Clarice Cliff pipe holder, modelled as a small bird, with printed 'Clarice Cliff' script mark.

3in (7.5cm) high

£50-70   FLD

A Clarice Cliff tree stump planter, with two moulded budgerigars, and brown printed script signature, and small hairline crack to bowl.

10.75in (27.5cm) long

£45-55   FLD

A Clarice Cliff 'Circus' breakfast cup and saucer, with transfer-printed clown pattern designed by Laura Knight, and pink printed 'Laura Knight' signature and 'Bizarre' marks.

c1935

£200-250   FLD

ESSENTIAL REFERENCE - ART IN INDUSTRY

The influential 'Modern Art for the Table' exhibition held at Harrods department store, London in late 1934 aimed to showcase the work of leading artists in ceramic and glass. Dame Laura Knight's 'Circus' pattern was a central display and other contributors included Frank Brangwyn and Duncan Grant. All the earthenware was produced by Wilkinson's and unusually included Clarice's name alongside the artist's. Although many designs were shown again at the prominent Royal Academy 'Art In Industry' exhibition in 1935, they were not successful commercially and were withdrawn from sale.

A Clarice Cliff 'Circus' circular side plate, with transfer-printed clown pattern designed by Laura Knight, and pink printed 'Laura Knight' signature and 'Bizarre' marks, with two scuffs to banding.

c1935

6in (15cm) diam

£250-350   FLD

FIND OUT MORE...

Greg Slater and Jonathan Brough ' Comprehensively Clarice Cliff' . London: Thames & Hudson, 2005.

Sevi Guatelli, ' The Best of Clarice Cliff' . Edinburgh: Best 50 Limited, 2008; www.thebestofclaricecliff.com

A first edition Clarice Cliff 'Circus' circular side plate, with transfer-printed horse pattern designed by Laura Knight, and pink printed 'Laura Knight' signature and 'Bizarre' marks.

1934

6.75in (17cm) diam

£250-350   FLD

QUICK REFERENCE – CUPS & SAUCERS

- Cups and saucers dating from the 1860s to the 1930s have risen in desirability again. Their popularity as part of 19thC tableware sets fell sharply for a few years as fashions moved away from a chintzy, floral look. As such, even fine quality sets could often be found at auction for under £100. Today the story is different, with people mixing patterns and shapes to create 'harlequin' sets to use at tea parties, causing a renewal in collecting interest.
- Look out first for major makers by checking marks on the base, as this will usually indicate fine quality. Pieces by factories such as Royal Doulton, Coalport, Royal Worcester, Hammersley, Paragon and Shelley will typically be priced at the higher end of the market. Many of these names have large and loyal bands of collectors, ensuring prices remain high. Popular designer names such as Susie Cooper, Clarice Cliff and others will also command higher prices.

- Always look for signs of quality in the decoration. Many pieces have hand-painted details, often highlighted in gilt – a fact that surprises many considering the time and skill required to decorate by hand. Sets with finely detailed and well-executed patterns will be more desirable and valuable, as will those that have shapes or patterns that exemplify the style of the day – for example, the Art Deco style of the 1920s and 30s.
- Many of the most decorative examples with gilt interiors were intended for display rather than use. These 'cabinet' cups are also rising in desirability again, although not as sharply as examples that can be used. Always examine the pieces closely – items that were in regular use may have been damaged over time. Worn patterns or gilding, and particularly cracks and chips, will reduce desirability and value.

An Aynsley cup and saucer, with gilt rim.

Saucer 4.5in (11cm) diam

£30-50   MA

A 1920s Aynsley transfer and hand-painted teacup and saucer, decorated with orange flowers and cobalt and orange panels.

Saucer 5.25in (13.5cm) diam

£20-25   W&L

An Aynsley teacup and saucer, with pink transfer-printed flowers and yellow hand-painted butterfly handle, the back with printed marks.

Saucer 5.25in (13.5cm) diam

£100-150   BEV

An Aynsley bone china transfer-printed tea cup and saucer, with blue cornflower or love-in-a-mist flowers, and lavender scalloped rim, with yellow butterfly handle, the back with reg no.765788 for 1931.

Saucer 5.25in (13.5cm) diam

£120-160   BEV

An Aynsley teacup and saucer, with yellow exterior, gilt rim and hand-painted butterfly handle, the back with printed marks and registered no.705789 for 1924.

Saucer 5in (13cm) diam

£120-180   BEV

CERAMICS

A CLOSER LOOK AT AN AYNSLEY CUP & SAUCER

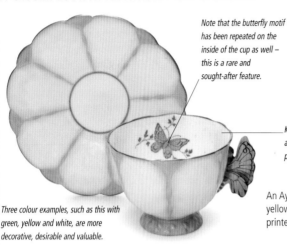

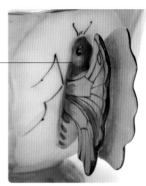

Note that the butterfly motif has been repeated on the inside of the cup as well – this is a rare and sought-after feature.

The butterfly handle is very well painted and detailed, with its legs and antennae painted onto the bowl.

Known as the 'Tulip' shape, the cup and saucer are moulded to represent petals or leaves.

Three colour examples, such as this with green, yellow and white, are more decorative, desirable and valuable.

An Aynsley 'Tulip' shape teacup and saucer, moulded and painted in white, yellow and green, and with hand-painted butterfly handle, the base with printed marks and registered no.765788 for 1931.

Saucer 5.25in (13.5cm) diam

£180-220　　　　　　　　　　　　　　**BEV**

A 1920s Royal Bayreuth teacup and saucer, with transfer-printed sprays of flowers in panels, and green ground with gilt floral, scrolling and hatched pattern.

Saucer 5in (12.5cm) diam

£50-70　　　**BAD**

A Brown Westhead Moore & Co. Cauldon Ware cup and saucer, with a yellow scalloped border with scrolling birds and flower garlands.

Saucer 4.75in (12cm) diam

£70-90　　　**BEV**

A 1930s Burleigh 'Belvedere' shape teacup and saucer, with hand-painted green band and sprays of multicoloured flowers on a cream background, marked 'no.309992 MADE IN ENGLAND BELVEDERE REGD'.

Saucer 5.75in (14.5cm) diam

£30-50　　　**BEV**

A 1930s Burleigh Zenith shape teacup and saucer, with hand-painted 'Lemon Tree' pattern with blue border, the cup with angular and shaped handle, the base with printed marks and registered no.769495, for 1931.

This is a rare and desirable pattern, on a quintessential Art Deco shape.

5.75in (14.5cm) diam

£55-65　　　**BEV**

A 1930s Burleigh Ware Imperial shape teacup and saucer, with hand-painted floral and foliate design and shaped handle.

5.75in (14.5cm) diam

£30-40　　　**BEV**

QUICK REFERENCE – BURGESS & LEIGH

Founded in 1851 as Hulme & Booth, the company became Burgess & Leigh (later shortened to Burleigh) in 1877. It was known for toilet sets and tablewares until the 1920s, when the focus moved to tea sets and tablewares. During the 1920s and 1930s, it became associated with brightly hand-painted tea sets and jugs, which often had shaped or figural handles as on this teacup. Many shapes were designed by Ernest Bailey, with patterns by Harold Bennett. Charlotte Rhead also produced designs from 1926-31. The company remained in the family of the co-founding Leigh family until 1999, when it was rescued from bankruptcy by the Dorling family, and was renamed Burgess, Dorling & Leigh.

A W&L teacup and saucer, with transfer-printed foliate and floral pattern on a mottled blue band, with scrolling and panels, the back with factory mark and registered no.152134 for 1890.

5.5in (14cm) diam

£18-22   **W&L**

A Carltonware Rita shape teacup and saucer, decorated with green raised dots on a cream ground, and with gilt interior.

This pattern, no.4225, can be found in a number of different colour combinations including white on Rouge Royale.

Saucer 4.5in (11.5cm) diam

£80-120   **BEV**

A 1930s Burleigh Ware Imperial shape teacup and saucer, designed by Ernest Bailey, with hand-painted garden scene with balustrade, the back painted with no.11516 and with printed factory and Australian registration marks.

5.75in (14.5cm) diam

£30-40   **BEV**

A 1930s Carltonware blue 'Barge' pattern Rita shape cabinet cup and saucer, with gilt interior.

Exotic hand-painted patterns on lustre grounds were first introduced in the 1920s.

Saucer 4.5in (11.5cm) diam

£100-150   **BEV**

A 1920s Carltonware yellow 'Mikado' pattern coffee can and saucer, with gilt interior, with 'W&R' printed mark.

The presence of the Wiltshaw & Robinson mark indicates that this is an early piece from the 1920s.

Saucer 4.25in (10.5cm) diam

£80-120   **BEV**

A Coalport quatrefoil-shaped cabinet teacup and saucer, with gilt interior, with panels of red with raised applied gilt with turquoise glazed dots, and hand-painted landscapes, with some wear.

Saucer 4.75in (12cm) wide

£80-120   **BAD**

A Copeland Spode cup and saucer, of scalloped form, with hand-painted and transfer-printed flowers inside and out, gilt scallop edged rim and reeded bodies, with printed mark and painted mark '571'.

Saucer 4.75in (12cm) diam

£40-60   **BEV**

A Davenport Imari-style hand-painted and transfer-printed teacup and saucer, with gilt highlights.

Imari is the name given to a type of porcelain made at Arita in Japan, and exported via the port of Imari. Cobalt blue, red and gilt are characteristic colours, often arranged in panels containing stylised natural motifs.

c1880s   Saucer 5.5in (14cm) diam

£60-80   **BEV**

A 1920s Crown Staffordshire teacup and saucer, with hand-painted and transfer-printed green mottled rim and pagoda on a cliff design, and with black handle.

Saucer 5.5in (14cm) diam

£30-35   **W&L**

A 1930s Royal Doulton hand-painted 'Aspen' pattern teacup and saucer.

The style of this tree, cliff and sea landscape was clearly inspired by Clarice Cliff's landscape patterns. However, note that the shape was not, being much more traditional.

5.25in (13.5cm) diam

£25-35   **BEV**

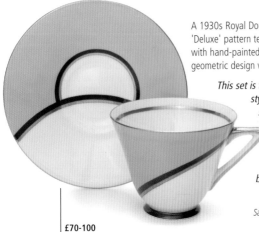

A 1930s Royal Doulton Art Deco 'Deluxe' pattern teacup and saucer, with hand-painted green and black geometric design with silver details.

This set is typically Art Deco in style, from the conical shape of the cup, to the angular handle and geometric pattern in light green and black and picked out in silver.

Saucer 5.5in (14cm) diam

£70-100   **BAD**

An Art Deco Fielding's Crown Devon fully hand-painted cup and saucer, decorated with arrows and sun design on a beige ground, the back with printed mark and painted 'A195'.

Saucer 4.5in (11.5cm) diam

£75-85   **BEV**

A Foley cup and saucer, with transfer-printed chintz pattern on a green ground, the base painted 'V1770' and printed 'English Bone China FB7 '.

c1932 5.5in (14cm) diam

£30-40   **BEV**

A Foley China octagonal cup and saucer, with blue transfer-printed pattern of urns and scrolling vines, the back with printed factory mark, painted '10024' and with registered no.447136 for December 1904.

c1895-97   5.25in (13.5cm) diam

£55-65   **W&L**

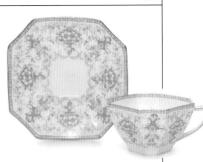

A CLOSER LOOK AT A ROYAL WINTON TEACUP AND SAUCER

A Foley Bone China 'Montrose' pattern teacup and saucer, with blue panels with pheasant and gold scrolling pattern, and sprays of pink roses, with shaped and gilded handle.

Saucer 5.75in (14.5cm) diam

£15-20   **W&L**

A Grafton China teacup and saucer, with hand-painted orange four-leaf clovers and clumps of primroses amid trees, the back with printed marks and painted '5432' pattern number.

5.5in (14cm) diam

£20-25   **W&L**

Royal Winton became renowned for their transfer-printed chintz wares after they developed a process allowing the transfer to be applied to a complex curving surface.

Chintzware was inspired by paisley and similar patterned textiles being imported during the 19thC. It enjoyed two heights of popularity, during the 1930s and the 1950s. The shape and mark can often help date a piece, with this ornate handle signifying an early date.

Hazel is a desirable and comparatively scarce pattern. Other patterns with black backgrounds include 'Black Crocus', 'Cromer' and James Kent's 'Florita'.

A 1930s Grimwades Royal Winton chintzware teacup and saucer, with transfer-printed 'Hazel' pattern and printed marks to reverse.

5.75in (14.5cm) diam

£55-65   **W&L**

An A.B. Jones & Sons Ltd Royal Grafton Bone China light blue transfer-printed cup and saucer, with scrolling rim, decorated with beige/gold diagonal leaf shapes containing sprays of pink and purple roses.

Saucer 5.5in (14cm) diam

£20-25   **W&L**

A Hammersley scalloped edge teacup and saucer, with ornate handle and transfer-printed and hand-painted scene of flowers in front of trellis, with printed marks to base.

6in (15cm) diam

£25-35   **W&L**

A Hammersley & Co. cylindrical coffee can and saucer, with floral gilt border and large pink roses.

1900-18   *Saucer 4.5in (11.5cm) diam*

£45-55   **BEV**

CERAMICS

A Haviland & Co. Limoges teacup and saucer, with moulded panels and transfer-printed blue cornflowers and corn ears.

1876-79   *Saucer 4.75in (12cm) diam*

£20-30   BEV

A George Jones & Sons 'Abbey 1790' blue and white transfer-printed teacup and saucer, with printed marks to reverse.

Saucer 5.75in (14.5cm) diam

£30-40   BEV

A C.T. Maling cup and saucer, with pink fringed gilt scrolls, transfer-printed pink roses, with printed tower mark and painted 'A3122/4'. c1895 Saucer

5.5in (14cm) diam

£30-50   BAD

A Midwinter Fashion shape cup and saucer, with transfer-printed 'Bali H'ai' pattern on saucer, designed by John Russell in 1960.

Saucer 4.75in (12cm) wide

£15-18   RET

A Noritake Imari-style teacup and saucer, decorated with orange chrysanthemums and foliage in panels, with gilt detailing, the back with printed leaf marks.

This is both an early mark and an early pattern based on traditional Japanese ceramics, but modified for Western tastes.

c1908   *Saucer 5.25in (13.5cm) diam*

£30-40   W&L

A Minton Haddon Hall pattern ribbed teacup and saucer, designed by John Wadworth, pattern B4451, with green vines with pink and blue flowers, with printed mark to back.

The double 'S' mark through the factory mark on the back indicates that this was a factory second. Other factories, such as Royal Doulton, score marks through with lines. Be aware of how factories identify seconds, as they will never be as desirable or valuable as first quality pieces in the same condition.

Saucer 4.5in (11.5cm) diam

£18-22   W&L

A 1980s Paragon teacup and saucer, with the transfer-printed and hand-painted 'Rockingham' pattern of floral sprays surrounded by a burgundy border with gold scrolling patterns.

6in (15cm) diam

£22-28   W&L

A Paragon double-handled teacup and saucer, with transfer-printed sprays of flowers in panels surrounded by gold flowers on a burgundy background, with scrolling patterns around, the back with printed marks.

c1939   5.75in (14cm) diam

£20-25   **W&L**

A CLOSER LOOK AT A SHELLEY CUP AND SAUCER

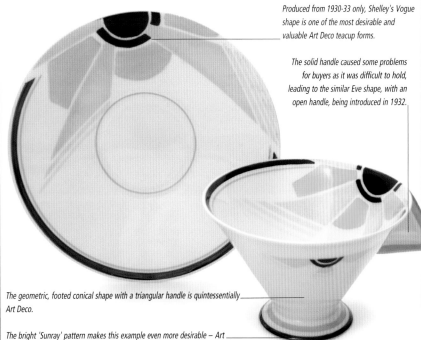

Produced from 1930-33 only, Shelley's Vogue shape is one of the most desirable and valuable Art Deco teacup forms.

The solid handle caused some problems for buyers as it was difficult to hold, leading to the similar Eve shape, with an open handle, being introduced in 1932.

The geometric, footed conical shape with a triangular handle is quintessentially Art Deco.

The bright 'Sunray' pattern makes this example even more desirable – Art Deco patterns on Art Deco shapes are highly sought after.

A 1930s Paragon Art Deco hand-painted china cup and saucer, decorated with yellow crocuses, the base with registration no.766514 for 1931.

Saucer 5.25in (13.5cm) diam

£30-40   **BEV**

A 1930s Shelley Art Deco Vogue shape teacup and saucer, with the hand-painted 'Sunray' pattern, no.11742, the base with printed factory mark and registered design no.756538 for 1930.

5.5in (14cm) diam

£80-120   **BEV**

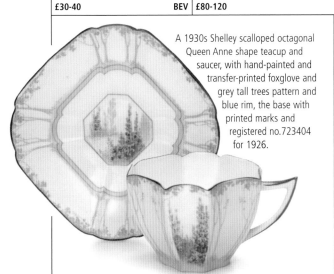

A 1930s Shelley scalloped octagonal Queen Anne shape teacup and saucer, with hand-painted and transfer-printed foxglove and grey tall trees pattern and blue rim, the base with printed marks and registered no.723404 for 1926.

This popular shape was produced from 1926-33, and again in the 1950s, and can be found with over 170 different patterns.

Saucer 5.25in (13.5cm) wide

£40-60   **BAD**

A 1920s-30s Rosenthal teacup and saucer, with the transfer-printed 'Donatello' pattern of flowers and a gilt scrolling border.

4.25in (11cm) diam

£55-65   **BEV**

An R.H. & S.L. Plant 'Tuscan China' teacup and saucer, with hand-painted and transfer-printed pattern of foxgloves, flowers and a garden wall.

5.5in (14cm) diam

£20-25   **W&L**

CERAMICS

An R.H. & S.L. Plant Ltd 'Tuscan China' trio set, decorated with a transfer-printed and hand-painted pattern of garlands and plums, with a black edged rim.

Saucer 6.75in (17cm) diam

£22-28 W&L

A late 1930s R.H. & S.L. Plant 'Tuscan China' teacup and saucer, with transfer-printed and hand-painted flowers and blue rim, the base with printed marks and registered no.771590 for 1932.

5.75in (14.5cm) diam

£20-25 W&L

A late 19thC H.M. Williamson & Sons 'Kaiser' pattern teacup and saucer, with hand-painted and transfer-printed scrolling and mottled pattern with blue, yellow and pink flowers, with 'W & Sons' printed marks.

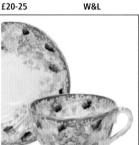

Saucer 5.25in (13.5cm) diam

£18-22 W&L

A Royal Worcester armorial cup and saucer, decorated with gilded panels containing a coat of arms, a monogram, butterflies and flower sprays, printed marks and date codes, the saucer with a restored stress crack.

1895   Saucer 6.25in (16cm) diam

£55-65 WW

A 1930s Sampson Smith Ltd 'Wetley China' cup and saucer, with hand-painted pattern of irises and blue rim, the back with printed marks and registered no.731211 for 1927.

Saucer 4.25in (11cm) diam

£30-50 BEV

A 1920s Royal Worcester cabinet teacup and saucer, with hand-painted flowers and transfer-printed green bows and flowers, with gilt interior, with printed factory mark.

Saucer 3.75in (9.5cm) diam

£80-120 BEV

A Royal Worcester teacup and saucer, pattern no.333, decorated with blue Classical panels and laurel rim.

Saucer 5in (13cm) diam

£30-40 W&L

QUICK REFERENCE

- Founded in 1815 by John Doulton, Martha Jones and John Watts in Lambeth, south London, Doulton initially produced utilitarian ceramics, such as chimney pots and pipes. The company began producing decorative wares from around 1871. Many of these pieces were designed and decorated by students from the nearby Lambeth School of Art. Look for the typical motifs and artists' monograms of notable artists, including Lambeth-trained sisters Florence and Hannah Barlow, and brothers Arthur and George Tinworth. These 'Doulton Lambeth' pieces included stoneware, which was often made in the Art Nouveau style, a 'faience' range, which featured naturalistic hand painting, and a 'Silicon' ware range.

- In 1877, Doulton took over the Pinder, Bourne & Co. factory in Burslem, Staffordshire, which produced earthenware and bone china. Its name was changed to Doulton and Company Ltd in 1882, and the company soon became known for fine porcelain. The title 'royal' was granted in 1901 by Edward VII and 'Royal Doulton' marks appeared in 1902. The Lambeth factory closed in 1956, but production continues at Burslem.

- The production of figures, for which Royal Doulton is now well known, took off in 1913, under the direction of modeller Charles Noke. These figures were all given an individual 'HN' number, after Harry Nixon, then manager of the painting department. More than 4,000 of these numbers have subsequently been assigned to different models and colourways, many of which were designed by Leslie Harradine. In general, the most desirable figures are those produced for a short time only, usually before WWII, particularly if finely modelled and in a rare colourway.

- Vases are often worth more than bowls or jardinières. Pairs are more desirable than singles or matched pairs. Those in a High Victorian style typical of the factory and period, like the piece shown bottom right, may be worth investing in as prices are lower than 10 years ago and quality is high.

- Condition is important, particularly with figures, as damage reduces value considerably, so check all over for chips, scratches and cracks. Over the past decade, value and demand for Doulton pieces have declined, though the finest pieces, particularly stoneware and very rare figurines, are still sought after. Now may, therefore, be a good time to buy, as a potential revival in the future would cause prices to rise.

A Doulton Lambeth stoneware ovoid vase, by Hannah Barlow, sgraffito-decorated with ponies and sheep in a landscape with oxide tint between repeat carved foliate borders in tan and tonal blue, impressed and incised marks.

10.5in (27cm) high

£600-900　　　　**FLD**

A Doulton Lambeth stoneware ovoid vase, by Hannah Barlow, sgraffito-decorated with ponies and sheep in a landscape setting, between carved foliate borders, with impressed and incised marks, restored neck.

10.5in (27cm) high

£200-300　　　　**FLD**

A pair of Doulton Lambeth stoneware pedestal vases, by Louisa Edwards, carved with a stylised Classical-inspired stiff leaf design within repeat borders, the base with impressed and incised marks.

11in (27.5cm) high

£500-700　　　　**FLD**

A Doulton Lambeth vase, by Hannah Barlow, sgraffito-decorated with a deep band of ponies and cattle with oxide glaze between carved borders with a repeat palmette design, impressed and incised marks.

11in (28cm) high

£600-900　　　　**FLD**

A Doulton Lambeth stoneware vase, by Elisa Simmance, incised and applied with scrolling flowers and foliage with beadwork decoration, the base with impressed mark, incised monogram, damaged.

18.5in (47cm) high

£150-200　　　　**WW**

CERAMICS

A pair of Doulton Lambeth stoneware vases, by Hannah Barlow, incised with a continuous band of horses between stiff and scrolling leaf collars, the bases with incised marks.

9.25in (23.5cm) high

£700-1,000   FLD

A pair of Doulton Lambeth waisted and footed vases, bearing monograms for Frank Butler, Ernest Bishop and Elizabeth Atkins, and incised '524' and '523', decorated with stylised, entwined foliage and flower heads.

1879   *10.25in (26cm) high*

£300-500   HALL

A CLOSER LOOK AT A DOULTON VASE

The vase was decorated by Hannah Barlow (1851-1916), who is celebrated for her lively and life-like animal designs.

Barlow used the sgrafitto technique, where a sharp point scratches a design into the wet clay – the body is then wiped with an oxide stain, which settles in the lines to highlight them.

It is an unusually large size, and would have cost a considerable sum in its day, making it rare today.

The price would have more than doubled if it was part of an original, matching pair.

A Doulton Lambeth stoneware floor vase, by Hannah Barlow, decorated with a deep sgraffito band of sheep in a highland setting with oxide tint between carved and tube-line foliate borders, the base with incised and impressed marks.

18in (46cm) high

£800-1,200   FLD

A pair of Doulton Lambeth stoneware vases, by Hannah Barlow, each incised with a continuous band of cows in pasture between stiff and scrolling leaf collars, the bases with incised marks.

9.25in (23.5cm) high

£700-1,000   FLD

A pair of Doutlon Lambeth vases, by George Tinworth, incised with scrolling and raised beads, on a shaded brown glaze, signed with initials on the body, one with a firing crack.

11.75in (30cm) diam

£600-800   SWO

A Victorian Doulton Lambeth stoneware vase, by Emily Stormer, decorated overall with raised rosettes, beading and stylised leaves, impressed marks and signature to base.

6in (15cm) high

£400-600   DUK

A Royal Doulton 'Brangwyn Ware' slender ovoid vase, designed by Frank Brangwyn, numbered 'D5081', incised with stylised leaves and buds, the base with printed mark, moulded '7936'.

Sir Frank William Brangwyn (1867-1956) was a progressive artist, illustrator, and designer, who was a member of the Royal Academy and the Royal Watercolour Society.

11.5in (29.5cm) high

£200-300   **DN**

A CLOSER LOOK AT A ROYAL DOULTON VASE

The Titanian range used titanium oxide to give a green or blue glaze ranging from light grey-blue to a deep royal blue – it is typically speckled, cloudy or streaked.

Birds are typical motifs, as are Oriental figures, and the treatment was used by Harry Tittensor, Harry Allen and other notable decorators.

This range was produced from 1915-c1930. Look out for Egpyptian motifs inspired by the discovery of Tutankhamun's tomb in 1922 as these fetch higher sums than birds.

Bases are generally marked with the factory mark and also the name of the range.

A Royal Doulton blue 'Titanian' cylindrical vase, decorated and gilded with a perched peacock and peahen, with printed mark to base.

10.25in (26cm) high

£400-600   **DA&H**

A Royal Doulton Veined Flambé vase, the ovoid body decorated with cobalt over red glazes, numbered '1622'.

15.75in (40cm) high

£150-250   **FLD**

A Royal Doulton porcelain twin-handled ovoid vase, with transfer-printed scene titled 'Ophelia', and printed factory mark to base.

8.25in (21cm) high

£70-100   **SAS**

A Royal Doulton bottle neck bulbous jug, of green ground with incised leaf decoration in brown and incised initials 'JB', with impressed mark to base with decorator's initials 'MVM'.

9in (23cm) high

£250-300   **LOC**

A Royal Doulton 'Titanian' vase, painted with a young coal tit on a green ground, signed 'H. Allen' for Harry Allen.

Although this example is hand-painted, not all Titanian wares were – many were transfer-printed and highlighted in gilt.

3.5in (9cm) high

£200-300   **LT**

CERAMICS

A Royal Doulton 'Titanian' large bowl, the mottled grey-green ground decorated with gilt exotic birds on branches of chrysanthemums, with jewelled rim with additional floral sprays.

14.5in (37cm) diam

£450-550   LT

A Royal Doulton plate, decorated with a portrait of an Art Nouveau maiden, the back with impressed and printed marks.

9.25in (23.5cm) diam

£70-100   WW

A Royal Doulton 'John Peel' loving cup, with fox and whip handles, numbered 293 from a limited edition of 500, moulded on one side with figures, on the other with hounds.

1923   9in (23cm) high

£400-600   BE

A Royal Doulton Robin Hood loving cup, designed by Charles Noke and Harry Fenton, numbered 393 from a limited edition of 600, relief decorated with scenes in Sherwood Forest, with printed marks to base.

Introduced in 1938, this was part of a range of limited edition jugs or cups produced from 1930-38.

8.5in (21.5cm) high

£650-750   LT

A Royal Doulton large 'Bacchus' character jug, D6499, designed by Max Henk, with rare City of Stoke-on-Trent Jubilee Year backstamp.

1959   7in (18cm) high

£700-1,000   TOV

A CLOSER LOOK AT A DOULTON CHARACTER JUG

This example can be identified as a prototype rather than a variation as the base is printed ' Design Original Sample and Decorating Sample 1' .

The handle on this prototype is modelled slightly differently to the production piece, and has the Flag of St. George to the reverse of the Union Jack.

The production model had a beige, not green, balaclava, the coat was brown not buff, and the face was painted differently.

Prices for trials and unique pieces have remained strong, despite the general downturn in the Doulton market.

A Royal Doulton prototype 'Captain Scott of the Antarctic' large character jug, similar to D7116, wearing olive green balaclava and buff coat, with printing to base.

7in (18cm) high

£3,000-5,000   LT

A Royal Doulton 'King Charles' figure, HN404, designed by Charles Noke and Harry Tittensor, with an unusual buff base, the base with printed green mark and initialled 'PS'.

Note the large size of this desirable figurine, which is valuable in all three of its variations.

1920-51 *16.75in (42.5cm) high*

£750-950 **TEN**

A Royal Doulton 'Sir Walter Raleigh' figure, HN1751, designed by Leslie Harradine, with printed marks to base.

1936-49 *12.25in (31cm) high*

£400-500 **A&G**

A Royal Doulton 'Vice Admiral Lord Nelson' figure, HN3489, designed by Alan Maslankowski, numbered 351 from a limited edition of 950, with certificate.

1993 *12.5in (31.5cm) high*

£500-700 **LT**

A Royal Doulton 'The Moor' large figurine, HN3642, with a flambé glaze, designed by Charles Noke in 1929.

1994-95 *17.25in (44cm) high*

£800-1,200 **FLD**

A CLOSER LOOK AT A ROYAL DOULTON FIGURINE

Figures produced for long periods of time are usually the most affordable and have also have fallen in value recently, as so many exist.

This example has a grey skirt, violet blouse and green and purple tartan shawl, all of which are different to the standard production model.

The biggest difference between this and the standard model is the fact that she is meant to be a balloon seller, but here she has no balloons.

She has a hairline crack to her skirt, but this does not deter collectors who are keen to collect as many rare variations as possible.

A Royal Doulton 'In the Stocks' figure, HN1474, designed by Leslie Harradine, some restoration.

1931-38 *5in (12.5cm) high*

£600-800 **LT**

A Royal Doulton 'Biddy Penny Farthing' figure, HN1843 without balloons, designed by Leslie Harradine (1938-present).

9in (23cm) high

£2,000-3,000 **LT**

CERAMICS

A Royal Doulton 'Pierette' figure, HN1749, designed by Leslie Harradine.

Although she can also be found with a red skirt, (HN1391), values are roughly the same.

1936-49   9.5in (24cm) high
£600-800   LT

A Royal Doulton protoype 'Charity' figure, HN3087, designed by Eric Griffiths, with a different purple blanket and yellow dress, Lawley's in a limited edition of 9,500 for the NSPCC.

1987   8.5in (21.5cm) high
£80-120   SAS

A Royal Doulton protoype 'Faith' figure, HN3082, designed by Eric Griffiths, with a different coloured pink and red coat, commissioned by Lawley's in a limited edition of 9,500 for the NSPCC.

8.5in (21.5cm) high
£80-120   SAS

A Royal Doulton 'Lambing Time' figure, HN1890, designed by W.M. Chance, with printed marks to base.

1938-81   9.25in (23.5cm) high
£35-45   SAS

A Royal Doulton 'Gandalf' figurine, HN2911, with blue cloak, designed by D. Lyttleton, from the Middle Earth series.

1980-84   7in (18cm) high
£40-60   PC

A Royal Doulton 'The Homecoming' figure, HN3295, and a 'Welcome Home' figure, HN3299, designed by A. Hughes from the Children of the Blitz series, both numbered 1944 from a limited edition of 9,500.
1990-91   Tallest 8.5in (21.5cm) high
£150-200   HT

A Royal Doulton 'The Boy Evacuee' figure, HN3202, and a 'The Girl Evacuee' figure, HN3203, designed by A. Hughes from the Children of the Blitz series, both numbered 7809 from a limited edition of 9,500.
1989   Tallest 8.25in (21cm) high
£250-350   HT

A Royal Doulton Archives Collection 'T'ang Horse' figurine, BA25, with flambé glaze, designed by Alan Maslankowski from a limited edition of 250 from the Burslem Artwares series.

2001   *10.5in (27cm) high*

£250-300   **FLD**

A Royal Doulton Archives Collection 'Hebei Goat', BA36, in a flambé glaze, designed by Alan Maslankowski from a limited edition of 250 from the Burslem Artwares Collection.

2002   *10.5in (26.5cm) high*

£200-250   **FLD**

QUICK REFERENCE - DOULTON FLAMBÉ GLAZE

The ancient Chinese 'sang-de-boeuf' glaze was much admired by John Slater and Charles Noke, who attempted to copy it in the 1890s. Cuthbert Bailey joined Doulton in 1901 and Bernard Moore, in 1902. Together they made a breakthrough and their results won prizes when first exhibited at the St Louis World's Fair in 1904, and the glaze is still popular and desirable today. Animals are highly sought after, particularly those designed by Noke. This is the largest elephant from a series of three, and also the most valuable.

A Royal Doulton frog, with a flambé Sung glaze, mottled crimson, green, yellow glazes, impressed '1162'.

The Sung glaze is highly sought after, particularly in combination with the flambé glaze. This shape is different from the standard frog numbered HN1162, more closely resembling HN905. This combination also suggests an early date.

4.5in (11.5cm) wide

£3,200-3,800   **LT**

A Royal Doulton large elephant, HN1121, with flambé glaze and trunk down, designed by Charles Noke.

c1938-57   *13in (33cm) wide*

£2,000-3,000   **LT**

A Royal Doulton 'Lop Eared Rabbit', HN1165B, with flambé and Sung glazes, the base impressed '1165B' and dated.

1923   *4in (10cm) long*

£3,000-4,000   **LT**

A Royal Doulton 'Bulldog with Tam O'Shanter & Haversack', HN153, designed by an unknown modeller, and with khaki glaze and printed registered no.663408 for 1918, one fore paw re-glued and chipped.

A Royal Doulton 'Lion on rock' figurine, HN2641, designed by Charles Noke from the Prestige series.

1952-92   *10.25in (26cm) wide*

£150-250   **FLD**

The values for these wartime commemoratives have fallen, and continue to do so, as highly accurate, very good quality reproductions are being made. Look out for the examples in the Titanian glaze, as values for these are holding strong.

1918-c1925

£250-300   **DN**

CERAMICS

QUICK REFERENCE

- The Fulper Pottery Co. was founded in 1814 in Flemington, New Jersey by Samuel Hill. It operated until 1935, when it was acquired by Stangl. It initially produced utilitarian wares, introducing art pottery in 1909. Wares were slip-moulded and Fulper became renowned for its varied range of rich glazes.
- Their first art pottery line, produced from 1909 until WWI, was known as 'Vasecraft'. Many forms were Germanic in their solid and architectural feel, and glazes were of a particularly high quality. Production from this early period is usually the most sought-after and valuable.
- After c1914, shapes became more curved, with inspiration drawn from Oriental forms. Glaze quality began to deteriorate gradually, particularly during the late 1920s. From the late 1920s until the factory closed, the Art Deco movement influenced forms, and glazes were of considerably poorer quality.
- Bodies also became lighter in weight over time, and although heavy examples are not always better quality, light examples are almost always lower quality. Always consider the glaze as every piece was glazed by a skilled decorator, making each unique. The more complex and interesting the glaze and shape, the better the piece is likely to be.

A Fulper corseted two-handled vase, with frothy Copperdust Crystalline glaze over Flemington Green flambé, with vertical mark.

9.5in (24cm) high

£250-350   **DRA**

A Fulper two-handled vase, covered in Copperdust Crystalline and Mirrored Black flambé glaze, with paper label over vertical mark.

9.75in (25cm) high

£350-450   **DRA**

A Fulper two-handled urn, of hammered texture covered in frothy Chinese Blue and Amber flambé glaze, with horizontal mark and '490'.

12.5in (32cm) high

£500-700   **DRA**

A large Fulper bullet vase, covered with a dripped Cat's Eye flambé glaze, the base with factory mark.

10in (25.5cm) high

£250-350   **DRA**

A Fulper baluster vase, covered in a fine frothy Cucumber Matt glaze, with vertical mark.

12in (30.5cm) high

£700-900   **DRA**

A Fulper melon-shaped vase, covered in a Cat's Eye flambé glaze, with vertical mark.

7in (18cm) high

£300-400 DRA

An early Fulper lamp base, covered in Mouse Grey to blue flambé glaze, the base with '17' ink stamp.

Fulper lamps were only made for a short period from c1910-15, making them scarce today. They were produced under the strictest production standards, meaning quality was high. Lamps with their original shades with glass inserts are particularly prized, even more so if they have geometric or natural motifs.

17.25in (44cm) high

£800-1,200 DRA

A large Fulper squat vessel, covered in brown crystalline glaze dripping over Mustard Matt, small chip to foot ring, with vertical mark.

10in (25.5cm) wide

£800-1,200 DRA

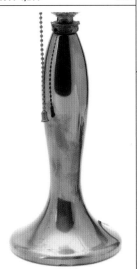

A rare Fulper factory lamp base, in Cat's Eye flambé glaze, with vertical mark and numbered '107'.

11.25in (28.5cm) high

£300-400 DRA

A CLOSER LOOK AT A FULPER VASE

At 16in (40.5cm) high, this is a large piece, with superb visual impact.

The form was inspired by Chinese ceramics, and can be dated to a period from the late 1910s to the mid-1920s.

Fulper is known for its complex, specially produced glazes that vary from being 'mirrored' to mottled to micro-crystalline – the former and the latter effects are particularly desirable.

Although some examples from this period do not bear the highest quality glazes, this example is very well-glazed.

A tall Fulper ovoid vase, covered in Cucumber Crystalline glaze, the base with raised racetrack mark.

16in (40.5cm) high

£1,500-2,500 DRA

A Fulper cat figure, in White Matt glaze, with horizontal mark.

8.5in (21.5cm) high

£500-700 DRA

CERAMICS

QUICK REFERENCE – HORNSEA

Hornsea Pottery was founded by Colin and Desmond Rawson in a large house in East Riding, Yorkshire in 1949. In 1954, the successful pottery moved into an old brick factory. Around this time, they also began to employ designers, including John Clappison, the son of an investor in the company. Hornsea's success grew into the 1960s with ranges such as 'Home Decor' (introduced 1960-62), 'Slipware' (introduced 1963), 'Heirloom' (1967-87), and others, all designed by Clappison, who was appointed chief designer in 1958 and continued to be so until the company closed in 1984. Some ranges, such as 'Heirloom', were so successful that the many examples on the market mean that prices are low. Rarer ranges and unusual colourways or shapes tend to fetch higher prices.

A mid-late 1960s Hornsea grey glazed 'Slipware' jardiniere, designed by John Clappison in 1963, the base with printed mark.

10in (25.5cm) wide

£70-100   GC

A mid-late 1960s Hornsea Mustard glazed 'Slipware' jardiniere, designed by John Clappison in 1963, the base with printed mark.

10in (25.5cm) wide

£70-100   GC

A mid-late 1960s Hornsea mauve glazed 'Slipware' baluster vase, designed by John Clappison in 1963, the base with printed mark.

Always examine these appealing period pieces all over as the glaze can craze easily, and small chips or glaze flakes are often found on the rim or base. Both factors devalue a piece considerably.

9.25in (23.5cm) high

£60-80   GC

A mid-late 1960s Hornsea light green glazed 'Slipware' baluster vase, designed by John Clappison in 1963, the base with printed mark.

7.5in (19cm) high

£40-60   GC

A mid-late 1960s Hornsea light blue glazed 'Slipware' squat baluster vase, designed by John Clappison in 1963, the base with printed mark.

4in (10cm) high

£20-30   GC

A small Hornsea pottery 'White Bud' jardinière, from the Home Decor range designed by John Clappison c1961, with moulded spot design.

9.5in (24cm) wide

£35-45   SAS

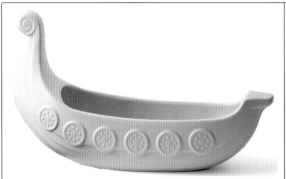

A Hornsea Pottery dish, in the form of a Viking longboat, from the Home Decor range designed by John Clappison c1961, with a cream glaze and printed Studiocraft marks.

c1965 · 11in (28cm) wide

£50-70 **MHT**

A Hornsea Pottery 'Coastline' pattern sugar bowl, with white crackle glaze on a black ground.

The curving asymmetric form is typical of the 1950s, and the pattern is very similar to the 'Cortina' range released in 1955 by West German factory Jasba.

c1957 · 3.35 in (8.5cm) high

£18-22 **PC**

A Hornsea Pottery cruet set on tray, comprising a salt and pepper shaker, mustard pot and oil bottle, lacking mustard-spoon, the base with black printed factory marks.

9in (23cm) long

£40-50 **RET**

A Hornsea black and white cruet set, on a black dish, designed by John Clappison.

c1962 · 5.25in (13.5cm) high

£10-15 **TCM**

A Hornsea Pottery tapering vase with moulded stylised foliate design on a grey ground, with printed Hornsea mark, and impressed '422'.

6.75in (17cm) high

£28-32 **RET**

A late 1960s Hornsea Pottery 'Springtime' pattern white square box with beige impressed flower design and turquoise lid, designed by John Clappison in 1964, the base impressed '280', and with printed factory and 'SPRINGTIME' marks.

3.25in (8cm) high

£18-22 **RET**

A rare 1960s Hornsea Pottery 'Studiocraft' waisted vase, designed by John Clappison in 1966, with screen-printed stylised leaves and printed marks to base.

This is a very rare range and is not connected with the earlier Studio Craft range of 1960-62.

7.75in (19.5cm) high

£40-60 **RET**

CERAMICS

QUICK REFERENCE

- Addis Emmett Hull founded the A.E. Hull Pottery in Crooksville, Ohio in 1905. Initially he produced utilitarian stonewares, and from 1907, dinnerwares, following the purchase of the Acme Pottery Co. Although some decorative vases were produced in the 1920s, it is the colourful matte glazed art pottery introduced in the 1930s that is collected today.

- Using moulds, wares were mass-produced with floral patterns. Although gloss glazes were produced, glazes are typically soft and matte, and were sprayed on to give a graduated effect. Colours are typically light and pastel-based, although a vibrant pink is commonly found.

- In 1950, the pottery burnt down and was rebuilt, opening again in 1952. The new machinery could not replicate the matte glazes, so the company was forced to concentrate on gloss glazes. By the late 1970s, the focus of production had moved to dinnerware, which was made until the company closed in 1986.

- Look out for well-moulded forms with even, graduated effects to the glazes. Glazes should be free of crazing. Inspect pieces all-over for any damage such as cracks or chips as this reduces value considerably. Pieces produced before 1950 tend to be the most desirable, with sought-after ranges including 'Calla Lily', 'Woodland' and 'Tokay'.

A Hull 'Water Lily' pattern double-handled vase, in pink and green, marked 'Hull Art USA L-4-6 1/2'.

6.75in (17cm) high

£30-40   BEL

A Hull 'Magnolia' pattern matte graduated pink and blue double handled urn vase, the base molded 'Hull Art U.S.A. 46 1/4'.

6.5in (16.5cm) high

£30-40   AEM

A Hull 'Calla Lily' pattern graduated light green and cream glazed vase, the base marked '340/33-6'.

6.25in (16cm) high

£70-90   BEL

A Hull pink 'Magnolia' pattern vase, with blue flowers, the base impressed 'H-13-10 1/2'.

11in (28cm) high

£30-40   TSIS

A Hull 'Magnolia' pattern matte glazed cornucopia, the base marked 'Hull Art USA 19-8 1/2"'.

8.75in (22cm) high

£20-30   BEL

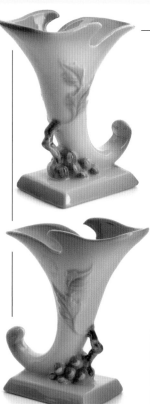

A CLOSER LOOK AT A HULL LITTLE RED RIDING HOOD BUTTER DISH

A range of Little Red Riding Hood items was produced during the 1940s and early 50s, including a lamp, salt and pepper shakers and the famous cookie jar.

This range is very popular and fakes are known – these are often made from a brighter white ceramic, and have larger flower transfers and more heavily applied gilt, than originals.

The butter dish, with Little Red Riding Hood appearing to curtsey, is among the rarest items in the range.

Look out for different transfers on this range as the value can be affected – poinsettia transfers are particularly desirable and valuable.

A very rare Hull Little Red Riding Hood butterdish, the base marked 'Pat. Des. No. 135889'.

Most pieces from this range were made by Hull and decorated by Royal China (part of Regal China), before being sent back to Hull for sale, but Regal also produced examples themselves.

7in (17.5cm) long

£300-400   **BB**

A pair of Hull 'Tokay' pattern gloss glazed cornucopia vases, the bases impressed 'Tokay U.S.A.'.

The 'Tokay' range, with its grapes and moulded vine-like handles, was introduced in 1958.

6.25in (16cm) high

£50-70   **AEM**

A Hull double handled urn vase, with green dripped glaze, the base unmarked.

This is a typical Arts & Crafts form and glaze.

4.75in (12cm) high

£50-70   **TSIS**

A Hull 'Water Lily' pattern flower pot with attached saucer, the base marked 'Hull Art USA L-25-5 3/4"', in mint condition.

5.75in (14.5cm) high

£30-50   **BEL**

A Hull 'Tokay' pattern pink and green glazed fruit bowl, the base marked '7 Tokay USA', with restored rim.

9.75in (24.5cm) wide

£30-50   **BEL**

A rare Hull 'Little Red Riding Hood' teapot, with transfer-printed daisy and poppy pattern and gilt and hand-painted detailing, the base moulded 'U.S.A.'.

1943-57   *8in (20cm) long*

£200-250   **BB**

QUICK REFERENCE

- Italian ceramics of the 1950s and 1960s have risen in popularity in recent years, and are colourful and relatively affordable. They can be found anywhere from car boot sales to specialist auctions, and prices range from a few pounds to over £2,000. The highest prices tend to be paid for pieces by notable designers such as Guide Gambone (1909-1969) and Marcello Fantoni (b.1915).

- After WWII Italy enjoyed an influx of money and a renewal of confidence that caused a boom in many industries. A large number of potteries produced affordable decorative ceramics for export. Forms were moulded, but decorated by hand. Colours are typically bright with abstract, stylised designs, and the influence of contemporary modern art can be seen in geometric and figurative patterns.

- Shapes included vases, lampbases, dishes and bowls and, depending on the quality and price, were sold in a range of

shops from discount outlets to high end department stores such as Macy's or Heal's. Distributors included Raymor in the US and Hutcheson & Son Ltd in the UK. Many distributors applied their own labels to pieces.

- Look out for well-formed, well-decorated examples that show skill in execution and detail in design. Colours and patterns should be representative of the period and style. Larger pieces are usually worth more, particularly if they are well made, and damage reduces value dramatically.

- Currently, very little is known about the majority of designers or factories. Bases are marked only 'Italy' followed by a number, possibly indicating the pattern, shape, or order number. Many names indicate towns, with these pieces being sold as tourist souvenirs. Bitossi's 'Rimini Blue' range, designed by Aldo Londi in 1953, is currently popular with collectors, particularly animal forms.

A 1950s-60s Italian vase with hand-painted multi-coloured squares and random white streaks on a textured pink ground, the base painted 'ITALY 6801'

8in (20.5cm) high

£40-60   GC

A 1950s-60s Italian vase with hand-painted multi-coloured squares and random white streaks on a textured light blue ground, the base painted 'ITALY 6514'

9in (23cm) high

£60-80   GC

A 1950s-60s Italian large conical vase, the body decorated with a panel of a sgraffito design of a stylised musician, the top and base covered with a beige lava-like glaze, the base inscribed 'Sestri Levante'.

A 1950s-60s Italian floor vase, hand-painted with lozenges in different colours, the base painted 'ITALY 40/200 56'.

16.25in (41cm) high

£60-80   M20C

A 1950s-60s Italian large bottle vase, the body decorated with a sgraffito design of stylised people, the top and base covered with a beige lava-like glaze, the base inscribed 'Sestri Levante'.

16.25in (41.5cm) high

£150-200   GC

Sestri Levante is a seaside resort and fishing port on the Italian Riviera. It is likely that these bottles were tourist souvenirs.

15.75in (40cm) high

£150-200   GC

A 1960s Italian vase, with hand-painted stylised flowers or peacock feather eyes, and trefoil rim, the base painted 'ITALY 5Z'.

9.75in (24.5cm) high

£60-80   **GC**

A 1950s Italian vase, hand-painted and sgraffito image of two women, the base painted 'ITALY 692'.

The asymmetric shape is typically 1950s. The figures are very similar to those used by Marcello Fantoni, as seen on the vase above.

12in (30.5cm) high

£60-100   **GROB**

A CLOSER LOOK AT A FANTONI VASE

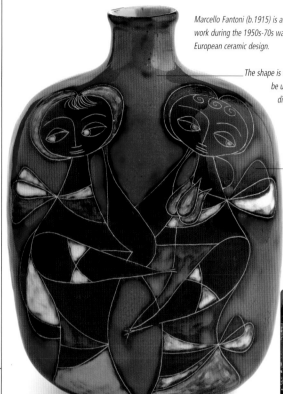

Marcello Fantoni (b.1915) is an important Italian ceramicist whose work during the 1950s-70s was particularly influential on European ceramic design.

The shape is clean-lined and modern, and although it can be used as a vase, it is primarily intended as a display piece.

The angular figural design is typical of Fantoni's work and Italian pottery of the period, with its inscribed sgraffito outlines and brightly glazed geometric shapes.

It is signed on the base, but is unlikely to have been made by Fantoni himself – the company produced a large number of ceramics that were exported widely, including to the US via Raymor.

An Italian Fantoni bottle vase, with a sgraffito and glazed gossiping women design on a glossy red glazed background, with turquoise glazed interior, the base painted 'Fantoni Italy', with hairline crack to rim.

6.75in (17cm) high

£300-500   **W&W**

A 1960s-70s Italian Bitossi green glazed footed cylindrical vase, impressed with geometric and runic symbols, the base painted '711 ITALY'

10in (25cm) high

£40-60   **RET**

A 1950s-70s Italian blue glazed torpedo vase, impressed with geometric symbols, probably by Bitossi.

10in (25cm) high

£40-60   **RET**

A 1960s-70s Italian Bitossi dark blue glazed low vase, impressed with geomtric and runic symbols, the base painted 'H-67/72 ITALY'.

£20-30   **RET**

CERAMICS

A 1950s Italian jug, with diagonally ribbed body, applied angled handle, textured white glaze and hand-painted yellow and brown design of umbrellas, leaping stags and baskets of flowers amid sprigs of leaves and star shapes, the base painted '6057 ITALY'.

9.25in (23cm) high

£30-40 **PC**

A CLOSER LOOK AT A CANTAGALLI DISH

Cantagalli was founded by Ulisse Cantagalli (1839-1901) in Florence in 1877 and is renowned for its reproductions of 16thC maiolica and other historic ceramics.

The curving, asymmetric shape, which is made more asymmetric with the addition of two small feet, is typical of 1950s forms.

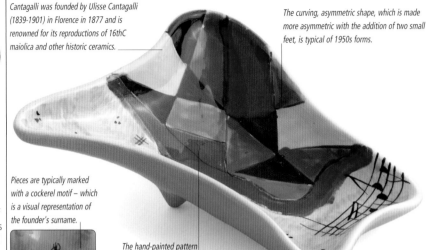

Pieces are typically marked with a cockerel motif – which is a visual representation of the founder's surname.

The hand-painted pattern includes multi-coloured geometric shapes, reminiscent of a harlequin, and musical notes – both are typical 1950s motifs.

A 1950s Italian Cantagalli dish, with hand-painted harlequin and musical notes pattern, the back with painted cockerel mark.

6.25in (16cm) longest

£30-40 **PC**

A 1950s-60s Italian clown jug, with applied handle and strap, the base painted '14708/162/1' and stamped 'MADE IN ITALY'.

Cheerful novelty designs such as this are popular with collectors.

3.5in (9cm) high

£20-30 **MA**

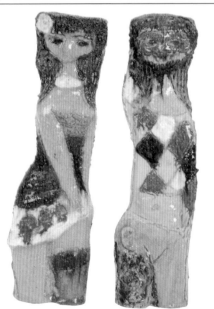

A pair of Italian Fantoni for Raymor figural abstract vases, modelled as a man and woman with hand-modelled features picked out in bright polychrome glazes, the base with hand-painted marks.

11.5in (29.5cm) high

£800-1,200 **FLD**

A 1950s-60s Italian jug, with multi-coloured spots, applied white knobbles, blue glazed interior and gilt details, the base painted '14794/27E ITALY'.

This is probably from a factory in or around Deruta.

8in (20.5cm) high

£18-22 **RET**

A 1950s-60s Italian Bitossi 'Rimini Blu' bull, designed by Aldo Londi in 1953, impressed with runic and geometric motifs and covered with a blue-green glaze.

This form is not part of the animal range still being made by Bitossi today.

12in (30.5cm) long

£180-200 **GC**

QUICK REFERENCE – LLADRO

Lladro was founded in Spain in 1953, and has since produced over 4,000 different designs. Elongated figurines, decorated in pastel colours with a high gloss glaze are typical. 'Gres' is similar to the earthy tones of stoneware, and comprises a sub-range of its own. Until 1971, when the blue printed mark was introduced, impressed or incised marks were used. Beware of fakes, with one key indicator being that Lladro never uses black for eyes. Look out for small limited editions, or models that were only produced for a short period of time. Similarly, retired models are likely to fetch higher values.

A Lladro 'Nurse' porcelain figure, no.4603, designed by Salvador Furío, in excellent condition.

1970-90   *15.75in (40cm) high*

£60-80   **SAS**

A Lladro 'Nuns' porcelain figure, no.4611, designed by Fulgencia García, in excellent condition.

1970-2005   *13in (33cm) high*

£35-45   **SAS**

A Lladro 'Woman with dog' porcelain figure, no.4761, designed by Vincente Martínez, in excellent condition.

1971-94   *13.75in (35cm) high*

£120-180   **SAS**

A Lladro 'Hawaiian Flower Vendor' Gres figure, no.2154, designed by Jose Puché, in excellent condition.

1985-2001   *11in (28cm) high*

£100-150   **SAS**

A Lladro 'Monks at Prayer' Gres figure, no.5155, designed by Salvador Debón, in excellent condition.

1982-2003   *14.5in (37cm) high*

£60-80   **SAS**

A Lladro 'Couple From The Arctic' Gres figure, no.2038, designed by Juan Herta, in excellent condition.

1971-2000   *13in (33cm) high*

£100-150   **SAS**

A Lladro 'Typical Peddler' porcelain figure, no.4859, designed by Salvador Furío, in excellent condition.

1974-85   *10.25in (26cm) high*

£150-200   **SAS**

QUICK REFERENCE

- The Lotus Pottery was founded in Devon by Michael and Elizabeth Skipwith in 1958 after they met at the Leeds College of Art. Initially known as Loversal Pottery, after Michael's birthplace in Doncaster, the couple changed the name when they moved to Old Stoke Farm in Stoke Gabriel in Devon. Although some decorative wares were made, the mainstay of production was kitchen and tablewares.

- By 1968, a number of glazes were in use, the most popular of which was the then-fashionable olive green shown here. Patterns differed widely and were based on natural themes, with the stylised daisy being the most popular, and the most common today. Other glazes included 'Dartside Green', white on red, and the blue on white 'Loire' range introduced in 1974. Look out for unusual glazes and patterns, as these tend to be popular.

- Bulls and larger decorative wares tend to fetch the highest prices, with tableware being generally affordable – few items fetch over £80 and most are under £30. Look out for the 'Alpine' range, decorated in sage green at the top and white at the bottom and inside. Introduced in 1966, it was accepted for the Design Council's Index of British Design.

- Most examples are marked around the base with the impressed 'LP' pottery monogram, although this is rarely found on the smallest pieces. The company prospered in the early 1970s, but suffered from increased competition from other potteries later in the decade. The Lotus Pottery closed in 1982, but Michael and Elizabeth Skipwith continued to pot individually.

A Lotus Pottery medium sized bull, designed by Elizabeth Skipwith, with a pattern of repeated g's or circles with curves on an olive green glaze, and with moulded hair to head.

Note the moulded hair on this example – not all Lotus bulls have this feature.

9in (22.5cm) long

£30-40　　　　　　　　　　　　　　　M20C

A Lotus Pottery small bull, designed by Elizabeth Skipwith, with mottled cream circle design on an olive green glaze.

6in (15cm) long

£20-30　　　　　　　　　　　　　　　DSC

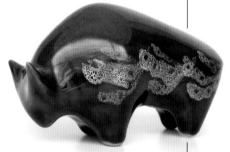

A Lotus Pottery small bull, designed by Elizabeth Skipwith, with a hand-painted foliate seaweed-like design on an olive green glaze.

3in (7.5cm) high

£10-15　　　　　　　　　　　　　　　M20C

A Lotus Pottery small bull, designed by Elizabeth Skipwith, with a cream flower on an olive green glossy glaze.

5in (12.5cm) long

£20-25　　　　　　　　　　　　　　　M20C

A Lotus Pottery large bull, designed by Elizabeth Skipwith, with star-like stylised flower on an olive green glaze.

12.75in (32.5cm) long

£50-70　　　　　　　　　　　　　　　M20C

QUICK REFERENCE – LOTUS POTTERY BULLS

The bull is the most collectable and best-loved form produced by the pottery. It was made from the late 1960s to the mid-1970s in four different sizes from 5in (12.5cm) long to 13in (32.5cm) long. Stylised bulls in general from this period have become highly desirable. Lotus bulls can be differentiated from those produced by Bitossi, Beswick (see p41) and other makers by their glazes and bulky form, even though they are typically unmarked. This is a very unusual and scarce glaze that recalls patterns used by Briglin (see p43). If it was in a more common glaze, such as the typical flower on an olive ground, the value would be around £20-30.

A Lotus Pottery bird figurine, with mottled cream flower on an olive green glaze.

This is a rare shape, and very similar to 'folk art' pottery whistles produced in US states such as Pennsylvania by early settlers.

6.25in (16cm) high

£30-40   DSC

A Lotus Pottery medium sized bull, designed by Elizabeth Skipwith, with wax-resist spirals and a cream glaze.

6.25in (16cm) long

£30-40   M20C

A Lotus Pottery vase, with a mottled cream flower on an olive green glaze, the side with impressed marks.

8in (20cm) high

£25-35   DSC

A Lotus Pottery triangular dish, with stylised flower motif on a glossy olive glaze.

4.5in (11.5cm) wide

£7-10   RET

A Lotus Pottery salt shaker, with mottled cream flower on an olive green glaze.

3.25in (8cm) high

£3-5   DSC

A Lotus Pottery pebble-shaped sugar sifter, with mottled cream flower on an olive green glaze, the centre with holes.

3.5in (8cm) diam

£8-12   DSC

QUICK REFERENCE

- The eccentric Martin Brothers are best known for their pottery bird-shaped jars, which can fetch anything from around £10,000 upwards at auction today. As well as these, they also produced salt-glazed stoneware pottery, including vases, jugs and dishes, which can be more affordable. Damage and restoration reduces values considerably, with pieces often being available for under £1,000.
- Robert Wallace Martin founded his first pottery in the 1860s, making terracotta sculpture. In 1873, he opened a new pottery in Fulham, London with his brothers Charles, Walter and Edwin. In 1877, they moved to Southall where most of their work was produced. The pottery prospered producing Gothic Revival style wares until the 1910s when deaths in the family left it foundering, until it closed in 1915.
- Look for the complex, unusual and sometimes 'grotesque' patterns and forms based on natural and mythological themes for which the brothers are best known. Robert Wallace was responsible for most of the grotesque figural jars and face jugs, Charles managed the business, Walter brought technical expertise, particularly with glazes, and Edwin was the thrower and decorator, having previously worked at Doulton.
- The brothers often signed the pieces they were responsible for, and most pieces are also dated. Marks can also help date pieces. From 1873-74 marks included the Fulham address, from 1874-78 the mark was simply 'London', from 1878-79 it was 'Southall', and from 1879-1915 it included 'London' and 'Southall'. The word 'Bros' or 'Brothers' was used after 1882.

A Martin Brothers stoneware miniature vase, incised and painted with blossom in white and brown on a buff ground, the base incised 'Martin London'.

2.25in (6cm) high

£350-450 WW

A Martin Brothers stoneware vase, by Robert Wallace Martin, with flowering plants, the base incised 'R W Martin & Bros., London & Southall 2.1886', extensive cracking.

Undamaged this vase may have fetched over three times as much.

1886 9.5in (24cm) high

£280-320 DN

A Martin Brothers stoneware vase, incised with scrolling foliage, painted in shades of brown and ochre, incised '9-1890, Martin Bros, London & Southall', cracked.

8.5in (21.5cm) high

£500-700 WW

A pair of early Martin Brothers stoneware vases, by Robert Wallace Martin, incised with simple foliage and berries on a banded design, incised 'R W Martin Southall, 1878', hairline crack to one, repair to rim of other.

1878 10in (25.5cm) high

£600-900 WW

A tall Martin Brothers stoneware vase, of slender form, incised and painted with simple grasses, the base incised 'Martin Bros, London & Southall, 10-1903', hairline crack to top rim.

1903 9.25in (23.5cm) high

£300-500 WW

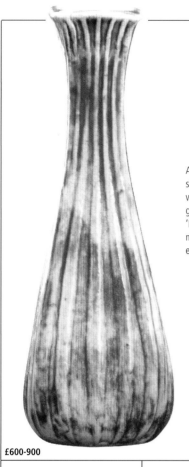

A Martin Brothers ribbed stoneware gourd vase, with mottled green glazes, the base incised 'Martinware Southall', minor restoration to exterior of top rim.

9in (23cm) high

£600-900   **WW**

A CLOSER LOOK AT A MARTIN BROTHERS JUG

The decoration is typical in terms of its concern with the Medieval 'grotesque', as well as the Far and Middle Eastern influences seen in the curling arabesques.

As well as being well-potted, the inscribed and painted design is extremely well-executed.

Although jugs are less popular than vases, particularly birds and figural forms, they are becoming more sought after as prices for the best pieces continue to rise.

It dates from 1895, which can be considered a highpoint of the brothers' output.

A Martin Brothers square section stoneware dragon jug, each side incised and painted with a ferocious dragon on an ochre ground, the base incised 'Martin Brothers London & Southall, 4-1895', professional restoration to the top rim.

1895   *9.75in (24.5cm) high*

£2,000-3,000   **WW**

A large Martin Brothers footed vase, with a tall collar neck incised with humming birds and lilies over a tonal blue ground, incised mark and date to base, restored.

1898   *12.5in (32cm) high*

£300-500   **FLD**

A small Martin Brothers stoneware bottle vase, incised with a ruffle shoulder band in green with a blue neck and brown body, the base incised 'Martin London'.

5in (12.5cm) high

£300-500   **DN**

A Martin Brothers stoneware vase, by Robert Wallace Martin, of lobed form with four cylindrical necks, incised with weave decoration, the base incised 'R W Martin D38', chips.

6in (15cm) high

£400-600   **WW**

A Martin Brothers stoneware jug, incised with finches flying and resting in boughs, incised 'R W Martin & Bros, London & Southall, 1-1887', restored base rim.

1887   *8.75in (22cm) high*

£400-600   **WW**

CERAMICS

QUICK REFERENCE

- William Moorcroft (1872–1945) began working as a designer at James MacIntyre & Company, Burslem in 1897, and was promoted to Manager of Ornamental Ware in 1898. His first designs were the 'Florian' and 'Aurelian' ranges, typified by their complex Moorish-inspired symmetrical patterns of natural themes including leaves and flowers. Highly stylised, they are typical of the Art Nouveau style prevalent at the time.

- Moorcroft's hand-thrown shapes were decorated with a tube-lining process, where an outline of liquid clay was piped onto the surface and then filled with liquid glaze. After great success, Moorcroft left MacIntyre in 1912 in order to found his own company with backing from London retailer Liberty. His success continued and, in 1929, Moorcroft was awarded the Royal Warrant.

- Colours are typically rich and deep, and patterns continued to be inspired by the natural world, although as the Art Nouveau style went out of fashion new ranges were created. After William's death, his son Walter took over and continued many of his father's designs, as well as introducing some of his own.

- The most desirable and valuable ranges tend to be early, from 1900–20s, and include 'Florian', 'Aurelian' and any of the landscape or mushroom patterns. However, more modern ranges produced by designers including Sally Tuffin (at Moorcroft from 1986–92) and Rachel Bishop (joined 1993) are also growing in value on the 'secondary market', particularly if they are from a limited edition or in an unusual colour or pattern variation.

- Patterns produced for long periods tend to be the most affordable, particularly if the piece is small. The pattern, shape, size and type of marks on the base can help to date a piece, and always examine the entire body for signs of damage.

A Macintyre & Co. 'Aurelian' pattern part tea service, designed by William Moorcroft, comprising a hot water jug, two plates, three saucers and five cups, the bases with registration no.314901 for 1898, and 308931 for 1897.

c1899   *Jug 5.75in (14.5cm) high*

£250-350   **DN**

A Moorcroft 'Flamminian' pattern small baluster vase, for Liberty & Co., designed by William Moorcroft, the red ground with foliate roundels, with incised signature and printed marks.

1906-1913   *4.75in (14.5cm) high*

£200-300   **DN**

A Macintyre & Co. twin-handled jar, with blue Forget-me-not flower pattern, designed by William Moorcroft, printed mark, missing lid.

c1903   *4.25in (11cm) high*

£70-100   **SAS**

A MacIntyre & Co. miniature vase, with the 'Poppy' design, designed by William Moorcroft, the base impressed '28', and brown printed 'MacIntyre' mark and 'WM' in green.

Probably produced from c1910-20 as salesman's samples, miniatures are very rare and desirable. The idea was revived in the 1970s, but backstamps and patterns differ. These later pieces are worth from around a tenth of this value.

           2.25in (6cm) high

£1,000-1,500   **SWO**

An MacIntyre & Co. Florian ware 'Seaweed' pattern biscuit barrel and cover, designed by William Moorcroft, the base with script 'WM' mark.

c1902   *6.25in (16cm) high*

£300-500   **SWO**

QUICK REFERENCE – POMEGRANATE

'Pomegranate' was designed by William Moorcroft and introduced in 1910. Along with 'Pansy', introduced a year later, it marked a sea-change in Moorcroft's designs. Background colours were mottled and merged together, and motifs were limited to one area of the piece, usually arranged in a band around the body – often the shoulder. First retailed by Liberty & Co., it became Moorcroft's most successful design by the 1920s, sold around the world. Examples made from 1910-c1919 had yellow or green backgrounds, while later examples had deeper blue and purple backgrounds.

A Moorcroft 'Pomegranate' pattern baluster vase, designed by William Moorcroft, on a dark blue and green ground, with signed and printed marks to base.

7in (17.5cm) high

£50-80   SAS

A Moorcroft 'Celadon Pomegranate' pattern large bowl, designed by William Moorcroft, with a pale green glazed ground, the base with painted signature.

10.25in (26cm) diam

£1,800-2,200   FLD

A Moorcroft 'Pomegranate' pattern spherical vase, designed by William Moorcroft, on a blue ground, with impressed signature and 'Potter to H M The Queen', with blue painted initials.

5.25in (13.5cm) high

£400-600   DN

A Moorcroft 'Pomegranate' pattern slender ovoid tall vase, designed by William Moorcroft, on a shaded blue ground, with impressed mark, cracked.

12.5in (31.5cm) high

£200-300   DN

A Moorcroft 'Pomegranate' pattern trumpet-shaped vase, designed by William Moorcroft, the base impressed 'Moorcroft Made in England' and with painted signature.

c1937   7.25in (18.5cm) high

£400-600   SWO

A miniature William Moorcroft pomegranate and berry pattern vase, with a dark blue ground, green initials and impressed marks.

3.5in (9cm) high

£150-200   SWO

CERAMICS

A Moorcroft 'Amazon Twilight' pattern ovoid vase, designed by Nicola Slaney, with impressed mark, artist signed and dated '17.9.98'.

This was Slaney's first design for Moorcroft; it was enormously successful.

1998   8.25in (21cm) high

£300-500   DN

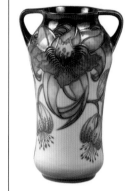

A Moorcroft 'Anna Lily' pattern double-handled vase, designed by Nicola Slaney, the base with printed and script marks.

1998   10.25in (26cm) high

£300-500   SWO

A Moorcroft 'Coneflower' pattern vase, designed by Anji Davenport, the base with factory and artist's marks, paw stamp, and mushroom stamp.

2001   7.5in (19cm) tall

£80-100   BEL

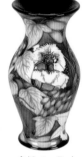

A Moorcroft 'Cotton Top' pattern baluster vase, designed by Sian Leeper, with impressed and painted marks, numbered 111 from a limited edition of 150.

2002   8.75in (22.5cm) high

£150-250   DN

A Moorcroft trial 'D'Larch' pattern ginger jar and cover, with stylised trees in yellow and green, on a graduated navy blue ground, initialled to reverse, dated '3.10.2000'.

2000

£350-450   LT

A Moorcroft 'Finches' pattern baluster vase, designed by Sally Tuffin, on a blue ground, with painted initials and date code.

1993   7.25in (18.5cm) high

£200-300   DN

A Moorcroft 'Kyoto' pattern vase, designed by Rachel Bishop, numbered 70 from a limited edition of 100, the base with printed and painted marks, and with certificate.

The design is based on that found on the gate to the Imperial Palace in the ancient Japanese capital of Kyoto. Along with Sally Tuffin, Bishop is one of Moorcroft's most sought-after contemporary designers.

c1994/95   24in (61cm) high

£1,200-1,800   LT

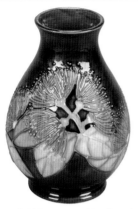

A Moorcroft 'Pohutukawa' pattern baluster vase, designed by Sally Tuffin, from a limited edition of 100 for Tanfield Potter, with impressed mark and date code, with Tanfield Potter retailer's label.

Tanfield Potter are a historic and respected ceramics and glass retailer in Auckland, New Zealand. They commissioned this design, which was also produced on a charger made in 1992 in a limited edition of 220. Related to the myrtle, the evergreen flowering Pohutukawa is also called the 'New Zealand Christmas Tree'.

1900   13in (33cm) high

£150-200   **DN**

QUICK REFERENCE – SALLY TUFFIN

Sally Tuffin (b.1938) studied at the Royal College of Art's fashion school before co-founding the fashion and textile design company 'Tuffin & Foale' that became synonymous with fashion during the Swinging Sixties. In 1986, after bringing up two children, she returned to design as Moorcroft's third ever designer – and the first from outside the Moorcroft family. She remained there until 1993, when she founded the Dennis Chinaworks with her husband Richard Dennis, a thriving company that she still runs today. From 1995-98, she also designed for Poole Pottery. Her work is hotly sought after by collectors, with five figure prices being paid for unique items and scarce, desirable ranges.

A Moorcroft 'Raincloud' pattern vase, designed by Sally Tuffin, numbered 147 from a limited edition of 150, initialled and dated 'Sally Tuffin' and signed 'J. Moorcroft' 1993'.

1993 16.75in (45.5cm) high

£1,000-1,500   **LT**

A Moorcroft 'Siberian Iris' pattern vase, designed by Sian Leeper, numbered 208 from a limited edition of 250, the base with impressed and painted marks.

2003   8.75in (22cm) high

£250-350   **DN**

A Moorcroft 'Torridon' pattern ovoid vase, designed by Philip Gibson, with impressed and painted marks.

2004   8in (20.5cm) high

£250-350   **DN**

A Moorcroft 'H.M.S. Sirius' pattern charger, designed by Sally Tuffin, numbered 9 from a limited edition of 150, together with original box.

This pattern was originally made to commemorate the Australian Bicentenary in 1988, but opened up to a wider audience later. The edition size was 250, with 100 being made specially for the Australian market.

1988   14in (35.5cm) diam

£350-450   **WW**

A Moorcroft 'Underwood' pattern ovoid vase, designed and decorated by Debbie Hancock, numbered 235 from a limited edition of 350 produced for MacIntyre of Leeds, with impressed and printed marks, and painted initials.

7in (18cm) high

£200-300   **DN**

FIND OUT MORE...

Paul Atterbury ' Moorcroft' , *published by Richard Dennis, 1996*

CERAMICS

QUICK REFERENCE

- Nursery ware ceramics, such as plates, mugs and other tableware, was made for children. The first examples appeared in the early 19thC, when surfaces were decorated with colour transfers, depicting moral and educational images and mottos. The idea was that, as the child ate, they could be educated or instructed on their moral code.
- By the early 20thC, nursery ware moved away from these serious themes and became more playful. Scenes from nature, animals, children's stories and nursery rhymes were all used. Related figurines were also produced.

- Many charming designs were produced by Grimwades Ltd (sometimes known under their brand name, Royal Winton). These are decorated with characters, such as Pip the Panda.
- In general, look out for popular images, such as the 'Man in the Moon'. Be aware that wear to transfers, as well as chips or cracks, will reduce the value of any piece. These pieces were made to be used by children, so pieces in mint condition will command a premium.
- Fakes have been produced. Be wary of any examples with transfers over the glaze, rather than under it.

A 1930s Grimwades 'The Circus' child's oval bowl, with printed 'Baby's Plate' mark, with some wear to transfers and chip to base.

Without the wear and damage, this dish could have fetched up to twice this value.

8in (20.5cm) diam

£30-40   BAD

A 1930s Grimwades 'Old Country Nursery Rhymes' child's dish, with a transfer-printed design of an elf and a sheep, the back with printed globe factory mark.

7in (17.5cm) diam

£40-60   BAD

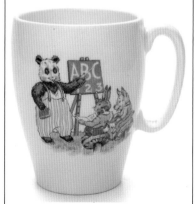

A 1920s-30s Grimwades 'Baa Baa Black Sheep' oval child's dish, the back with printed marks and registered no.554903 or 557903 for 1910.

8in (20.5cm) wide

£30-40   BAD

A Royal Winton child's mug, with a transfer-printed rabbit drummer, a pig playing trumpet and a panda conducting.

3.75in (9.5cm) high

£30-50   BAD

A 1950s Royal Winton child's mug, with a transfer-printed scene of a panda teaching a rabbit and pig, the base with printed mark.

3.75in (9.5cm) high

£35-45   BAD

A Royal Winton 'Bunny's Playtime' transfer-printed child's dinner or pudding bowl.

6.25in (16cm) diam

£25-35 **BAD**

A large Royal Winton 'Bunny's Playtime' circular bowl, with a transfer-printed design of a rabbit watering plants.

6.75in (17cm) diam

£30-40 **BAD**

A Royal Winton 'Bunny's Playtime' transfer-printed double-handled nursery mug, with a rabbit painting a chick's portrait.

3.25in (8.5cm) high

£30-50 **BAD**

A Royal Winton 'Bunny's Playtime' transfer-printed nursery wall clock, with six vignettes of rabbits at play.

This was made by drilling a standard plate and fitting it with a clock mechanism. Note how an 'adult' sized and more ornate dinner plate has been used. Always examine the mechanism and particularly the hands to ensure they are original. Wall clocks are much harder to find than cups, bowls and dishes.

8.75in (22.5cm) wide

£60-90 **BAD**

A Royal Winton 'Pip The Panda' transfer-printed cup and saucer, the back and base with printed mark.

6in (15cm) diam

£30-50 **BAD**

CERAMICS

QUICK REFERENCE – MABEL LUCIE ATTWELL

Artist and illustrator Mabel Lucie Attwell (1879-1964) rose to prominence in the early years of the 20thC with drawings of fairies and children. After designing posters and producing book illustrations, she turned to ceramic design, registering her first designs for children's ware for Shelley in 1926. These usually incorporated her hallmark chubby children, reputedly inspired by her daughter Peggy, and her 'Boo Boo' elf characters. Produced into the 1930s, they are highly popular with collectors today. Nearly all pieces are 'signed' with her printed name, and bear a green shield Shelley mark on the bases or backs. Beware of fakes made from original Shelley pieces, which are either all hand-painted or bear transfer-printed designs over the glaze. Also look at the Shelley marks carefully, as entirely faked ceramics and designs are known. Attwell did not design for Susie Cooper, despite the rise in supposedly 'rare' Cooper ceramics bearing designs like Attwell's.

A Shelley 'Boo Boo' teaset, designed by Mabel Lucie Attwell, comprising a milk jug in the form of a saluting elf, a teapot in the form of a toadstool house, and a toadstool-shaped sugar bowl, each with facsimile name printing, and factory printed marks to base.

Milk jug 6.5in (16.5cm) high

£400-600   HT

A Shelley 'Boo Boo' Nursery ware teapot and cover, designed by Mabel Lucie Attwell, printed and enamelled in colours, printed factory mark.

4.5in (11.5cm) high

£120-180   WW

A 1930s Shelley nursery ware saluting 'Boo Boo' elf-shaped milk jug, designed by Mabel Lucie Attwell, the base with printed marks and registered no.724421 for 1926.

6in (15.5cm) high

£100-150   BAD

A 1930s Shelley nurseryware child's mug, with transfer-printed scene of a baby with elves seated on a crescent moon, designed by Mabel Lucie Attwell, the back with printed factory marks.

2.75in (7cm) high

£120-180   PC

A 1930s Shelley nurseryware child's mug, with transfer-printed design of a child with a bunny seated on a caravan, with animals and elves around him, designed by Mabel Lucie Attwell, with printed marks to back.

2.75in (7cm) high

£120-180   PC

A Shelley nurseryware child's plate, designed by Mabel Lucie Attwell, with a transfer-printed scene of a little girl pushing animals in a wheelbarrow, with light blue rim, and printed factory marks to back.

6in (15cm) diam

£80-120   BAD

A 1930s Shelley child's dish, with a transfer-printed and hand-painted pattern of elves in a plane and parachuting elves, the back with printed factory marks.

6in (15cm) diam

£120-180   PC

A 1940s-50s Simpsons Pottery Ambassador Ware bowl, designed by Mabel Lucie Attwell, with transfer-printed cart, pixie, donkey and little girl pattern and pink rim, the back with printed marks.

Despite being an authentic Attwell design, as it is not Shelley this is less desirable to collectors. Ambassador ware was a higher quality range from Stafforshire's Soho Pottery, which was known as Simpson's from 1944.

5.25in (13.5cm) diam

£30-50   BAD

QUICK REFERENCE

- In summer 1946, Pablo Picasso (1881–1973) went to the annual Vallauris pottery festival during a holiday in the South of France. While he was there he met Suzanne and George Ramié, owners of the Madoura pottery. Later he visited their pottery and created three of his own pieces.
- Upon his return to the town a year later, he revisited the pottery and was given an area to produce his own designs. Between then and 1971, he created over 3,500 designs in the stylised, abstract and avant garde style of his paintings. Although many unique items were created, the vast majority of examples that can be found today will be from the limited edition ranges produced from his originals by a team of potters at Madoura.
- The limited editions were produced either by directly copying Picasso's form and design, or by using a plaster

mould that had been carved or decorated by Picasso himself. Each example from a limited edition was then stamped with a mark in French meaning 'Original Print of Picasso', often together with other information such as the size of the edition.
- Designs focus on the subjects typically found in his paintings such as mythology, Classical subjects, animals, faces and bull-fighting. Picasso also worked the clay surface, creating texture and raised, moulded motifs.
- When buying it is best to learn about the marks used as these will help you identify the best pieces, and spot fakes. All pieces are marked in some way, but always look for the official pottery mark. The appeal of the design, the size of the edition and the condition will all affect value. Values range from as little as £400 to over £20,000.

A Madoura glazed faience earthenware 'Visage No.72' plate, designed by Pablo Picasso, painted with abstract face, marked 'No. 72 EDITION PICASSO 120/150 MADOURA'.

This design was conceived in 1963 and produced in a limited edition of 150.

10.25in (26cm) high

£1,800-2,200   SDR

A Madoura faience plate, designed by Pablo Picasso on 10th March 1953, hand-painted with face and sunray motif and 'Vallauris 10 3 53', stamped 'Plein Feu Empreinte Originale De Picasso'.

8in (20.5cm) diam

£1,500-2,000   DRA

A Madoura faience plate, from the 'Service Visage Noir', designed by Pablo Picasso, with abstract face on black ground, signed 'EDITION PICASSO', stamped 'EDITION PICASSO MADOURA PLEIN FEU'.

This design, from the 'Black Face Service', was conceived in 1948.

9.25in (23.5cm) diam

£2,000-3,000   DRA

A glazed Madoura faience plate, designed by Pablo Picasso, depicting a goat, stamped 'Madoura Plein Feu Empreinte Originale De Picasso'.

10in (25.5cm) wide

£2,000-3,000   DRA

A Madoura faience wall plaque, designed by Pablo Picasso, moulded with four dancing figures in black on a white ground, the back with impressed 'Madoura/ Plein Feu/ Empreinte/ Originale De/ Picasso' marks.

9.75in (25cm) diam

£1,200-1,800   L&T

CERAMICS

A glazed Madoura faience plate, designed by Pablo Picasso, with still-life, stamped 'Madoura'.

This example is valuable because the design is close to Picasso's stylised, abstract painting. It is truly a 'painting on clay'.

1956   9.5in (24cm) wide

£3,000-4,000   DRA

A CLOSER LOOK AT A PICASSO PITCHER

Picasso's animal and anthropomorphic pottery forms are particularly sought after by collectors, and tend to be valuable.

Pitchers are typically modelled as stylised birds, usually known as a 'chouette', the French word for 'owl', and were produced in many variations from the 1950s onwards.

The hand-painted design on this example is comparatively simple – had it been more decorative, it could have been worth more.

Its three-dimensional form was entirely handmade, rather than being moulded from a carved plaster cast, and is more appealing than a dish.

A Madoura faience pitcher, designed by Pablo Picasso, with design of abstract faces, spots and a stylised branch, signed and stamped 'EDITION PICASSO MADOURA'.

6.25in (16cm) wide

£2,000-3,000   DRA

A Madoura faience pitcher, designed by Pablo Picasso, with abstract masks, signed 'EDITION PICASSO MADOURA'.

6in (15cm) wide

£1,500-2,500   DRA

A Madoura faience pitcher, designed by Pablo Picasso, with abstract bird design, signed 'EDITION PICASSO MADOURA'.

11.5in (29cm) high

£4,000-5,000   DRA

A Madoura faience pitcher, designed by Pablo Picasso, with wax-resist image of Don Quixote and bull, the back with impressed edition mark.

5in (12.5cm) wide

£450-650   GORL

A Madoura ceramic water pitcher, designed by Pablo Picasso, no. 276 from an edition of 300, of abstract bird form, signed 'Edition Picasso 276/300 Madoura Plein Feu'.

9.5in (24cm) high

£3,000-4,000   SDR

A 1930s Poole Pottery bowl, shape no.434, decorated in a stylised floral and foliate pattern designed by Truda Carter, with decorator's monogram 'UA'.

9.5in (24cm) diam

£150-200 BAD

A 1930s Poole Pottery vase, of shouldered ovoid form decorated in the VY 'Blue bell' pattern designed by Truda Carter, the base with impressed and painted marks.

8in (20.5cm) high

£70-100 FLD

QUICK REFERENCE – POOLE POTTERY

The world famous Poole Pottery began as a subsidiary acquired in 1921 by the Carter, Stabler & Adams pottery. The pottery's fame grew during the 1920s with the introduction of a range of hand painted Art Deco stylised floral and foliate patterns designed by Truda Carter, which dominated production into the 1950s. During the 1950s, the 'Contemporary' and 'Freefrom' ranges were introduced, designed by Alfred Read and Ruth Pavely. The employment of Robert Jefferson as designer in 1958 led to the introduction of the experimental Poole Studio, whose work led to the 'Delphis' range. The 1960s and 70s were dominated by 'Delphis', and by the 'Aegean', 'Ionian' and 'Atlantis' ranges that were developed within the innovative new Craft Section. The fashionable oranges, reds and greens of the period were typical. This important vase bears a label showing it was exhibited at the Royal Academy Exhibition of British Art & Industry. Being such an important piece, it is likely that Carter painted, as well as designed, the pattern.

A Carter, Stabler & Adams (Poole Pottery) vase, shape no.946, designed and probably painted by Truda Carter, the base with impressed factory marks, applied exhibition and auction paper labels, firing fault to top rim.

c1934 15.75in (40cm) high

£1,000-1,500 WW

A Carter Stabler & Adams Poole Pottery 'Mary Mary, Quite Contrary' hand painted plate, from the Nursery Rhymes range, designed by Dora Batty, the back with impressed and painted marks.

8in (20.5cm) diam

£30-40 W&W

A 1950s Poole Pottery 'Contemporary' range vase, shape 722 designed by Alfred Read, with PV pattern designed by Ruth Pavely, the base with printed and painted marks.

9.5in (24cm) high

£180-220 WW

A 1950s Poole Pottery 'Contemporary' range vase, pattern PKC, designed by Alfred Read, the base with printed and painted marks.

6in (15cm) high

£180-220 WW

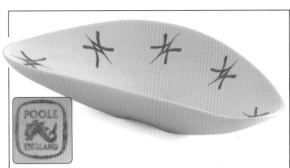

A 1950s Poole Pottery 'Contemporary' range bowl, shape 338 designed by Alfred Read, decorated with the FSU pattern designed by Ruth Pavely, the base with printed mark.

This mark was used from 1955-59. A more rectangular version was used 1959-67.

17.5in (44cm) wide

£60-90   **WW**

A Poole Pottery mottled brown and yellow 'Aegean' large spear dish, with printed black POOLE dolphin mark, stamped 'AEGEAN' and '82', and with painted 'iY or CY' monogram.

17.5in (44cm) long

£40-50   **M20C**

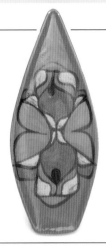

A Poole Pottery orange, green and yellow 'Delphis' large spear dish, with printed black POOLE dolphin mark, stamped '82', and with painted 'iY or CY' monogram.

17.5in (44cm) long

£40-50   **M20C**

A Poole Pottery mottled brown and yellow 'Aegean' spear dish, with printed black POOLE dolphin mark, stamped 'AEGEAN' and '91', and with painted scrolling 'AF' monogram.

12in (30.5cm) long

£30-40   **M20C**

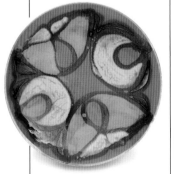

A Poole Pottery 'Delphis' bowl, with printed factory mark, stamped '3', and with painted 'MA' monogram for Mary Albon.

1972-74   8in (20.5cm) diam

£30-40   **M20C**

A Poole Pottery white glazed vase with wax resist band of a spiralling pattern, covered all over with a glossy transparent glaze, the base with black printed 'POOLE ENGLAND' mark, with painted ABC monogram and painted JM monogram for Jacqueline MacKenzie.

1972-77   12in (30.5cm) high

£30-40   **M20C**

A Poole Pottery stoneware 'Grouse' group figurine, designed by Barbara Linley Adams, together with a bird on a pinecone figurine, each with impressed and printed marks.

These figurines are believed to have been produced as test samples, and are in addition to the limited edtion of 1,000 pieces. From the collection of Roy Holland, Managing Director of Poole Pottery.

13in (33cm) wide

£150-250   **W&W**

QUICK REFERENCE

- Rookwood was founded in Cincinnati, Ohio in 1880 by Maria Longworth Nichols, a wealthy heiress who decorated ceramics as a hobby. Initially, the pottery lost money, until Nichols invited William Watts Tyler to run the company in 1883. Tyler set about organising the structure of the company and standardising lines. When Nichols moved abroad in 1890, Tyler took over the now profitable pottery.

- Well-proportioned and balanced shapes were thrown and decorated by hand. These shapes were then glazed with one of the many different glazes developed by Rookwood from the mid-1880s onwards. Tyler encouraged experimentation: glaze technicians were employed to reproduce ancient techniques and glazes, and develop new ones. The first to be produced is known as Standard, which is typified by a graduated brown background, usually painted with flowers. Portraits are rare and desirable.

- Much of the interest for collectors lies in Rookwood's glazes, many of which were inspired by Japanese ceramics. Following the success of Standard, the clear, glossy Iris glaze and the green-tinted Sea Green glaze were introduced in 1894. Vellum, which creates an Impressionistic appearance by diffusing the painted decoration (usually plants or landscapes) it covers, was launched in 1900. Matte glazes followed in 1901. As the glaze is so important, crazing (a fine network of lines) will reduce value, as will damage that detracts from the glaze or design.

- Rookwood employed many highly skilled decorators, such as Matthew Daly, Sara Sax and Maria Storer, and their work can be highly desirable. Pieces tend to be signed, so look out for marks.

A Rookwood Standard glaze vase, decorated by Edith Felten with floral decoration, marked with Rookwood logo, 'IV', shape no.914F and the artist's initials, restored top rim.

1904   *4.25in (11cm) high*

£100-150   **BEL**

A rare tall Rookwood Standard glaze vase, decorated by Sallie Toohey, with poppies on a graduated brown and beige ground, the base with flame mark, '856B' and artist's cipher.

1899   *15.5in (39.5cm) high*

£2,500-3,500   **DRA**

A Rookwood Iris Glaze vase, by Lenore Asbury, with white clematis, the base with flame mark and 'VI/951C/W./L.A'.

Rookwood's 'Iris' glaze was introduced in 1894, and was exhibited at the 1900 Paris Exposition.

1906   *9.5in (24cm) high*

£2,000-3,000   **DRA**

A Rookwood vase, decorated by Carl Schmidt with white roses, the base with the Rookwood flame mark, dated 'IV', impressed '612EZ', and artist's initials 'CS'.

7.75in (19.5cm) high

£800-1,200   **JDJ**

A Rookwood Iris glaze bulbous vase, decorated by Clara Lindeman with a branch of pink apple blossoms on shaded ground, the base with flame mark and 'VIII/654C/C.C.L.'

1908   *5in (12.5cm) high*

£800-1,200   **DRA**

A Rookwood Scenic Vellum vase, painted by E.T. Hurley, with a misty forest landscape, with flame mark and 'VIII/904D/V/E.T.H'.

1908   *8.5in (21.5cm) high*

£1,500-2,500   **DRA**

A Rookwood Scenic Vellum vase, painted by M.G. Denzler, with a bucolic landscape, with flame mark and 'XVI/9232E/V/MGD', some pitting around shoulder.

1916   *8in (20.5cm) high*

£1,000-1,500   **DRA**

A Rookwood Scenic Vellum ovoid vase, decorated by Ed Diers with tall trees, the base with flame mark 'XVII/30D/ED', restored chip at rim.

1917   *10in (25.5cm) high*

£800-1,200   **DRA**

A Rookwood Scenic Vellum vase, decorated by Lenore Asbury with a lake scene, the base with Rookwood flame logo, shape no.1661, and 'L.A.' artist initials.

8.75in (22.25cm) high

£1,000-1,500   **POOK**

A Rookwood Vellum vase, decorated by Fred Rothenbusch with white petunias on a graduated blue and white ground, with flame mark and 'XXV/2262E/FR'.

1925   *5.5in (14cm) high*

£800-1,200   **DRA**

QUICK REFERENCE – VELLUM GLAZE

The 'Vellum' glaze range was introduced at the St Louis exposition in 1904, and grew to become highly successful. It was developed by Stanley Burt, Rookwood's chemist and superintendant, who joined Rookwood in 1892. The matt outer glaze diffused the painted design beneath, giving a pleasing hazy effect. Most pieces were produced before 1915 – many have a fine network of cracks (crazing) today, which reduces the value. After 1915, Rookwood changed its clay composition so crazing is not found on these later Vellum pieces – however, they are rare. Flowers are the most common design, followed by landscapes. Look out for pastel tones and greens, as these are scarcer. Large sizes over 10in (20.5cm) in height, like this, are also rare. The vase shown below is also considerably more valuable because it was decorated by Rookwood's best and most famous decorator, Kataro Shirayamadani (1865-1948).

A Rookwood Scenic Vellum vase, decorated by Kataro Shirayamadani, with a scene of a wooded pond, marked with the Rookwood logo, 'XII', shape no.1369B, the letter 'V' for vellum and the artist's incised Japanese signature, minor nick to the glaze.

1912   *15in (38cm) high*

£8,000-12,000   **BEL**

QUICK REFERENCE

- The Roseville Pottery company was founded in the 'pottery state' of Ohio in 1890, and began by producing utilitarian stoneware. Its output included flowerpots, cuspidors (spittoons) and umbrella stands. The company's success allowed it to buy other potteries and, by 1910, production had been relocated to Zanesville, Ohio.
- Jumping on the art pottery 'bandwagon' in 1900, Roseville released 'Rozane', a range that mimicked the highly successful 'Standard Glaze' series by Rookwood (see p93). By 1908, the demand for expensive, hand-decorated art pottery had ebbed, and all but one range was discontinued at Roseville in favour of mass-produced moulded wares, which the company produced until it closed in 1954.
- Moulded designs were typically based on natural motifs, such as flowers and leaves. Although the coloured glazes were still applied by hand, the designs were much quicker and easier to decorate. Notable designers at Roseville include Frederick Rhead from 1904-08, Frank Ferrell from 1917-54, and George Krause, who worked on glazes from 1915-54. Ferrell in particular was responsible for the most successful mass-produced art pottery ranges.
- Value is determined by a combination of range, shape, colour, size and quality of decoration. More common and less desirable ranges from the 1940s, such as 'Bittersweet', tend to be less valuable. However, the similarly common ranges of 'Dahlrose' and 'Pine Cone' are widely collected and tend to be more valuable.
- Look out for large sizes or shapes that were easily damaged but in excellent condition. Always look closely at protruding parts such as handles and examine the glaze all over the piece. Chips, restoration, glaze skips and other factory flaws reduce value considerably.
- Consider how well the decoration is applied. As moulds wore down through use, look for well-detailed, sharply moulded patterns, with glazes correctly applied. Carelessly applied glazes reduce the value.

A Roseville brown 'Fuchsia' pattern vase, marked '901-10' and with a silver foil factory label to base.

10.25in (26cm) high

£150-250   BEL

A Roseville green and brown Fuchsia pattern vase, with two handles, marked '891-6'.

6.25in (16cm) high

£120-180   BEL

A Roseville brown 'Fuchsia' pattern ovoid vase, marked '347-6', with a small glaze skip to the white of one flower.

8.5in (21.5cm) wide

£120-180   BEL

A Roseville blue 'Fuchsia' vase, with impressed '904-15' mark, and restoration to rim.

15in (38cm) high

£250-350   DRA

A Roseville 'Fuchsia' pattern floor vase, with two handles, the base impressed '905-18'.

The large size, full range of vibrant colours, and excellent moulded detail make this piece particularly desirable. Fuchsia was introduced in 1938 in a variety of tones based on brown, blue and green.

18.25in (46.5cm) high

£2,000-3,000   BEL

CERAMICS

A Roseville 'Futura' range Bamboo Leaf Ball vase, no.387-7", with professional restoration between base and body, unmarked.

7.25in (18.5cm) high

£250-350   **BEL**

A Roseville 'Futura' Twist vase, 398-6 1/2", with a small area of professional restoration to the rim.

6.75in (17cm) high

£200-300   **BEL**

A CLOSER LOOK AT A ROSEVILLE FUTURA VASE

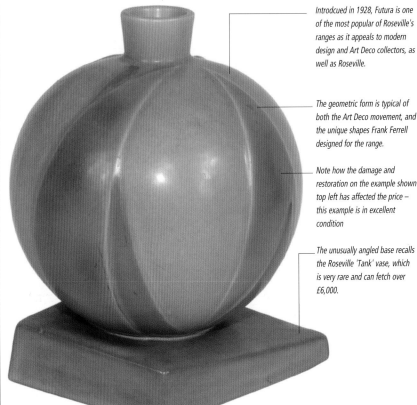

Introdcued in 1928, Futura is one of the most popular of Roseville's ranges as it appeals to modern design and Art Deco collectors, as well as Roseville.

The geometric form is typical of both the Art Deco movement, and the unique shapes Frank Ferrell designed for the range.

Note how the damage and restoration on the example shown top left has affected the price – this example is in excellent condition

The unusually angled base recalls the Roseville 'Tank' vase, which is very rare and can fetch over £6,000.

A Roseville 'Futura' range Bamboo Leaf Ball vase, 387-7", in blue with dark blue and green stylised leaves.

7.5in (19cm) high

£700-1,000   **BEL**

A Roseville 'Futura' range four-footed four-sided vase, with stylised floral pattern on a burgundy ground, with small glazed-over chip to inner foot.

9in (23cm) high

£800-1,200   **DRA**

A Roseville 'Futura' range handled urn vase, no.382-7", in excellent condition.

7.25in (18.5cm) high

£250-350   **BEL**

A Roseville blue 'Futura' range hibachi footed dish, no.198-5", repairs to two areas of the rim and two darkened lines at the rim among the crazing.

A hibachi is a traditional Japanese heating or cooking bowl filled with hot charcoal.

5.25in (13.5cm) wide

£250-350   **BEL**

A large Roseville brown 'Pine Cone' urn, no.912-15", the base with impressed mark.

With its origins in Classical architecture, this is a rare shape.

15.25in (39cm) high

£1,000-1,500 **DRA**

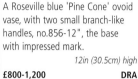

A Roseville blue 'Pine Cone' ovoid vase, with two small branch-like handles, no.856-12", the base with impressed mark.

12in (30.5cm) high

£800-1,200 **DRA**

QUICK REFERENCE – ROSEVILLE PINE CONE

'Pine Cone' was introduced in 1935 and went on to become one of the company's best-selling ranges. Designed by Frank Ferrell, it probably saved the company during the Depression. More than 150 shapes were produced. It was made in green, blue, brown and pink colourways, with blue usually being the most desirable and pink extremely rare. This particular piece displays well-placed colouring as well as crisp moulding. Complete and undamaged jardinières are hard to find, and are usually valuable in any range.

A Roseville green 'Pine Cone' footed bowl, 261-6", with original foil label to base.

6.5in (16.5cm) high

£150-250 **BEL**

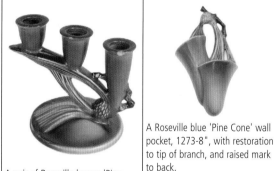

A pair of Roseville brown 'Pine Cone' triple candleholders, no.1106, the bases marked '1106-5 1/2"', each with a number of small chips.

5.5in (14cm) high

£100-150 **BEL**

A Roseville blue 'Pine Cone' wall pocket, 1273-8", with restoration to tip of branch, and raised mark to back.

Wallpockets are a popular theme for many Roseville collectors, so are often comparatively highly priced.

8in (20.5cm) high

£300-400 **DRA**

A Roseville blue 'Pine Cone' jardinière and pedestal, the jardinière marked 'Roseville USA 403-10"' and the pedestal marked 'Roseville USA 406-10", with one chip to the inside of the foot and slight wear to the top surface.

28.5in (72cm) high

£1,000-1,500 **BEL**

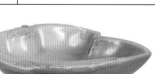

A Roseville blue 'Pine Cone' candy dish, no.497, the base marked 'Roseville USA 497"'

7in (18cm) high

£60-80 **BEL**

CERAMICS

QUICK REFERENCE – ROSEVILLE MARKS

Roseville used many different marks over time, but many pieces were left unmarked. The word 'USA' was only used on raised, moulded marks. Beware of faintly moulded examples, as these may be fakes. Also consider the style of the wording and individual letters, as this can help identify fakes made primarily in the Far East. If in doubt, compare to a piece you are sure is original, also taking the colours and form of the body into account.

Early Rozane Ware 'wafer' mark with 'Woodland' range name.

Stamped 'RV' ink mark, c1923-c1927.

Foil or paper label and handwritten shape number, c1927-35.

Impressed Roseville mark and shape number, 1936-40.

Moulded Roseville USA mark, shape number and size, 1940 onwards.

A 1940s-Roseville pink 'Apple Blossom' basket, 309-8", marked 'Roseville USA 309-8"'.

8.5in (20.5cm) high

£150-250   BEL

A Roseville blue 'Bleeding Heart' vase, 961-4", marked 'Roseville USA 961-4"'.

4.75in (12cm) wide.

£100-150   BEL

A Roseville 'Blackberry' vase, 567-4", with glaze flake and an area of branch handle repaired.

4in (10cm) high

£200-300   BEL

A Roseville blue 'Bushberry' vase, marked 'USA 32-7'.

7.25in (18.5cm) high

£180-220   BEL

QUICK REFERENCE – ROYAL COPENHAGEN

Royal Copenhagen was founded under Danish Royal patronage in 1775. Although it is well known for its fine tableware (such as 'Flora Danica'), it is 20thC decorative wares that attract the most interest from collectors today. Important designers include Axel Salto, Knud Kyhn, Arnold Krog, Johanne Gerber, and the long-serving Nils Thorsson. Forms tend to be simple, with much inspiration for the pattern taken from nature. The pieces are subject to strongly modern stylisation. The base of the popular 'Baca' and similar ranges of the 1950s-70s bear monograms for each designer, which are known as 'chop' marks. The one shown here is for Johanne Gerber.

A Royal Copenhagen Baca Fajance bottle vase, with a handpainted pattern of leaves and branches, no.780/3259, designed by Johanne Gerber, the base with printed and painted marks.

7.75in (19.5cm) high

£50-80   GC

A Danish Royal Copenhagen Fajance vase, no. 711/3755, designed by Nils Thorsson, with painted and printed factory marks to base.

7.5in (19cm) high

£40-60   RET

A Royal Copenhagen Fajance pottery vase, no.726/3259, designed by Nils Thorsson, with painted and printed factory marks to base.

8.75in (22.5cm) high

£60-80   SAS

A Danish Royal Copenhagen Baca Fajance chimney vase, no. 635/3121, designed by Ellen Malmer, with printed and painted marks to base.

7.75in (19.5cm) high

£50-60   M20C

A Danish Royal Copenhagen Baca Fajance dish, no.730/2883, designed by Nils Thorsson, the base with printed factory marks.

6.75in (17cm) wide

£30-40   RET

A Royal Copenhagen Fajance square dish, no.704/2883, designed by Nils Thorsson, with painted and printed factory marks to base.

6.5in (16.5cm) wide

£50-70   SAS

A Royal Copenhagen celadon lidded fluted bowl, no.457/2939, the finial modelled as a seated figure and with crackle glaze, with gilt highlights, the base with printed and painted marks.

6in (15.5cm) high

£80-120　　　W&W

A Royal Copenhagen spherical stoneware vase, designed by Axel Salto, embossed with a tree pattern under black and mahogany glaze, the base incised 'Salto 1243 'with factory mark.

7.75in (19.5cm) high

£2,000-2,500　　　DRA

A Royal Copenhagen bear cub, no. 21434, designed by Knud Kyhn.

Earlier glazes are lighter in tone, being more creamy in colour, sometimes with green tones.

3.25in (8cm) high

£50-80　　　WW

An Art Deco Royal Copenhagan celadon glaze free standing mask, 'Medusa', designed by Hans Henrik Hansen in 1927, model no. 1/2950, the base with impressed and painted marks.

1927　　　*10.5in (27cm) high*

£500-700　　　WW

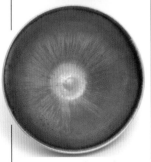

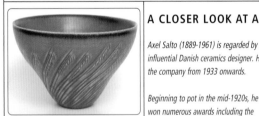

A 1950s-60s Royal Copenhagen bowl, designed by Gerd Bogelund, the interior decorated with a fine brown haresfur glaze, the exterior with impressed and sgrafitto stylised motifs of ears of wheat, the base with printed three wave mark and painted 'GB'.

4.75in (12cm) high

£120-180　　　UCT

A CLOSER LOOK AT AN AXEL SALTO ROYAL COPENHAGEN VASE

Axel Salto (1889-1961) is regarded by many as most influential Danish ceramics designer. He worked for the company from 1933 onwards.

Beginning to pot in the mid-1920s, he won numerous awards including the Grand Prix at the Milan Triennale 1951.

Salto' s powerfully modelled 'budding', 'sprouting' or 'living' themed stonewares were inspired by organic forms such as buds and tree cones. They cross the boundary between functional vase and decorative sculpture.

His dark and rich glazes match the natural form perfectly, and were inspired by ancient Chinese examples such as Sung period wares.

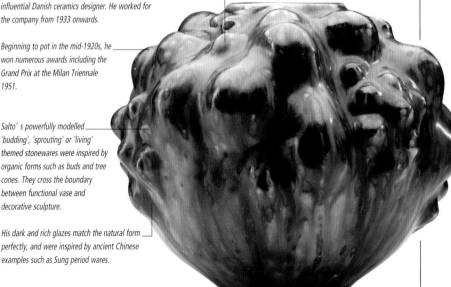

A Royal Copenhagen stoneware 'budding' vase, designed by Axel Salto, covered in mottled brown glaze, the base incised 'SALTO', with factory marks, and numbered '20559'.

10in (25.5cm) wide

£6,000-8,000　　　DRA

QUICK REFERENCE

- The Worcester porcelain factory (established in 1751) first began operating under the name Worcester Royal Porcelain Company in 1862. George III had granted the first of several royal warrants in Worcester's illustrious history in 1789.
- The late Victorian period was very successful for Royal Worcester. The company became known for the colour of its porcelain: soft ivory and pink tints, which echoed art glass. Key designers include George Owen and James Hadley.
- The early years of 20thC saw a simplification of forms and decorative styles. There was a greater output of everyday ware, but hand-painted porcelain was still produced and contributed to the company's success. Vases, plates and other forms were decorated by well-known painters, including Harry Davies and the Stinton family (the best known are Harry Stinton, his father John Stinton Jnr., and uncle James Stinton). By this time all major Royal Worcester artists were signing their work, so look for marks, as a well-known artist may add value.

- Naturalistically painted, modelled ceramic sculptures were introduced in the 1930s. Dorothy Doughty's bird and flower models (produced from 1935) are popular with collectors, as are Doris Lindner's animal figures. Look for small limited editions, as these may be rare and desirable.
- Royal Worcester became a public company in 1954 and merged with Spode in 1978. From this period, Royal Worcester stopped their decorative pieces, focusing on high-quality tableware and figure modelling. In 2009, having gone into administration, Royal Worcester was bought by rival company, Portmeirion Pottery.
- Pieces are marked 'Royal Worcester', with a dot added to this mark for every year between 1892 and 1916. After this, an asterisk was added to the dots.

A Royal Worcester miniature vase, painted by James Stinton with a pheasant in a landscape, with gilt scrolling handles, puce mark to the base and no.'287'.

5.5in (14cm) high

£250-350 DUK

A Royal Worcester 'blush' double-handled vase, with pierced collar and painted with flowers and a butterfly, on gilt-painted and moulded base.

13.5in (38.5cm) high

£180-220 A&G

A Royal Worcester porcelain two-handled pedestal ovoid vase, shape no.2277, painted by Ernest Philips with two panels of summer flowers and a pink ribbon bow, within blue and gilt striped bands, signed, printed mark in puce, date cipher.

1912

£350-450 TEN

A Royal Worcester prismatic enamel pedestal urn, decorated with trailing gilt blossom and enamelled flowers on pink-blush-tinted ivory ground below mask head handles strung with 'silk' swags below short pierced neck, restored.

11.75in (30cm) high

£300-400 FLD

A Royal Worcester two-handled pedestal vase, shape 998/G, painted by G.H. Cole with lilies within green and gilt stiff-leaf band borders, with green printed marks, dated.

£300-500 DN

A Royal Worcester pedestal vase, the globular body decorated with brightly coloured clover, buttercups and forget-me-nots, the base with printed mark and date code.

1903   *9.75in (25cm) high*

£180-220   **WW**

A CLOSER LOOK AT A PAIR OF ROYAL WORCESTER VASES

Miniature vases are scarce and desirable. The fact that they are an original pair adds to the value.

They required great skill to decorate due to their size. This traditional shape shows off the pattern very well.

They were decorated by Harry Stinton (1883-1968), who is considered to be the best of the famed Stinton family of decorators at Worcester.

Stinton is particularly celebrated for his Highland cattle scenes, which were similar to those produced by his father John, but use a more purple palette.

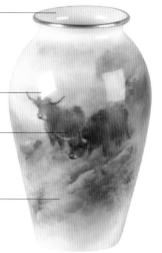
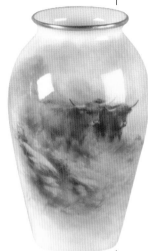

A pair of Royal Worcester baluster vases, shape no.461, painted with Highland cattle in a mountainous setting by Harry Stinton, signed 'H. Stinton', green mark, bearing retailer's stamp of John Ford & Co., 39 Princes Street, Edinburgh.

4in (10cm) high

£800-1,000   **A&G**

A Royal Worcester trumpet vase, painted with roses and buds by Millie Hunt, signed 'M Hunt', within sponged gold borders, dated.

1931

£220-280   **FLD**

A pair of Royal Worcester trumpet vases, each painted with pink and claret roses by Millie Hunt, signed 'M Hunt', within gilt sponged collars, dated, 1934 and 1937

7.5in (19cm) high

£500-600   **FLD**

A pair of Royal Worcester small baluster vases, painted with fruit by Albert J. Shuck, shape no.2491, one with two apples and blackberries with reverse blackberries vignette, the other with two apples and cherries, the reverse with fruiting strawberry vignette, both signed, one with indistinct date code.

c1937   *4in (10cm) high*

£600-700   **TEN**

An early 20thC Royal Worcester footed vase, painted by James Stinton with a cock pheasant and flying hen bird in a landscape setting, with pierced collar, signed, green printed mark, pattern '42/G'.

5.75in (14.5cm) high

£250-350   **L&T**

A Royal Worcester porcelain 'Warwick Vase', shape 2130, painted with landscape scenes and signed 'H. Davies' within raised gilt pendant husk and floral swag borders on a white and apple green ground, dated, restored.

9.75in (25cm) diam

£400-500　　　　　　　　　　　　　　　　　　**FLD**

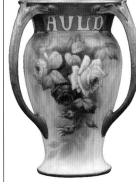

A Royal Worcester tyg, painted with pink and claret rose sprays below a moulded border reading 'Auld Lang Syne', restored.

9.5in (24cm) high

£300-400　　　　　　　　　　　　**FLD**

A Royal Worcester jug, with hand-painted floral pattern and gilded dragon-shaped handle, the base with printed factory marks, also printed '11048' and with registered no.21627 for 1893.

6in (15.5cm) high

£100-150　　　　　　　　　　　　**BAD**

A late 20thC Royal Worcester teapot, painted by Terence Nutt on one side with two apples and blackberries, on the other with a peach, blackberries and green grapes, with gilded and gadrooned rim, spout, handle and circular foot, printed crown and wheel mark in black, initialled 'RB/BB', signed.

6in (15cm) high

£1,000-1,500　　　　　　**TEN**

A late 19thC Royal Worcester Persian-style ewer, painted with a study of an owl on a branch and moonlit clouds by Charles Baldwyn, restored.

10.25in (26cm) high

£100-150　　　　　　　　　　　　**FLD**

A late 19thC Royal Worcester sugar bowl and sparrow beak milk jug, hand-decorated with bamboo and geometric Oriental motifs in floral blue and gilt.

3.5in (9cm) high

£120-180　　　　　　　　　　　　**LOC**

A Royal Worcester bonbon dish, in the form of a conch shell, with coral and weed stem with a circular base, in gilt, bronze and ivory effect, puce printed mark to the base, with impressed mark and 'no. 94'.

8.75in (22cm) high

£250-300　　　　　　　　　　　　**DUK**

A Royal Worcester 'British Friesian bull', RW3746, modelled by Doris Lindner, numbered 268 from a limited edition of 500, with black printed marks, wood stand and certificate.

Issued 1962

£450-550   **DN**

A Royal Worcester 'Dairy Shorthorn bull', RW3781, modelled by Doris Lindner, numbered 106 from a limited edition of 500, with black printed marks, wood stand and certificate.

Issued 1965

£450-550   **DN**

A Royal Worcester 'Jersey bull', RW3776, modelled by Doris Lindner, numbered 167 from an edition of 500, with black printed marks, wood stand and certificate.

£450-550   **DN**

QUICK REFERENCE – DORIS LINDNER

Sculptor Doris Lindner (1896-1979) became one of Royal Worcester's most notable modellers after she was asked to contribute to an exhibition in London in 1931. Her first model was of a polar bear, followed by dogs and other animals such as foxes, some in the Art Deco style of the day. In 1935, she began modelling horses and produced her first limited edition, of 'Princess Elizabeth on Tommy', in 1948. The 1960s were her heyday, and she produced more than 20 limited edition figurines, modelled from life. Most edition sizes were 500, with a few smaller (and scarcer) editions of 100 or 150. Today, her work is sought after by a dedicated group of collectors, meaning prices have remained strong, even during the economic downturn. The model should retain its wooden plinth and certificate.

A Royal Worcester 'Aberdeen Angus' bull, RW3697, modelled by Doris Lindner, numbered '286' from a limited edition of 500, with wooden stand and certificate. Issued

1959   *7.5in (19cm) high*

£700-900   **LOC**

A Royal Worcester 'Jersey Cow', modelled by Doris Lindner, numbered 357 from a limited edition of 500, with stand and certificate.

7in (18cm) high

£400-600   **LOC**

A Royal Worcester 'Dairy Shorthorn Bull', modelled by Doris Lindner, numbered 250 from a limited edition of 500, with stand and certificate.

8.75in (22cm) high

£350-450   **LOC**

A Royal Worcester model 'Laurieston & Richard Meade OBE', modelled by Doris Lindner, numbered 13 from a limited edition of 500, on a wooden plinth and in a glass case with certificate.

14.25in (36cm) wide

£600-800   **LOC**

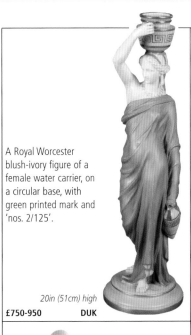

A Royal Worcester blush-ivory figure of a female water carrier, on a circular base, with green printed mark and 'nos. 2/125'.

20in (51cm) high

£750-950   **DUK**

A Royal Worcester 'The Tea Party' figure group, RW3700, modelled by Ruth Esther van Ruyckevelt, from a limited edition of 250, from the Victorian Figures series, in colours and gilt, black printed crown and wheel mark, title and facsimile signature, impressed '42', in original box with certificate.

1960   *8in (20cm) high*

£700-1,000   **TEN**

A Royal Worcester candle snuffer, modelled as a nun, with printed mark and date code.

1924   *4in (10cm) high*

£70-100   **WW**

A Royal Worcester blush-ivory figure of a rustic girl at a spring, model no.1810, partially coloured and gilt, with green marks.

1900   *6.75in (17cm) high*

£200-300   **DN**

A Royal Worcester 'Mephistopheles' Toby jug, shape 2850, the base with printed marks.

3.25in (8.5cm) high

£50-60   **FLD**

A Royal Worcester 'Spitfire' figure group, RW3352, designed by Eileen Soper from the Wartime series, dated, minor restoration.

This is the rare coloured version, which is worth considerably more than plain white. During the war, when this was produced, raw materials were strictly limited and could not generally be used on decorative pieces.

1941

£1,000-1,500   **FLD**

A pair of late 19thC Royal Worcester 'Irish Navvy and Wife' figures, by James Hadley, shape no.1810, typically modelled, in shades of green and pink, printed and impressed marked.

Tallest 7in (18cm) high

£300-400   **HT**

CERAMICS

A pair of Finnish Arabia salt and pepper shakers, designed by Kaj Franck in 1955, glazed in glossy black or red.

2.75in (7cm) high

£40-60   **QU**

A Danish Soholm Stentoj rectangular wall plaque, with stylised floral design, designed by Joseph Simmonds, with impressed mark on back, numbered '3540', and with painted 'LE' monogram.

17.5in (44.5cm) long

£100-150   **RET**

A 1970s Swedish Elbogen Pottery 'Marg' figure, the base with painted marks.

This was part of a range of different handmade female figures, each with its own name.

13.5in (34cm) high

£80-120   **M20C**

A CLOSER LOOK AT BJORN WIINBLAD CANDELABRA

Bjorn Wiinblad (1918-2006) was a Danish artist, illustrator, designer and ceramicist whose work has attracted a worldwide reputation and group of collectors.

Bjørn Wiinblad was born in Copenhagen and was educated at the Royal Academy of Arts in Copenhagen. He first started working with ceramics at Lars Syberg's studio, and set up his own studio in 1952.

From 1946, he worked at (and subsequently owned) the Danish factory Nymolle, and also worked with Germany's Rosenthal from 1956 onwards. He designed mass-produced transfer printed ceramics for both companies. He also ran his own pottery studio, from 1952, and it was there that these handmade, hand-painted candelabra were made.

His work is inspired by traditional Danish myths, music and nature, and often features whimsical characters in his individual and eccentric style.

A Norwegian Figgjo Flint Turi Design 'Lotte' pattern transfer-printed and painted beaker, with printed marks to base.

3in (7.5cm) high

£12-18   **RET**

A Swedish Gustavsberg stoneware poodle, from the 'Kennel' series designed by Lisa Larson in 1972, with painted and impressed marks to base.

3.5in (9cm) high

£50-70   **SAS**

Two Danish studio earthenware candelabra, by Bjorn Winblad, each of conical form, modelled as figures beneath a bowl and sconces, dated.

1972   *Tallest 15.75in (40cm) high*

£500-700   **SWO**

QUICK REFERENCE

- The Shelley brand was devised c1910 by the Wileman & Co. pottery in Staffordshire, England, but was not used officially until 1925. The company was founded c1892 and became known for its art pottery. However, it became world famous for its tea and tablewares during the 1920s and '30s. The pottery closed in 1966.
- Notable designers who produced important ranges which are sought after by collectors today, include Frederick Alfred Rhead, Walter Slater and his son Eric; and illustrators Hilda Cowham and Mabel Lucie Attwell, who are known for their desirable nursery ware (see p86-88).
- Among the most collectable and valuable Shelley designs are the two Art Deco geometric teaware ranges, 'Mode' and 'Vogue' designed by Eric Slater, and produced from 1930-33. The teacups had solid handles, which made them difficult to hold, and this led to the development of the hollow-handled 'Eve' shape in 1932. Also look out for the 'Queen Anne'

shape, which was decorated with over 170 different patterns, and the popular 'Dainty' shape, which was designed in 1896.
- The most desirable and valuable patterns are Art Deco in style, typically executed in the bright colours typical of the era. Values vary depending on the pattern. Desirability is maximised when these are found on a strongly Art Deco shape, such as 'Vogue' or 'Mode'. Transfer-printed floral 'chintz' wares are also sought after, but values for them have fallen over the past five years. More attention is being paid to Eric Slater's banded and dripped 'Harmony' ranges.
- Look out for complete teasets as these tend to fetch the largest sums. Teapots and individual teacups are also desirable, and are always worth considering when undamaged. Rhead's late 19thC art pottery ranges are also well worth looking out for as prices tend to be high due to their scarcity and his increased popularity among collectors in the UK and the US.

A Shelley blue lustre vase, designed by Walter Slater, printed and painted with a Chinese dragon, highlighted in gilt, with printed mark and facsimile signature to base.

Walter Slater replaced F. A. Rhead as Art Director, working there from 1905-37.

15in (38cm) high

£1,200-1,800　　　WW

A very rare Shelley Intarsio range 'Pomegranate' pattern vase, with printed marks to base.

Shelley were forced to withdraw this pattern by Moorcroft as it was similar to their Pomegranate pattern. A ginger jar in the same pattern can fetch up to £1,800.

8in (20.5cm) high

£700-1,000　　　GOL

A Shelley Intarsio range 'Native Americans' pattern vase, no.3411, with printed marks to base.

This stylised pattern is extremely rare on any form, and is especially desirable on large impressive vase forms such as this.

11in (28cm) high

£2,800-3,300　　　GOL

A Wileman & Co. Intarsio range temple jar, with the 'Rabbits' pattern, designed by Frederick Alfred Rhead.

Notable ceramics designer Frederick Alfred Rhead (1856-1933) was Art Director at Wileman & Co. from 1896-1905. He produced a number of innovative ranges, the most desirable of which was Intarsio. This is a very scarce pattern on a rare and highly desirable form.

c1900

£2,000-2,500　　　GOL

CERAMICS

A 1930s Shelley cake stand with handpainted circle design and shaped chrome stand, the base with green printed factory mark.

10in (25.5cm) high

£50-60 RET

A 1930s Shelley Vogue shape part coffee set, comprising coffee pot, four cups and saucers and milk jug, handpainted with the very rare 'Coral Martian' pattern, no.11867, with printed marks to bases.

The pattern name has been applied by collectors, and was not the original name. The pattern was also available in green, which is worth around the same amount.

1931-33 *7in (18cm) high*

£2,000-2,500 GOL

A very scarce Shelley lemonade set, with jug and six beakers, decorated with the 'Apples' pattern, with printed marks to the base.

The jug is very similar to Clarice Cliff's iconic Art Deco 'Conical' shape, showing how popular styles were reproduced by different makers.

8in (23cm) high

£800-1,200 GOL

A 1930s Shelley Mode shape teaset for two, hand-painted with the yellow butterfly wing pattern, no.11758, with printed marks to base.

Teapot 5in (12.5cm) high

£2,000-2,500 GOL

A Shelley Harmony waisted vase, with dripping bands of orange and green.

c1930 *21cm high*

£130-160 BEV

FIND OUT MORE...

'Shelley Potteries', by Chris Watkins, William Harvey and Robert Senft, published by Barrie & Jenkins, 1980. The Shelley Group, www.shelley.co.uk or The National Shelley Club, www.nationalshelleychinaclub.com

A CLOSER LOOK AT A SHELLEY TEA SERVICE

The Harmony range of Dripware was discovered 'by accident' when Eric Slater mixed too much turpentine in glazes, which dripped in an attractive manner.

Evenly distributed banding is highly desirable, particularly on the desirable Art Deco 'Eve' shape.

Purple Harmony is very rare – yellows, blues and greens are more common.

Slater accentuated the effects and widened it into a range of decorative wares – tablewares are harder to find, particularly in sets.

A 1930s Shelley 'Harmony' range Eve shape teaset, designed by Eric Slater, comprising teapot, six cups and saucers, milk jug and sugar bowl, decorated with the purple Harmony pattern no.12084.

Teapot 7in (18cm) high

£2,500-3,000 GOL

A Stangl Pottery 'Bluebird', no.3276, with 'STANGL' brown oval mark, incised '3276' and with artist's initials 'ES'.

5.25in (13.5cm) high

£50-70   **BEL**

A Stangl Pottery 'Western Bluebird' figurine, no.3815, with printed factory marks and decorator's initials.

7in (17.5cm) high

£75-95   **BH**

A Stangl Pottery 'Key West Quail Dove', no.3454, marked 'STANGL 3454' in blue ink and artist signed 'RV' initials.

9.25in (23.5cm) high

£150-200   **BEL**

A Stangl Pottery 'Cardinal' in matte finish, no.3444, with small brown oval 'STANGL' mark, incised '3444' and with artist's initials, a small glaze flaw at the tip of the tail.

6.75in (17cm) high

£100-150   **BEL**

QUICK REFERENCE – STANGL BIRDS

Partly inspired by Audubon's famous 'Birds of America', Stangl's birds were originally produced from 1940-72. Values are based on the size and complexity of the figurine, and how well it has been decorated. Decorators, whose numbers were swelled with homeworkers at busy times, were able to choose their own colours, and their level of skill varied widely. Even though artists often signed their work with initials, the work of individual artists does not really affect value, so this information is only of use for dating. In 1972, some models were re-released, and these are often signed and dated. As with 'vintage' Stangl, they can still be desirable and valuable if they are well decorated. This pair of woodpeckers is an excellent example of a good design that has been well decorated.

A Stangl Pottery 'Gray Cardinal', no.3596, marked with partial small black 'STANGL POTTERY BIRDS' mark, incised '3596' and with 'BM' artist's initials.

4.75in (12cm) high

£45-55   **BEL**

A Stangl Pottery large 'Cockatoo', no.3584, with large black oval 'STANGL POTTERY BIRDS' mark and '3584' in black.

12.25in (31cm) high

£150-200   **BEL**

A Stangl 'Woodpeckers' figurine, no.8752, with inscribed number and printed factory mark.

8in (20.5cm) high

£300-400   **BH**

CERAMICS

QUICK REFERENCE

- The term 'studio pottery' is used to describe pottery made by the owner of an independent pottery, or under their supervision. Quantities are typically limited, and each piece is, in effect, unique as it was handmade or hand-decorated. Although some studio pottery was made in the 19thC, it developed into a movement of its own after World War II.
- Key figures include forerunners Bernard Leach, his colleague Shoji Hamada, Lucie Rie, and Hans Coper. Later names, many of whom studied with or were inspired by one of these influential potters, include Alan Caiger-Smith, David Leach, Marianne de Trey and John Maltby. In the US, leading potters such as the Natzlers, Peter Voulkos, Maija Grotell, Beatrice Wood and others were also highly influential.

- Although the work of these important potters is usually very expensive, look out for the work of their students, as this is often more affordable and just as important when put in context. Similarly, the work of many potters is yet to be 'discovered'. Learn how to recognise styles of certain potters and find out a little about their backgrounds.
- Always consider the form, glaze and size. Look for pieces that are well made, and of good quality. Collecting by theme, such as glaze, is often rewarding as there are many variations to be found. Consider a potter's work in context of his time – those that innovated or led a new style, or exemplified the 'look' of the day, are often worth considering. Invest in a book of marks (often called 'seals') to help you learn how to identify particular potters.

An Aldermaston Pottery bowl, by Alan Caiger-Smith, with green, blue and black curving lines and painted monogram.

10.75in (27.5cm) diam

£500-700   **WW**

An Aldermaston Pottery bowl, by Alan Caiger-Smith, the interior with stylised panels in blue and ochre, the exterior with a simple blue band, the base with painted marks.

11.75in (30cm) diam

£300-500   **WW**

An Aldermaston Pottery waisted cylindrical vase, by Alan Caiger-Smith, with red lustre panels and printed and painted marks to base.

Caiger-Smith founded the Aldermaston Pottery in 1955. Considered a key training ground for a new generation of potters, it closed in 2006 when he retired. He is known for his tin and lustre glazes, which are often combined with Hispano-Moresque patterns and styles.

An 1960s Ambleside footed vase, designed and possibly made by George Cook, with sgrafitto geometric pattern, the base inscribed 'Ambleside'.

4.75in (12cm) high

£30-50   **GC**

A Richard Batterham stoneware jar, in a pale celadon glaze over impressed dot and line decoration.

9.75in (25cm) high

£150-200   **WW**

9.25in (23.5cm) high

£350-450   **WW**

A Carn Pottery fan vase, with low relief moulded curving and circular design to one side and stylised flower design to the other, the base with factory black printed mark.

Along with cats, fan vases are the most desirable shapes.

6in (15cm) high

£20-30 UCT

A Seth Cardew stoneware jug, with a tenmoku gaze and inscribed with bands and wavy lines, with impressed 'SC' seal mark.

6.25in (16cm) high

£30-50 W&W

A Carn Pottery asymmetric vase, with moulded low relief stylised designs, the base with black printed factory mark.

5.25in (13cm) high

£15-25 UCT

A Michael Casson basket, with a mottled brown salt glaze, the base with impressed seal.

13.25in (33.5cm) high

£120-180 W&W

A Deichman Pottery jardinière bowl, decorated with fish in a green glaze on a cream ground, the base painted with 'EKD' and 'NB' monograms.

Danish-born Kjeld and Erica Deichmann founded a pottery in New Brunswick, Canada in 1935. Inspired by Scandinavian pottery they had grown up around, they pioneered studio pottery and the craft tradition in Canada. Erica was responsible for the glazes, whilst Kjeld produced the forms. The pottery closed in 1963, when Kjeld died. This pattern is unusual, most pieces are plain.

6in (15cm) high CAD

£700-1,000 TAC

A Coldrum Pottery baluster vase, by Reginald Wells, covered with a mottled blue and lavender glaze, the base stamped 'Coldrum'.

9.25in (23.5cm) high

£100-150 W&W

A Canadian Deichmann mug, with green dripped glaze, the base inscribed 'Deichmann 45' and with 'NB' monogram, damaged handle.

5.25in (13cm) high CAD

£80-120 TAC

CERAMICS

An earthenware animal-shaped shower caddy, by Deborah Halpern, with painted 'Deborah D Halpern' signature.

Australian artist and ceramicist Halpern (b.1957) is known for her quirky and colourful animals inspired by Picasso.

14.25in (36cm) high

£300-500 JA

A Farnham Pottery owl money bank, with incised and applied decoration and green glaze, minor chips.

Founded in Surrey in 1872, the company produced art pottery from 1880 onwards. Typically covered in a green glaze, wares were sold by Liberty and Heal's among others. Owls are typical motifs, but jugs are more common and were produced into the 1950s.

2.25in (6cm) high

£300-400 WW

A large David Leach Lowerdown Pottery cut-sided vase, covered in a dolomite glaze, with impressed seal marks.

7.5in (19cm) high

£450-550 WW

An early St Ives stoneware bowl, by Bernard Leach, incised to interior and exterior with cloud motif under an ash glaze, impressed 'St Ives' and 'BL' script seal marks.

5.5in (14cm) diam

£300-500 WW

A CLOSER LOOK AT A STUDIO POTTERY SCULPTURE

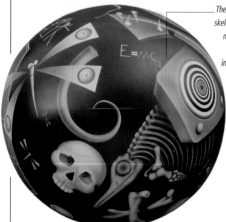

The skull and dinosaur skeleton are 'momento mori', hinting at the passing of life and inevitability of death – a theme used in art since the Renaissance.

The spherical form suggests the world, with objects in it showing developments across time, such as bacteria under a microscope, and a television.

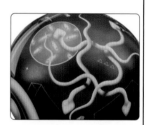

It is well-designed and finely painted, being an excellent example of ceramics used as an art form to convey a message.

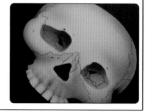

A Steven Gunderson ceramic sphere, decorated with geometric biological forms in black, white and red, with ball inside.

19in (48cm) diam

£800-1,200 SK

A Bernard Leach stoneware tea bowl, with tenmoku glaze outside and khaki glaze inside, and impressed 'BL' and 'St Ives' seals.

Pieces by Leach (1887-1979) are highly sought after. Generally considered to be the 'father' of studio ceramics, he founded the influential St Ives pottery with Shoji Hamada in 1910, from where he trained many of the great names in studio pottery.

4.75in (12cm) diam

£700-1,000   **TEN**

A Bernard Leach stoneware tea bowl, blue glaze with khaki on one side, with impressed 'BL' and 'St Ives' seals.

c1960   *3.25in (8.5cm) high*

£500-600   **TEN**

A John Maltby stoneware unomi, octagonal with painted panels, impressed seal.

Born in 1936, Maltby is one of the UK's most celebrated living studio potters. He trained in sculpture under David Leach and founded his own pottery in 1964. He is known today for his unique sculptural forms, simple geometric motifs and creating contrasts between light and dark. A unomi is a traditional Japanese tea bowl.

3.75in (9.5cm) high

£250-300   **WW**

A Bernard Leach earthenware mug, inscribed 'S.S. White Heather 1921' and decorated with a view of the boat with an 'X4' brown glaze, incised 'BL' and 'St Ives'.

The S.S. White Heather was a herring boat. This mug was made by Leach as part of a set.

4.25in (10.5cm) high

£200–300   **TEN**

One of a pair of Lorenzen salt and pepper shakers, decorated with abstract fish and waves on a mottled grey ground, the bases inscribed 'Lorenzen's Lanz Nova Scotia'.

c1960   *2.25in (5.5cm) high*

£20-30 PAIR   **MHC**

A John Maltby stoneware elliptical vase, decorated with diamond motifs, with impressed seal mark.

5in (12.5cm) high

£80-120   **WW**

A Paul Metcalfe early figural bottle vase, decorated with a stylised figure of a robed lady in green and white oxide glazes, the base with painted monogram and date.

1962   *17in (44.5cm) high*

£100-150   **FLD**

CERAMICS

QUICK REFERENCE – NATZLER

Viennese born Otto (b.1908) and Gertrud (1908-71) Natzler founded their pottery in Los Angeles upon their arrival in the US in 1938. Forms, produced by Gertrud, were typically simple with bowls being the first shapes produced. Otto devised the glazes, and it is primarily for these that the couple have become celebrated. The most desirable (and valuable) glazes resemble bubbled and cratered lava, but complex crystalline glazes, as seen on this bowl, are also sought after. The Natzler name is typically inscribed into the base.

A Natzler earthenware footed small bowl, in a blue and brown glaze, signed on the base.

4.5in (11.5cm) diam

£2,000-3,000   DRA

A Natzler footed bowl, in olive-green, turquoise and brown mottled semi-matte glaze, the base signed 'NATZLER'.

8.5in (21.5cm) diam

£1,200-1,800   DRA

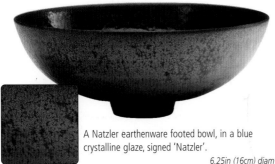

A Natzler earthenware footed bowl, in a blue crystalline glaze, signed 'Natzler'.

6.25in (16cm) diam

£7,000-10,000   SDR

A Natzler free-form earthenware bowl, covered in matte stone grey glaze, signed 'Natzler'.

This mottled and striated glaze, and the one on the blue bowl above, bear many similarities to the 'hare' s-fur' glazes used by Scandinavian ceramics companies such as Palshus and Gustavsberg.

6.25in (16cm) high

£3,000-4,000   SDR

A Natzler beaker-shaped earthenware vase, with indented lip, covered in grey sea glaze, signed 'Natzler'.

5.5in (14cm) high

£3,500-4,500   SDR

A Natzler earthenware cup, covered in glossy mottled turquoise and lavender glazes, signed 'Natzler'.

c1962   3.75in (9.5cm) high

£2,500-3,500   SDR

A William Newland earthenware bull, slip-trailed with geometric motifs in cream on an ochre ground, with painted signature and dated '58', repaired horn.

Newland (1919-98), along with Margaret Hine and Nicola Vergette, was part of a group known as the 'Picassoettes' since they took their inspiration from Picasso. Bulls and other animal forms, decorated with exotic motifs, are typical.

1958   12.25in (31cm) wide

£700-900   **WW**

A CLOSER LOOK AT A PARKINSON SCULPTURE

Parkinson pottery, which is hard to find, has become highly sought-after since a book and exhibition in 2004.

It has a surreal appearance, recalling glove display hands in department stores, and accentuated by the chess board design.

Black and white painted slip-cast domestic and sculptural animals and figures are typical – this is an extremely rare design.

Susan studied at the Royal College of Art. The pottery was active for only eleven years from 1952-63.

A Richard Parkinson Ltd 'Hand in Glove' sculpture, designed by Susan Parkinson, painted with geometric panels of chess pieces, minor restoration on base rim.

13.75in (35cm) high

£1,000-1,500   **WW**

A Richard Parkinson Ltd slip cast porcelain bust of schoolboy, designed by Susan Parkinson, with black enamel decoration, the base with impressed marks.

6in (15cm) high

£550-650   **FLD**

A Richard Parkinson Ltd heraldic lion, designed by Susan Parkinson, painted in dark grey-blue on a white ground, with impressed mark.

9.5in (24cm) wide

£380-420   **WW**

A Katharine Pleydell-Bouverie stoneware cut-sided vase, covered in a green glaze, impressed seal mark, painted 'BX'.

2.25in (5.5cm) high

£100-150   **WW**

A tin-glazed earthenware jug, decorated by Alfred Powell with a lakeside landscape scene in blue, the reverse with a similar scene of a country house, the base with painted monogram.

Although better known for his work with Wedgwood, Powell and his wife Louise also decorated a series of blanks.

5.25in (13.5cm) high

£150-200   **W&W**

CERAMICS

A CLOSER LOOK AT A SUSIE COOPER VASE

This spherical shape is typical of the geometricity of the Art Deco movement. This shape was hard to make and is rare today.

The right angles and straight lines of the hand-painted pattern contrast against the curving shape, but are also typical of the Art Deco movement.

This is typical of Cooper's most desirable Art Deco designs from c1928-30. Had it been in brighter colours and not cracked, it would have fetched more

The mark on the base shows a galleon amidst waves with yellow sails – this style of mark was used from 1921-31.

A Gray's Pottery ball vase, designed by Susie Cooper, pattern no.8215, painted with geometric design in shades of yellow, black and grey, printed factory mark, painted number, hairline crack to base.

c1929   7in (18cm) high

£450-650   **WW**

A late 1930s Susie Cooper Kestrel shape coffee set for six, decorated in the 'Crescents' pattern, no.1543, comprising coffee pot, milk jug, sugar bowl, ten cups, saucers and side plates and others, the bases with printed and painted marks, minor damages.

Coffee Pot 7.5in (19cm) high

£100-150   **WW**

A late 1930s Susie Cooper 'Panel Spray' part service, pattern no.1690, comprising milk jug and sugar bowl, six cups, saucers and side plates and a sandwich plate, the bases with printed marks.

This is a very rare pattern, probably as production was interrupted by the onset of war in 1939. Each of the six ' trio ' sets, which comprise a cup and saucer and side plate, are commercial and collectable. The scarcer milk jug and sugar bowl are an additional bonus.

£1,000-1,500   **WW**

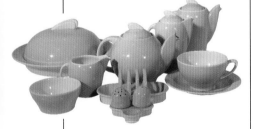

A late 1930s Susie Cooper 'Blue Crescent' Kestrel bachelor set, comprising teapot, two hot-water pots, milk jug and sugar basin, cup, saucer and side plate, a muffin dish and cover, cruet and a toast rack, the bases with printed factory marks, minor damages.

Teapot 5in (12.5cm) high

£200-300   **WW**

A Grays Pottery hand painted circular plate, designed by Susie Cooper, with an abstract geometric pattern in yellow, black and red with overlapping geometric forms.

c1929   10in (25.5cm) diam

£80-120   **FLD**

A Susie Cooper 'Endon' pattern 'Spiral' shape dinner service, comprising six dinner plates, six dessert plates, six side plates, two meat plates, five side plates, five dessert plates, six fruit bowls, six saucers and two tureens, one lidded.

The 'Spiral' shape was introduced in 1938, and the 'Endon' pattern dates from a similar time.

£120-180   **SWO**

CERAMICS

QUICK REFERENCE

- Joseph Szeiler (1924–1986) was born in Hungary and studied to become a veterinary surgeon before emigrating to England, via Austria, in 1948. He first worked for J&G Meakin as a mould runner, later gaining more experience at Wade Heath & Co. In 1951, he took the decision to found his own company, renting a room in Hanley, Staffordshire. His first production included animals and figures: Szeiler created the designs and moulds, then made and glazed the figurines.

- In 1955, his business had expanded enough to allow him to buy larger premises in Burslem, where his company remained until his death and its closure in 1986.
- Animal figurines are the most common and most desirable designs, with many being highly stylised and elongated. Fawn and cream, sometimes with a light blue, are typical colours. Prices have begun to rise, as more collectors are drawn to Szeiler's work, but rarely fetch over £50.

A Szeiler elongated dog figurine, with printed mark to base.

3in (7.5cm) high

£7-10   DSC

A Szeiler sleeping dog in a basket.

Animals in woven baskets are a hallmark range for Szeiler, and can be found in many different variations.

Basket 1.5in (4cm) high

£5-8   DSC

A Szeiler long-eared small donkey figurine in repose, with printed mark to base.

The long ears are a typical feature of many Szeiler animals. The mark is earlier in date, although no precise date ranges are yet known.

3.25in (8cm) long

£8-10   DSC

A Szeiler-type 'Bengo' figurine, with blue collar and tag, the base with 'UNIVERSAL MADE IN ENGLAND' printed mark.

This figurine is worth more as it represents Bengo, a popular cartoon character. Universal and Zalpark marks indicate that a piece may have been made as part of a joint venture.

3.25in (8.2cm) high

£20-25   DSC

A Szeiler blue and white donkey figurine, with elongated ears, the base with printed mark.

4.75in (12cm) high

£25-30   DSC

A Szeiler donkey and cart figurine, with printed mark to base.

6in (15cm) long

£15-20   DSC

A Szeiler koala and cub figurine, with printed mark to base.

3.5in (9cm) high

£15-20   DSC

CERAMICS

A Copeland Spode blue and white transfer printed 'Italian' pattern teapot.

9.75in (24.5cm) long

£60-80   BAD

QUICK REFERENCE – SADLER CAR TEAPOTS

Sadler's car teapots were first released in 1937 and produced again after WWII. Green, cream or yellow are the most commonly found single colours. Produced in the 1930s only, black, grey, maroon, blue or pink are scarcer colours. They have platinum luste details. The rarest variation from the 1930s has transfer-printed patterns of pixies and animals in the style of (but not by) Mabel Lucie Attwell, along with orange detailing, and can fetch over £500. When present, the numberplate is 'OKT42' indicating 'Okay, tea for two', but this was generally only applied to pre-war examples. After the war, single colour and mottled examples were produced, and impressed marks included the Sadler name. Prices have remained stable, due to their appeal to collectors of teapots and automobilia.

A 1920s-30s handpainted 'cottage ware' teapot, unmarked but possibly by Price Bros., with two chips to the corner of the lid and knob.

c1930s   *8.5in (21.5cm) wide*

£7-10   PC

A 1930s Royal Doulton handpainted 'Aspen' pattern teapot, with gilded foot, handle, rim and spout.

5.25in (13.5cm) diam

£50-60   BEV

A 1930s-50s Sadler novelty motor car teapot, with a green glaze, the base with impressed marks and registered number 820236 for 1937.

8.75in (22.5cm) wide

£30-50   WW

A 1930s Royal Doulton teapot, with handpainted arabesque pattern in green yellow, black and gold, the base marked 'V.1289'.

c1934   *5in (12.5cm) high*

£80-100   BEV

A Shelley 'Mode' shape teapot and cover, pattern number 11754, in green and gold, the base with printed and painted marks.

Designed by Eric Slater and produced from 1930-33, Mode is one of Shelley's two strongest Art Deco forms. This popular pattern was also available in yellow, red, black, blue or pink – all with similar gold handles and details.

5in (13cm) high

£300-400   WW

A Shelley fine bone china transfer printed 'Anemone' pattern 35oz teapot.

7in (17.5cm) high

£70-100   W&L

A Royal Grafton Fine Bone China teapot, handpainted with large brown flower and blue leaves.

7in (17.5cm) high

£20-30 **W&L**

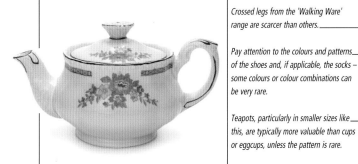

A Grindley small teapot, transfer printed with sprays of colourful flowers, with black detail and rims.

3.5in (9cm) high

£25-35 **W&L**

A CLOSER LOOK AT A TEAPOT

Crossed legs from the 'Walking Ware' range are scarcer than others.

Pay attention to the colours and patterns of the shoes and, if applicable, the socks – some colours or colour combinations can be very rare.

Teapots, particularly in smaller sizes like this, are typically more valuable than cups or eggcups, unless the pattern is rare.

The bodies are usually white, those with transfer printed patterns, such as tropical islands, are rarer.

A Carltonware 'crossed legs' teapot with yellow shoes and green and brown socks, designed by Roger Michell of the Lustre Pottery, with printed marks to base.

1978 *8.25in (21cm) high*

£100-150 **BEV**

A 1950s Sadler teapot, with sprial ribbed body and transfer printed with roses, with impressed marks to base.

4.75in (12cm) high

£18-22 **W&L**

A Midwinter 'Fashion' shape coffee pot, with the transfer-printed 'Bali H'ai' design, designed by John Russell, with printed marks to base.

7.5in (19cm) high

£40-60 **RET**

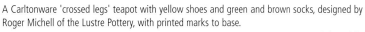

A Midwinter 'HMS Mary' novelty teapot and cover, the base with impressed and printed marks.

c1940 *9.5in (24cm) wide*

£250-350 **WW**

CERAMICS

A Grueby tile, decorated in cuenca with a yellow tulip and green leaves on a green ground, marked 'KY', with two corner chips.

6in (15cm) wide

£1,000-1,500   DRA

A W.B. Simpson tile panel of a knight, painted in colours, the back with impressed marks and paper label, cracked into twopieces.

24.5in (62cm) high

£280-320   WW

A Batchelder horizontal tile, depicting a Dutch boy and girl with dog-drawn carriage in typical Dutch landscape, the back covered with grout, hiding probable mark.

17.75in (45cm) wide

£450-550   DRA

A CLOSER LOOK AT A SET OF EAST GERMAN TILES

This set, and the others on this page, were part of a series produced for an East German holiday home as part of a series showing the power and modernity of the Communist block.

Communist bloc.
The angular, brightly coloured design is appealing and typical of the period – the shapes of the tiles themselves echo and creatre the lines of the design.

The design includes a TV tower, which were considered important statement buildings – examples were built in Moscow, Stuttgart, Riga and Berlin amongst other cities.

The sputnik satellite can also be seen amid the dots that represent stars in outer space – furthermore, the sun shines on the

A set of East German enamelled copper wall tiles, showing the Alexander TV tower in Berlin, the Sputnik satellite, and a radiating sun, framed in metal.

c1975   *28in (71cm) high*

£700-900   VZ

A set of East German enamelled copper wall tiles, showing an idyllic countryside landscape in the background with a dam, power station and a crane, framed in metal.

c1975   *30.5in (76.5cm) wide*

£650-750   VZ

A set of East German enamelled copper wall tiles, showing an industrial landscape with factory chimneys, a chemical plant, a modern high speed train and a flowery meadow with trees, framed in metal.

c1975   *40in (101cm) wide*

£650-750   VZ

QUICK REFERENCE

- The Troika Pottery was founded in 1963, at the Wells Pottery in Wheal Dream, St Ives, Cornwall, by potter Benny Sirota, painter Leslie Illsley and architect Jan Thompson (who left in 1965). Early pieces were smooth and glossy, often in white. Shapes were slip-moulded using liquid clay poured into moulds to ensure uniformity and ease of production.
- New shapes were introduced 1965. Illsley was influenced by Scandinavian ceramics as well as the work of Paul Klee and Constantin Brancusi, therefore circle and geometric designs in earthy muted colours were common. Success followed, due in part to the tourist industry, and in part because several high-profile London stores began stocking Troika wares.
- In 1970 the pottery expanded and moved to Newlyn. The characteristic matte, textured glaze became the main glaze around 1974.
- Consider the form, size, colours and the style of decoration. Practical, rectangular vases were produced in large numbers and are more common today. Meanwhile, scarcer hallmark shapes, such as 'wheel', 'anvil' and 'chimney' vases, remain popular with collectors. Well-executed, complex geometric patterns are desirable. Figural and pictorial images are extremely rare. Damage will reduce value considerably.
- From 1963 to 1967, pieces were usually marked 'St Ives' with a stylised trident in a square. The trident was phased out after 1967, and when the pottery moved to Newlyn, the 'St Ives' was also dropped.

A rare early Troika St Ives rectangular wall plaque, with abstract geometric decoration of squares and raised circles within a black border, with printed Trident mark.

7.5in (19cm) high

£200-300   GORL

A Troika St Ives 'Thames' wall plaque, modelled with a stylised curve of the river with two dimensional buildings surrounding, with Trident mark.

9.75in (25cm) high

£800-1,200   GORL

SPITALFIELDS
ANTIQUE MARKET
Commercial Street, London E1 ■ EVERY THURSDAY from 7am

COVENT GARDEN
ANTIQUE MARKET
The Jubilee Hall, Southampton St, Covent Garden WC2
EVERY MONDAY from 6am

STRATFORD-UPON-AVON
ANTIQUE CENTRE
60 Ely St, Stratford-upon-Avon ■ 7 DAYS A WEEK 10am - 5pm

YORK
ANTIQUE CENTRE
2a Lendel, York ■ MONDAY - SATURDAY 10am - 5pm

Tel: 020 7240 7405 - Sherman & Waterman Associates

A Troika 'Chimney' vase, relief decorated to each side with abstract carved motifs, and with white tin-glazed sides, painted mark and initialled for Avril Bennett.

1973-79   *8in (20.5cm) high*

£250-350   **FLD**

A Troika St Ives 'Chimney' vase, decorated with a gingerbread man in black oxide over a blue ground with an abstract pattern, with a black oxide glazed shoulder, hand painted St Ives mark.

7.75in (20cm) high

£300-500   **FLD**

A Troika Pottery 'Chimney' vase, incised with sun and keypad motif, with a panel of 'Studio St Ives' stamped decoration, glazed in purple, blue and bronze, the base with painted marks and unidentified decorator's monogram.

7.75in (20cm) high

£350-450   **WW**

A Troika Pottery 'Rectangle' vase, decorated by Avril Bennett in relief and washed with oxide glazes in a palette of green and brown, the base with painted marks.

1973-79   *12.75in (33cm) high*

£280-320   **FLD**

A CLOSER LOOK AT A TROIKA MASK

Troika's masks are rare because they were complex to make and took up space in the kiln, making them expensive to buy and so comparatively few were sold.

Always inspect the corners and the base, which are often cracked or chipped. Prices have fallen slightly over the past few years, even for those in mint condition.

They were inspired by the work of artist Paul Klee, Aztec designs and also sometimes African or Oceanic tribal art and masks.

The backs of these masks are also decorated, but any decoration is usually much simpler than on the front.

A rare Troika pottery mask, doubled sided with typical geometric moulded decoration, with a brown ground, the base with painted mark and indistinct decorator's initials.

10in (25.5cm) high

£600-900   **GORL**

A Troika Pottery square jardinière, decorated by Louise Jinks, the base with painted factory marks, and with hairline crack to the rim.

Jinks was a senior decorator from 1979-81.

1976-81   *7.5in (19cm) high*

£180-220   **GHOU**

www.kcsceramics.co.uk

CERAMICS

Visit our Secure ON-LINE shop

**• Specialists in Troika Pottery • Poole Pottery
• Retired Lladro • Royal Doulton • Tiles**

We sell and also buy collections

Valid insurance valuations and certificates charged at only 2%

Credit & Debit Cards Accepted • Professional packing & shipping worldwide

Mrs Karen Parker – Based in West London
Tel: +44 (0) 20 8384 8981 • Email: karen@kcsceramics.co.uk
Internet shop: www.kcsceramics.co.uk

CERAMICS

ESSENTIAL REFERENCE

- Wade was founded by Henry Hallam in 1810, and produced industrial ceramic fittings. In 1867, it moved to Burslem, Staffordshire, becoming known as Wade & Colcough. By the mid-1940s, the three Wade brothers each owned a factory in England; a fourth was founded in Ireland in the 1950s. In 1958, the three factories were combined into Wade Potteries Ltd by Sir George Wade. The company still exists, although the Irish factory closed in the 1990s.
- Wade is perhaps best known for its ranges of miniature, moulded porcelain figurines known as 'Whimsies'. The company had produced miniature figurines since the 1930s, and Whimsies were introduced in 1954. Sold in boxed sets, they were available until 1959, when they were given away as free gifts with products such as Red Rose tea or Christmas crackers. They were offered as premiums in Canada from 1967, and the US from 1983.
- In 1971, they were re-introduced for sale, but were sold individually in boxes. This continued until 1984, when they were withdrawn once again, to be re-introduced recently. Although millions have been made, they have become highly sought-after, with higher prices paid for scarcer,

earlier examples, or unusual variations in glaze or form. Excepting the most recent release, earlier examples are considered as being more finely modelled and decorated.
- The company also produced other ranges of figurines, trays and small ceramic items from the mid-1950s into the 1980s, which are also collectable. These include 'Minikins', 'Whoppas', and the two very popular 'Hat Box' ranges of cartoon film characters, licensed by Disney. Available from 1956-65 and again from 1981-85, the ranges also attract interest from Disney collectors.
- Always consider condition, as this is important to value, as so many examples exist. Run your fingers all over a Whimsie to check for chips and examine them closely to look for repair – either can reduce value by as much as 70 per cent or more. Excellent condition original boxes can double the value.
- In the selection shown here, range names and numbers have been taken from the Charlton Standard Catalogue and, unless otherwise indicated, precise date ranges given refer to the range, or a combination between a figure's introduction date and the production dates of the range.

A Wade 'St Bernard' Whimsie, from Set Seven, the Pedigree Dogs range.

Many early Whimsies have separate legs – these were abandoned on later examples, presumably as they were too fragile and easily broken.

1957-61   1.75in (4.5cm) long

£25-30   **DSC**

A Wade 'Collie' Whimsie, from the English Whimsies range, complete with original box.

The figure on its own is usually worth around £3-4.

1975-84   1.5in (3.5cm) high

£5-8   **DSC**

A Wade 'Alsatian' Whimsie, from Set Seven, the Pedigree Dogs range.

1957-61   1.5in (4cm) long

£20-25   **DSC**

A Wade 'Spaniel With Ball' Whimsie, finished in white, from Set One, the English Animals range.

A rarer variation has a beige glazed rump. Perhaps made as protoypes, examples can fetch twice this value or more.

1954-58   2in (5cm) long

£15-20   **DSC**

A Wade 'Jock' figurine, with green tartan coat, from Set One of the original Disney 'Lady and the Tramp' Hat Box range.
1956-65   *1.75in (4.5cm) high*
£15-20   **DSC**

A Wade 'Jock' figurine, with blue tartan coat, from Set One of the original Disney 'Lady and the Tramp' Hat Box range.
1956-65   *1.75in (4.5cm) high*
£15-20   **DSC**

A Wade 'Scamp' figurine, from the re-issued Disney 'Lady and the Tramp' Hat Box range, with original plastic 'hat box' with paper labels.
1981-85   *1.75in (4cm) long*
£20-25   **DSC**

A Wade 'Jock' figurine, with no tartan coat, from Set One of the original Disney 'Lady and the Tramp' Hat Box range.

This is the rarest and most valuable variation of the three Jocks from the first issue of this range.
1956-65   *1.75in (4.5cm) high*
£30-35   **DSC**

MILLERS COMPARES

This is the first version of Tramp. In the second version he is seated, as the legs on the earlier version proved fragile and easily broken.

Like many Whimsies, the modelling and painting on this earlier version are better.

This simpler second version was introduced in 1985 to complete the re-issued set in the last year of its production.

The base is ridged, which is a hallmark of authentic Whimsies, and this style of label was used 1981-1985.

A Wade 'Lady' figurine from the re-issued Disney 'Lady and the Tramp' Hat Box series, with gilt label to stomach and plastic 'hat box' with paper labels.

Original moulds were used for many figurines in the second series, and it can be hard to tell which period they were made in without the box. However, as some moulds were worn through use, details on re-issues can be flatter. Painted details may also differ e.g. later versions of Lady (like this one) lack a blue collar.
1981-85   *1.75in (4cm) long*
£20-25   **DSC**

A Wade 'Tramp' figurine, from Set One of the original Disney 'Lady and the Tramp' Hat Box range.
1956-6   *52.25in (5.5cm) high*
£20-25   **DSC**

A Wade 'Tramp' figurine, from the re-issued Disney 'Lady and the Tramp' Hat Box range, the base with gilt label.
1985   *2in (5cm) high*
£15-20   **DSC**

CERAMICS

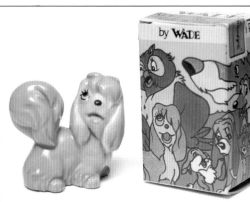

A Wade 'Peg' figurine, from the re-issued Disney 'Lady and the Tramp' Hat Box range, with original printed card box.

Card boxes replaced plastic 'hat boxes' towards the end of the production period, with Peg only being sold in a card box.

1985	1.75in (4cm) long
£20-25	**DSC**

A Wade 'Si' figurine from Set Two of the Disney 'Lady and the Tramp' Hat Box range.

1956-65	2in (5cm) high
£30-35	**DSC**

A Wade 'Am' figurine from Set Two of the Disney 'Lady and the Tramp' Hat Box range.

1956-65	2in (5cm) high
£30-35	**DSC**

A rare Wade 'Tod' figurine from the re-issued Disney 'Fox & The Hound' Hat Box range.

Tod was not as popular as other characters with buyers at the time, making him rare today.

1982-85	2in (5cm) high
£40-50	**DSC**

A Wade 'Dumbo' figurine, from Set Two of the the Disney Hat Box range.

As well as being a desirable character, undamaged examples of ' Dumbo' are scarce.

1956-65	1.5in (4cm) high
£30-35	**DSC**

A Wade 'Pegasus' figurine, from Set Two of the Disney Hat Box range.

Always examine the wings carefully as they are often damaged. Pegasus is from Dinsey's 'Fantasia'.

1956-65	2in (5cm) high
£40-50	**DSC**

A Wade 'Bambi' figurine from the first issue of Set Two of the Disney 'Bambi' Hat Box range, with original printed card 'hat box'.

This is the original card 'hat box' packaging from the 1950s and 60s.

1956-65	1.75in (4cm) high
£30-35	**DSC**

ESSENTIAL REFERENCE – MINIKINS

A Wade 'Cow' Minikin, from Series Two, with 'L-plate' motif to front and musical notes to back.

Minikins were issued from 1955-58 in three different series, each comprising differently shaped figurines modelled by William Harper. All are unmarked and covered in a glossy white glaze, but bear different combinations of motifs and coloured facial features. In all, these differences created 48 variations per set. At an original cost of 1/- each, they were sold to retailers in boxes of 48. With its 'L' plate and musical notes on a cow, this model is a scarce combination.

1956-58   1.25in 93cm) long

£20-25   DSC

A Wade 'Cat Walking' Minikin, from Series One, with blue tail and ears.
1955-58   1.5in (4cm) long
£10-15   DSC

A Wade 'Cat Standing' Minikin, from Series One, with green star and yellow ears.
1955-58   1.25in (3cm) high
£10-15   DSC

A Wade 'Dog' Minikin, from Series Three, with red collar and yellow ears.
1957-58   1.25in 93cm) high
£20-25   DSC

A Wade 'Mouse' Minikin, from Series Two, with blue spot.

1956-58   1in (2.5cm) high
£10-15   DSC

A Wade 'Rabbit' Minikin, from Series Two, with musical note decoration.

1956-58   1.25in (3cm) long
£10-15   DSC

A Wade 'Fawn' Minikin, from Series Three, with flower to chest and pink ears.

This model is quite rare as it was only produced for one year. Note the oversized head, which is typically 1950s in style and also hinted at Disney's 'Bambi'.
1957-58   1.25in (3cm) high
£25-30   DSC

A very rare Wade 'Pelican' Minikin, from Series Three, with anchor decoration.

This is rare as it was produced for only one year before the Minikin range was discontinued. The Pelican was also less popular than other more 'cuddly' and collected animals such as dogs and cats.
1957-58   1.25in (3cm) high
£30-35   DSC

A CLOSER LOOK AT A NATWEST PIGGY BANK

Many believe these unmarked Woody versions are fakes – all Wade banks are marked 'WADE ENGLAND' on the base.

The deeper pink skin colour and the unmarked base indicate that this example was made by Sunshine Ceramics.

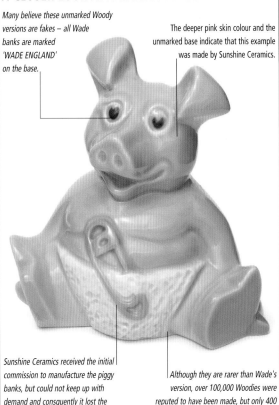

Sunshine Ceramics received the initial commission to manufacture the piggy banks, but could not keep up with demand and consquently it lost the commission to Wade in 1983.

Although they are rarer than Wade's version, over 100,000 Woodies were reputed to have been made, but only 400 full sets of the family were made.

A Sunshine Ceramics 'Woody' piggy bank, modelled by Paul Cardew, and produced for the National Westminster Bank, the base unmarked.

1982   *5.25in (13cm) high*

£5-8   **DSC**

A Wade 'Woody' piggy bank, modelled by Paul Cardew, produced for the National Westminster Bank, the base moulded 'WADE ENGLAND'.

1983-88   *5.25in (13cm) high*

£10-15   **DSC**

A Wade 'Annabel' piggy bank, modelled by Paul Cardew, produced for the National Westminster Bank, the base moulded 'WADE ENGLAND'.

1983-88   *6in (15cm) high*

£15-20   **DSC**

A Wade 'Maxwell' piggy bank, modelled by Paul Cardew, produced for the National Westminster Bank, the base moulded 'WADE ENGLAND'.

1983-88   *6.5in (16cm) high*

£25-30   **DSC**

A Wade 'Lady Hilary' piggy bank, modelled by Paul Cardew, produced for the National Westminster Bank, the base moulded 'WADE ENGLAND'.

1983-88   *6.75in (17cm) high*

£35-40   **DSC**

ESSENTIAL REFERENCE: NATWEST PIGGY BANKS

A Wade 'Sir Nathaniel' piggy bank, modelled by Paul Cardew, produced for the National Westminster Bank, the base moulded 'WADE ENGLAND'.

The National Westminster bank offered these piggy banks from 1982-88 as an incentive for children to save. Woody was given when a child opened an account, with Annabel being given when the balance had reached £25, Maxwell when the balance reached £50, Lady Hilary when it reached £75, and Sir Nathaniel when it reached £100. As £100 was a large sum of money for a child in the 1980s, far fewer examples of Sir Nathaniel were given away compared to Woody. 'Cousin Wesley', modelled by Ken Holmes, was given away in 1998, expanding the family to six. Only 5,000 examples were made and he can fetch £300 or more today with box and slip. Also look out for the 'Gold Woody', decorated with 22 carat gold leaf, of which only only around 30 examples were made, each accompanied by a certificate of authenticty. Fakes are known. These include the 'Gold Woody', and a 'Gold Annabel' which was never made by Wade. Sir Nathaniel banks in white coats are also fakes. In 2007, Paul Cardew's Rame Pottery re-released the pig family with silver detailing to celebrate its 25th anniversary. A new full set costs £200.

1983-88   *7in (17.5cm) high*

£50-60   **DSC**

A 1950s Wade set of four transfer printed ballet dancer dishes, complete with original box.

Dishes 4.75in (10.5cm) wide

£30-40   DSC

A Wade 'Alsation Puppy Lying' pup in a basket dish, with an Alsatian Puppy Lying Whimsy figurine, from the Cat and Puppy Dishes range.

1974-8   1 3.25in (8cm) wide

£10-15   DSC

A 1950s-60s Wade Viking longboat dish, with green and beige glazes and moulded marks to base.

7.5in (19cm) long

£10-15   DSC

A 1950s Wade Mermaid vase, with moulded mermaids on two sides.

The shape and design was perhaps inspired by similar 1930s Art Deco pressed glass vases from Czechoslovakia, Germany and England.

4.25in (10.5cm) wide

£20-25   DSC

A 1950s-60s posy vase, with a Koala on a branch.

2.5in (6.5cm) high

£20-25   DSC

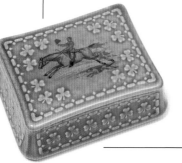

An Irish Wade trinket box, with moulded shamrocks and transfer printed horse racing scene, with moulded marks and grey-blue glaze to base.

The grey glaze, often with greeny-blue tones, is typical of Wade's Irish production.

5in (12.5cm) wide

£15-20   DSC

A 1930s Wade jug vase, in the form of a budgerigar perched on a branch curling up a column, the base printed 'WADE ENGLAND'.

10.25in (26cm) high

£25-30   DSC

FIND OUT MORE...

www.wade.co.uk – *the official company website*

Pat Murray, Wade Whimsical Collectable, *The Charlton Press, 2004*

CERAMICS

QUICK REFERENCE

- Wedgwood was founded by Josiah Wedgwood (1730-1796) in Burslem, Staffordshire in 1759. Success came quickly, and he expanded in 1764, and again in 1768. After meeting the businessman Thomas Bentley, who became his partner in 1769, Wedgwood became fascinated by Classical Greek and Roman designs, and these influenced the company's designs from then on. Although all types of pottery were made, the company is famous for its matte Jasper ware developed c1774-75 and produced in blue, black or green with applied white friezes of Classical scenes.

- The company continued to be an important and innovative pottery during the 20th century, and employed a number of notable designers from the 1930s onwards. Perhaps the most important of these was New Zealand architect and Modernist designer Keith Murray (1892-1981). His geometric Art Deco designs in cool, Classical matte glazes have become highly sought after today. Forms are simple, with moulded ribs, or plain bands cut into the bodies with a lathe. They were produced in a range of colours including 'Moonstone' white, 'Straw Yellow' and green.

- Other notable designers included Daisy Makeig-Jones (1881-1945) who is known for her complex 'Fairyland Lustre' range of the late 1910s and 1920s, and illustrator Eric Ravilious (1903-42) who designed nursery and table ware from c1936 to 1940. Norman Wilson (1902-85), John Skeaping (1901-80) and Millicent Taplin (1902-80) are other notable names whose various designs from the 1920-60s are worth looking out for.

- Wedgwood has attracted a huge following of collectors, and prices are strong, particularly for 20thC designs. It will be interesting to see how the company's recent insolvency affects values over the coming years.

A Wedgwood matte green ball vase, shape 4197, designed by Keith Murray, the base with printed full signature mark.

6in (15.5cm) high

£350-400   BEV

A Wedgwood Straw yellow tapering cylindrical vase, shape 4315, designed by Keith Murray, the base with printed 'KM' mark.

7.5in (19cm) high

£450-550   BEV

A Wedgwood Straw yellow ball vase, shape 4197, designed by Keith Murray, the base with printed full signature mark.

This mark was introduced 1932.

6in (15cm) high

£350-450   BEV

A 1930s Wedgwood matte green horizontally fluted globe vase, shape 4324, designed by Keith Murray, the base with impressed 'KM' mark.

This is an extremely rare design. This mark was introduced in 1934. It is more commonly seen printed, rather than impressed.

7in (17.5cm) high

£500-700   PC

A Wedgwood bowl, designed by Norman Wilson, of fluted form, glazed black and white, impressed marks, printed 'NW'.

Here, a Black Basalt slip has been applied to a Moonstone white glazed body, which has then been cut back on a lathe to reveal the underlying colour.

10.75in (27cm) diam

£280-380   WW

A Wedgwood Black Basalt bowl, by Norman Wilson, of fluted form, glazed black, impressed marks, minor chips to top rim.

10in (25.5cm) diam

£380-480   WW

A rare Wedgwood earthenware bowl, by Norman Wilson, sky blue cut back to black, the interior black, impressed marks, 'NW' monogram.

6.25in (16cm) diam

£420-480   WW

QUICK REFERENCE – NORMAN WILSON

Norman Wilson (1902-1985) was invited to join Wedgwood as Works Manager in 1926. Part of a young, dynamic team, he became Production Director in 1946, having introduced new production processes including the installation of a tunnel kiln. Among collectors, he is best known for his glaze experiments, and matte glazes that were used by Keith Murray. After studying ancient Chinese Sung glazes, Wilson developed a range of unique experimental glazes that were applied to production and specially commissioned forms. Known as 'Norman Wilson Unique Ware', these were produced erratically from 1928-63, with no two pieces being exactly the same.

A Wedgwood Dragon Lustre dish, designed by Daisy Makeig-Jones, with mythical beast printed in gilt on a pearl lustre ground, the base with printed and painted marks.

3.5in (9cm) diam

£100-150   WW

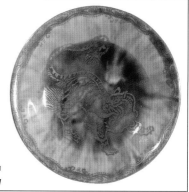

A Wedgwood earthenware bowl, designed by Norman Wilson, the exterior salmon pink, the interior mottled pink, the base with impressed marks and 'NM' monogram.

8in (20.5cm) diam

£400-500   WW

A Wedgwood Fairyland Lustre 'Candlemas' pattern vase, designed by Daisy Makeig-Jones, shape 2410, printed and painted in colours and gilt on a black ground, the base with printed factory mark, and 'NJW Baker' retailer's paper label.

'Candlemas' was introduced in 1918, and was based on the ritual ceremony of the blessing of candles, which would then be carried in a procession. Produced in four different colour variations, it was made until 1929.

7.5in (19.5cm) high

£800-1,200   WW

A Wedgwood part tea set, retailed by Thomas Goode & Co., painted with a trailing fruiting vine, pattern no. A5061, comprising eight cups, eight saucers, eleven tea plates, two bread and butter plates, a sugar bowl and a milk jug.

£150-200   **DA&H**

A Wedgwood 'Persephone' pattern oval meat dish, designed by Eric Ravilious with chip and some wear to glaze and pattern.

c1938   *16.75in (42.5cm) wide*

£70-100   **SWO**

A CLOSER LOOK AT A WEDGWOOD FAIRYLAND LUSTRE BOWL

Bowls are particularly popular with collectors – as they are decorated both inside and out, you get a lot of 'pattern for your pound'.

Wedgwood's Fairyland Lustre range has risen in price over the past few years, primarily due to interest from American collectors. However, prices may be peaking.

The 'Dana – Castle on a Road' pattern was designed in 1917 and released in the same year – it was popular and soon became a bestseller.

Makeig-Jones' innovative and complex designs were highly influential and expensive in their day. Carltonware and Crown Devon produced similar, more affordable ranges, but none matched the quality of Fairyland Lustre.

A Wedgwood Fairyland Lustre 'Dana - Castle on a Road' pattern octagonal punch bowl, designed by Daisy Makeig Jones, printed and painted in gilt and enamels, the base with printed and painted marks to base including the 'Z5125' pattern number.

9in (23cm) wide

£1,000-1,500   **L&T**

A Wedgwood 'Persephone' pattern six place dinner service, designed by Eric Ravilious, comprising six each of four sizes of plates, six handled bowls, two lidded tureens, an oval bowls and a gravy boat and stand, each with transfer-printed design.

c1938   *Plates 9in (23cm) diam*

£400-600   **SWO**

A rare Wedgwood 'Garden Implements' pattern Liverpool-shape lemonade jug and four beakers, designed by Eric Ravilious in c1938, printed in black and pink lustre, the bases with printed factory marks.

Jug 7.75in (20cm) high

£1,200-1,800 (SET)   **WW**

FIND OUT MORE…

Maureen Batkin ' Wedgwood Ceramics 1846-1959' . *Ilminster: Richard Dennis Publications, 1982.*

Robin Reilly and George Savage ' Wedgwood – The New Illustrated Dictionary' . *London: The Antique Collectors' Club, 1999.*

QUICK REFERENCE

- Samuel Weller (1851-1925) founded Weller in Fultonham, Ohio in 1872, and moved the company to Zanesville in 1888. Like local rival Roseville, it initially produced utilitarian wares, before moving into the art pottery market.
- Weller bought W. A. Long's Lonhuda Pottery in 1894. Within a year, he had learned Long's special glazing techniques, which had been developed by ex-Rookwood decorator Laura Fry, and the partnership between Long and Weller was dissolved. The Lonhuda range, which featured hand-painted natural motifs on brown glossy background, much like Rookwood's Standard Glazed pieces, was re-launched by Weller as Louwelsa. Although competition was strong, Weller prospered and by 1904 had become the largest art pottery in the world.
- Weller continued to produce high-quality hand-decorated ranges at affordable prices. These included Aurelian (c1897), Eocean (1898), Dickensware (1900) and Sicardo (1902). Designers included Charles Upjohn (working 1895-1904),

Jacques Sicard (1902-07) and Frederick Rhead (1903-04).
- Many factories stopped producing hand-decorated ranges as the 1920s approached, turning to faster and less expensive moulded wares. Weller reacted against this by releasing the hand-painted Hudson range in 1917, but the Great Depression after 1929 forced even Weller to move to entirely moulded wares by 1935. Much was designed by Rudolph Lorber and his assistant, Dorothy England Laughead. These pieces were of good quality and new glazes, such as 'Burnt Wood' and 'Graystone', were still being developed.
- Hand-decorated lines, such as Louwelsa, Eocean and Hudson, usually command the highest prices, particularly large examples with all-over surface decoration. Look for artists' signature as this will usually add value. Later moulded forms are generally not as valuable, though the most complex or rarest ranges by notable designers can be desirable. Be sure to look for damage on all examples, as this always reduces value, especially on the moulded ranges.

A Weller 'Louwelsa' large baluster vase, decorated by Sarah McLaughlin, the base with a partial Louwelsa stamp and numbered, with glaze flake to base and hairline to rim.

11in (28cm) high

£150-200   BEL

A Weller 'Hudson' vase, painted by Ruth Axline, with a branch of yellow, blue and pink dogwood blossoms around the upper body, and with kiln stamp/artist's cipher.

9in (23cm) high

£300-400   DRA

A Weller 'Hudson' vase, painted by Sarah McLaughlin with irises, with circular factory ink stamp and artist's mark to base.

9.25in (23.5cm) high

£600-800   DRA

A Weller 'Hudson Light' tapered vase, painted with pink and yellow columbine, the base stamped 'WELLER'.

13.75in (35cm) high

£300-400   DRA

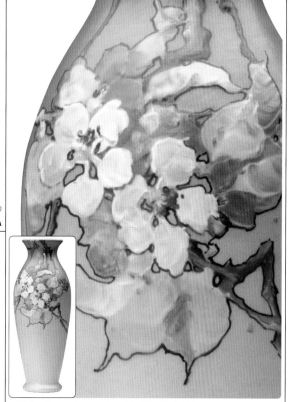

A Weller 'Hudson' vase, painted by Mae Timberlake, with nasturtium blossoms, stamped kiln mark and signed 'Timberlake'.

12.75in (33.5cm) high

£600-800   DRA

CERAMICS

A Weller scenic 'Hudson' vase, painted by Hester Pillsbury with a cabin in the woods, against a mountainous landscape, repair to two cracks through body, kiln stamp.

Scenic Hudson vases are scarcer than floral patterns. Had this vase not been cracked it might have been worth double this price.

9in (23cm) high

£600-800   **CRA**

A CLOSER LOOK AT A WELLER VASE

The Sicard range was designed by Frenchman Jacques Sicard, who had previously worked for notable French potter Clement Massier.

Developed under great secrecy with the aim of putting Weller back among the top pottery companies in the US, the range was sold from 1902-12.

The range is typified by iridescent glazes and motifs derived from nature. This example displays a superb range of colours and a complex and detailed pattern.

One of Weller's most sought-after ranges among collectors, this example is enhanced by a decorative shape typical of the period.

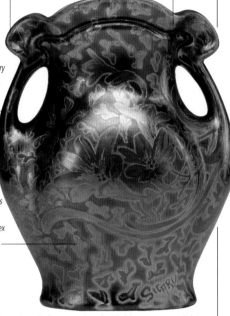

A Weller 'Sicard' two-handled vase, painted with blossoms on a rich purple lustred ground, signed 'Weller Sicard'.

9in (23cm) high

£1,500-2,500   **DRA**

A Weller 'Etna' vase, moulded with pink daisies against a shaded dark grey ground, the base stamped 'WELLER WARE ETNA'.

10.75in (27.5cm) high

£250-350   **DRA**

A Weller 'Sicard' vase with scrolling leaf and daisy pattern, the base with script factory mark, glaze chip to bottom, possibly from grinding.

5.5in (14cm) high

£450-550   **DRA**

A Weller 'Turada' bowl, with heavy slip decoration and black glaze, the base marked 'Weller Turada 44'.

Turada was designed by Samuel Weller.

c1898

4.5in (11.4cm) diam

£60-80   **BEL**

A Weller 'Sicard' cabinet vase, decorated with an all-over star pattern, the base stamped '6'.

4in (10cm) high

£350-450   **DRA**

A Weller 'Knifewood' vase, with owls, squirrels and birds on oak branches, the base stamped 'Weller'.

7in (18cm) high

£450-550   **DRA**

A rare Weller Matt Green-glazed basket vase, on a 'Silvertone' blank, crisply decorated, unmarked, and with restoration to handle.

Such green glazes were typical of Arts and Crafts potteries, and are desirable among collectors today.

9in (23cm) high

£200-300   **DRA**

A rare Weller 'Fru Russett' tapering vase, with pierced rim, large applied yellow flowers and green leaves on a pale purple ground, restored rim, the base with impressed mark.

The Arts and Crafts style Fru Russett range was introduced in 1905 and is very rare today. Typical colours include matte green, brown, or blue and motifs are usually floral.

10.5in (26.5cm) high

£1,200-1,800   **CRA**

A very rare Weller 'Muskota' wall hanging 'Tree Squirrel', with restored paws.

The Muskota line of animals was produced from 1915-28 and is very popular with collectors today. The range also included butterflies, birds and fish, with this form being very scarce.

13.75in (35cm) long

£450-550   **BH**

A Weller 'Tutone' chalice vase, with green highlights, the base with Weller Pottery full kiln stamp, and three tight lines at the rim.

5.5in (14cm) high

£15-25   **BEL**

A Weller 'Velva' vase, in brown with floral panel, the base with script Weller Pottery mark.

7.5in (19cm) high

£60-80   **BEL**

A Weller 'Woodcraft' tree-shaped vase, with climbing squirrel and owl, with tight crack to rim, and second restored crack.

18in (45.5cm) high

£600-800   **DRA**

A rare Weller Art Deco owl figurine, in a semi-matte blue glaze, the Greek letters 'Kappa Kappa Gamma' on the base.

9.75in (25cm) high

£400-600   **BEL**

QUICK REFERENCE

- Wemyss ware was produced by the Fife Pottery in Kirkaldy Scotland from 1882, after the owner's son, Robert Methven Heron, invited Bohemian decorators to join the pottery. The pottery had its origins in the 18thC producing objects in muted colours, but when Karel Nekola, one of the new staff, decorated pieces with flowers and leaves inspired by his love of nature, production changed direction and Wemyss ware was born.
- Popularity grew rapidly, and pieces were sold by top London retailer Thomas Goode & Son, whose marks can often be found on pieces.
- Following Nekola's death in 1915. Edwin Sandland took over decoration. After his death in 1928 he was in turn succeeded by Nekola's son Joe. A loss in popularity due to changing public tastes forced the pottery to close in 1930. Joe Nekola moved to the Bovey Tracey pottery in Devon, taking the Wemyss moulds with him. After his death in 1952, Esther Weeks took over until 1957. She is still decorating Wemyss today at the Griselda Pottery, Fife (established 1985).
- The colourful, cheery and quirky style of Wemyss ware has attracted a legion of loyal collectors, including personalities such as Elton John, the late HM Queen Elizabeth the Queen Mother, and HRH Prince Charles. Most collectors collect Wemyss ware by pattern and some patterns and shapes are more desirable than others. The work of Karel Nekola is particularly sought after.
- Examine pieces all over for signs of damage, as this reduces value dramatically. Wares made in Fife are particularly prone to crazing and chipping. Devon-produced pieces have a cleaner white 'glassy' glaze, and are lighter in weight than examples from Fife. They are also generally less valuable, giving a more affordable entry point to the market.

An early 20thC Wemyss dog bowl, decorated with cabbage roses and inscription 'Plus je connais les hommes/Plus j'admire les chiens', with painted and impressed marks 'Wemyss', restoration to rim, cracks.

The charming inscription means "The more I know [about] men, the more I admire dogs." Dog bowls are scarce and valuable.

4.25in (11cm) diam

£300-500   **L&T**

A Wemyss basket jardinière, decorated with cabbage roses, the base with impressed 'Wemyss' mark.

c1900   11.5in (29.5cm) diam

£280-320   **L&T**

A small Wemyss loving cup, decorated with dog roses, with impressed 'Wemyss Ware R. H. & S.' mark, and 'T. Goode & Co.' retailer's mark, glaze losses on rim.

c1900   4.25in (10.5cm) high

£280-320   **L&T**

A small Wemyss basket, decorated with cabbage roses, with impressed 'Wemyss Ware R. H. & S.' mark, and 'T Goode & Co.' retailer's mark.

c1900   8in (20.5cm) long

£250-300   **L&T**

An early 20thC Wemyss low pomade and cover, with dog roses, possibly by Karel Nekola, with impressed and painted 'Wemyss' mark, chip to rim.

3.75in (9.5cm) diam

£350-400   **L&T**

A 1920s Wemyss biscuit barrel and cover, decorated in the 'Jazzy' pattern with cabbage roses, the cover inscribed 'Biscuits', with painted 'Wemyss 213' mark.

'Jazzy' is the name given to the multi-coloured, brushed background, which replaces the standard white on other pieces.

4.75in (12cm) diam

£250-350   L&T

A Wemyss 'Cabbage Rose' biscuit box and cover, painted in colours, impressed and painted 'Wemyss' painted and printed marks.

5in (12.5cm) diam

£220-280   WW

A large early 20thC Wemyss mug, decorated with cabbage roses, with impressed mark 'Wemyss'.

5.5in (14cm) high

£280-320   L&T

A Wemyss 'Cabbage Rose' jug and a basin, painted in colours, the bases with various marks, damaged.

Had this not been damaged, it may have fetched over £800.

Jug 6.25in (16cm) high

£150-200   WW

An early 20thC Wemyss pin tray, decorated by Karel Nekola with dog roses and bearing the inscription "Sois satisfait des fruits, des fleurs, même des feuilles/ Si c'est dans ton jardin à toi que tu les cueilles", impressed and painted mark "Wemyss", hairline crack.

The wording reads, 'Be satisfied with the fruits, flowers, and same with the leaves/If it is in your garden that you picked them'. Plaques are scarce and desirable.

5.75in (14.5cm) wide

£500-700   L&T

A CLOSER LOOK AT A WEMYSS GOBLET

The rose, shamrock and thistle motifs are typical of decoration on Wemyss, but are rarely found together on one piece.

The rose can be read as indicating England, the thistle Scotland, and the shamrock Ireland.

The goblet bears the VR monogram for 'Victoria Regina' – royal commemoratives are widely collected, which widens the market.

The goblet shape is appealing, and the decoration is very detailed.

A small Wemyss Victoria goblet, with decoration of roses, thistles and shamrock, and bearing crown and cipher, impressed mark 'Wemyss Ware R. H. & S.', 'T. Goode & Co.' retailer's mark.

c1900

5.5in (14cm) high

£200-300   L&T

CERAMICS

A small early 20thC Wemyss pig, covered in a green glaze.

6.25in (16cm) long

£350-450   L&T

A Wemyss pottery pig, covered in a pink glaze, with impressed mark.

6.25in (16cm) high

£320-380   WW

A small Wemyss pig figure, covered in a white glaze, with impressed 'Wemyss' mark.

c1900   6.25in (16cm) long

£350-450   L&T

A Wemyss pig, painted in shades of black and white, its snout and toes painted pink, painted 'Wemyss', and printed 'Made in England'.

6.5in (16.5cm) wide

£350-450   WW

A CLOSER LOOK AT A WEMYSS PIG

Pigs can be found in a number of different patterns and plain glazes, but beware of fakes which have glossier glazes in different tones when compared to authentic examples.

Plump seated pigs are perhaps the most celebrated and recognisable of Wemyss' shapes and are highly sought after.

Smaller Plichta pigs dating from after 1930, such as this one, tend to be more affordable than earlier examples.

In 2004, Sotheby's sold a rare sleeping piglet painted with roses for a record price of £34,800.

A small post-1930 Wemyss pig figure, decorated by Joe Nekola with shamrocks, printed marks 'Plichta London England', painted marks 'Nekola/pinx'.

6.25in (16cm) long

£320-380   L&T

A Wemyss goose flower holder, naturalistically painted in typical colours, on an oval foot, impressed 'Wemyss Ware R.H. & S.' and a pink stamped mark for T. Goode & Co.

c1900   8in (20.5cm) high

£320-380   DN

QUICK REFERENCE

- West German ceramics from the 1950s-1970s have recently become highly collectable. Interest in this field is understandable, as this period enjoyed an explosion of innovation and design in West German pottery, which changed dramatically from decade to decade. Established companies, such as Bay Keramik, Dümler & Breiden, Emons & Söhne and Ruscha, underwent a revival, as new companies, such as Scheurich and Otto Keramik, opened.
- The ceramics of the 1950s are typified by curving, organic or geometric forms, and painted in bright, primary colours, often outlined in black. Patterns comprised ovals, circles, lines and stylised, curving, natural motifs. Angled or asymmetric curving handles or rims were common. Largely ornamental, jug vases with handles were particularly popular. These handles were often strongly angled in the 1950s, taking on ring forms in the 1960s.

- There was a complete change of style in the 1960s-70s. Colour and texture became extremely important. Rather than forming planned patterns, glazes were trailed, dripped or daubed over the body of the piece. Many of these glazes were thick 'lava' glazes, arranged in bands or stripes of bright colours, such as orange or red.
- Look for wilder, thick glazes, known by collectors as 'Fat Lava', as these tend to be more desirable, particularly in unusual forms. Many 'Fat Lava' pieces were produced in limited numbers, as opposed to tamer designs in less exuberant colours, which are more common.
- Makers can be identified by considering shape, colour, type of glaze and style of moulded marks on the base. Some pieces were inscribed or had impressed marks: some even have labels. Handle as many identified pieces, ideally those with labels, as possible.

A 1950s Marzi & Remi 'sugarglaze' vase, with inscribed curving lines through a brick coloured glaze, the base marked '2015-50'.

19.75in (50cm) high

£80-120   OUT

A 1960s Bay Keramik floor vase, with hand-painted cell-like design, introduced in 1961, the base with moulded numbers.

Many have attributed this design to Bodo Mans due to the abstract nature and bright colours of the design, but this has not been confirmed.

£100-150   OUT

A 1950s West German Conradt Gebrüder vase, with hand-painted round and curving line design, the base marked "100/5".

10in (25cm) high

£40-60   OUT

A 1950s West German Bay Keramik torpedo vase, with white textured glaze and hand-decorated multicoloured crescent and curving line decoration, the base moulded '529 38'.

15.25in (38.5cm) high

£20-30   RET

A 1950s West German Bay Keramik baluster vase, with hand-painted yellow and blue bands and black dashes, designed by Bodo Mans, the base moulded '584-25'.

10in (25cm) high

£30-50   OUT

CERAMICS

A 1950s West German Fürstenberg porcelain bull, with black glaze, the base marked 'F'.

6in (15cm) high

£40-60   **OUT**

A 1950s Keto 'Komposition' vase, with hand-painted multicoloured triangles and inscribed lines, the base printed 'Keto Keramik Handarbeit Komposition 1004'.

9in (23cm) high

£40-60   **OUT**

A CLOSER LOOK AT A BAY VASE

Defined areas of bright, saturated colour combined with inscribed 'sgrafitto' or painted lines are typical of 1950s designs.

Patterns were often named after romantic, foreign places as the 1950s was the age of the jet plane and an increase in foreign travel.

Bodo Mans was one of the most notable designers during the 1950s, and produced many similar designs inspired by modern art.

Despite the pattern being modern, the shape is more traditional – had that been more modern as well, the value would have been higher.

A West German Bay Keramik 'Paris' pattern urn vase, designed by Bodo Mans in 1960, the base moulded '1014-25 WEST-GERMANY'.

10in (25cm) high

£30-40   **MA**

A 1960s West German Marzi & Remy blue and white arabesque patterned jug vase, with impressed 'MR' monogram used from 1960-67, numbered '2027/32A'.

Marzi & Remy (1879-1994) are best known for their beer steins, which were mostly decorated with the design protruding through the coloured glaze, as in this example. This moulded pattern recalls tiles of the Arts and Crafts movement of the late 19thC and early 20thC.

1960-67   *12.5in (32cm) high*

£20-30   **M20C**

A 1970s Ruscha wall plate, decorated with a sgraffito and glazed design of grazing fawns on a mottled cream ground, the back printed 'RUSCHA HANDARBEIT' and moulded '717/1'.

1969-78   *7.25in (18.5cm) diam*

£22-28   **RET**

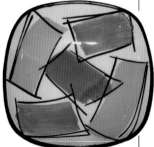

A 1950s West German Schramberg Majolika Fabrik hand-painted 'Cuba' pattern dish, the base marked '4370 Cuba'.

5in (12cm) wide

£15-20   **OUT**

A CLOSER LOOK AT A SCHEURICH VASE

Known to collectors as the 'Flame' pattern, the range was actually called 'Lora'.

This is a comparatively large size, had it been a floor vase, the value could have been doubled.

This particular colour combination is very unusual, particularly the green.

Before firing, layers of glaze are cut away by hand to reveal underlying colours, making the pattern on each unique.

A West German Scheurich floor vase, the grey bubbly 'lava' glaze cut through to reveal the red underglaze in the form of horses, the base with moulded marks.

18in (46cm) high

£100-150   **WW**

A West German Scheurich 'Lora' pattern floor vase, with a copper-coloured micro-crystalline glaze over a glossy red glaze, the base moulded '517 45 W.GERMANY'.

This type of coppery micro-crystalline glaze was developed by Oswald Kleudgen and became a signature glaze of his.

17in (43cm) high

£80-100   **M20C**

A West German Scheurich 'Lora' pattern floor vase with three layers of glaze, comprising a beige lava glaze over glossy orange over glossy green, the base with indistinct numbering.

15in (38cm) high

£70-100   **M20C**

A 1970s West German Scheurich torpedo vase, with thin grey lava glaze and glossy white and dripped blue bands, the base moulded '522-20'.

8in (20cm) high

£40-60   **OUT**

A West German Scheurich floor vase, with banded orange and green design and tube-lined curlicue designs in a lava glaze.

20in (51cm) high

£30-50   **SAS**

A 1970s Scheurich cylinder vase with orange band and tube-lined grey 'lava' glaze design, with beige and grey 'lava' glaze top and base, the base moulded '231 15 W GERMANY'.

This form number was used on three different shapes by Scheurich, showing how shape numbers were reused at different times.

6in (15cm) high

£15-20   **RET**

CERAMICS

A 1970s Scheurich 'Wien' series bulb vase, designed by A. Seide, with lava glazed ribbed top and dripped glazed body designed by Oswald Kleudgen, the base with indistinct moulded marks.

7in (17.5cm) high

£20-30   RET

A 1970s West-German Scheurich 'Wien' series jug vase, designed by A. Seide, covered with a dripped orangey red glaze over a bronze-brown ground, the base numbered '269-27'.

10.5in (27cm) high

£40-60   OUT

A mid-late 1970s West German Scheurich jug vase, with glossy orange and brown glazes, the base moulded 400-22 W.GERMANY.

8.75in (22cm) high

£15-20   M20C

A West German Scheurich jug vase, with glossy mottled red central band and cream foamy glaze over a brown ground, the base moulded 400-22 W.GERMANY.

8.75in (22cm) high

£20-25   M20C

QUICK REFERENCE - GLAZES AND SHAPES

Ruscha were one of the many companies to produce one shape and then apply a myriad of different glaze treatments, known as the 'decor' to collectors, with the famed 313 jug designed by Kurt Tschörner in 1954. The practice was taken up by many other companies, with Scheurich being a the most prolific practitioner. Given the vast choice available in the marketplace, many collectors choose to focus on one shape by one maker and then aim to collect as many different variations on the decor as possible. This particular example is more valuable than the other two on this page as it has the most appealing lava glaze. In many cases, shapes can fetch more if they have been focused on by a large number of collectors.

A West German Scheurich jug vase, with heavy cream and brown lava glaze over a matte cobalt blue ground, the base moulded '400-22 W.GERMANY'.

8.75in (22cm) high

£25-30   M20C

A 1970s West German Scheurich 'Montignac' pattern, Linie 72 series bottle vase, with bull outlined in a lava glaze, the base moulded 281-19.

By the 1950s, ceramic design began to show the influence of the prehistoric cave paintings found in the Lascaux caves, France, 1940. Montignac is the nearest town to the caves. The decoration is rare.

7.5 (19cm) high

£40-60   OUT

A 1970s Bay cylindrical footed vase, moulded decoration, blue glaze, base moulded '604-11 BAY W.-GERMANY', with silver foil manufacturer's label.

This design imitates Aldo Londi's popular 1953 'Rimini Blue' design for Bitossi, although the pattern is moulded, not impressed.

7in (17.5cm) high

£20-25   RET

A 1970s West German Bay Keramik jug vase, with white speckled glaze and orange and brown 'lava' glazed band, the base moulded 'W.-GERMANY 2 20'.

8in (20.5cm) high

£25-30   RET

A 1970s Carstens Luxus series vase, with green, orange and red glazes and stylised floral design, designed by Dieter Peter, the base with moulded factory logo and numbered '7692-45 W.-GERMANY'.

17.75in (45cm) high

£100-150   RET

A Carstens glossy lime green footed cylinder vase, with grey salt glaze swirls, the base moulded '147-28' and with printed white semi-circular 'WEST-GERMANY' mark.

11.5in (29cm) high

£30-40   RET

A 1970s Austrian Carstens small handled jug vase, with orange, beige and green glazes and stylised floral design, designed by Dieter Peter, the base moulded '3967-18 AUSTRIA'.

7.25in (18.5cm) high

£35-45   RET

A West German Carstens waisted vase, with alternating bands of a brown glaze with copper inclusions and orange salt-glaze, with factory silver foil label, the base moulded '3643-30 W.-GERMANY'.

12in (30.5cm) high

£30-35   RET

A 1960s West German Carstens 'Ankara' pattern vase, designed by Scholtis, the base with moulded Carstens mark, numbered '1236-23'.

Although prices for many West German ceramics of this period can vary widely, this design seems to fetch consistently good prices when offered at modern design auctions.

9in (23cm) high

£40-60   OUT

CERAMICS

A 1970s West German Roth Keramik double-handled disc vase, shape no.314, with glossy red and black lava glazes, base unmarked.

This is also found in a smaller size.

15.5in (39cm) high

£300-350   **GC**

An extremely rare 1970s Roth Keramik red dish, with red glossy curving shapes between black 'lava' glazes, unmarked.

8in (20cm) long

£300-500   **OUT**

A CLOSER LOOK AT A ROTH VASE

Known as the 'Guitar' to collectors, this is arguably the rarest and most dramatic of Roth's designs, with no clear precedent.

It can be found in a number of different colours, including red, purple, yellow, blue, and different green tones – values rise in that order to as much as £600.

An extremely rare 'reverse' variation is also known, with glossy red glazed lines between 'lava' glazed shapes.

Roth's pieces are not marked with the company name on the base, but are sometimes labelled.

A 1970s West German Roth Keramik orange and black lava glaze 'guitar' vase, shape no.312, by an unknown designer, the base unmarked.

12.25in (31cm) high

£250-300   **GC**

A 1970s West German Ruscha no.717 dish, with red stylised flower pattern, crystalline copper glaze and tubelined lava glaze, the base moulded '717/2'.

11in (27.5cm) diam

£40-50   **M20C**

A late 1970s-early 1980s West German Ruscha no.717 dish, with orange stylised flower and leaf pattern and tube-lined lava glaze, the base moulded '717/2'.

11in (27.5cm) diam

£35-45   **M20C**

A 1970s Ruscha wall charger with applied discs and rectangles and mottled and cloudy brown, beige and orange glazes, inscribed on back '717/2'.

The 717 dish is one of the most common dish shapes found today, and was produced from the 1950s onwards in a variety of decor types. This design is not too hard to find. The discs are often raised, almost resembling mushrooms.

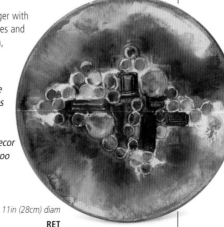

11in (28cm) diam

£50-70   **RET**

An extremely rare Ruscha vase, shape 816/1, with tube-lined gun-metal grey lava glaze in a grid pattern, and a glossy turquoise glaze, the base unmarked.

Both the glaze and the shape are very hard to find – this combination is extremely rare.

8.5in (21.5cm) high

£120-180   MHC

QUICK REFERENCE - RUSCHA'S VULKANO GLAZE

The 'Vulkano' glaze marks the turning point in West German ceramics design between the linear, abstract designs in primary colours of the 1950s, and the freely applied, dripping and 'volcanic' lava glazes of the 1960s and 70s. Designed for leading factory Ruscha by talented glaze technician Otto Gerharz Snr in 1959, the focus became the glaze itself, rather than the patterns that could be created with it. Look out for a good variety of strong colours including green, as shown here, as these tend to be popular with collectors.

A 1960s West German Ruscha 'Vulkano' glaze vase, the shape designed by Kurt Tscörner, the glaze by Otto Gerharz Snr, the base marked 320/2.

7in (18cm) high

£30-50   OUT

A 1960s Ruscha 'Vulkano' glaze jug, the form designed by Kurt Tschörner, the glaze by Otto Gerharz Snr, the base moulded '314/2'.

10.75in (27cm) high

£80-100   GC

A 1970s West German Ruscha 'Antique' vase with a moulded pattern of charioteers, and red glaze over a brown background, the base marked '508-18'.

7in (18cm) high

£40-60   OUT

A 1970s East German Strehla waisted, footed vase with tube-lined lava glaze on a red ground, unmarked.

East German companies were keen to cash in on the success of West German ceramics, and produced their own, very similar, versions.

8.25in (21cm) high

£22-28   RET

A 1960s West German Übelacker Keramik jug vase, with mottled blue glaze and red and green band, the base impressed with an Ü motif and numbered 1628/30, and with silver manufacturer's label.

12in (30.5cm) high

£35-45   RET

FIND OUT MORE...

Fat Lava: West German Pottery From the 1960s & 70s, by Mark Hill, published by www.markhillpublishing.com

From Spritzdekor to Fat Lava and West & East German Pottery: Makers' Marks & Form Numbers, by Kevin Graham, published privately, kj_graham@gmx.de

QUICK REFERENCE

- This section is arranged alphabetically by manufacturer, with the final page comprising ceramics by as yet unidentified factories. Unlike glass, most ceramics are marked on the base. Marks may include the factory name, and possibly the designer's name as well, although this generally only appears on 20thC ceramics. Other marks may include an impressed number identifying the shape, and a painted or printed number or name to indicate the pattern or range.
- In 1890, the American McKinley Tariff Act required the name of the country of orgin to be marked on goods, including ceramics. This lead to the appearance of marks such as 'England', 'Bavaria' and 'Nippon' (Japan). In 1921 the act was amended, requiring the words 'Made in' to appear before the country. There are some exceptions, including Wedgwood, who used 'Made in England' from 1898.

- Other marks can help identify a country of origin. For example, 'Déposé would indicate manufacture in France and 'Gesetzlich Geschütz' (Ges.Gesch) in Germany. Look out for 'Reg'd' (registered) design numbers and diamond marks as these can both supply further information when researched in reference books. 'Trademark' and 'Limited' or 'Ltd' were not used before c1861-62, and are often much later.
- Be aware that the styles and shapes of marks often changed over time, which can help with dating. If a piece is unmarked, consider the way it was made: was it hand-potted or moulded, or decorated by hand? Compare the style of the form and the decoration with examples in reference books or on websites, but always cross-reference any possible identifications with other sources, particularly if found online.

A Canadian Beauce Pottery wine carafe, shape G-121, and four goblets, shape G-119, with ribbed cog-like decoration and green glaze, designed by Jacques Garnier in 1964, the base with 'arrow heads' factory mark.

This is typical of the geometric, almost Modernist, solid forms produced by Garnier.

9in (23cm) high

£50-80   TWF

A 1960s-70s Canadian Blue Mountain Pottery jug, with a dripped and mottled cobalt and light blue glaze, the base with moulded three tree mark.

10.25in (26.5cm) high

£30-50   TWF

An Arequipa ovoid vase, finely carved with an iris under a matte green glaze, the base with stamped mark, restoration to a small area at rim.

7.75in (19.5cm) high

£800-1,200   DRA

An early 1970s Canadian Blue Mountain Pottery tall bottle vase with flared neck and rim, with 'Flame' glaze with some orange dripping/mottling, the base with moulded 'three tree' mark.

8.25in (21cm) high

£20-40   TWF

A 1970s Canadian Blue Mountain Pottery 'Spitoon' vase, shape 32A, with scarce brown glaze overlaid with randomly trailed foam-effect white glaze.

5.25in (13cm) high

£20-40   TWF

A modern Burleigh Ware 'Guardsmen' jug, modelled in low relief with marching guardsmen and a sentry box, the base with printed factory marks.

This stunning jug was designed and first released in the early 1930s. Very few original examples survive today, and these can fetch over £1,000 in undamaged condition. Beware, as reproductions have been made since the late 1970s, and are considerably less valuable. Authentic Burleigh reproductions like this, which are better painted and moulded than copies by other factories, are more desirable.

7.75in (20cm) high

£120-180   WW

A Bursley Ware rectangular tray, designed by Charlotte Rhead, pattern TL43, painted with flower designs in pastel shades.

13in (33cm) wide

£150-200   GHOU

A C. & Co. Ltd slip decorated planter, painted with white 'Glasgow Rose' motif, on a green ground, printed mark.

7.5in (19cm) diam

£80-120   WW

A 19thC Capo di Monte oval box and cover, with gilt-metal mounts, decorated with moulded cherubs at play.

5in (13cm) wide

£80-120   L&T

A Cauldon 'Chariots' pattern blue and white transfer-printed octagonal vase.

5in (12.5cm) high

£75-85   BAD

QUICK REFERENCE - CANDY WARE

Candy & Co. Ltd was founded in 1875 in Newton Abbott in Devon, England and began by producing bricks and tiles. In 1922, it launched its 'Wescontree Ware' range of art pottery, changing the name to 'Candy Ware' in 1936. Comprising vases, jugs, bowls, lamp bases, chargers, ashtrays and others, a hand-thrown and hand-decorated range was introduced in 1936. Primarily filling the kiln around the core production of utilitarian products, the art pottery range was discontinued in the 1950s when a new kiln was installed. The company itself closed in 1998.

A Clermont Fine China limited edition model of the Cleveland Bay stallion 'Mulgrave Supreme', modelled by Robert Donaldson, numbered 17/100, contained in a mahogany and glazed display case, together with certificate.

12in (30.5cm) high

£700-900   A&G

A late 1930s Candy Ware ribbed vase, with light blue and beige dripped glaze, silver embossed Candy Ware label and indistinct circular printed mark to the base.

7.5in (19cm) high

£20-30   M20C

CERAMICS

A 1920s Clews & Co. Ltd 'Chameleon Ware' vase with hand-painted stylised leaf design.

Chameleon ware was designed by David Capper, Works Manager at Clews. Introduced from 1913-14, Capper developed experimental semi-matte glazes to imitate the popular Ruskin art pottery glazes, and applied them to Oriental inspired forms. The affordable range won a gold medal at the Philadelphia Exposition in 1926, and grew to make up 80 per cent of the factory's output. Look out for Egyptian, Middle Eastern and Oriental patterns, inspired by archaeological finds at the time.

6.25in (15.5cm) high

£40-60   P&I

A 1930s Clews & Co. 'Chameleon Ware' squat vase with mottled blue and green glaze, with tripod firing mark to base.

4in (10cm) diam

£20-30   P&I

A Crown Devon 'Delph' vase, pattern no. 2055, painted in colours with factory marks to base.

8.75in (22cm) high

£30-40   WW

A 1960s Crown Devon ovoid jardinière, handpainted with a geometric design possibly designed by Colin Melbourne, the base impressed '1508'.

9in (23cm) long

£8-10   M20C

A CLOSER LOOK AT A COWAN PLATE

Viktor Schreckengost (1906-2008) was an important American artist, industrial designer and ceramics designer who worked through the Art Deco and mid-century modern styles.

His best known work is the 'Jazz Bowl' created in 1930 for Eleanor Roosevelt which is now considered an Art Deco masterpiece, and an example is in the Cleveland Museum of Art.

This hand-painted charger is also recognisably Art Deco, and was part of a series of similar designs showing sporting activities that also includes 'Polo'.

Large, visually impressive and typical of his style, they are sought-after and hard to find.

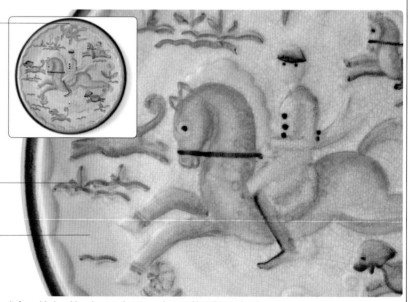

A Cowan 'The Hunt' wall plate, with low-relief moulded and hand-painted pattern, designed by Viktor Schreckengost.

1930-31

11.5in (28.5cm) diam

£700-1,000   ANT

QUICK REFERENCE - COLIN MELBOURNE

Colin Melbourne is arguably one of the most ignored British modernist ceramic designers. A graduate of the Royal College of Art, he produced highly modern, stylised animal figurines for Beswick from 1955. Known as the 'CM' range, produced from 1956-66, their avant garde style was unpopular at the time, and they are comparatively rare today. In 1954, he formed a design consultancy with David Queensberry called Drumlanrig Melbourne, and also worked for Crown Devon, where he continued to produce highly modern designs. His work is still underrated today, and represents an excellent opportunity for collectors with an eye for the future.

A Crown Ducal 'Rhodian' pattern shape 150 ovoid vase, pattern no. 3272, designed by Charlotte Rhead, the base with printed and painted marks.

c1933   4.5in (11.5cm) high

£80-120   GHOU

A pair of Crown Ducal vases, of bulbous cylindrical form, with red glazed interior, cream ground with piped panels containing red and brown leaves, with printed mark.

6in (15cm) high

£60-80   LOC

A Crown Devon 'Memphis' range vase, designed by Colin Melbourne, with a gilt chevron transfer pattern over a black glazed ground, the base with printed and impressed marks.

7.75in (20cm) high

£80-120   FLD

A Crown Devon 'Memphis' range vase, designed by Colin Melbourne, with a gilt chevron transfer pattern over a black glazed ground, printed marks.

10.25in (26cm) high

£80-120   FLD

A Crown Lynn vase, by Frank Carpay, the vase thrown by Daniel Steenstra, decorated with bands of forest green, orange, black and teal, with stylised celestial spheres representing the Sputnik, and silver lustre glaze at the rim.

Crown Lynn was founded near Auckland, New Zealand, in 1854. Tableware production began in 1941, and the company produced wares for the war effort and for New Zealand railways. The company still produces table and decorative wares today. Dutchman Frank Carpay (1917-1985) studied under Picasso at Madoura in France, and also Roger Capron at Vallauris. He worked for Crown Lynn's 'Specials Department' from 1953-56, producing designs such as this, which was commissioned by the vendor during a visit to the pottery.

c1955   9.75in (25cm) high

£700-900   WEB

A late 1950s Denby Pottery 'Crystalline' range two-handled vase, designed by Glynn Colledge, hand-painted with a stylised floral sprig and bands to the base, the base with printed mark.

7.25in (18.5cm) high

£40-60   GC

CERAMICS

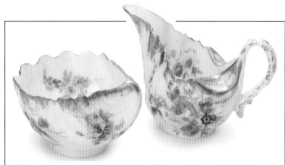

A Hammersley scalloped and gilded milk jug and sugar bowl, with hand-painted flowers.

The teacups are in the same shape as the sugar bowl.

c1900-14   *Milk jug 3in (7.5cm) high*

£40-60   **BAD**

A Haviland porcelain cake plate, decorated by Anna B. Leonard, with gourds and leaves in orange and green, stamped 'Haviland France' and painted 'Anna B. Leonard'.

14in (35.5cm) diam

£300-500   **DRA**

A 1970s Honiton Pottery rectangular dish with a hand-painted fish design, the base impressed 'HONITON ENGLAND' and painted 'DC'.

11.25in (27cm) long

£15-20   **M20C**

A 1960s-70s Dutch Jema bull, impressed with runic and geometric symbols and covered with a blue-green glaze, the stomach impressed 'JEMA HOLLAND 79'.

14.5in (36.5cm) long

£50-70   **M20C**

A tall Kenton Hills vase, with pink blossoms on pearl grey ground, the base drilled probably at the factory, with leaf stamp and '176'.

12.5in (32cm) high

£300-500   **DRA**

A Kenton Hills 'Unica' vase, by Alza Stratton, in brown butterfat on white ground, signed 'Alza Stratton Unica', stamped mark, restoration.

8.25in (21cm) high

£200-300   **DRA**

A large Katshutte Pottery figure of a Spanish dancer, painted in colours, printed factory mark, paper label, repaired fan.

20in (51cm) high

£400-600   **WW**

A Robert Lallemant elliptical pottery vase, blue and black painted marks, with damage.

Lallemant (1902-1954) studied at the Ecole des Beaux-Arts in Dijon and at Lachenal c1921, founding a pottery in Paris in 1923 producing modern and stylised patterns on clean-lined angular forms. If it had not been damaged, it may have fetched over three times this value.

6.75in (17cm) high

£100-150   **WW**

CERAMICS

A Langley Pottery vase, designed by Glynn Colledge and hand-painted with a stylised foliate design, the base with printed windmill mark.

8in (20.5cm) high

£30-40   M20C

A 1960s-70s Langley Pottery bulbous vase hand-painted with a stylised natural motif in green, brown and orange glazes, designed by Glynn Colledge, the base with printed windmill factory mark and painted 'J.M.'.

Staffordshire based firm Lovatt & Lovatt, who made Langley pottery, was acquired by Denby in 1959, which explains how Denby designer Glynn Colledge came to design for them. This is a scarce shape and a desirable pattern.

7.75in (19.5cm) high

£80-120   GC

A 1960s-70s Langley Pottery footed cylindrical vase, hand-painted with a stylised natural motif, designed by Glynn Colledge, printed windmill factory mark.

7.75in (19.5cm) high

£50-70   GC

A Canadian Laurentian Pottery sculptural jug vase, with integral handle, organic curving rim and orange and brown dripped glaze.

11.75in (29.5cm) high

£20-40   TWF

A McCoy 'Loy-Nel-Art' vase, with loop handles and floral decoration, marked '02' on the base, glaze slightly scratched and flaked at base.

12.25in (31cm) high

£100-150   BEL

A French Longwy vase, the base painted 'F=3024-D:56907', with printed green factory mark.

4.5in (11cm) high

£80-120   BEV

A 19thC Meissen box and cover, painted with flowers, the cover formed as a shell with a cartouche of figures standing on the docks to the interior, cancelled crossed swords mark, damage and restoration.

4.75in (12cm) wide

£80-120   WW

A 20thC Meissen group of two songbirds, modelled perched on a stump, with blue crossed swords mark, incised '3071'.

£180-220   DN

CERAMICS

A 1960s Midwinter Fashion shape transfer-printed 'Petite Rose' cake stand, with chrome plated fittings, designed by John Russell.

9in (23cm) high

£20-30   RET

A Minton cabinet plate, with pierced Greek key gilt border and pâte-sur-pâte style border of dolphins and shells on a pale blue ground, with printed mark.

1891-1902   9.5in (24cm) diam

£30-40   LOC

A pair of Minton models of cockatoos, each perched on a branch.

£320-380   L&T

A Myott & Sons hand-painted 'Diamond' vase, with original flower frog, the base with gold printed factory mark and painted '9185' pattern mark.

6in (15cm) high

£120-180   BAD

A CLOSER LOOK AT A MYOTT JUG

Myott was founded in 1898 but is best known for its colorful Art Deco ceramics produced in the 1930s. Records were destroyed in a fire in 1949, making it hard for collectors to find out more.

Autumnal oranges and browns are typical of Myott - red, blue and green are rarer - but watch out for flaking to the orange. Printed gold marks were used from 1930-42.

Prices are currently considerably lower than those for other Art Deco ceramics by Susie Cooper and Clarice Cliff – this is an area to watch as their appeal is obvious.

Pieces bearing the 'B.A.G.' mark were made for export by British American Glass. The quality of the design and painting is usually higher on such pieces, and the patterns may have been exclusive to them.

A 1930s Myott 'Squareneck' jug, painted in beige, yellow, orange green and brown tones with a fruiting pattern, the base with gold printed mark, painted 9104 pattern mark and registered no. 739316 for 1928.

8.75in (22.5cm) high

£80-120   BAD

A 1930s Myott baluster shaped jug, with a hand-painted green and orange floral and geometric design, the base with gold printed 'BAG Co Ltd, HAND PAINTED' mark and stamped 'B.G 76'.

7.75in (19.5cm) high

£100-150   BAD

A 1960s-70s French Vallauris blue glazed mussel-shaped dish, with orange glazed spot.

13in (33cm) long

£15-25   M20C

A Volkmar three-handled vase, covered in mottled indigo matte glaze, incised 'V'.

7in (18cm) high

£600-900   DRA

A CLOSER LOOK AT A VALLAURIS VASE

The town of Vallauris is well-known for its many potteries which have attracted notable artists and designers, including Pablo Picasso who worked at the Madoura pottery from 1948-55.

Other designers include Roger Capron and Charles Voltz – the designer of this piece is not yet known, but the glaze type and colours link it to a Vallauris pottery.

The curving, asymmetric form, that even extends to the the shape of the rim and the body, which curves backwards, is typical of the period.

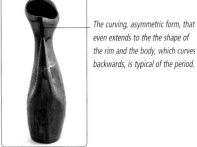

The base is unmarked but the light weight and clay type indicate that it was made by pouring liquid clay, known as slip, into a mould rather than being hand potted.

A late 1950s/early 1960s French Vallauris large floor vase, with curving asymmetric form, handle and rim.

15.5in (40cm) high

£40-60   MHC

A 1930s Wade Heath waisted cylindrical jug, handpainted with orange flowers, green leaves and grey and yellow patches, the base with printed lion mark, and impressed '127'.

7.75in (19.5cm) high

£30-50   BAD

A Watcombe Pottery terracotta jug, designed by Dr Christopher Dresser, of angular form with three serrated bands, printed "Watcombe Torquay" with registered diamond for 3rd June 1872.

8in (20.5cm) high

£120-180   WW

A Watcombe pottery model of a winking cat with long neck, covered in an ochre glaze and with one glass eye, the base with inscribed marks.

12in (30.5cm) high

£180-220   BE

CERAMICS

A Wheatley vase, with four buttressed feet, the top embossed with leaves and buds, covered in matte green glaze, marked 'WP' and 'C102'.

10in (25.5cm) high

£1,000-1,500   DRA

A Wheatley tall tapering cylindrical vase, covered in a fine feathered matte green glaze, and with 'WP' mark.

10in (25.5cm) high

£800-1,200   DRA

A CLOSER LOOK AT A WALLEY VASE

William J. Walley (1852-1919) was born the son of a potter in Ohio. He travelled to England to study at Minton in the 1860s before founding his first pottery in Maine in 1873.

Hand-sculpted motifs are also typical and range from leaves in the manner of Grueby, to this famous and highly sought-after devil's head.

Following an important aspect of the Arts and Crafts movement, he believed that every pot should be made and decorated by hand rather than being moulded and produced on a factory production line.

Simple but strong greens and blue matte glazes are typical, gloss glazes are more unusual – particularly with this amount of colour variation.

A W.J. Walley vase with devil mask, losses and crude repair to glaze flaking, the base stamped 'WJW'.

12in (30.5cm) high

£1,700-2,000   DRA

A T.J. Wheatley 'Albertine' vase, modelled with applied hibiscus on a barbotine painted ground, stamped 'WHEATLEY' and artist signed 'KW', a few minor losses and touch-ups.

The three-dimensional underglaze slip decoration, called 'Barbotine', was derived from Limoges faience, and became extremely popular in the US, and particularly in Cincinnati. Thomas Jerome Wheatley was involved in several Cincinnati pottery businesses between 1879 and 1882. The Cincinnati Art Pottery was incorporated in Ohio at the end of 1880 with Wheatley as a partner, and operated under the name T. J. Wheatley & Company until he left the business in 1882. This particular example, from the range often known as 'Albertine', was exhibited in "From Our Native Clay," held by the American Ceramic Arts Society in New York in 1987.

c1880   *19in (28cm) high*

£600-900   CRA

A T.J. Wheatley vase with applied thistle, under matte green glaze, no visible mark, several flecks and nicks.

11.5in (29cm) high

£500-800   DRA

A late 19thC Hungarian Zsolnay Pecs earthenware vase, decorated with hand-painted red, green and blue Moorish or Turkish style flowers on a mustard ground.

10.25in (26cm) tall

£50-80   LOC

A Hungarian Zsolnay Pecs heart-shaped dish, painted with a central bird within Persian style foliage, in geometric borders, the back with printed spire mark.

10in (25.5cm) diam

£280-320   **GORL**

An Arts and Crafts earthenware charger, painted with a bird in a landscape in shades of blue and yellow, painted marks, dated, hairline crack to rim.

1881   *12in (30.5cm) diam*

£150-200   **WW**

A Continental tin-glazed earthenware Gallé-style seated cat figurine, probably Mosanic, painted with honey-coloured fur patches and green eyes, and pseudo 'De Roos' mark to base.

The shape is also very similar to figures by Wemyss.

c1900   *11.75in (30cm) high*

£500-800   **TOV**

An early 20thC Continental porcelain tazza, applied with flowers, the base mounted with a maiden.

Despite the large amount of skill and time that went into creating such a detailed piece, fashions and tastes have moved away from ornate, floral designs such as this. Tazzas are also largely impractical today. Considering its size and obvious decorative appeal, its price seems very reasonable.

13.25in (34cm) high

£50-80   **WW**

A 19thC majolica figure, possibly Vesta, wearing a laurel wreath and carrying an eternal flame.

10.25in (26cm) high

£120-180   **FLD**

A late 19thC Staffordshire copper lustre jug with moulded and hand-painted flowers, unmarked.

7.75in (19.5cm) high

£20-30   **BAD**

An early 20thC French beeware basket, with bee on handle, handpainted with people in a row holding hands in landscape, with an 'X' on the base, the side signed 'I Berty Nice'.

6in (15cm) high

£50-70   **BAD**

QUICK REFERENCE

- Collectors look for characters associated with happy times in their own childhood or those that are widely popular. Pieces associated with comic books, TV programmes and films, or those by major brands, are usually popular. Official, licensed products are usually more desirable and more accurately modelled.
- Famous characters will usually have enthusiastic collecting bases and therefore will often fetch the largest sums. Look for typical clothes, poses, accessories or phrases associated with that character. Pieces produced before a character became well known are typically rare and desirable, as they would have been made in smaller numbers. Do not ignore minor characters as these can be rarer than more popular characters, and collectors will often want to complete a set.

- Many character items were intended for promotional use. Most were not made to last and few pieces are likely to have survived in good condition, making a truly mint example highly desirable.
- Limited editions may become valuable if the demand exceeds supply. For this reason, it is preferable to invest in pieces from small production runs (for example, under 1,000). The maker and quality of moulding and decoration will add desirability, as will an accurate depiction of the character. Limited editions should ideally come with mint condition boxes and paperwork.
- With the nostalgic nature of the market, demand ebbs and flows as generations mature. It is therefore a good idea to hunt for new collectable characters. For example, Buzz Lightyear is likely to be popular in the future.

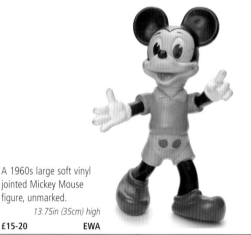

A 1960s large soft vinyl jointed Mickey Mouse figure, unmarked.

13.75in (35cm) high

£15-20   EWA

A 1960s Walt Disney Productions soft vinyl Mickey Mouse figure, with tail, marked 'C WALT DISNEY PRODUCTION MADE IN ITALY'.

9.75in (25cm) high

£20-25   EWA

A 1970s Walt Disney Productions Mickey Mouse poseable vinyl advertising figurine, in yellow shirt and red and white polka dot shorts, marked 'C WALT DISNEY PRODUCTIONS MADE IN HONG KONG', with woven tag.

7.5in (19cm) high

£10-15   EWA

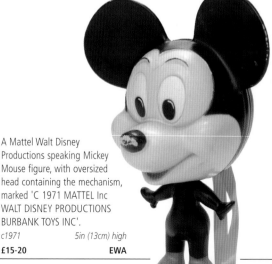

A Mattel Walt Disney Productions speaking Mickey Mouse figure, with oversized head containing the mechanism, marked 'C 1971 MATTEL Inc WALT DISNEY PRODUCTIONS BURBANK TOYS INC'.

c1971   *5in (13cm) high*

£15-20   EWA

A Playcraft 'Squeeze 'N Squeak' Mickey Mouse figure, marked 'C WALT DISNEY PRODUCTION 1979'.

5in (12.5cm) high

£10-15   EWA

A Kohner plastic 'Mickey Mouse' Peppy Puppet, marked 'Walt Disney Productions', mint and unopened with original bubble packaging.

1970   *11in (28cm) high*

£25-35   **MTB**

A 1930s Britains 'Minnie Mouse' and 'Clarabelle', each with detachable heads, paintwork in fair condition, one head pin replaced by matchstick.

Britains' lead figures of Disney characters are hard to find. Minnie is scarcer than Mickey, and Clarabelle is even rarer. Although she was created in 1928, the same year Mickey Mouse made his debut in 'Steamboat Willie', she only appeared as a bit-character on screen afterwards. She was originally paired with Horace Horsecollar, Mickey's friend, but was later seen stepping out with Goofy. After 1942, she almost faded into obscurity, appearing in only four films. However, she appeared more frequently in Disney's comics.

£300-500   **SAS**

A Walt Disney Productions Pinocchio vinyl figure, marked 'WALT DISNEY PRODUCTIONS' on shoes and impressed on back of hat, with woven Ingersoll Marketing tag.

8in (20.5cm) high

£20-30   **EWA**

A scarce 1930s Wadeheath 'Donald Duck' child's teapot and cover, hand-painted in characteristic yellow, blue and black.

5in (12.5cm) long

£400-600   **LT**

A Walt Disney Productions Goofy vinyl figure, marked 'C WALT DISNEY PRODUCTIONS MADE IN HONG KONG' and 'MADE FOR INGERSOLL MARKETING LTD'.

Ingersoll (now part of Timex) made its first Disney watch, featuring Mickey Mouse, in 1933. Since then it has been in continuous production, being made by a number of different watchmakers. This figurine is likely to have been made as part of a promotional countertop display. Well made, licenced and relatively detailed with his clothing, he seems likely to be a great bet for the future.

8.75in (22cm) high

£20-30   **EWA**

A Snow White and the Seven Dwarfs ceramic musician band, of unidentified manufacture, each individually modelled, Doc has repaired left foot, otherwise minor chips and scratches.

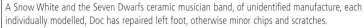

Snow White 8in (20cm) high

£70-100 THE SET   **VEC**

CHARACTER COLLECTABLES

A Hanna-Barbera 'The Banana Splits Annual'.

10.5in (27cm) high

£10-15 MTS

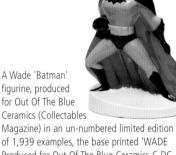

A Wade 'Batman' figurine, produced for Out Of The Blue Ceramics (Collectables Magazine) in an un-numbered limited edition of 1,939 examples, the base printed 'WADE Produced for Out Of The Blue Ceramics C DC Comics 1999 Limited Edition 1,939'.

7.25in (19cm) high

£35-45 DSC

A 1930s W.Goebel decanter, probably depicting Andy Capp, with hand-painted details and removeable head stopper, the base with impressed Crown mark and 'K.L. 904'.

10in (25cm) high

£180-220 BAD

A Wade 'Betty Boop' figurine, produced for C&S Collectables in a limited edition of 1,500 pieces, the base with 'C King Features Syndicate INC Fleischer Studios INC Wade Limited Edition' printed mark.

1996 *3.75in (9cm) high*

£50-80 DSC

'The Bonzooloo Book', by G.E. Studdy, printed in London, with colour pictorial bands, 12 colour plates, and other illustrations.

Illustrator George Ernest Studdy (1878-1848) developed his small dog character in the late 1910s, and he first appeared in a comic strip in The Sketch as 'Studdy Dog' in 1918. In 1922, he was renamed 'Bonzo' and a legend was born.

c1928

£200-300 FRE

A 1970s Nayytex child's Charlie Brown printed t-shirt,with Charlie Brown on the Apollo rocket.

c1970 *16.5in (42cm) high*

£15-20 CANS

A 'Dan Dare, Pilot of the Future' book, published by Juvenile Productions Ltd., with realistic pop-up pictures, with pencil annotations from Christmas 1953.

1953 *10.5in (21cm) wide*

£50-80 GAZE

A 1950s Marx TV-Tinykins 'Huckleberry Hound' miniature figurine, made and hand-painted in Hong Kong, mint and boxed.

2.5 (6.5cm) high

£8-12   **MTB**

A Marx Fairykins 'Jack Be Nimble' miniature figurine, mint and boxed.

2.25in (5.5cm) high

£8-12   **MTB**

A CLOSER LOOK AT A POPEYE DOORSTOP

Painted cast iron doorstops are highly sought after in the US, and in 2006 a very rare Littco doorstop of a girl dressed as a 'ghost' and holding a pumpkin made over $70,000 at auction.

Hubley is a prolific and collectable maker, and are also known for its cast iron cars and other toys.

Bunches or pots of flowers are more common forms – this is a rare and desirable cartoon character, so would appeal to both Popeye and character collectors.

It is in unusually excellent condition for a doorstop, with nearly all of its original paint intact and in bright condition, and as a result has fetched a high price.

A 1960s Combex soft vinyl Noddy advertising doll, marked 'COMBEX MADE IN ENGLAND NSRCL 1960 4563'.

8.75in (22cm) high

£20-25   **EWA**

A rare Hubley cast iron 'Popeye' doorstop, full figure, with vibrant colours, in near mint condition.

9in (23cm) high

£10,000-15,000   **BER**

A complete set of five Einson-Freeman Co. colour lithographed paper 'Par-T-Masks' of the major characters from 'The Wizard of Oz' (Dorothy shown here), with minor creases but with intact original rubber bands.

These MGM licensed character masks are rare. They were issued in September 1939 in time for Hallowe'en, and given away by department stores as free premiums during the holiday season.

1939

£200-280   **BLNY**

A rare colour lithographed 'The Tin Woodman of the Magical Land of Oz announces Jean Gros' French Marionettes' die-cut bookmark, with advertisement for American Seating Co. to back, published by Schroeder & Gunther, Inc.

This advertised a play by Ruth Plumly Thompson. The picture of the Tin Woodman was reprinted from the endpaper in ' The Patchwork Girl of Oz' (1913). A list of the Oz Books through ' The Giant Horse of Oz' (1928) appears on the verso of this bookmark.

1932

£400-600   **BLNY**

Three American Colourtype Co. MGM 'Wizard of Oz' colour lithograph valentine cards.

1940

£100-150   **BLNY**

An A.A. Burnstein Sales Organisation MGM rubber 'Tin Man' toy, the back marked 'JACK HALEY/WIZARD OF OZ', nose chipped and body partially compressed with some flaking of colour.

It is suspected that most of these figures were destroyed when children donated them to World War scrap drives.

1939   *6.5in (16.5cm) high*

£280-330   **BLNY**

A CLOSER LOOK AT A SUPERMAN FIGURINE

The production of this figurine was beset with problems, such as the 'S' transfer bubbling after application.

A number of these licensed figurines were also stolen from the pottery and the actual release date was 2001, not 1999 as printed.

Due to these problems, the official edition size was reduced to only 250 examples, rather than the originally planned 1,938.

Of these, 61 examples came in a special presentation box, with a certificate and special backstamp – these can fetch over 25 per cent more.

A Wade 'Superman' figurine, produced for Out Of The Blue Ceramics (Collectables Magazine) in a limited edition of 250, the base printed 'WADE Produced for Out Of The Blue Ceramics C DC Comics 1999', and numbered '066/189'.

7.25in (19cm) high

£120-180   **DSC**

A rare unused free gift from Pow! comic of an iron-on Spiderman transfer sheet, with ink stamp for '28th January 1957'.

As a transfer, the image is obviously viewed in reverse before application.

1957   *8.75in (22cm) high*

£10-20   **SAS**

A Wade 'Tom' figurine, the base moulded 'WADE ENGLAND C M.G.M.'

1973-79   *3.5in (9cm) high*

£20-25   **DSC**

A Wade 'Jerry' figurine, the base moulded 'WADE ENGLAND C M.G.M.'

1973-79   *2in (5cm) high*

£20-25   **DSC**

A 1970s Japense Tokyo Takei chromed plastic pedestal alarm clock, the blue face marked '2 JEWELS JAPAN'.

8in (20.5cm) high

£30-40   M20C

A 1960s-70s Coral chrome plated plastic pedestal 2 jewel alarm clock, with silver face and chrome plated metal ring-shaped stand.

6.25in (16cm) high

£30-40   M20C

A late 1960s Western Germany Westra red and white plastic pedestal alarm clock, with black snooze button.

8in (20.5cm) high

£40-50   M20C

A late 1960s West German Kaiser chrome plated plastic alarm clock with blue face.

Note the 'space age' disc-shaped design of the alarm indicator on the left of the face.

4in (10cm) high

£20-30   M20C

A 1970s Japanese model no.51113 alarm clock, with blue dial and silver hands with luminous lines, and red and silver markers.

5.5in (14cm) high

£40-50   M20C

A 1970s Japanese red and white plastic rounded cube-shaped Rhythm transistor alarm clock, model no.7RA032.

5.5in (14cm) high

£40-50   M20C

A 1970s-80s AP plastic clock and barometer.

9.25in (23cm) high

£50-60   MTS

A 1960s-70s Western German Uwestra red plastic triangular alarm clock.

3.5in (9cm) high

£20-30   M20C

COMMEMORATIVES

QUICK REFERENCE

- Although royal commemorative ware was made before Queen Victoria's reign, it was not until then that production boomed. Ceramics (the first and most common kind of royal memorabilia) could be produced and distributed economically due to the advent of transfer printing, canals and the railways. Popularity grew during the late 19thC and the early 20thC, and memorabilia is still produced today.

- As so much memorabilia was produced, collectors tend to focus on one monarch, or one event. Queen Victoria and the current Queen are among the most popular subjects, partly because of the number and variety of pieces produced during their long reigns. Some events commemorated within these reigns are scarcer than others. For example, many more pieces commemorating Queen Victoria's Golden Jubilee were produced than for her marriage. Interest in items celebrating the lives of younger members of current royal family is also growing.

- Value typically depends on the quality and maker of the piece. Well-known, high quality manufacturers, such as Royal Worcester, Royal Crown Derby, Minton and Copeland are consistently popular. You should also look out for the work of popular 20th century designers such as Eric Ravilious, Charlotte Rhead and Richard Guyatt. However, well decorated pieces that are not by major makers or designers are also often desirable. Brightly coloured and detailed pieces appeal are likely to appeal to a wide range of collectors.

- Look for limited editions, particularly pieces from editions of less than 250. Keep all paperwork and boxes as these are essential to value.

- Condition is very important. Many 19thC pieces were not made to last, so some wear is acceptable. However cracks and chips will reduce desirability. Damage on recent pieces reduces value considerably.

A Copeland & Garrett '1837/38 Victoria' miniature pottery plate, printed with a named portrait surmounted by flowers of the Union within a scrolling border, the reverse with impressed and printed marks.

4.25in (11cm) diam

£580-680   SAS

A Wedgwood & Co. earthenware tea bowl and saucer, printed in black and enamelled in colours, the reverse named 'Victoria', with impressed and printed marks.

c1838

£180-220   SAS

An '1840 Victoria & Albert Wedding' blue printed pottery jug, with named portraits, the reverse with a crown centred by the date.

4.5in (11.5cm) high

£100-150   SAS

An '1838 Victoria' commemorative octagonal nursery plate.

The portrait on this desirable plate was developed after a portrait painted by Sir George Hayter.

c1838

£200-300   SAS

A Hines Bros '1887 Victoria's Jubilee' octagonal pottery plate, printed in black, with gilt lined rim.

c1887   *9.75in (24.5cm) wide*

£50-70   SAS

A Doulton Lambeth '1897 Diamond Jubilee' blue glazed stoneware jug, moulded with green young and old oval portraits of Queen Victoria.

8.75in (22cm) high

£120-180 SAS

A CLOSER LOOK AT A TILE

Founded in 1877, Sherwin & Cotton of Staffordshire was a well-known tile producer until its take-over by Johnsons in 1911, which continued to use the name for some time.

This was designed by George Cartlidge, and was part of a series of 'photographic' tiles he produced. Cartlidge also designed some Morrisware for S.Hancock & Sons.

Showing Victoria as most imagine her to have appeared, this was made to commemorate the Diamond Jubilee.

This series of tiles was renowned at the time for its translucent glazes and three-dimensional appearance.

An Adderley '1937 George VI Coronation' loving cup, printed in colours with St. George slaying the dragon.

1936   *4.75in (12cm) high*

£200-250 SAS

A Sherwin & Cotton relief and intaglio moulded photographic dust-pressed tile panel, depicting Queen Victoria in sepia glaze, framed.

c1897   *9in (23cm) high*

£100-150 FLD

A Paragon '1937 Edward VIII Coronation' loving cup, with twin gilt lion handles, numbered 562 from an edition of 1,000.

Memorabilia for Edward VIII's (better known as the Duke of Windsor) proposed coronation is not as rare as many think. Although he abdicated in December 1936, manufacturers had nearly a year, from George V's death in January 1936, to produce commemorative wares.

1936   *4.5in (11.5cm) high*

£70-100 GHOU

A Copeland for Goode '1937 George VI Coronation' pottery tyg, printed with sepia portraits and decorated in colours, small hairline crack.

£200-300 SAS

A small Shelley George VI and Queen Elizabeth '1939 Visit to America' loving cup, decorated in colours and gilt, with printed marks to the base.

1939   *3.5in (8.5cm) high*

£120-180 SAS

A Crown Devon '1937 George VI Coronation' musical tankard, moulded with superimposed portraits oval flags and flowers in colours, playing 'Here's a Health unto His Majesty'.

c1937   6in (15.5cm) high

£80-120   **SAS**

A transfer printed 'George VI Coronation' mug designed by Dame Laura Knight, the base with printed mark reading 'R.R. No.814375/6 DESIGNED & MODELLED BY DAME LAURA KNIGHT D.B.E. R.A.' and with GR cypher and facsimile Laura Knight signature, the inside of the rim printed 'PRESENTED ON CORONATION DAY BY SIR ARTHUR STANLEY TREASURER OF ST THOMAS HOSPITAL'.

1937   3.25in (8cm) high

£35-40   **CARS**

An Aynsley '1953 Elizabeth II Coronation' plate, with central printed portrait flanked by flags and flowers and inscribed border.

c1953   9in (23cm) diam

£200-300   **SAS**

An Aynsley '1953 Elizabeth II Coronation' plate, with printed colour portrait and profuse gilt decoration.

c1953   9in (23cm) diam

£100-150   **SAS**

A Paragon '1953 Elizabeth II Coronation' limited edition loving cup, set with twin gilt lion handles, numbered 555 from an edition of 1,000.

4.75in (12cm) high

£120-180   **SAS**

A Spode '1981 Price Charles & Lady Diana Wedding' limited edition loving cup, with sepia portrait ovals decorated in colors with flowers on a gilded cobalt blue ground, numbered 229 from an edition of 250, with certificate.

6.25in (16cm) high

£60-90   **SAS**

A Wedgwood '1953 Elizabeth II Coronation' mug, with printed design designed by Eric Ravilious, the base with printed factory mark.

c1953   4.25in (10.5cm) high

£180-220   **WW**

An '1805 Nelson' death of Nelson pearlware jug, printed in brown and highlighted in colours with an inscribed portrait oval and on the reverse HMS Victory centred by an oval cartouche inscribed with honours, restored.

6.75in (17cm) high

£350-450 SAS

A 'Nelson in Memoriam' commemorative reverse handpainted glass picture, depicting Britannia with an oval portrait of Nelson beneath his battle honours with dates, framed.

c1805 *16.25in (41cm) high*

£2,500-3,500 SAS

An unusual '1812 Constitution and Russian Campaign' silver lustre decorated pearlware jug, printed with loyal cartouche flanked by a lion and unicorn and on the reverse 'A. Cossack of the Oural Mountains'.

1812 *5.25in (13.5cm) high*

£250-350 SAS

A Copeland for Goode 'Transvaal Tyg', subscriber's copy, decorated in colours and gilt, cracked.

c1900 *5.5in (14cm) high*

£150-200 SAS

An Elliot pottery jug, commemorating the relief of 'Mafeking' on May 17th 1900, applied with monograms of Queen Victoria and Baden-Powell, hound handle.

1900 *6.75in (17.5cm) high*

£120-180 FLD

SPECIAL AUCTION SERVICES
ESTABLISHED 1991

For the only regular specialist auctions of

COMMEMORATIVES

including Royalty, Political, Exhibition & War

POT LIDS & PRATTWARE
Fairings, Goss & Crested China
Baxter & Le Blond Prints

Forthcoming auction dates
6th March 2010
5th June 2010
4th September 2010
27th November 2010
(Please check prior to each auction for exact details).

In these specialised auctions items are offered **individually** and not group lotted, **there is no minimum or lotting charge.** Auctions are held at **weekends** for the convenience of **collectors** in our purpose-built permanent auction gallery. **Contact Andrew Hilton** for a sample catalogue.

SPECIAL AUCTION SERVICES
Kennetholme, Midgham, Reading RG7 5UX
Telephone 0118 971 2949
www.specialauctionservices.com
(North side of the A4, 8 miles west of junction 12 on M4/A4)

CERAMICS

A Booth '1914 Great War' cylindrical mug, printed in grey and decorated in colours with servicemen from the allied forces.

£80-120   SAS

A Paragon '1938 Munich Peace Conference' plate, printed with a named portrait of Chamberlain and inscribed on the reverse.

1938   *9in (21cm) diam*

£100-150   SAS

A Wilkinson Ltd. 'Admiral Beatty - Dread Nought' character jug, designed by Sir Francis Carruthers Gould, decorated in underglaze colours, enamelled and gilded, the underside with printed manufacturer's and retailer's mark and facsimile signature of Carruthers Gould.

Issued by Soane & Smith Ltd during World War I.

10.75in (27cm) high

£250-350   SAS

A Wilkinson Ltd Marechal Foch toby jug, designed by Sir Francis Carruthers Gould, seated with a glass of champagne, the bottle inscribed 'Au Diable Le Kaiser' (The Kaiser to the devil), the plinth with animals, the base with black printed marks and Carruthers Gould's facsimile signature.

This jug was produced for and distributed by Soane & Smith as a limited edition along with ten others to celebrate the allied leaders of World War I. The rarest is of General Louis Botha, as only 150 examples were produced. An example fetched over £1,500 at auction in 2005, and a complete set fetched £9,000 at auction in 2009.

1918   *11.75in (30cm) high*

£400-600   DN

A CLOSER LOOK AT A WINSTON CHURCHILL TOBY JUG

Churchill is an iconic British figure and commemorative pieces are still highly sought after by specialist collectors, especially items produced in his lifetime.

This is made more appealing due to the well-modelled, characterful face and his fingers which are posed in his famous 'V' for victory sign.

It is modelled and glazed in the manner of Ralph Wood, and is considered one of the best traditional toby jugs made in the 20thC, so it appeals to toby jug collectors too.

Examples are known decorated in more colours. In 2008 an undamaged, more finely decorated, example sold for over £1,800 at auction.

A 'The Rt Hon Winston S Churchill OM CH FRS MP' pottery toby jug, by Leonard Jarvis, modelled in relief and painted in colours, incised marks, chips to paint brushes.

c1946   *7in (18cm) high*

£350-450   WW

An Annalee Gulf War commemorative 'Desert Storm' mouse, in mint condition with card tag, clothing and flag.

1991   *8.25in (21cm) high*

£20-30   BH

SPRING SUMMER WINTER

A

Antiques
for Everyone

THE NEC BIRMINGHAM
HALLS 17-19

Free Car Parking • Vetted for Authenticity

For ticket bookings call: 0844 581 0827
or Book Online

www.antiquesforeveryone.co.uk

All bookings are subject to a single transaction fee
Rights of admission reserved. Security searches in operation. Visitors are not permitted to bring antiques into the fair.

CLARION ARTS   HOMES & ANTIQUES

CERAMICS

COSTUME JEWELLERY

QUICK REFERENCE

- Costume jewellery has risen dramatically in popularity over the last ten years, and values have risen accordingly. However, while iconic pieces by well-known designers are now commanding prices close to those paid for precious jewellery, much costume jewellery is still comparatively affordable. With a great variety of pieces available, there is a look for every taste and occasion.
- Desirable makers include Trifari, Chanel, Christian Dior, Stanley Hagler, Schiaparelli, Miriam Haskell and Joseff of Hollywood, and their names are usually marked on the back of their pieces. Copies are becoming more common, particularly at the upper end of the market, so learn to recognise marks and the quality of materials.
- Style and eye-appeal are also very important to value. As many buy costume jewellery to wear, a great design with the 'sparkle' factor will generally be desirable and valuable, even without a renowned maker's name.

- During the 1930s and 1940s, many pieces were made from solid silver, sometimes plated with gold, and these are usually marked 'Sterling' to the reverse.
- The quality, colour and size of the stones are important to value: look out for chunky 'baroque' faux pearls, and Murano or Czech glass beads. The way the stones are set also helps indicate a piece's quality. The best examples are held in place with metal prongs, with work done by hand. Much costume jewellery has three-dimensional effects that may be hand-wired onto frame, and these pieces are particularly desirable.
- Missing stones will reduce value. Although they can be replaced, it is often hard to find an exact match of size or colour. The beads and faux pearls, used by designers like Miriam Haskell are even more difficult to find as they were exclusive designs and are no longer made to the same quality.

A mid-1950s Art wreath pin, gold tone metal set with pastel Lucite flowers and aurora borealis highlights, marked "Art".

1.75in (4.5cm) diam

£40-60   PC

A pair of Boucher holly wreath Christmas earrings, set with green and gold glass spheres.

1in (2.5cm) diam

£6-8 PAIR   AEM

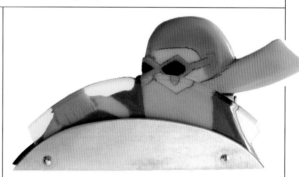

A very rare 1980s Butler & Wilson Amy Johnson pin, plastic and chrome, the back with white painted "Butler & Wilson" mark.

2.75in (7cm) wide

£100-150   TDG

Cristobal

Antiques, decorative objects
Furniture and
Period costume jewellery

Tel 020 77247230
Mob 07956 388194
Mob 07900 880909
e-mail sminers@aol.com
www.cristobal.co.uk

26 Church Street, London NW8 8EP

A Robert DeMario gilt metal flower and leaf pin, set with faux anthracite and pearls, some stones missing, the back marked "DeMario N.Y".

2.5in (6.5cm) wide

£10-15   PC

A pair of Kramer clip-on earrings, with red, colourless and purple rhinestones, and faux pearls, the clip impressed KRAMER.

1in (2.5cm) high

£15-20   PC

A 1980s Christian Lacroix 'Rococo' gold-plated heart shaped pin, set with shocking pink glass and with Lacroix's entwined CL logo, marked "CL Paris Christian Lacroix".

2.75in (7cm) wide

£30-50   TDG

A 1950s pair of earrings, attributed to Rousselet, comprised of multicoloured glass drops set on gold tone chains.

2.75in (7cm) long

£50-80   PC

A 1960s pair of Schreiner faux aquamarine earrings, the large central stones surrounded by circular and teardrop shaped rhinestones.

1.25in (3cm) high

£50-70 PAIR   CRIS

A Lea Stein Rhodoid small scottie dog pin, with applied black bow and eye and nose details, the clip marked 'LEA STEIN PARIS'

1.5in (3.5cm) high

£25-35   PC

A CLOSER LOOK AT A ROBERT NECKLACE AND EARRINGS

There are a number of different types of cut rhinestones, including the rectangular 'baguette', which also have many facets – both are signs of quality.

Blue is a very desirable colour, and the different, complimentary tones of blue add visual appeal.

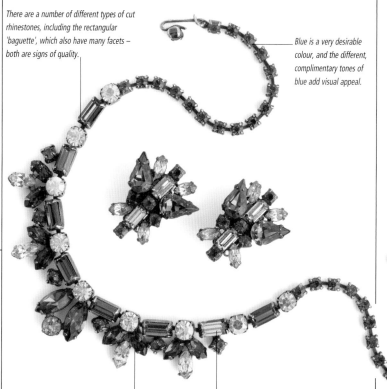

The lighter blue stones are 'aurora borealis' stones, which have an applied iridescence that changes and sparkles as they move in the light.

The rhinestones are 'prong set', rather than being glued into a moulded setting – this is another sign of quality and also allows more light to enter the rhinestones.

A Robert necklace and pair of earrings, set with aquamarine and cobalt blue cut fax stones.

Earrings 1.25in (3cm) wide

£100-150   PC

COSTUME JEWELLERY

A 1950s Trifari gold-plated butterfly pin, the wings inset with 'plique à jour' style coloured glass ovoid beads.

2in (5cm) wide

£50-80   PC

A mid-1950s Trifari gold-plated pin in the form of a basket of flowers, the flowers inset with coloured rhinestones.

1.75in (4.5cm) high

£40-60   PC

A 1940s Trifari vermeil bow-shaped pin, with red ruby baguette and colourless pavé-set rhinestones.

3.5in (9cm) wide

£300-500   PC

A 1990s Vivienne Westwood silver tone metal bow and orb pin, pavé set with clear rhinestones.

1.5in (3.5cm) long

£50-80   PC

A late 1950s Trifari gold plated pin in the form of three fish, the eyes with inset ruby red cabouchon rhinestones.

2.25in (6.5cm) high

£70-100   ROX

A Vivienne Westwood gold-tone metal heart-shaped perfume holder pin, surmounted by a trademark orb and ribbon, with red enamel, and ring fitting to transform into necklace/choker, containing Boudoir perfume.

c2000   *2in (5cm) high*

£40-60   TDG

QUICK REFERENCE – TRIFARI

Trifari's origins lay in a company founded by Italian emigré Gustavo Trifari in New York around 1910. Success first came when sales manager Leo Krussman joined in 1917, and grew when salesman Carl Fishel joined in 1923, and 'Trifari, Krussman & Fishel (TKF) was founded in 1925. Designer Alfred Philippe joined in 1930, and his designs are amongst the most sought-after today. During the 1930s, the company designed pieces for a number of Broadway musicals, as well as for film and theatre stars, which cemented its success. Quality was always high, even after World War II, with only the best rhinestones being used in good quality settings. During the 1940s, a number of gold-plated sterling silver (vermeil) pieces were made, which are usually valuable. The company continues to produce innovative and sought-after designs today. This brightly coloured set has further appeal due to the patriotic colours used, as well as the all-important 'sparkle' factor, enhanced by the differently cut rhinestones.

A 1950s Trifari pin and earrings, set with colourless and blue baguette cut rhinestones and light blue rectangular rhinestones, the backs stamped 'TRIFARI PAT PEND'.

Pin 2.25in (5.5cm) high

£150-200   PC

A pair of unmarked clip earrings, set with cut faux aquamarines and teardrop shaped brown glass stones, in a gold tone mount.

1.25in (3cm) high

£20-25   PC

A pair of unmarked earrings, the gold tone mounts set with faceted aurora borealis stones and large faux amber teardrops.

1.25in (3cm) high

£30-40   PC

A pair of unmarked earrings, with vintage stones prong-set in a modern matte gold-tone metal mount.

1.5in (4cm) high

£20-30   PC

A pair of unmarked earrings and matching leaf shaped pin, the gold tone metal mounts with prong set striped 'tiger's eye' rhinestones.

Pin 2.75in (7cm) high

£70-90   PC

A 1920s unmarked cold enamelled orchid-shaped pin, set with faceted diamanté.

2in (5cm) high

£20-30   PC

A 1950s unmarked vintage gold plated patriotic US flag pin, prong-set with red, colourless and blue rhinestones.

1.5in (3.5cm) high

£5-8   AEM

A 1930s Art Deco Continental silver clip, with red plastic bar and inset diamanté, the back with Continental control marks, and stamped 'MD'.

1.5in (3.5cm) high

£50-80   PC

QUICK REFERENCE – SINDY

- Sindy was launched by Pedigree in 1963 as a competitor to Mattel's Barbie fashion doll. Rather than produce Barbie under license, Sindy was modelled on another American doll, Ideal's Tammy. Her 'girl next door' look made her instantly more popular than Barbie in Britain, and she became a bestseller in 1968 and 1970. Initially, Pedigree also produced a wider range of clothing and accessories than Mattel.

- In 1978 Sindy was launched in the US by Marx Toys, but as the company went into receivership in 1980, was discontinued. Fashions were updated in the 1980s, and in 1989 she was redesigned to look more like Barbie, who dominated the market during the late 1980s and '90s. In 1997, Sindy was removed from major retailers after a law suit from Mattel, until her successful relaunch in 1999.

- Look out for early dolls and outfits from the late 1960s and early 1970s. Some accessories were lost, making them rare today, and some outfits and dolls are more desirable than others. As with most plastic fashion and similar dolls, items must be in as close to shop-bought condition as possible. Stains, fading and cut or messy hair, reduce value. Although 'the doll you love to dress' is usually the most valuable item, values for some outfits can match those paid for the dolls.

A Pedigree Sindy doll, first issue with original 'Weekenders' outfit, with original original box.

First issue Sindy dolls are becoming increasingly hard to find, particularly with their original boxes and clothes. On this example, the original pink card band adds value as it is usually missing. This outfit was designed by Foale & Tuffin. Sally Tuffin went on to produce ceramic desgns for Poole and, ultimately, her own company.

c1964   12in (30.5cm) high

£120-180   **MTB**

A 1970s Pedigree 'Funtime' blonde Sindy doll, with original clothing, in mint, unopened condition in original window box.

12in (30.48cm) high

£100-150   **MTB**

A Pedigree 'Sweet Dreams' Sindy doll, with sleeping eyes, twist neck, twist body, bending knees, and original 'Good Morning' clothes, in mint condition in unopened card window box.

1978   12in (30.48cm) high

£100-150   **MTB**

A Marx Toys Sindy doll, with original clothes, in mint condition in unopened, worn card window box.

1978   13in (33cm) high

£50-80   **MTB**

A 1980s Pedigree 'Ballerina' Sindy doll, with original clothes, in mint condition, in unopened card window box.

13in (33cm) high

£50-70   **MTB**

A Pedigree Sindy 'Party Time' doll, with original blue dress and shoes and 'We're Havin' a Party' 45rpm record, in mint condition in unopened card window box.

'Party Time' Sindy was only sold with blonde hair and a choice of three coloured outfits in royal blue, yellow and pink.

1981   12in (30.5cm) high

£120-180   **MTB**

A CLOSER LOOK AT A PAUL SINDY DOLL

The first issue Paul from 1965 had moulded hair. This second issue, with rooted hair, was introduced in 1966.

He was named after Paul McCartney, since The Beatles were the most popular band at the time, and even his hair mimics the famous 'mop top'.

Even though he was also dubbed 'the well-dressed young man', Paul didn't sell well and was withdrawn shortly after his introduction.

Paul's white sneakers are rare as they were usually lost, as was his plastic stand.

A Pedigree Paul doll, in mint condition with original 'Casuals' clothing, plastic stand and box.

1966   12in (30.5cm) high

£100-150   **MTB**

A Hasbro 'Rainbow Sindy' doll, with multicoloured hair, original clothes and hair styling guide, in mint condition in unopened, original card window box.

1992

£20-25   **MTB**

A Pedigree 'Patch' doll, with original schoolgirl outfit with plastic satchel, complete and in mint condition.

Patch is Sindy's little sister.

1966   9in (23cm) high

£50-60   **DSC**

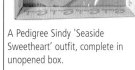

A Pedigree Sindy 'Seaside Sweetheart' outfit, complete in unopened box.

1964   12.5in (31.5cm) wide

£100-150   **MTB**

A Pedigree Sindy 'Country Walk' outfit, complete in unopened box.

This early set, which originally retailed for £19/11d, is sought after because it still has the original bone and dog bowl. A similar set was issued by Mattel for Barbie, but the dog was a terrier rather than a poodle.

1963   12.5in (31.5cm) high

£120-180   **MTB**

QUICK REFERENCE – DAISY DOLLS

The Daisy doll range was produced from 1973-83 in Hong Kong and distributed and marketed by Flair Toys in the UK, the US and Europe. Her unique selling point was that her clothes were designed by top fashion designer Mary Quant, with her name being taken from Quant's orange and white daisy company logo. Her outfits were themed around a world trip, and many were given names of activities associated with cities or named after the cities themselves. There are several variations: a budget 'Dizzy Daisy' without bendable legs or a twisting waist; a version with both features; and 'Dashing Daisy' with bendable waist and curved hands enabling her to hold things. From 1979, Daisy had centre-parted hair and rooted eyelashes. The small-headed version is preferred by collectors to the later large head, and this coloured leotard is a hard-to-find variant on the standard one.

A 1970s Flair Toys Ltd 'Daisy Long Legs' doll, complete with original clothes, stand, booklet and badge, and in mint condition in original card window box.

Daisy Long Legs was released in 1978, and at 15in (38cm) high, is taller than the standard 9in (23cm) high Daisy. As she was taller, a special range of clothes was produced to fit her.

1978-83   17in (43cm) high

£80-120   **MTB**

A 1970s American Gabriel Industries Inc. 'Dotty' Daisy doll, with large head, blonde hair, and original clothing, in complete and mint condition, in unopened original box.

10.5in (26.5cm) high

£65-75   **MTB**

An American Gabriel Industries Inc. 'St. Tropez' Daisy doll, with medium-sized head and original clothes, in complete and mint condition, in original unopened card window box.

10.5in (26.5cm) high

£120-180   **MTB**

A 1970s Flair Toys Ltd 'Dizzy Daisy' doll, with small head, blonde hair and original clothing, in complete and mint condition in unopened card window box.

9.5in (24cm) high

£100-150   **MTB**

A late 1970s Flair Toys Ltd 'Dashing Daisy' 'Skidoo' doll, complete with original clothes and skateboard, in mint condition in slightly damaged original card window box.

The back of the box shows a number of the accessories and different outfits designed by Mary Quant to accompany Daisy. As would be expected from such a fashion designer, she really was 'on trend' for her time!

12in (30.5cm) high

£150-200   **MTB**

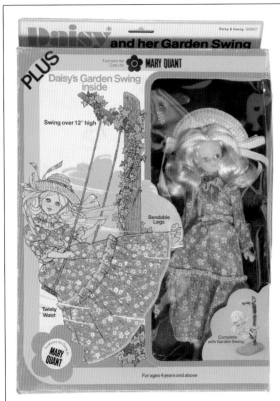

A 1970s Flair Toys Ltd Daisy 'Fandango' outfit, designed by Mary Quant, complete and in mint condition with original packaging.

8in (20cm) high

£35-45   **MTB**

A 1970s Flair Toys Ltd Daisy 'Bee-Bop' outfit, designed by Mary Quant, complete and in mint condition with original packaging.

8in (20cm) high

£30-40   **MTB**

A 1970s Flair Toys Ltd 'Daisy & Swing' doll playset, complete with Daisy doll with bendable legs, clothes, and plastic garden swing, in mint condition in original card window box.

This set is hard to find, particularly complete and in its original box.

12in (30.5cm) high

£120-180   **MTB**

A 1970s Flair Toys Ltd Daisy 'Hoedown' outfit, designed by Mary Quant, complete and in mint condition with original packaging.

11.5in (29cm) high

£32-38   **MTB**

A 1970s Flair Toys Ltd Daisy 'Guinevere' outfit, designed by Mary Quant, complete and in mint condition with original packaging.

12in (30.5cm) high

£32-38   **MTB**

A 1970s Flair Toys Ltd Daisy 'Showbiz' outfit, designed by Mary Quant, complete and in mint condition with original packaging.

12.5in (31.75cm) high

£20-30   **MTB**

A 1970s Flair Toys Ltd Daisy 'St. Moritz' outfit, designed by Mary Quant, complete and in mint condition with original packaging.

12in (30.5cm) high

£25-35   **MTB**

QUICK REFERENCE - PIPPA

Pippa, 'the pocket sized fashion doll' was produced by Palitoy from 1972-80. At only 7in (18cm) in height, she was smaller than her more famous competitors Barbie or Sindy, allowing little girls to carry her around in their pockets or bags. A couple of hundred different, colourful outfits were produced and these have become collectable today, particularly if complete, as many small pieces were lost. Pippa's condition is important to collectors. As she was carried around, she is often worn, and her honey blonde hair tended to yellow unappealingly with age. In 1979, this fourth issue was released and had much fairier hair. As with other variations, these can be of more interest to collectors looking to complete a collection. This particular dress (right) is also hard to find. Mint and boxed examples will fetch the higher values.

A Palitoy Pippa doll, fourth issue in multicoloured daisy print yellow dress, in mint condition in original card window box.

1979   *7in (18cm) high*

£150-200   **MTB**

A Palitoy Princess Pippa doll, in mint condition, in unopened card window box.

c1974   *7in (18cm) high*

£200-250   **MTB**

A Palitoy Pippa's friend 'Tammie' doll, third issue in gingham dress, in complete and mint condition, in original card window box.

Tammie's first issue outfit (1972) of blue trousers and a top printed with vines and leaves in blue tones is very hard to find.

1975   *7in (18cm) high*

£100-150   **MTB**

A rare Palitoy Pippa's friend 'Penny' doll, first issue with dungarees, in mint condition, in original card window box.

1976   *7in (18cm) high*

£200-300   **MTB**

A Palitoy Pippa's friend 'Mandy' doll, first issue with red pocket on dress, in complete and mint condition, in original card window box.

1976   *7in (18cm) high*

£100-150   **MTB**

A late 1970s Palitoy Princess Pippa doll, complete and in mint condition, in original card window box.

With long hair down to her feet, Princess Pippa was introduced in 1974, with this dancing version arriving in 1975. Look out for the almost 'Arctic blonde' fair-haired variation, which is very rare.

c1976   *7in (18cm) h*

£200-300   **MTB**

A Palitoy Pippa's friend 'Pete' doll, with original clothes, in mint and complete condition, in original card window box.

Pete is virtually identical to Topper's 'Gary' doll.

c1977   7in (18cm) high
£70-90   **MTB**

A Palitoy Pippa 'In the Pink' outfit from the Vienna Collection, in complete and mint condition in original box.

1974   8in (20cm) wide
£45-50   **MTB**

A Palitoy Pippa 'Monaco Collection' outfit, complete and in mint condition with original box.

The white, wide-brimmed hat is the rarest part as it was usually lost.

1976   8in (20cm) wide
£20-25   **MTB**

A Palitoy Pippa 'Riviera Collection' outfit, in complete and mint condition, in unopened original card box.

c1976   8in (20cm) wide
£45-50   **MTB**

A Palitoy Pippa 'Holiday Girl' clothing set, comprising three outfits, in complete and mint condition with original box.

The 'Disco Fan' set released in the same year also contained three outfits.

1975   9in (23cm) high
£100-150   **MTB**

A Palitoy Pippa 'Oriental Collection' outfit, with fan, in complete and mint condition in original, unopened box.

c1977   7in (18cm) wide
£45-50   **MTB**

A Meccano Pippa 'Holiday Collection' outfit, for the French market, complete and in mint condition with unopened box.

1978   8in (20cm) wide
£40-50   **MTB**

A Mattel 'bubble-cut' Barbie doll, with blond hair, model 850, with original red swimsuit, stand and leaflet, in very good condition with original box.

Released in 1959, the ever youthful Barbie celebrated her 50th birthday last year. Vintage, pre-1973, dolls are as sought after today as they were by the little girls who played with Barbie originally.

1962-67   *12in (30.5cm) high*

£150-200   **MTB**

A Mattel Barbie doll, with 'Twist 'n Turn' waist, produced for the European market, in mint condition, in unopened slightly worn box.

A Mattel black 'Tropical Barbie', model 1022, with long hair and original clothes, in mint condition in unopened, original box.

A Mattel 'Midge' doll, with 'brownette' hair, 'bendable' legs and original clothing, complete and unopened in original card box.

This was the most expensive Midge doll produced, and is scarce today as she was also not as popular as Barbie herself. Midge is Barbie's best friend.

1964   *12in (30.5cm) high*

£400-500   **MTB**

These inexpensive versions of Barbie were bagged inside the box, but sold in the US without the box, leading to them being called 'baggies' by collectors.

1973   *12in (30.5cm)*

£40-60   **MTB**

Sold 'with the longest hair ever', she cost $6.99, and was a variant of the white Tropical Barbie released in the same year.

1985   *12in (30.5cm) high*

£20-30   **MTB**

A Mattel Barbie 'Solo in the Spotlight' special edition reproduction doll, model 13534, with brunette hair, in mint condition in unopened mint condition box.

This doll was also retailed in Hallmark card stores.

1994   *13in (33cm) high*

£40-60   **MTB**

A Mattel 'Skipper' doll, model 950, blonde hair, original swimsuit and shoes, card box with taped ends.

Although the doll is in very good condition overall, the box has been repaired, which reduces the overall value, which may have topped £150 in mint condition.

1964-66   *10in (25.4cm) high*

£80-120   **MTB**

A Mattel 'Talking Ken' doll, model 1111, with original red outfit, and sealed in original card window box.

1968   *13in (33cm) high*

£70-100   **MTB**

A scarce Mattel 'Barbie Ponytail' printed vinyl carrying case.

1961   *10.75in (27cm) wide*

£30-50   **BH**

DOLLS

QUICK REFERENCE - TRESSY

Released in 1964, Tressy's unique feature was her 'growing' hair, operated by pushing a button on her stomach, and wound back in using a key in a slot in her back. She was made by Palitoy in the UK, American Character in the US and Bella in France. Her sister was Toots (Cricket in the US), her friend was Mary Make-Up, and her clothing line was 'Budget Fashions'. This first issue had sideways glancing eyes and was boxed in a fragile, and now very rare, triangular box.

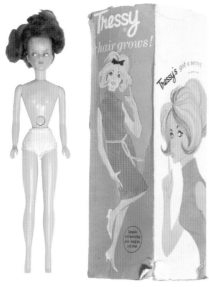

A Palitoy Tressy, first issue, with brown hair, and knickers, together with an original triangular cardboard box.
c1965   15in (38cm) high
£60-90   MTB

A Palitoy Tressy doll, fourth issue, with original clothing, in mint condition in unopened card window box.

Released in the mid-1970s, this version had gripping hands and a built-in key in her back to wind her hair. She was also available in an identical blue outfit.
15in (38cm) high
£100-150   MTB

A French Bella Tressy doll, with original clothing, in mint condition in unopened card window box.
c1966   14in (35.5cm) high
£55-65   MTB

A Palitoy 'Toots' doll, complete with ballet dress, style book and hairgrips, with rare red triangular box.
c1966   10.5in (26.5cm) high
£80-120   MTB

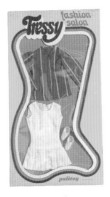

A late 1960s-70s Palitoy Tressy tennis or sports outfit, in complete and mint condition in original packaging.
12in (30.5cm) high
£10-15   MTB

A late 1960s Tressy 'Emerald Princess' outfit, in complete and mint condition in original packaging.
10.5in (26.5cm) high
£50-80   MTB

A 1960s Palitoy Tressy 'Mix n' Match' outfit, complete and in mint condition in original packaging.
9.5in (24cm) high
£15-20   MTB

DOLLS

An Ideal Tammy doll, first issue, with original skiing outfit and skis, complete with original card box.

Tammy was produced from 1962-66. This is and example of the first issue, with a first issue box. Intended as a competitor to the wildly successful Barbie, she also had an extensive wardrobe, and a set of friends and accessories, but was more wholesome than Barbie.

1962   *13in (33cm) high*

£100-150   **MTB**

An Ideal Tammy doll, with original blue jumpsuit and stand, in original card box.

c1964   *13in (33cm) high*

£100-150   **MTB**

An Ideal Dad doll, complete with original clothes, rare shoes and stand, and original card box.

Tammy's Mom is much harder to find than her Dad.

c1964   *13in (33cm) high*

£70-100   **MTB**

An American Mattel Rock Flowers 'Rosemary' doll, complete with original clothes, record and card window box.

8in (20.5cm)

£60-80   **MTB**

An Ideal Ted doll, complete with original clothes and stand, and original card box.

Ted was Tammy's brother, and is very similar to Tammy's boyfriend Bud. However, Bud has darker eyebrows and is the hardest doll of Tammy's friends and family to find.

c1964   *13in (33cm) high*

£70-100   **MTB**

An American Mattel Rock Flowers 'Heather' doll, complete with original clothes, record and card window box.

Produced from 1971-74, Mattel's Rock Flowers series were similar to Dawn dolls and had bendy bodies, rooted hair and painted faces. In total, five dolls, including Doug, were produced. The record played two songs that were typical of the period.

8in (20.5cm) high

£50-70   **MTB**

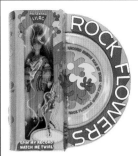

An American Mattel Rock Flowers 'Lilac' doll, complete with original clothes, record and card window box.

8in (20.5cm) high

£50-80 · MTB

A Palitoy 'Dancing Tammie' pocket-sized doll, complete with original clothing, in mint condition in unopened original card window box.

7in (18cm) high

£50-80 · MTB

A Palitoy 'Dancing Marie' pocket-sized doll, complete with original clothing, in mint condition in unopened original card window box.

Marie was one of Palitoy's miniature fashion dolls, like Pippa. Her novelty lies in her ability to dance – if her arms were moved, her body twisted.

7in (18cm) high

£160-180 · MTB

A Dutch Otto Simon Fleur 'Showjumper' doll, with riding outfit, in complete and mint condition, in original card window box.

Fleur was a European 'clone' of Sindy, released in 1978 after Pedigree ceased sales of Sindy in the Netherlands. She proved to be highly successful in her home country and, although she met with some success internationally from 1983, sales were highest in the Netherlands. Fleur was redesigned in the late 1980s, and discontinued in 1988. This doll was one of the less expensive in the range, and packaged in a box to mimic Sindy.

14in (35.5cm) high

£20-30 · MTB

An American Mattel 'Twiggy' doll, with twisting waist, and original clothes and plastic boots.

The boots in particular are scarce. Without the original clothing, the doll alone is usually worth up to £30.

1966-67 · *11in (28cm) high*

£40-50 · DSC

A Dutch Otto Simon & B.T. Toys International Fleur 'Mount Everest' doll, with mountain climbing outfit, in complete and mint condition, in original card window box.

14in (35.5cm) high

£20-30 · MTB

An Ideal Dorothy Hamill doll, with original clothes and medal, in mint condition in original card window box.

Dorothy Hamill was the US Olympic figure skating champion who won a gold medal in the 1976 Innsbruck Winter Olympics.

1977 · *13in (33cm) high*

£40-60 · MTB

An Armand Marseille AM 996 doll, with sleeping blue eyes, painted eyebrows and eyelashes, open mouth with two teeth, and jointed composition body.

20in (51cm) high

£100-150　　　　**SAS**

An Armand Marseille AM 996 doll, with sleeping blue eyes, painted eyebrows, hair eyelashes, open mouth with flicking tongue, two teeth, brown wig, and jointed composition body.

20in (51cm) high

£100-150　　　　**SAS**

An Armand Marseille AM 351 'Dream Baby', with sleeping blue eyes, painted eyelashes, open mouth with two teeth, and composition body.

9.75in (25cm) high

£50-80　　　　**SAS**

A Simon & Halbig 1078 doll, with sleeping blue eyes, painted eyebrows and eyelashes, open mouth with four teeth, pierced ear-lobes, and jointed composition body.

18in (46cm) high

£180-220　　　　**SAS**

A Robert Carl 25 doll, with sleeping brown eyes, painted eyebrows and eyelashes, open mouth with four teeth, jointed composition body, dressed as a nurse.

16.25in (41cm) high

£80-120　　　　**SAS**

A Bruno Schmidt 2097.2 baby doll, with sleeping blue eyes, painted eyebrows and eyelashes, open mouth with two teeth, joined composition body.

14.25in (36cm) high

£100-150　　　　**SAS**

A Simon & Halbig 949 doll, with fixed blue eyes, painted eyebrows and eyelashes, closed mouth, pierced ear lobes, kid body with porcelain lower arms, four fingers incomplete, in original box.

18.5in (47cm) high

£250-350　　　　**SAS**

A 1930s American sprayed composition 'Topsy' doll, with floral printed red clothing, unmarked.

9in (23cm) high

£30-40   **DSC**

A 1930s Canadian Reliable sprayed composition black doll, with later blue knitted cardigan, nappy and socks.

Many of Reliable's dolls were exported, including to the UK.

11in (28cm) high

£25-30   **DSC**

A 1930s American sprayed composition 'Topsy' doll, with cotton dress and woven socks, unmarked.

Composition is a hard material made up of glue, resin and wood particles. More resistant to damage and cheaper to produce than bisque, surfaces are often spray painted. Topsy dolls, with their hallmark top knots of hair, were popular in the US during the 1930s. The value depends on the maker, expression on the face, size and condition.

11in (28cm) high

£40-50   **DSC**

A Norah Wellings 'Welsh Girl' fabric doll, with original clothing, in mint condition with card tag.

As well as being desirable to Norah Wellings collectors, these are also sought after by costume doll collectors.

9in (23cm) high

£50-60   **DSC**

A 1920s-30s Norah Wellings 'Island Girl' fabric doll, with original clothes, in good condition, with some wear.

14.25in (36cm) high

£20-30   **DSC**

A 1930s Chad Valley 'Greek Boy' fabric doll, in original clothes, with red embroidered label to sole of left foot, very slight discoloration, otherwise in excellent condition.

17in (33cm) high

£100-150   **VEC**

A German Steiff 'Musician' brown felt 1911 replica doll, from a limited edition 1,200, with white tag numbered '411915', tags and certificate, in mint condition, with original box.

1997-98   *17in (43cm) high*

£50-80   **VEC**

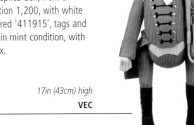

DOLLS

A 1950s Amanda Jane 'Jinx' hard plastic doll, dressed as a sailor, in complete condition.

7.5in (19cm) high

£40-50   DSC

A 1950s Rosebud 'Miss Rosebud' hard plastic doll, with polka dot printed dress, the back moulded 'Miss Rosebud MADE IN ENGLAND'.

As well as considering condition, look at the clothes, as these make a difference to value. For example, the complete fairy outfit can mean the same doll may fetch around £150.

7.5in (19cm) high

£40-50   DSC

A 1950s Linda hard plastic doll, with red corduroy dress and bonnet, the back moulded 'MADE IN HONG KONG', in original and excellent condition.

These dolls were copies of the popular, but comparatively expensive, Miss Rosebud dolls. They were sold in cornershops at prices which were more affordable to children saving pocket money. The style of bonnet and dress is a typical feature.

8in (20.5cm) high

£15-20   DSC

A 1950s Palitoy hard plastic 'Marcher' doll, in complete original condition with printed floral skirt, socks and plastic shoes.

This doll gained its name due to her unusual walking movement, which looks almost like marching.

19.25in (49cm) high

£40-50   DSC

A 1950s Welsh Tudor Rose hard plastic 'Island Girl' Topsy-style black doll, with grass skirt and ribbons tied in her three hair knots.

Tudor Rose dolls have been increasing in value over the past few years.

8in (20.5cm) high

£25-30   DSC

A 1950-53 Vogue hard plastic Ginny, with factory purple ribbon trimmed dress and painted lashes.

7.5in (19cm) high

£120-180   BH

A 1950s hard plastic Roberta Walker, wearing a pink dress with grey trim.

8in (20cm) high

£20-30   BH

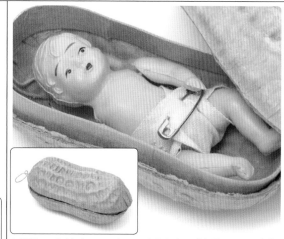

A late 19thC to early 20thC 'Smallest Doll In The World', the fully jointed, carved wooden miniature doll contained inside a wooden egg.

Despite its tiny size, the doll's feet are painted, as are her facial features and her hair.

Doll 0.5in (1.5cm) high

£80-120   DSC

A 1930s probably Japanese 'peanut baby', the celluloid miniature doll with fabric nappy contained inside a pressed pulp peanut shell.

Peanut 4in (10cm) high

£20-25   DSC

A 1920s Japanese painted moulded solid bisque 'My Little Pet' miniature doll, with felt clothes, mounted on original printed sales card.

Card 4.5in (11.5cm) high

£20-30   DSC

A 1930s Japanese 'Bathing Set' celluloid miniature doll, with celluloid bath, oversized dummy, and section of fabric, contained in a matchbox with original printed label.

Bath 1.5in (3.5cm) long

£25-30   DSC

A 1950s 'Smallest Baby In The World' plastic miniature doll, with red plastic bath and original box.

Bath 1.25in (3cm) long

£10-15   DSC

A 1950s Rodnoid hard plastic miniature doll, with jointed arms and legs.

The Rodnoid name could only be used for one year, as the company found that it was already in use by another company for one of its products.

2.75in (7cm) high

£10-15   DSC

A CLOSER LOOK AT MINIATURE DOLLS

The box is rare as most would have been thrown away as these were inexpensive dolls at the time.

These were often used in doll houses, due to their small size.

Note the wild statements about the dolls printed on the box.

On its own, each doll is worth around £5.

A 1950s boxed set of three Japanese moulded rubber 'Three Little Sisters' miniature dolls, imported by CODEG, complete with original box.

Dolls 2.25in (5.5cm) high

£25-30   DSC

TOYS & DOLLS

QUICK REFERENCE

- Shallowpool Handicrafts were produced by Peggy Pryce, Joan Rickarby and Muriel Fogarty in Devon, England. After World War II, the three women bought a rural cottage and set up a business in fabric homewares, producing items such as rugs and lampshades. They began making dolls during the mid-1950s. Rickarby designed the painted plaster heads and hands, former hairdresser Pryce produced the wigs, and Fogarty assembled the dolls on wire armatures, and handled business matters.
- Dolls were based on Cornish or historical characters, painstakingly researched to ensure that costumes were as accurate and detailed as possible. They were sold in local shops, and gift and souvenir shops in Cornwall for tourists.

- The company grew to be very successful, employing 16 doll makers and exporting to shops in the US as well as around the UK. In the late 1970s, Pryce married and left the business, with Rickarby and Fogarty carrying on with production until the mid-1980s, when they both retired and Shallowpool Handicrafts was closed.
- To ensure you are buying a complete doll, it is helpful to familiarise yourself with the dolls produced, including their clothes and accessories. There may be variations, particularly in fabrics used for clothing, but this does not usually affect value. Avoid staining, fading, tears, or damage to the paint, especially on the faces, as these will reduce the desirability.

A Shallowpool 'Cornish Pasty Seller' doll, with painted plaster Cornish pasties on a plate and printed poem about pasties in her apron pocket.

This is one of the most commonly found dolls, undoubtedly due to the popularity of Cornish pasties.

8in (20.5cm) high

£15-20   DSC

A Shallowpool 'Bal Maiden' doll, with cane and plaster long-handled hammer stick and knitting in her apron pocket.

This Cornish character broke up rocks dug out of copper or tin mines, an activity known as 'spalling', to earn a living.

7.5in (19cm) high

£25-30   DSC

A Shallowpool 'Old Mother Hubbard' doll, with white painted plaster dog on a fabric ribbon.

9in (23cm) high

£40-50   DSC

A Shallowpool 'Fanny Wheeler' doll, holding a painted plaster lantern.

Fanny Wheeler assisted her father in his smuggling activities, taking a boat to France with him to bring back kegs of illicit spirits.

7.75in (19.5cm) high

£40-50   DSC

A Shallowpool 'Cornish Lady' dressed in early 17thC riding costume, with a feathered hat.

This figure was inspired by Lady Howard of Fitzford from Daphne du Maurier's 1964 novel 'The King's General'.

8in (20.5cm) high

£20-25   DSC

QUICK REFERENCE

- Although there are still collectors who buy vintage eyewear as a record of optical developments and changing styles, most of today's buyers are looking to wear their new purchases. The most popular frames are colourful and date from the 1950s onwards. Value depends on style, condition, the name of the maker or designer, and materials used.
- Frames that effectively represent their period are particularly desirable, with the 'cat's eye' style of the 1950s and oversized rounded frames of the 1960s being widely sought after. Rare 'wild' styles in bright or clashing colours and shapes that might have been unpopular or expensive at time are often the most valuable.
- Consider the material and work that has gone into making the frames. Hand-crafted elements, such as enamelling, painting or complex laminating or cutting, will generally add value.
- Look for the names or monograms of famous designers, as these will generally add value. Notable eyewear designers include Alain Mikli and Emmanuelle Khanh; frames were also designed for or by Christian Dior, Emilio Pucci and Pierre Cardin. Some designers' monograms changed over time, which can help with dating.
- Always examine frames for burn marks, cracks or splits, which cannot be repaired easily and will make the frames less attractive to prospective buyers. Warped or bent plastic can sometimes be corrected by professionals and is therefore often less problematic. Look for 'dead' unused shop stock, which is usually unworn.
- Scratched, cracked, or even missing lenses do not typically affect value, as buyers often intend to fit their own lenses. Unusual original lenses, such as those with a graduated tint in matching or contrasting colour, may add value, however, and should be kept even if they are replaced.

A pair of 1930s-40s clear pink tinged plastic half-hexagonal frames, unmarked.

5in (12.5cm) wide

£40-60   VE

A pair of 1940s-60s small tortoiseshell plastic frames, with half hexagonal rims and curved arms.

Retro styles such as this, particularly in tortoiseshell, have recently become fashionable again, after years of modern styles being popular.

5in (12.5cm) wide

£70-100   VE

A pair of 1960s French black plastic sunglasses with half hexagonal-shaped top rims, curved arms and "VERGO FILTRANT FRANCE" oval sticker on the original lenses.

5in (12.5cm) wide

£70-100   VE

A pair of 1950s plastic sunglasses, the frames of transparent light blue over opaque white.

5in (13cm) wide

£30-40   CANS

A pair of 1950s brown and white laminated plastic sunglasses.

5in (13cm) wide

£30-50   CANS

A 1960s pair of red and white over clear laminated plastic frames, with inset diamond pattern, unmarked.

5.75in (14.5cm) wide

£70-100 **VE**

A pair of 1960s French grey pearlescent and white laminated plastic frames, the upper layer cut through with dots, lines and curls, marked "France WOC".

5.25in (13.5cm) wide

£120-180 **VE**

A 1960s pair of American Renauld metal-framed angular rectangular sunglasses, with white enamel detailing.

During the early and mid 1960s, Renauld advertised a wide range of avant garde, futuristically shaped sunglasses.

6in (15.5cm) wide

£120-180 **VE**

A 1960s pair of carved red pearlescent plastic frames, marked "AM 26".

6in (15.5cm) wide

£120-180 **VE**

A pair of 1960s-70s brown and white moulded plastic imitation bamboo frames, marked "Frame France Made in France".

Bamboo-style frames became highly fashionable during the 1970s. The classic frame shape, typical of the late 1940s-50s, is given extra life by the shaped arms.

5.5in (14cm) wide

£120-180 **VE**

A 1960s-70s pair of French black and white laminated plastic 'swirl' frames, marked "Frame France".

6in (15cm) wide

£100-150 **VE**

A pair of late 1960s-70s Italian transparent pink plastic frames, marked "FRAME ITALY 820".

5.75in (14.5cm) wide

£25-35 **BB**

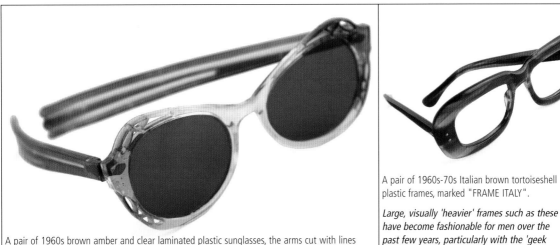

A pair of 1960s brown amber and clear laminated plastic sunglasses, the arms cut with lines through the brown layer, the frames pierced with geometric and curving shapes, unmarked.

5in (13cm) wide

£80-120   VE

A pair of 1960s-70s Italian brown tortoiseshell plastic frames, marked "FRAME ITALY".

Large, visually 'heavier' frames such as these have become fashionable for men over the past few years, particularly with the 'geek chic' trend.

5.75in (14.5cm) wide

£25-35   BB

A pair of 1960s American laminated purple and light blue plastic frames, marked "Graceline USA

5in (12.5cm) wide

£20-25   BB

A pair of 1980s French blue and black back laminated plastic frames, marked "FRAME FRANCE STEPPE".

Popularised by films in the 1980s, such as 'Top Gun' starring Tom Cruise, the 'aviator' frame shape championed by RayBan has become popular again recently.

5.25in (13.5cm) wide

£15-20   BB

A pair of 1980s 'Les Halles Espace' blue aluminium frames.

5.75in (14.5cm) wide

£40-60   VE

A CLOSER LOOK AT A PAIR OF GLASSES

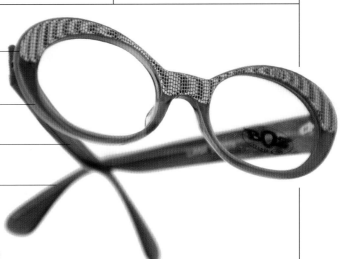

These frames clearly look back to the large, oval 'bug eye' styles of the 1960s; eyewear designers often look to the past for inspiration.

The award-winning 'Boz' brand was led by Jean Francois Rey from 1991. He was inspired by African and Asian cultures, which can be seen here in the snakeskin effect.

The son of eyewear designers, Rey is considered by many to be one of the best avant garde eyewear designers today.

The eclectic choice of colours and patterns is typical of his creativity. He also draws inspiration from Japan and its culture.

A pair of 1990s French Boz 'Frames And Fun' snakeskin effect and red laminated plastic frames, marked "Made in France Lana SA/274", with lens sticker.

5.25in (13.5cm) wide

£80-120   VE

FASHION

QUICK REFERENCE

- Vintage fashion is still a hot collecting area. Examples are not only sought after by collectors, but also by fashionistas who follow the trend for wearing vintage set by celebrities such as Kate Moss and Sarah Jessica Parker. Although this rise in popularity has meant prices have risen too, there's plenty still available to suit every budget. Pieces can be found at auctions, vintage fashion dealers and even in charity shops.
- The top end of the market is dominated by the work of leading 20thC designers such as Christian Dior, Gianni Versace and Coco Chanel. These pieces can be divided into two categories: couture, made in limited quantities after pieces from seasonal collections, and 'diffusion' ranges that can be bought 'off the peg'. Couture examples are usually more desirable, particularly if they are from notable collections, and fetch higher sums. Learn to recognise the difference by researching the different labels used.
- Although the top end of the market may be the most stable area in terms of value, the middle and lower ends have seen similar rises, and can be more fun to collect. Clothes often cost the same as, or even less than, something from the high street. Currently, the 1950s, 60s and 70s are the most popular decades. Always check the label as some makers may have been 'cult' names. Look out for prestigious locations which can indicate good quality makers or retailers.
- Look for pieces that are well cut, made from high grade materials, well finished and which have good stitching. Avoid pieces that are torn or stained – unless this is intentional. Examine vintage photographs and fashion books to learn more about the styles of the period you are interested in. After the work of leading designers, pieces that epitomise the fashion of the age are the most sought after by collectors.

An early 20thC American cotton and lace day dress, with tapework and lace panels and trim, and embroidered flowers and leaves, with elasticated waist.

Dresses from this period are scarcer than most, due to their age and fragile material. The style came back into fashion in the 1970s, with names such as Gunne Saxe. More common in the US than the UK, if the condition is as good as this, it should make an excellent buy.

c1915   41.5in (105cm) high

£100-150   **CANS**

A 1920s brown corduroy coat, with a a detachable fox fur collar or stole, lined in cotton, and with ruched sleeves, unlabelled.

45.75in (116cm) high

£200-250   **CANS**

A 1930s-40s black crepe dress, with red and white beaded pockets with stylized flower within a shield design, in excellent condition.

As well as the dress fabric being in perfect condition, there is, surprisingly, no damage to the beaded pockets. Damage to beaded designs like these is almost impossible to repair satisfactorily and can reduce value by over 75 per cent.

39.5in (100cm) long

£80-120   **CANS**

A 1930s yellow chiffon or georgette tea dress, printed with red and yellow flowers and green leaves, with ruffled neck.

42.25in (107cm) long

£100-150   **CANS**

A 1940s green cotton dress, printed with black and white flowers, with bow to front, and matching jacket with cream lapels, unlabelled.

58in (147cm) long

£100-150 CANS

A late 1940s burgundy crushed velvet belted dress, with ruched shoulders and glass buttons, unlabelled.

£80-120 CANS

A late 1940s-50s Canadian Sty-Val silver-grey acetate dress, woven with roses in silver and gold coloured thread, labelled.

38.25in (97cm) high

£80-100 CANS

A 1940s black crepe dress, with pleated fan effect to front, scooped neck line, and high split skirt.

47in (119cm) high

£60-80 CANS

A 1940s American Brookmar day dress, printed with red berries, purple leaves and green flowers, with torn label.

42.25in (107cm) long

£60-80 CANS

A 1940s Utility houndstooth coat with attached hood, original Bakelite buttons, matching belt, and deep cuffs.

41in (104cm) high

£180-220 CANS

FASHION

A 1950s 'London Town MADE IN MAYFAIR LONDON ENGLAND' purple, orange, brown and green floral printed halterneck dress, with boned and structured inside mesh petticoat underneath, and trail to the scoop back.

37in (94cm) long

£80-100 **CANS**

A CLOSER LOOK AT A 1950S DRESS

The bright colours reflect the change from the austerity of wartime and post-war 1940s utility-wear.

The stylised pink rose and polka dot motifs are also typical of the period and add a whimsical touch.

The condition is excellent, making it very wearable today – an important factor in its valuation.

The cut of the dress with its full skirt and bolero jacket, is typical of the 1950s.

A 1950s American sleeveless halterneck cotton dress and matching bolero jacket, printed with pink roses in white wavy bands, and white polka dots on blue, with label reading 'LO ROCO MODEL in Marchington'.

45in (114cm) long

£80-100 **CANS**

A 1950s cotton belted dress, printed with roses and polka dots, the pockets with black trim, unlabelled.

34.75in (88cm) long

£70-90 **CANS**

A 1950s green cotton belted maxi-dress, printed with white flowers and with 'angel' or 'flutter' sleeves.

51.75in (131cm) long

£40-50 **CANS**

A 1950s white cotton shirtwaister dress, printed with polka dots and with spherical buttons inset with rhinestones, unlabelled.

40.5in (103cm) long

£60-80 **CANS**

A 1950s American Kabro of Houston tonal blue, grey and purple cotton shirtwaister dress, with Tiki style print.

As American GIs returned to the US from overseas, Hawaiian inspired Tiki prints underwent a style revival in the 1950s and 60s, affecting everything from barware to fashion.

43.75in (111cm) long

£60-80   CANS

A 1950s ball gown, the cream ground embroidered with a floral pattern in green tones, with two green pleats and small bow to chest, unlabelled.

45.25in (115cm) long

£100-150   CANS

A mid-1950s Jeanne Lanvin black Chantilly lace cocktail dress, with boned strapless bodice, bouffant tiered skirt, large silk rose, horse-hair stiffened petticoat, bearing large woven label.

£420-480   KT

A 1950s jade green halterneck ball gown, woven with a vein-like design and bow to chest, with stiffened calico petticoat and and hooped layer underneath.

Ball gowns of this period make superb buys, as they are generally not hard to find, often of very good quality and are considerably less expensive than modern dresses. They also add a certain vintage style to an occasion. The pattern on this vibrantly coloured example is unusual.

47.75in (121cm) long

£150-200   CANS

QUICK REFERENCE - CHRISTIAN DIOR

On February 12th 1947, a 42 year old Christian Dior (1905-57) exploded onto the international fashion scene with his first collection. Named 'Corolle', it brought elegance back to fashion with wasp-like waists, longer fuller skirts, a high bust and rounded shoulders. Within months the curvaceous style had become known as the 'New Look', and it went on to be copied across the world. Although the waist on this example is more relaxed, it still bears many of the hallmarks of Dior's original designs.

A Christian Dior Export slubbed silk cocktail dress, no.25713, with curving shoulders, boat neckline, large fringed bow to one hip, labelled 'Christian Dior Europe, manufacturé par Christian Dior Export'.

c1956–7

Bust 34in (86cm)

£380-420   KT

A 1950s Liberty of London waisted Astrakhan collar wool coat, with 'Liberty of London' label to inside.

The waisted shape, buttons and Astrakhan collar give this a Victorian or Edwardian feel. Asktrakhan is the tightly curled fur from Persian or kerakul lambs.

39.5in (100cm) long

£150-200   CANS

A CLOSER LOOK AT A DOLLYROCKERS DRESS

DollyRockers was designed by Samuel Sherman, also known as 'Sambo' and was active from c1963-75.

They were promoted in conjunction with Dolcis shoes by Smith's Crisps model Pattie Boyd (b.1944), who married Beatle George Harrison and Eric Clapton.

Look out for dresses that are made from Liberty print, a fact indicated on the label, as these can fetch over £100.

Labels reading 'Dollyrockers London' are different, being new clothes made from vintage fabric, and sold today through London retailers.

A 1960s DollyRockers cotton dress, printed with brown, yellow and orange repeated flowers and foliage on a bright blue ground, with frill under bust, labelled.

32.75in (83cm) long

£60-80　　　　　　　　　　　　　　　**CANS**

An Ossie Clark printed velvet coat, with Russian-style button closure down one side, printed with multicoloured flowers designed by Celia Birtwell, with black on white printed label.

c1970　　　　　　*Bust 34in (86cm)*

£450-550　　　　　　　　　　**KT**

A late 1960s Pucci printed silk jersey evening gown, printed in shades of blue and green over a turquoise skirt, labelled.

Bust 36in (92cm)

£280-320　　　　　　　　　　**KT**

A 1970s Emilio Pucci Kelly green cotton poplin skirt and blouse, printed with violet and blue floral pattern, with twill A-line skirt with welt pockets, with 'Emilio Pucci' label.

Now owned by luxury goods group LVMH, the Pucci name has never been out of fashion for long. Always look for the 'Emilio' name in the print as the company's classic 1960s and ' 70s look was widely copied. The colour and pattern of this suit are typical of Pucci's look.

size 6-8

£280-320　　　　　　　　　**FRE**

An early 1960s HF Couture of London pink cotton dress, printed with a green, black and white curving abstract pattern.

Despite dating from the 1960s, the shape is very 1950s and the pattern recalls the Art Deco period of the 1930s.

36in (91cm) long

£50-60　　　　　　**CANS**

A 1960s Shifts International of Miami cotton dress, printed with blue fish and lime green seahorses on a white background, trimmed with lace.

The colours, pattern and shape are similar to dresses by Lily Pulitzer, which were also popular.

35in (89cm) long

£50-60　　　　　　**CANS**

A 1950s Kittiwake swimsuit, with purple-brown and white wicker-like pattern, unworn.

22.75in (57.5cm) long

£30-40 CANS

An early 1960s Slix navy blue swimsuit, with diagonal red and white stripes, unworn.

18.5in (47cm) long

£40-50 CANS

ESSENTIAL REFERENCE - 1940S UTILITY CLOTHING

Utility clothing is the term used to describe clothes produced in Britain during the war, when materials were rationed and skilled labour was limited. The range was introduced in 1941, and bore the 'CC41' label shown here, which stood for Civilian Clothing 1941'. The government regulated the import, distribution and use of cloth, limiting the 'austere' styles and the range itself. They also controlled the price to ensure people could afford clothing of suitable quality. Much was worn out or altered, making surviving intact examples rare. Initial dislike turned into apathy, and the range was withdrawn in 1952.

A 1940s Capstan utility-wear woven pink cotton swimsuit, printed with seashells and fish, size 36, with Capstan and Utility labels.

18.5in (47cm) long

£60-80 CANS

An early 1960s Slix brown and white swimsuit, with diagonal stripe of alternating coloured leaves.

18.5in (47cm) long

£40-60 CANS

A mid 1960s Slix light blue swimsuit, with horizontal red stripe with woven white flowers, unworn.

18.5in (47cm) long

£35-45 CANS

A 1950s British Kittiwake swimsuit, with folded 'V' shape to front, unworn, size 34.

The label indicates that the elasticated material was tested by Courtaulds.

22.75in (57.5cm) high

£40-60 CANS

FASHION

A 1960s-70s Jon Wood polyester and acrylic long-sleeved men's shirt, printed with motifs of a lady and a spinning wheel and a man and a pipe organ.

£25-35   **CANS**

A 1970s Jaytex blue cotton long-sleeved men's shirt printed with light blue horses and jockeys.

£25-30   **CANS**

Two 1960s-70s Nayytex 100% acrylic ladies' sweaters, printed with flower motifs, unworn and with original card tags.

19.75in (50cm) high

£22-28 EACH   **CANS**

A 1970s Marshall Lester cotton t-shirt, printed with multi-coloured advertising style designs.

24in (61cm) long

£25-30   **CANS**

A 1960s Japanese printed and PVC-coated cotton rainmac with stylised floral pattern, unworn, with matching hat.

This fetches as much as this due to the fact that it is complete and entirely unworn.

34.75in (88cm) high

£65-75   **CANS**

A 1960s psychedelic printed nylon slip, with black piping and straps.

Although it looks like a floral design, on closer inspection it is made up of faces. Spot the Twiggy-like face with the side parting.

23.25in (59cm) long

£15-20   **CANS**

A 1960s yellow elasticated roll-on girdle, with suspenders.

1950s examples usually have metal clips.

12.5in (31.5cm) high

£15-20   **CANS**

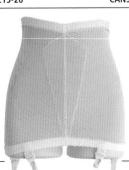

QUICK REFERENCE

- Along with handbags, vintage shoes have become hotly sought after over the past few years. Although some collect for historical reasons, most buy to wear. As a result, shoes from before the Second World War tend to be less desirable due to their fragility and, often, their small sizes. Shoes from before the 20thC, and particularly those from before the 19thC, are scarce and typically very valuable.

- The most popular period is currently the 1950s-60s, when shoe designs became fun and elegant after wartime restrictions. While 1940s shoes can also be sought after, they are too austere for many. Shoes and boots from the 1970s and 80s are growing in popularity, particularly

examples that are evocative of the 'disco' period. In general, look for bright colours, and shapes and materials that are typical of any given period.

- Famous designer names, such as Salvatore Ferragamo, will add value. Also look for notable store locations, such as London's Bond Street or New York's Fifth Avenue, as these usually indicate a good retailer and therefore high quality. The quality of the decoration also adds to value.

- Condition is all-important, particularly to collectors who buy to wear. Examine the soles and uppers carefully looking for wear, splits or missing decoration. While some shoes can be resoled and repaired, this may reduce their resale value.

A pair of 1940s black mesh and black and white leather shoes, marked 'Carmellites Shoes for the Lovely Nahm's Shoe Store 205 West Fox Street Carlsbad New Mexico'.

£150-200   **LDY**

A pair of 1940s 'Styleez Selby Shoe Flare Fit' black suede shoes with pierced sides and curl detail to upper.

£30-50   **CANS**

A pair of 1940s Palter de Liso navy leather platform shoes, with peep-toe and cut decoration, styled by Wexee.

£120-180   **GCHI**

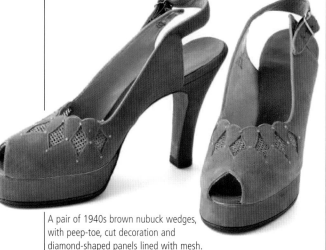

A pair of 1940s brown nubuck wedges, with peep-toe, cut decoration and diamond-shaped panels lined with mesh.

£80-120   **CANS**

A pair of 1940s white nubuck and brown leather brogue-style shoes.

£35-45   **CANS**

A pair of 1940s cork wedges with leopardskin fabric uppers, marked 'La Rose Jacksonville Florida'.

£150-200   **GCHI**

A 1950s blue leather shoe by Rayne, with leather tassel decoration, marked 'Rayne by Appointment'.

£20-30   **LDY**

One of a pair of 1950s brown suede peep-toe court shoes, with brown leather strapped decoration.

£20-30   **LDY**

A 1940s pair of mules, with burgundy suede uppers with embroidered flowers, and carved-wood platform soles, made in the Philippines.

Sometimes known as 'sweetheart souvenirs', these were sent or taken home to wives and girlfriends by American GIs stationed in the Philippines during and after WWII. Houses, foliage and flowers painted in bright colours are typical motifs. The use of coloured woven raffia is another common feature.

£150-200   **GCHI**

QUICK REFERENCE – SALVATORE FERRAGAMO

Salvatore Ferragamo (1898-1960) was one of the greatest innovators in shoe design. After an apprenticeship in Italy, he moved to Southern California in 1914, where he studied anatomy to ensure his shoes were comfortable. His handmade, innovative designs combined function with ornamental forms, and he rapidly gained a celebrity following including Rudolph Valentino and Mary Pickford. In 1927, he returned to Italy, where he continued his innovative work, introducing new materials such as the cork wedge, which was patented in 1937. He continued to attract celebrity clients, including Eva Peron and Marilyn Monroe, after the war. His reputation as a visionary designer of elegant and innovative shoes continued until his death.

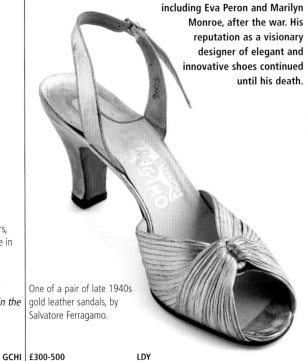

One of a pair of late 1940s gold leather sandals, by Salvatore Ferragamo.

£300-500   **LDY**

A CLOSER LOOK AT A PAIR OF 1950S SHOES

The uppers and strap are made from clear flexible Perspex – plastics such as this were new and fashionable in the 1950s.

The choice of pink and the added sparkle from the diamanté complemented the fashions of the day.

The glamorous design contrasts with the austere fashions of the 1940s, which saw restrictions and rationing.

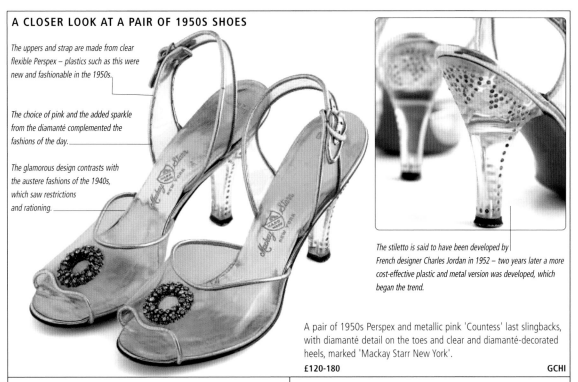

The stiletto is said to have been developed by French designer Charles Jordan in 1952 – two years later a more cost-effective plastic and metal version was developed, which began the trend.

A pair of 1950s Perspex and metallic pink 'Countess' last slingbacks, with diamanté detail on the toes and clear and diamanté-decorated heels, marked 'Mackay Starr New York'.

£120-180   GCHI

A pair of 1950s black suede court shoes, the toes decorated with red velvet ribbon bows, marked 'Michelé Fifth Avenue Paris custom made'.

£150-200   GCHI

A pair of 1950s Danbarale blue leather stilettos, with diamanté and fan detail.

£150-200   IVD

A pair of 1950s unworn American peep-toe slingbacks, with knot detail, marked 'The Guarantee Shoe Store'.

£35-45   CANS

A pair of 1950s flexible Perspex slingbacks, with Perspex 'bows', the painted heels decorated with diamanté, the shoes marked 'Jacqueline designed by Wohl'.

£70-100   GCHI

A pair of 1950s mink and black velvet slippers, marked 'Mandel's fascinating slippers' and 'Genuine Mink'.

£120-180   GCHI

FASHION

A pair of 1950s Nina Original gold-coloured wood paltform mules, with black lace-effect plastic uppers.

£100-150   **GCHI**

A pair of 1950s faux-leopard skin fabric mules, with wing-shaped uppers.

£150-200   **GCHI**

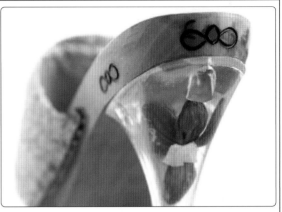

A pair of 1950s straw mules with wooden soles and Perspex heels, the heels inset with raffia flowers.

Always examine raffia closely, as it can be damaged very easily.

£200-250   **GCHI**

A pair of 1950s Nylonette waterproof shoe protectors/galoshes, with black suedette flaps and a fastening button.

The hollow heels allowed the wearer to slip these over their shoes for protection.

£40-60   **CANS**

A pair of 1950s black suede zipped boots, with fur trim, marked 'Kickerino Alaskans', in excellent condition.

£100-150   **GCHI**

A pair of 1980s French Cassis, Cote d'Azur, black suede and gold leather court shoes, with chain detail at heel.

£70-100   LDY

QUICK REFERENCE - 1980S SHOES

The bold style of these shoes matches the dominant style of the period – power dressing. As more women entered executive jobs and strived for ever-increasing success in the working world, their clothes began to reflect their determination and power. Shoulder pads and suits in bold colours and patterns were typical. Examples include Signourney Weaver's character Katharine Parker in the 1988 film 'Working Girl', Prime Minister Margaret Thatcher, and Alexis Colby from the TV series 'Dynasty'. As many of today's designers are already beginning to look back to 1980s fashions, it will be interesting to see how this affects the value and desirability of original shoes and clothes.

A pair of 1980s R.P. Ellen green, white and navy blue slingbacks.

£20-30   CANS

A pair of 1980s 'Wild Pair' black sequin stilettos.

£45-55   IVD

A pair of 1980s Corsina grey leather peep-toe shoes, with applied cream leather butterfly detail.

£45-55   IVD

A 1980s Yves Saint Laurent suede and leather laced court shoe.

A pair of 1980s black and white swirl leather heels, by Gina.

£30-50   CANS

Saint Laurent updated the classic, clumpy brogue of the 1970s and devised a shoe that looks back to the early 20thC, reflects period fashions and is supremely elegant, with great proportions. With the Yves Saint Laurent label and high quality materials, these shoes are desirable and valuable.

£150-200   LDY

QUICK REFERENCE

- It's not just collectors who are snapping up vintage handbags. With the surge of interest in vintage clothing seen over the past decade, fashionable people of all ages are buying handbags to give an individual touch.
- Prices range from as little as £20 to over £5,000 for a highly desirable Hermès 'Kelly' bag. However, most bags can be found for under £100 at vintage clothing stores, auctions, car boot sales and charity shops. When buying always look inside for designer labels, and examine a bag all over to assess its condition.
- Value depends on a number of factors including desirability, the maker, the quality of construction and the materials used, age and condition. Bags made from leather and the rarer animal skins are usually the most

valuable, although bags made of other materials that exemplify the style of the day or have novelty appeal can be equally valuable.
- Away from the best names such as Chanel, Hermès and Gucci, look out for labels of makers in desirable locations, such as Fifth Avenue, New York or Bond Street, London, as this usually indicates a high quality bag.
- Condition is very important. A bag in truly mint, shop-bought, condition will fetch a considerable premium over one that shows signs of use. Look inside as torn or stained interiors reduce desirability and value. Although bags from the 1950s and 60s are currently the most popular, iconic bags from the 1980s are beginning to see a surge of interest, so could be a good investment.

A 1920s Whiting & Davis chain mesh bag with embroidered pink fabric lining, metal frame, stamped inside.

Whiting & Davis, founded in 1876 in Massachusetts, is synonymous with high quality mesh bags. It made bags printed with brightly coloured Art Deco patterns. Although the company fell out of fashion in the mid20thC, it returned briefly during the 'disco' age in the 1970s. The companys's bags remain popular with collectors.

5in (12.5cm) wide

£70-100   CANS

A 1930s brown silk Art Deco bag, the clasp set with cut steel rhinestones, cream silk lined interior, metal frame, marked 'Made in England'.

6in (15cm) high

£30-40   CANS

A 1930s brown ruffled silk bag, pink satin lining, with original mirror, rhinestone clasp, marked 'Made in England'.

The quality and condition of the bag contribute to its value.

8.5in (22cm) wide

£40-60   CANS

A 1930s Art Deco woven Corde handbag, with brass fittings and frame covered with cream bakelite panels, marked 'Made in England'.

8.25in (21cm) high

£50-80   CANS

A 1930s woven silk clutch bag, the silk hand-printed with ducks and birds, with black silk lining and gold piping in and out, bevelled hand mirror and an Art Deco clasp.

7.5in (19.5cm) wide

£40-60   CANS

A 1930s Art Deco iridescent beaded bag, with black Lucite and chromed metal frame.

7in (18cm) wide

£120-180   **GCHI**

A 1940s bag, with a hand-painted and beaded garden and floral design, the padded handle with small floral motifs.

9in (23cm) wide

£150-200   **AHL**

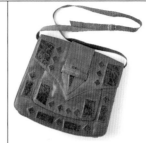

A 1940s brown leather bag with crocodile skin panel decoration, with expandable front pocket and arrow-shaped catch.

10.5in (26.5cm) high

£60-90   **CANS**

A CLOSER LOOK AT A 1940S HANDBAG

During the post-war period, when many materials were expensive and hard to obtain, bags were decorated with all manner of different materials, such as telephone cable.

Box bags are also typical of the period. The bright, jaunty colours and pattern of the telephone cables added colour and cheer at a time of great austerity.

A 1940s-50s British faux-snakeskin bag with wrist handle and purse.

6.75in (17cm) high

£30-50   **CANS**

Avoid dirty or stained examples as they are hard to clean. Breaks in the cord also reduce value.

These bags were made in a variety of patterns and colour combinations – generally the more complex the pattern and the more colours are present, the better.

A 1940s blue felt bag, with applied posy of felt flowers and hearts.

15in (38cm) wide

£60-80   **GCHI**

A 1940s telephone cable covered box bag, lined with red woven fabric on a frame.

7.25in (18.5cm) wide

£60-80   **CANS**

FASHION

A CLOSER LOOK AT AN ENID COLLINS HANDBAG

Enid Collins founded her company in 1959 in Texas and quickly became a popular name with fashionable young women into the 1970s.

The most collectable and desirable bags are sturdy wooden box bags decorated with painted designs highlighted with rhinestones, faux jewels, sequins and other materials.

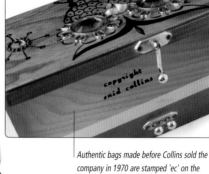

Authentic bags made before Collins sold the company in 1970 are stamped 'ec' on the outside, together with the name of the design, and also bear a stamp on the interior.

The more detailed and amusing the design, and the more materials and colours used, the more the bag is likely to be worth – but check carefully for missing parts.

A 1950s-60s woven box bag, white plastic and yellow and black straw, metal clasp, unmarked.

11in (28cm) wide

£30-50   **CANS**

A 1960s Enid Collins 'Night Owl' box bag, decorated with rhinestones, marked inside, with plastic handle.

8.5in (22cm) wide

£50-70   **CANS**

A 1960s basketwork box handbag, with applied plastic fruit and woven wool leaves and faux-leather handles, in excellent condition.

10.25in (26cm) high

£100-150   **GCHI**

A 1950s Hovland Swanson woven raffia drawstring bag, with applied raffia covered fruits and raffia 'grass', with original price and shop tickets.

8in (20cm) high

A 1950s-60s Souré Bag of New York, of plastic-covered printed cotton, decorated with embroidered multicoloured gloves, applied rhinestones and faux pearls.

15.25in (38.5cm) long

£220-280   **GCHI**

£50-70   **GCHI**

A set of 1950/60s Manderin Jiffy Juvenile Product elasticated permanently knotted ties for boys, in original shop display box.

Box 12.5in (32cm) wide

£40-60   CANS

A 1980s enamelled 'kissing fish' belt buckle, with grey woven belt.

5in (12.5cm) wide

£15-20   CANS

A 1980s embossed metal buckle in the shape of a large fish eating a small fish, on a red elasticated belt.

5in (13cm) wide

£20-30   CANS

A 1980s Valentino red and black chequered dyed fox stole, fully articulated with rhinestone eyes, labelled "Valentino Night/Made in Italy".

£75-95   FRE

A pair of 1930s Plaza silk stockings, in original, unopened packaging with dog shaped card, marked 'Made in England'.

The scarcity of an unopened pack, the dog motif and Art Deco font that make these appealing – some collectors even specialise in stockings.

6.75in (17cm) wide

£20-25   CANS

A set of six 1950s handpainted plastic Bobby Pins hairpins, on original shop display card.

Card 4.75in (12cm) high

£10-15   CANS

A set of six 1950s handpainted plastic Bobby Pins hairpins, on original shop display card.

Card 4.75in (12cm) high

£10-15   CANS

A 1950s handpainted solid plaster girl wall mask, with ponytail and inset rhinestones, in mint condition.

9.5in (24cm) high

£40-50   **MA**

A 1950s-60s Japanese moulded and handpainted miniature lady head vase, for cacti or hairpins.

This small size is unusual.

3.25in (8cm) high

£20-30   **MA**

A 1950s handpainted solid plaster Chinese girl wall mask, in mint condition.

Always examine these very closely. Any paint loss, even if 'touched up' reduces value dramatically. Only those in truly mint condition will fetch such high sums.

11in (28cm) high

£50-60   **MA**

A 1950s slip-moulded cat figurine, with handpainted leaf designs, unmarked.

12in (30.5cm) high

£25-35   **RET**

A 1950s printed vinyl portable record case.

10.5in (27cm) high

£20-30   **CANS**

An early 1950s guitar-shaped wall mirror, with handpainted floral decoration, mounted on wood.

Ignoring the chintzy floral decoration, this shows the beginning of the rock 'n roll movement. These are hard to find in such good condition.

An early 1950s 'Crinoline Lady' fabric, netting and painted plaster dressing table lamp, with wire frame to support her dress.

Considered 'kitsch' by many, always look at the doll, as good quality 19thC bisque 'half dolls' can fetch over £100. Complete examples, such as this, are scarce.

15in (38cm) high

£20-30   **MA**

17in (43cm) high

£50-70   **MA**

ESSENTIAL REFERENCE – SHATTALINE PRODUCTS

Shattaline Products produced a range of resin lampbases, paperweights, pen deskbases and small tables from the mid-1960s until the mid-1970s. The crackle effect was gained by using a catalyst in the resin which caused random internal cracks. Colours included orange, yellow, green, blue and red, but tones can vary as the colourant was applied to batches by hand. Pieces were then sanded and polished by hand. The range was sold by Selfridges, Liberty and other major department stores in the UK, with candleholders being sold through Price's candles. Contrary to popular belief, British Home Stores did not sell this product, but rather a similar, competitive product. The production process was designed by retired army Major turned sculptor Lewen Tugwell during the mid 1960s and pieces were first made in Surrey, with production moving to Scotland in the early 1970s.

A 1960s-70s Shattaline green resin small cylindrical lampbase, with original textured cream fibreglass shade.

Base 5.5in (13.5cm) high

£30-40   M20C

A 1960s-70s Shattaline red resin square section lampbase, with original textured amber fibreglass shade.

Base 11.5in (29cm) high

£60-70   M20C

A 1960s-70s orange and red resin cylindrical lampbase, with original textured cream fibreglass shade.

The different colours used, and the fact that the inside of the base appears to be made up of chunks of resin, rather than a single block of internally cracked resin, indicates that this was made to imitate Shattaline products. A number of imitators existed at the time, one based in Germany (Solarstein) and another using the name 'Scatterlite'.

Base 11.5in (29cm) high

£60-70   M20C

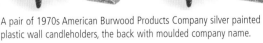

A pair of 1970s American Burwood Products Company silver painted plastic wall candleholders, the back with moulded company name.

The textured, almost space age, design was also reflected in jewellery from the period – particularly that made in Scandinavia.

15.5in (39.5cm) high

£80-100   M20C

A 1950s-60s teak framed table lamp, with brass fitments and textured pink shade.

Pink shades are rare, they are usually orange or off-white in colour. This is the smallest of three sizes of this lamp.

10in (25.5cm) high

£30-40   M20C

A 1970s plastic reclining nude pink and black plastic letter rack.

6in (15.5cm) long

£15-20   MA

QUICK REFERENCE

- Caithness glass was founded near John O'Groats in Scotland in June 1961, primarily to create employment for local people. Talented Irish designer Domnhall O'Broin co-founded the company, and became its technical director and designer from 1961-1966, being responsible for many of their most successful designs. The company is now owned by Dartington Glass.

- O'Broin is arguably one of the over-looked names in 20th century glass design. He trained under Helen Monroe Turner at the Edinburgh College of Art and was one of the first apprentices at Waterford Crystal from 1950, where he worked under Miroslav Havel, and designed patterns such as 'Colleen'. O'Broin left Caithness in 1966, moving to the US where he worked for Pilgrim and Fenton before setting up on his own.

- His designs are typified by modern, yet elegant, shapes with clean lines. Scandinavian glass, being imported into Britain at the time in large numbers, was a strong inspiration. Rims were machine cut and the bases heavily cased in clear glass which 'lifted' and contrasted with the colour. Pieces were spun at high speed in moulds, giving an even, rounded base with a smooth central depression.

- The jewel-like colours used were inspired by the Scottish landscape, gaining patriotic and evocative names such as 'Loch Blue', 'moss' (green), 'Peat' and 'Heather' (purple). Pieces are generally unmarked, although 'CG' paper, or later 'Caithness Glass' labels may have survived.

- Avoid examples that are chipped or scuffed or have internal bubbles or limescale from water, as these factors detract from the purity of the colour and form. After O'Broin left, other designers worked for the company, including Charles Orr from 1967-72 and, notably, Colin Terris from 1972 onwards. Along with O'Broin's, their designs are becoming increasingly sought-after.

A 1960s-90s Caithness Glass footed fruit bowl, designed by Domnhall O'Broin in 1961.

7in (17.5cm) high

£20-30   GC

A 1960s-70s Caithness Glass Heather purple 'Cased' vase, no.4010/M, designed by Domnhall O'Broin in 1961.

7in (17.5cm) high

£30-50   GC

A 1960s-80s Caithness Glass small Loch blue 'Barrel' vase, no.4019/115, designed by Domnhall O'Broin in 1961.

5in (12.5cm) high

£15-20   GC

A Caithness Glass cased 'Moss Green' posy vase, by Domnhall O'Broin, factory and 'Design Centre London' paper labels.

4in (10cm) high

£10-15   MHC

A Caithness Glass Loch Blue 'Stroma' rose bowl, designed by Domnhall O'Broin in 1961.

The colour variation is brought about by the thickness of the glass – near the rim it is extremely thin.

XXin (XXcm) high

£20-30   GC

A 1960s Caithness Glass Loch Blue tall cylindrical mould blown vase, designed by Domhnall O'Broin in 1963, with paper label.

10.5in (26.5cm) high

£80-120   **GC**

A 1960s-70s Caithness Glass Peat brown 'Barrel' vase, no.4019/235, designed by Domhnall O'Broin in 1961.

9in (23cm) high

£50-70   **GC**

A 1960s-70s Caithness Glass Moss green lamp base, designed by Domhnall O'Broin in 1961, with original 'CG' paper label.

This was featured in the influential book 'Modern Glass' by Geoffrey Beard, as an example of a very modern design for the period. Larger pieces such as this are harder to find than smaller vases.

7.25in (18.5cm) high

£80-120   **GC**

A 1960s-70s Caithness Glass Heather lamp base, no.4010/LL, designed by Domhnall O'Broin in 1961.

10in (25.5cm) high

£70-100   **GC**

A 1960s-70s Caithness Glass Peat brown decanter with hollow blown stopper, designed by Domhnall O'Broin in 1961.

11.25in (28.5cm) high

£40-60   **GC**

A 1960s-70s Caithness Glass Heather cased purple decanter, with hollow stopper, designed by Domhnall O'Broin.

Colour tones can vary widely, and it can be hard to tell which colour a piece was intended to be. Clearly identifiable colours such as this are the most desirable.

11.25in (28.5cm) high

£60-80   **GC**

A Caithness Glass Peat brown Morven decanter, shape no.4025/D, designed by Domhnall O'Broin in 1961, with hollow stopper.

This starkly modern, squared off form is typical of O'Broin's forms. Unusually for a decanter, the inside of the rim is not ground, with the seal coming only from the weight of the well-fitted blown stopper.

9.75in (24cm) high

£30-40   **M20C**

A Caithness Glass Heather purple 'Morven' decanter, shape no.4025/D, designed by Domhnall O'Broin in 1961.

9.75in (25cm) high

£40-50 GAZE

A 1990s Caithness Glass cased mottled jade green 'Concerto' rose vase, with ribbed base and cellophane label.

Concerto was available in three colourways: Blue, Jade and Pink.

7in (17.5cm) high

£20-25 GC

A Caithness Glass 'Xanadu' range ovoid vase, designed by Colin Terris in 1996, with layers of pulverised coloured enamel over an opaque white core and an applied blue trail.

7.25in (18.5cm) high

£70-100 GC

A Caithness Glass graduated purple vase, engraved with a bird perched on a thorny branch.

A cutting and engraving department was founded at Caithness by Colin Terris in 1968, meaning all cut or engraved ranges date from after this year. Natural or animal motifs, and commemorative designs, are typical. Designs commemorating personal events, such as a wedding, usually devalue a piece.

9in (23cm) high

£10-15 GC

A Caithness Glass colourless cylindrical 'Oban' vase, designed by Charles Orr, with applied green and blue ribbon trails.

7in (17.5cm) high

£20-30 GC

A CLOSER LOOK AT A CAITHNESS GLASS VASE

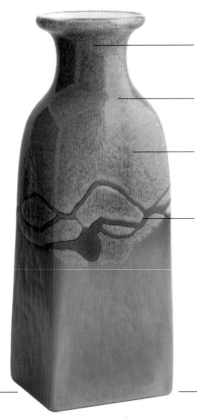

Xanadu uses many layers of glass over an opaque white base to create a mottled, stone-like effect, and can be found in triangular, ovoid, rectangular and hexagonal forms.

The pattern was created by hand in a time-consuming process using coloured enamel frit and randomly applied hot glass trails, making each piece unique.

This range was expensive and comparatively unpopular at the time, so was withdrawn from sale only a few years after being introduced, meaning that it is comparatively scarce today.

It can be found in a range of colours including orange and red, green and blue, and purple and grey.

A Caithness Glass 'Xanadu' range bottle vase, designed by Colin Terris in 1996, with layers of pulverised coloured enamel over an opaque white core and an applied blue trail.

10in (25.5cm) high

£100-150 GC

QUICK REFERENCE

- Wines from the Champagne region have been prized since Roman times, and were often used at royal ceremonies. In 1662, English scientist Christopher Merret developed the first intentionally sparkling wine, although French Benedictine monk Dom Perignon is usually credited with this achievement. However, his version was developed some 40 years after Merret's.
- From the 17thC to the 20thC, champagne was sweet, often being served as a dessert. Dry 'brut' champagne only became popular in the late 19thC.
- Two types of glass are used to serve champagne: a tall flute with a rim that may curve slightly inwards, and a low, saucer-shaped dish. Both are mounted on stems to keep the hand from touching the bowl and warming the wine. The taller version is preferred by connoisseurs.
- The saucer, known as a 'coupe', was reputedly developed in 1663, although facts are scarce. Legend has it that its form

was based on the shape of the breasts of Madame de Pompadour or Queen Marie Antoinette. This is almost certainly false, as examples exist that predate both women. The style saw peaks in popularity during the mid-19thC and during the 1920s and 30s, when it was also used for cocktails.

- Value depends on the maker, glass, and the style and quality of any decoration. Prices for vintage examples can be lower than those for brand new glasses. Although unusual motifs can make a glass desirable, simple and almost 'modern', geometric cuts are often the most popular with collectors.
- Edwardian acid-etched examples are currently very affordable, and are typically made from a delicate, thin glass. Look for simpler classical or geometric patterns, as these may rise in value over time. Owning vintage glasses can add a stylish dash of originality to entertaining.

A 1930s-50s coupe champagne glass, cut with a pattern of stylised leaves and flowers.

Patterns like this tend to be less popular and desirable. The stem is also not cut.

4.5in (11.5cm) high

£10-12   GROB

A 19thC coupe champagne glass, the bowl copper wheel-cut with a pattern of leaves and ferns, with plain, waisted cylindrical stem.

4.5in (11.5cm) high

£12-15   GROB

A 19thC or early 20thC coupe champagne glass, the bowl cut with thistles and leaves, with straight faceted stem.

This is possibly by notable company Edinburgh & Leith.

4.75in (12cm) high

£20-25   GROB

A late 19thC or early 20thC coupe champagne glass, the bowl with acid-etched stylised floral swag and scrolling motif, with hatched band with stylised roses.

4.5in (11.5cm) high

£10-12   GROB

A mid 20thC coupe champagne glass, the bowl cut with trailing strawberry plants and strawberries, with conical baluster stem.

Strawberries are popular motifs – probably because of the luxurious association of strawberries and champagne.

4.5in (11.5cm) high

£10-12   GROB

GLASS

A late 19thC or early 20thC coupe champagne glass, with acid-etched bands of loops and interlaced circles, and tapering cylindrical stem.

4.75in (12cm) high

£8-12   **GROB**

A mid-20thC Continental coupe champagne glass, the bowl cut with a curving pattern of 'thumbprint' ovals, with conical baluster stem.

4.75in (12cm) high

£10-15   **GROB**

An early 20thC Continental coupe champagne glass, the bowl cut with a curving pattern of 'thumbprint' ovals, with conical baluster stem.

4.75in (12cm) high

£10-15   **GROB**

A late 19thC cut crystal coupe champagne glass, cut with diamonds and fans, and faceted, slightly waisted stem.

5in (12.5cm) high

£25-35   **W&L**

A 20thC Continental coupe champagne glass, the bowl cut with 'thumbprint' ovals and trefoil cuts, the conical baluster stem with annulated knop above.

Although this stem is comparatively complex compared with some examples, buyers often prefer the simpler, less ornate examples.

4.75in (12cm) high

£12-15   **GROB**

A 1920s-30s coupe champagne glass, the bowl with criss-cross diamond and star patterns, with facet-cut stem.

4.75in (12cm) high

£10-12   **GROB**

A 19thC coupe champagne glass, with heavy, hollow baluster stem, and bowl cut with large facets.

4.5in (11.5cm) high

£15-18   **GROB**

A 19thC coupe champagne glass, the hollow stem and base of the bowl cut with facets.

The hollow stem is a desirable feature for collectors.

5in (12.5cm) high

£25-30   **GROB**

QUICK REFERENCE - CHANCE GLASS

Chance Brothers, founded in 1824 outside Birmingham, produced its first tableware in the 1930s. Its varied Fiesta range was introduced in 1951, and became immensely popular. Plate glass was heated until it 'slumped' into a mould, or over an object, to take its form. The 'handkerchief' vase was one of their most prolific and popular ranges. Look out for the rare reversed version of the pattern below, with red dots on a white background, as this can fetch over three times the value of this one. As with Gingham, the pattern continued to be produced by Fiesta Glass (successor to Chance Glass) from 1981.

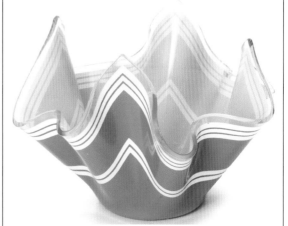

A 1970s Chance Glass light blue 'Bandel II' pattern screen-printed small handkerchief vase.

4in (10cm) high

£7-10   **RET**

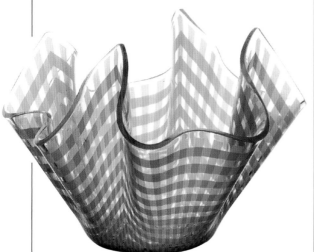

A Chance Glass small red 'Polka Dot' transfer-printed handkerchief vase.
1974-81   *4in (10cm) high*

£10-15   **GC**

A Chance Glass 'Large Flemish' handkerchief vase.

The lightly textured 'Large Flemish' pattern had been used for window glass at Chance since the late 19thC. It was allegedly inspired by the rippling effect of canals that ran through the factory.

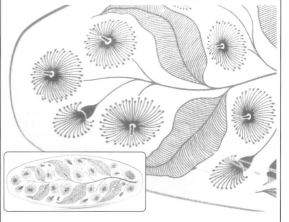

7in (18cm) high

£15-25   **GC**

A 1980s Chance Glass small green and white 'Gingham' pattern transfer-printed handkerchief vase.
1978-81   *4in (10cm) high*

£15-20   **GC**

A 1970s Chance Glass screen-printed gold 'Calytpo' pattern ovoid tray, the pattern designed by Michael Harris in 1959.

The popularity of Calypto was long-lived as it was produced until at least 2000. Usually found in white, the gold colourway was introduced after 1970.

13.5in (34cm) long

£10-15   **RET**

QUICK REFERENCE

- The areas that make up much of today's Czech Republic have been renowned for glass design and production for centuries. The late 19thC and early 20thC saw much glass in the dominant Art Nouveau style being produced. Most pieces are commonly attributed to the company Loetz, but recent research has revealed that companies such as Kralik and Rindskopf also had a large output.

- As the country was 'behind the Iron Curtain' from 1945 until 1989, the major revolution in design has been largely ignored. As glass collectors and researchers have found more, prices have begun to rise.

- Complexity and rarity are currently the main indicators to value. The designer is also important, but as the market is so new many names are yet to become widely known. Hot-worked, enamelled and cut and engraved pieces that are unique and influential tend to fetch the highest sums.

- However, such pieces often inspired ranges that were mass-produced, and are more affordable.

- Many of these are hot-worked or pressed glass designs, and the modern, avant garde style developed from the late 1950s to the early 1970s are the most desirable. Leading designers, whose work is sought after by collectors, include Adolf Matura, Frantisek Vizner, and Frantisek Zemek, as well as the influential names known for producing more unique works such as Stanislav Libensky, Pavel Hlava, René Roubícek and Jirí Harcuba.

- As much glass is unmarked, it is best to consult a reference book to learn how to recognise designs. Many pieces are currently mistaken for the work of factories on Murano or in Scandinavia. A considerable amount of research is yet to be undertaken, and the area looks set to grow in importance over the next few years.

A Kralik 'Silveria' vase, the textured, mould blown lobed body with applied pink enamel to the base and randomly applied green trails, with a light iridescent surface.

c1900

£280-320   MDM

A Kralik red 'Banded' near-spherical vase, with pulled rim, reddish-pink enamel spots, and applied and melted in white trail and heavily iridised surface.

c1905

£350-450   MDM

A Czechoslovakian Kralik gold and amber 'Silberband' vase, with melted-in light green trails and heavy iridescent surface.

Both 'Silberband' and 'Silveria' (see right) are terms given by a collector, rather than the official range names. There are two variations: those with a combination of either cranberry and amber, or of green and amber, spots.

c1905   *6in (15cm) diam*

£350-450   MDM

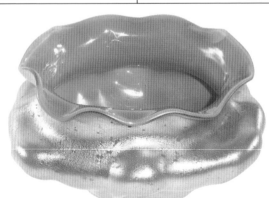

A pair of tiny Kralik salts, in the 'Wavy' pattern, with silver rims.

1905

£140-160   MDM

A Kralik rare opalescent pink lobed bowl, of organic form, the exterior with heavy silvery iridescence.

c1905   *6.5in (16.5cm) diam*

£350-450   MDM

A Kralik 'Corrugated' tapered vase, with wavy rim, pulled pattern and heavy iridescent surface.

c1905

£350-450 MDM

A Kralik 'King Tut' vase, with green mottles and applied and pulled dark blue trails melted into the body.

c1905

£300-400 MDM

A Rindskopf waisted vase, applied pulled, 'feathered' trails over opaque body, iridescent surface.

c1900

£350-450 MDM

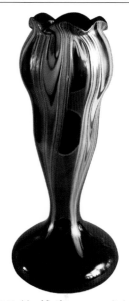

A Rindskopf floriform vase, applied, melted-in pulled and feathered white trails, and an iridised surface.

c1900

£450-550 MDM

A large tumbler vase, designed by Karel Poner, with hand-enamelled with Classically dressed female figures over a white cloudy ground, with engraved and enamelled signature with date.

Little is known about Poner, apart from that he studied under Professor Kysela at the School of Applied Arts in Prague. During the late 1930s and early 1940s he produced enamelled vessels in a modern, painterly style, featuring Classically dressed characters, or people going about their lives. Examples can be found in the Museum of Decorative Arts in Prague.

1941 11.75in (30cm) high

£350-450 FLD

A CLOSER LOOK AT A LOETZ VASE

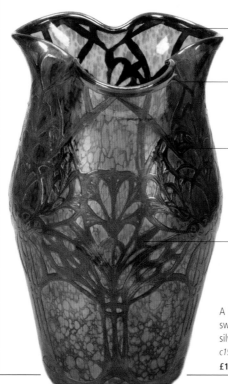

The organic form and colour are typical of the Art Nouveau movement, and much of the glass produced by Loetz.

The iridescent, mottled green finish identifies it as being part of the successful 'Papillon' range, which was produced in quantity and was more affordable than other ranges.

It is further embellished with silver overlay, which was complex to apply. The overlay is also in the Art Nouveau style and is itself embellished with engravings.

This particular piece is visually stunning and would have been expensive and highly fashionable in its day.

A Loetz Creta 'Papillion' glass vase, swollen with a trefoil neck, the floral silver overlay with engraving.

c1900 8.25in (21cm) high

£1,000-1,500 DN

GLASS

A 1960s-70s Czechoslovakian Zelezny Brod Citrine tapered vase, with applied brown trails, designed by Frantisek Zemek.

This form was designed by Zemek in 1957 and was shown in the landmark publication 'Modern Bohemian Glass' by Josef Raban. The design, whilst typical of the 1950s obsession with curving organic forms, also hints at machinery, reminiscent of a screw or propeller.

8.25in (21cm) high

£50-70   MHC

A 1960s Czechoslovakian Msistov glassworks 'Rhapsody' range large vase, designed by Frantisek Zemek in 1960.

15.25in (38.5cm) high

£120-180   TCF

A Czechoslovakian Novy Bor mould blown ball vase, with optic moulded columns and iridescent surface effect, machine cut rim.

8.25in (22cm) high

£70-90   GC

A Czechoslovakian Moser vase, no.54303, designed by Jiri Suhajek in 1976, with applied light green side casing and stylised red and green flower to centre.

8.5in (21.5cm) high

£300-400   VZ

A Czechoslovakian Skrdlovice glassworks teardrop shaped vase, designed by Vladimir Jelinek or Zdenka Strobachovà, with graduated blue bands fading to rose pink, and 'kicked up' conical base.

c1960   *11.5in (29cm) high*

£1,200-1,800   QU

A CLOSER LOOK AT A CHLUM U TREBONE GLASS VASE

The colour variation is created by heating this heat-sensitive glass for different periods of time.

This type of glass was a speciality of the factory, with and orange-red 'Garnet' colourway being much more commonly found.

The UFO form is typical of its time, and the protrusion in the base recalls studio glass by fellow Czech designer Pavel Hlava.

The glass is blown into a ribbed mould before being blown to shape, which gives the linear optical effect.

A Czechoslovakian Chlum u Trebone glassworks optic mould blown 'Garnet & Blue' glass vase, designed by Jan Gabrhel in 1962, with protrusion in base.

4.5in (11.5cm) high

£100-150   PC

A 1970s Czechoslovakian Prachen glassworks amber glass cylindrical vase, applied blue prunts stamped with stylised floral motifs, designed by Josef Hospodka in 1969.

Although blue, the prunts appear green due to the transmitted light through the yellow-amber body.

9.75in (25cm) high

£80-120 **SAS**

A CLOSER LOOK AT A VÌZNER VASE

Frantisek Vizner (b.1936) is one of Czechoslovakia's most influential and famous glass designers, with a global reputation.

Vìzner's forms tend to be solid, with a monumental and almost industrial or architectural feel. They also hint at his later, simpler cut and polished studio works.

It was made using the challenging 'gathering on the post' technique, where the partially blown body is used to gather a second mass of differently coloured glass.

The 'peg' cased in a heavy base is recurring form in Vìzner's work for Skrdlovice at the time – after 1977 he produced his own studio works.

A late 1970s Skrdlovice glassworks vase, no.7410 designed by Frantisek Vìzner in 1974, the ribbed colourless body cased with a heavy green base, unmarked.

This design was produced in at least three sizes, being roughly 25cm, 19cm or 15cm in height, although sizes do vary as each piece was handmade.

£200-300 **PC**

A 1960s Borské Sklo colourless cased pink torpedo vase, with polished pontil to base.

9in (23cm) high

£22-28 **RET**

A 1960s-70s Czechoslovakian Skrdlovice glassworks cased bottle vase, with internal air bubbles, designed by Jaroslav Svoboda.

12in (30.5cm) high

£300-400 **GC**

A late 1960s-70s Czechoslovakian Borské Sklo green vase, designed by Pavel Hlava in 1967, with colourless casing.

Pavel Hlava (1924-2003) was one of the most notable Czech post-war glass designers. It is likely that this design was produced by blowing the molten glass into a modified wire cage, creating the undulating and warped bulges. It shows how his studio glass techniques were translated into glass produced in a factory.

10.25in (26cm) high

£70-100 **M20C**

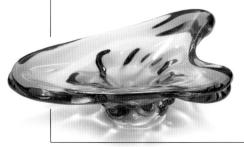

A 1970s Czechoslovakian Berànek or Chribskà glassworks 'Niagara' range amber and blue bowl, with pulled rim and lobes.

9in (23cm) long

£25-30 **RET**

A 1990s-2000s Czechoslovakian Bohemia Glass cased pink bowl, with pulled rim, polished base and blue foil factory label.

Although hot-worked bowls such as these have been produced since the late 1950s, this example can be dated to after 1990 as the label reads 'Czech Republic', not 'Czechoslovakia'.

7in (17.5cm) diam

£10-15   M20C

A Czechoslovakian stylised owl lampworked cylindrical jug, designed by Vera Liskova, with some applied features.

5.25in (13.5cm) high

£15-20   GC

A Czechoslovakian blown and lampworked glass bird pourer, with applied eyes and legs, designed by Vera Liskova.

3.75in (9.5cm) high

£25-30   GC

A Czechoslovakian blown and lampworked glass bird, designed by Vera Liskova.

Vera Liskova (1924-1985) is renowned for her lampworked abstract forms and animals formed from borosilicate glass. Each fragile piece is finely blown and formed by hand over a gas burner. Liskova elevated Lampworking to an art form in her larger abstract works, which can fetch many thousands of pounds.

3.75in (9.5cm) high

£20-25   GC

A Czechoslovakian Zelezny Brod Alexandrite glass vase, designed by Miroslav Klinger, engraved with a stylised, geometric heron standing amidst grasses, possibly by J. Maresova, signed 'JM 64'.

Alexandrite (or Neodymium) glass changes colour from a pale ice blue under flourescent lighting to this colour under incandescent lighting. The presence and style of any engraved design affects value considerably. Modern, stylised designs like this are much more desirable than simple, naturalistic renderings of flowers.

1964   *6.75in (17cm) high*

£100-150   PC

A 1970s Czechoslovakian Podebrady glassworks paperweight, with internal trapped rings of air, designed by Josef Svarc in 1968.

2.5in (6.5cm) high

£70-100   PC

A Rudolfova glassworks green pressed glass vase, no.13157, designed by Rudolf Jurnikl and produced from 1963.

8in (23cm) high

£70-100   GC

A Rudolfova glassworks blue pressed glass vase, no.12992, designed by Vaclav Hanus and produced from 1957.

This is often incorrectly attributed to the Art Deco period.

10in (25cm) high

£40-60   GC

A late 1950s-80s Czechoslovakian Rosice glassworks large blue 'Lens' vase, no.914, designed by Rudolf Schrötter in 1955.

8in (20.5cm) high

£30-40   RET

A Hermanova glassworks colourless pressed glass vase, no.20307, designed by Frantisek Peceny and produced from 1979.

6in (15.5cm) high

£15-25   GC

A Libochovice glassworks colourless pressed glass vase, no.3236, designed by Frantisek Vizner and produced from 1965.

In 1965 the numerous factories producing pressed glass in Czechoslovakia were amaglamated under the umbrella name 'Sklo Union' – it is by this name that the glass is known to collectors today. This is typical of Vìzner's pressed glass designs, with its heavy moulded motifs on a simple cylinder. Lenses were a motif commonly used in Czech cut and pressed glass.

11in (28cm) high

£80-120   GC

A Hermanova glassworks large colourless 'Dragon's Head' colourless pressed glass large vase, no.20235, designed by Frantisek Peceny and produced from 1972.

Note how the form resembles the head of a dragon costume that may be seen at Chinese street celebrations. Unusually, this gives the vase a definitive 'front', which is shown here.

9.75in (25cm) high

£60-80   GC

A Rosice glassworks blue pressed glass ashtray, from the 'Praha' range of kitchen and tablewares designed by Adolf Matura from 1968-71.

5.25in (13cm) diam

£22-28   RET

GLASS

QUICK REFERENCE

- Dartington Glass was founded in 1966 in Torrington, Devon by the Dartington Hall Trust, who aimed to bring work and prosperity to area by introducing a new industry. The chief designer was Frank Thrower, who had worked alongside Ronald Stennett-Willson (who was later to found King's Lynn Glass) at British importers, Wuidart from 1953 to 1960. Thrower had also designed for Portmeirion, and his work at both these companies had taught him about Scandinavian designs, which greatly influenced his work. Dartington also employed Scandinavian blowers, including master glassmaker and factory manager, Eskil Vilhelmsson.
- Thrower was responsible for over 500 designs, most of which have concave and convex moulded decoration. The output was dominated by tablewares and Dartington decanters attract interest from dedicated group of collectors. In general, however, decorative pieces, such as

vases, are more popular with collectors. Shape, colour and size are all important. The textured range is especially popular, and collectors often aim to own an example of every shape in every colour.

- Smokey grey 'Midnight' and clear glass are the most common colours. Rarer colours, such as 'Flame' red and 'Kingfisher' blue are more desirable. Look out for liming from water, as this detracts from the colour, and other damage as this will decrease value.
- Until an exhibition book in 2007, Thrower's work was largely ignored by collectors, but it is becoming sought after, particularly his hallmark late 1960s and early 1970s designs. Wedgwood acquired 50 per cent of Dartington in 1982 and Thrower continued to design ranges for them, until he died in 1987. These later designs are currently less popular, so it may be a good time to buy them.

A 1970s Dartington Glass Clear FT60 candleholder or vase, designed by Frank Thrower in 1968.

4.75in (12cm) high

£15-25   **RET**

1968-c1973   £25-30   **RET**

A Dartington Glass Kingfisher blue FT60 candleholder or vase, designed by Frank Thrower in 1968, with red cellophane label.

Kingfisher was discontinued c1973. The red label indicates this was a 'first' quality piece.

4.75in (12cm) high

RET

A Dartington Glass Kingfisher blue FT66 vase with abstract moulded designs and flared rim, designed by Frank Thrower in 1968.

5in (12.5cm) high

£25-35   **GC**

A 1970s Dartington Glass Midnight grey FT62 'hyacinth vase', designed by Frank Thrower in 1968.

6in (15cm) high

£20-30   **GC**

A Dartington Glass Kingfisher blue FT2 posy vase, designed by Frank Thrower in 1967.

This shape went out of production after a few years and the number was re-used for small circular paperweights.

c1970   *3.25in (8.5cm) high*

£20-25   **RET**

A Dartington Glass cobalt blue FT58 'Greek Key' small vase, designed by Frank Thrower in 1968.

This popular shape was produced in cobalt blue glass for only six months in 1994.

5.5in (14cm) high

£80-120   **GC**

A very rare Dartington Glass mould blown Smokey 'Candy Jar', no.FT223 designed by Frank Thrower in 1979.

This vase was part of a range manufactured at Woods Brothers near Barnsley for Dartington Glass. The range was only available for six months, with only a single shipment being delivered. Colours included Amber, Green, Smokey and Jet. Smokey and Jet are the rarest colours.

11in (28cm) high

£50-70   **PC**

A CLOSER LOOK AT A DARTINGTON GLASS VASE

These are known by collectors as 'Stig' vases as they were developed by Thrower with Dartington's master glassmaker Stig Peterssen.

Peterssen was also reputedly one of the few glassmakers skilled enough to roll the lip tightly over.

These are rare as they were only made for two years. They were also produced in a lower, wider shape numbered FT75.

Produced in Kingfisher blue, Midnight grey and colourless, the rarest colour of all is Flame red – an example may fetch over £500.

A Dartington Glass Kingfisher blue large FT76 'Polo Neck' vase, with hand-rolled rim.

1968-70   9in (23cm) high

£250-350   **GC**

An extremely rare Dartington Glass Kingfisher blue FT85 decanter, designed by Frank Thrower in 1968.

The Kingfisher blue colour is the rarest colour for this shape – most are found in colourless or the scarcer Midnight grey glass.

1968-70   10.25in (26cm) high

£180-220   **GC**

A Wedgwood Crystal Midnight grey FJT15 'Marcel' decanter, by Frank Thrower in 1982.

1982-87   13.5in (34cm) high

£40-60   **RET**

A pair of Dartington Glass pressed glass FT137 avocado dishes in a later box, designed by Frank Thrower in 1971.

These were promoted as 'Avocado Pair', showing Thrower and his team's gentle sense of humour. They also demonstrated Thrower's skill at creating products that mirrored fashions of the day – avocados were an exotic dinner party favourite of the 1970s.

5.5in (14cm) wide

£15-25   **RET**

GLASS

QUICK REFERENCE - GALLÉ

Emile Gallé founded a glass decorating workshop in Nancy, France, in 1873. In 1874, he took over his father's glass and ceramics business and began producing his own designs, which won gold medals when exhibited at the International Exposition in Paris in 1878. His love of nature can be seen in his high quality floral and foliate designs which became the epitomy of the Art Nouveau style. The popularity of his work expanded, leading him to produce commercial cameo designs from 1899, which were made using acid-etched techniques. Gallé died in 1904, and from then a star was added next to his signature until 1914. The factory closed in 1936.

A Gallé cameo glass solifleur vase, purple overlay with wisteria flowers, cameo signature.

8.75in (22cm) high

£600-800   WW

A Gallé carved crystal Jack-in-the-Pulpit vase, etched 'Modèle et Decor Deposés Cristallerie Emile Gallé Nancy'.

13.25in (33.5cm) high

£1,200-1,500   DRA

An Emile Gallé vase, of colourless glass, with all-round opaque yellow and pink overlay decoration, etched five times, showing wisteria in bloom, relief-engraved 'Gallé' with three dots on side.

1904   *13.5in (34.5cm) high*

£3,500-4,500   WKA

A tall Gallé cameo glass vase, with amber nasturtium over a graduated yellow to amber and clear ground, signed 'Gallé' on body.

18in (46cm) high

£1,200-1,800   DRA

A Gallé cameo glass vase, with blue and purple dogwood blossoms on a frosted blue and yellow mottled ground, minor burst to rim.

10.75in (27.5cm) high

£1,200-1,800   DRA

A tall post-1904 Gallé cameo glass barrel vase, yellow tinted with pink berried branches, signed 'Gallé' and with a star, small chip to foot.

12.25in (31cm) high

£500-700   DN

QUICK REFERENCE

- Founded in Zealand, Denmark in 1825, Holmegaard initially produced bottles and other functional pieces. Early designers included Oluf Jensen and Orla Juul Nielsen, whose designs for tableware were exhibited at the 1925 Paris Exposition. However, it was the work of three designers who changed the company's fortunes.
- The first, Jacob Bang (1899-1965) joined Holmegaard in 1927, and was partly inspired by Nielsen's designs. His designs were predominantly period Modernist and austere in style with minimal surface decoration. Bang left Holmegaard in 1941 to design ceramics, but returned to glass in 1957 when he joined Kastrup, Holmegaard's sister company.
- The second was Per Lütken (1916-98), whose designs are the focus of many collectors today. Recruited from art school in 1942, Lütken is known for his asymmetric, organic and flowing designs from the 1950s. Curving bud-

like or teardrop forms with heavy walls in grey or blue are typical of his work. Many of his designs are signed with a PL monogram, and dates were included up until 1962.
- In contrast to these, Lütken also designed the Carnaby range, which has a strong 'Pop Art' plastic appearance. This is similar to the 'Palet' range designed by the third key designer, Michael Bang (b1944), son of Jacob. Also popular are the 'Gulvvase' bottles, designed by Otto Brauer.
- The Kastrup factory was founded in 1847 to augment production at Holmegaard, and had a sister factory at Odense. In 1873, Kastrup was sold, but was merged with Holmegaard again in 1965. Generically, all pieces are known to collectors as 'Holmegaard'. Demand and prices for smaller and more common pieces have remained static, but unique pieces by the Bangs and designers other than Lütken may rise as more information is uncovered.

A Danish Kastrup Holmegaard 'Gulvvase', no. 540021, with transparent red cased opaque white body, designed by Otto Brauer in 1962.

Cased examples with opaque white interiors are the most desirable and valuable versions – red in particular. Transparent colours include cobalt blue, brown and olive green.

1965-80   17in (43cm) high

£180-220   **QU**

A 1970s English Cascade Glass kingfisher blue bottle, after Otto Brauer's 1962 Gulvvase.

This design was produced during the late 1970s. Cascade Glass can be identified by colour – this blue, colourless, pewter grey and smokey topaz.

10in (25.5cm) high

£10-15   **M20C**

A 1960s Danish Kastrup Glas blue bottle vase, from the Capri series designed by Jacob Bang in 1961, with original label.

6in (15cm) high

£30-50   **ZI**

A Danish Kastrup cobalt blue mid-size Gulvvase no.40230, designed by Otto Brauer in 1962.

12in (30.5cm) high

£50-70   **M20C**

A Danish Kastrup 'Capri' blue bottle vase, with applied prunt impressed 'JB', designed by Jacob Bang in 1961, catalogue number 32652.

8.75in (22cm) high

£50-70   **ZI**

GLASS

A Danish Kastrup vase from the 'Antik Grøn' series, with applied prunt with impressed head, design no.32708 by Jacob Bang in 1964.

1964-70   *6in (15cm) high*
£50-70   **ZI**

A Danish Kastrup-Holmegaard candleholder from the 'Napoli' series, designed by Michael Bang in 1969.

1969-71   *4in (10cm) high*
£40-60   **ZI**

A 1960s Danish Holmegaard Majgron (May-Green) vase, no.46022, designed by Per Lütken, the base with inscribed factory marks.

11.5in (29cm) high
£40-60   **GC**

QUICK REFERENCE – KASTRUP

This design is often incorrectly attributed to Per Lütken and described as a 'Duckling' or 'Naebvase' (Beak vase). The designer of this piece is not known and, like the vase to the right, it is typical of a number of 'generic' vases produced by the company in response to popular tastes. This particular design can be found with this model number in the 1960 Kastrup catalogue, and was discontinued in 1965 after the company's merger with Holmegaard.

A Danish Holmegaard torpedo-shaped mould blown vase from the Grønland series, catalogue no.17706, designed by Per Lütken in 1960, the base signed 'Holmegaard 1961 PL'.

1961-64   *9.75in (24.5cm) high*
£70-90   **ZI**

A Danish Kastrup cased blue large 'Orchidevase', shape no.32003, with internal controlled spiral of bubbles, designed by an unknown designer.

c1954-65   *12.5in (32cm) high*
£50-80   **M20C**

A Danish Kastrup small double cased swung-out vase, with opaque opal glass sandwiched between two layers of transparent sapphire blue, by an unknown designer.

c1960   *9in (23cm) high*
£50-80   **ZI**

A Danish Holmegaard light green 'Duckling' vase, cat. no. 14405, by Per Lütken in 1952, base signed 'Holmegaard 1954 PL'.

Produced from 1950 into the 1970s, these are wrongly called 'Naebvase' (Beak vases), which was a Danish nickname. Available in a range of sizes, colours include colourless, smoke grey and light green.

1954   8in (20cm) high

£30-50   **ZI**

A CLOSER LOOK AT A HOLMEGAARD VASE

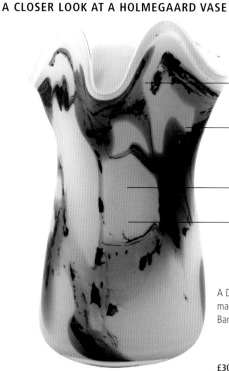

This is a protype piece produced during the development of the 'Atlantis' range.

It was produced when the designer Michael Bang was discussing his ideas for the range with master glassblower Emanuel Anderson.

As it is freeblown with random patterning, it is unique – such early protype examples are higly desirable.

These colours went on to be included in the 'Atlantis' factory production range.

A Danish Holmegaard free-blown test-piece vase made by Emanuel Andersen, designed by Michael Bang and Emanuel Andersen c1981.

8.25in (21cm) high

£300-350   **ZI**

A Danish Kastrup Holmegaard unique, free-blown abstract vase or sculpture, form no.2386, designed by Per Lütken for an exhibition in November 1970, the foot signed 'Holmegaard 2386 PL'.

1970   18.75in (47.5cm) high

£800-1,200   **ZI**

A Danish Holmegaard colourless cased green orchid vase, from the 'Flamingo' series, catalogue no.16028, designed by Per Lütken in 1956, the base inscribed 'Holmegaard 1958 PL'.

1958   6.25in (16cm) high

£80-£120   **ZI**

A 1960s Danish Kastrup Natblå (Night Blue) mould blown vase, catalogue no.32315, designed by Jacob Bang in 1959.

9in (23cm) high

£50-80   **ZI**

A Danish Holmegaard Sapphire blue large folded vase, designed by Per Lütken in 1955, the base signed 'Holmegaard 1955 PL'.

1955 8.25in (21cm) high

£150-200   **ZI**

GLASS

QUICK REFERENCE - CARNABY & PALET

There is much confusion over which brightly coloured opaque cased glass forms are from the 'Carnaby' and 'Palet' ranges, and which are by Holmegaard. Many examples attributed to Holmegaard are in fact by German factories such as Hirschberg or Friedrich. The 'Carnaby' range comprises only 16 shapes, which are vases, except for one pitcher (shown on this page), whilst the 'Palet' range is an extensive set of tablewares. Rims on 'Carnaby' pieces are not machine-cut, but are rounded. Values for 'Palet' vary widely, and depend on condition. As it was made to be used, it is often damaged or stained, meaning value is reduced.

A 1970s Kastrup-Holmegaard Coral Opal vase from the Carnaby series, designed by Per Lütken in 1969, catalogue no.341 10 94.

1969-76   *4in (10cm) high*

£50-80   ZI

A 1970s Kastrup-Holmegaard Coral Opal ball vase from the Carnaby series, catalogue no.56 03 16, designed by Per Lütken in 1969.

1969-76   *5.25in (13.5cm) high*

£80-120   ZI

A 1970s Danish Kastrup-Holmegaard Yellow Opal vase from the Carnaby series, catalogue no.341 10 67, designed by Per Lütken in 1969.

1969-76   *5in (12.5cm) high*

£50-80   ZI

A 1970s Danish Kastrup-Holmegaard Yellow Opal 120cl pitcher from the Palet series, catalogue no. 331 24 02, designed by Michael Bang in 1970.

The yellow colourway was introduced to the series in 1971.

8in (20.5cm) high

£50-70   ZI

A 1970s Kastrup-Holmegaard Opal Blue sugar shaker, no. 392183, with cork stopper, designed by Michael Bang in 1970.

The use of a large cork stops the contents from falling out and also acts as a cushioned base for the thin glass body.

1970-75   *5.5in (14cm) high*

£40-60   UCT

A 1970s Kastrup-Holmegaard Jade Grøn 2.2ltr Cheese Jar from the Palet series, catalogue no.351 26 32, with applied prunt impressed 'OST', designed by Michael Bang in 1970.

6in (15cm) high

£150-200   ZI

A 1970s Kastrup-Holmegaard Blue Opal pitcher, from the Carnaby series, designed by Per Lütken in 1969, catalogue no.39 13 00.

8in (20.5cm) high

£80-120   ZI

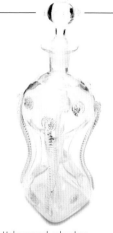

A Holmegaard colourless 'Klukflaske' or 'Kuttrolf' decanter, with applied vines and rosettes, catalogue no.186, designed by an unknown designer.

c1900   *11in (28cm) high*

£80-120   **ZI**

A Danish Holmegaard colourless 'Klukflaske' or 'Kuttrolf' decanter from the Viol series, with black crown-shaped stopper, designed by Jacob Bang in 1938.

                         10in (25cm) high

£50-80   **ZI**

A CLOSER LOOK AT A HOLMEGAARD DECANTER

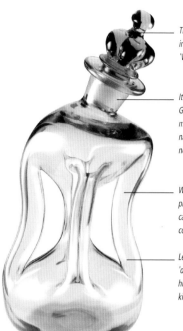

The crown-shaped stopper indicates that this was from the 'Viol' series.

It is based on the traditional German 'kluk kluk' decanter made for centuries and so-named due to the glugging noise it makes when pouring.

With its crimped form, it is very practical to grip and handle. It can also be found with blue or colourless bodies.

Legend has it that the leaning 'drunken' form and crown hinted at an alcoholic Swedish king.

A 1950s-70s Danish Holmegaard Smoke grey 'tired' Klukflaske decanter from the Viol series, with crown-shaped knop, based on a design by Jacob Bang from 1928.

                         10in (25cm) high

£30-40   **ZI**

A 1990s Danish Holmegaard decanter, designed by Michael Bang, from the 'Amateur Schnappsmaker' series, with screen-printed 'Prunus spinosa L' sloe berry decoration designed by Finn Clausen in 1989, catalogue no.4 240 005.

1989-2005   *6.5in (16.5cm) high*

£20-30   **ZI**

A Holmegaard 'Skaal' decanter and matching shot glasses, with handpainted sailor motif and 'Skaal' wording, catalogue no.M256, designed by Jacob Bang in 1937.

'Skaal!' is Danish for 'Cheers!' This schnapps set was also available with other hand-painted designs and finishes, including sandblasting.

1937-57   *7.75in (19.5cm) high*

£100-150   **ZI**

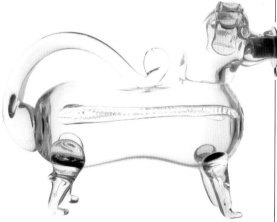

A Danish Holmegaard 'Fyldehund' or 'Snapsehund' decanter, in the form of a dog, with stoppered nose and tail handle, marked 'HG7'.

With its origins in the late 19thC, Holmegaard produced this form during the 1920s, reviving it again in the mid-1970s.

1977   *9in (23cm) long*

£60-90   **ZI**

GLASS

A Danish Kastrup pitcher from the Grøn Series, designed by Jacob Bang in 1960, catalogue no.7178.

This form was also available with a bamboo wrapping (cat. no. 7278). These examples are harder to find intact as the bamboo often becomes loose and damaged. When intact, these usually fetch a little more.

9.75in (24.5cm) high

£40-60   **ZI**

A CLOSER LOOK AT A HOLMEGAARD DECANTER

The impressed viking's head seal indicates this was made for Danish wine company Torben Anton. Other seals can be found; a CE under a crown for Cherry Elsinore, and with the logo of British wine merchants Stowells of Chelsea.

A taller blue version was also produced in 1955 – both have a hand-finished rim giving the effect that each is hand-blown.

The glasses are harder to find than the decanter.

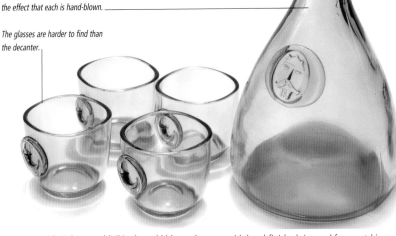

A 1960s Danish Holmegaard 'Viking' mould blown decanter with hand-finished rim, and four matching glasses, designed by Ole Winther.

1962-70   *9in (23cm) high*

£25-35   **M20C**

One of a set of six Holmegaard 'Labrador' grey sherry glasses, 'Atlantic' range, by Per Lütken, 1962.

'Labrador' was a favourite colour of of Lütken's from the 1950s.

4.25in (11cm) high

£30-50 SET   **ZI**

One of a set of six Holmegaard Smoke grey Dutch Cordial glasses.

Available in delgrun (Dark Green), Smoke (grey), clear and violet. Frequently found with klukflaskes on the secondary market, but they were not originally sold combined as sets.

c1958   *5.75in (14.5cm) high*

£30-50 SET   **ZI**

A 1950s Danish Holmegaard cordial or schnapps glass from the Mercur series, designed by Per Lütken in 1948.

2in (5cm) high

£50-80 FOR A SET OF SIX   **ZI**

A Danish Holmegaard blue-green sugar bowl and creamer from the 'Baltica' series, catalogue no.s 19765 and 19764 respectively.

The Mocca creamer set is available in blue-green, cobalt blue, ruby and clear glass.

Largest 2.75in (7cm) high

£30-50 PAIR   **ZI**

A Danish Holmegaard Sapphire blue mould-blown goblet-shaped vase, from the Saphir series, catalogue no.18163, designed by Per Lütken c1960, the base marked 'Holmegaard 18163 PL'.

3.5in (9cm) high

£40-60   **ZI**

A Danish Holmegaard Smoke grey ashtray, with pulled rim, catalogue no.16517, designed by Per Lütken c1960, the base inscribed 'Holmegaard 1962 PL'.

1962   *6in (15cm) long*

£30-50   **ZI**

A Danish Kastrup-Holmegaard 24% lead crystal fish sculpture, catalogue no.341 45 06, designed by Michael Bang c1974, marked 'HG5 MB'.

1975   *3.5in (9cm) long*

£30-50   **ZI**

A Danish Kastrup-Holmegaard furnace-worked bowl with random scalloped rim and knobbles, catalogue no.620719, from the Rosalin series, designed by Christer Holmgren in 1968, the base inscribed 'Holmegaard C. 620719'.

5.75in (14.5cm) diam

£40-60   **ZI**

An early 1970s Danish Kastrup-Holmegaard novelty bird figurine.

Sold as novelties through the shop in large quantities, these can be identified as Holmegaard by the colours used.

A Holmegaard bottle or decanter from the 'Apotekerflasker' series, with transfer printed design, marked 'HG80'.

2.5in (6cm) high

£30-50   **ZI**

Each year from 1975-99, Holmegaard produced a limited production copy of an late 18thC apothecary bottle from the Thisted Apotek (now Svane Apoteket) in Denmark. Each piece is marked 'HG for Holmegaard, followed by two digits for the year. As commissioned objects, they were not sold through Holmegaard's distributors.

1980   *6.5in (16.5cm) high*

£50-70   **ZI**

A Danish Kastrup-Holmegaard Smoke grey suncatcher with probably unique impressed abstract patterns, created using tools and objects in the factory.

c1970   *4.75in (12cm) diam*

£20-30   **ZI**

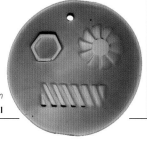

FIND OUT MORE...

www.holmegaardresource.com - *an independent online resource to vintage designs.*

www.glashistoriskselskab.dk - *Danish site providing a useful visual resource.*

QUICK REFERENCE - LALIQUE

René Lalique (1860-1945) began his career designing and making jewellery in the 1880s, turning to glass through perfume bottles he designed for Coty around 1906. By 1918, success led him to buy and to move into larger premises, where he designed quintessentially Art Deco style vases, bowls, lamps and perfume bottles using the mass-production techniques of pressing and moulding. Despite using these techniques, quality was high and Lalique's products were expensive. Over 150 designs were produced from 1920-30, with motifs focusing on stylised natural forms, animals and nudes. Lalique died in 1945, and from then all marks comprised his surname only, without the 'R' initial. The company still produces many of his original designs today.

A René Lalique 'Dentelle' clear and frosted vase, no.943, moulded 'R. LALIQUE', with chip to one rib.

c1912   7.5in (19cm) high

£400-600   DRA

A René Lalique 'Chamonix' opalescent vase, no.1090, stencilled 'R. LALIQUE FRANCE', with small nicks to buttresses.

c1933   6in (15cm) high

£500-800   DRA

A René Lalique 'Domremy' green vase, no. 979, moulded with thistles, etched mark 'R Lalique France No. 979', minor rim fault.

Green is a rarer colour than the much more common opalescent.

8.5in (21.5cm) high

£1,200-1,800   TEN

A Lalique 'Domremy' opalescent glass vase, no. 979, designed by René Lalique, stencil 'R Lalique', etched 'France'.

8.75in (22cm) high

£700-1,000   WW

A René Lalique 'Grenade' dark amber vase, no.1045, the base engraved 'R. Lalique France'.

4.5in (11.5cm) high

£1,500-2,000   DRA

A Lalique 'Nymphale' deep blue glass vase, the base engraved 'Lalique France'.

8.5in (21.5cm) high

£350-550   DN

A Lalique 'Rampillon' clear, frosted and blue-stained vase, no.991, the base with stencilled 'R Lalique' signature.

5in (13cm) high

£700-1,000   **WW**

A CLOSER LOOK AT A LALIQUE VASE

This is a comparatively scarce design, perhaps as it was less popular at the time meaning fewer were sold.

It retains some of its white patina, which helps to highlight the moulded pattern of peppercorns.

The dark topaz colour, which appears black here, is also scarce.

The shouldered urn shape and clean-lined form is typical of the Art Deco period.

A René Lalique deep topaz 'Poivre' vase, no.901, with whitish patina, the base moulded 'R. Lalique'.

c1921   *9.5in (24cm) high*

£2,000-3,000   **DRA**

A 1930s Lalique 'Saint Tropez' pattern blue-tinted opalescent glass vase, the tapering cylindrical body moulded with stems and berries, acid-etched mark 'R. Lalique, France' to base, minor chip to one berry.

7.5in (19cm) high

£1,500-2,000   **TOV**

A René Lalique 'Sauge' vase, no.1014, of clear and frosted glass with green patina, the base engraved 'R. Lalique'.

c1927   *9in (23cm) high*

£1,200-1,800   **DRA**

A René Lalique 'Sirenes' opalescent and blue stained glass perfume atomiser, no.660, the base marked 'R Lalique', metal fittings missing.

5.5in (14cm) high

£800-1,200   **WW**

A Lalique blue glass decanter, the reeded body with a blue glass stopper, marked 'Lalique made in France'.

11.25in (28.5cm) high

£150-250   **SWO**

A René Lalique 'Danseuses Egyptiennes no. 1' perfume burner, for Marcas et Bardel, with orange enamel and original chromium cap, moulded 'R. Lalique FRANCE'.

c1926   *5.25in (13.5cm) high*

£800-1,200   **DRA**

Two René Lalique 'Perles' clear and frosted glass perfume bottles, no.602, with brown patina, and moulded marks.

c1926   *5.75in (14.5cm) high*

£400-600   **DRA**

GLASS

QUICK REFERENCE

- Mdina Glass was founded on Malta in 1968 by Michael Harris, an ex-Royal College of Art glass tutor. At Mdina Harris adapted new studio glass techniques acquired in the USA in 1966 to commercial production of art glass. His designs, often shallow dishes and bottle shaped vases, were made from thick glass and in colours that evoked the sea and the beach: turquoise, tan, aqua, greens and blues. Each piece is unique, as it was handmade.

- Production was aimed at the tourist and international gift market. Typical pieces were inexpensive and small, as these were easier to transport. Although much of Mdina's success was due to the tourist industry, it was helped by export sales to the UK, USA and Germany.

- Harris left Malta in 1972 and set up a glass factory on the Isle of Wight. Early pieces were similar to Mdina, but more finely blown. In 1978, saw the introduction of the Azurene range, designed by Harris and William Walker. It featured 22ct gold and silver leaf on coloured glass bodies. It was successful and continues to be desirable. Other popular ranges are Meadow Garden, Kyoto and Golden Peacock.

- Mdina pieces have 'Mdina' inscribed on their bases. Some may have their original stickers: paper stickers were earlier than plastic ones. Isle of Wight pieces can also be identified by a signature on the base or a sticker.

- Prices are rising, though affordable. Large, unusual designs and those signed by Michael Harris are the most desirable.

A Mdina Glass large stoppered bottle, designed by Michael Harris, of cylindrical form with swollen neck and spherical stopper with internal blue green and sandy ochre swirl, the base inscribed 'Mdina'.

Note the large size of this piece. These are considerably rarer than smaller examples, and seem only to have been produced until the mid-1970s.

16.25in (41cm) high

£350-450   FLD

A 1980s Mdina Glass bottle, the mottled ochre body with randomly applied green trails, the base inscribed 'Mdina'.

8in (20cm) high

£30-40   M20C

A 1980s Mdina Glass large bottle, with ochre mottling and applied colourless trails, the base inscirbed 'Mdina'.

13.5in (34cm) high

£40-60   M20C

A Mdina Glass 'Tiger' ovoid vase with flared neck, the base inscribed 'Mdina 1987'.

1987   6in (15.5cm) high

£50-70   VZ

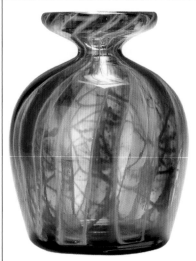

A Mdina Glass vase, with flared rim and horizontal green trails outlined in sand brown over a colourless base with a fine network of ochre crackle lines, the base inscribed 'Mdina 1987'.

6in (15cm) high

£50-70   VZ

A 1970s Mdina Glass disc-shaped vase, with elongated neck and blue and green striated band, the base inscribed 'Mdina'.

6in (15.5cm) high

£50-70   GC

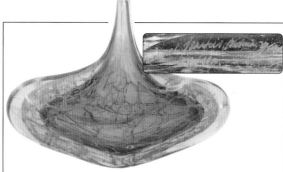

An extremely rare Mdina Glass 'Crizzle Stone', designed, made and signed by Michael Harris, with iridescent streak of silver chloride around the body, the base signed 'Michael Harris Mdina Glass Malta'.

Derived from his iconic 'Fish' vases, these are the rarest and most complex forms produced by Michael Harris at Mdina. See p.233 ' Miller's Collectables Price Guide 2009' for an example valued at £1,200-1,800 but unsigned by Harris – only two other signed examples are known.

7.5in (19cm) high

£2,800-3,400   ART

A large Mdina 'Cut Ice' Fish vase, designed by Michael Harris, the randomly strapped interior cased in colourless glass with two polished facets to one side.

c1971   9in (23cm) high

£250-350   FLD

A 1970s Mdina Glass 'Lollipop' vase, designed by Michael Harris, with green and blue curving forms with silver chloride colouring, cased in colourless glass, the base inscribed 'Mdina 1985', and with studio paper label.

1985   6.75in (17cm) high

£70-100   VZ

A mid-1970s Mdina 'Fish' vase, designed by Michael Harris, the purple and ochre core with silver chloride, cased in colourless glass with straps.

8.75in (22cm) high

£150-250   FLD

A 1980s Mdina Glass 'Fish' vase, with squared transparent blue wings over a mottled pink core, the base inscribed 'Mdina'.

7in (17.5cm) high

£40-60   VZ

A Mdina Glass object, comprising a 'Side Stripe' bottle vase embedded in a 'Sculpture' with green and ochre trails, the base signed 'Michael Harris Mdina Glass Malta', with annealing crack.

It is difficult to work out why this unusual and experimental piece was produced, and even more difficult to work out why it was signed by Michael Harris!

c1970   11in (28cm) long

£250-350   SAS

A Mdina Glass 'Tricorn' vase, designed by Michael Harris, with a mottled green and ochre body with silver chloride colouring, the base inscirbed 'Mdina'.

c1970-74   10.5in (27cm) diam

£250-350   FLD

GLASS

A Mdina Glass goblet, with blue straps applied over a mottled orange and yellow bowl, the foot engraved 'Mdina 1980'.

1980 6.5in (16.5cm) high

£40-50 **M20C**

A late 1970s-80s Mdina Glass random sculpture, with colourless and blue trails, the base inscribed 'Mdina'.

8.5in (21.5cm) high

£30-50 **M20C**

A CLOSER LOOK AT A MDINA GLASS BOTTLE

These are often mistaken for a Geoffrey Baxter design for Whitefriars due to the bark texture – Harris knew Baxter and had discussed the idea of a bark textured range with him around 1964.

It was made using the 'gathering on the post' technique, where the part blown neck was used to gather more glass, which was then blown into a mould to form the body.

These bottles are usually tall and thin, this wide form is very rare.

These bark textured bottles were only made from c1970, when metal moulds made in England had arrived in Malta, until c1972, when Harris left Mdina Glass.

A Mdina Glass mould blown bark textured bottle vase, designed by Michael Harris, the base with concave polished pontil mark.

c1971 8.75in (22.5cm) high

£150-200 **GC**

An Isle of Wight Studio Glass 'Tortoiseshell' low bottle vase, designed, made and signed by Michael Harris, the base with 'coachbolt' pontil mark and engraved 'Michael Harris Isle of Wight England'.

Although the Tortoiseshell range was produced from 1973-c82, the presence of a plain, concave 'coachbolt' pontil mark identifies this as coming from 1973.

1973 6in (15cm) diam

£180-220 **FLD**

An Isle of Wight Studio Glass 'Tortoiseshell' bell vase, designed by Michael Harris, with impressed 'flame' pontil mark to base and black triangular studio sticker.

c1978-80 8in (20.5cm) high

£120-180 **VZ**

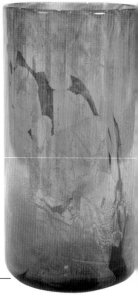

An Isle of Wight Studio Glass 'Pink Azurene' cylinder vase, the mottled pink body overlaid with silver and 22ct gold leaf, the base engraved 'Michael Harris ENGLAND 11/500'.

This 'limited edition' style of signature shows that it was made for export to US department stores, such as JC Penney.

11.5in (29cm) high

£300-400 **FLD**

QUICK REFERENCE

- Glass has made on Murano since the 13thC, when glassmakers moved from Venice to protect the wealthy city from furnace fires. For centuries, traditional glass-making techniques were handed down through families and though design underwent a radical transformation in the 1950s, these historic techniques were simply used in new, innovative ways. Colours became brighter and exuberant, while forms became more abstract and sculptural. New designers were invited to the island and by the end of the decade the new movement was in full swing.

- The most desirable and valuable pieces are the work of influential designers, such as Paolo Venini, Fulvio Bianconi, Flavio Poli, Ercole Barovier and Dino Martens. As well as the designer, the factory is important. Notable factories include Venini (founded 1921), Seguso Vetri D'Arte (1933-92), Barovier & Toso (founded 1942) and A.V.E.M (founded

1932). Landmark designs include Dino Martens's 'Oriente', Flavio Poli's Sommerso, and Venini's 'fazzoletto' vases.

- Many pieces are not signed, so check reference books to help you identify the work of these factories and designers. Original labels will also help with identification, though these have usually been removed. Successful designs were widely copied or imitated by other designers and glass factories, so it is also advisable to study as many identified examples as you can, to get a feel for authentic pieces.

- Consider the technique used – the more visually appealing and complex it is, the more desirable your piece is likely to be. For example, with sommerso designs, brightly coloured, well-balanced forms with clearly demarcated layers are usually desirable. Bear in mind that the market is wider and often more affordable away from major designers, with some pieces available for £20.

A Seguso Vetri D'Arte sommerso glass vase, no.12024, with a brown core covered with a heavily ribbed honey yellow casing.

c1970   *12.75in (32cm) high*
£400-600   **VZ**

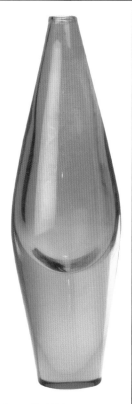

A Seguso Vetri d'Arte sommerso glass vase, designed by Flavio Poli, with graduated pink/red core, covered with layer of green and yellow glass and an outer layer of colourless glass.

c1965   *14in (35.5cm) high*
£1,800-2,200   **DOR**

A Seguso Vetri D'Arte sommerso torpedo shaped vase, designed by Flavio Poli, the light green core overlaid with an ice blue layer also forming the base, with factory label to base.

c1960   *17.5in (44.5cm) high*
£800-1,200   **VZ**

A Seguso Vetri D'Arte sommerso glass vase, designed by Flavio Poli, the tapering cylindrical green core cased in bright yellow, with heavy base.

c1960   *11.25in (28.5cm) high*
£300-500   **GC**

A Seguso Vetri D'Arte sommerso bottle vase with cylindrical neck, designed by Flavio Poli, the purple core covered with a light violet layer.

c1960   *10in (25.5cm) high*
£800-1,200   **VZ**

A Seguso Vetri D'Arte sommerso vase, designed by Flavio Poli, the ovoid form triple cased in green, blue, red and colourless glass.

c1955   *7in (18cm) high*

£600-800   **QU**

A Seguso Vetri D'Arte sommerso vase, designed by Flavio Poli, of flattened conical form, the base of the blue core cased in a layer or pinky-red and with an outer layer of colourless glass.

c1958   *10.75in (27.5cm) high*

£800-1,200   **VZ**

A CLOSER LOOK AT A SEGUSO VASE

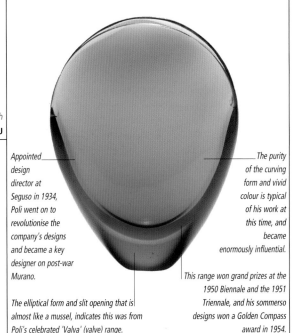

Appointed design director at Seguso in 1934, Poli went on to revolutionise the company's designs and became a key designer on post-war Murano.

The elliptical form and slit opening that is almost like a mussel, indicates this was from Poli's celebrated 'Valva' (valve) range.

The purity of the curving form and vivid colour is typical of his work at this time, and became enormously influential.

This range won grand prizes at the 1950 Biennale and the 1951 Triennale, and his sommerso designs won a Golden Compass award in 1954.

A Seguso Vetri D'Arte 'Valva' vase, designed by Flavio Poli, the light turquoise-blue core overlaid with two layers of different tones of violet glass, with outer colourless layer.

c1952   *9.75in (24.5cm) high*

£3,500-4,500   **VZ**

A Seguso Vetri D'Arte sommerso bowl, the pink core cased with a layer of yellow and with a thick colourless outer layer, with pulled rim.

c1950   *13.75in (35cm) high*

£300-500   **DOR**

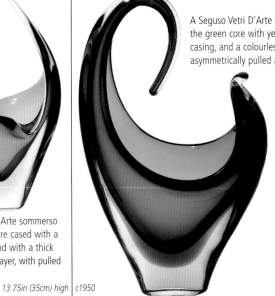

A Seguso Vetri D'Arte sommerso bowl, the green core with yellow and orange casing, and a colourless outer layer, with asymmetrically pulled and curled rim.

c1950   *11.5in (29cm) high*

£1,200-1,800   **DOR**

A Seguso Vetri D'Arte textured light blue glass cubic paperweight, in the form of an ice block, with manufacturer's model number label reading '54461'.

c1978   *3.5in (9cm) high*

£250-300   **VZ**

A Barovier & Toso 'Crepuscolo' lampbase, the shaped clear glass body with iron wool inclusions, the applied foot and rings with gold foil inclusions, designed by Ercole Barovier.

c1950   *13.5in (34cm) high*
£400-600   **QU**

A CLOSER LOOK AT AN A.V.E.M. JUG

The Ansa Volante range of jugs was exhibited at the 1952 Biennale exhibition in Venice, and the asymmetric form is a typical feature.

The term means 'flying handle', referring to the integral handle and dynamic form wih its sweeping lines – some have two handles.

The range was produced in red or green glass, both with an iridescent surface created by 'fuming' the piece in metallic salts.

A scarcer variation also included randomly placed aventurine filament inclusions.

An A.V.E.M. 'Ansa Volante' jug vase, designed by Giorgio Ferro in 1952, the organic, pulled deep red glass with a heavily iridised surface.

Ferro worked for A.V.E.M. from 1951-55 before leaving for Ferro Galliano.

13in (33cm) high
£800-1,200   **VZ**

A Barovier & Toso 'Neolitico' bowl, bands of trapped air bubbles and dark brown trails combed into columns, designed by Ercole Barovier.

The pattern is created by applying trails which are melted into the body and then 'combed' with tools in a similar way to Art Nouveau glass designs by Louis Comfort Tiffany.

1954   *10.5in (26.5cm) diam*
£800-1,200   **QU**

A Cenedese sommerso glass vase, the graduated blue and yellow core with layers of yellow, light blue and colourless glass.

c1950   *23in (60cm) h*
£1,000-1,500   **DOR**

A Barovier & Toso 'Cordonato Oro' ovoid vase with pulled and curled rim, designed by Ercole Barovier, the red core with gold foil inclusions, covered with a colourless layer of ribbed glass, the ribs containing rope-twist effect gold foil inclusions, the base with factory label.

This range was shown by Barovier & Toso in the 1950 Biennale in Venice, and is a fusion between modern and traditional techniques and styles.

1950   *11.25in (28cm) high*
£450-550   **VZ**

A Cenedese sommerso vase, designed by Antonia da Ros, with cylindrical and flared neck and yellow casing over a blue core, the base inscribed 'Cenedese'.

c1968   *8.75in (22cm) high*
£700-1,000   **VZ**

GLASS

QUICK REFERENCE - MURRINES

A murrine is the term given to a small glass tile cut from a rod containing a pattern, typically in the form of a flower (for example a millefiori, or 'a thousand flowers'), lines, or other motifs. These are arranged in a pattern like a mosaic on a glassblower's table, and the part-blown hot glass body is rolled over them, picking them up. The whole is then inserted in the furnace, all the parts are melted together and the body finally blown into shape. The technique dates back to the Roman era, but in the post-war period it was revised and updated. Vittorio Ferro (b.1932) is one of the leading modern exponents of the style, and was the maestro at Fratelli Toso until the 1980s. Following his 'retirement', he continued to design and produce his individual style of murrines at the De Majo and Fratelli Pagnin factories. The brightly coloured, black-lined murrines and almost iridescent effect are hallmarks of his style, which is increasingly popular with collectors and looks to be a good bet for the future.

A Cenedese sommerso cylindrical vase, designed by Antonia da Ros, with cylindrical and flared neck and yellow casing over a green core, the base inscribed 'Cenedese'.

c1968   *12.5in (32cm) high*

£1,200-1,800   **VZ**

An Alberto Donà vase, of flattened ovoid form with pulled, curving neck, with yellow and turquoise green vertical stripes covered with a layer of colourless glass, the surface cut with shallow slices, the base signed 'Alberto Donà Murano 1993'.

1993   *19.5in (49.5cm) high*

£1,200-1,800   **VZ**

A De Majo 'Estate' baluster vase, designed and made by Vittorio Ferro, with grey and green murrines with internal black iridised veins, and red 'rose' murrines, the base inscribed 'Vittorio Ferro 1998'.

10.75in (27cm) high

£800-1,200   **VZ**

A Carlo Moretti ruby red glass vase, of double conical form, with applied rectangular shards of colourless glass with white stripes.

c1970   *6.5in (16.5cm) high*

£550-650   **DOR**

A 1950s Pustetto Zanetti 'Arte Nuova' sommerso glass vase, probably designed by Aldo Fuga, with green, yellow and colourless layers, with factory foil label.

The Arte Nuova glassworks was founded in 1954 by Itamo Pustetto and Mario Fuga and known for its sommerso designs, many by Pustetto and Nino D' Este. Designs by Aldo Fuga were acclaimed at the Brussels Exposition 1958. It closed in the mid-1960s. Works are often misattributed to Seguso.

11.75in (30cm) high

£400-600   **DOR**

A Fratelli Toso vase, the colourless glass body covered with stylised flower murrines with white metals and orange centres, designed by Ermanno Toso, with applied orange rim.

c1960   *6.75in (17cm) high*

£1,000-1,500   **VZ**

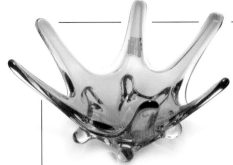

A 1950s-60s Fratelli Toso large cased blue 'splash' vase, with pulled arms and nodules, with 'MURANO CHAMBORD' gold foil label.

Chambord was a trade name used by Fratelli Toso, whose name appears at the bottom of the (usually) shield-shaped label, which is damaged on this example.

17in (43cm) diam

£120-180　　　　　　　　　　　　　　　　　　　　GC

A Venini & C. 'Corroso' amber glass vase, in the form of a double-handled urn, with acid-etched textured surface, the base with three line 'venini murano italia' acid stamp.

The surface of this vase is treated with acid to give a mottled, lightly textured surface.

c1940　　　　9.75in (24.5cm) h

£800-1,200　　　　　　　VZ

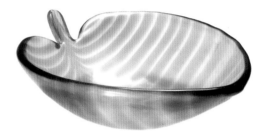

A scarce Venini & C. 'Foglia' leaf-shaped bowl, designed by Tyra Lundgren, the colourless glass with blue stripes, and iridescent surface, the base with 'venini murano MADE IN ITALY' three line mark.

Swedish glass designer Lundgren produced a number of prize-winning designs for Venini shortly before the war, which were exhibited in both Murano and Sweden.

c1938　　　　8.8in (22cm) long

£1,200-1,800　　　　　　VZ

A Venini & C. 'corroso' bowl, designed by Carlo Scarpa, of clear and turquoise-blue cased glass, with frosted exterior.

Corroso indicates a lightly textured matt exterior treated with acid.

c1940　　　　7.8in (19.5cm) wide

£200-250　　　　　　　　VZ

A Venini & C 'Tuuli' bottle, designed by Timo Sarpaneva, with opaque yellow and black bands, and black stopper, the base inscribed 'venini 90 Sarpaneva'.

This 'Tuuli' range was created using the complex and challenging 'incalmo' technique, where separate gathers of different glass were blown to precise sizes and joined together while hot. The austerity of design is typical of Sarpaneva's Finnish aesthetic.

1990　　　　12.25in (31cm) high

£1,000-1,500　　　　　　VZ

A Venini & C. 'Tuuli' bowl, designed by Timo Sarpaneva in 1988, the cylindrical form with applied opaque red and dark violet bands, with light violet tinted central band, the base inscribed 'venini 91 Sarpaneva'.

1991　　　5.25in (13.cm) high

£800-1,200　　　　　VZ

A Vittorio Zuffi & C. murrine vase, the urn-shaped colourless body with applied green handles and alternating columns of green star murrines and colourless glass with heavy aventurine inclusions.

c1895　　　5.25in (13cm) high

£400-500　　　　　QU

GLASS

QUICK REFERENCE - MEMPHIS AND MURANO

Eccentric and geometric forms in bright colours are typical of the Postmodern style promoted by the Memphis group in the 1980s. Although other designers and artists contributed to the group, Ettore Sottsass is considered their notional leader. Complex to make, and as much a piece of decorative sculpture as a functional form, each component of this bowl was separately blown before being joined together. Compagnia Vetreria Muranese produced Memphis glass designs from 1982 until c1992, becoming known as Toso Vetri D'Arte from 1982-90. Examples can be quite scarce as these were never mass-produced or inexpensive, and may be a good tip for the future if the style is re-appraised by more design collectors.

A Compagnia Vetreria Muranese 'Sol' bowl, designed by Ettore Sottsass for Memphis in 1982, comprised of transparent red, blue and green components, with an opaque lining, the base inscribed 'E. SOTTSASS PER MEMPHIS by COMPAGNIA VETRERIA MURANESE'.

8.5in (21.5cm) high

£1,000-1,500   **VZ**

A Compagnia Vetreria Murano for Memphis 'Erinna' vase, designed by Ettore Sottsass, with pink, blue and orange components, the base inscribed 'E. SOTTSASS PER MEMPHIS'.

1986   19in (48cm) high

£1,000-1,500   **VZ**

A Compagnia Vetreria Muranese 'Pasifila' glass vase, designed by Ettore Sottsass in 1986, comprised of cone forms in blue, translucent white, pink and opal green, the base inscribed 'E.SOTTSASS PER MEMPHIS'.

18.25in (46cm) high

£1,000-1,500   **VZ**

A Vistosi limited edition 'Pink Cigar' table centrepiece, designed by Peter Shire, the asymmetric form comprised of blue, black (dark violet), pink and yellow geometric forms, the base inscribed 'PETER SHIRE X VISTOSI 2/4'.

c1985   16.5in (42cm) high

£1,000-1,500   **VZ**

A Vistosi limited edition table centrepiece, designed by Peter Shire, with green conical and light and dark blue disc and spherical forms on a colourless column with a brown spiralling trail, the base inscribed 'PETER SHIRE X VISTOSI 4/6'.

c1985   24in (61cm) high

£800-1,200   **VZ**

A Vistosi 'Faleria' limited edition lidded jar, designed by Ettore Sottsass in 1980, the yellow body with green hemispherical lid and lined in black, the base engraved 'E.SOTTSASS 150-250 VISTOSI'.

c1981 10.75in (27cm) high

£2,500-3,500   **QU**

A 1950s-60s Murano glass yellow cased red 'sommerso' bottle, with attenuated neck and remains of foil label to neck.

The elongated neck of this bottle, shouldered body and vibrant colours suggest Seguso as a maker. However, this cannot be confirmed by the label despite the quality being suitably high. The interior of the neck has also not been ground to hold a stopper.

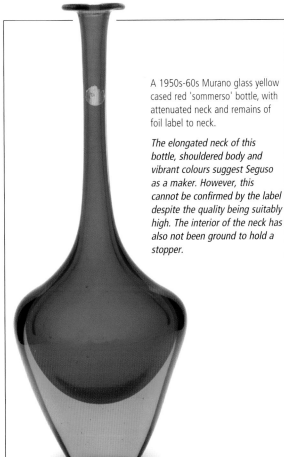

14.25in (36cm) high

£80-120　　　　RET

A 1960s Murano glass yellow cased brown vase with colourless outer layer, elongated neck and winged body.

7.25in (18.5cm) high

£22-28　　　　RET

A 1960s Murano 'sommerso' glass green cased red vase, with elongated neck and colourless outer casing.

17in (43cm) high

£60-80　　　　RET

A 1960s Murano glass yellow cased green 'sommerso' vase with outer colourless casing, pulled rim and winged body.

These forms are often misattributed to Flavio Poli. A company called 'Turca' produced similar forms, and their link with Poli has not been confirmed.

11in (27.5cm) high

£65-75　　　　RET

A 1960s Murano glass red and yellow cased bowl with curved and pulled rim.

13.5in (34cm) high

£45-55　　　　RET

A 1960s Murano 'sommerso' glass yellow cased red bowl, with cut and pulled rim and 'MURANO MADE IN ITALY' red and silver foil label.

Similarly coloured circular foil labels with the same wording and scalloped edging can be attributed to Seguso during the 1950s.

11.25in (27cm) high

£45-55　　　　RET

GLASS

A 1950s-60s Murano sommerso glass yellow cased green bowl, with wavy and pulled rim.

12.5in (31.5cm) wide

£20-30   **RET**

A 1960s-70s Murano glass colourless cased orange-red heat sensitive glass bowl with pulled rim.

Here, a special chemical has been added to the glass so that it changes colour from orange to deep red when reheated in the furnace. The blue casing is unusual, as it would usually be colourless.

6in (15cm) diam

£30-40   **RET**

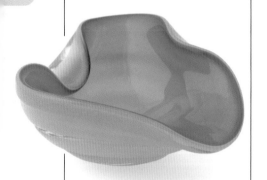

A 1950s-60s Murano glass green 'Opaline' ashtray, with pulled and folded rim.

7.25in (18cm) high

£30-50   **MHT**

A 1960s Murano sommerso glass yellow cased green oval bowl, with pinched thick rim.

These heavily rendered, vibrantly coloured bowls are sometimes known as 'geode' bowls after the geological rock forms containing crystal-lined cavities.

7.25in (18.5cm) high

£30-40   **RET**

A 1960s Murano glass sommerso bowl with a red core, a layer of controlled bubbles and aventurine inclusions, cased with green tinged clear glass with pulled wings.

4.5in (11.5cm) diam

£30-40   **RET**

A 1960s Murano glass aqua green ashtray with colourless casing and pulled lobes.

9in (23cm) diam

£20-25   **RET**

A 1950s-70s Murano glass cased green and yellow ashtray, with pulled rim and network of controlled internal bubbles.

6.75in (17cm) diam

£10-15   **M20C**

A 1960s Murano glass yellow tinted cased red 'sommerso' bowl, cut with facets, the base cut with a hobnail pattern.

5.25in (13cm) wide

£35-45   **RET**

A 1960s-70s Murano 'sommerso' glass green and blue faceted ashtray, the outer layer tinged with violet.

A Murano glass dish, the graduated violet and colourless glass with applied cobalt blue abstract splash motif, and heavy colourless base.

The designer and maker of this bowl remain unknown. Some collectors have attributed it to Czechoslovakia, although this has not been confirmed and a Muranese origin is more likely. Regardless, it would have been very complex and hard to make.

c1960   *6.75in (17cm) diam*

£120-180   **QU**

5.25in (13cm) wide

£30-50   **TGM**

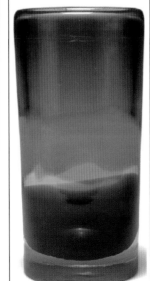

A 1970s Murano glass cylinder vase, the graduated blue to colourless body overlaid with multicoloured star murrines, unmarked.

9.25in (23.5cm) high

£300-500   **QU**

A Murano glass cylinder vase, the colourless body with graduated violet, yellow and purple bands.

c1965   *9.5in (24cm) high*

£300-500   **QU**

A Murano glass footed vase, the conical form with cylindrical neck and flared rim overlaid with multicoloured millefiori murrines.

c1910   *5.5in (14cm) high*

£300-400   **QU**

A small Murano glass teardrop shaped vase, the colourless glass overlaid with columns of zanfirico canes and multicoloured ribbon twist canes, unmarked.

5.5in (14cm) high

£100-150   **QU**

GLASS

A Cenedese sommerso glass vase in the form of a bird, the tail forming the vase, designed by Antonia da Ros, the blue core covered with a layer of colourless glass and an outer layer of green glass.
c1961   *10.75in (27cm) high*
£80-120   **VZ**

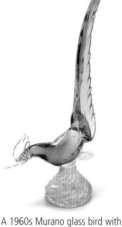

A 1960s Murano glass bird with applied and hot-worked features, on a spiralling base containing aventurine inclusions.
                          17.25in (44cm) high
£40-60   **RET**

A 1950s-60s Murano glass sommerso bird, the red core cased with uranium glass, unsigned.

Although unsigned, the way the tail and beak are handled is indicative of Seguso.
                              6in (15cm) long
£20-30   **TGM**

A Seguso Vetri d'Arte yellow glass cockerel, designed by Flavio Poli.

                            7in (18cm) wide
£1,000-1,500   **DOR**

QUICK REFERENCE - MURANO GLASS ANIMALS

An entire zoo of glass animals has been produced on Murano since the 1950s. Although leading designers and factories produced examples, the many smaller factories produced their own versions copied from, or inspired by, the works of the masters. There is an enormous gap in values, with most copies or pieces by smaller factories being worth under £150, and usually under £80. The work of a master can fetch many thousands. The key is to study original factory catalogues and books, and identify items by their shape and colour. The work of leading factories is also very well executed, sometimes using complex techniques that require skill, experience and time. Size can also indicate a finer quality piece. This fish is a good example. Antonio da Ros joined Cenedese in 1958, where he was encouraged to experiment by Gino Cenedese. His early works were thickly blown, with simple forms. He explored colour by using one or two colours in different tones, usually in different internal layers.

A Cenedese sommerso glass fish, designed by by Antonio Da Ros, with cobalt blue core overlaid with dark violet and light blue layers.
1962   *6in (15cm) wide*
£600-800   **DOR**

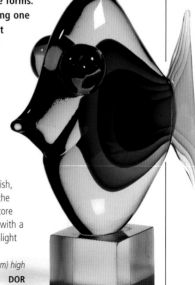

A Cenedese sommerso glass fish, designed by Antonio Da Ros, the multi-layered deep rose pink core overlaid with light blue glass, with a rose pink tail and a matching light blue cube pedestal.
1965-66   *10.5in (27cm) high*
£1,800-2,200   **DOR**

QUICK REFERENCE

- Post WWII Scandinavian glass has increased in popularity and value, as glass collectors re-evaluate its importance to 20thC glass design, due to a widening knowledge base.
- 1950s pieces were predominantly asymmetric, with curving forms and cool colours. Designers took their inspiration from natural forms. By the 1960s, this became a clean-lined, geometric, brightly coloured Modern style. Textured forms became popular and continued to be so into the 1970s.
- Both the factory and the designer are important in determining value and desirability. Factories include Orrefors, Kosta Boda and Iittala, with stylish pieces by Riihimäen Lasi Oy and Orrefors currently proving popular. Look for the work of leading designers, who influenced others and helped define the movement, such as Vicke Lindstrand, Simon Gate, Tapio Wirkkala, Sven Palmqvist, Tamara Aladin and Nanny Still. This can seem confusing, because some designers, such as Lindstrand, moved between factories, or the factories merged. Examination of the engraved marks on its base may identify the designer or, if unmarked, the designer and maker may be identified from the style, colour and way it was made.
- Investigate the secondary factories, designers or ranges that are still being researched. These include John Orwar Lake for Ekenas, Strömbergshyttan, and Erik Höglund for Boda. Now may be the time to buy, as these designers may become more collectable and valuable later.
- Consider how a piece was made and its colour, as some techniques and colours are rare. Unique vases are usually worth more than mould-blown pieces. Condition and 'eye appeal' are a major factors in determining desirability. Examine pieces for damage which detracts from the purity of colour and form that is typical of Scandinavian glass.

A mid-late 1970s Finnish Riihimäen Lasi Oy green footed waisted cylindrical vase, by an unknown designer and produced from 1976 as part of the 'Export Collection'.

10in (25cm) high

£20-30   M20C

A mid 1960s-70s Finnish Riihimäen Lasi Oy green footed vase, with trumpet neck, by an unknown designer.

10in (25cm) high

£20-30   M20C

A 1960s-70s Finnish Riihimaki Lasi Oy mould blown cased green tapered 'Stromboli' vase, designed by Aimo Okkolin in 1963.

7in (18cm) high

£20-30   NPC

A 1960s Finnish Riihimäen Lasi Oy green 'Chimney' vase, designed by Aimo Okkolin in 1960.

10in (25cm) high

£20-30   M20C

A Finnish Riihimäen Lasi Oy cased green vase, with solid, heavy foot, by an unknown designer.

4.5in (11.5cm) high

£20-30   M20C

GLASS

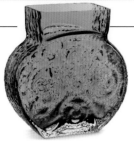

A 1960s-70s Finnish Riihimäen Lasi Oy mould blown cased green vase, designed by Helena Tynell.

7in (18cm) high

£80-120   **GC**

A Finnish Riihimäen Lasi Oy cased blue large vase, with disc centre and waisted neck and base, by an unidentified designer.

10.5in (26.5cm) high

£30-50   **M20C**

A Finnish Riihimäen Lasi Oy green mould blown vase from the 'Fossil' range, designed by Helena Tynell.

8.75in (22.5cm) high

£100-150   **GC**

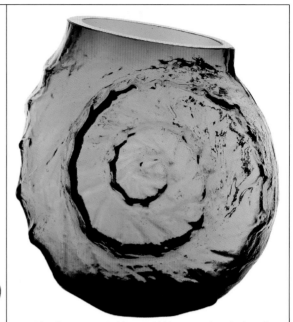

A Finnish Riihimäen Lasi Oy blue mould blown vase from the 'Fossil' range, designed by Helena Tynell.

In taking its inspiration from natural history rather than the drawing board and geometry set, the Fossil range is very rare.

6.25in (16cm) high

£100-150   **GC**

A Finnish Riihimäen Lasi Oy blue 'Safari' textured vase, no.1495, designed by Tamara Aladin in 1970.

Unusually for Riihimaki, this was machine blown into a mould, rather than being spun to create the textured finish. As such, a mould line appears down each side of the vase. It was produced in three sizes, of which this is the medium. Colours include green, dark blue, this blue and colourless.

10in (25cm) high

£40-50   **M20C**

A Riihimäen Lasi Oy mould blown blue decanter, the front and back with a moulded stylised flower design, designed by Helena Tynell.

6.75in (17cm) high

£60-90   **UCT**

A Riihimäen Lasi Oy, blue mould blown 'Pala' vase, with textured surface, designed by Helena Tynell in 1964.

1964-76   *2.75in (7cm) high*

£15-18   **UCT**

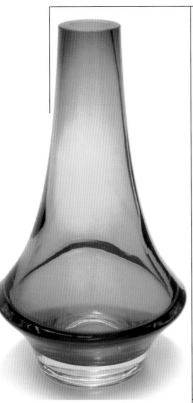

A CLOSER LOOK AT A RIIHIMAKI VASE

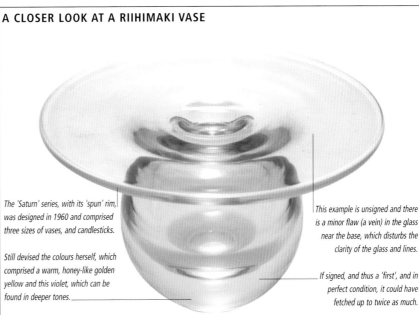

The 'Saturn' series, with its 'spun' rim, was designed in 1960 and comprised three sizes of vases, and candlesticks.

Still devised the colours herself, which comprised a warm, honey-like golden yellow and this violet, which can be found in deeper tones.

This example is unsigned and there is a minor flaw (a vein) in the glass near the base, which disturbs the clarity of the glass and lines.

If signed, and thus a 'first', and in perfect condition, it could have fetched up to twice as much.

A Finnish Riihimäen Lasi Oy 'Saturn' light violet vase, designed by Nanny Still in 1960.

3.25in (8cm) high

£50-80   UCT

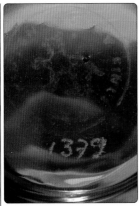

A 1960s Finnish Riihimäen Lasi Oy cased yellow vase, no.1379, the design attributed to Tamara Aladin, the base with acid etched mark and engraved '1379'.

The presence of the mark indicates this was produced for the mainland European market: examples intended for the UK market are generally unmarked.

8in (20cm) high

£30-40   M20C

A Finnish Riihimäen Lasi Oy yellow vase, the design attributed to Tamara Aladin.

1965-1971   11in (28cm) high

£40-50   M20C

A 1980s Finnish Riihimäen Lasi Oy red waisted and tapered vase, shape no.6012, designed by Aimo Okkolin in 1982.

10in (25cm) high

£20-30   M20C

A Finnish Riihimäen Lasi Oy 'Tuulikki' range red vase, designed by Tamara Aladin in 1972.

1972-76   8in (20cm) high

£20-25   M20C

GLASS

A Swedish Orrefors cut and fire-polished vase, by an unknown designer, the base inscribed 'Orrefors'.

After being cut, the body was reheated and the edges of the facets were smoothed off and rounded using a fire torch, or by inserting the piece back into the glory hole for a short time.

9in (23cm high

£80-120   **GC**

An Orrefors '1000 Windows' series glass vase, cut with semi-circular lenses, by Simon Gate, the base inscribed 'Orrefors 90895/211'.

Gate designed this Regency style pattern in 1934. Sales remained strong and this vase, modified from earlier vase shapes, was still sold by Orrefors in 2003.

7.75in (19.5cm) high

£20-30   **AEM**

A Swedish Orrefors 'Selina' opalescent bowl, designed by Sven Palmqvist from 1954, the base engraved 'Orrefors Pu XXXX'.

8in (20.5cm) diam

£80-120   **PC**

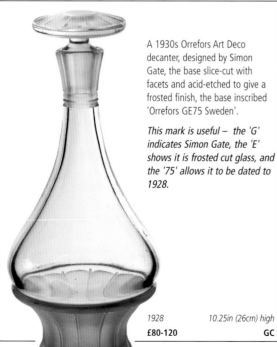

A 1930s Orrefors Art Deco decanter, designed by Simon Gate, the base slice-cut with facets and acid-etched to give a frosted finish, the base inscribed 'Orrefors GE75 Sweden'.

This mark is useful – the 'G' indicates Simon Gate, the 'E' shows it is frosted cut glass, and the '75' allows it to be dated to 1928.

1928   10.25in (26cm) high

£80-120   **GC**

A CLOSER LOOK AT AN ORREFORS GOBLET

Designed in 1957, the Tulpan series won a gold medal at the important Milan Triennale exhibition in 1957, the year this piece was made. It has become an icon of Scandinavian glass design.

Tulpan is Swedish for 'tulip', the form of the flower being echoed in the gently curving bowl.

At 17in (27cm) high, the size is important – larger examples do exist, but are very rare.

This required great skill to create, particularly the regularity of the form and the hollow conical foot. Landberg is known for his elegant, classical shapes at this time.

An Orrefors ruby red 'Tulpanglass' vase, designed by Nils Landberg in 1954, the base engraved 'Orrefors Expo Nu 312-57'.

1957   17in (43cm) high

£1,200-1,800   **DRA**

An Orrefors colourless glass seated polar bear, the base inscribed 'Orrefors CB4354 - 1/1'.

3.75in (9cm) high

£35-40   **TGM**

A Kosta Boda 'October' bowl with applied enamelled trees and birds and multicoloured chips to form the flowery meadow, designed by Kjell Engmann in 1983, the base signed 'Bow 68628 K. Engmann'.

6.25in (15.5cm) high

£50-70   **TGM**

A 1930s Kosta colourless optic tapering cylindrical vase, designed by Elis Bergh, with an applied black foot.

10in (25.5cm) high

£120-180   **UCT**

A 1990s Kosta Boda vase, designed by Göran Wärff, with cut panel to front, and low-relief, moulded star shape surrounded by applied powdered enamels to the reverse, the base engraved 'KOSTA 47317 WARFF', and with cellophane label.

4.5in (11.5cm) high

£70-90   **TGM**

A Swedish Kosta bottle vase, with randomly applied coloured trails and chips, designed by Bertil Vallien, the base with broken pontil mark, unsigned.

9in (23cm) high

£80-100   **GC**

A 1970s-80s Kosta Boda bowl, designed by Göran Wärff in 1973, the exterior with applied purple and black enamels over a colourless base, with star and irregular shaped exclusions, the rim signed 'KOSTA 56773 WARFF'.

Five digit numbers have been used for designs from the 1970s onwards, with the last two numbers indicating the year of design rather than production of that piece. Wärff joined Orrefors from Pukeberg in 1964, before leaving to travel and teach in 1974. He returned in 1984 and still produces organic, earthy inspired designs, that accentuate the qualities of glass.

6in (15cm) diam

£70-100   **TGM**

A Kosta solifleur vase, designed by Vicke Lindstrand, of tapered cylindrical form, cased in clear over a graduated colour ground, with a single tear-shaped bubble to the base, the base with full engraved signature.

11in (28cm) high

£100-150   **FLD**

A Swedish Kosta carafe or decanter, with applied spout, designed by Vicke Lindstrand in 1959, the base inscribed 'Kosta LH1463'.

11.5in (29cm) high

£60-80   **GC**

GLASS

A Swedish Flygsfors cased vase, with angled cut rim, designed by Paul Kedelv, the base inscribed 'Flygsfors 63'.

11in (28cm) high

£50-70   RET

A 1960s Boda orange goblet, designed by Eric Hoglund, with random internal bubbles.

6.75in (17cm) high

£30-50   GC

A 1960s Swedish Gullaskruf mould blown teal blue bottle vase, designed by Arthur Percy.

Percy (1886-1976) worked for Gullaskruf from 1951-70.

9.75in (24.5cm) high

£8-12   M20C

A Norwegian Hadeland cased olive green tapering vase, possibly designed by Willy Johansson.

6.5in (15cm) high

£20-30   M20C

A 1970s Hadeland ovoid vase with acid etched and sandblasted design of a little girl seated and hugging a doll, with factory foil labels, unsigned.

7.5in (19cm) high

£60-80   GC

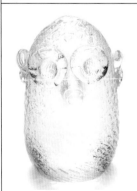

A 1970s Norwegian Hadeland troll, with applied ears, nose and eyes, the base acid stamped 'Hadeland'.

3in (7.5cm) high

£22-28   RET

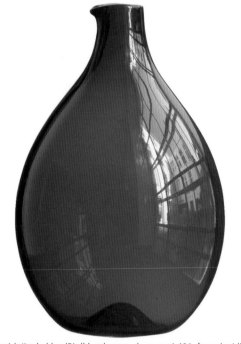

A Finnish Iittala blue 'Bird' bottle vase, shape no. i-401, from the i-line range, designed by Timo Sarpaneva in 1956.

1957-68   *6.75in (17cm) high*

£80-120   QU

A Finnish Nuutajarvi Nostjo cased blue footed vase, with heavy colourless foot and machine-cut rim, designed by Kaj Franck in 1962, the base inscribed 'KF Nuutajarvi Nostjo-62'.

The restrained, sombre colour and austere form with its clean lines are typical of Franck's Modernist designs.

6.25in (16cm) high

£280-320   **UCT**

A CLOSER LOOK AT A RUDA VASE

Ruda Glasbruk was based near other Swedish glass factories Orrefors and Kosta from 1910-72 - their decorative glass was always secondary to their industrial glass.

Augustsson was designer from 1947-72 and most of his designs are textured, having been blown into a mould, before being finished by hand.

This was from a range that also included tankards, jugs and other vase shapes.

'Kobolt' Blue is the most common colour found, with green (known as 'Turkos') and an amber-brown (known as 'Orient') being harder to find.

A 1960s Swedish Ruda Glasbruk mould-blown textured blue 'Kobalt' vase, designed by Göte Augustsson, with factory label, the base with polished concave pontil mark.

6.5in (16.5cm) high

£30-50   **M20C**

A 1970s Swedish Reijmyre colourless cased purple vase, with tapering neck, machine-cut rim and base moulded with concentric circles.

10in (25.5cm) high

£40-50   **UCT**

A 1960s Swedish Ruda Glasbruk mould blown textured blue 'Kobalt' bottle vase, designed by Göte Augustssen, the base with polished concave pontil mark.

8.75in (22cm) high

£30-50   **M20C**

A Swedish Skruf tapering cylindrical glass vase, by Bengt Edenfalk, cased in colourless glass with applied ribbon trail decoration, the base etched 'Edenfalk Skruf'.

This range can be found in a number of shapes and colours, including grey, brown and sage green. A vase from this range was included in an exhibition of modern glass at the Corning Glass Museum in 1959. Edenfalk (b.1924) worked for Skruf from 1953-78, leaving to produce designs for Kosta.

13in (33cm) high

£120-180   **WW**

A 1930s Strömbergshyttan brown vase with scalloped rim, the base with polished pontil mark.

These were imported into the UK by Elfverson & Co., run by H.J. Dunne Cooke. This shape, available in 6in, 8in, 10in and 12in sizes, was numbered 3055A.

8.25in (21cm) high

£60-90   **GC**

QUICK REFERENCE

- Peter Layton was born in Prague in 1937, and brought up in England. He studied ceramics at the Central School of Art and Design in London, before discovering glassblowing while teaching at the University of Iowa in the 1970s.
- Largely self-taught, he established his own glass studio at his pottery at Morar in the Highlands of Scotland, before moving to Rotherhithe in London. He went on to establish a glass department at Hornsey College of Art (Middlesex University), and founded the influential London Glassblowing Workshop in 1976.
- Layton has since played a major role in the development of studio glass in Britain. As well as mentoring many new glassmakers and designers, helping them mould their style, identity and confidence, he has offered facilities enabling them to work.
- His designs are inspired by the fluidity of molten glass, vivid colour and controlled yet asymmetric form. Nature

and landscape are also influences. Pieces are typically built up using a number of layers of glass, with patterns being created with applied coloured swirls, speckles and trails.
- Smooth, rounded forms inspired by pebbles are typical, and the 'dropper bottle', with its thin, elongated neck, is a hallmark form that can be found in many of his ranges. As each piece is handmade and freeblown, each one is unique in terms of its precise form and patterning. Values depend on the size, range, colour and complexity of the design, and range from as little as £150 to over £5,000.
- Layton has also produced a number of unique, individual works for exhibitions that explore themes such as the human body, life and death. These usually incorporate other materials such a metal piping and even medical equipment. He is also known for his architectural commissions in association with Simon Moss. Layton's designs can be found in many private and public collections across the world.

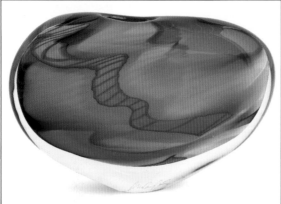

A Peter Layton 'Turquoise Paradiso' stone form vase, the graduated sky blue, yellow, green and cream core with a diagonal black striped orange zig-zag, the base signed 'Peter Layton'.

2007   6.75in (17cm) high

£800-1,200   **GC**

A Peter Layton 'Aeriel' stone form vase, the blue core overlaid with ochre and cream swirls, and cased in colourless glass, the base signed 'Peter Layton'.

2006   7in (18cm) high

£300-400   **GC**

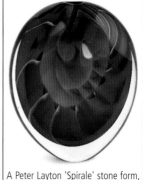

A Peter Layton 'Spirale' stone form, the spiralling burgundy and blue and yellow striped core overlaid with a colourless layer, the base signed 'Peter Layton'.

8in (20.5cm) high

£700-1,000   **GC**

A unique Peter Layton stone form vase, the buff-grey core with a yellow grid-like pattern and applied large yellow stylised floral murrines with orange stripes, the base signed 'Peter Layton'.

The murrines have been applied to a colourless layer over the core, giving depth to the design, which is further highlighted by the yellow and grey grid pattern of the core.

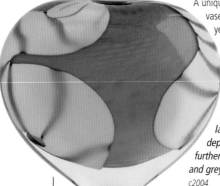

c2004   7.5in (19cm) high

£1,000-1,500   **GC**

A Peter Layton 'Forest Floor' stone form vase, the core with applied multi-coloured chips, and cased in colourless glass, the base signed 'Peter Layton'.

2006   7in (18cm) high

£300-400   **GC**

A Peter Layton 'Yellow Paradiso' large flattened bottle, the base signed 'Peter Layton'.

2006   11.25in (28.5cm) high

£1,000-1,500   **GC**

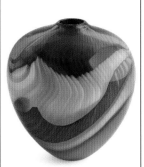

A Peter Layton 'Turquoise Paradiso' ovoid vase, the base signed 'Peter Layton'.

c2007   *6.5in (17.5cm) high*

£800-1,000   **GC**

A Peter Layton 'Aurora' ovoid vase, the base signed 'Peter Layton'.

c2005   *9.5in (24cm) high*

£300-500   **GC**

A Peter Layton 'Kimono' ovoid vase, with matte finish, the base signed 'Peter Layton'.

1989   *8in (20.5cm) high*

£400-600   **GC**

A Peter Layton 'Landscape' dropper bottle, the base signed 'Peter Layton'.

1995   *9in (23cm) high*

£250-350   **GC**

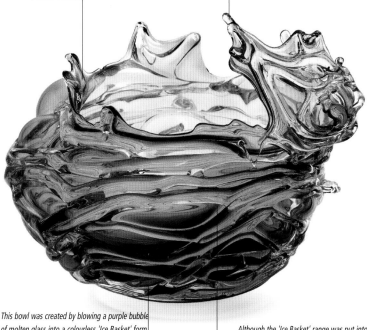

A CLOSER LOOK AT A PETER LAYTON BLOWN BASKET

This unique bowl is related to the 'Ice Basket' range, like the vase shown on the left, but colours were not used in the 'Ice Basket' range.

The random rim and trails on the body give a sense of great movement, and suggests water, or glass in a molten state.

This bowl was created by blowing a purple bubble of molten glass into a colourless 'Ice Basket' form, causing it to open up in a random manner.

Although the 'Ice Basket' range was put into production, these 'blown out' pieces were not – to date only three pieces are known.

A Peter Layton 'Ice Basket', the colourless glass cage form with acid-etched surface, the base signed 'Peter Layton'.

2003   *9in (23cm) high*

£600-800   **GC**

A Peter Layton 'Blown Basket', the purple core overlaid with colourless random trails, the base signed 'Peter Layton'.

2006   *7in (17.5cm) high*

£800-1,200   **GC**

GLASS

QUICK REFERENCE

- Studio glass is glass produced by individual glass artists working outside a factory environment. This became possible after Americans, Harvey Littleton and Dominick Labino developed a process in the early 1960s by which individuals could melt, form and blow glass. Artists could work alone, although many still chose to work in teams. The movement spread to Europe in the late 1960s-70s.
- As artists developed and shared skills, pieces became more complex and appealing. Glass began to be considered an art form and has developed into a vibrant movement, with major museums exhibiting studio glass by the 1980s.
- Be aware that with studio glass, date is not always a good indicator of value. Some early examples of styles are crude, although they do represent notable developments. Learning about key makers and styles helps with identification.
- Pieces by major names, such as Dale Chihuly and Marvin Lipofsky, already make high sums. However, works by those they taught, or those by lesser-known makers, are usually more affordable and may appreciate in value, as more people become aware of these artists and start collecting their work. Learn about your chosen artist's background, whom they studied with, and their style, to help you identify their work. Many pieces are signed but are often hard to read; others may be unsigned.
- Study how glass is made, so you can spot complex pieces, that would have been time-consuming to make and therefore expensive at the time. Such pieces may be rare today as fewer were made. Large pieces, and pieces by well-known makers may make good investments as more collectors are drawn to the area and demand rises.

A 1980s Iestyn Davies cased cylindrical vase, cut with windows containing Japanese symbols and with mottled black and white surface, applied gold and silver leaf and red trailed band, the base signed.

This heavy vase was complex to produce, and incorporates a number of hot and cold working steps including cutting and The application of gold and silver foil and hot red trails. The Japanese symbols are typical of 1980s and early 1990s fashions.

13.5in (34cm) high

£600-800   **GC**

A Glasform bowl, designed by John Ditchfield, no.1917, of compressed spherical form with a swirled tonal green to blue body, engraved to the base and with foil label.

5in (13cm) high

£150-250   **FLD**

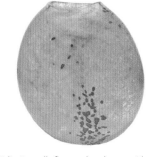

A Julia Donnelly flattened oval vase, with mottled surface of coloured chips, signed 'Julia Donnelly 1990'.

Julia Donnelly worked for Siddy Langley from 1987-2002 - pieces produced during this period are signed with her initials only.

1990   *6in (15cm) high*

£30-40   **TGM**

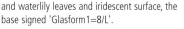

A Glasform 'Lily pad' pebble shaped vase, designed by John Ditchfield, with applied trails and waterlily leaves and iridescent surface, the base signed 'Glasform1=8/L'.

4.25in (11cm) high

£70-100   **GAZE**

A Carin von Druhle tall ovoid vase, the exterior with applied random trails and strong iridescence, the base signed 'Carin von Druhle 1990'.

1990   *7in (17.5cm) high*

£80-120   **TGM**

A Robert Eickholdt studio glass vase, the cobalt blue body overlaid with fragmented silver foil, cased in clear glass and then with a layer of fragmented gold foil and a final layer of colourless glass, the base signed 'Eickholdt 1996'.

1996   *10.25in (26cm) high*

£120-180   **TGM**

An Island Glass vase, with mottled blue and violet decoration, green trail and lobed rim, the base with impressed three lion pontil mark.

Island Glass was co-founded by Michael Harris in the early 1980s on the island of Guernsey in the Channel Islands. The mottled effects, and particularly the lobed rim, are style hallmarks.

6.75in (17cm) high

£25-30   **GC**

A CLOSER LOOK AT A SAM HERMAN VASE

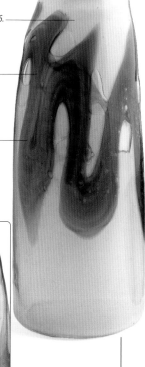

Sam Herman (b.1936) is considered by many to be the father of the British studio glass movement, introducing studio glass techniques to the UK in 1966.

This is a very early piece and was made at either the Royal College of Art in London, where Herman was tutor in glass, or at the newly founded Glasshouse.

This style of applied trailing is very similar to designs produced for Herman's exhibition at the Victoria & Albert Museum, London in 1971.

One side appears cracked, but this contains silver chloride and is completely fused, leaving just a line – it is likely that the piece cooled slightly when being made.

A Sam Herman studio glass vase, with applied purple trail and silver chloride decoration on a translucent white base, trapped air bubbles and colourless outer casing, the base inscribed 'Samuel J. Herman 1970'.

1970   *9.75in (24.5cm) high*

£300-400   **PC**

A Sam Herman for Val St. Lambert studio glass sculpture, with heavily cased wings, the base inscribed 'Val 212 Samuel Herman 1979'.

Herman worked at Val St Lambert over a number of years, becoming a consultant in 1990. Although he produced the designs, not all the pieces were produced by him.

1979   *15.75in (40cm) high*

£1,500-2,000   **GC**

A Sam Herman for Val St Lambert glass vase, of swollen cylindrical form with tapering shoulder, signed in script 'Samuel Herman 1979 VAL 88'.

1979   *12.25in (31cm) high*

£650-850   **L&T**

A 1970s Scottish Kirkhill Glass blue vase with random applied trails, designed and made by John Airlie, the base with broken pontil mark, unsigned.

5.5in (14cm) high

£40-60   **GC**

An Isgard Moje glass arm ring, with diagonal light blue stripes and painted with horizontal coloured bands, the rims gilded.

c1975   *2in (5cm) deep*

£300-500   **QU**

An Okra Glass iridised vase, with pulled feather pattern, the base inscribed 'Okra GLASS GUILD FOUNDER MEMBER 1997/1998 No.847'.

These vases were given by Okra Glass to founder members of the Guild collectors' club in 1997 and '98.

1997   *4.5in (11.5cm) high*

£70-100   **TGM**

A Pauline Solven glass vase, with mottled pink and green pattern, signed and dated.

Pauline Solven was part of the first wave of studio glassmakers, studying at the Royal College of Art under Michael Harris and Sam Herman. She continues to blow glass today.

1980   *6in (15cm) high*

£100-150   **SAS**

An Anthony Stern ovoid vase, the red body with an applied white stripe cased in colourless glass, the base signed 'Anthony Stern'.

c2000   *7.25in (18.5cm) high*

£70-100   **TGM**

An Anthony Stern studio glass bowl, the colourless bowl with an iridised exterior, the applied black foot signed 'Anthony Stern'.

3in (7.5cm) high

£20-30   **TGM**

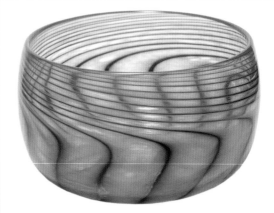

An Anthony Stern studio glass bowl, the mottled translucent blue body with wide, then tight reversed spiralling design, the base signed 'Anthony Stern'.

6in (15cm) high

£50-70   **TGM**

QUICK REFERENCE - WEBB'S FLAIR RANGE

Long established Stourbridge glassmakers such as Webb (est.1802) approached post-war modern design cautiously, preferring to stick with trusted cut designs. During the late 1950s, works manager Sven Fogelburg encouraged designers to travel to the innovative Scandinavian factories, whose work was becoming increasingly popular. Following a visit in 1959, designer David Hammond and technician Stanley Eveson began to produce sculptural forms by shaping molten glass with wet pads and piercing them with a metal spike to create an aperture. Pieces were also swung and spun while molten to give dramatic winged and lobed forms. Bubbles were added using a mould, and colours cased in colourless glass. The progressive resultant 'Flair' range was produced in limited numbers and can be hard to find today, particularly in large sizes.

A 1960s Thomas Webb large 'Flair' vase, designed by David Hammond and Stan Eveson in 1961, with yellow rim and amber base with controlled internal air bubbles.

13in (33cm) high

£120-150   GC

A Thomas Webb 'Flair' cased blue oval bowl with swungout rim, the base with internal controlled air bubbles, designed by David Hammond and Stanley Eveson in 1961.

13in (33cm) wide

£80-120   GC

A 1930s Webb vase, with moulded lobes, internal green swirls and air bubbles, the base with broken pontil mark.

8in (20.5cm) high

£50-70   GC

A Thomas Webb 'Flair' cased blue tall vase, with swungout rim, the base with internal controlled air bubbles, designed by David Hammond and Stanley Eveson in 1961.

6in (15cm) high

£80-100   GC

A 1960s Thomas Webb 'Flair' small vase, designed by David Hammond and Stanley Eveson in 1961, with swung rim and green base with internal bubbles.

8in (20.5cm) high

£60-80   GC

A Thomas Webb Domino pattern cut glass vase, with alternating acid-etched frosted and clear panels, designed by David Hammond, the base with acid stamp.

10in (25.5cm) high

£200-250   GC

QUICK REFERENCE

- Whitefriars glass has become a sought-after name in 20th century glass design on both sides of the Atlantic over the past few years. The most popular and desirable range is currently the 'Textured' range, designed by Geoffrey Baxter in 1966 and produced into the 1970s. Royal College of Art graduate Baxter, who joined the company in 1954 as designer, also contributed many other designs, many of which were inspired by Scandinavian designs.

- The company was founded in 1680, in London. It was originally called Powell & Sons, but as it was founded on the site of a monastery, it was more commonly known as Whitefriars. In 1923, the company moved to Wealdstone, Harrow, in North-west London, and in 1962, it took on the Whitefriars name officially. The company closed in 1980 due to competition from abroad.

- During the late 19thC, it produced glass in the Art Nouveau style, and glass inspired by Venetian designs. Although collected, these finely crafted designs are not currently as popular with collectors. During the 1920s and '30s, it produced fashionable art glass, some in the Art Deco style. Interest in this area has remained stable, although bargains may be found as many overlook this period.

- Consider the form, colour and size of pieces, as these factors affect value considerably. Some colours and shapes, and combinations of them, are rare. For example, the value of an iconic 'Drunken Bricklayer' can nearly double for a large example in an unusual colour such as Meadow Green or Kingfisher.

- With the textured range, look for crisp moulded details as moulds wore down over time, leaving lower levels of texture. As demand and prices have risen, fakes have begun to appear. Three of these, along with guidance on how to identify them are shown on page 260. Whitefriars enjoys a lively and stable market, particularly on the internet, and looks set to remain a collector's favourite in years to come as research uncovers more information.

A Whitefriars cased green 'Teardrop' vase, no.9572, designed by Geoffrey Baxter in 1966.

5.5in (14cm) high

£20-30   RET

A Whitefriars tall cased green 'Teardrop' vase, no.9571, designed by Geoffrey Baxter in 1966.

8in (20.5cm) high

£30-40   RET

A Whitefriars cased Ruby red 'Teardrop' vase, no.9572, designed by Geoffrey Baxter in 1966.

5.5in (14cm) high

£20-30   RET

A Whitefriars Willow cased glass vase, designed by Geoffrey Baxter. in 1965.

9.75in (25cm) high

£150-250   WW

A Whitefriars Cinnamon cased vase, no.9651, designed by Geoffrey Baxter in 1965.

An elongated version of this form, produced at the same time, and seen on the next page, was created by swinging the molten glass and using gravity to elongate it. In this colourway, it is no. 9650.

1965-69   *9.5in 24.5cm) high*

£200-250   GC

A CLOSER LOOK AT A WHITEFRIARS VASE

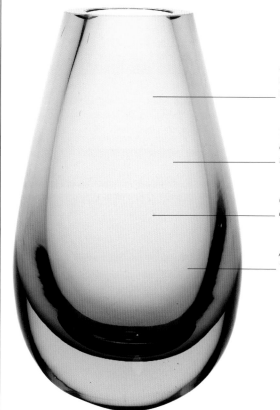

Look closely at the base – this vase is made from two contrasting colours of glass, rather than the usual single colour.

The green and blue glasses used were not compatible in the furnace, meaning examples tended to crack into pieces after manufacture.

Only around five successful examples are currently known to collectors.

Another variation was the blue and pink cased 'Evening Sky', which is similarly very rare.

A Whitefriars Willow 'Swungout' vase, no.9650, designed by Geoffrey Baxter in 1965.

This is the elongated version of the shape shown in Cinnamon on the previous page.

c1966   15.75in (40cm) high

£500-600   GC

A very rare Whitefriars Aquamarine double colour cased vase, designed by Geoffrey Baxter in 1957.

3.75in (9.5cm) high

£700-800   GC

A Whitefriars Arctic Blue glass vase with cut and polished rim, no.9557, the design attributed to Geoffrey Baxter c1956.

c1957-60   6in (15.5cm) high

£25-35   GC

A Whitefriars cased Indigo blue tapering oval section ovoid vase, designed by Geoffrey Baxter in 1961.

9.75in (24.5cm) high

£50-60   GC

A very rare Whitefriars 'Lichen' cased vase, designed by Geoffrey Baxter.

Lichen is a rare combination of pewter and green, and was only available in 1970.

c1970   6.75in (17cm) high

£200-300   GC

A Whitefriars Arctic Blue ovoid vase, no.9495, by Geoffrey Baxter in 1957, cut rim, polished pontil.

The design features in the 1957 catalogue but Arctic Blue was introduced in 1959.

8in (20.5cm) high

£30-50   M20C

GLASS

QUICK REFERENCE - FAKES

Over the past few years, as prices for Whitefriars' Textured range have risen, a number of fakes, produced in the Far East or Eastern Europe, have appeared. The iconic 'Drunken Bricklayer' was the first, but others from the range are now being made. These fakes can be identified from a number of features that differ from those on authentic examples. These features comprise colour, texture, the pontil mark, and the general feel and appearance. The glass used for most fakes has an almost waxy feel, and the colourless casing is different, not being as well balanced or executed as on authentic examples. The next page features authentic examples of the 'Drunken Bricklayer' and 'Hoop' vases.

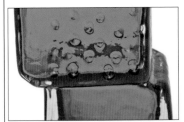

The colours are wrong – colours of fakes currently comprise red, green, cobalt blue and a strong amber. In cases where Whitefriars used these colours, the fakes are the wrong tone.

There is a moulded long, shallow trench on the top of the bottom brick – this does not appear on originals.

The middle brick has more dimples (28) than authentic examples, and they are also in a different formation.

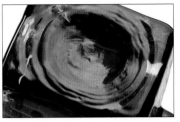

The concave pontil mark is a part of the moulded design, rather than being polished out by a machine as with authentic examples.

A modern fake Whitefriars cased Ruby red 'Drunken Bricklayer' vase, copied from pattern no.9673 designed by Geoffrey Baxter in 1966.

c2008   *8.25in (21cm) high*

£15-20   **GC**

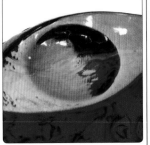

A fake Whitefriars cased red 'Onion' vase, copied from pattern no.9758 designed by Geoffrey Baxter in 1972.

This vase was not originally produced in this colour, the polished pontil mark is a part of the moulded design, and the textured design is smoother and less detailed than on originals.

c2008   *5.5in (14cm) high*

£8-12   **GC**

A fake Whitefriars cased Ruby red 'Hoop' vase, copied from pattern no.9680, designed by Geoffrey Baxter in 1966.

Of all the identified Whitefriars fakes, this is the perhaps the easiest to spot as the textured pattern is completely different to the original. The red tone is also wrong, and this shape was never made in red.

12in (30.5cm) high

£20-30   **GC**

A Whitefriars Willow 'Totem' vase, no.9671 from the 'Textured' range designed by Geoffrey Baxter in 1966.
1967-72   10.25in (26cm) high
£120-180   **FLD**

A Whitefriars Willow 'Cucumber' vase, no.9679 from the 'Textured' range designed by Geoffrey Baxter in 1967.
1967-73   12in (30.5cm) high
£120-180   **RET**

A Whitefriars Tangerine 'Hoop' vase, no.9680 from the 'Textured' range designed by Geoffrey Baxter in 1966.

1967-73 11.5in (29.5cm) high
£200-250   **WW**

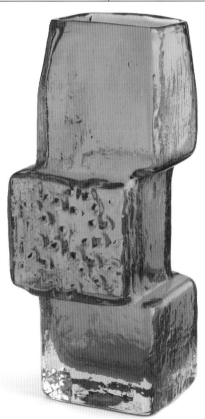

A Whitefriars Tangerine 'Drunken Bricklayer' vase, no.9672 from the 'Textured' range designed by Geoffrey Baxter in 1966.
1967-74   8.25in (21cm) high
£200-300   **WW**

A Whitefriars cased Cinnamon brown 'Bark' vase, pattern no.9691 from the 'Textured' range designed by Geoffrey Baxter in 1966.
1966-69   7.75in (18.5cm) high
£60-80   **M20C**

A Whitefriars cased Kingfisher blue 'Bottle' vase, pattern no. 9730 from the 'Textured' range, designed by Geoffrey Baxter in 1969.
1969-72   8in (20.5cm) high
£50-70   **M20C**

A Whitefriars Aubergine 'Stitched Square' vase, no.9811, from the 'Late Textured' range, designed by Geoffrey Baxter in 1972.

6in (15cm) high
£120-160   **GC**

GLASS

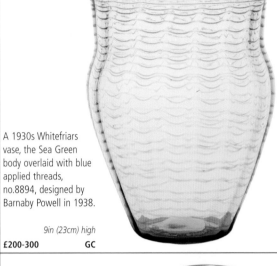

A Whitefriars Sea Green vase with applied band of swags, pattern no.9004, designed by William Wilson in 1938, the base with broken pontil mark.

7.25in (18.5cm) high

£60-80   **GC**

A late 1920s-30s Whitefriars green and blue 'Cloudy' glass vase, no.8608, with white and air bubble inclusions, cased in clear glass.

9in (23cm) high

£280-320   **WW**

A 1930s Whitefriars vase, the Sea Green body overlaid with blue applied threads, no.8894, designed by Barnaby Powell in 1938.

9in (23cm) high

£200-300   **GC**

A Whitefriars Ruby red three-cornered bowl, no.9588 designed by Geoffrey Baxter.

1964-70   9.5in (24cm) widest

£35-50   **RET**

An extremely rare Whitefriars Ruby red eight-lobed 'Tricorn' vase, no.9570 designed by Geoffrey Baxter in 1961.

As its name suggests, these vases usually have three lobes. Only one or two examples with more than three lobes have been found, and were probably prototypes.

A Whitefriars flared vase, with a Tangerine swirl applied on a Pewter grey body, no.9708 designed by Geoffrey Baxter in 1969.

1969-71   8in (20.5cm) high

£50-70   **MHC**

A Whitefriars 'Antique' baluster vase, with blue, brown and purple random streaks, no.9784, designed by Geoffrey Baxter.

c1972   7in (18cm) high

£80-120   **GC**

FIND OUT MORE...

Lesley Jackson, Whitefriars Glass: Art of James Powell & Sons *Richard Dennis, 1996*

Wendy Evan, Catherine Ross and Alex Werner, Whitefriars Glass: *James Powell & Sons of London, Art Books International, 1996*

1962-78   8in (20.5cm) high

£80-100   **GC**

An Anchor Hocking Forest Green 'Shell' Depression glass dish.

7in (17.5cm) wide

£3-5   AEM

An Imperial 'Heavy Grape' pattern purple or amethyst Carnival glass bowl.

4.5in (11.5cm) diam

£12-18   AEM

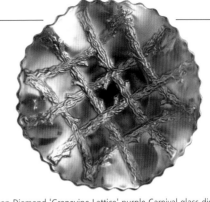

A Dugan-Diamond 'Grapevine Lattice' purple Carnival glass dish.

7in (17.5cm) diam

£60-100   BH

A Northwood 'Singing Birds' pattern marigold Carnival glass mug.

3.75in (9.5cm) high

£20-40   AEM

A set of six amorphous glass bottles, screen-printed with Surrealist designs after Salvador Dali, each with facsimile 'Dali' signature.

Tallest 13.5in (34cm) high

£100-150   WW

A rare Davidson orange cloud glass powder jar.

Red is even rarer and more valuable.

1933-35   *5.5in (14cm) high*

£80-120   BAD

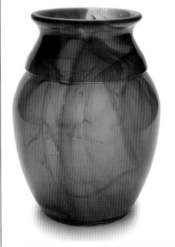

An unusual Davidson brown cloud glass ovoid vase, pattern no.34 SVG.

This shape is comparatively hard to find.

1934-41   *7.5in (19cm) h*

£70-100   BAD

A Duncan Miller 'Sandwich' pattern Crystal Depression glass 9oz (255g) goblet.

Note the difference in the design to Anchor Hocking's version. Coloured examples by Duncan Miller are harder to find than colourless 'Crystal'.

1924-55   6in (15cm) high

£7-12   AEM

A CLOSER LOOK AT A HARTLEY WOOD VASE

Hartley Wood was founded in 1837 in Sunderland, and produced 'crown' window and other similar types of glass. It produced limited quantities of decorative wares from the 1930s onwards.

The bright colours that had been used for the company's stained glass windows were emulated. The larger or more colours a piece has, the more desirable it will be.

Known as 'Antique Glass', each piece is unique as it was handmade, charming, slightly off-centre and uneven forms are typical.

Earlier pieces from the 1930s have an oily feel to the thickly blown glass, later pieces are thinner and lighter in weight, and were often blown into moulds so are more regular in form.

A 1930s Hartley Wood hollow-footed 'Antique Glass' vase with flared rim, and random green, yellow, blue, purple and red swirling pattern, the base with broken pontil mark.

8in (20cm) high

£80-120   GC

A Fenton hand painted pink graduated vase, the base with a square Fenton label and signed 'handpainted by A Findlay' and 'W.C. Fenton'.

5.75in (14.5cm) high

£50-80   TSIS

A Fenton Topaz 'Coin Dot' ruffled vase, shape no.1441.

Made for only a short period of time, Topaz Coin Dot is hotly sought after.

1959-61   7in (17.5cm) high

£50-80   TSIS

A 1990s Gozo Glass 'Sea Collection' perfume bottle, with deep internal pulled swirls, inscribed "Gozo Glass" on the base.

5.25in (13cm) high

£28-32   TGM

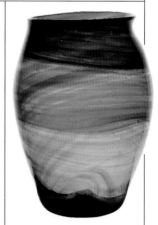

A 1930s Hartley Wood 'Antique Glass' vase, with random green, yellow and orange swirling pattern, the base with broken pontil mark.

9.5in (24cm) high

£100-150   GC

A very rare Stevens & Williams (Royal Brierley) two colour, lens-cut 'Rainbow' vase, pattern no.68307.

This scarce range was only produced for a few years from 1938 due to the onset of war. Most examples bear cut features, with the lenses here adding an interesting optical effect.

c1939 *10in (25.5cm) high*

£800-1,200 **GC**

A 1930s Stevens & Williams (Royal Brierley) pink glass vase with random internal bubbles, designed by Keith Murray, on an applied colourless pad foot.

Known as 'Cased Bubbly', pink and blue were the first colours to be produced in this scarce range, and were followed by amethyst and green. Some pieces bear acid etched marks with Murray's name.

c1938-39 *8.5in (22cm) high*

£300-400 **GC**

A CLOSER LOOK AT A STEVENS & WILLIAMS VASE

The bubbly, mottled design follows the 1930s fashion for bubbly glass, such as that produced by Monart, Graystan and Walsh Walsh.

The surface is rough to the touch, and may have been treated with chemicals or coloured enamels to further the 'ancient' feel.

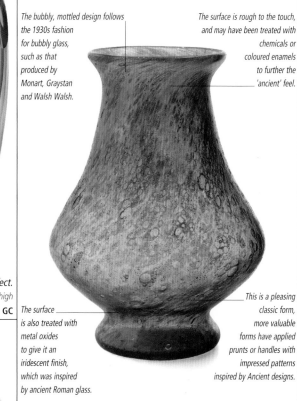

The surface is also treated with metal oxides to give it an iridescent finish, which was inspired by ancient Roman glass.

This is a pleasing classic form, more valuable forms have applied prunts or handles with impressed patterns inspired by Ancient designs.

A 1930s Stevens & Williams 'Caerleon' range baluster vase, with random internal air bubbles, blue and yellow powdered enamel mottled design and iridescent surface, the base with broken pontil mark.

8in (20.5cm) high

£200-250 **GC**

A Strathearn cylindrical vase sand-blasted and vibropen etched with a fisherman and net, the base signed in vibropen 'STRATHEARN 1978'.

1978 *7.75in (19.5cm) high*

£70-100 **GC**

A 1980s Stuart 'Dark Crystal' rectangular vase, designed by Iestyn Davis, with mottled red textured surface and machine-cut rim.

3.75in (9.5cm) high

£20-30 **MHC**

A 1980s Stuart 'Dark Crystal' baluster vase, designed by Iestyn Davis, with mottled red textured surface and machine-cut rim.

Introduced in 1982 along with 'Ebony & Gold', Dark Crystal is much harder to find today. Both ranges were only produced for a few years, and Dark Crystal appears to have sold in much lower quantities at the time.

5.25in (13.5cm) high

£40-60 **GC**

GLASS

A 1980s Stuart Strathearn 'Ebony & Gold' baluster vase, shape no.SS001.

The horizontal scratch in the gold leaf was probably created when the gold leaf was being applied and smoothed onto the surface. Note the similarity between Michael Harris' Azurene and this short-lived range by Iestyn Davies. These are entirely mould blown, so light in weight. Such large sizes are hard to find.

9.25in (23.5cm) high

£70-100　　　　**PC**

A 1970s Wedgwood Glass purple 'Sheringham' glass candleholder, with three discs, shape no.RSW13 designed by Ronald Stennett-Willson in 1967 for King's Lynn Glass.

6.25in (16cm) high

£35-40　　　　**SAS**

A CLOSER LOOK AT A BUBBLY GLASS VASE

Bubbly glass was fashionable during the 1930s, with many makers producing it, often with a 'waxy feel' and an unfinished pontil mark. As there were several producers, identification can be hard.

The shape and colour hint at Walsh Walsh's 'Pompeiian' range, released in 1929 as an inexpensive art glass range – if so, its value would be around £80-120.

Under ultraviolet light, the yellow glass glows bright green, showing that it is 'uranium' glass – this is unusual for Walsh Walsh.

The pontil mark on the base is polished and finished off well, which is typical of Walsh Walsh's high quality production, but it does not bear their acid etched mark.

A 1930s uranium glass spherical vase, probably by Walsh Walsh, with random pattern of integral bubbles of different sizes, the base with polished concave pontil mark.

6in (15cm) high

£40-60　　　　**PC**

A German Vereinigte Lausitzer Glaswerke grey-blue ovoid footed vase, designed by Wilhelm Wagenfeld, with oval cut lenses designed by Erich Jachmann.

Jachmann (b.1925) also later produced cut and optic-blown designs for WMF. Bauhaus designer Wagenfeld worked as Art Director for VLG from 1935-47.

c1950　　　　*6.25in (16cm) high*

£300-400　　　　**VZ**

A late 1970s Wedgwood Glass purple moulded textured bowl, no.RSW267, designed by Ronald Stennett-Willson in 1975.

6.75in (17cm) diam

£50-60　　　　**RET**

A Wedgwood Glass colourless glass squirrel, shape no.SG410, the base with factory acid stamp.

4in (10cm) high

£22-28　　　　**TGM**

An American pressed and flashed ruby souvenir glass creamer, etched 'Gettysburg 1863'.

4in (10cm) high

£20-30   BH

An American pressed and flashed ruby souvenir glass small mug or handled toothpick holder, etched 'Atlantic City Edna Heck'.

2.5in (6cm) high

£20-40   BH

A 19thC Bohemian ruby flashed tankard, with a slice cut body, loop handle and thumb lift cover, cut and engraved with deer in a wooded landscape.

7in (18cm) high

£100-150   FLD

A 19thC Stourbridge crystal oil lamp, with a wide fluted ruby base rising to a wrythen fluted column with applied crystal trim below a ruby cased and flash cut paraffin reservoir fitted with a 'Messengers Patent' fitment.

16.25in (41cm) high

£180-220   FLD

A late 19thC Stourbridge crystal water jug, of footed ovoid form, collar neck, loop handle decorated with a cranberry threading over clear crystal ground, with a matched wine goblet.

£180-220   FLD

A mid-20thC art glass vase, of tumbler form with a mottled and fissured air bubble ground, in tonal pink over clear.

9.5in (24cm) high

£50-80   FLD

A great place for everyone to visit...

HEMSWELL ANTIQUE CENTRES

Europe's largest choice of antiques & collectables is just a few clicks away...

Why not check out our extensive selection online or visit our centres, which include over 300 dealers in 3 buildings. With the largest choice of antiques and collectables in Europe, we have something of interest for everyone...

Period Furniture ❖ Clocks ❖ Prints
Pine Furniture ❖ Mirrors ❖ Books
Lighting ❖ Linen & Lace ❖ Silver
Fireplaces ❖ Pictures ❖ Jewellery
Ceramics ❖ French Beds
Paintings ❖ Collectables
Architectural Objects

We have ample car parking and a licensed coffee shop and we are open 7 days a week throughout the year. You will easily find us only 10 miles north of Lincoln on the A631.

T: 01427 668389
E: enquiries@hemswell-antiques.com

www.hemswell-antiques.com

GLASS

A green beeer bottle, Brown & Plummer, Swindon.

8in (20.5cm) high.

£2-5   BS

A green half pint beer bottle, Marchants, Reading.

8in (20.5cm) high.

£2-5   BS

A late Georgian blue spirit bottle, Bristol, with wheel engraving 'Speed of the Plough', dedicated to M. Dickson Aug 1832.

11in (28cm) high

£200-250   AG

A Ye Olde Fulham Pottery stoneware bottle, with original top.

9in (23cm) high.

£50-60   BS

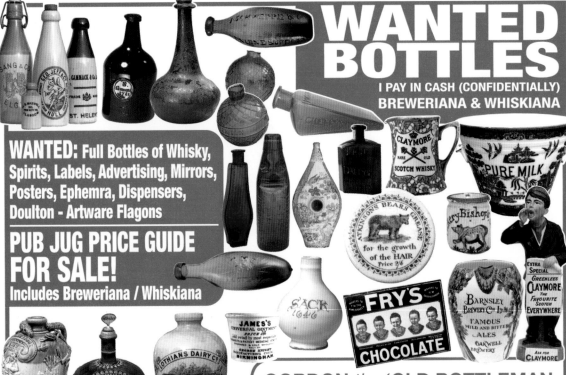

WANTED BOTTLES
I PAY IN CASH (CONFIDENTIALLY)
BREWERIANA & WHISKIANA

WANTED: Full Bottles of Whisky, Spirits, Labels, Advertising, Mirrors, Posters, Ephemra, Dispensers, Doulton - Artware Flagons

PUB JUG PRICE GUIDE FOR SALE!
Includes Breweriana / Whiskiana

GORDON *the* 'OLD BOTTLEMAN
25 Stapenhill Road • Burton-on-Trent • DE15 9AE
Tel: 01283•567•213 • Mobile: 07952•118•987

QUICK REFERENCE

- Though the Inuit art heritage goes back to the Athabascan and Thule cultures of 10thC Alaska and Northern Canada, most collectable Inuit art dates from the 1950s onwards. It first came to prominence in 1949 after James Houston, a young Canadian artist, visited the Canadian Arctic with the intention of finding out whether the native art was appealing and could be sold. Creation and trade became increasingly organised in the 1950s and 1960s. Interest has subsequently grown across the world, with the market seeing rapid development in the last 25 years.
- Most works are sculptural and created from the native soft yet durable soapstone. Soapstone ranges in colour from deep grey through to green and can be polished to a high shine, earning it a reputation as 'Canadian jade'. Drawings, textiles and prints are also collected. Subjects include scenes from Inuit daily life as well as myths, Shamanism and abstract ideas. Well-executed, stylised or even abstract designs, particularly those displaying wit or humour, find the most favour with collectors. Polar bears, real and mythical creatures and 'transformation' sculptures are also desirable.
- Influential artists such as John Pangnark, Osuitok Ipeelee, Pauta Saila, Jessie Oonark and Judas Ullulaq are the most collectable. A large proportion of the most valuable pieces were made by these artists, many of whom are now dead. The growing popularity of Inuit art has resulted in many pieces of average or poor quality coming onto the market. Of the many contemporary artists working today, only a few will come to be considered masters of the form. Research artists and market trends in reference books, or visit dealers and auction to inspect desirable examples yourself.
- Many pieces are signed on the bottom with syllabics (the Inuit form of verbal lettering), or with a disc number beginning with an E or W, which can be used to identify the artist by consulting an online reference guide. Look out for the Canadian government sticker on more contemporary Inuit pieces.

A stone 'Embracing Mother, Child and Bird' figure, by Kenojuak Ashevak, E7-1035, from Cape Dorset.

9.75in (25cm) high

£4,500-5,500 WAD

A stone 'Mother Holding Children' group, by Miaiji Uitangi Usaitaijuk (1911-1965), E9-1174, from Salluit, signed in syllabics with disc number.

c1950 *6in (15cm) wide*

£2,200-2,800 WAD

A stone 'Mother and Child' figure, by Mannumi Shaqu, E7-824, from Cape Dorset.

Shaqu (1917-2000) is considered an early master of Cape Dorset sculpture. An example of his work is owned by HM The Queen, and has appeared on a postage stamp. His work has also been included in a large number of exhibitions in Canada, the UK and the US.

c1970 *12in (30.5cm) high*

£5,000-7,000 WAD

A stone 'Mother and Child' figure, by an unidentified artist, from Cape Dorset.

This early sculpture was acquired by Sir Norman Hartnell, the Queen's dressmaker, during one of his visits to Canada in the 1950s.

c1955 *9.5in (24cm) high*

£5,000-7,000 WAD

INUIT ART

QUICK REFERENCE – WHALEBONE

As well as various forms of soapstone, Inuit artists used materials found in the environment, such as this section of whale vertebra which has been cleverly used to form a body and arms. Bone is usually found in distressed condition, having been exposed to the weather and elements. It has been used for centuries by Inuit and pre-Inuit communities such as the Thule. Apart from considering the style and subject matter, dating a piece such as this is usually impossible. Also most are not signed by the sculptor. Collectors should find out about the import and export regulations that apply to this material before buying or selling.

A stone figure of a drummer, by Adamie Alariaq, (1930-1990), E7-1090, from Cape Dorset, signed in Roman.

16in (40.5cm) high

£450-550   **WAD**

A carved weathered bone 'Drum Dancer', the front and back with inset ivory discs carved with faces, and holding a carved bone drum and beater, by Hank Napuwatuk from Alaska.

3.5in (9cm) high

£300-400   **THG**

A carved whalebone bone 'Drum Dancer' figure, by an unidentified artist.

c1970   *20in (51cm) high*

£3,000-4,000   **WAD**

A stone and ivory 'Articulated Fisherman' figure, by Charlie Ugyuk, E4-341, from Spence Bay, signed in Roman.

Charlie Ugyuk (1931-1998) was the uncle of top-rated Inuit sculptor Karoo Ashevak. Typical of the Taloyoak (Spence Bay) style, this particular work is detailed and highly expressive, particularly the face. Ugyuk's work can be found in many private and public collections across the world.

18in (45.5cm) high

£15,000-25,000   **WAD**

A dark soapstone figure, by Annie Okalik (b.1927), E1350, from Arviat, with a multicoloured beaded coat.

4in (11cm) high

£400-500   **WAD**

A stone, sinew, antler and ivory figure of a shaman, by Judas Ullulaq, (1937-1998), E4-342, from Gjoa Haven.

The depiction of a mystical figure, the grotesque appearance and the use of inset bone or ivory teeth and eyes are all typical of Ullulaq, whose work is highly sought after.

c1980   7in (18cm) high

£3,000-5,000   **WAD**

A stone and antler 'Shaman' figure, by Josiah Nuilaalik (1928-2005), E2-385, from Baker Lake, signed in syllabics.

15in (38cm) high

£4,500-5,500   **WAD**

A stone 'Shaman Posing' figure, by Davie Atchealak (1947-2006), E7-1182, from Iqaluit, signed in Roman.

12.5in (32cm) high

£4,000-5,000   **WAD**

A soapstone 'Shaman/Bird' figure, by Elizabeth Tunnuq (b.1928), E-2133, from Baker Lake.

c1968   7in (18cm) high

£1,500-2,500   **WAD**

A stone figure of Tupilak, from Cape Dan, unsigned and by an unknown artist.

A Tupilak is a mystical and gruesome 'doll' made from materials such as human hair, animal parts, and even parts of a dead child's body. Once carved, magic spells were chanted and the figure was imbued with power from its creator's sexual organs. The Tupilak was then cast into the sea to seek and destroy an enemy. However, if the enemy had greater powers than those of the person who created it, the Tupilak was reversed and could destroy its creator. As original Tupilaks were destroyed or lost, reproductions made for sale were carved in bone, horn or stone.

c1971   6.5in (16.5cm) high

£1,500-2,000   **WAD**

A CLOSER LOOK AT A JOHN PANGNARK FIGURE

Pangnark is known for his highly abstract forms that resemble hills or rocky outcrops, and have a monumental feel despite their small size.

Most are inscribed or carved with simple lines to form basic facial features.

The subject matter of a shaman transformation figure is very unusual for Pangnark, which adds value to this piece.

The Inuit believed that shamen gained many of their mystical powers from an animal 'familiar' (here it is a seal), which they could transform into at will.

A stone seal/shaman transformation figure, by John Pangnark, (1920-1980), E1-104, from Arviat.

7.5in (19cm) high

£12,000-15,000   **WAD**

An untitled coloured pencil drawing, by Luke Anguhadluq (1895-1982), signed in syllabics.

30in (75cm) wide

£400-500   **WAD**

A 'Sentient Owl' stonecut by Kenojuak Ashevak, (b.1927), E7-1035, from Cape Dorset.

1970   *33.5in (85cm) wide*

£1,000-1,500   **WAD**

A 'Loon Protects The Owl', limited edition stonecut, by Kenoujak Ashevak (b.1927), E7-1035, numbered 6 from an edition of 100, from Cape Dorset.

2002   *31in (78.5cm) wide*

£1,000-1,500   **WAD**

An untitled coloured pencil drawing by Luke Anguhadluq (1895-1982), signed in syllabics.

26in (66cm) high

£1,000-1,500   **WAD**

A limited edition 'Eskimo Boat in Ice' woodcut print, by James Houston (1921-2005), from Baffin Island, from an edition of 30, framed.

Artist James Houston 'discovered' Inuit art, and brought it to the world' s attention during the 1950s.

14.5in (37cm) wide

£700-1,000   **WAD**

An 'Angagok Conjuring Birds' stencil print, by Jessie Oonark (1906-1985), E2-384, from Baker Lake, from a limited edition of 45.

30in (76cm) high

£1,500-2,000   **WAD**

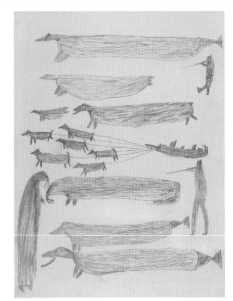

A graphite drawing, by Parr (1893-1969), E7-1022, from Cape Dorset, marked 'June 1961'.

1961   *24in (61cm) high*

£5,000-7,000   **WAD**

QUICK REFERENCE

- 'Casino Royale', the first novel to feature Ian Fleming's super spy James Bond, was first published in 1953. Fewer than 5,000 'true first editions' (first print run of the first edition) of the novel were printed and many went to libraries, leaving them in poor condition. This means good condition copies of this book are rare and sought after.
- In general, true firsts are most desirable, however, the first batch of Fleming's fifth Bond novel, 'From Russia, With Love' was sent to a book club due to their poor quality. The effective second printing (marked Cape) is therefore considered the true first edition. 'From Russia, With Love' is widely considered not only Fleming's best book but also the best film adaptation, and good condition copies are extremely sought after and valuable. A copy signed by Fleming, especially one dedicated to a close friend or colleague, will be particularly desirable. Other Bond authors, such as John Gardner who revived the Bond series in 1981, are also collectable.

- EON Productions were granted the film adaptation rights for all the Bond novels in the 1950s (except 'Casino Royale', which was only granted in the 1990s). The first adaptation, 'Dr. No', was released in 1962 and featured Sean Connery as Bond. The film launched Bond as a global phenomenon. Connery was followed in the role by George Lazenby (1969), Roger Moore (1973-1985), Timothy Dalton (1987-1989), Pierce Brosnan (1995-2000) and Daniel Craig (2006-). In general, merchandise from the immensely popular Sean Connery era is most desirable.
- James Bond's many cars and gadgets have been made into toys by a wide variety of manufacturers. Iconic cars, such as the Aston Martin, are likely to be most desirable. Condition is important, with mint condition examples usually commanding the highest prices. Models should also ideally be accompanied by their original boxes, which should also be in good condition. Always look for licensed products by known makers, although some unlicensed toys can be rare.

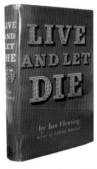

Ian Fleming, 'Live and Let Die', first edition of 7,500 copies, first impression, with original boards, first state dust jacket, price-clipped and slightly rubbed at corners.
1954
£5,000-7,000 BLO

Ian Fleming, 'From Russia, With Love', first edition of 15,000 copies, with original boards, dust jacket with small tear to head of spine, otherwise a very good copy.
1957
£1,200-1,800 BLO

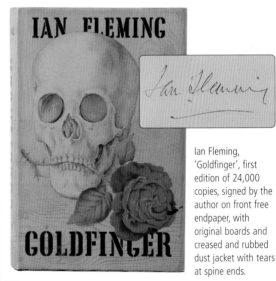

Ian Fleming, 'Goldfinger', first edition of 24,000 copies, signed by the author on front free endpaper, with original boards and creased and rubbed dust jacket with tears at spine ends.
1959
£3,500-4,500 BLO

Ian Fleming, 'Moonraker', first edition, first impression, with original boards and price-clipped dust jacket, with some browning, rubbed at edges, and spine slightly dulled.

The first print run comprised 9,900 copies. The word 'shoot' on p.10 is sometimes misspelt 'shoo' in the first edition. In general, the correct spelling (in this example) is preferred.
1955
£1,500-2,000 BLO

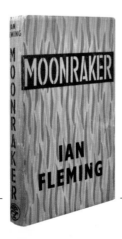

Ian Fleming, 'Dr No', first edition of 20,000 copies, first impression, with small contemporary ink name on front free endpaper, original plain first state boards, dust jacket, rubbed at corner tips and spine ends.
1958
£800-1,200 BLO

JAMES BOND

Ian Fleming, 'Goldfinger' paperback, published by Pan Books Ltd., a reprint with the same cover as the first paperback edition.
1962

£7-10   **PC**

Ian Fleming, 'On Her Majesty's Secret Service', first edition, numbered 151 from a limited edition of 250 copies signed by the author, with colour portrait by Amherst Villiers, original vellum-backed black buckram boards and original glassine plastic jacket.
1963

£3,800-4,800   **BLO**

A CLOSER LOOK AT A JAMES BOND FIRST EDITION

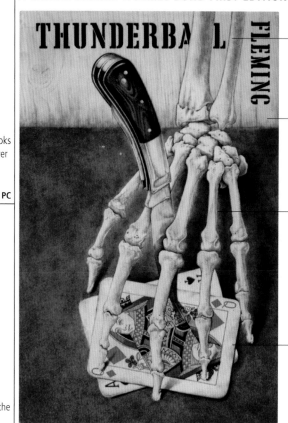

Thunderball was the ninth Bond book, and was written with the intention of being turned into a film, making it the first novelisation of a Bond screenplay.

The cover design was by illustrator and artist Richard Chopping (1917-2008) who produced a number of cover designs for Bond books, typically in a trompe l'oeil style.

Fleming's signature automatically adds value, but the witty and Secret Intelligence Service (MI6) related inscription adds even more interest and value.

More importantly, 'Jack' may be Jack Whittingham, who worked with Fleming on the initial screenplay for the film, before a legal case erupted, making this an important dedication.

Ian Fleming, 'Thunderball', first edition of 50,398 copies, near full-page inscription from the author on front free endpaper that reads 'To Jack, By appointment, M.O. to the SIS!, Ian', original boards, dust jacket, slightly rubbed at tips of corners.
1961

£8,000-12,000   **BLO**

Ian Fleming, 'You Only Live Twice', first edition, signed and dedicated 'To Julie...' on the front free endpaper, minor spotting to extreme edges, with original boards and dust jacket, in excellent condition.

Julie was the lady who hand-rolled Fleming's cigarettes – dedications connected with Fleming's life or work are sought after. Although Bond smokes rarely on screen, the character in the novels was a heavy smoker, puffing his way through some 60 cigarettes a day.
1964

£3,500-4,500   **BLO**

A 'The James Bond Annual', including pictures from 'Goldfinger' and 'You Only Live Twice', and with Sean Connery cover.
1968   *10.75in (27cm) high*

£20-30   **PC**

Peter Haining, 'James Bond: A Celebration', published by Planet, page 187 with a dedication and Desmond Llewelyn (Q) signature.
1987   *10.75in (27cm) high*

£70-100   **SAS**

An American 'Dr. No' one sheet poster, linen-backed.
1962   41in (102cm) high
£1,200-1,800   ATM

An American 'From Russia with Love', one sheet poster, linen-backed.

This was chosen as the second 007 film after President John F. Kennedy listed the book among his top ten favourite novels.
1964   40in (101.5cm) high
£600-900   ATM

An Italian 'Dalla Russia Con Amore' ('From Russia With Love') locandino poster, linen-backed.
1964   26.75in (68cm) wide
£200-300   ON

An American 'Goldfinger' one sheet poster, linen-backed.
1965   41in (104cm) high
£1,200-1,500   P

A CLOSER LOOK AT A JAMES BOND POSTER

It was designed by notable poster artists Robert McGinnis (b.1926) and Frank McCarthy (1924-2002), who designed a number of Bond posters, with McGinnis also designing the famous 'Breakfast At Tiffany's' poster.

This scene, with Bond taking a bath with exotic women, is the desirable style C version of the poster.

Style A shows Blofeld's volcano lair from the film, and Style B featured Bond's 'Little Nellie' mini-helicopter in a mid-air fight.

International versions of this poster usually used the Little Nellie image, with only a few exceptions.

An American 'Diamonds Are Forever' three sheet poster produced for the foreign market, with blue ink Dutch stamp, with folds and minor holes, dated.
1971   74.75in (190cm) high
£120-180   SAS

A British 'You Only Live Twice', style 'C' one sheet poster, linen-backed.
1967   40in (101.5cm) high
£1,000-1,500   ATM

A Corgi James Bond silver Aston Martin, no.270, with gold bumpers, revolving number plates and tyre slashers, in excellent condition, with unopened packet, in good condition original window box.

This type of box is particularly scarce, and the envelope of accessories is unopened – both contribute to the price.
1968-73

£300-500   SAS

A Corgi James Bond silver Aston Martin, no.270, with lapel badge, unused number plate labels, instructions and spare assassin, in excellent condition, in excellent condition original striped window box.
1973-76

£250-300   SAS

A Corgi James Bond Lotus Esprit, no.269, with nine rockets on sprue, in excellent condition, in very good condition original box.
1977-83

£40-60   SAS

A CLOSER LOOK AT A CORGI ASTON MARTIN

This model is complete with all its accessories, including the spare assassin and the sticky lapel badge, which was usually used and lost.

It is important that the model, box, and accessories are all in the best condition possible.

This was released to coincide with the release of 'Goldfinger' in 1964 and dominated Christmas sales in December 1965.

It also includes the catalogue, which indicates an early example from the four year production run.

A Corgi James Bond gold Aston Martin DB5, no.261, with two assassins, lapel badge, instructions, packets, with 'Car Makers To James Bond' catalogue, in very good condition with original box in very good condition.
1965-69

£180-220   SAS

A Corgi James Bond CC07505 'Die Another Day' Aston Martin Vanquish, in original box, signed by Barbara Broccoli and Michael G. Wilson.
c2003

£1,000-1,500   SAS

A Corgi Rockets D928 James Bond 'On Her Majesty's Secret Service' Spectre Mercedes-Benz 280 SL, in unopened vacuform packaging.
1970-72

£250-300   SAS

An A.C. Gilbert James Bond 'Action Toy Set 5', no.16565, in excellent condition, in original box.

£70-100 SAS

An A.C. Gilbert James Bond 'Action Toy Set 4', no.16564, in original box, lacking cellophane, one ankle fractured.

£35-45 SAS

QUICK REFERENCE - A.C. GILBERT & JAMES BOND

The A.C. Gilbert Co. was founded in 1909 and grew to be one of the largest American toys companies. It is best known for its Erector Set, similar to Britain's Meccano, and also produced model trains. After the death of founder Alfred Gilbert in 1961, the company struggled financially but won the license to produce James Bond toys in 1965. A large number of figures and toys were produced, and are hotly sought after by collectors today. In 1966, the company's fortunes took a turn for the worst when large numbers of their hastily produced 'James Bond Road Race Set' were returned to retailer Sears due to poor quality. In 1967, they went out of business, and lost the license, with companies such as Mego stepping in to create licensed Bond toys. This desirable set contains all ten small figurines produced by Gilbert and is complete with the speargun, rifle and breathing tank accessories, which are often lost.

An A.C. Gilbert James Bond 'Ten Movie Characters' set, no.16525, in excellent condition, in original box.

£120-180 SAS

An A.C. Gilbert James Bond figurine.

This figurine is from the boxed sets also shown on this page. When the Gilbert company went bankrupt, all remaining stocks were sold off by Sears individually or in sets, usually without the original boxes.

3.5in (9cm) high

£7-11 KNK

A late 1960s A.C. Gilbert James Bond Auric Goldfinger figurine.

3.25in (8.5cm) high

£6-9 KNK

A Triang TG4 James Bond 'Thunderball' '007 Underwater Battle Game', with frogmen figures, strip catalogue, in excellent condition in fair condition original box.

£350-450 SAS

An American MB Games 'James Bond 007 Secret Agent' game, with original box in very good condition.

c1964   19in (48cm) wide

£70-100   **NOR**

An Australian Milton Bradley 'James Bond 007 Thunderball' game.

c1966   19in (48cm) wide

£40-60   **GAZE**

A Spears 'James Bond 007 Secret Service Game' board game, in excellent condition, in very good condition box.

1966   19in (48cm) wide

£15-25   **SAS**

A late 1960s Jumbo Games 'James Bond 007' game, with instructions in Dutch, in original 'snakeskin' look attaché case box, some graffiti.

£25-35   **SAS**

A 1980s Coibel 186 'Official James Bond 007 Secret Agent Set', in original box.

£180-220   **SAS**

An Arrows 'James Bond Thunderball' jigsaw, in near mint to mint complete condition, in good condition picture boxes.

c1966

£70-100   **VEC**

A Lone Star James Bond 'Super Action Set', no.1210, in excellent condition in original window box.

1973

£300-500   **SAS**

A Multiple Toymakers James Bond 'Bond-X Automatic Shooting Camera', no.3021, in worn original box.

Multiple Toymakers made a number of James Bond toys and were a major producer of toys in the 1970s.

1966

£350-450   **SAS**

MARBLES

QUICK REFERENCE

- Interest in marbles is increasing as yesterday's children become today's collectors. Collectable marbles can be divided into three groups: handmade, machine-made and artist marbles.
- The earliest marbles were handmade, primarily in Germany from the 1860s to the 1920s. M. F. Christensen developed a marble-making machine in 1905, and companies in the USA began to produce machine-made marbles. Production of this sort of marble peaked in the 1920s and 1930s.
- Handmade marbles can be identified by the presence of rough pontil marks, where they were broken away from the glass rod to form a sphere. Rarer marbles such as the opaque Indians and 'sulphides' (which have internal white porcelain-like forms) are the most sought after, as are large marbles and those in truly mint condition. Handmade marbles are typically the most desirable, but they have become so hard to find and valuable that many collectors' interest has shifted to the best machine-made marbles.
- By the 1950s and 1960s, poorer quality machine-made marbles, such as 'cat's eyes', were being produced in large numbers. These are generally of little interest to collectors.
- Machine-made marbles have no pontil mark. Makers to look out for are Christensen Agate (1905-1917) and the largest USA producer, Akro Agate, which produced marbles from 1910 until 1951, when the factory closed.
- Several artists, including Mark Matthews, still produce contemporary pieces, which are often collectable. Many are made from dichroic glass, which contains micro-layers of metal oxide, creating an iridescent effect. When viewed from different angles and under different lighting conditions, the marble's colours appear to shift and change.
- The type of marble affects value: pattern, colour and size are important, with symmetry in design, and unusual or very bright colours typically popular with collectors. 'Eye appeal' will also determine value, as what may appeal to one collector may not appeal to another. Mint condition marbles can often be worth twice as much as a damaged version. Chips, scuffs, marks and wear will reduce value, particularly of machine-made marbles. Chips are less important on handmade-marbles, unless the pattern is affected. Packaging can also be desirable, as so much was thrown away.

A German handmade 'Mist' marble, with translucent and transparent blue and yellow strands over a transparent core.

Note the rough top area of the marble, which shows where it was broken off the rod before being formed and finished.

c1860-c1920   0.5in (1.5cm) diam

£30-40   **AB**

A German handmade solid core 'lobed swirl' marble.

c1860-c1920   0.75in (2cm) diam

£30-40   **AB**

An American Akro Agate Company 'Popeye Corkscrew' machine-made marble.

c1927-35   0.5in (1.5cm) diam

£15-25   **AB**

An American Peltier Glass Company National Line Rainbo 'Burnt Christmas Tree' machine-made marble.

c1925-32   0.5in (1.5cm) diam

£60-100   **AB**

An American Champion Agate Company Furnace 'Scraping Swirl' machine-made marble.

c1980-1990   0.5in (1.5cm) diam

£15-25   **AB**

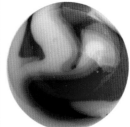

An American Christensen Agate Company 'Bloodie' machine-made marble.

c1927-28   0.5in (1.5cm) diam

£25-35   **AB**

MARBLES

An Eddie Seese six-panel swirl marble, with alternating bands of dichroic glass and multicoloured swirling bands over a cobalt blue ground, signed.

1.5in (4cm) diam

£40-60   BGL

A Shane Caswell dichroic blue and green 'vortex' marble, the back with torchwork 'rake pull' decoration, signed.

1.75in (4.5cm) diam

£30-40   BGL

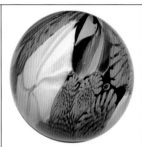

A Francis Coupal limited edition floral marble, with stretched and pulled murrine canes, signed.

2in (5cm) diam

£200-300   BGL

A Bobbie Seese multicoloured Onionskin marble, with pulled multicoloured caned and dichroic glass over an opaque white base, signed.

1.75in (4.5cm) diam

£40-60   BGL

A CLOSER LOOK AT A JOSH SIMPSON MARBLE

Simpson's immensely popular 'Planet' range began in 1976 when he was demonstrating glassmaking to school children, who reacted better to stories about imaginary planets than to goblets and vases.

Each element is hand-applied, making every planet unique and creating complex patterns mimicking land masses, deep seas and even cities that draw the eye in.

Traditional techniques associated with Murano glass, such as ' millefiori' and sections of twisted 'filigrana' canes, are combined with more modern innovations such as dichroic glass.

The presence of an 'orbiting spaceship', here a section of ' filigrana' cane, show that this planet is 'inhabited'.

A Josh Simpson 'Inhabited Planet' marble, containing canes, murrines, dichroic 'gold glass' and a 'spaceship' on a blue ground, signed.

1.75in (4.5cm)

£120-180   BGL

A Julie Powell translucent purple marble, with a hand-painted overlay of a hummingbird, flowers and leaves, signed.

Powell designed Fenton glass before she began producing these unique works.

1.5in (4cm) diam

£60-80   BGL

A Milon Townsend studio glass sphere or marble, with lampworked three-dimensional horse and paddock enclosed within colourless glass.

Townsend is a key American studio glass artist, who specialises in lampworked designs. This piece crosses the boundary between studio glass and contemporary marble making. His marbles containing human figural forms are particularly sought after.

1.5in (4cm) diam

£100-120   BGL

METALWARE

QUICK REFERENCE – CONRAH

The Conrah range was designed by Ronald Hughes in 1967, and produced in south Wales during the 1970s. The range of vases, bowls and candlesticks was made from anodised aluminium in bright colours, which were cut through by machine, leaving reflective sparkling geometric patterns arranged in wide bands around the bodies. Fine lines may also be found in addition to the main pattern. Often misread as 'Conran', marks were tooled or printed on to a plastic disc set into the base. The range was also known as 'Cristillium'. Currently, prices and understanding of the area are low, but this may change as the vases are both visually appealing and typical of the time they were produced. Avoid scratched, and especially dented, examples as damage is impossible to restore.

A Conrah pink anodised aluminium large cylinder vase, cut with a faceted lattice design, the base with inscribed Conrah mark.

10in (25.5cm) high

£60-80   GC

A Conrah gold-finish anodised aluminium small cylinder vase, cut with a faceted lattice design, the base with inset black plastic Conrah mark.

8in (20.5cm) high

£30-40   GC

A 1970s Conrah anodised aluminium medium cylinder vase, finely cut with horizontal lines and cut with faceted lozenge shapes, the base with inset plastic disc.

9in (23cm) high

£60-80   GC

A Conrah black anodised aluminium candlestick, cut with a faceted lattice design, the base with inset black plastic Cristillium mark.

6.75in (17cm) high

£20-25   GC

A Conrah green anodised aluminium large cylinder vase, cut with faceted lozenge motifs, the base with inset black plastic Conrah mark.

10in (25.5cm) high

£60-80   GC

A Conrah blue anodised aluminium flower pot, cut with a faceted lattice design, the base with inset black plastic Conrah mark.

3.75in (9.5cm) high

£15-20   GC

A Conrah black anodised aluminium bowl, cut with a faceted lattice design, the base with inset black plastic Conrah mark.

5.25in (13cm) diam

£20-25   GC

QUICK REFERENCE – VINERS & STUART DEVLIN

Stuart Devlin (b.1931) is one of the most innovative British silversmiths and metalworkers of the late 20thC, and was awarded a Royal Warrant in 1982. He is best known for his silver and gold designs, which contrast shiny silver with textured gold areas. Viners commissioned Devlin to produce a range of stainless steel tableware in the early 1970s, following the success of, among others, Robert Welch's stainless steel designs for Old Hall. Nine shapes were produced, including the iconic spherical 'rose bowl' below, which was said to have been inspired by the 1969 moon landing. A limited number of pieces were produced in solid silver, but are very rare today. The range was phased out in 1979, and prices are much more affordable than for his solid silver and gold designs, allowing collectors to buy into the classic Devlin look at a much lower price.

A 1970s Viners 'Devlin Collection' stainless steel and gold plated metal tall wine goblet, designed by Stuart Devlin, the base with inset plastic disc.

7in (18cm) high

£25-35   GC

A 1970s Viners 'Devlin Collection' stainless steel and gold plated metal champagne goblet, designed by Stuart Devlin, the base with inset plastic disc.

4.5in (11.5cm) high

£15-20   GC

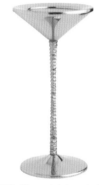

A 1970s Viners stainless steel and gold-plated metal candleholder, designed by Stuart Devlin, the base with inset plastic disc.

£20-30   GC

A 1970s Viners 'Devlin Collection' stainless steel and gold-plated metal nut dishes or candleholders, designed by Stuart Devlin.

5in (13cm) diam

£20-30   GC

A 1970s Viners 'Devlin Collection' stainless steel and gold-plated metal small wine or water goblet, designed by Stuart Devlin, the base with inset plastic disc.

5.25in (13.5cm) high

£25-35   GC

A 1970s Viners 'Devlin Collection' stainless steel and gold-plated metal 'Violet Bowl', designed by Stuart Devlin, with pull-off, friction fit textured, domed top.

3.25in (8cm) high

£40-50   GC

QUICK REFERENCE – OLD HALL

Old Hall stainless steel tablewares were produced by J. & J. Wiggin Ltd from 1934-84, and have become highly collectable. The mark can help to date a piece: 'Staybrite' marks date from before WWII, 'Olde Hall' was used from 1928-59, 'Ye Olde Hall' in 1934-35 only, with 'Old Hall' being used from 1959-84. Pieces designed by Robert Welch after 1955 are perhaps the most desirable today due to their fashionable modern styling, but look out for pre-war designs such as those by Dr Harold Stabler. Quality was very high and ranges to look out for include 'Cottage', 'Avon', 'Alveston' and 'Campden'.

An Olde Hall 'Cottage' range stainless steel one-pint teapot, with 'Staycool' handle, designed by Nellie Wiggin, the base with registered design no.828398 for 1938.

1938-59   *6in (15cm) high*

£25-30   **GC**

A 1950s Olde Hall honey or conserve pot, with lid attached to the geometric handle, the base with registered design no.627169 for 1949.

3.5in (9cm) high

£15-20   **GC**

An Old Hall 'Avon' range stainless steel teapot, designed by Robert Welch in 1966, the base with registered no.928252 for 1966.

5.75in (14.5cm) high

£45-50   **GC**

An Old Hall 'Avon' range stainless steel milk jug, designed by Robert Welch in 1966, the base with registered no.928252 for 1966.

4in (10cm) high

£10-15   **GC**

An Old Hall 'Oriana' range stainless steel milk jug, with angled handle, designed by Robert Welch in 1958.

3.5in (9cm) high

£8-12   **GC**

An Old Hall 'Avon' range stainless steel coffee pot, designed by Robert Welch in 1966, the base with registered no.928252 for 1966.

7in (17.5cm) high

£45-50   **GC**

An Old Hall 'Oriana' range stainless steel teapot, with angled handle and 180 degree flip lid, designed by Robert Welch in 1958.

This range was designed for the P&O cruise liner 'Oriana', although examples were also sold commercially. Those produced for use on the ship were marked 'P&O Line' or 'ShipCo' on the base.

5.75in (14.5cm) high

£35-40   **GC**

QUICK REFERENCE – OKIMONO

An okimono is the Japanese term given to small or medium sized ornamental objects placed near altars or in the traditional 'tokonoma' display alcove. The name means 'object for placement on display', and okimono are larger than netsuke, which saw their origins as functional toggles in traditional Japanese dress. They are carved in ivory, but may also be found in wood, bronze or stone. The late 19thC until the 1920s saw a boom in the production of okimono, with many being exported to the West. Human figures or animals are the most commonly found subjects, and they may show scenes from Japanese life or mythology. Value is determined by the carver, the skill of the carver, and the subject, size, date and complexity of the piece itself. Those that are well-detailed, with realistic, expressive features are usually the most desirable and valuable.

A Japanese Meiji period ivory okimono of a basket maker, carrying various baskets in both hands and on his back, his clothing decorated with red, green and mother-of-pearl inset roundels, with red seal mark.

5.75in (14.5cm) high

£800-1,200   L&T

A Japanese Meiji period carved ivory figure of a father, feeding grapes to his two small boys, cracks and chips.

10in (25.5cm) high

£280-320   WW

A Japanese late Meiji period one piece carved ivory figure of a hunter, standing with one foot on a cut tree stump, holding a matchlock gun, wearing straw hood and outer jacket and stockings, game birds hanging from his belt, with three character engraved mark on the base.

8in (20.5cm) high

£550-750   TEN

A Japanese one piece carved ivory figure of a poultryman, standing full length and smiling, holding a chick in his upheld right hand, a hen beneath his left arm, a cockerel at his feet, incised two character mark on inset red kakihan.

c1900   *6.75in (17.5cm) high*

£500-700   TEN

A Japanese one piece carved ivory figure group, with bijin standing wearing a kimono and elaborate chignon, the base with inset rectangular kakihan with incised two character mark, and with rustically carved shaped oval wood base.

c1920   *7.25in (18.5cm) high*

£300-500   TEN

A Japanese Meiji period one piece carved ivory mythological scroll painter figurine, a figure of Hotei on horseback appears magically from mist issuing from the scroll, the base with inset red kakihan with incised two character mask.

A kakihan is an artist's mark.

9.25in (23.5cm) high

£250-350   TEN

A Chinese jade carving of an elephant, with three boys scrambling on its back, two holding onto a string of cash, one pouring water out of a cornucopia, a figure to the reverse holding up a tall lingzhi fungus.

3in (7.5cm) high

£120-180   **WW**

A Chinese pale celadon jade carving of a recumbent hound, its neck twisted and looking back, raised on a wood stand.

In 2009, an 18thC spinach green jade water buffalo made for a Qing dynasty Japanese emperor, and with an all-important impeccable noble provenance, sold for £3.4 million at the same salerooms as this later piece. The quality and expressive nature of a piece of carved jade, together with a cast-iron provenance allowing it to be dated and identified, are key factors for value.

5.5in (14cm) wide

£180-220   **WW**

A Chinese pale celadon jade carving of a boy, dancing and wearing flowing robes.

2.5in (6.5cm) high

£120-180   **WW**

A 19thC/20thC Chinese jade Buddhistic lion, with areas of rust coloured stone.

4.25in (11cm) wide

£120-180   **WW**

A 17th or 18thC Chinese bronze model of a crouching horned lion dog, baring its teeth.

5.5in (14cm) high

£450-550   **WW**

A 19thC Chinese bronze censer, cast in relief with scaly dragons highlighted in gold, the base with a Qianlong mark.

6.75in (17cm) wide

£150-250   **WW**

A 19thC Japanese Meiji period bronze figure of a rat, the crouching animal holding a nut between its front feet, signed to base.

2.75in (6.75cm) high

£400-600   **JA**

A Baccarat pansy paperweight, with a millefiori garland and a star cut base.

c1850   *2.5in (6.5cm) diam*

£1,000-1,500   **DCP**

A Baccarat butterfly paperweight, with millefiori wings, surrounded by a millefiori garland, and with a star cut base.

c1850   *3in (7.5cm) diam*

£1,300-1,600   **DCP**

A Baccarat flat bouquet paperweight, with a pansy, red double clematis and three forget-me-nots.

This contains a larger number of different flowers, hence the higher value. Each element of the flowers was made when the glass was hot, using a 'lampworking' technique. The bunch was encased in colourless glass when finished. The glassmaker had to be skilled enough to ensure no air bubbles are trapped under this layer.

c1850   *2.5in (6.5cm) diam*

£4,000-5,000   **DCP**

A Baccarat red 'thousand petalled; rose paperweight, with a star cut base.

c1850   *3in (7.5cm) diam*

£2,500-3,000   **DCP**

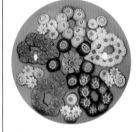

A Clichy concentric millefiori paperweight, the petalled design set on an opaque turquoise ground.

c1850   *3in (7.5cm) diam*

£1,000-1,500   **DCP**

A Clichy swirl paperweight, with an opaque light blue and white swirl emanating from a single large millefioricentral cane.

c1850   *3in (7.5cm) diam*

£1,300-1,600   **DCP**

A CLOSER LOOK AT A CLICHY PAPERWEIGHT

This is known as a 'barber pole' design due to the blue and white spiral pattern canes, which resemble barber's poles – some collectors call them 'candy cane'.

The design, with its sectioned-off millefiori, is also known as a 'chequer' pattern, and is time-consuming to make.

Clichy is famous for its trademark rose millefiori, of which there are three different examples in this weight.

This example is regular, colourful and well organised, and would have been made by a skilled glassmaker.

A Clichy 'barber pole' chequer paperweight, with three different roses.

c1850   *2.75in (7cm) diam*

£2,000-3,000   **DCP**

A mid-19thC Clichy 'scramble' paperweight, the jumble of canes including pink, yellow and white roses, some scratching.

'Scramble' designs include many different types and colours of millefiori and canes, arranged and melted together in a random pattern. They tend not to be as valuable as complex set-ups.

2.25in (6cm) diam

£250-350   **WW**

A St. Louis mixed fruit paperweight, with two pears and two cherries, on an opaque white double swirl ground.

c1850   *2.75in (7cm) diam*

£600-800   **DCP**

A Pantin paperweight with a bunch of grapes and vine leaves on a plain white ground.

c1878   *3in (7.5cm) diam*

£4,000-5,000   **DCP**

A 1930s Scottish paper weight, in the style of Paul Ysart for Monart, with a radial star formation of ruffle and cog millefiori canes on a turquoise powder ground, the base with rough pontil.

3in (7.5cm) diam

£180-220   **FLD**

QUICK REFERENCE – ST LOUIS

St Louis was founded in French Alsace-Lorraine in 1767 and, like other French makers, produced paperweights from the mid 19thC. Single flower or fruit designs are typical of its weights, which also often have higher domes than those of its competitors. Swirling white or pink grounds are another hallmark feature. Some weights have been found with date canes, these usually read 1848, with dates of 1845 and 1849 being much rarer.

A St. Louis purple dahlia paperweight, with striped petals, a millefiori centre, and green leaves.

c1850   *2.25in (6cm) diam*

£1,300-1,600   **DCP**

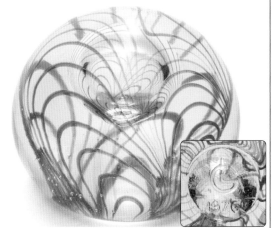

A Liskeard Glass paperweight, with blue internal swirls over a trappped air bubble, designed by John Randle, the base with impressed stamp and dated 1976.

3.25in (8cm) diam

£20-25   **GC**

A Caithness Glass paperweight with opaque multi-coloured internal swirl core under a curtain of trapped air bubbles, the base with acid mark.

The mark on the base is 'CIIG', with the 'II' mark indicating this is a second. Looking closely, there is a piece of grit or other material from the manufacturing process trapped inside.

3.25in (8cm) diam.

£10-15   **GC**

QUICK REFERENCE

- The collector's market for vintage fountain pens began in the late 1970s, and grew throughout the 1980s and 1990s. The most sought after pens are still those produced by the three big brands: Parker, Waterman and Montblanc. Dunhill Namiki maki-e lacquer models from the 1930s are also extremely desirable and usually command the highest prices.
- While collectors have traditionally been interested in pens from their own countries, this has changed. The Internet allows collectors a wider choice than ever before, and pens (unlike larger objects) can be shipped quickly and easily. Consequently, formerly less widely appreciated brands, such as England's Conway Stewart, are now proving popular across the world.
- As well as the brand, size, rarity and quality count. Many pen collectors are men and therefore favour larger pens that fit their hands. Also desirable are those pens with high immediate visual impact, and those with gold-plated overlays, lacquerwork designs or unusual, brightly coloured celluloids.
- Pens should be in working order, as many collectors intend to use them for writing. Condition is also extremely important. Avoid cracked or chipped examples and ensure that replaceable parts, such as nibs and clips, are correct for that model.
- Fountain pens were mass-produced before the ballpoint took over in the 1960s and, with so many on the market, standard pens are often worth under £50, even with original gold nibs. However, these pens can often make useful and interesting writing instruments.
- Modern limited editions are often produced in large numbers and are only of value if kept in unused condition, with boxes and paperwork. Used examples are usually much less desirable, unless extremely rare. Look for early editions, such as Montblanc's 'Lorenzo de Medici', or those pens from small editions (ideally under 1,000).

An 'S. Mordan & Co.' silver pencil, with rare large foliate, agate set terminal revealing lead storage, engraved with presentation engraving 'H.T. Lister' in script, with 'SM' hallmarks for London 1859.

1859   *4in (10cm) long*

£120-180   **PC**

A very rare Sampson Mordan and Gabriel Riddle silver pencil, with crown-like terminal, with 'SM*GR' hallmarks for London 1825, and marked 'S.MORDAN & CO'S PATENT'.

The propelling pencil was patented by Hawkins and Mordan in 1822, and so this is an early and very scarce example. It was produced under the partnership of Mordan and the wealthy stationer Riddle.

4in (10cm) long

£250-300   **PC**

A Sampson Mordan ivory cased pen, pencil and folding knife combination, with two gold butterfly collars sliding down to operate the pen holder and pencil, marked 'S.MORDAN & CO.'.

c1880

£180-220   **BLO**

An S. Mordan & Co. silver telescopic propelling pencil in the form of a champagne bottle.

During the late 19thC, Mordan & Co. produced a wide range of novelty shaped pencils, many of which are detailed in the only surviving Mordan catalogue, dating from 1897. Shapes include a cross, a pistol and an owl, all of which are popular with collectors.

c1890

£250-350   **AMER**

PENS & PENCILS

QUICK REFERENCE – THE DUOFOLD

Designed in 1919 by Parker employee Lewis Tebbel, the Duofold was launched in late 1921 amid scepticism about its high price of $7. It met with great success, and has since become the company's 'flagship' model. Many collectors know the original Duofold as the 'Big Red', due to its bright orangey red colour, which was a novelty at a time when nearly all pens were black. From 1922 onwards, the Duofold was almost constantly modified in some way, meaning collectors can usually date pens to within a few years. A number of different colours and sizes can be found, including the large 'Senior', the smaller 'Junior' and 'Lady', the slimmer 'Special' and the tiny 'Vest Pocket'. During the 1930s, both ends of the pen became slightly tapered, or 'streamlined'. When it was reintroduced after WWII, it was largely mass-produced as a more affordable pen, only becoming a top-of-the-range model again when it was reintroduced again in 1988 to celebrate Parker's centenary.

A 1940s English Parker red and black marbled Duofold Senior, with Canadian Duofold Pen nib.

These high quality 1930s-style English Duofolds are hard to find. c1945

£200-300 PC

A 1930s Parker Lapis 'Blue on Blue' Duofold Junior Streamline, with Duofold nib.

£300-350 BPH

An American Parker Lucky Curve Duofold Senior, with a fine P. Duofold Pen USA nib.
c1927

£120-180 HSR

A 1920s Parker Mandarin Yellow Lucky Curve Duofold Senior button-filler, with Duofold USA nib.

'Mandarin Yellow' is the rarest and most valuable colour for a 1920s-30s Duofold. Always examine the barrel and cap closely, as they are prone to cracking, with cracks showing up as grey.

£500-700 BPH

A 1930s Parker 'Pearl & Black' Duofold Senior Streamline, with Canadian Parker Duofold nib.

The discolouring of the barrel is the result of sulphur leaching out from the internal rubber ink sac, which causes the plastic to darken or take on amber tones.

£150-200 BPH

A 1990s Parker Duofold Centennial Mark I blue marbled convertor/cartridge-filler, with gold-filled trim, with 18k Parker Duofold two colour nib.

£150-200 BPH

A 1950s English Parker Duofold burgundy aerometric-filler, with Duofold Parker 14ct nib, in excellent condition.

£20-30 PC

An American Parker red Super 21 aerometric-filler, with Lustraloy cap, fine octanium nib, and original nib grade label.

1956

£35-45 HSR

A 1950s-1970s English Parker Teal blue 51 Classic aerometric-filler, with medium nib and Lustraloy cap.

£30-50 PC

A Parker 61 'Heirloom' green pencil, with two-colour 'Heirloom' cap.

This is a very rare cap finish, as it tended to wear away with use and polishing.

£60-80 BPH

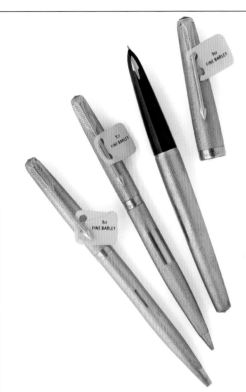

An English Parker 61 'Presidential' 9ct solid gold trio set, comprising capillary-filling pen, twist-action pencil and push action ball-pen, with fine barley pattern, with London hallmark for 1974, in original presentation box, with instructions and two pouches, with original clip labels in place.

Introduced in 1956, the 61 used a special spongey material in a tube to absorb and hold the ink. If clogged with dry ink, they are almost impossible to repair. The solid gold 'Presidential' was the most expensive model in the line.

£1,000-1,500 HSR

A 1950s American Parker 51 'Signet' aerometric-filler and Clutch pencil, with gold-plated barrels and caps.

c1952

£150-200 BPH

A CLOSER LOOK AT A PARKER 51 DEMONSTRATOR

Introduced in 1941, Parker's modern, rocket-shaped 51 was revolutionary – its hooded nib allowed the use of a special, quick drying ink known as 'Quink'.

This example shows Parker's 'Vacumatic' system, which was introduced in 1932 and uses a plunger and diaphragm to create a vacuum in the body, sucking in the ink.

The plastic plunger on this example dates it to after 1941. Examples made from 1948 onwards used Parker's 'Aerometric' squeezable tube system.

Transparent 'Demonstrator' pens were used by pen salesmen to show retailers how the mechanism worked, with shop owners also often using them to show customers.

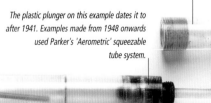

A Parker 51 Vacumatic Lucite 'Demonstrator' pen, with medium nib and Lustraloy cap.

1945

£150-200 PC

A Parker Lucky Curve Pastel Green Moiré ring-top button-filler, with a Lucky Curve nib and engraved barrel.
c1927

£40-60 AMER

A Parker Gold Pearl Vacumatic Standard, with later English Parker nib.
c1942

£120-180 AMER

A Parker Lucky Curve 'True Blue' ring-top button-filler, with Canadian Lucky Curve nib.

This example has a very good colour, the white often goes yellow due to the internal rubber ink sac degrading.
1928

£150-200 BPH

A Parker Silver Pearl Vacumatic Maxima, with matching cap and barrel end 'jewels', and two-colour Parker Arrow fine nib.

The Maxima was the largest and most expensive model in the Vacumatic series. The partly transparent hallmark ' Vacumatic' striped plastic barrel allowed the ink level to be seen.
c1936

£220-280 HSR

A 1980s French Parker 75 gold plated 'Cisele' convertor/cartridge-filler, in mint condition.

£70-100 BPH

A 1980s Parker 45 'Grey Shield' Harlequin convertor/cartridge-filler, with medium nib.

£30-40 PC

A Parker limited edition 'RMS Queen Elizabeth' convertor/cartridge-filler, numbered 1558 from an edition of 5,000, with fine nib, wooden presentation box, card outer, certificate, instructions, guarantee card, nib adjuster, two cartridges and convertor.

These pens were made from brass taken from the propeller of this luxury liner, which sank in Hong Kong harbour in 1972. Each pen is numbered. Ensure that the accessories are complete and the packaging and certificate bear matching numbers.
1977

£650-750 HSR

A Parker 180 'Bark-finish' silver-plate convertor/cartridge-filler, with two sided gold medium nib, with shop tag, boxed.

£50-80 HSR

A rare early Waterman's chased black hard rubber No.22 'Taper Cap' eyedropper pen, with glass and rubber eyedropper.

c1904

£60-80   PC

A 1910s-20s Waterman's chased black hard rubber no.12 eyedropper, with crisp barrel imprint and Waterman's Ideal no.2 nib, and box, in near mint condition.

£30-50   PC

A Waterman's chased black hard rubber no.12P pump-filler, with Waterman's Ideal Reg US Pat Off 2 nib and added accommodation clip.

Introduced in 1903, this used a piston mechanism to fill the pen. It was not very successful, so was discontinued soon after.

c1904

£100-150   AMER

A 1920s Waterman's chased black hard rubber 42 1/2 V safety pen, with two 9ct gold bands with London hallmarks for 1929 and marked 'F.D.W.', with Watermans Ideal no.2 nib, in excellent condition.

£40-60   PC

A CLOSER LOOK AT THE SMALLEST PEN IN THE WORLD

A Waterman's red and black 'Woodgrain' mottled hard rubber No. 16 eydropper, with Waterman's Ideal New York no.6 nib.

The final number in a Waterman's model number indicates the size of the nib, and so the size of the pen. A 6 is larger than a 2.

c1915

£180-220   AMER

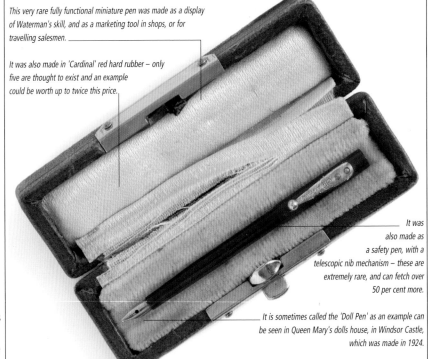

This very rare fully functional miniature pen was made as a display of Waterman's skill, and as a marketing tool in shops, or for travelling salesmen.

It was also made in 'Cardinal' red hard rubber – only five are thought to exist and an example could be worth up to twice this price.

It was also made as a safety pen, with a telescopic nib mechanism – these are extremely rare, and can fetch over 50 per cent more.

It is sometimes called the 'Doll Pen' as an example can be seen in Queen Mary's dolls house, in Windsor Castle, which was made in 1924.

A Waterman's 'Smallest Pen in the World' black hard rubber eyedropper pen, with plain gold nib with circular vent, slit and iridium point, in an original plush and satin lined case, with metal clasp.

c1914

Pen 1.5in (4cm) long

£2,000-2,500   AMER

A 1920s American Waterman's red and black Ripple no.42 safety pen, with Italian scrolling hexagonal gold-plated overlay, and Waterman's no.2 nib.

£200-300   PC

A 1920s Italian Waterman's rolled gold overlaid no.42 safety pen, with alternating engine turned, wavy line and plain panels, ivy motif barrel and cap band, marked 'Waterman's Ideal 18KR' with a Waterman's No.2 nib, initialled and dated by turning screw.

Most Waterman safety pens with fancy rolled gold overlays marked as this example were made in Italy.

£300-400   AMER

An American Waterman's no.0552 lever-filler, with gold filled 'Pansy Panel' overlay and Waterman's Canada no.2 Ideal nib.
c1925

£200-250   HSR

A Waterman's black hard rubber 552 lever-filler, with 9ct gold 'Gothic' overlay with London halllmarks for 1923 and marked F.D.W., with Waterman's no.2 Ideal nib, the barrel with engraved name.

Engraved names and initials usually reduce desirability, unless the name is famous, or the initials are exceptionally beautiful.
1923

£120-180   AMER

A 1920s Waterman's red and black 'Ripple' hard rubber no.52V lever-filler, with ring-top cap, and fine Waterman's Ideal no.2 nib.

£200-250   PENF

A Waterman's 'Turquoise' Lady Patricia lever-filler, with gold plated trim, initialled and dated, with Canadian Waterman's no.2 nib.

This is a scarce colour in excellent condition.
c1932

£100-150   AMER

QUICK REFERENCE – WATERMAN'S RIPPLE SERIES

With its bright orange colour, the 1921 Parker Duofold revolutionised pen design at a time when most pens were black. In answer to this, Waterman's released its 'Ripple' range in 1923. The pattern on each pen is unique due to the way the plastics were mixed. Resistant to staining, colours comprised orangey red and black, green and blue, and red and tan. Produced until the 1930s, they are popular with collectors today. Look out for the scarce no.5 and no.7 series, which were fitted with special nibs for specific tasks such as 'stiff fine' for accountants. The different nib grades were indicated by coloured cap bands.

A Canadian Waterman's no.56 red and black Ripple hard rubber lever-filler, with matching Ripple feed and Waterman's New York no.6 nib, with replaced lever.

c1923

£220-280   HSR

A 1920s Conway Stewart black hard rubber 'The Duro' lever-filler, with early lever and clip, and medium Conway Stewart 14ct nib.

The large size of this pen adds to its desirability.

£220-280   BPH

A 1920s Conway Stewart red and black mottled hard rubber Lady-sized lever-filler, with Conway Stewart 14ct nib.

£60-80   BPH

A Conway Stewart no.388 light and dark pink pearl and black marbled lever-filler, with a medium 14ct Conway Stewart nib.
c1939

£50-80   HSR

QUICK REFERENCE – THE 'CRACKED ICE' SERIES

The 1930s and the 1950s saw Conway Stewart using a wide variety of different types of coloured plastic for their pens. Marbled plastics are the most common, and alternatives sometimes very scarce. Perhaps the most desirable is this black plastic shot through with silver veins, which has been dubbed the 'Cracked Ice' by collectors. Larger-sized examples with evenly distributed, bright silver veins will be more desirable than those with duller, uneven veins. Version from the 1950s, recognised by their tapered ends, are often brighter and more visually appealing. Also look out for the rare 'Reverse Cracked Ice' plastic, with silver marbling shot through with black veins, as these can fetch around 25 per cent more.

A Conway Stewart no.15 black veined light and dark green pearl lever-filler, with a medium 14ct Conway Stewart nib.
c1953

£40-60   HSR

A Conway Stewart No. 22 'Floral' lever-filler, with Conway Stewart no.5 nib.

The pattern is printed on paper, sandwiched between two layers of celluloid. Over time, the paper discolours from cream to yellow, reducing the value. It was generally believed that this pen had a limited production run of 200 examples, but this is not true, although it is hard to find.

£120-180   PC

A 1930s Conway Stewart No.475 'Cracked Ice' celluloid lever-filler, with a medium Conway Stewart 14ct nib.

£120-180   BPH

A De La Rue 'Onoto' chased black hard rubber Self-Filling Pen, with four wide gold bands, one with initials, with Onoto medium nib.

c1912

£50-80 AMER

A De La Rue 'Onoto The Pen' Regina blue plunger-filler, with wide oblique Onoto no.3 nib.

c1935

£80-120 AMER

An De La Rue 'Onoto The Pen' No.3234 burgundy pearl and black marbled plunger-filler, with Onoto medium no.5 two tone nib.

These handsome and elegant marbled pens, dating from the 1940s and early 1950s, are of high quality and have become very desirable over the past few years.

c1948

£120-180 HSR

A De La Rue Onoto 'Magna' No.1873 piston-filler, with engine-turned wavy line decoration and Onoto two-tone no.7 nib, in excellent condition.

As its name suggests, the 'Magna' was De La Rue's largest standard production pen, and is sought after today. The hallmark plunger mechanism and 'Onoto' brand name were developed in 1905. The name Onoto was chosen because it had no meaning and the pronunciation was similar in all languages.

c1947

£250-350 PC

A De La Rue 'Onoto' green pearl and black marble lever-filler, with Onoto fine no.3ST nib.

c1950

£60-90 HSR

The Battersea Pen Home
Vintage and Modern Pen Specialists

PO Box 6128, Epping CM16 4GG
Phone: 01992-578 885   Fax 01992-578 485
Email admin@penhome.co.uk
www.penhome.co.uk

Authorised repairers for Parker and Waterman pens and recommended by Sheaffer UK

"One of Britain's leading retailers and repairers of vintage pens and pencils"
The Daily Telegraph

"The nation's most specialist small business"
Royal Mail

Please note that we are unable to provide valuations for pens over the phone as value is highly contingent on the pens condition. If you would like a valuation, please post the pen to us by Royal Mail Special Delivery

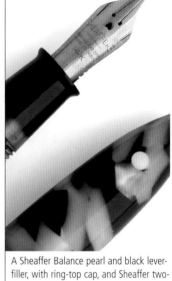

A 1920s Sheaffer 'Secretary' bright red flat top lever-filler, stamped 'C' on the barrel end, with a Sheaffer Secretary nib.

£80-120   AMER

A 1950s Sheaffer green Sentinel snorkel-filler, with silver tone cap, and Sheaffer two-colour 14k nib.

£40-60   BPH

c1930

A Sheaffer Balance pearl and black lever-filler, with ring-top cap, and Sheaffer two-tone 15k nib.

£80-120   BPH

QUICK REFERENCE – SHEAFFER'S PFM

PFM stands for 'Pen For Men', and is often said to have been the last great design of the golden age of the fountain pen. Introduced in 1959, it came in five different models, ranging from the PFM I, with a plastic barrel, stainless steel clip and palladium silver nib, upwards. All were set with Sheaffer's new 'inlaid' nib that has since become a hallmark of the company. Despite being popular with collectors today, it was not successful at the time. By 1963, the range was cut down to the III and V, and the model was phased out in 1968. This PFM V fountain pen retailed at £15 in 1959, and was marketed as having a 'man-sized barrel' with 'the only inlaid point in the world...built to take man-sized pressure'.

An American Sheaffer PFM V snorkel-filler, with gold-filled cap and burgundy barrel, and medium Sheaffer 14K inlaid nib.
1955

£60-90   HSR

A 1980s Sheaffer Targa convertor/cartridge-filler, with 18k Sheaffer inset nib.

£100-150   BPH

An American Sheaffer PFM V blue snorkel-filler and ballpen set, with gold-filled caps, and with Sheaffer fine 14ct inlaid nib.
1959-68

£200-250   HSR

A Sheaffer limited edition Lifetime Balance lever-filler, from an edition of 6,000.

This is a faithful copy of Sheaffer's 1929 Balance pen.
1997

£500-700   PC

An English Mabie Todd & Co. Swan chased black hard rubber eyedropper 'Chatelaine' pen, with scroll embossed gold-plated cap and barrel ends and chain.
c1905

£80-120   PC

A Mabie, Todd & Co. Swan black hard rubber eyedropper pen, with gold-filled scrolling filigree overlay, metal overfeed and a medium flexible Mabie, Todd & Co. nib, the barrel engraved 'H.H.S'.

It is rare to find Swan pens with gold-plated filigree overlays from this period in such excellent condition.
c1910

£320-380   HSR

A late 1920s Mabie, Todd & Co. Swan Eternal no.644B/61 red and black mottled hard rubber lever-filling pen, with Swan no.8 nib.

This is a scarce large no.8 size pen, and is highly desirable.

£200-300   PC

Two Mabie Todd & Co 'Blackbird' lever-filling pens one in green, the other in blue, in mint condition, with original price bands.
c1948

£50-80   BPH

A Mabie Todd & Co 'Blackbird' red lever-filler, with Blackbird nib and period box.

The Blackbird range was the company's mid-range brand, and was sold at more affordable prices. This bright, pillar box red is the rarest colour in the series.
c1948

£50-70   BPH

A CLOSER LOOK AT A SWAN PEN SET

Swan's Leverless pens were introduced in 1932 and were filled by twisting the bottom part of the barrel, which moved an internal metal bar to compress the ink sack and draw in ink when released.

This model is rare, and it is even harder to find a pen and pencil set in such excellent condition.

The Art Deco styling with its flat-top, which is typical of the period, and repeated gold plated band design, is appealing.

The pen became even more desirable after it was featured on the cover of the landmark book 'Fountain Pens Vintage & Modern' by Andreas Lambrou.

A Mabie Todd Swan no.275/60 Leverless pen and Fyne Poynt pencil set, with rolled gold overlay and bands to cap and barrel, with broad Swan no.2 nib.
c1934

£400-500   HSR

A 1920s Montblanc smooth black hard rubber 4B safety pen, with Montblanc 14ct no.4 nib.

The barrel is marked Simplo, which was the original brand name used by the company founded in Hamburg, Germany in 1908 that became Montblanc. Many early Montblanc, and all Simplo 'Rouge et Noir' pens were safety pens.

£300-400   AMER

A 1930s Montblanc 333 1/2 EF black celluloid piston-filler, with plain ink window and Montblanc 3 1/2 14ct nib, in excellent condition.

£200-300   AMER

A 1950s Montblanc Meisterstück 144G-F black celluloid piston-filler, with striped ink window and two-colour Montblanc 14ct fine nib.

£150-200   AMER

A Montblanc 254 black celluloid piston-filling pen, with gold plated trim, clear ink window and Montblanc medium 14ct nib.
c1955

£70-100   PC

A Montblanc 'Peter I The Great' fountain pen, numbered 412 from a limited edition of 888, in dark green resin with white gold overlay, the cap top set with emeralds, with a Montblanc 18k medium nib, in presentation box, with paperwork and card outer box.

Montblanc has become known for its limited-edition pens, which must be in unused, mint condition and complete with their boxes and paperwork to fetch high values. This was the sixth pen in the 'Patrons of Art' series. A version with a gold-plated overlay was made in an edition size of 4810, which corresponds with the height of Mont Blanc in metres.
1997

£2,000-2,500   AMER

A CLOSER LOOK AT A MONTBLANC PEN

This rare and unusual model is not recorded in any Montblanc reference book. The steel nib and brass trim indicate that this was a budget 3-series pen.

Montblanc often sold branded components, such as nibs, to factories in countries such as Spain, Denmark and Italy, where they would be assembled.

Spanish and Italian examples are often marked with the country of manufacture, but this simply bears the Montblanc cap star and the Montblanc name and mountain logo.

It is likely that this was made in France, as the size, clip style, and torpedo shape bear similarities to pens made in France at the time.

A 1940s probably French Montblanc black celluloid button-filler, with brass trim and a medium-oblique Montblanc no.3 steel nib.

£100-150   PC

A rare 18thC rootwood inkhorn, with screw-off cover over the inkwell, and screw-off base with pierced wooden plate for pounce, in excellent condition.

Pounce was a powder sprinkled over a newly written document to dry the ink. Once it was dry, the pounce was poured back into its container.

3.5in (9cm) high

£100-150   **BLO**

An unusual late 19thC spelter inkwell, probably Scandinavian, the hinged cover with mask of a Green Man, the body decorated with female heads at each corner, lion maks and floral garlands, the legs decorated with lion masks and pad feet, with ceramic liner.

4in (10cm) wide

£70-90   **BLO**

A German Soennecken black hard rubber füllflacshe (inkflask) Nr 902, in original card box, together with a Montblanc-style black hard rubber inkbottle with cracked cap and oxidation.

c1920

£70-100   **BLO**

A rare English travelling writing compendium, the rectangular red morocco leather case in two parts to hold quill pens, with a Sheffield Plate inkwell with screw-off cover, and a similar pounce pot, in excellent condition.

c1810-20   *7.25in (18.5cm) long closed*

£350-450   **BLO**

A 'Parker Quink Ink' ceramic jar, designed by Hobbs Welch, with printed mark and Design Centre paper label.

Modelled on the famous Quink bottle, these were typically used as countertop displays and storage jars in shops. This is a particularly strong price for one of these, as they often fetch around half this price or under. Always look out for cracks, as they were easily damaged.

c1982   *7.75in (20cm) high*

£70-100   **WW**

A 1920-1930s Stephens' travelling ink bottle case, the top embossed 'Stephens', with an empty bottle of Stephens red ink.

£20-30   **PC**

A 1980s English Parker Duofold-style ceramic oversized display pen, with lift-off lid.

These were also used as counter top displays in shop.

£20-30   **PC**

QUICK REFERENCE – BAKELITE

- In 1907 Belgian chemist Dr Leo Baekeland developed the first entirely synthetic plastic, known as Bakelite. Cheap to produce and extremely versatile, it became known as 'the material of 1,000 uses' and was used both in industry and for decorative and functional purposes in the home.
- Bakelite was produced in a range of different colours with black and brown being the most common. Rarer colours were red, green and blue.
- The development of Bakelite prompted a boom in the plastics industry that led to many variants being produced. Although these are slightly different materials, the name 'bakelite' is commonly used to refer to many early plastics.

A 1930s brown Bakelite inkwell and pen box, marked 'INSURE WITH THE BRITISH GENERAL INSURANCE COMPANY'.

The well proportioned, rounded form is particularly well made.

6in (15.5cm) long

£50-60   **P&I**

A 1920s Linsden multicoloured mottled Bakelite box, with revolving compartmentalised tray, the base moulded 'Linsden'.

These can also be found in mottled brown Bakelite, which is less desirable. This example is unfaded, with even the outside retaining its variety of strong colours. The Bakelite around the metal pins that allows the panel to revolve, and between the top and sides, is also not damaged. Although it is often mistaken for a stationery box, this was actually a smoker's companion.

3.75in (9.5cm) high

£30-50   **P&I**

A rare 1930s Bonbons Martougin mottled brown Bakelite box, the top with moulded head of Minerva.

6.25in (15.5cm) diam

£70-100   **P&I**

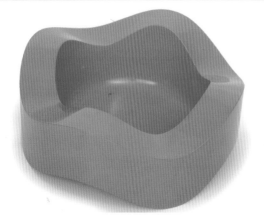

A 1960s-70s German Helit '11 Sinus' orange Melamine stacking ashtray, designed by Walter Zeischegg in 1966, the base moulded 'HELIT 84005 MADE IN GERMANY'.

This famous ashtray can be found in a range of colours, and the form was also produced in Bakelite by Kartro in Brazil. Walter Zeischegg (1917-1983) studied sculpture in Vienna, and was one of the founders and lecturers of the Ulm School of Design. Devoting himself to design from 1950 onwards, he followed the work of Max Bill and worked with Carl Aubock, before designing primarily for Helit.

5.25in (13cm) diam

£10-15   **M20C**

Four 1970s Pentagram stacking and interlocking plastic dishes or ashtrays, the bases moulded 'DO REG.NO.954,589 PENTAGRAM'.

The design registration number dates from late 1971.

4.25in (10.5cm) diam

£20-25 EACH   **M20C**

A rare brown Bakelite miniature quaitch, marked 'MADE IN SCOTLAND'.

Scottish-made Bakelite is scarce.

4.25in (11cm) long

£8-12   **P&I**

A French Art Nouveau glamour postcard, by Raphael Kirchner.

£40-60　　　　　　　MCS

I'm sure it's going to rain · my seaweed's quite wet

A comic postcard, by Donald McGill.

£4-5　　　　　　　MCS

A 'The Bully' cat postcard, by Louis Wain.

Louis Wain (1860-1939) was an English artist, known for his illustrations of cats with personality. In 1917, he began to suffer from schizophrenia and was admitted to a mental hospital in 1924.

5in (12.5cm) high.

£25-35　　　　　M&C

A hand embroidered silk postcard, of the kind made by Second World War troops.

£5-7　　　　　　　MCS

A black and white photographic postcard, depicting the Cairngorm Mountains, from The Best of All Series, published by J. B. White, Dundee.

50P-£1　　　　　　SOR

T. Vennett-Smith
AUCTIONEERS & VALUERS Est. 1989

One of the Country's leading Collectors Auctions

FOR

Postcards, Cigarette & Trade Cards,
Theatre Programmes,
Cinema Memorabilia & Ephemera
1800 lots per Auction

also Postal Auctions with over 1000 lots
and Specialist Sports Auctions

**We travel the Country and are pleased to call to pick up collections and lots for our auctions
We also undertake valuations for Insurance,
Probate and Family division**

VENDORS COMMISSION 15% + VAT (inc. insurance)

**** SEE www.vennett-smith.com
for all our auctions ****

**T. Vennett-Smith
11 Nottingham Road, Gotham, Notts. NG11 0HE
Tel: +44 (0)115 9830541 Fax: +44 (0)115 9830114
Email: info@vennett-smith.com**

QUICK REFERENCE

- Promotional film posters come in many shapes and sizes, ranging from small glossy stills for display inside cinemas to 24-sheet billposters. The most popular of these are the more easily displayed US one-sheet 27in (68.5cm) by 41in (104cm) size and the UK quad 30in (76cm) by 40in (84cm) size.
- Posters for popular films, classic and cult favourites are usually desirable, particularly those with an appealing image or style. Little-known films are generally less sought after, unless the poster was created by a famous artist, such as Robert Peal, Giuliano Nistri or Saul Bass.
- Different promotional posters are produced for each country the film is released in. Apart from being in a foreign language, they can also have different artwork and vary from the original in other ways. For example, Belgian posters tend to be smaller but often have visually stunning artwork, while Australian posters are larger but sometimes have weaker artwork. In general, you should look out for original posters

produced for the film's country of origin, as these are usually most popular.
- Posters may be re-issued if a film is re-released or has won an award, or following its release on video or DVD. These re-releases should not be confused with the originals, which are usually more valuable. Reproductions (photographic images of the original, printed on shiny poster paper) are also common, as are fakes. In forged or reproduced posters, the image may be pixelated or in different tones of colour. The best way to avoid buying a fake is to gain familiarity with originals from reputable dealers or auction houses.
- Condition is important, with folding, tears and stains reducing value, particularly if the surface of the image is affected. However, mint condition examples can be hard to find, and some damage can be restored. Posters can also be professionally backed onto linen or other materials. This does not reduce value and can enhance desirability.

'Batman', American one sheet, framed and glazed, in very good condition.

1966   40in (101.5cm) high
£500-750   MAS

'A Bigger Splash', by David Hockney (b.1937), printed by Nonsdale & Bartholomew, Nottingham, original UK quad, in near mint condition, linen-backed.
1974   40in (102cm) wide
£200-300   BLNY

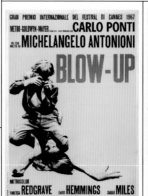

'A Clockwork Orange', designed by Philip Castle, printed by W.E. Barry, Ltd., Bradford, original UK quad, linen-backed.

1971   40in (102cm)
£300-450   BLNY

'Blow-Up', printed by Rotolito, original Italian due-foglio (two-sheet), linen-backed.

1967   55in (140cm) high
£550-750   BLNY

'Charlie Chan I London', Swedish film poster by Rohman, lithograph in colours printed by J. Olsens, linen-backed.

1934   39in (99cm) high
£300-500   BLNY

WANTED
1960's and 1970's
CONCERT POSTERS

FLYERS, HANDBILLS,
PROGRAMMES, TICKETS,
PERSONAL EFFECTS,
SIGNED ITEMS, DOCUMENTS,
ANYTHING UNUSUAL OR
ASSOCIATED 1960's AND 1970's
ROCK AND POP MEMORABILIA.

WE PAY
THE BEST PRICES

We will pay up to **£6,000** for an
original concert poster for **THE
BEATLES**, **£4,000** for **THE
ROLLING STONES** and **THE
WHO**, **£2,000** for **LED ZEPPELIN**
and **JIMI HENDRIX**, as well as
very high prices for other 1960's
and 1970's Rock and Pop
Memorabilia.

FREE VALUATIONS
CASH PAID INSTANTLY

Tel: 01494 436644 or
07890 626840

Email: music@usebriggs.com

BRIGGS ROCK AND POP
MEMORABILIA
Loudwater House,
London Road, Loudwater,
High Wycombe,
Buckinghamshire, HP10 9TL

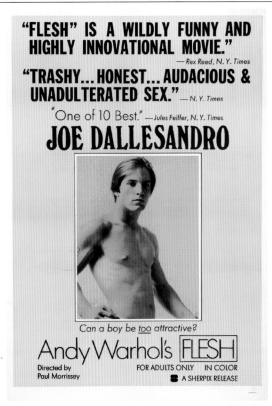

'Andy Warhol's Flesh', American one sheet, in near mint condition, linen-backed.

Directed by Joe Morrissey, the controversial 'Flesh' was one of the first general release films to objectify the naked male body, in this case that of the New York hustler, Joe Dallesandro.

1970   *41in (104cm)*

£300-450   **BLNY**

'Jour de Fête', by Rene Péron,
French issue for the 16mm release,
lithograph in colours, linen-backed.

1948   *47in (119cm) high*

£450-550   **BLNY**

'The Godfather', American one
sheet, offset lithograph in black
and white, in near mint condition,
linen-backed.

1972   *41in (104cm)*

£150-250   **BLNY**

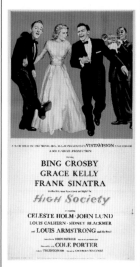

'High Society', by an unknown designer, American one sheet, linen-backed.

1956   81in (206cm)

£500-750   BLNY

'The Lord of the Rings', British one sheet artists' poster, printed by Berry Ltd, folded.

The first film produced from Tolkien's famous series is best known for its use of 'Rotoscope' animation, where live-action film images are traced over into animation. Although a financial success, it was panned by many critics and the second half was never made.

1978   40in (101.5cm) wide

£80-120   GORL

'Manhattan', American one sheet, Style B, in near mint condition, linen-backed.

This Style B version is considered scarcer and more desirable than others.

1979   41in (104cm) high

£150-200   BLNY

For Selling Vintage Posters Contact Onslows Market leaders for 20 years

Email: onslow.auctions@btinternet.com
Website: www.onslows.co.uk
Telephone: 01258 488838

Regular auctions with a World-wide audience

H G Gawthorn (1879-1941)
Lithograph poster circa 1928
Sold for £7500 June 2008

'Evanjelium Sv. Matusa' Czech one sheet, by Josef Vyletal, lithograph in colours, linen-backed.

Vyletal is considered a leading and innovative designer, working from the 1960s onwards.

1967   33in (84cm) high

£200-300   **BLNY**

'Wakacje Pana Hulot' (Mr Hulot's Holiday), by Zbigniew Lengren (1919-2003), original Polish issue, offset lithograph in colours, linen-backed.

1953   33in (84cm)

£350-450   **BLNY**

QUICK REFERENCE – EASTERN EUROPEAN POSTERS

Poster design from the former Eastern Block, particularly the Czech Republic and Poland, has become highly desirable over the past decade. Innovative artists produced startling designs that often incorporated unusual visual elements, such as photomontage, collage and a dynamic use of composition, colour, perspective and typography. This Russian poster, by the noted Stenberg brothers, is typical. The Stenbergs, who created most of their work in Moscow from 1924-33 following the principles of Russian avant garde art, are considered forerunners of this diverse and increasingly popular style.

'Mabul', by Vladimir & Georgii Stenberg, Russian lithograph in colours, linen backed.

1927   28in (71.5cm) high

£2,000-3,000   **BLNY**

'Moulin Rouge', by Rosie, East German lithograph poster in colours, linen-backed.

This design clearly uses Toulouse Lautrec as inspiration, a theme that marries up with the title of the film perfectly.

1952   33in (84cm) high

£1,000-1,500   **BLNY**

'Vecírek' (The Party), Czechoslovakian poster, by an unknown designer, linen-backed.

1970   33in (84cm) high

£150-200   **BLNY**

'Takoví Jsme Byli' (The Way We Were), by an unknown designer, Czechoslovakian poster, in near mint condition, linen-backed.

1973   33in (84cm)

£150-200   **BLNY**

QUICK REFERENCE

- By the mid20thC, travel was available and cheap enough to be a viable option for more people than ever before. As more people took holidays, travel posters began to rapidly increase in popularity. The earliest and most prolific of these were ocean-liner and railway company posters, and these continue to be the most popular with collectors. Airlines began to compete commercially with cruise liners from the 1950s onwards and, despite the arrival of television advertising, many appealing and collectable posters were produced during this period.

- Many railway posters did not feature images of trains or railways. Instead, most aimed at luring people away from their everyday lives by displaying brightly-coloured, exotic scenes, unlike any to be seen in the busting city. These included ships, golfing scenes or hotels, and town, seaside an countryside views. Images of green, rolling hills in England tend to be particularly popular with collectors.

- Artwork by popular designers, such as Cassandre (Adolphe Mouron), Frank Brangwyn and Tom Purvis, will usually be desirable, as will major names in travel, such as White Star, BOAC, Air France and Canadian Pacific. However, the 'eye appeal' of the image is often the primary indicator to value, because many buyers will wish to display these posters in their homes. Striking, brightly coloured designs that display the excitement and glamour of travel are desirable, particularly those in popular styles, such as Art Deco or 1950s.

- As aesthetic appeal is paramount, condition is important. Many posters were folded in storage before they became popular collectables, so folds are acceptable and can often easily be removed by a professional restorer. However, tears that extend into the image and any damage that seriously mars the surface of the image will reduce a poster's value and desirability considerably.

'Helensburgh', by Frank H Mason, railway poster printed for LNER by McCorquodale & Co Ltd.

1941   40in (102cm)
£350-450   ON

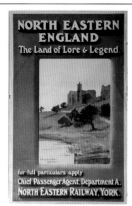

'North East England Warksworth Castle', railway poster printed for the North Eastern Railways by Albery & Co., with small losses to margins.

40in (102cm) high
£150-200   ON

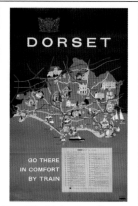

'Dorset' by Eric Lander, railway poster printed for the Southern Railway (British Rail) by Leonard Ripley & Co Ltd.

40in (102cm) high
£120-180   ON

'Great Western Railway, Sunny South Wales', by an anonymous designer, with vignettes showing golf, tennis, yachting and a map of the system, printed by Felix J Pole.

40in (102cm) high
£250-350   ON

A Longman Facts and Figures 1 Passenger Services poster, printed for BR(WR) by Stafford & Co Ltd.

40in (102cm) high
£150-200   ON

POSTERS

'Brides les Bains', by Leon Benigni, for PLM railways, lithograph in colours, linen-backed.

1929   *39in (99cm) high*

£1,200-1,500   **BLNY**

A CLOSER LOOK AT A FRENCH RAILWAY POSTER

The flat planes of colour and limited palette recall the work of the famous French Art Deco poster designer Adolphe Mouron, known as 'Cassandre', whose work can fetch thousands of pounds.

The use of the railway, and the sharp angle and sense of perspective it gives, are also hallmarks of Cassandre, and many of the best Art Deco travel posters.

PLM was the Paris to Lyon and the Mediterranean railway. Its appealing posters for desirable holiday spots along its routes are highly sought after.

This poster can be found in three different colourways, this purple, green, and white and light blue – there is little difference in the price.

VERS LE MONT.BLANC
PAR St GERVAIS LES BAINS
ET LE COL DE VOZA

'Vers le Mont Blanc', by George Dorival, printed by Lucien Serre & Cie for PLM railways, linen-backed.

1928   *41in (104cm) high*

£1,500-2,000   **BLNY**

'Val D'Esquières', by Michel Bouchaud, printed by Lucien Serre & Cie for PLM railways, linen-backed.

c1930   *39in (99cm)*

£1,000-1,500   **BLNY**

'Saint Raphaël', by J. Munier, lithograph in colours printed by Moullot for SNCF, linen backed.

As well as railway collectors, this colourful and attractive French poster would also appeal to tennis memorabilia collectors, and posters with this theme are hard to find.

c1925   *39in (100cm) high*

£600-950   **BLNY**

'Paris Tanger Casablanca Par Marseille, Cie de Navigation Paquet', by Hardy, lithograph in colours printed by M. Dechaux for PLM railways, linen-backed.

1933   *39.5in (100cm) high*

£600-950   **BLNY**

'The Ancient Theatre at Arles' by Leopold Lelée, printed by Lucien Serre & cie for PLM railways, with folds.

39.5in (100cm) high

£40-60   **ON**

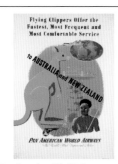

'Pan American World Airways to Australia and New Zealand', by an anonymous designer, lithograph in colours, linen-backed.
c1950   39.5in (101cm) high
£450-550   BLNY

'Fly BEA to Spain for Silver Wing Holidays', colour photographic poster by an anonymous designer.
c1965   40in (102cm) high
£30-40   ON

A CLOSER LOOK AT AN AIRLINE POSTER

Award-winning artist Weimer Pursell (1906-1974) produced poster designs for major companies including Coca Cola, Standard Oil and American Airlines.

The use of geometric forms and lines in bright colours contrasted against black is typical of Pursell's work, and reflect his interest in modern abstract art.

The abstract forms are buildings in Manhattan, with the lines on the 'pavement' hinting at people going places, or even the subway system.

He is also known for his Art Deco poster designs for the 1933 Chicago World's Fair. His work is sought after and can be hard to find.

'American Airlines to New York', designed by Weimer Pursell, with minor wrinkles.
c1956   39.75in (101cm) high
£3,000-5,000   SWA

'Pan Am's Supersonic Clipper' photographic poster featuring Concorde, printed in America.
c1965   111.5in (283cm) wide
£120-180   VSA

'Blue Star Line to South America', by Norman Wilson, lithograph in colours, printed by McCorquodale & Co., London, linen-backed.
c1930   40in (102cm) high
£600-950   BLNY

'Blue Star Line A Europa', by an anonymous designer, lithograph in colours printed by John Waddington, London, linen-backed.
c1925   40in (102cm) high
£1,500-2,000   BLNY

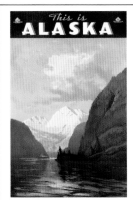

'This Is Alaska', by an anonymous designer, lithograph in colours printed for the Alaska Steamship Line, backed on linen.

c1950   34in (86cm) high

£300-400   **BLNY**

'Spiez', by Otto Baumberger, lithograph in colours, printed by Fretz & Frères, Zurich, backed on Japan paper.

1938   40in (102cm) high

£400-500   **BLNY**

'Route des Pyrènnées, Services d'autocar de la Cie du Midi', by Roger Soubie, printed by Baudelot, with tears, folds and losses.

                40.5in (103cm)

£300-400   **ON**

'Roman & Mediaeval France', coaching poster by Lajos Marton, printed by McCorquodale for PLM Autocars.

1935   39.5in (100cm) high

£40-60   **ON**

'Avranches Baie de Mont St Michel', by Albert Bergevin for the Avranches Syndicat D'Initiative, lithograph in colours, linen-backed.

Bergevin (1887-1974) lived in Avranches, a hillside town that overlooks the bay of Mont St Michel. The colourful Art Nouveau style, very much inspired by Henri de Toulouse Lautrec, is appealing.

c1920   42in (107cm) high

£1,200-1,500   **BLNY**

'Play Golf in Germany', by Osswald, lithograph in colours, printed by Oscar Consee, Munich, linen-backed.

As with the tennis-themed poster on a previous page, the golfing theme adds value to this poster.

1930   39in (99cm) high

£800-1,000   **BLNY**

'Coq Sur Mer', tourism poster by Martin Melsen, printed by Henri Melsen, Brussels, linen-backed.

1923   39in (99cm) high

£500-700   **BLNY**

QUICK REFERENCE

- Pictorial posters advertising products enjoyed a golden age that began in the late 19thC and lasted for almost a century. The 1920s and 1930s saw particularly innovative posters, as influential and prolific designers pushed boundaries to see what they could create. Although the advent of television largely took over the advertising market, product posters are still sought after today due to their visual appeal and their importance to the 20thC poster and graphic design.
- Always consider the brand and the item depicted. Certain long-lived brands have become 'household names' and these are usually desirable and often valuable as they have a large following of collectors. Meanwhile, posters advertising smoking are becoming more sought-after, partly as a document of social history as the habit becomes less popular. Smoking posters also have cross-market interest (as they appeal to collectors of smoking memorabilia as well as poster collectors), and other products with cross-market

interest, such as cars or cycling, may also prove to be desirable. It is also worth considering 1970s posters advertising brands that are now popular. Posters from this era onwards are usually not as highly priced as earlier posters, and may be worth investing in, particularly if nostalgia for the brand grows in the future.
- In general, look for striking images with bold, bright colours, and designs that are typical of the period – Art Nouveau and Art Deco posters are sought after, as are those from the 1950s. A strong design by a notable designer, such as Jean Carlu, Paul Colin or Bernard Villemot, will also be desirable. However, visual appeal is paramount – an attractive poster for an unknown brand will usually prove popular.
- Condition is very important, so avoid those examples with tears and damage. This is particularly true of posters from the 1970s onwards, which you should buy in as close to mint condition as possible.

'Lefèvre-Utile Gaufrettes Vanille', biscuit poster by Alphonse Mucha, lithograph in colours, framed and glazed.

c1890   8in (20cm) high

£350-450   **BLNY**

A CLOSER LOOK AT A LEFEVRE-UTILE POSTER

French biscuit maker Lefèvre Utile is a collectable name, particularly designs by notable Art Nouveau designer Alphonse Mucha like the one on the left.

This is a complex and highly detailed image, printed with many different colours and tones, that gives a superb period feel.

Bocchino produced a number of designs for Lefevre-Utile, all with a wholesome feel that has led to him being dubbed the 'Norman Rockwell of the biscuit world'.

'Lefèvre-Utile', by Vincent Bocchino, printed by F. Champenois, Paris, lithograph in colours, in near mint condition, backed on card.

1911   27in (68cm) wide

£1,000-1,500   **BLNY**

'Caramel Klaus' by Giovanni Bonfatti, printed by Raimondi & Zaccardi, Milan, in very good condition, linen-backed.

c1920   55in (140cm) high

£800-1,200   **BLNY**

'Souriez Madame! C'est du Cleret' by Jean d'Ylen, printed by Vercasson, mounted on linen with restoration.

15.75in (40cm) high

£150-250   **ON**

'Mazawatte Tea', by an unknown designer, printed by Stafford & Co., two sheet poster, lithograph in colours, mint condition, linen-backed.

c1920   40in (102cm)

£600-900   **BLNY**

'Monet Goyon', by P.D., printed by Affiches Gaillard, Paris, lithograph in colours, linen-backed.

c1930   *43.5in (110cm) high*

£1,000-1,500   **BLNY**

'Monet Goyon', by P.D., printed by Affiches Gaillard, Paris, lithograph in colours, in near mint condition, linen-backed.

Art Deco and later posters that hint at the speed of cars or motorcycles, as here, are usually highly sought after.

c1930   *44in (112cm)*

£1,200-1,600   **BLNY**

A CLOSER LOOK AT A SHELL POSTER

This is executed in the typical muted colour palette found on many Shell posters of the 1930s-50s, and is titled in the same way as much of the rest of the series.

Mann is not considered one of the most sought after designers in the series, but the angular, abstract and modern style is appealing.

The campaign, aimed at making people drive more, included designs by leading and innovative modern artists including Edward McKnight Kauffer and Hans Schleger.

Cathleen Mann (1896-1959) studied at the notable Slade School of Fine Art and produced a number of designs for Shell, British Petroleum and the London Underground.

'Film Stars use Shell', by Cathleen Mann, printed by The Baynard Press, lithograph in colours, in near mint condition, linen-backed.

1938   *45in (114cm) wide*

£800-1,200   **BLNY**

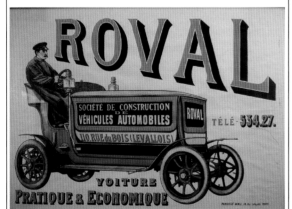

'Roval Voiture Pratique & Economique' by an anonymous designer, printed by Wall, Paris,, mounted on linen.

40in (102cm) wide

£500-700   **ON**

'Eco-Pneus', by an anonymous designer, lithograph in colours printed by Havas, Caen, linen-backed.

c1930   *46in (117cm) high*

£300-400   **BLNY**

'Pneu-Velo Continental', by an anonymous designer, printed by Editions & Publicité, Paris, linen-backed.

c1910   *30.5in (77cm) high*

£800-1,200   **BLNY**

POSTERS

'Starlight Savon', by Henri Meunier, lithograph in colours, printed by O. de Rycker, Brussels, linen-backed.

1899   *34in (87cm) high*

£1,000-1,500   **BLNY**

'Ripolin' paint advertising poster, by Jean d'Ylen, printed by Vercasson, mounted on linen with restoration.

          29.5in (75cm) high

£400-600   **ON**

'Lord' hat advertising poster, by Paolo Federico Garretto, Alfieri & Lacroix S.A.-Milano, in excellent condition, linen-backed.

1930   *36in (91.5cm) high*

£150-250   **SAS**

'Splendid' cigar advertising poster, by Fred Neukomm (1905-1988), printed by Kummerly & Frey, Berne, lithograph in colours, linen-backed.

c1930   *50in (127cm) high*

£800-1,200   **BLNY**

QUICK REFERENCE - BERNARD VILLEMOT

French artist, illustrator and poster designer Bernard Villemot (1911-89) is considered one of the most important French post-war poster designers. He created his first poster for Bally in 1967 and worked with them for 22 years until his death. His first poster, known as 'Legs', won the Martini Prize Gold Medal, and subsequent designs went on to win the Grand Prix for poster design more than five times. This design, released during the peak of his skills, is known as 'Bally Kick'. He also worked for Air France, Orangina, and other companies. Influenced by the Bauhaus, his hallmark style uses flat planes of bold, contrasted colours, thin outlines and stylised abstracted forms. The result is a simple, yet highly feminine image that promotes Bally shoes as being glamourous and modern, and having great flair.

'Bally' shoe advertising poster, by Bernard Villemot, offset lithograph in colours, printed by A. Kacher, Paris, linen-backed.

1972   65in (166cm) high

£300-400   **BLNY**

'Vichy', by Bernard Villemot, lithograph in colours, printed by S.A. Courbet, Paris, linen-backed.

1953   *39.5in (100cm) high*

£500-600   **BLNY**

QUICK REFERENCE

- One of the first kinds of attractive packaging, these ceramic lids were used to cover pots containing products such as food, bear's grease (a hair product), or toothpaste. They were manufactured in Staffordshire, by companies including F. & R. Pratt, who were granted a related patent in 1848, T. J. & J. Mayer and J. Ridgway.
- The first pot lids were produced in the 1820s, and were transfer printed in blue and white, or black and white. By the 1830s they were being produced in bulk. Coloured lids appeared in the early 1840s. Over 350 images are known, some of which featured bears, which indicated bear's grease in the pot below. Some collectors choose to collect by image type, with bears and scenes of Pegwell Bay most popular.
- Before 1860, lids were flat and lightweight, and had a screw thread. The quality of these early pieces was high, and so they are usually the most desirable. The lids became heavier and convex between 1860 and 1875, and heavier still with flat tops after 1875. It is a good idea to handle as many lids

as you can to get a feel for these weights.

- It is not possible to narrow down the date of most pot lids beyond these periods, as most are not dated and many images were produced for long periods. Examples that commemorate specific event, such as the Great Exhibition in 1851, can be dated c1851 as it is unlikely they were produced for long afterwards. Changes to design and some maker's marks can also help with dating.
- Collectors look for examples in excellent condition or those with unusual variations in design or borders. Always examine a scene carefully to identify any variations. Chips to flange and rim do not seriously affect value, but chips to design can cause a drop of 50-75 per cent. Be aware of reproductions – run your finger over a lid. If you feel the transfer, the piece is likely to be a later reproduction.
- The numbers given are used in K. V. Mortimer's 'Pot Lids Reference & Price Guide', the current standard reference guide for pot lids.

A Staffordshire 'The Volunteers' pot lid, no.217, probably produced by the Bates, Brown-Westhead, Moore & Co. factory from 1859.

£120-180   SAS

A Staffordshire 'The Wolf And The Lamb' pot lid, no.343, produced by the Pratt factory.

4.25in (10.5cm) diam

£25-35   SAS

A Staffordshire 'Our Pets' pot lid, no.330, with glaze flaking, produced by the Pratt factory, with registration diamond for March 1852 near the horse's tail.

4in (10cm) diam

£120-180   SAS

A Staffordshire 'On Guard' pot lid, no.334, with dog under the bench, produced by the Pratt factory.

On some lids, the dog is replaced by a bucket, but this does not usually affect the value.

4.25in (10.5cm) diam

£40-60   SAS

A Staffordshire 'The Snow-drift' pot lid, no.267, with a line and dot border.

The scene was based on Sir Edwin Landseer's oil painting 'Highland Shepherd's Dog In The Snow'.

4.25in (10.5cm) diam

£30-40   SAS

POT LIDS

A large Staffordshire 'Drayton Manor' pot lid, no.102, with gilt-lined border, produced by the Mayer factory.

Showing the residence of politician and Prime Minister Sir Robert Peel, this lid was reproduced up to the 1960s by Mayer and Kirkhams, explaining its low value.

A Staffordshire 'Albert Memorial' pot lid, no.241, produced by the Pratt factory.

This variation with the carriage is slightly less valuable than the one without. Earlier examples have green, rather than brown, trees.

A Staffordshire 'New Houses of Parliament, Westminster' later issue pot lid, no.232, produced by the Pratt factory.

5.25in (13cm) diam

£100-150   **SAS**

4.25in (10.5cm) diam

£70-90   **SAS**

£50-70   **SAS**

A Staffordshire 'Great Exhibition 1851' pot lid, no.142, produced by the Mayer factory, restored.

4.25in (10.5cm) diam

£40-60   **SAS**

A Staffordshire 'Windsor Castle and St. George's Chapel' pot lid, no.175, without wording, damaged.

A variation with advertising wording for Royal Windsor Toilet Cream can fetch over five times the price of this damaged example.

3.5in (9.5cm) diam

£60-80   **SAS**

A very rare Staffordshire 'Holy Trinity Church' pot lid, no. 229, with leaf and scroll border, produced by the William Pratt factory, restored.

This is the rarest of the series of lids showing buildings associated with Shakespeare.

5in (13cm) diam

£650-750   **SAS**

A Staffordshire 'Paris Exhibition 1878' pot lid, no.153, produced by the Pratt factory, with a dotted border and hairline crack.

4.5in (11cm) diam

£40-60   **SAS**

A Staffordshire 'The Administration Building World's Fair, Chicago 1893' pot lid, no.156, with a grey print.

Look out for other colours such as buff or a yellowy brown as these are extremely rare and may fetch over five times this sum.

4.25in (10.5cm) diam

£350-450   **SAS**

A Staffordshire 'The Ins' pot lid, no.15.

Produced as a pair with 'The Outs' shown below, examples with fancy borders fetch more. For an example, see 'Miller's Collectables Price Guide 2009', p.371.

3.5in (8cm) diam

£250-300 **SAS**

A Staffordshire 'The Village Wakes' pot lid, no.321, with fancy border, produced by the Pratt factory.

A very rare variation lacking the title, two children and the monkey can fetch over four times the value of this standard scene.

4in (10cm) diam

£450-550 **SAS**

A Staffordshire 'Bears on Rock' pot lid, no.10, with brown bears and gold banded border and flange, produced by the Mayer factory.

Brown bears on this early and small lid are very rare – black is more common.

3.25in (8cm) diam

£700-1,000 **SAS**

A Staffordshire 'The Outs' pot lid, no.16, by the Pratt or Ridgway factory.

3.5in (9cm) diam

£150-250 **SAS**

A CLOSER LOOK AT A POT LID

This is part of a popular trio of lids which includes 'The Village Wakes'.

Bear subjects are sought after, and this has a green printed base, as well as an unusual and fancy border which adds value.

'The Village Wakes' was taken from a watercolour by Jesse Austin. This was taken from a painting by the notable painter David Wilkie RA (1785-1845).

This lid bears a diamond registration mark near the roof of the house, showing it was registered in July 1852.

A Staffordshire 'The Bear Pit' pot lid, no.6, with wavy line border and without the dome on the left, produced by the Pratt factory.

3in (7.5cm) diam

£120-180 **SAS**

A Staffordshire 'The Parish Beadle' pot lid, no.322, complete with green printed Punch base.

4in (10cm) diam

£1,000-1,500 **SAS**

POT LIDS

A Staffordshire 'Balaklava, Inkerman, Alma' pot lid, no.204, depicting the Earl of Cardigan, Lord Raglan, General Simpson and the Duke of Cambridge, produced by the Mayer factory, restored.

Later issues have poorer colours and are worth less than strongly coloured early examples, which can fetch around £600 or more.

5in (12.5cm) diam

£250-350 **SAS**

A Staffordshire 'Wellington with Cocked Hat' late issue pot lid, no.182, without lettering on the border, produced by the Mayer factory.

5.25in (13.5cm) diam

£400-600 **SAS**

A CLOSER LOOK AT A POT LID

This rare lid was made by Bates, Walker & Co. around 1876 to commemorate the centenary of the War of Independence.

Hand-coloured examples are much rarer than monochrome lids and can fetch around twice this amount.

Exhibition lids are a collectable subject area, and the American War of Independence theme is also highly desirable.

A medium Staffordshire 'Tria Juncta in Uno' pot lid, no.202, depicting Queen Victoria, Napoleon II and Sultan Abd-ul-Majid, produced by the Mayer factory.

5in (13cm) diam

£350-450 **SAS**

A Staffordshire 'Napoleon III and Empress Eugenie' pot lid, no.181, with double line, laurel and berry border.

5.25in (13cm) diam

£200-300 **SAS**

A Staffordshire 'Queen Victoria and the Prince Consort' pot lid, no.167, almost certainly by the Pratt factory.

Look out for the extremely rare variation where Queen Victoria has no earring in her left ear.

5in (13cm) diam

£280-320 **SAS**

It was probably produced for sale at H.P. & W.C. Taylor's stand at the Philadelphia Exhibition – look out for larger sizes as these are even rarer.

A Staffordshire 'Washington Crossing the Delaware' pot lid, no.157, smaller size, monochrome version, with base.

3.5in (9cm) diam

£1,500-2,500 **SAS**

A rare Staffordshire 'The Matador' pot lid, no.78, probably produced by the Mayer factory.

This very rare lid was also produced in an even smaller size.

3.5in (8.5cm) diam

£700-900 SAS

A Staffordshire 'Lady Brushing Hair' pot lid, no.111, with purple bodice and yellow skirt, produced by the Pratt factory.

Look out for a differently coloured variation with a bare breast – deemed too risqué for Victorian tastes it was withdrawn and is rare today. However, the rarest variation features the lady wearing a yellow bodice and short sleeves – this can fetch over three times the value of this example.

3in (7.5cm) diam

£200-300 SAS

A very rare Staffordshire 'The Kingfisher' pot lid, no.286, with gold line border, produced by the Mayer factory, restored.

5.25in (13cm) diam

£650-850 SAS

A Staffordshire 'The Swallow' pot lid, no.129, produced by the Bates, Elliott & Co. factory, restored.

3.75in (9.5cm) diam

£100-150 SAS

A Staffordshire 'Shells' pot lid, no.73, restored.

3.25in (8cm) diam

£50-80 SAS

A Staffordshire 'Rose & Convulvulus' pot lid, no.401, with gold line border, produced by the Pratt factory.

4in (10cm) diam

£180-220 SAS

A Staffordshire 'Royal Coat of Arms' pot lid, no.173, with blank blue panel beneath, restored.

Look out for the name 'J.N. Osborn' in the panel, as this can increase value by at least half.

4in (10cm) diam

£300-400 SAS

QUICK REFERENCE

- Surprisingly, the most important factor to consider is the case, as to most collectors the style and colour matter more than the internal radio mechanism. The golden age of radio design lasted from the 1930s until the late 1950s, with pre-war radios generally the most valuable.
- Most examples from the 1930s are in the Art Deco style. Look for strong geometric or stepped forms and designs influenced by architecture such as skyscrapers. Grilles were the first feature to change in the early 1930s, and examples with decorative grilles are worth looking out for. During the 1950s, shapes generally became more streamlined and curved.
- As well as the form consider the material. The first radios were housed in simple wooden cases, but during the late 1920s inlays and other materials were used, with plastics such as Bakelite and Catalin beginning to appear in the

1930s. Although most Bakelite examples are found in brown, plastics freed radios from the dull monotony of woods.
- Bright colours such as red, green and blue are therefore highly desirable, but the classic Art Deco combination of black and chrome is also sought after. Coloured British radios are particularly scarce. Brand names are another important factor, with desirable names including FADA, EKCO, Philco and Emerson.
- The highest prices paid today are for classic Art Deco radios in brightly coloured Catalin by American makers. In 2007, a very rare baby blue 'Air King' fetched $51,000 at auction.
- However, as few can afford to buy at this level, and examples in good condition are limited, many collectors look elsewhere. Appealing radios in wooden cases that represent the style of the 1930s represent the largest part of the market, and prices look set to remain strong.

A Philips model 2531 radio and separate hexagonal speaker, with brown Bakelite cases and stylised floral grille.

c1930   *19in (48cm) high*

£150-250   OTA

A German Mende radio, with black Bakelite case and original grille cloth.

German sets from this period are not common.

c1933

£400-600   OTA

An E.K. Cole Ltd Ekco SH25 radio, designed by J.K. White, with brown Bakelite case, anodised copper grille, and original grille cloth.

This classic design incorporates some of the Egyptian references found in the Art Deco style of the period.

1932   *18in (45.5cm) high*

£450-650   OTA

A Co-operative Wholesale Society 'Defiant' radio, model M900, with brown bakelite case and printed factory label.

A rare Zetavox model ST radio, with stepped and geometric brown Bakelite case and geometric speaker panel.

1933

£400-600   OTA

This is the most desirable Co-operative Society Defiant radio, due to the shaped case, as well as the rarest model. The 'Defiant' name was used as the company was defying industry rules concerning the minimum cost of a radio at the time.

1935   *13.25in (34cm) high*

£1,000-1,500   WW

A Philco 'People's Set' radio, model no. 444, with mottled dark brown Bakelite case, applied factory labels.

This was designed purely for the UK market and was sold at a very low price, hence the 'People's Set'.

1936   *16.5in (42cm) high*

£320-380   **WW**

A CLOSER LOOK AT AN EKCO RADIO

Originally released as an economy radio, this was available in black and chrome or brown Bakelite versions.

Although the black and chrome version was only slightly more expensive, it is usually worth up to double the value of the brown today!

Wells Coates (1895-1958) was an important Modernist designer, best known for his architecture, which included London's Isokon Building.

There were five models of round EKCO radio, each with different front designs – this is one of the most popular.

An E.K. Cole Ltd Ekco AD36 black Bakelite radio, designed by Wells Coates, with chrome detailing.

1935   *14.5in (37cm) high*

£450-650   **OTA**

A German model VE301 DYN radio, from the 'Volksempfänger' (People's Radios) range commissioned by the National Socialist government, with brown Bakelite case.

1936

£100-200   **OTA**

An E.K. Cole Ltd Ekco AC97 black Bakelite radio, with chrome and ivory Bakelite detailing and original grille cloth.

The striking Modernist design of this radio was also available in brown, which is less desirable to collectors today.

1937   *21in (53cm) high*

£700-1,000   **OTA**

A Murphy Radio Ltd model AD94 radio, with black Bakelite cabinet.

This was Murphy's first bakelite cabinet, and was produced to meet wartime conditions.

1940   *13.5in (34cm) high*

£80-150   **OTA**

A Fada Streamliner Model 1000 'Bullet' radio, with Butterscotch Catalin case and knobs.

1940   *10.25in (26cm) wide*

£300-400   **OTA**

A Raymond 'Minit' radio, with red bakelite case and grille.

1949   *10in (25cm) long*

£70-150   **OTA**

A scarce 1950s French Marquett type 63 radio receiver, with brown and cream bakelite case, and applied factory label to base.

8.25in (21cm) wide

£120-180   **WW**

A CLOSER LOOK AT A PYE RADIO

A newer type of valve developed during the war enabled small battery powered radios to be made for 'personal' portable use.

Also available in black and cream Perspex, this model was unsuccessful, largely due to poor construction.

The Pye 'Sunrise' trademark (used since 1929) was similar to the Japanese flag – as news came in of prisoners of war being ill-treated in Japanese camps it fell in popularity.

This model is made of flimsy Perspex, and examples in perfect condition are rare, particularly with an original instruction booklet.

A Pye model M78F battery powered portable radio, with light green and pinky-cream Perspex case, and original instruction leaflet.

7.25in (18.5cm) high

1948

£300-850   **OTA**

A Murphy Model A3A radio, with walnut veneered wooden case designed by R.D. Russell, and original stand and grille cloth.

The stand is rare and worth £50-80 alone. At the time, detractors called the radio the 'Pentonville Special', as the grille bars resemble those of a prison cell.

1932   *18.5in (47cm) high*

£150-250   **OTA**

A late 1950s Czechoslovakian Tesla Talisman, no.308U, with streamlined brown bakelite case, designed in 1956.

This stylish design was made under licence in Czechoslovakia. Once considered vary rare, after the fall of the Berlin wall many examples were suddenly found on street markets, severely reducing the value.

12.5in (32cm) long

£50-150   **OTA**

A rare Pye Model K radio, with a solid walnut case and 'Sunrise' design speaker grille.

1932   *15.5in (39cm) high*

£100-200   **OTA**

A Western Electric Co. Model 44001 crystal radio set with built-in 2-valve amplifier.

Most crystal sets were intended for headphone use and did not use any power source. This set had an optional amplifier to enable more headphones or a horn speaker to be used for family listening. This was an expensive extra for a cheap set, and few have survived.
1924   5in (12.5cm) high
£200-400   **OTA**

A Kenmac 'The Listener' crystal set, contained in a tortoiseshell effect celluloid case in the form of a book.

c1924   4.75in (12cm) high
£400-600   **OTA**

On The Air

The Vintage Technology Centre

We Buy

Old radios, televisions, gramophones and telephones.

Top Prices Paid

We Sell

To collectors, museums and dealers from all over the world.

Send a large S.A.E. for a sample copy of "AIRWAVES" -essential reading for anyone interested in Vintage Technology. Or visit us at:

www.vintageradio.co.uk

We have the reputation, experience and contacts to give you the best deal

On The Air Ltd

The Highway, Hawarden (nr.Chester) Deeside CH53DN
Tel/Fax 01244 530300

A Japanese Matsushita Electrical Industries Panasonic red plastic model R-70 Panapet transistor radio.

Examine the case as damage reduces the value considerably. The rarest colour is purple, which often fetches up to twice the value of more common colours such as red. The Panapet radio was made only for the Western market.
                                    4in (10cm) high
£30-40   **M20C**

An S.G. Brown Ltd model H2 black metal horn-shaped radio speaker.

As early radios had no built in speakers, many types of speaker were made, often using a horn to amplification. Value depends mainly on the appearance.
c1924
£60-80   **OTA**

FIND OUT MORE...

Jonathan Hill ' Radio! Radio!' . *Exeter: Sunrise Press, 1996*
Tony Thompson ' Collecting Vintage Radios' . *Marlborough: The Crowood Press Ltd, 2007*

A C/I 'Chelford No. 2' rectangular plate, face restored.

12in (30.5cm) wide

£50-60   GWRA

A Henschel & Sohn worksplate, kassel number "28977", dated.

Ex Malawi Railways G Class 2-8-2 Locomotive number 64.

1954

£400-500   GWRA

A Beyer Peacock & Co. 'Manchester' brass worksplate, dated.

Ex Bengal & Assam Railway 4-6-0 'RS' class in the range 31863 - 31870.

1914   *9.75in (25cm) wide*

£150-200   GWRA

A Hudswell Clark & Co Ltd Railway Foundry Leeds brass worksplate, number "D1254", in ex loco condition, "D10" stencilled onto reverse, dated.

Ex Manchester Ship Canal 204hp 0-6-0DM which was sold to Hunslet January 1976 where it was rebuilt under order HE 8522.

1962

£60-80   GWRA

A 'The Thames-Clyde Express' cast aluminium locomotive name plate, with letters in relief on red background.

40in (101.5cm) wide

£2,500-3,000   HT

A 'Melton Mowbray' enamelled totem station sign.

36.5in (92.5cm) wide

£500-700   HT

A British Railways E. R. 'Fairlop' enamelled station name board, in good condition, with two chips and some fading to background.

58in (147.5cm) wide

£80-100   W&W

A 'Road Narrows' alloy sign, fitted with reflective beads, all beads intact, stress cracks at the top of sign, one fixing bracket remains.

£50-70   GWRA

SHEFFIELD RAILWAYANA AUCTIONS

"Britain's leading Railwayana Auction House"
Steam World

Nameplates, Posters, Postcards, Clocks, Totems, White Star, Cast Iron Signs, Signalling Devices, Tickets, Lamps, China, Silver Plate, Antiquarian Railway Books, Anything related to Railways

DATES FOR 2010

March 13th, June 12th, September 11th, December 11th

Commission rate to vendors only 10% plus VAT (i.e. 11.75%) on single items, no other hidden charges. Illustrated catalogue in full colour £6 available 3 weeks prior to each auction. Free telephone valuations. Free collection of nameplates or collections. Why not telephone now?

SHEFFIELD RAILWAYANA AUCTIONS
4 The Glebe, Clapham, Bedford MK41 6GA
Tel/Fax: +44 (0)1234 325341
Email: SheffRailwayana@aol.com
Website: www.sheffieldrailwayana.co.uk

A brass plaque, with belt-shaped rim and raised lettering 'Great North Eastern Railway', two lion crests and Scottish Thistle and English Rose decoration.

23in (58.5cm) diam

£450-550   A&G

A Letterkenny railway gate crossing lamp, the interior stamped with the company initials 'L.R.', with brass plate marked 'SAXBY FARMER LTD SIGNALLING ENGINEERS LONDON'.

£80-120   GWRA

G. W. Railwayana Auctions Ltd

The Worldwide Specialist Auctioneers of Railway, Transport & Advertising Memorabilia

World Record Breakers

Flexible Vendor Commission Rates

Bredon Office Tony Hoskins 01684 773487 / Evesham Office Simon Turner 01386 760109
W: www.gwra.co.uk   E: master@gwra.co.uk   *10% Buyers Premium*

A Beatles metal lunchbox, by Aladdin Industries, with embossed 3-D portraits and signatures, with thermos flask.

This was the first metal box to feature pop music performers

Lunchbox 8in (20.5cm) wide

£200-250   HER

A Beatles unused diary, by Beat Productions, Glasgow, Scotland, the pages printed with 'fun Fab four facts'.

1965

£60-80   KA

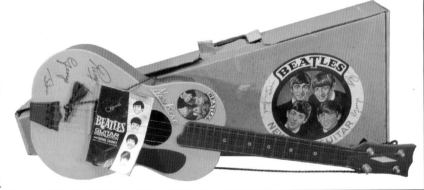

The Beatles 'New Beat Guitar', by Selcol Ltd., of orange and burgundy plastic with four strings, in original box with applied sticker of the band and facsimile signatures, with instructions and song chart.

£250-300   GORL

An American Beatles 1964 scrap book, published by Whitman (linked with NEMS Enterprises).

Originally sold for 29cents, filled with American newspaper clippings from August 1964 when "A Hard Day's Night" premiered at the Salem Paramount movie theatre (13 August 1964).

£70-80   KA

A Washington Pottery 'Beatles' plate, transfer printed with an image of the Beatles and their script signatures.

£40-50   KA

A set of four coloured plastic figures of The Beatles, made by Emirober.

£45-50   KA

Beatles
& Pop Memorabilia
WANTED

Any Pop Memorabilia Considered
Free Quotations

Thosands And Thousands Paid For Beatles, Stones, Zeppelin, Who, Hendrix & Floyd Concert Posters.

£25,000 to £60,000 Paid For Handwritten Beatles Lyrics

£8,000+ Paid For Signed Beatles Albums

£4,000+ Paid For Signed Beatles Photos & Programmes

£2,000 Paid For Beatles Autographs On One Page

£1,000 to £4,000 Paid For Handwritten Beatles Letters

we-buy-beatles.com

Tracks, PO Box 117, Chorley, Lancashire, PR6 0UU
TEL: 01257 269726 - FAX 01257 231340
e-mail: sales@tracks.co.uk

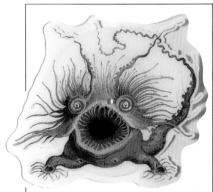

A CLOSER LOOK AT A PICTURE DISC

The value of picture discs is dependant on the recording artist, with popular artists, such as Madonna and Queen, commanding higher values.

Look for examples with high quality and appealing artwork that is typical of the artist or album. Some images are rare and, if desirable, may be valuable.

The sound quality produced by picture discs is typically poor, so visual appeal is perhaps the most important factor to value.

Picture discs were produced from the early 1930s, when they were made from a sheet of thin vinyl film placed over a thick paper print and pressed with grooves. Coloured vinyl picture discs were introduced in the 1970s by Metronome Records.

Queen, I'm Going Slightly Mad, EMI, shaped single picture disc.

SINGLE £25-30   PC

Queen, Innuendo, 12" single picture disc, EMI.

SINGLE £25-30   PC

A Bob Dylan 'The Freewheelin' Bob Dylan' US stereo LP, by CBS label, serial no BPG-62193.

£25-30   PC

A Manic Street Preachers 'You Love Us' UK stereo LP, by Heavenly, serial no. HVN 10.

£20-25   PC

An Oi Polloi 'Unite and Win!' UK LP, by Oi! records, serial no OIR-011.

£20-25   PC

A Pink Floyd 'The Best of Pink Floyd' stereo LP record, by Colombia.

£100-120   PC

WANTED
1960's and 1970's CONCERT POSTERS

FLYERS, HANDBILLS, PROGRAMMES, TICKETS, PERSONAL EFFECTS, SIGNED ITEMS, DOCUMENTS, ANYTHING UNUSUAL OR ASSOCIATED 1960's AND 1970's ROCK AND POP MEMORABILIA.

WE PAY THE BEST PRICES

We will pay up to **£6,000** for an original concert poster for **THE BEATLES**, **£4,000** for **THE ROLLING STONES** and **THE WHO**, **£2,000** for **LED ZEPPELIN** and **JIMI HENDRIX**, as well as very high prices for other 1960's and 1970's Rock and Pop Memorabilia.

FREE VALUATIONS
CASH PAID INSTANTLY

Tel: 01494 436644 or 07890 626840

Email: music@usebriggs.com

BRIGGS ROCK AND POP MEMORABILIA
Loudwater House,
London Road, Loudwater,
High Wycombe,
Buckinghamshire, HP10 9TL

A Michael Jackson vinyl doll, by Ljn, NY under licence from MJJ Productions Inc, in the `Beat It' outfit .

This is one of a series of four dolls, originally retailed for $14.99.

14in (35.56cm)

£70-90   MTB

BEATLES, POP AND ENTERTAINMENT MEMORABILIA WANTED!

TOP PRICES PAID! ANYTHING CONSIDERED!
CONCERT POSTERS, HANDBILLS, TICKETS, PROGRAMMES, NOVELTIES, TOYS, GUITARS, PROMO ITEMS, SIGNATURES, ETC.
E.G. BEATLES, STONES, THE WHO, LED ZEPPELIN, SEX PISTOLS, PUNK, PSYCHEDELIA, 60s, 70s, 80s, ETC.

PLEASE CONTACT:
**DAVE FOWELL
COLLECTORS CORNER
P.O. BOX 8, CONGLETON, CHESHIRE, CW12 4GD, ENGLAND**
TEL: 01260 270429 FAX: 01260 298996
EMAIL: dave.popcorner@ukonline.co.uk

SCIENTIFIC INSTRUMENTS

ANTIQUE SCIENTIFIC INSTRUMENTS

ANTIQUE MICROSCOPE SLIDES IN CABINETS AND BOXES QUALITY MICROSCOPES

I specialise in and wish to purchase unusual, interesting and early Rules, Slide Rules in Boxwood, Ivory or Brass, Pocket Calculators and unusual mechanical calculators by Fowler, Otis King, Curta, etc. Early and unusual Scientific Instruments, e.g. Microscopes, Telescopes, Theodolites, Compasses, etc. Early Drawing Instruments and Quality Cabinet Makers Tools

WANTED!
I wish to purchase Antique Microscope Slides and Quality Microscopes

HIGHEST PRICES PAID
Single items or collections

Charles Tomlinson
Tel/Fax: 01244 318395
Email: charles.tomlinson@lineone.net

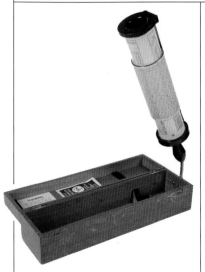

A Fuller calculator, by Stanley, London, with bakelite mounts, in a fitted bow with brass mounting arm, with copies of instructions.

£250-300　　　WW

A pair of 19thC apothecary's balance, by S. Mawson & Sons, with brass beam and pans, standing on stained wood base with two underlying drawers, with various weights.

Balances are a very specialised market, with few dedicated collectors. Value depends on the maker and the use: coin or cabinet scales can be more desirable.

£100-150　　　A&G

An 'Improved Patent Magneto-Electric Machine for Nervous Diseases', with a brass and steel frame and ebonised handled grips, with a printed label to the interior of the mahogany case, with winding handle.

10.25in (26cm) wide

£100-150　　　WW

An 18thC brass gunner's sector, divided in eight horizontal scales, including 'Paces Pynt Blanck, Bredth of the Ladell Waight of the Shot'.

8in (20.5cm) long

£350-400　　　WW

A silver pincushion shaped as a swimming duck, by Crisford & Norris of Birmingham, with textured plumage.

1908   2in (5.5cm) long

£150-200   **WW**

A silver plated pincushion, modelled as a pig, unmarked.

2in (5cm) long

£30-40   **SAS**

A pair of silver novelty pincushions, by Adie & Lovekin of Birmingham, in the form of a swimming swans.

Pairs of novelty pincushions by the same maker are rare, as most people only needed one pincushion.

1907   Larger 2.75in (7cm) wide

£300-400   **WW**

A CLOSER LOOK AT A NOVELTY PIN CUSHION

A silver pincushion shaped as a seated chick emerging from an egg, by S. Mordan & Co., with Chester hallmarks.

Sampson Mordan & Co. was a well known maker of fine silver and gold objects, as well as propelling pencils, whose work is sought after. The Chester assay office closed in 1962.

1906   1.75in (4.5cm) high

£120-180   **WW**

Rollerskating themed items are scarce, particularly of this early date.

The first recorded use of roller skates was in 1743, with the four wheeled version we know today being invented in the US in 1863 by James Leonard Plimpton.

Although Collins & Cook are not a major name, it is well made, with plenty of detailing from the toe cap to the serrated sole welt and wheel axles.

The shape and style of the boot is consistent with Edwardian fashions

An Edwardian silver novelty roller skate pin cushion, by Collins & Cook of Birmingham, with registered design number '535766' for 1909.

1909   2.75in (7cm) long

£180-220   **WW**

A silver pincushion in the shape of a small standing pig, by Henry Matthews of Birmingham.

1906   2in (5cm) long

£120-180   **WW**

An Edwardian silver novelty pin cushion, Saunders & Shepherd, Birmingham, in the form of a standing elephant.

1905   2in (5cm) wide

£100-150   **WW**

A pair of Russian silver multi-coloured, cloisonné enamel sugar tongs, by Mari Serrenova, with shaded floral designs.

1908-1917

£220-280 WW

A pair of late 19thC to early 20thC Russian silver gilt and cloisonné enamelled sugar tongs, initialled, with Russian state marks.

1896-1908

£250-350 WW

A late Victorian silver cigar cutter, by H. Matthews of Birmingham, in the form of a pair of scissor snuffers.

1894   4.5in (11.5cm) long

£150-200 WW

A set of four late Victorian silver menu holders, by S. Clifford of London, on a fox hunting theme.

Despite the recent ban in the UK, pieces related to fox hunting and country pursuits are sought after. Even though their use is now outdated, menu holders are strongly collectable.

1899

£250-350 WW

A Victorian silver heraldic menu holder, by Henry William Dee of London, in the form of a squirrel eating a nut, on a curved base.

Certain animals are more collectable than others, especially dogs and cats. Squirrels are comparatively rare, however, hence the higher price. This is also well made, with plenty of detail.

1877   2in (5cm) high

£320-380 WW

A silver commemorative model of a pile driving engine, by Sunard & Co., inscribed 'Rowden Barter & Co. presented to Sir George LE Hunt, as a memento of the ceremony of driving the first pile – outer Harbour S.A. 20/7/04'.

c1904   8.75in (22cm) high

£380-420 WW

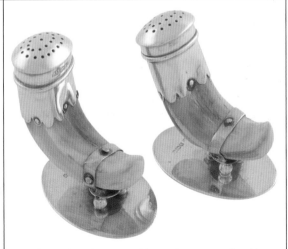

A pair of Edwardian silver mounted boar tusk pepperettes, by Atkin Brothers of Sheffield, mounted on oval bases.

1902   2.5in (6.5cm) high

£400-600 WW

QUICK REFERENCE – DUNHILL LIGHTERS

Dunhill are often called the 'Rolls Royce' of cigarette lighters, having produced some of the most luxurious models ever made. The 'Unique' lighter was developed by scientific instrument makers Wise & Greenwood in 1919. With its snuffer arm and a mechanism that allowed it to be operated with one hand, it became a bestseller. Look out for examples in precious metals, those with lacquered designs by Japanese company Namiki, or ones that contain hidden features, such as watches or compacts. Prices range from under £100 for a plated 'Unique', to over £10,000 for a rare watch lighter in a precious metal.

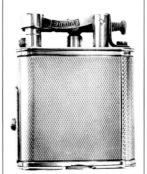

A late 1930s Dunhill silver plated 'Unique' pipe lighter, with extending wick and slider, engine turned design.

The slider moves a tube containing the wick up and down, allowing tobacco in a pipe bowl to be lit.

2.25in (5.5cm) high

£100-150   SAS

A 1970s Dunhill 70 gold plated 'Rollagas' rolled gold cigarette lighter, with engine turned pattern, impressed 'DUNHILL 70' and numbered 'BR889', with some wear from use.

2.25in (6cm) high

£30-40   CARS

A Dunhill 9ct gold 'Unique' lighter, with engine turned design, and control marks.

2.25in (5.5cm) high

£350-450   SAS

A 1950s Dunhill 'Aquarium' table lighter, with reverse-cut and painted underwater scene of tropical fish, and metal fittings.

Look out for the half-size 'Miniature', as this is rarer. If birds or other animals or motifs replace the fish, the price will also rise, as these can be very rare.

4in (10cm) high

£600-900   SWO

An Elisorm Auto-Tank 9ct gold lighter, with engine turned decoration to the body, marked '9ct' and with 'JP' owner's initials.

£35-45   SAS

An Art Deco 9ct gold vesta case, with hinged lid, engine turned centre and Greek key border, and with London hallmarks for 1923.

1923

£200-300   SAS

SMOKING MEMORABILIA

A silver circular vesta case, decorated in low relief with figures playing bowls on the lawn, maker's mark worn, with Birmingham hallmarks for 1907.

As well as appealing to vesta case collectors, the bowls theme is very rare and would appeal to collectors of sporting memorabilia, which is why this example has a high price.

1907   1.5in (4cm) diam

£500-700   **WW**

A Victorian silver novelty vesta and slow match holder, in the form of a carriage lamp with clear convex lens, with London hallmarks for H.W. Dee, 1870.

Railwayana attracts a greater number of buyers than bowls, the subject of the vesta shown above. This is also an appealing shape and of an early date.

1870   1.75in (4.5cm) high

£800-1,200   **WW**

An Art Deco silver cigarette box, with engine turned decoration, an ivory thumbpiece and an applied enamel plaque, with Birmingham hallmarks for Hassett & Harper Ltd, 1935.

1935   6.5in (17cm) long

£100-150   **WW**

A CLOSER LOOK AT A NAMIKI CIGARETTE CASE

Maki-e lacquer is a historic technique that takes many years to learn and designs can take weeks of painstaking work to create, layer by layer.

The right hand column of the mark reads 'Namiki kan', showing this to have been made in the 1930s. The left hand column is the artist's name and red 'kao' symbol, revealing that it was decorated by Maizawa Shobi.

Cigarette cases are scarce, but the value of this example is reduced by more than half because it is worn, bears a presentation engraving and the design is comparatively simple.

The goldfish design is one of the most commonly found on Namiki products, with the fish representing good fortune and luck.

A 1930s Japanese Namiki maki-e lacquer metal cigarette case, decorated with a goldfish and pondweed design by Maizawa Shobi, the gold washed interior inscribed 'Jose Pablo Costa 8-12-41'.

Shobi was a pupil of Shiroyama in 1899, on the staff of the Iwate Prefecture Technical High School in 1905, and worked as an independent lacquer artist after 1907. He was also one of the six committee members at the time of the establishment of the school of lacquer artists known as the Kokkokai. The year of the inscription is interesting as this was the year Japan bombed Pearl Harbor.

4in (10cm) high

£150-200   **MHC**

An oak Zebrano effect smoker's cabinet, with doors backed with pipe racks, the fitted interior with square cut crystal decanter to the right, blue and white tobacco jar to the centre, with three drawers, the base moulded to edge.

15.75in (40cm) wide

£180-220   **DA&H**

An Art Deco bronze penguin floor smoker's ashtray, with circular top fitted with a well and verdigris finish.

23.5in (59.5cm) high

£400-500   **SK**

QUICK REFERENCE

- Football's continued popularity creates a strong demand for memorabilia, particularly for items connected to famous teams, popular players or important matches.
- Memorabilia relating to Manchester United is among the most widely collected. Other popular teams include Liverpool, Chelsea and Arsenal. Well-known Arsenal players of the past include Charlie George, Frank McLintock and Peter Storey; modern players include Thierry Henry, Ian Wright and Patrick Vieira. Memorabilia connected to Arsenal's 'Double' win (premier league and FA Cup) in 1970-71 is desirable, as is that connected to the "Invincibles", who won the Premiership (2003-04) unbeaten.
- Shirts, boots and other equipment are all sought-after and can be extremely valuable, particularly if they were used during an important match or signed by the player and their team mates. Items connected with footballing

legends, such as Pelé, George Best, Bobby Charlton and Bobby Moore, are still in high demand, but today's football players and teams can attract equally significant sums.
- Medals, representing a team's success, are sought after with collectors, as are team caps.
- Programmes are another popular area of collecting. A large variety is available and values vary greatly. Programmes for FA and European Cup finals, international games and early, pre-WW1 games are typically the most desirable and valuable, but be aware that some matches (e.g. the 1966 World Cup) were are so obviously significant at the time that many programmes were stored in good condition keeping values low. Modern programmes are printed in large numbers and many fans keep them, meaning this is an affordable entry into collecting. Look for examples in clean condition.

A squad-signed red and white short-sleeved Tony Adams Arsenal no. 6 jersey, with Premier League flashes, 21 signatures in black marker pen, sold with a copy of Tony Adams' Testimonial programme.

£600-800   **GBA**

A long-sleeved yellow Arsenal no. 11 jersey from the 1969 League Cup final jersey worn by George Armstrong, embroidered club crest and inscribed 'WEMBLEY, 1969'.

Swindon Town defeated Arsenal 3-1 at Wembley. George Armstrong made 621 first-team appearances in a 15-year playing career.

c1969

£1,800-2,800   **GBA**

A signed short-sleeved white England no. 8 international jersey 1995 worn by Peter Beardsley, with a letter of authenticity signed by Peter Beardsley.

In his letter of authenticity Peter Beardsley states that he wore this jersey in a 1995 Umbro Cup match against Brazil.

£150-250   **GBA**

A white long-sleeved Real Madrid No.23 jersey worn by David Beckham in the Champions League match v Bayern Munich on the 10th March 2004, with UEFA Champions League flashes, dirt and blood stains; sold together with a certificate of authenticity issued by Star Chamber.

c2004

£800-1,200   **GBA**

An orange Holland no. 10 short-sleeved jersey worn by Dennis Bergkamp in the match v France at Euro 2000, embroidered with Dutch and French national flags and inscribed '21 JUNI 2000, Euro 2000 and Fair Play flashes.

In this group D match Holland beat France 3-2.

2000

£600-900   **GBA**

A short-sleeved red and white Arsenal no. 12 jersey worn by Martin Hayes in the 1988 Football League Cup final, inscribed '1988, WEMBLEY'.

Martin Hayes replaced Perry Groves and scored in the 74th minute. However, two late goals gave victory to Luton Town 3-2.

£1,000-1,500   **GBA**

A long-sleeved green Arsenal 1980 F.A. Cup final goalkeeping jersey worn by Pat Jennings, inscribed 'F.A. CUP FINAL, WEMBLEY 1980'.
1980

£1,500-2,000   **GBA**

A white short-sleeved Chelsea No.8 jersey worn by Frank Lampard during the season 2006-07 season , with Premier League flashes, the reverse lettered LAMPARD.

This jersey was gained as a swap by a West Ham United player after the match at Upton Park on 18th April 2007.
c2006

£300-400   **GBA**

A CLOSER LOOK AT AN ENGLAND FOOTBALL JERSEY

The Umbro diamond first appeared on England jerseys in the Greece match on 21st April 1971, with Banks wearing the yellow jersey in this and other 1971 matches.

Arguably the greatest goalkeeper England has ever produced, Banks is best remembered for saving Pele's header during the 1970 World Cup. He retired in 1973.

The jersey was purchased at a charity auction in 1971, an event which Gordon Banks attended.

As well as being worn by Banks, it is signed by him in a good, easily displayed position.

A signed long-sleeved yellow England international goalkeeping jersey worn by Gordon Banks, with Umbro diamond, three lions badge, the reverse with a red no. 1, signed by Gordon Banks in fine marker pen.
1971

£1,800-2,800   **GBA**

A short sleeved yellow and blue Arsenal no. 12 jersey worn by Paul Merson in the match v Manchester United 2nd April 1989.

In Arsenal's 1988-89 Championship winning season, this was the match when the famous Tony Adams' donkey chant' was first heard.
c1989

£400-600   **GBA**

A short-sleeved white England no. 19 World Youth Championship jersey 1993, inscribed 'WORLD YOUTH CHAMPIONSHIPS, AUSTRALIA 1993'.

Although Brazil won the 1993 tournament. England attained their best finishing position in the competition's history.

£60-90   **GBA**

A Liverpool v Woolwich Arsenal 9th programme for February 1907, a combined-issue also covering Everton Reserves v Barrow, in very good condition.

1907

£700-1,000   **GBA**

A Woolwich Arsenal v Birmingham programme from the first season at Highbury 1913-14, played on the 22nd November.
1913
£1,000-1,500   **GBA**

An Arsenal v Tufnell Park programme for 19th September 1914, first-team fixture in the London F.A. Challenge Cup, a combined issue also featuring the reserves fixtures v Swindon Town.

£600-800   **GBA**

An Arsenal v Bolton Wanderers four-page programme for 9th October 1920.

1920
£250-350   **GBA**

An F.A. Cup final programme for Arsenal v Huddersfield Town, on 26th April 1930.

The 1930 F.A. Cup Final was won by Arsenal who beat Huddersfield Town 2-0. This was the first cup final in which both teams entered the pitch side-by-side, and was in honour of Arsenal manager Herbert Chapman who had managed Huddersfield very successfully in the 1920s. The 1930 F.A. Cup Final is also remembered for the sinister image of the Graf Zeppelin looming over Wembley Stadium during the first half.
1930
£800-1,200   **GBA**

An Arsenal v Burnley four-page programme for 28th August 1922.
£250-350   **GBA**

A copy of the official programme for Arsenal v Tottenham Hotspur played at Highbury 29th August 1925, including an article titled 'Permit me to introduce Mr Herbert Chapman'.
£550-650   **GBA**

An F.A. Cup semi-final programme Arsenal v Manchester City played at Villa Park 12th March 1932, with Sellotaped repairs to centre pages.

1932
£300-500   **GBA**

An F.A. Cup final programme for Arsenal v Sheffield United, on 25th April 1936.

Although there is some staining through age, the blue and red are comparatively unfaded, and the inclusion of one of Wembley's famous 'twin towers' in an Art Deco-style design is appealing.
1936
£400-600   **GBA**

An F.A. Cup final programme for Huddersfield Town v Preston North End on 30th April 1938.

1938
£300-400   **GBA**

A European Cup final programme for Real Madrid v Stade Reims, played in Stuttgart on 3rd June 1959.
1959
£250-350   **GBA**

A Belgium v England international programme, played at the Heysel Stadium on 21st September 1947.

1947
£300-500   **GBA**

A souvenir tournament programme from the Campeonato Mundial de Futball in 1962 in Chile, the Spanish text by Bernard Joy and David Bravo, printed in Chile.
1962
£220-280   **GBA**

A 15ct gold London Football Combination winner's medal presented to Arsenal's R. Robinson, for the 1927-28 season, inscribed 'LONDON FOOTBALL COMBINATION, ARSENAL F.C., WINNERS, R. ROBINSON, 1927-28', in original fitted case.

£450-550 GBA

A silver and enamel medal for the 1930 World Cup finals, by Stefano Johnson of Milan, with enamelled obverse, the reverse inscribed '1ER CAMPEONATO MUNDIAL DE FOOTBALL, URUGUAY, MONTEVIDEO, 15 JULIO AGOSTO 15'.

The enamelled design is after Guillermo Laborde's official poster design for the 1930 World Cup.

£550-750 GBA

A 15ct gold F.A. Charity Shield medal presented to Arsenal's George Male in 1931, inscribed 'FOOTBALL ASSOCIATION CHARITY SHIELD', in replacement case.

Arsenal beat West Bromwich Albion 1-0.

£1,000-1,500 GBA

A CLOSER LOOK AT A MEDAL

Herbert 'Herbie' Roberts (1905-1944) was a serving police officer and played amateur football for his local side Oswestry Town.

In 1926, he was signed to Arsenal by Herbert Chapman for £200, and turned professional.

He was the team's first choice centre-half from 1930-37, and went on to win F.A. Cup runners-up and winner's medals in 1932 and 1936.

He retired after breaking his leg in 1938. He then trained the reserves team until war broke out. He died in 1944 while serving with the Royal Fusiliers.

A 9ct gold F.A. Cup runners-up medal for the 1931-32 season, awarded to Arsenal's Herbie Roberts, inscribed 'THE FOOTBALL ASSOCIATION CHALLENGE CUP, RUNNERS-UP', in original fitted case inscribed 'THE FOOTBALL ASSOCIATION CHALLENGE CUP, 1931-32'.

£2,000-3,000 GBA

A 14ct gold F.A. Cup winner's medal presented to Arsenal's goalkeeper Alex Wilson in 1936, inscribed 'THE FOOTBALL ASSOCIATION, WINNERS, ARSENAL F.C. 1935-36, A. WILSON', in fitted case.

Alexander Wilson (1908-1971) was signed by Arsenal in 1933.

£7,000-10,000 GBA

A 9ct gold and enamel Football League Division Three Championship medal awarded to Neil Webb, the obverse inscribed 'FOOTBALL LEAGUE CHAMPIONSHIP, DIVISION 3, WINNERS', the reverse inscribed 'SEASON 1982-83, N WEBB', in original fitted case.

Neil Web won this medal during his first season at Portsmouth. They finished the season with 91 points, five clear of their nearest rivals Cardiff City.

£1,000-1,500 GBA

A pair of Ashley Cole football boots, white, black and red Adidas Predators, the right tongue inscribed 'COLEY 3'.

£150-250   GBA

A pair of Saloman Kalou football boots, white and blue Adidas F50 boots, the tongue bearing the national flag of the Ivory Coast and inscribed 'KALOU' and 'JUNIOR'.

£150-250   GBA

A pair of Adidas football boots worn by Steven Gerrard in an England training session prior to the World Cup qualifier vs. Greece. Embroidered 'SG', signed by Gerrard, Nick Barmby and Sammy Lee, together with a letter of authenticity signed by Gerrard and a colour photograph of Gerrard wearing the boots and with Barmby and Lee.

2001

£350-450   GBA

A panelled leather football signed by the Celtic 1967 European Cup final team, with printed inscription, and eleven faded autographs in ink.

£150-200   GBA

A white Slazenger 25 Challenge leather football signed by the England 1966 World Cup winners, signed in pen by Sir Alf Ramsey, the 11 England finalists and additionally by squad members Greaves and Bonetti, with a programme for the final and a souvenir magazine.

£1,200-1,800   GBA

Jack Kelsey's last Wales international cap for season 1961-62, the red cap inscribed '1961-62, E, S, I, B, B'.

Kelsey is regarded as one of Wales' greatest goalkeepers. In the 1961-62 season, he played in the internationals v England, Scotland and Northern Ireland, and in the two friendlies against Brazil. He injured his back while trying to save at the feet of the Brazilian Vavà and, despite extensive attempts to rectify the problem, he was forced to retire a year later.

£1,500-2,000   GBA

An old Highbury red and white corner flag, lettered 'A.F.C.'

£650-750   GBA

A German stoneware half-litre stein with football decoration, inscribed "Hipp Hipp Hurrah".

7.25in (18.5cm) high

£80-120   **GBA**

A full-size silver plated replica of the Football Association Challenge Cup Trophy, the two-handled cup and cover realistically modelled and inscribed, fitted to ebonised plinths, with F. A. Cup ribbons, with a custom-built portable and lockable wooden cabinet.

27.25in (69cm) high

£5,000-7,000   **GBA**

Jimmy Dugdale's electroplated winner's tankard from the first Football League Cup final in 1961, engraved with the crest of the Football League and inscribed 'THE FOOTBALL LEAGUE CUP, 1960-61, WINNERS'.

5in (13cm) high

£1,000-1,500   **GBA**

A large Bohemian porcelain figure, decorated as a Uruguayan Olympic footballer in sky blue and white, in commemoration of their gold medal winning team at Amsterdam, the base inscribed 'OLYMPICOS', factory marks to underside of base, restored.

c1928

£450-650   **GBA**

An extremely rare Marx "World Cup Willie' Rollakin miniature figure, the base with ball-bearing to allow him to roll along.

With its original box, the value can rise to over £100.

1.5in (4cm) high

£60-70   **MTB**

A 1966 World Cup first day cover signed by Bobby Moore, postmarked Wembley 1st June 1966, signed in black biro.

1966

£300-500   **GBA**

An official poster for the England 1966 World Cup July 1966, after Carvosso, published by McCorquodale & Co. Ltd, framed and glazed.

26in (66cm) high

£600-800   **GBA**

QUICK REFERENCE

- Baseball cards were introduced in 1933 by the Goudey Gum Company to encourage children to buy more gum. This idea was copied from cigarette cards, which had been produced from the 19thC.
- By 1951 other companies, including Bowman Gum and Topps Chewing Gum, began producing collectable baseball cards. When Topps acquired Bowman in 1956, they became the world's largest sports card manufacturer.
- Collecting cards was largely a pastime for children until the early 1970s. Once adults began collecting too, prices for rare and desirable cards leapt in value. Only a few hundred

examples of the legendary 1909-1911 T206 Honus Wagner card were produced and only 57 examples are known today, one of which sold for £1.5 million in 2007. Backs and colours of backgrounds can differ.
- Aside from rarity, one of the most important indicators to value is 'centring'. The printed image should ideally be surrounded by an even amount of white space.
- Condition is also important. Creases, abrasions, folds, tears and other damage will lessen value.
- Fakes are common, but these can often be identified by a blurred or pixellated image and the thickness of the card.

An American Tobacco Co. Piedmont Cigarettes Albert (Chief) Bender baseball card, with trees in the background.

1909   *2.75in (6.8cm) high*

£100-150   **AEM**

A Crofts Candy 'Dots Miller Fielding' baseball card, E92, with rare red-printed back.

1909

£1,200-1,500   **MAS**

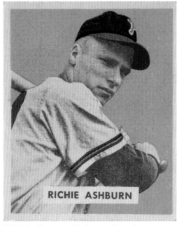

A Bowman Richie Ashburn rookie baseball card.

This very rare card is not in the best condition and is not well centred, hence its lower value. If in better condition, it could fetch well over twice this value.

1949   *2.5in (6.5cm) high*

£150-250   **BH**

A Topps 'Connie Mack's All-Stars Eddie Collins' baseball card, sealed in box with SGC rating of 40 (VG3).

1951

£100-150   **MAS**

A Topps 'Connie Mack's All-Stars, Jimmy Collins' baseball card, sealed in box with SGC rating of 60 (Ex5).

1951

£150-250   **MAS**

A Topps Rocco Colavito rookie baseball card.
1957   *3.5in (9cm) high*
£30-50   **BH**

A CLOSER LOOK AT A BASEBALL CARD

Mickey Mantle and Hank Aaron are two of baseball's greatest names. They are both depicted on this card.

The card is also signed by them. Had it not been signed, its value would have been around $200-400, depending on condition.

Showing switch-hitting Mantle, who was pitted against right-handed slugger Aaron in front of the Yankee stadium, this style was used again in 2006 with opponents Pujols and Ordonez.

The signatures have been certified as authentic by the official PSA/DNA authentication service, and the card has been sealed in a protective wallet.

A Topps 'World Series Batting Foes Mickey Mantle and Hank Aaron' baseball card, number 418, dual signed, PSA/DNA authenticated.
1958
£1,000-1,500   **MAS**

A Sport Magazine Willie Mays baseball card.
1959   *3.5in (9cm) high*
£20-30   **AEM**

A Topps Jim Palmer rookie card, priced according to condition.
1966   *3.5in (9cm) high*
£25-35   **BH**

A Topps Bob Clemente baseball card.
1964   *3.5in (9cm) high*
£50-70   **BH**

A Topps Hank Aaron baseball card.
1968   *3.5in (9cm) high*
£25-35   **AEM**

A Topps Willie Mays baseball card.

1968   *3.5in (9cm) high*

£25-35   **AEM**

1968 ROOKIE STARS

METS

JERRY KOOSMAN • P   **NOLAN RYAN • P**

A 1968 Rookie Stars baseball card featuring Jerry Koosman and Nolan Ryan.

This card, featuring Hall of Famer Nolan Ryan, is one of the iconic cards of the period. Koosman's appearance is considered less important by many and, although Ryan was not the greatest pitcher in baseball, he was considered dominant in his prime. Nevertheless, Koosman also made a number of high achievements, making this a superb example of a dual rookie card. Prices have fallen over the past few years, with this card once fetching around £1,000 in the 1990s.

1968   *3.5in (9cm) wide*

£250-350   **AEM**

A Topps Cal Ripken, Bob Bonner and Jeff Schneider baseball card.

This was Ripken's rookie card, with Ripken entering the Hall of Fame in 2007.

BOB BONNER   **CAL RIPKEN**   **JEFF SCHNEIDER**
Shortstop   3rd Base   Pitcher

BALTIMORE ORIOLES FUTURE STARS

1982   *3.5in (9cm) high*

£20-40   **BH**

A Score Joe DiMaggio signed baseball card, numbered 'JD18' from 56 examples from a limited edition of 2,500, with certificate of authenticity, from the DiMaggio estate.

1992 was the first year that baseball card companies began inserting signed cards into their packs. This was from a series of five, which is considered highly desirable as it features the legendary DiMaggio, has his signature on a card, and was one of the first signed series sold in this way.

1992   *3.5in (9cm) wide*

£200-300   **BH**

A Nabisco All Star Autographs Ernie Banks baseball card, signed by Banks, together with a certificate of authenticity.

1993   *3.5in (9cm) high*

£20-30   **BH**

An Upper Deck Brooks Robinson baseball card, signed in blue marker by Robinson.

1998   *3.5in (9cm) high*

£15-25   **BH**

A Hillerich & Bradsby & Co. 'The Famous Slugger Year Book', with Mize and Di Maggio '1939 Batting Champions' cover.

1940   6.5in (16.5cm) high

£40-60   **BH**

'Major League Baseball Facts & Figures', featuring Ted Williams on the cover, published by Whitman Publishing Company.

Williams was Player of the Year in 1941.

1942   6.75in (17cm) high

£10-15   **BH**

A 'The Official Encyclopedia of Baseball' book, first edition, published by A.S Barnes & Company.

1951   10in (25.5cm) high

£30-50   **BH**

A very rare early 1950s Babe Ruth photographic miniature Flip Book, with pictorial cover, with wear and damage.

4in (10cm) high

£100-150   **BH**

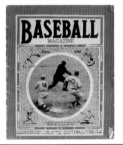

Baseball magazine, January 1937, with wear and damage.

1937   11.5in (29cm) high

£7-10   **BH**

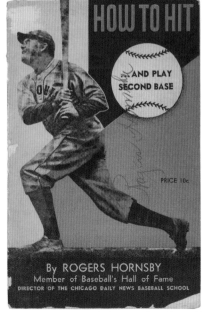

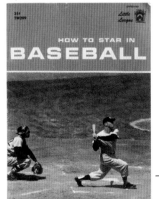

A Little League 'How To Star in Baseball' book, with Mickey Mantle photographic cover.

1961   8in (20.5cm) high

£5-7   **BH**

A Rogers Hornby 'How to Hit…And Play Second Base' signed booklet.

1945

£600-800   **MAS**

SPORTING

A very rare Babe Ruth Memorial Mission tract (and 1927 Yankee), published by Faith, Prayer & Tract League of Grand Rapids, Mich.

1948   *5.75in (14cm) high*

£20-30   **BH**

A 1924 World Series Washington Base Ball Club Pennant Winners program and score card.
1924

£200-300   **MAS**

A 1950 World Series Yankees vs Phillies multi-signed program, with ten signatures including Joe DiMaggio.

1950

£600-800   **MAS**

Two 1950s packs and a one dozen sales card sleeve of Champ condoms, with Ted Williams covers.

2in (5cm) high

£200-300 FOR THREE   **BH**

A Post Toasties corn flakes cereal box, complete and in mint condition with baseball cards back, framed and glazed.

1962

£450-550   **MAS**

A 1950s Dizzy Dean endorsed 'Falstaff Beer' advertising sign.

£250-350   **MAS**

A Ty Cobb Detriot American League printed felt B18 baseball blanket, issued as a cigarette premium.

This is in slightly poor condition, and has its top left margin cut off. In better and brighter condition, it can fetch up to £300 due to Cobb's popularity.

1914   *5.25in (13cm) wide*

£100-150   **BH**

MULLOCK'S
Specialist Auctioneers & Valuers

EUROPE'S NO.1
SPORTING MEMORABILIA SPECIALISTS

SPECIALISTS SALES OF
VINTAGE FISHING TACKLE,
GOLFING,
FOOTBALL AND RUGBY
MEMORABILIA
HELD REGULARLY
THROUGHOUT THE YEAR.
PLUS
BI-ANNUAL SALES OF
TENNIS, CRICKET,
OLYMPICS, MOTOR SPORTS,
SNOOKER, BILLIARDS ET AL.

THE OLD SHIPPON, WALL UNDER HEYWOOD,
CHURCH STRETTON, SHROPSHIRE, SY6 7DS
Tel: 01694 771 771 Fax: 01694 771 772
auctions@mullocksauctions.co.uk
www.mullocksauctions.co.uk

T. Vennett-Smith
AUCTIONEERS & VALUERS Est. 1989

One of the Country's leading Sports Auctions

FOR

**Cricket, Football, Tennis, Golf, Boxing, Rugby, Olympics, Motor & Horse Racing, etc.
Approx 2500 lots per Auction**

Special Services for ex-professional players and charities
Benefits & Testimonials undertaken

Illustrated Catalogue Available (over 150 pages)

VENDORS COMMISSION 15% + VAT (inc. insurance)

** SEE www.vennett-smith.com for all our auctions **

T. Vennett-Smith
11 Nottingham Road, Gotham, Notts. NG11 0HE
Tel: +44 (0)115 9830541 Fax: +44 (0)115 9830114
Email: info@vennett-smith.com

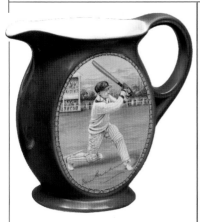

Two New Hall Pottery Staffordshire water jugs, both featuring an oval portrait of Don Bradman with printed oval signature, one white glazed, the other blue glazed, the reverse with a vignette of crossed bats, balls and stumps, chips and staining.

6.75in (17cm) high

£350-450 GBA

A sterling silver mounted cricket ball, with presentation inscription,

£300-400 GORL

A Bussey cricketers' tape measure.

4.5in (11.5cm) diam.

£80-120 MSA

A Victorian silver and enamel 'Cricket' fob, Robinson Brothers, Birmingham.
1889
£250-300   **BEX**

A silver snuff box, Edward Smith, with engine-turned decoration, the cover with cartouche engraved with the inscription 'Presented to John Sherman by Members of the Manchester Cricket Club, 1848'.

It was noted in Lillywhite's Cricketing Almanack of 1850, that John Sherman's 'slow bowling proved very effective against the Eleven of England in 1848', this at the age of 60.

7.75in (19.5cm) wide 3.31oz
£550-650   **BEA**

A silver 'S.B.S.' (Special Boat Service) inter-port cricket game medal, Phillips, Aldershot.
£50-80   **FOF**

QUICK REFERENCE – CRICKET

Apart from a move to straight bats from curved in the mid-18thC, cricket equipment has changed very little since the invention of the game in the 17thC. Collectors' interest is therefore largely focused on memorabilia connected to famous matches, events or players. Items connected or signed by players such as Dr. W. G. Grace (1848-1915), Gary Sobers (b1936), and Don Bradman (1908-2001) are usually extremely desirable, although firm provenance must be established. Items associated with popular modern players, such as Andrew Flintoff, also attract interest. A great deal of other memorabilia has been produced from the mid-19thC, including ceramics, programmes, tickets, photographs and accessories and, in good condition, these are all popular with collectors.

A Boy's Own Paper 'Famous English Cricketers' supplement print, mounted.
1880   *15in (38cm) wide*
£150-250   **GBA**

Grace, W. G., 'W G, Cricketing Reminiscences & Personal Recollections', published by James Bowden.

1899
£25-35   **GBA**

A Jack Hobs Press Club dinner menu profusely signed by guests, signatures in ink to the reverse.

£250-300   **GBA**

An autographed display for the 1957 West Indians to England, including the signatures of the touring squad on Surrey CCC headed paper, a tour brochure, dinner menu and squad photograph, mounted, framed and glazed.

34in (86.5cm) high
£300-400   **GBA**

A set of Stavros Niarchos racing colours signed by Cash Asmussen in 1993, Gibson (Saddlers) of Newmarket, the white cap signed in blue biro.

The most successful horse to carry Mr Niarchos' s familiar colours was the filly Miesque who won the English and French 1,000 Guineas, the Breeders' Cup Mile and many other important races. Mr Niarchos (1909-1996) was the leading owner in France on two occasions, and topped the breeders' list three times.

An antique dark green satinised cotton jockey's jacket and cap, Merry & Co. of St James's, cap and sleeves light green sleeves, in good condition.

c1900

£150-200   GBA

£450-550   GBA

A silver picture frame containing locks of mane hair from the 1989 Derby winner Nashwan and his half-brother Unfuwain, the hair mounted alongside colour portrait photographs of the two stallions.

The photos and mane hair were obtained at a Shadwell Stud open day in 2001.

8.5in (19cm) high

£150-200   GBA

An enamel stickpin, picturing the racehorse 'Spearmint'.

' Spearmint' won the 1906 Grand Prix de Paris - one of the most important horse races in France outside the Classics. ' Spearmint' also won the prestigious Derby in 1906. He was owned by Major Edmund Loder and trained by Peter Gilpin.

0.75in (2cm) diam.

£15-20   WORA

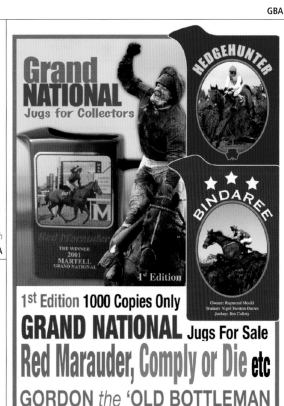

Grand NATIONAL Jugs for Collectors

HEDGEHUNTER

BINDAREE

Owner: Raymond Mould
Trainer: Nigel Twiston-Davies
Jockey: Jim Culloty

THE WINNER 2001 MARTELL GRAND NATIONAL

1st Edition

1st Edition 1000 Copies Only

GRAND NATIONAL Jugs For Sale

Red Marauder, Comply or Die etc

GORDON *the* **'OLD BOTTLEMAN**

25 Stapenhill Road • Burton-on-Trent • DE15 9AE

Tel: 01283·567·213 • Mobile: 07952·118·987

SPORTING

QUICK REFERENCE

- Golf probably originated in Scotland around the 12thC, with shepherds knocking stones into rabbit holes. The sport had grown in popularity by the 15thC, when the Scottish Parliament created two acts prohibiting "gowf," which was taking time away from the archery practice considered necessary for national defence.

- Golf memorabilia dating from the 15thC to the early 19thC is extremely rare and can be valuable. Late 19thC/early 20thC pieces are more plentiful and often more affordable. Golf clubs and balls are consistently sought after, with the most valuable pieces being early, rare or high-quality examples by renowned manufactures, such as Thomas Dunn, Douglas McEwan, Tom Morris and Robert Forgan. As most equipment is worn after being used, good condition pieces will typically be the most desirable. While golf is one of the oldest sports still played today, women did not generally participate until the early 20thC. Memorabilia featuring female players is therefore rare and sought after.

- The Victorian enthusiasm for the sport resulted in the production of a vast quantity of golfing themed metalware, glass, artwork and books, as well as ceramics, by factories such as Doulton, Shelley and Spode. Ephemera relating to games and tournaments, such as programs and tickets is also popular and can be affordable.

- Specialist golfing auctions are relatively common, with several in July around the time of the Open Championship.

A McEwan long nosed driver, in golden beech, hickory shaft, in good condition, with listing but lacking original grip.

c1885

£700-1,000   **GBA**

A B.G.I. Co. one piece wood, with leather insert to face, ebony sole plate, and lead counterweight.

£800-1,200   **L&T**

RHOD McEWAN GOLF

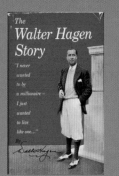

The **Walter Hagen Story**

"I never wanted to be a millionaire – I just wanted to live like one..."

Specialist bookseller in rare, elusive and out-of-print golf books and memorabilia.

I am always interested in purchasing books in any quantity, and memorabilia.

Free catalogue available

Glengarden, Ballater
Aberdeenshire AB35 5UB
Tel: (013397) 55429
www.rhodmcewan.com

QUICK REFERENCE – THE RYDER CUP

Held biannually, the first Ryder Cup competition was in 1927. Since then the US has won over 25 times, against Britain's three wins and Europe's seven wins. Memorabilia related to the event has risen in popularity over the past few years. Programmes are highly desirable, with 1959 being arguably the rarest, although a copy of the first, from 1927, would be the most valuable – if any exist. Values depend on the year, and the signatures that appear on the piece. Entire teams and key players are the most desirable. Won by the US in 1971, the value of this competition menu would have risen had it also been signed by British and American team captains Eric Brown and Jay Hebert. However, star players Arnold Palmer's and J.C. Snead's signatures are desirable.

A dinner menu, "Honouring the Ryder Cup Teams of the United States and Great Britain", held at the Waldorf Astoria on October 22nd, 1951.
1951
£400-500   L&T

A Ryder Cup dinner menu, held at the Marine Hotel, North Berwick, on 22nd September 1973, the cover signed by Joan Ryder.
£400-600   L&T

A Ryder Cup Victorian dinner menu, held at the Old Warson Country Club, Saint Louis, Missouri, on 18th September 1971, the cover signed by Arnold Palmer, Gene Littler, Gardner Dickinson, Charles Coody, and J.C. Snead.
£400-600   L&T

A Ryder Cup gala dinner menu, held at the Rochester Riverside Convention Centre, Rochester, New York, on Wednesday 20th September 1995.
1995
£150-250   L&T

A Ryder Cup welcoming dinner menu, held at The Greenbrier, White Sulphur Springs, West Virginia, on September 13th 1979.
1979
£200-300   L&T

A Ryder Cup gala dinner menu, held at The Omni Hotel, Charleston, South Carolina, on Wednesday 25th September 1991.
1991
£120-180   L&T

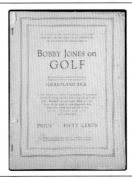

Jones, Bobby, 'Bobby Jones on Golf', with an introduction from Grantland Rice, published by One Time Publications, New York, numerous studies of the game by Jones, plus the rules of gold, lacking back wrapper.
c1930
£150-200   GBA

Walter Hagen, "The Walter Hagen Story" as told to Margaret Seaton Heck, published by Simon and Schuster, first edition, with dustwrapper, and a presentation inscription from Hagen.
1956

£300-400   L&T

A 1950s Walter Hagen black and white photograph, showing Hagen seated on a golf course with a club.

£80-120   MAS

After Michael Brown, 'Life Association of Scotland Calendar 1903', 'First International Golf Match – England v Scotland – Hoylake, 1902, framed.
21.75in (55cm) wide

£700-1,000   L&T

A silver-plated three-piece mesh pattern ball bachelor's tea set, comprising teapot, cream jug and sugar basin.

Had the golfing shape and theme not been here, a standard silver plated teaset would usually be worth under £100.

c1900

£2,000-2,500   L&T

A late Victorian electroplated inkstand, decorated with foliage engraving, crossed clubs and a mesh pattern ball, with hinged cover enclosing a glass liner, on four volute supports, bearing trade label for John Macfarlane, Alloa.
6.75in (17cm) long

£200-300   L&T

A silver golfing medal, one side with a scene of a golfer and inscribed Amateur Golf Championship, the other with a ribbon tied laurel wreath in relief, with ring suspension, no inscription, with Birmingham hallmarks for 1954.
1954   *1.75in (4.5cm)*

£800-1,200   L&T

An American Amateur Championship gilt metal and enamel contestant's badge, reading "September 1-6. 1913", centrally with the initials of "USGA", by The Whitehead & Hoag Company, lacks pin .
1.25in (3cm) wide

£800-1,200   L&T

A Michael Jordan North Carolina signed replica basketball jersey.

£300-400 MAS

An official Spalding basketball, signed by Wilt Chamberlain.

Wilton Norman Chamberlain, also known as 'Wilt The Stilt', was inducted into the Basketball Hall of Fame in 1978. Considered one of, if not the, best player in basketball to date, he had a good rapport with this fans. The fact that this is on a baseball is a nice touch.

£1,200-1,800 MAS

A Hawthorne Milk 'Jerry Sloan, Chicago Bulls' basketball card.
1970-1

£400-500 MAS

A bronze figure of an American footballer, with pale brown patina, mounted on a wooden plinth.
10.5in (27cm) high

£80-120 GBA

A rare Moyer football player ceramic money bank, with orange, black and white uniform, marked '© Moyer' on side of base, with some wear to the painting.

Mr. Moyer reportedly used his own face to model this player.
7.5in (19cm) high

£70-100 BEL

A 1970s Wilson OJ Simpson signature series plastic football and original box.
11.5in (29cm) high

£50-70 BH

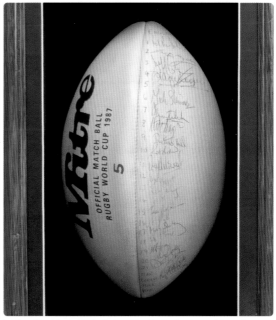

A Mitre '5' white rugby ball signed by the England squad from the inaugural Rugby World Cup in 1987, stamped 'OFFICIAL MATCH BALL, RUGBY WORLD CUP 1987', signed by the team manager Geoff Cooke, the coach, and a total of 21 players including Rendall, Moore, Probyn, Dooley, Skinner, and others, mounted in a wooden display case.
c1987

£500-600 GBA

An limited edition 1997 New Zealand 'All Blacks' rugby shirt display, numbered 59 from an edition of 300, the shirt with two columns of signatures, framed with certificate of authenticity taped to the backboard.

The signatures are of all the All Blacks who played in the undefeated run of eight test matches during 1997 season.

1997   42.5in (108cm) wide

£450-650   **GBA**

A Pennsylvania Resident Citizen's Fishing License pin, numbered 57318.

1941   1.75in diam

£20-25   **BH**

A Victorian brass paper holder, with spring-loaded crossed racquets and balls clip, on a shaped wooden base.

5in (13cm) wide

£120-180   **GBA**

A bronze figure of a boxer, with rich brown patina, mounted on a marble base.

8.5in (21.5cm) high

£120-180   **GBA**

Two Kinsella ceramic figures of boy cricketers, one titled 'The Hope of his Side', the other based on the Kinsella print 'Out First Ball', with the two Kinsella cricket prints that the figures were based on.

Largest 5in (13cm) high

£400-500   **GBA**

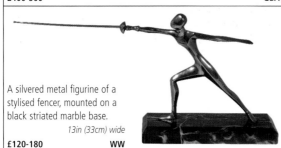

A silvered metal figurine of a stylised fencer, mounted on a black striated marble base.

13in (33cm) wide

£120-180   **WW**

A 1939 World Student Games poster, designed by Franz Kralicek, the colour lithograph printed by Christoph Reisser Sohne, Vienna.

Note the strong Fascist version of the Art Deco style.

1936   38.5in (98cm) high

£100-150   **GBA**

QUICK REFERENCE

- Teddy bears are named after American president, Theodore (Teddy) Roosevelt, who refused to shoot a bear-cub on a hunting trip in 1902. Morris Michtom (who later founded the Ideal Novelty and Toy Company) produced a soft toy 'teddy bear' to sell at his Brooklyn store. The bear was so popular that it started a craze, which is still with us today.
- Despite the teddy's American origin, German company, Steiff (founded 1886) are considered the best maker. Other collectable German makers include Gebrüder Hermann. Bing and Schreyer & Co. (Schuco). British companies to look out for include Farnell, Merrythought and Chad Valley. The American companies Ideal, Gund and Knickerbocker have also produced collectable bears.
- Bears can be identified and dated from labels, if they are still attached, or from their materials, colour and form. Before WWII, bears tended to have long limbs with large, upturned paw pads, pronounced snouts and humped backs. They were usually made from mohair and feel solid, as they were stuffed with wood shavings or kapok. Post-war bears usually have shorter limbs and plumper bodies, less pronounced snouts, and rounder heads. Synthetic materials were used from the 1960s. Try to handle as many bears as possible to get a feel for the different styles
- Large bears in unusual colours are often more desirable to collectors, as are those with 'eye appeal' – an appealing expression will always capture a collector's heart. A lot of damage can be restored, but tears, stains, replaced pads and worn fur will often reduce value.
- Bears by contemporary bear artists and modern limited edition bears, from notable makers such as Steiff, are beginning to fetch good prices on the secondary market. Always keep limited edition bears in mint condition, and retain the box and paperwork. Some limited editions, particularly those of Steiff, are replicas of older bears, and these should not be confused with the originals, which are usually worth more. If in doubt, smell a bear, as the scent of an old bear cannot be faked.

A Steiff blonde mohair bear, with boot button eyes, original pads and ear button.

This bear displays all of the features associated with pre-war bears, particularly those by Steiff, such as a hump and long limbs.

c1908   9.5in (24cm) high

£700-900   PC

A 1930s Steiff small blond 'Teddy Baby', with velvet fur, internal wire frame and large feet allowing him to stand, and ear button.

3in (7.5cm)

£300-400   PC

A 1930s-40s Steiff golden mohair small bear, with glass eyes and ear button, in very good condition.

5.25in (13.5cm) high

£350-400   PC

A late 1940s Steiff blond mohair bear, with glass eyes, original pads and stitching and ear button, lacking tag.

13.5in (34cm) high

£300-400   PC

A 1950s Steiff white mohair miniature bear, with original features, in excellent condition.

3.5in (9cm)

£60-80   PC

A 1950s Steiff bear, from the 'Original Teddy' range, bright golden mohair and original red ribbon, no button.

5.25in

£80-100   **PC**

A Steiff red and blue mohair 'Harlequin' teddy bear, from a limited edition of 6,850, with ceramic medallion, certificate, and white ear tag numbered '420214', in mint condition with box.

2000-2001   *14in (35.5cm) high*

£100-150   **VEC**

A Steiff 'Schwarzbar' black mohair bear, from a limited edition of 1,500 exclusive to the UK market, with certificate, in mint condition with box.

2001   *13.75in (35cm) high*

£100-150   **VEC**

A CLOSER LOOK AT A STEIFF ZOTTY BEAR

'Zotty' bears were introduced by Steiff in 1951, and are named after 'zottig', the German word for shaggy, due to their fur. They are currently less popular meaning prices have fallen – it is therefore a good time to buy.

As well as the distinctive fur, they typically have open felt-lined mouths, and they were copied by many makers including Hermann.

Steiff was the only company to use plain 'bibs' on their bears' chests, which helps with identification.

The fur is often tipped with a different tone – do not confuse these with the similar but rarer Steiff 'Petsy' bears from c1929, which have reddy-brown tipped blond mohair and closed mouths.

A 1950s-60s Steiff 'Zotty' bear, with tipped fur, original felt pads and mouth and original eyes and stitching, in excellent condition.

£100-150   **PC**

A Steiff '1908 Rosé Replica' bear, from a limited edition of 3,000, with felt paws, black glass eyes and growler, in presentation box with certificate.

In 1908 Steiff produced samples in black, pink, green or yellow mohair for the English market. No more were then produced. This is a replica of the pink sample bear.

2008   *13.75in (35cm)*

£120-160   **TBW**

A Steiff 'Henderson' bear, from a limited edition of 2,000, with long curled mohair and growler, together with a presentation box and certificate.

This bear was named after pioneer teddy bear collector and researcher Lt Col Bob Henderson, whose collection was sold at aution in 1994. The highest price was £110,000, paid for his life-long companion, a 1904 cinnamon mohair Steiff known as 'Teddy Girl'.

1997   *21.5in (55cm)*

£220-280   **TBW**

A 1930s Schuco gold mohair miniature bear, with a metal internal body and original eyes and stitching.

3.5in (9cm) high

£180-220   **BEJ**

A 1920s-30s Schuco orange mohair miniature bear, with original stitching, the head removing to reveal a glass perfume bottle, in excellent condition.

3.5in (9cm) high

£200-250   **PC**

A late 1920s Schuco brown mohair 'Piccolo' bear, with original foot pads, boot button eyes and stitching, with worn fur.

At a tiny 2.5in (6.5cm) high, this was the smallest bear produced by Schuco.

2.5in (6.5cm) high

£200-250   **PC**

QUICK REFERENCE – SCHUCO MINIATURES

Along with Steiff, Schuco are well-known for their miniature bears, which were produced in large numbers during the 1920-70s. The most commonly found are in gold mohair, but look out for a number of unusual variations, as these can fetch higher values. The rarest colour is purple, but examples were also produced in other colours including red, orange, peach, green, grey and pink. Some also hide a secret, having removable heads, or opening to reveal accessories such as perfume bottles, or compacts. These are particularly sought after, and can fetch over £500 in complete and excellent condition.

A 1920s-30s Schuco gold mohair miniature bear, with removeable head, which conceals a glass perfume bottle, in excellent condition.

5in (12.5cm) high

£500-700   **PC**

Three miniature Schuco bears, in red, green and pink mohair, each wearing knitted tunics, possibly given them by their original owner.

3.5in (9cm) high

£450-550 EACH   **PC**

TEDDY BEARS

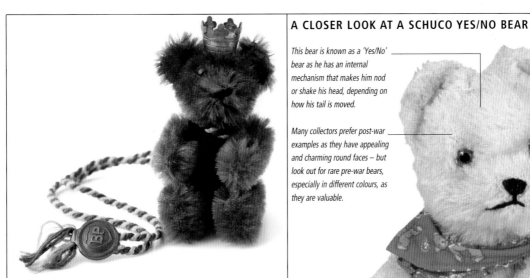

A Schuco brown mohair miniature bear, with metal crown, and a green and yellow cord with 'BP' embossed tinplate button.

This bear was given away as a promotional present at BP petrol station from 1958-60. Complete examples are rare today.

1958-1960   *5in (12.5cm) high*

£100-150   **PC**

A CLOSER LOOK AT A SCHUCO YES/NO BEAR

This bear is known as a 'Yes/No' bear as he has an internal mechanism that makes him nod or shake his head, depending on how his tail is moved.

Many collectors prefer post-war examples as they have appealing and charming round faces – but look out for rare pre-war bears, especially in different colours, as they are valuable.

Schuco were better known for producing a large range of clockwork metal toys, enabling them to make such mechanisms. This type of bear was introduced in 1921.

Post-war bears also have downturned paws on longer limbs, and flat feet, allowing them to stand.

A 1920s-30s Schuco gold mohair tumbling miniature bear, with working clockwork mechanism that moves his long arms.

5in (12.5cm) high

£650-750   **PC**

A 1950s Schuco gold mohair small 'Yes/No' bear, with working tail mechanism to nod and shake head.

5in (13cm)

£250-350   **PC**

A 1950s Schuco gold mohair 'Yes/No' bear, with original stitching, pads and glass eyes, and later neckerchief, with internal mechanical.

9in (29cm) high

£400-600   **TED**

A 1960s-70s Schuco 'footballer' bear, with golden mohair head and 'pipe cleaner' body and limbs, in original woven football kit with plastic boots.

3.75in (9.5cm)

£150-200   **PC**

An early Schuco gold mohair plush bear, with a home-knitted dress, with re-covered felt pads and wear to fur.

10in (25.5cm) high

£250-300   **BEJ**

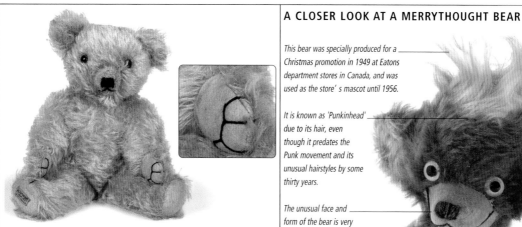

A 1930s Merrythought bear, with long golden mohair and kapok and excelsior stuffing, felt paw pads, stitched nose, amber and black glass eyes, celluloid button in the ear and fabric label to foot.

This bear can be identified from the the foot label and ear button. Had these not been present, the characteristic paw stitching combined with the shape of the body and his head would have helped indicate the maker. Only Farnell and Merrythought used this style of stitching, but their bears are different in form.

19in (45.5cm) high

£600-800 PC

A CLOSER LOOK AT A MERRYTHOUGHT BEAR

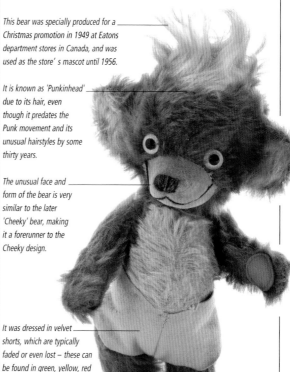

This bear was specially produced for a Christmas promotion in 1949 at Eatons department stores in Canada, and was used as the store's mascot until 1956.

It is known as 'Punkinhead' due to its hair, even though it predates the Punk movement and its unusual hairstyles by some thirty years.

The unusual face and form of the bear is very similar to the later 'Cheeky' bear, making it a forerunner to the Cheeky design.

It was dressed in velvet shorts, which are typically faded or even lost – these can be found in green, yellow, red or blue.

A Merrythought 'Punkinhead' bear, with brown mohair body and pale chest and ear linings, sewn-on velvet shorts, fully jointed, in good condition.

c1950

16in (40.5cm) high

£800-1,000 TBW

A Merrythought 'Cheeky' gold mohair bear, the large ears with bells sewn inside them, one foot with 'Regd. Design' Merrythought fabric label.

1960

£300-400 PC

A rare Merrythought gold mohair and fabric 'Mr Twisty Cheeky' bear, with internal wire frame.

Look out for rare Mrs Cheeky.

1966-68 *11in (28cm)*

£200-250 TBW

A 1960s Merrythought gold mohair 'Cheeky' bear, with bells in his ears, and original pads and stitching in excellent condition, with 'Reg'd Design' Merrythought label to foot.

The instantly recognisable 'Cheeky' bear with bells in its ears was released in 1957. Labels typically carry 'registered design' wording as this popular design was distinctive enough to be registered, and therefore protected.

10in (25.5cm) high

£150-200 PC

A late 1960s-70s Merrythought 'Cheeky' rare blue plush bear, in very good condition, with original stitching, eyes and label to foot pad.

18.25in (46cm) high seated

£380-420 LHT

A 1970s Merrythought gold mohair bear, with original stitching and plastic eyes, and label on the right foot.

10in (25.5cm) high

£30-40 **PC**

A Merrythought 'Little Patchwork Punkie' limited edition pellet-filled mohair bear, from a limited edition of 150, with 23 patches in different colours, felt paws, glass eyes, and certificate.

8in (20cm) high

£65-85 **TBW**

A Merrythought brown tipped cream mohair 'Happy Cheeky' bear, from a limited edition of 50.

2009 *25.25in (38cm)*

£150-180 **TBW**

QUICK REFERENCE - DATING MERRYTHOUGHT

Before 1945, Merrythought usually marked its bears with a metal button. Often missing, other hallmarks such as claw style can help with identification. Also look out for remains of labels or stitching or a lack of fading or wear in a label-sized area, as the position and size of this are also useful. After WWII, Merrythought bears were labelled, and the style of the label will help with dating.

A 1990s Merrythought golden mohair bear, with leather paw pads and original labels, in mint condition.

£200-300 **BEJ**

From 1945-56, an embroidered fabric label with the company name and 'Hygenic Toys' wording was used.

From 1957 until 1991, a printed fabric label was used, including the wording 'Ironbridge Shropshire'.

From 1991 onwards, the label included a 'wishbone' motif as well as wording.

A limited edition Merrythought 'Cheeky Toggles' bear, in felt duffel coat.

2009 *11.5in (29cm) high*

£100-150 **TBW**

A limited edition Merrythought bear, 'Sleepy Cheeky', in matching nightshirt and cap.

2009 *25.25in (38cm)*

£80-120 **TBW**

A scarce Farnell white or blond mohair 'Alpha' bear, with pale brown rectangular vertically stitched nose, webbed paw stitching and flat foot pads.
c1925

£1,000-1,500   **TBW**

A 1930s Farnell rare blue mohair bear, with original glass eyes, pale brown facial stitching and pads, with some wear to his fur.

9.25in (23.5cm) high

£1,800-2,200   **PC**

A 1930s Farnell bear, with wool plush fur and replaced pads, wearing a later leather collar, with patches of wear to his fur.

20in (50.5cm) high

£200-300   **PC**

A 1930s Farnell bear, with blond mohair head and paws and blue and red plush integral clothing, with original blue eyes and stitching.

10in (25.5cm) high

£100-120   **PC**

A Farnell red mohair 'soldier' miniature bear, with original eyes.

These were often sold as gifts for sweethearts to take with them during WWI, their upturned faces allowing them to peek out of the breast pocket of a soldier's uniform. They were made in patriotic colours of red, white and blue, as well as the traditional gold colour.
1915   *3.75in (9.5cm)*

£300-400   **TBW**

A CLOSER LOOK AT A FARNELL BEAR

This bear is large and of very high quality – this has led to Farnell being dubbed the 'English Steiff'.

Gold mohair is the most common colour, with blond, blue or red being much scarcer. Blond bears should have light brown nose and mouth stitching.

The long limbs, shaved protruding snout, large flat foot pads, rounded face and humped back are typical features of pre-war Farnell bears.

The paw stitching is a characteristic feature of Farnell bears made before 1930 – it was also used by Merrythought, which hired one of Farnell's directors in 1920.

A late 1920s Farnell gold mohair large bear, with original stitching and eyes and webbed claws, with broken growler.

25in (63.5cm) high

£1,500-2,000   **PC**

TEDDY BEARS

A 1930s-40s Chiltern pale gold mohair 'Hugmee' bear, with original velvet paw pads, stitching and amber and black glass eyes.

Chiltern released the 'Hugmee' bear in 1923, and it became extremely popular. Note the shape of the head, and the size and length of the arms and legs –these are all typical of features of Hugmee bears from the 1930s onwards.

15in (38cm) high

£350-450   BEJ

A 1950s Chiltern golden moahir 'Ting-a-Ling Bruin' musical bear, with Rexine pads and original pads, stitching and eyes.

The Ting-a-Ling Bruin bear was introduced by Chiltern after WWII, and contained a mechanism that produced a musical tinkling sound when moved.

12in (30.5cm) high

£250-350   PC

A late 1940s/50s Chiltern gold mohair bear, with original paw pads, stitching, woven nose and glass eyes, in excellent condition.

The thick-thighed 'drumstick' legs are characteristic of Chiltern bears from the 1930s onwards.

£200-250   TBW

A Chiltern gold mohair 'Hugmee' teddy bear, with original foot pads, woven nose, glass eyes and original tag.

1930s-40s   *13in (33cm) high*

£400-500   LHT

A late 1940s-early 1950s Chiltern small gold mohair 'Hugmee' bear, with card-lined paws, velvet pads and original stitching and eyes.

8in (20cm) high

£200-300   PC

A late 1950s Chiltern large blond mohair 'Hugmee' bear, with original stitching, eyes and paw pads, lacking label.

This was the largest standard production size in the Hugmee range.

26in (66cm) high

£400-600   PC

A 1960s Chiltern 'Ting-a-Ling' musical bear, with gold, light blue and pink plush, and original stitching, plastic label and card label, in mint condition.

7in (17.5cm) high

£200-250   PC

QUICK REFERENCE – AMERICAN TEDDY BEARS

Many US bears were not labelled and so identification is difficult for today's collectors. A great many factories sprang up during the teddy bear 'fever' of the 1910s and 20s, including Ideal, Knickerbocker, Bruin, Aetna and Gund. However, many were short-lived and most did not mark or label their bears. Typical features of pre-war American bears include a wide, triangular head, large ears at the corners, arms slung lower down on the body and the bodily shape of German bears. This example, by market leader Ideal, is typical.

An early American gold mohair bear, with replaced foot pads, original stitching and boot button eyes, with some wear to the fur.

1905-06   *18in*

£300-400   **PC**

An early American pale gold plush bear, with original nose stitching, boot button eyes, and 'pinched' ears, paw pads re-covered in chamois.

c1910   *20in (51cm) high*

£700-800   **BEJ**

An American gold mohair 'sleepy eye' bear, with original stitching and celluloid spherical eyes, one paw pad recovered, with wear to his fur.

Rather than the standard boot button or two-colour glass eyes, these eyes are made from celluloid balls fixed in a metal mounting. The balls are weighted so that when the bear is laid down on its back, they roll down showing a plain side, thus appearing 'closed'.

1910-12

£800-1,000   **PC**

A 1920s American Ideal cinnamon mohair bear, with large flat feet, felt paw pads, small amber coloured glass eyes and a long snout.

15in (38cm) high

£700-800   **BEJ**

A 1950s American gold mohair 'mascot' bear, made for the University of California, with matching blue felt paw pads, sewn-on 'C' and 'California' badge, with original light blue eyes and stitching.

£40-50   **TBW**

An American bear-on-wheels, with fixed head position, original tail and metal frame and wheels.

American bears-on-wheels are more unusual than German.

1900-10

£300-500   **PC**

A Chad Valley blond alpaca fur 'Cubby' bear, with original stitching, eyes and original label to foot pad.

c1954   9.5in (24cm) high

£150-250   **PC**

A 1950s Chad Valley golden mohair 'Bear Brand' shop display large bear, with original paw pads, stitching and glass eyes, with panel where a label was once sewn on.

This enormous bear was originally part of a display selling women's stockings.

       45in (114cm) high

£450-550   **PC**

A CLOSER LOOK AT A CHAD VALLEY BEAR

Chad Valley, founded in 1820, produced its first bears in 1915 and became very successful. Many British children of the 1940s-60s grew up with a Chad Valley bear.

This is characteristic of post-war Chad Valley bears, with ears placed flat on its head, a vertically stitched bulbous nose and long, curving arms.

Its fur and stitching is in excellent condition, if it had enjoyed years of love and wear, value would plummet to around £30 or less.

It still bears the company label on its foot pad. The label wording can help to date the bear, as it refers to Elizabeth Queen Consort of King George VI as 'Her Majesty the Queen', and can therefore be dated to before the 1953 Coronation of Queen Elizabeth II, when wording changed to 'Queen Mother'.

A late 1940s-early 1950s Chad Valley golden mohair small bear, with original paw pads, stitching and eyes, with label to right-hand paw pad.

£500-700   **TED**

A 1930s Chad Valley white mohair polar bear, with down-turned paws, original stitching and eyes, and Chad Valley label on left foot pad.

Polar bears were popular from the 1930s onwards, but grew again in popularity in the 1950s after the birth of a polar bear cub named Brumas in London Zoo in 1949.

£600-800   **PC**

A rare German Eduard Cramer musical bear, with internal mechanism operated by moving the neck up and down, with original stitched woollen nose and claws.

c1930   18in (45.5cm) high

£2,200-2,800   **TCT**

A 1930s Dean's Rag Book Co. rare blue mohair bear, with original paw pads, shaved snout and original stitching and eyes, and cupped ears.

c1926

£400-500   **TBW**

A 1950s German Diem yellow mohair bear, with short plush mohair on snout and paws, with internal growler.

£200-250 PC

A 1930s French Faye gold silk plush teddy, with original eyes and stitching, in excellent condition.

6.5in (16.5cm) high

£120-180 BEJ

A rare Einco white mohair bear, with side-glancing 'googly' type eyes, and original paw pads, in good condition.

Einco was the trade name used by Eisenmann & Co., a toy import company based in London. Founded in the late 19thC by brothers Josef and Gabriel Eisenmann, the company had an office in Germany and distributed bisque dolls, teddies and other toys. In 1908, Josef and Leon Rees founded the Chiltern Toy Works in Buckinghamshire, producing their first bear (Master Teddy) in 1915. This 'mousey' look is unusual, and is even more rodent-like than Deans' bears.

1915-20

£400-600 TBW

A 1960s German Grisly Spielwaren blond bear, with synthetic plush fur, open mouth, original eyes, and manufacturer's button to chest.

Grisly Spielwaren was founded In Germany in 1954, and saw a peak in sales during the 1960s and 70s. The company is still active today.

£80-120 PC

A 1930s German Hermann pin-jointed blond mohair bear, in period South German style woven wool outfit, with original stitching, eyes and paw pads.

6.75in (17cm) high

£200-300 PC

A 1930s German Hermann 'Helvetic' pale gold plush bear, with Rexine pads and original eyes, stitching and paw pads.

The term 'Helvetic' is used to describe a mechanical music box, usually Swiss, inside the bear.

18in (46cm) high

£700-900 BEJ

A 1950s Australian Joy Toys bright gold mohair plush bear, with original paw pads and eyes.

£200-300 TBW

A British Gabrielle Designs 'Paddington' bear, designed by Shirley Clarkson in 1972, with hat, duffel coat, Wellingtons and luggage tag.

The earliest versions from around 1973 have no hint of a foot inside their child's Dunlop wellington boots.

£40-60   PC

A Gabrielle Designs 'Aunt Lucy' bear, complete with clothing and accessories, including Peruvian coins in a pocket in her petticoat.

As she was not as popular as Paddington, Aunt Lucy is much harder to find today.

£150-200   PC

An American R. John Wright alpaca plush Paddington Bear, with 'Please look after this bear' label to neck, leather suitcase complete with marmalade, from a limited edition 2,500, in mint condition and with box in excellent condition.

R. John Wright is a noted American bear and doll artist whose work, often produced under license from Disney and others, is highly sought after by collectors.

2001   *13.5in (34cm) high*

£380-420   VEC

A Steiff 'Rupert Bear', with white alpaca fur, wearing traditional outfit, with stitch-sculpted fingers and thumb, from a limited edition.

2008   *11in (28cm) high*

£100-150   TBW

An unusual cotton plush 'Rupert Bear' style bear, with pale gold mohair head and paws, with wooden mechanism that opens the mouth when the tummy is squeezed.

c1930

£300-400   BEJ

A 1960s Chad Valley plush 'Sooty' teddy bear, wearing red dungarees, with original paw pads.

£15-20   PC

A Steiff 'Karl Lagerfeld' white alpaca fur bear, designed by Karl Lagerfeld, with Italian wool jacket over striped denims, a black silk cravat set with a Swarovski crystal, miniature Lagerfeld Eyewear Collection glasses, and exclusive white gold ear button, from a limited edition of 2,500, with box and certificate.

2008   *15.5cm (40cm)*

£600-800   TBW

TEDDY BEARS
of Witney

In 1989 Ian Pout of Teddy Bears gave £12,100 (a world record price) for Alfonzo, a red Steiff bear owned by a Russian princess. In 1996 Ian gave a higher amount for Aloysius, the star of 'Brideshead Revisited'. These were exceptional prices for exceptional bears.

We are always keen to offer a fair price for old bears, especially by **Steiff, Merrythought, Farnell, Deans, Chiltern and Chad Valley.**

Old bears always wanted

SHOP OPEN 7 DAYS A WEEK.
Please contact Ian Pout at
Teddy Bears, 99 High Street, Witney, Oxfordshire OX28 6HY
Tel: 01993 706616 Email: bears@witneybears.co.uk
Collectors catalogue of new bears (£5)
www.teddybears.co.uk

A British 'Brennus' (King) artist bear, by Jean and Bill Ashburner, jointed at the wrists and with two joints to the neck, with a needle sculpted nose and realistic three-dimensional polymer pads on unltrasuede paws, numbered five from a limited edition of eight.

18in (46cm)

£320-370

A German Freche Früchte Bären 'pumpkin' bear, by Kerstin Jeske, with label at the back in seam.

4in (10cm) high seated

£90-110　　PC

A German 'Freche Früchte Bären' 'cake' bear, by Kerstin Jeske, with label at the back in seam.

5in (12cm) high seated

£80-90　　PC

A British 'Gabriel Oak' artist bear, by June Kendall, with gold mohair and ultrasuede paws, glass eyes, and green-checked scarf, part filled with steel shot for weight, numbered six from a limited edition of twelve.

June Kendall is based in Hampshire, England, and was inspired to make bears at a time when she was involved in events in Dorset celebrating the 150th anniversary of Thomas Hardy. As a result she named her creations ' Hardy Bears' . This bear is themed on a character from ' Far From the Madding Crowd' .

2008   *4.25in (11cm) high*

£40-60   **TBW**

A Dany-Bären Riualdo artist bear, by Danielo-Rebecca Melse, in red aged mohair, with tags, black glass eyes, black vertically stitched nose, felt pads, and black claw stitching, numbered one from a limited edition of two, in near mint condition.

                                              16in (41cm) high

£300-500   **VEC**

An American 'Stella' artist bear, by Sue Lain, made with dusky pink mohair, and wearing a vintage broderie anglaise dress, numbered four from a limited edition of eight.

2008   *12in (30cm)*

£120-180   **TBW**

An English miniature 'Mikey' artist bear, by Elisabeth Marsden, with knitted wool golly doll and yellow cardigan, and split pin joints and glass eyes.

                                              2.75in (7cm) high

£45-50   **PC**

A Japanese 'Puu' artist bear, by Yuki Yamanaka, made of aged viscose, with a gingham patch and 'replaced' footpad, numbered four from a limited edition of ten.

Yuki Yamanaka, from Chiba, Japan, designed clothes after leaving university. She was inspired to start making bears in 1997 by an antique teddy that she particularly loved. The large head and tiny eyes are typical of contemporary Japanese animated and cartoon characters.

2007   *8in (20cm)*

£80-120   **TBW**

A British 'Miranda' artist bear, by Elizabeth Leggat, made from antique short pile plush mohair, and wearing a 1920s-style silk dress trimmed with vintage ribbon, with silver purse made from vintage material, weighted with steel shot, from a limited edition of six.

The purse is made from pieces of an original Edwardian purse.

2008   *4in (10cm)*

£450-500   **TBW**

An American 'Algernon' artist bear, by Jeanette Warner, made of sparse cinnamon mohair with black glass bead eyes and aged felt paws.

2008/09   *13in (33cm) high*

£100-140   **TBW**

A Swedish L. M. Ericsson telephone, the black tinplate body with gilt transfer decoration, nickel-plated cradle, and original cable.

c1910   *13.25in (33cm) high*

£100-150   **WDL**

A 1960s replica of the famous 'candlestick' telephone, originally manufactured by GEFA A.G. of Vienna in the 1920s.

c1965

£250-350   **ATK**

A 1930s black bakelite 200 series telephone.

8in (20cm) wide

£180-220   **L**

A 1950s black bakelite 300 series telephone, with original lead.

6in (15cm) wide

£100-150   **L**

A 1960s red plastic telephone, by the Reliance Telephone Co.

5in (12.5cm) wide

£40-60   **L**

A 1970s cream plastic Ericofon telephone, by Ericsson.

8.25in (21cm) high

£70-100   **L**

CANDLESTICK
&
BAKELITE
TELEPHONES FROM
THE 1920s to 70s,
for candlestick and classic black phones.

(Shown here ivory coloured 332)

www.candlestickandbakelite.co.uk

Call or e mail for a free catalogue, or download it from our web site.
020 8467 3743
candlestick.bakelite@mac.com

P.O. Box 308, Orpington, Kent, BR5 1TB

**See a selection of phones at
"The Beehive",
22, Station Square, Petts Wood,
Kent.**

Telephone Lines Ltd

ANTIQUE, BAKELITE, DESIGNER PHONES

KIOSKS AND A B BOXES

REPAIR SERVICE

HIRE SERVICE

SPARES AVAILABLE

EXPORT ENQUIRIES INVITED

If you are buying or selling ring or visit

**TELEPHONE LINES LTD
304 HIGH STREET
CHELTENHAM
GLOS GL50 3JF**

www.telephonelines.net
**TEL: +44 (0)1242 583699
FAX: +44 (0)1242 690033**
info@telephonelines.net

TELEPHONES

A Northern Telecom moulded plastic airplane telephone, in two tones of orange, with rotary dial and large Lucite 'propeller', embossed mark and foil label.

9in (23cm) wide

£50-80   **CRA**

A blue plastic 'Ola' T1000GD telephone, by Thomson, designed by Phillipe Starck.

11in (28cm) long

£50-60   **L**

An American candlestick telephone, with 'Stars & Stripes' decoration.

c1974   *11in (28.5cm) high*

£70-100   **NOR**

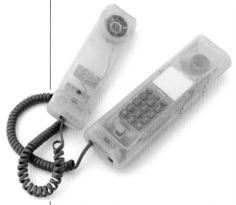

A Swatch Twinphone transparent green plastic telephone, Deluxe model.

9.5in (24cm) long

£30-50   **MHT**

A wooden Trub telephone, by gfeller, designed in the 1970s.

c1994   *8.25in (21cm) wide*

£70-90   **L**

A 1980s red plastic 'Hot Lips' telephone.

8.5in (21.5cm) wide

£35-45   **L**

QUICK REFERENCE

- Corgi toys were first produced in 1956 by Welsh toy company Mettoy, founded in 1933 by Phillip Ullman of the German toymaker Tipp & Co. Corgi toys were released to compete with Dinky's successful range of diecast toys, including the new Supertoys range. However, Corgi's vehicles featured exciting additions, such as plastic windows, and doors and boots that opened.
- Suspension, marketed as 'Glidamatic' was introduced in 1959. Clockwork, self-propelled versions were also introduced and are generally worth more than 'free-wheeling' models today. Innovations continued during the 1960s, including steering and jewelled head lights. Faceted ruby rear lights were introduced on a Bentley Continental released in 1961. 'Trans-o-lite' headlamps that transmitted daylight to give the appearance of illumination were introduced in 1963.
- The 1960s and 70s also saw a range of models tied in with popular TV programmes and films. These included Batman's Batmobile, James Bond's Aston Martin and Chitty Chitty Bang Bang. These models were enormously popular at the time, and remain so with collectors today. Other popular ranges include Chipperfields Circus, and boxed gift sets which have seen an enormous rise in popularity over the past few years.
- As with other diecast toys, look out for variations by considering the colour, decals or stickers and other features such as the interior or wheels. To fetch the best prices, models should be accompanied by their boxes and any accessories they were sold with. The inclusion of the inner packaging is also a desirable feature. Always look for models in mint condition, and avoid pieces with repainting.

A Corgi No.351 Land Rover 'RAF' Vehicle, greyish blue, spun hubs, tow hook, in near mint condition, with good condition carded box.

The version of this model with suspension is worth roughly 25 per cent more.

1958-62

£100-150 VEC

A Corgi No.472 Land Rover public address vehicle 'Vote for Corgi', with spun hubs and two figures, in near mint condition, with good condition carded box.

1964-66

£100-150 VEC

A Corgi No.438 Land Rover 'Lepra', metallic green, cream plastic canopy, lemon interior, cast hubs, silver plastic tow hook, in mint condition, with mint condition window box.

This is a scarce variation with different coloured canopy. It is usually found with a green canopy and no decal, which would usually be worth under £100 in excellent, boxed condition.

1963-77

£650-850 VEC

A Corgi No.417 Land Rover 'Breakdown Service', red, yellow tin canopy, spun hubs, in mint condition, with mint condition, inner carded packing Collectors Club leaflet, in good condition box.

1960-62

£120-180 VEC

A Corgi No.487 Land Rover 'Chipperfield Circus' parade vehicle, red, blue, lemon interior, spun hubs, clown and monkey figures, in excellent condition, with good condition carded box.

1965-69

£80-120 VEC

A Corgi No.348 Ford Mustang Fastback, in lilac with a pale green interior, cast hubs, psychedelic 'flower power' decals with racing number 20 to doors, in near mint condition, with near mint carded box, with Collectors Club leaflet.

Produced for only a short period of time, this a very rare model in mint condition. The 'Pop Art' decoration is also obviously of its time and, along with that on a Mini Cooper, has become sought after in recent years.
1968-69
£1,000-1,500   **VEC**

A Corgi No.233 Heinkel Trojan Economy Car, red body, lemon interior, flat spun hubs, in mint condition, with mint condition carded box complete with Collectors Club folded leaflet.
1962-72
£70-100   **VEC**

A Corgi No.341 Mini Marcos GT850, maroon body, grey chassis, cream interior, golden jack take-off wheels, in mint condition, with near mint condition box, with Collectors Club folded leaflet.
1968-70
£50-70   **VEC**

A Corgi No.474 Ford Thames 'Walls Ice-cream' Van, with musical chimes and spun hubs, in excellent condition, with good condition carded box.
1965-68
£150-200   **VEC**

A Corgi No.437 Cadillac Superior 'Ambulance', with battery operated red roof-light and cast hubs, in mint condition, with inner packing card and Collectors Club leaflet, with excellent condition carded box.
1965-68
£120-180   **VEC**

A Corgi No.431 VW Pick-up, with plastic canopy and spun hubs, in mint condition, with mint condition Collectors Club leaflet and carded box.

The variation with a metallic gold body and red VW emblem can be worth around 50 per cent more.
1964-66
£100-150   **VEC**

A Corgi No.490 VW Breakdown Truck, with tan body, spun hubs, in mint condition, with good condition carded box with Collectors Club leaflet.
1967-69
£100-150   **VEC**

A Corgi No.1121 'Chipperfield Circus' six-wheel Crane Truck, with chrome jib, lacking hook and string but otherwise in excellent condition, with good condition carded picture box.

1963-69

£70-100   VEC

A Corgi No.1142 Ford Holmes Wrecker Truck, with unpainted booms, in excellent condition with two figures and instruction sheet, with excellent condition inner tray, and good condition outer window box.

1967-74

£150-200   VEC

A Corgi No.1120 Midland Red Motorway Express Coach, with yellow interior and flat spun hubs, in mint condition, with near mint condition box with Collectors Club leaflet.

£120-180   VEC

A Corgi No.50 Massey Ferguson 65 Tractor, with excellent condition carded box with inner packing card.

1959-66

£100-150   VEC

A Corgi Major Toys gift set no. 28, 'Car Transporter with four cars', comprising a Bedford TK cab transporter in red with mid and light blue trailer, Fiat 2100 (232), Renault Floride (222), Ford Consul Classic (234) and a Mercedes Benz 220 SE couple (230), vehicles in mint condition, with Corgi dog dummy boxes, box complete with internal packaging and instructions, minor wear to lid.

This is a very rare and desirable set and is in superb condition. Corgi gift sets in similar condition have been rising rapidly in value over the past few years.

1963-65

£600-800   W&W

A CLOSER LOOK AT A CORGI TANKER

The dark blue colour and decals on this model were produced as a special promotion for Shell Chemicallen of Holland c1963-64 only.

The variation of the lighter blue 1129 'Milk' Bedford tanker with an S-Type cab produced from 1962-65 is more common and worth around £150-200.

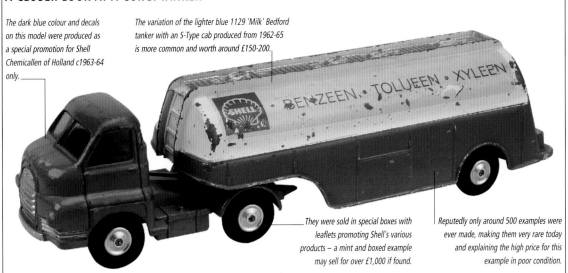

They were sold in special boxes with leaflets promoting Shell's various products – a mint and boxed example may sell for over £1,000 if found.

Reputedly only around 500 examples were ever made, making them very rare today and explaining the high price for this example in poor condition.

A Corgi 1129 blue and white Bedford S-Type 'Shell Petrol' Tanker, in poor condition.

c1963-64

£250-350   SAS

A Corgi 'Batman' 107 Batboat, in excellent condition, in excellent condition original striped window box.
1974-81
£70-100 SAS

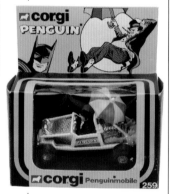

A Corgi 259 Penguinmobile, in excellent condition, in excellent condition original striped window box.
1979-80
£50-70 SAS

A CLOSER LOOK AT A BATMOBILE

Corgi released the Batmobile for Christmas 1966, having dominated the Christmas market in 1965 with James Bond's Aston Martin – the Batmobile proved just as popular.

It was produced in different variations until 1979, but the rarest examples are the first issues from 1966-67, of which this is one.

This example is rarer still as it has a matte, not gloss, black body and is in excellent condition.

Although it retains its appealing pictorial box, it is not in great condition, and some of the many accessories are missing, which reduces the value by as much as a third.

A Corgi matte black 267 Batmobile, with three rockets and Club Slip, in excellent condition, in fair condition original box, inner plinth slightly torn.
1966-67
£600-800 SAS

A Corgi 647 'Buck Rogers' Starfighter, with Wilma and Tweaky plastic figurines, in excellent condition, in very good condition original striped window box.
1980-83
£50-70 SAS

A Corgi 434 'Charlie's Angels' Van, in excellent condition, in very good condition original pictorial window box.
1978-80
£30-40 SAS

A Corgi 342 'The Professionals' Ford Capri, in excellent condition, in very good condition original box.
1980-82
£80-120 SAS

A Corgi 320 'The Saint' Jaguar XJS, in excellent condition, in excellent condition original striped pictorial window box.
1978-81

£20-30   SAS

A Corgi 436 Spidervan, in excellent condition, in excellent condition original striped pictorial window box.
1979-80

£25-35   SAS

A CLOSER LOOK AT NODDY'S CAR

This model is hard to find, particularly in such excellent condition, as it was produced for only one year.

Always look closely at the Golly's face – the value can nearly double if Golly has a tan face, and can triple if he has a black face.

At the time, Noddy's popularity was waning, meaning fewer were sold and the model was discontinued relatively quickly.

If Golly has been replaced by a brown Master Tubby, the value falls to around half this price.

A Corgi 801 Noddy's Car, with Noddy, Big Ears, and a grey-faced Golly, in excellent condition, in excellent condition original box.
1969

£300-400   SAS

A Corgi 292 'Starsky & Hutch' Ford Torino, in excellent condition, in very good condition original box.

Unusually, an export model (produced in 1986) is worth around a tenth of this value – mainly as it was made in a run of 20,000 and was generally kept in mint condition by many collectors.
1977-82

£80-120   SAS

A Corgi 348 Vegas Ford Thunderbird, with Dan Tanner as driver, in excellent condition, in excellent condition original striped pictoral box.

1980-81

£30-40   SAS

A Corgi 497 'The Man From U.N.C.L.E.' Thrush-Buster, with purplish-blue body, Waverly Ring, Club Slip, packing disc, packing ring and corrugated packing piece, in excellent condition, in very good condition original box.

To fetch this price, the model must have the ring and both internal card packing components. Look out for the white finished body, which was produced in the first year only (1966) and can fetch over twice this price.
1966-69

£300-400   SAS

QUICK REFERENCE

- Dinky toys were first produced in 1933 by Meccano Ltd as accessories to their popular range of Hornby model railways. They originated in a range known as 'Model Miniatures' introduced in 1931, which comprised 22 sets including one of model vehicles. In 1934, this set became the first set of 'Meccano Dinky Toys', intended to compete with America's Tootsie Toys, which were being imported into the UK and proving very popular with children.
- Dinky toys were made in Liverpool until 1979, and also at Bobigny in France from 1937–72. Following the closure of the Liverpool factory in 1979 the name was acquired by Matchbox in 1987, and then Mattel, who have not used it since 2001.
- Collectors consider the 'golden age' of Dinky to be the 1930s. By 1935, over 200 models were made, and examples are usually highly sought after. Survivors are rare as many pre-war models were made from a metallic alloy that tends to crumble over time.
- In 1947 the smaller scale 'Supertoys' range was released, followed by the 'Speedwheels' range in 1969. These are easier to find, and often less expensive to collect. Supertoys are particularly sought after by collectors.
- When buying, look for models in good condition, and beware of any repainting, even in small areas, as this reduces desirability considerably. If the original box is present and in good condition it can add over 40 per cent to the value.
- Look out for variations in paint colour, details such as cab stripes and hubs, and even plastic interiors. Some variations may indicate special models that were exported to certain countries in limited numbers, and can fetch high prices today.

A Dinky No.110 Aston Martin DB3S, mid-green, red seats, ridged hubs, white driver, racing number 22, in excellent condition, with good condition correct colour spot card picture box.
1956-59

£180-220   VEC

A Dinky No.176 Austin A105 Saloon, grey body, red side flash and ridged hubs, in near mint condition, with near mint condition correct colour spot card picture box.
1958-59

£100-150   VEC

A Dinky No.167 A.C. Aceca Coupé, grey body, red roof, shaped spun hubs, in excellent condition, with excellent condition incorrect colour spot card picture box.

The colour of the car on the box does not match the colour of the model. For some collectors, this makes this example less desirable. This is more valuable than the example with matching red hubs.
1958-63

£100-150   VEC

A Dinky No.112 Austin Healey Sprite MkII, red body, cream interior, spun hubs, in near mint condition, with good condition card picture box.

Look out for the South African export variation with a turquoise, pink, light blue or dark blue body, as this can fetch around four times as much as this.
1961-66

£80-120   VEC

A Dinky No.38A Frazer Nash BMW Car, grey, red seats and ridged hubs, in excellent condition, needs cleaning.

Frazer Nash were a British car manufacturer who were active from 1922-c1957. From 1934-39, they were the offical importer and assembler for BMW in the UK.
1947-50

£220-280   VEC

A French Dinky No.500 Citroen 2CV, orange body, plastic open-top, cream interior, shaped spun hubs, near mint condition, with near mint condition colour card picture box.

£100-150   VEC

A Dinky No.515 Ferrari 250GT 2 + 2, red body, white interior, concave spun hubs, in near mint condition, with near mint condition full colour card picture box.

£100-150   VEC

A Dinky No.1408 Honda S800, yellow body, red interior, concave spun hubs, in excellent condition, with near mint condition card picture box.

£80-120   C

A Dinky No.57/005 Ford Thunderbird, mid blue body, white roof, shaped cast wheels, plated bumpers, red interior, in near mint condition, with excellent condition card picture box.

This number indicates this model was made in Hong Kong, and is one of the more desirable and valuable of the small range made there from 1965-80. Yellow 'see-through' window boxes for Hong Kong models are scarce.
1965-67

£150-200   VEC

A Dinky No.165 Humber Hawk, maroon roof, lower body, cream middle, shaped spun hubs, slight spotting to roof, otherwise excellent condition, with excellent condition correct colour spot card picture box.
1959-60

£100-150   VEC

A CLOSER LOOK AT A DINKY CAR

This model was also produced from 1950-54 numbered 139b.

Many colour variations of this model number are sought after. Cream bodies with dark maroon roofs are more affordable at around half this value.

This colour variation with a 'lowline' long-slung configuration and blue hubs was only available from 1958-59, making it rarer than other variations.

As this is an American car, it has appeal to diecast collectors on both sides of the Atlantic, widening demand.

A Dinky No.171 Hudson Commodore Sedan, lowline, light grey body, mid blue upper and ridged hubs, factory paint touch-in to bonnet, in excellent condition, with near mint condition correct colour spot card picture box.
1958-59

£200-300   VEC

A Dinky no.157 Jaguar XK120, turquoise lower body, cerise upper body, red ridged hubs, in excellent condition.
1957-59

£100-150   VEC

A Dinky No.22A Maserati Sport 2000, dark red, plated convex hubs, white driver, in excellent condition, with good condition yellow card picture box.

£70-100   VEC

A Dinky No.108 MG Midget Sports Car, red body and ridged hubs, tan interior, racing number 24, white driver, in excellent condition, with excellent condition white colour spot card picture box.

This is a desirable car and is in red, rather than the plainer white.
1955-59

£200-300   VEC

A French Dinky Simca 8 Sport, pale duck egg green, red interior, chromed convex hubs, white tyres, in near mint condition.

£300-500   VEC

A Dinky pre-war No.22G Streamlined Tourer, dark blue body and smooth hubs, white tyres, upper windscreen missing, steering wheel complete, some light play wear but in overall good condition.
1935-41

£120-180   VEC

A rare Dinky no.105 Triumph TR2 touring with spun hubs, in light grey, with red interior, spun hubs with black knobbly tyres, includes driver, in excellent condition.

This variation, with its spun hubs, is usually worth up to twice the amount of the more common version with red cast hubs.
1957-60

£180-220   VEC

A Dinky No.254 Austin Taxi, green lower body, yellow upper and ridged hubs, black interior and baseplate, in near mint condition, with excellent condition correct colour spot card picture box.

Look out for the rarer blue variation, with matching blue hubs, as this can be worth over three times the value of this two-tone variation.
1956-59

£100-150   VEC

A Dinky No.273 Mini Van 'RAC Road Service', blue, white roof, red interior, in near mint condition, with good condition carded box.
1965-70

£100-150   VEC

SAS

Collecting or selling...we provide professional and sound advice for both large and small accumulations and collections (including a pick-up service) and hold regular auctions of Diecast, Toys, Trains, Toy Figures, Dolls and Teddy Bears.

For free sample catalogue, information and valuations contact

SPECIAL AUCTION SERVICES
Tel: 0118 971 2949
Kennetholme, Midgham, Near Reading, Berkshire RG7 5UX
www.specialauctionservices.com
mail@specialauctionservices.com

A Dinky No.987 Mobile Control Room 'ABC Television', blue, grey, red, plastic hubs, in excellent condition, complete with cameraman and camera, with good condition lift-off-lid box.

1962-69

£150-200   VEC

A Dinky No.491 'Jobs Dairy' Van, cream, red chassis and ridged hubs, black knobbly tyres, in excellent condition, with excellent condition correct colour spot yellow card box.

This model was made for promotional purposes, and is rare today. Always check the transfers, as wear reduces value. Job's Dairy was founded in 1819 in Middlesex, London and is still selling milk today.

£150-200   VEC

TOYS & GAMES

A Dinky No.923 Big Bedford Van 'Heinz', red cab, chassis, yellow back, hubs, replacement decals.

The Heinz transfers on this rare model have been replaced. Had they been original and the model in mint condition and complete with its box in similar condition, the value could have been £2,000.

1958-59

£80-120   VEC

A CLOSER LOOK AT A DINKY VAN

Dinky's ranges of delivery vans are one of the most collectable Dinky areas, with the '28' series being highly popular.

Pre-war models are harder to find, particularly in excellent or mint condition, and most were only produced for short time periods of a few years or less.

Values depend on the 'decal' transfers. Other desirable examples include 'Pickfords', 'Wakefield's Castrol' and 'Hornby Trains'.

Learn the differences between the three different shapes, or 'types', as this affects value. Early 'type one' shapes are usually the most valuable.

A Dinky No.28L 'Crawfords' Delivery Van, type one, red body, metal wheels, solid casting, some traces of original green lacquer, slightly distorted, some restoration to paint and decals on rear section, otherwise in good condition.

1934-35

£300-500   VEC

A Dinky No.25B Covered Wagon, type four, black chassis, cream cab, back, red tin tilt, ridged hubs, chrome loss to grille assembly, otherwise in excellent condition.

1947-50

£180-220   VEC

A Dinky No.575 Panhard SNCF Semi Trailer, dark blue cab, trailer, concave metal hubs, tin tilt with printing to both sides, in near mint condition, with fair condition complete card picture box.

£150-200   VEC

A Dinky No.502 Foden Flat Truck, green cab, flatbed, ridged hubs, black chassis, silver flash, black herringbone tyres, overall in good condition.

Foden flatbed trucks are popular with collectors, with rare export models in mint condition sometimes fetching over £10,000.

1947-48

£80-120   VEC

A Dinky No.434 Bedford TK Crash Truck 'Auto Services', metallic red cab, deep red interior and plastic hubs, grey back, in excellent condition, with good condition carded picture box.

The 'Auto Services' transfer is rarer than the 'Top Rank Motorway Services', although values do not differ too much.

1966-70

£80-120   VEC

A Dinky No.430 Breakdown Lorry, dark tan cab and chassis, green back, red ridged hubs, 'Dinky Service' in black to sides, in excellent condition, with excellent condition blue and white striped lidded box.

The most valuable variation has a red, glazed cab and a pale grey back, and can fetch over double the value of this colourway.

1954-64

£180-220   VEC

Wallis & Wallis

Est. 1928

International Specialist Toy & Model Auctioneers

e-mail:auctions@wallisandwallis.org   www.wallisandwallis.org

The Longest Established Toy Auction House in the UK

A rare Dinky Supertoys Foden Flat
Truck with chains (505) – Sold for £3,100

2010 SALES

SALE	DAYS	CLOSING DATE
162	March 22nd	February 20th
163	May 4th	March 27th
164	June 7th	May 8th
165	July 19th	June 12th
166	August 22nd	July 24th
167	October 4th	August 28th
168	November 15th	October 9th

We offer…

- *25 years experience with toys*
- *Personal attention with no consultation fees*
- *Five experienced cataloguers*
- *Valuations for probate*

Fine single items and collections welcome –
introductory commission for new customers

*"Whether buying or selling – it
pays to come to the specialists."*

A rare Dinky American issue post WWII Gift Set
No6 Commerical Vehicles – Sold for £1,450

Catalogues £8.00. Overseas £8.50. Back numbers, with prices realised, are available price 10 for £22 or
£4.50 each. (All prices include postage)

West Street Auction Galleries, Lewes, Sussex, England BN7 2NJ
Tel: +44 (0) 1273 480208   Fax: +44 (0) 1273 476562

QUICK REFERENCE

- A nostalgic name from many childhoods, Matchbox toys were produced by Lesney Products. Founded in London in 1947, the company produced its first toys in 1949. Aiming to produce pocket-sized toys for pocket money prices, its first major success was a coronation coach, produced from 1952 for the coronation of Queen Elizabeth II. The 'Matchbox' name was registered in 1954, and was used on base plates from 1955.

- Although no consistent scale was used, the most common was the 1-75 range, launched in 1953. This forms the core of most collections, along with the 'Models of Yesteryear' range launched in 1967. From 1953–69, Lesney's toys were distributed by Moko, whose name appeared on packaging, with Lesney acquiring the company in 1959. Metal wheels were discontinued in 1958 and were replaced with plastic.

- The 1960s were a 'golden age' for Matchbox, and by 1966 the company was producing 100 million models per year. In 1969, the 'Superfast' range, with suspension, was launched to compete with 'faster' cars such as those made by Corgi, or Mattel's 'Hot Wheels'. 'Superfast' cars were made until 1983.

- Later ranges, from c1971 onwards, include 'Super-Kings' and 'Speed Kings', although these are not currently as popular with collectors, they may prove to be an area to watch for the future. Lesney closed in 1982, with the brand being acquired by Tyco in 1992. Modern limited editions 'collectors' models may turn out to be a very long term investment, as so many have been kept mint and boxed.

- The majority of examples to be found cost under £30 and allow a collection to be built up affordably. However, look out for rare variations, considering features such as colours, decals, wheels, base plates and the interior, which can fetch hundreds of pounds. Always aim to buy in mint condition, as this is most likely to ensure an item holds or increases its value.

A Matchbox 'Regular Wheels' No.65b Jaguar 3.8 Saloon, in red, with a silver base and black plastic wheels, in near mint condition, with box in excellent condition.

Check the wheels, as the same model and colour with silver plastic wheels can be worth over twice the value of this version.
Introduced in 1962

£120-180 VEC

A Matchbox 8e Ford Mustang, in orange with red interior and solid chrome hubs, in very good condition, with good condition original box.

The orange body is the most valuable variation, white bodies are usually worth roughly a tenth of this value if they are in similar condition.

Introduced in 1966

£280-320 SAS

A Matchbox 31b Ford Station Wagon, in yellow with maroon baseplate, with windows and silver plastic wheels, in excellent condition, in good condition original box.
Introduced in 1960

£150-200 SAS

A Matchbox 'Models of Yesteryear' No.Y5-2 1929 Bentley 4.5 litre, metallic apple green, red seats and tonneau, racing number 5, Union Jack decals to both side doors, in excellent condition, unboxed.
1963

£70-100 VEC

A Matchbox Superfast No.57f Range Rover Carmichael Rescue Vehicle, finished in yellow with black base and trim.

The yellow body and lack of decals indicate that this is a very rare pre-production model – production models were in red or white and had 'Police Rescue' or 'Fire' decals.
c1982

£200-300 VEC

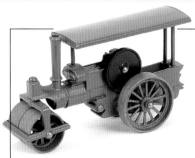

A Matchbox 'Models of Yesteryear' No.Y11 Aveling and Porter Road Roller, green, red, gold trim and maker's plate, in near mint condition, unboxed.

The gold maker's plate on this example makes it around twice as valuable as those without.

1958

£100-150   VEC

A Matchbox 'Models of Yesteryear' No.Y9 Fowler Showman's Engine in bright red with 'Lesney Modern Amusements' decal, with white roof, yellow wheels, in excellent condition, with box in near mint condition.

1965

£40-60   VEC

A Matchbox 'Regular Wheels' No.G3 'Farm' gift set, containing No.4 Dodge Stake Truck, No.12 Land Rover Safari, No.37 Dodge Cattle Truck, No.39 Ford Tractor, No.40 Hay Trailer, No.43 Pony Trailer, No.65 Claas Combine Harvester and No.72 Standard Jeep, all in mint condition, with near mint blue and yellow window box with detailed picture, still shrink-wrapped.

1968

£200-300   VEC

A Matchbox No.G1 'Auto Transporter' gift set, comprising five cars and car transporter, overall conditions are generally near mint, with good condition presentation window box, inner plastic tray is in near mint condition.

£25-35   VEC

A Matchbox 'Kingsize' No.G8 gift set, containing No.K1 Foden 'Hoveringham' Tipper, No.K11 Fordson Super Major Tractor with Farm Tipping Trailer, No.K12 Foden Wreck Truck and No.K15 Merryweather Turntable Fire Engine, in mint condition, with inner plastic tray, near mint condition outer blue and yellow window box, still shrink-wrapped, with original Sellotape marks to window.

The addition of the K1 Foden tipper is unusual.

c1965

£280-320   VEC

A Matchbox 'Kingsize' No.G8 'Construction' gift set, containing No.K1 Foden 'Hoveringham' Tipper, No.K7 'Curtiss' Rear Dumper, No.K10 'Aveling Barford' Tractor Shovel, No.K13 ERF Concrete Mixer and No.K14 'Taylor' Jumbo Crane, in mint condition, with excellent condition box.

The inner plastic tray is both rare and in excellent condition. The pictorial sleeve is also in unusually excellent condition. This example shows how the combination of models and a box in mint condition can push up the price for desirable gift sets.

£750-850   VEC

A Matchbox 'Leslie Smith OBE' poseable figure, no.186 of only up to 500 produced, dressed in grey suit and holding Matchbox book, in mint condition, with carded box.

Smith (1918-2005) was the co-founder of Lesney in 1947. This model was produced in 1990 to commemorate the Matchbox MICA UK Convention on the 24th March 1990.

1990

£70-100   VEC

TOYS & GAMES

QUICK REFERENCE

- Tinplate toys are made from sheets of steel plated with tin. These sheets were painted by hand, or decorated with lithographic transfers, and cut into shapes, bent, embossed and fixed together to form toys. Tinplate became popular in the mid-19thC and replaced wood and cast iron as it was more economical and provided wider scope for manufacture.

- Germany was the 'home' of the tin toy, with factories exporting toys around the world. Notable makers include Märklin (founded 1856), Gebrüder Bing (1863-1933), and Schreyer & Co (1912-78), whose Schuco name is still used for toys today. Toys by these companies are particularly popular. The US became a secondary centre from the 1880s onwards, with names such as Marx (1896-c1982) and Ferdinand Strauss (c1914-42) being sought after.

- From the late 19thC-1930s, production focused on cars, trucks, zeppelin airships and aircraft. The earliest examples from the mid-late19thC were hand-painted. Look closely to see brush marks, especially on details.

- After WWII, the centre of production moved to Japan and names such as Horikawa (SH), Nomura (TN Toys) and Yonizawa are sought after. The development of the battery allowed for novelty features such as flashing lights and sounds; the more numerous and bizarre the 'actions' the more a toy is likely to be worth. Robots and spacecraft also became popular reflecting the excitement of the 'Space Race' to the moon in the 1950s and 60s.

- Value is dependent on the type of toy, the maker, the size, the date and the condition. Scratched transfers are almost impossible to restore, although shallow dents can sometimes be fixed. Early hand-painted pieces are highly sought after, but the desirability of humorous features in later toys should not be underestimated. Large, early ships or zeppelins by Märklin can fetch over £20,000, while a simple 1960s Japanese spacecraft can be found for under £50.

A 1920s-30s Bing black lithographed tinplate clockwork 19872 Model T Ford, with driver.

6.25in (16cm) long

£300-500   SAS

A late 20thC reproduction JB Carette-style navy blue non-powered painted tinplate Limousine, with bisque driver and passenger, in excellent condition.

If this were an original Carette limousine, it could have fetched over £3,000.

12.5in (32cm) long

£30-50   SAS

A 1920s German Gebrüder Bing red lithographed tinplate clockwork tourer, with driver, in good condition, but lacking rear seat.

5.5in (14cm) long

£120-180   SAS

A US Zone German Schuco Kommando Anno 2000, red, plated radiator, opening bonnet to reveal engine, paint finish crazed overall, otherwise in excellent condition, with good condition box and instructions.

c1946-c1949   6in (15cm) long

£80-120   VEC

A US Zone German Schuco Varianto-Limo 3041, red tinplate clockwork car, complete with control wire, very minor wear to edges, otherwise in excellent condition, with fair condition box and instructions.

The 'US Zone' wording refers to the period from 1945-49, when Western Germany was divided into administrative zones by the Allies, following WWII.

c1946-c1949

£100-150   VEC

A US Zone German Schuco Fex 1111, green bodywork with plated radiator and windscreen, red wheel hubs, very minor chips, wear to edges, otherwise in good condition, boxed.

c1946-c1949   *6in (15cm) long*

£80-120   VEC

A rare French CIJ clockwork tinplate Renault Fregate, finished in greyish-green, with electric head lights, opening driver's door, steerable front wheels, plated bumpers and grille, lacking rear seat assembly, otherwise in good condition.

CIJ is a sought-after name, and this is very good quality car.

                                                12.5in (32cm) long

£350-450   VEC

A 1950s German Tipp & Co. US Navy Staff Car, tinplate friction drive car in dark green, with US Navy 63 transfers, plastic hubs and tyres, plated parts, in near mint condition.

                                                7.5in (19cm) long

£60-90   VEC

A rare French CIJ two tone friction drive Renault Dauphine, with detailed printing, rubber wheels, and registration number '5-56', light scratching on roof, otherwise in excellent condition.

                                                8.75in (22cm) long

£250-350   VEC

A Japanese TN Toys tinplate 'Sonic Dodge Charger', battery operated, with passenger detail to interior, rubber tyres, whistle and aerial accessory, in generally excellent condition, with good condition card box.

                                                16in (41cm) long

£80-120   VEC

A rare Japanese Modern Toys large tinplate American Car, finished in red, battery-operated, with steerable front wheels, rubber tyres, some discolouration to plated parts, lacks aerial, in good condition, with some wear.

                                                14in (36cm) long

£70-100   VEC

A late 1960s Japanese Ichiko friction-powered lithographed tinplate pop-art Jaguar Saloon, in good condition, headlamps replaced.

It's the fabulous graphics that make this car so desirable and valuable, as well as the fact that it is a Jaguar.

                                                7.75in (20cm) long

£150-200   SAS

QUICK REFERENCE - FIRE ENGINES

Fire engines and vehicles are as popular with today's grown-up collectors as they were with the young boys who played with them originally. Nostalgia plays a key part, perhaps as so many wanted to be firemen when they were young. Fire engines also form an easily definable collecting area, yet still give a challenge to collect as many different types as possible from the 1900s-70s. Key makers' names, such as Märklin, Bing or Arnold, are important, but also look out for examples with an excellent level of detail to the transfer printing. Other desirable features include separately modelled firemen, such as on the example below, and extra actions such as an extending and elevating ladder. The more complex and large an engine is, the more valuable it is likely to be.

A rare French Unis tinplate clockwork Fire Engine, red, with detailed tin-printing, two tinplate firemen, elevating ladder, with permanent key and grey tinplate wheels, revolving turntable, in generally excellent condition.

8.25in (21cm) long

£120-£180   **VEC**

A rare Wells or similar tinplate clockwork Fire Engine, red, with extending and elevating cream tinplate ladder, revolving turntable, permanent key, with three seated firemen figures, tinplate balloon wheels, slight creasing to ladder, otherwise in excellent condition.

12in (30cm) long

£100-150   **VEC**

A rare early Spanish Paya tinplate miniature Fire Engine, in red with detailed printing including fireman, with ladder and black wheels, in good condition.

Paya were founded near Alicante in 1902, and have been making toys ever since. During the mid-1980s they began to re-release many of their earlier classic toys in limited editions. These are accompanied by certificates and appealingly colourful boxes.

4.25in (11cm) long

£40-60   **VEC**

A French tinplate clockwork Fire Engine, red, with plated ladder and wheels, and elevating single section ladder with revolving turntable, in good condition.

10in (25cm)

£50-70   **VEC**

A German tinplate clockwork Fire Engine, red, with silver rear platform, wheels and single elevating ladder, permanent key, in excellent condition.

6in (15cm) long

£40-60   **VEC**

A German Goso tinplate Turntable Fire Escape, red, with silver ladder and grille, plated hub caps, rubber tyres, single section ladder, some wear to top of cab, otherwise in good condition.

10.25in (26cm) long

£80-120   **VEC**

A rare German Wimmer articulated Aerial Fire Truck, brick red bakelite cab, with clockwork motor, tinplate trailer with single elevating ladder, and rubber wheels, in good condition.

9in (23cm) long

£50-80   **VEC**

An unusual 1960s European tinplate large Fire Truck, with friction drive and ladder, with beige roof and fittings, some plated parts and two firemen figures in rear, in good condition.

13.5in (34cm) long

£50-80   **VEC**

A Märklin late edition 1991 clockwork tinplate Fire Engine, with certificate, in excellent condition, in excellent condition original box.
1991

£100-150   **SAS**

A CLOSER LOOK AT AN ARNOLD FIRE ENGINE

Arnold was founded in Nürnberg, Germany by Karl Arnold in 1906. Arnold tinplate toys are sought after, especially if they date from before WWII like this one.

The box is original, rather than reproduction, and in very good condition, which adds to the desirability, particularly as it has such charming artwork.

As the clockwork motor drives the car along, a mechanism in the 'boiler' causes sparks to fly out – actions like this are desirable.

The transfers are detailed and in largely excellent condition.

A German Arnold No.640 clockwork Steam Fire Engine, in red, with detailed printing, with driver figure and boiler to rear, with key, in excellent condition, with good condition box.

4.75in (12cm) long

£200-300   **VEC**

A 1930s French RL Toys tinplate clockwork Fire Car, with detailed printing, green tinplate wheels, with '1946' registration number, some wear otherwise in good condition.

5.5in (14cm) long

£50-80   **VEC**

A German KD tinplate Fire Engine, with friction drive and opening rear door, detailed tinprinting including firemen, aerial and beacon to roof, in excellent condition, with excellent condition red card box.

6.25in (16cm) long

£60-90   **VEC**

A German Gama large tinplate Tipper, with orange tipping body and lower cab, hub caps, beige cab roof, black trim, opening rear tailgate and steerable front wheels, in good condition but some wear to edges.

14in (36cm) long

£120-180   **VEC**

A German Gama Articulated Transport Truck, with detailed interior, steerable front wheels, silver trailer with 'International Transport' to sides, detailed tin-printing, drop-down rear door, rubber tyres, in overall good condition, but lacking spare wheel.

19in (48cm) long

£150-250   **VEC**

A CLOSER LOOK AT A RICH TOYS VAN

The Rich Manufacturing Company was founded in Illinois in 1915 and produced toys until 1962, being known as 'Rich Toys Inc' from 1935 when the company moved to Clinton, Iowa.

This example retains many of its original accessories, including wooden and glass milk bottles and carriers, and has a driver and opening doors – all are desirable features.

Their pre-war toys are prized and comparatively scarce. Most were pull-along and made of wood, or where tinplate was used, they were usually horse-drawn.

Advertising toys can be scarce and also appeal to collectors of advertising memorabilia, a factor which often drives prices up.

A rare Rich Toys lithographed tin 'Bordens' delivery van, with yellow wooden roof and wooden bonnet, stencilled 'Bordens', with seated driver and two cases of milk bottles, one with four glass bottles, the other two wooden bottles, rear doors open, in good condition.

13.5in (34cm) long

£4,500-6,000   **BER**

A German Arnold large tinplate Tipper Truck, with friction drive, orange chassis and hub caps, detailed tin-printed interior and steering wheel, yellow tipping body with opening tailgate, in good condition but lacking driver.

11in (28cm) long

£250-350   **VEC**

A rare German Gama No.291/1 'International Express' Van, with opening rear door, friction drive, detailed cab interior, lacking one rear door handle, head light lenses and front hub caps, otherwise in good condition.

13.75in (35cm) long

£100-150   **VEC**

A rare German Goso miniature clockwork Breakdown Truck, with blue cab, silver chassis, brick red jib and rubber wheels, in excellent condition.

5.25in (13cm) long

£40-60   **VEC**

A 1950s German Tipp & Co. transfer-printed tinplate motorcycle and rider, the rider wearing a red jacket and plus fours, marked 'MADE IN U.S. ZONE GERMANY' and with 'TCO' maker's monogram.

Known for their motorbikes, Tipp & Co. (1912-71) are a sought-after name. The Ullman Brothers, who owned Tipp & Co., fled Germany during WWII after the government seized their company, and founded Mettoy in Britain. After the war, both companies ran concurrently.

7.5in (19cm) long

£250-350　　　　　　　　　　　　　　QU

A Spanish Rico clockwork Touring Motorcyclist, with brown and red rider with white helmet on blue bike, plain brown tinplate wheels and stabilisers, clockwork inoperable, otherwise in good condition.

£120-180　　　　　　　　　　VEC

A US Zone German Huki clockwork red and white motorbike with sidecar, with brown and grey rider, registration 'K-1021', sidecar with number '21', in excellent condition.

c1946-c1949　　6.25in (16cm) long

£250-350　　　　　　　　　　VEC

A German Günthermann tinplate Crawler Tractor, with driver, orange wheels, working motor, lacking tracks, otherwise in excellent condition.

7in (18cm) long

£60-£80　　VEC

A 1960s Japanese Marusan friction-powered lithographed 'Silver Pigeon' Motorcycle, in good condition, part of base-plate overpainted.

5.25in (13.5cm) long

£200-300　　　　　　　　　　SAS

A CLOSER LOOK AT A FISCHER MOTORCYCLE

This toy's small size indicates that it is a penny toy, an inexpensive toy sold for a penny in stores and by street vendors.

Despite so many having been made and sold, few have survived the ravages of a child's attention as they are so small and fragile, making them scarce today.

Fischer is a notable German maker and their unusual, amusing toys, such as this example, are sought after.

Value also depends on the level of detail and the condition. Although this piece is well-detailed, it is worn; had it been in mint condition it may have fetched up to twice as much.

A Fischer penny toy red and gold motorcycle, with rider and passenger in front chair, in fair condition, slight varnishing to wheels.

3.5in (8.5cm) long

£400-600　　　　　　SAS

A Gama lithographed tinplate clockwork tractor and trailer, with plastic driver, lacks clockwork motor.

1937   *12in (30.5cm) long*

£50-80   **VEC**

A Marx clockwork crawler tractor, finished in orange with yellow detailing, with silver metal wheels and black rubber tracks, lacking seat and chimney stack, otherwise in good condition.

£25-35   **VEC**

A 1920s German Lehmann 651 EPL 1 Zeppelin, lacking celluloid blades and in poor condition, bent at back, scratched surface and rusting.

This very worn example is worth as much as this due to the notable maker and the subject matter. Zeppelins are highly sought after.

£120-180   **SAS**

A clockwork painted tinplate airship, finished in grey and red.

By an unknown maker, the form of this example is not as realistic or detailed as the one above.

                                    7.75in (20cm) long

£60-80   **SAS**

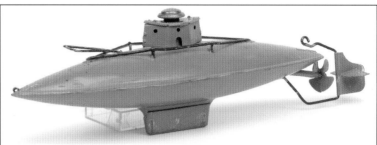

A tinplate clockwork submarine, possibly by Bing, finished in grey, with black hand-rails, brass screw on cap, propeller and rudder, in good condition.

                                        10in (25cm)

£150-200   **VEC**

A 1920s German Fischer yellow and blue speedboat penny toy, numbered '5', lacking rear flag, wheels overpainted, otherwise in good condition.

The overpainting and missing part reduce the value of this whimsical wheeled boat.

                                    6.25in (16cm) long

£180-220   **SAS**

A rare 1930s German Günthermann acrobatic aircraft, in dark blue and grey, with clockwork motor and flip-over acrobatic action, lacks tailfin and rear jockey wheel but includes pilot, permanent key, in fair condition.

                                7.75in (20cm) wingspan

£80-120   **VEC**

A CLOSER LOOK AT A LEHMANN TOY

Lehmann were founded in Nuremberg in 1881 and produced often complexly constructed lightweight tinplate toys that were exported across the world.

Along with Günthermann, their toys are loved for their fun and inventive forms, often with a bizarre sense of humour – the Balky Mule is typical.

The clown is well dressed and the mule has a textured finish. When wound the clown rocks back and forth as the mule bucks.

A French JRD novelty character driving a clockwork eccentric action tinplate car, with logo to bonnet and boot '1949 RF', the driver with moustache and bowler hat, blue jacket, yellow waistocat and red bow tie, in good condition with some wear to finish.

7in (18cm) long

£80-£120   VEC

A Greppert & Kelch 552 clockwork lithographed tinplate red, white and blue three-wheel trolley car, with lady driver, dog and boy.

6in (15cm) high

£100-150   SAS

The theme and unusual action were popular with children and this toy was made for decades from the early 1900s, making it one of the more common and affordable of Lehmann's toys.

A Lehmann transfer-printed tinplate EPL 245 Balky Mule, in good condition.

7.5in (19cm) long

£280-320   SAS

A 1950s American Marx 'Milton Berle' lithographed tinplate 'Crazy Car', with vivid and colourful illustrations and catchphrases, revolving head and 'eccentric' movements, in fair condition with some wear and damage.

Milton Berle (1908-2002) was a famous 1950s US radio and television star known to millions as 'Uncle Miltie'. The damage and lack of a box has reduced the value, although he does retain his plastic hat, which is often missing.

7in (18cm) long

£60-90   VEC

A 1960s Japanese Masutoku Toy Factory M-T Co Hand Car, no.3296, battery operated, three actions, in near mint condition, with good condition illustrated box.

£70-£100   VEC

A Lehmann transfer-printed tinplate Sea Lion, with key, in very good condition.

Lehmann's animal toys are highly collectable. Including a climbing monkey and a walking crocodile, they were often inspired by German colonial activities in Africa.

7.25in (18.5cm) long

£250-350   SAS

A Schuco clockwork pig violinist, complete with sailor's uniform, cap, violin and bow, in good condition.

5.5in (14cm) high

£80-120   **SAS**

QUICK REFERENCE - SCHUCO FIGURES

Schuco was the tradename used by Schreyer & Co., founded in Nuremberg, Germany in 1912, until 1921 when the company was renamed Schuco. Their mechanical toys were loved before and after the war, and included bears (such as the famous Yes-No teddy bear) and cars. These small clockwork figures form a collecting area of their own – many are animals that play instruments or perform acrobatics. Look out for unusual figures that may not have appealed at the time so would have sold in fewer numbers making them rarer today. One example is a monk with a beer tankard, or 'Mr Atom' who can fetch over £500. Unless very rare, to be of interest the clockwork mechanism must work, accessories should be complete and the clothes must not be faded.

A Schuco clockwork Pig drummer, complete with drum, sticks, hat and clothes, in good condition.

5.5in (14cm) high

£80-120   **SAS**

A Schuco 882 clockwork acrobatic 'Turn Clown', in fair condition with original clothes by wear to his face, in poor condition original box.

£60-80   **SAS**

A Schuco 986 'Solisto' clockwork monkey drummer, complete with drum, sticks, hat and clothes, in good condition.

5.5in (14cm) high

£60-80   **SAS**

A Japanese 1950s-60s Nomura 'TN Toys' transfer-printed tinplate, fabric and soft vinyl bartender clockwork toy in mint condition.

11.5in (29cm) high

£50-80   **MA**

A British lithographed tinplate lever-action red, blue and yellow minstrel dancer, in good condition.

£40-60   **SAS**

A 1950s Japanese grey transfer-printed tinplate clockwork robot.

5in (12cm) high

£150-180   QU

A 1960s Japanese Yonezawa transfer-printed tinplate and plastic robot, marked 'MADE IN JAPAN'.

8in (20cm) high

£500-700   QU

A Mainland battery operated 99/30 dark metallic grey painted and lithographed tinplate 'Moon Explorer', in good condition, in good original box.

£70-100   SAS

A 1950s-60s Japanese TM Modern Toys tinplate and plastic 'Mischief Monkey' clockwork toy, in mint condition.

The scarce box refers to this toy as 'Mischievous Monkey' and can add more than 50 per cent to the value.

8in (20cm) long

£20-30   MA

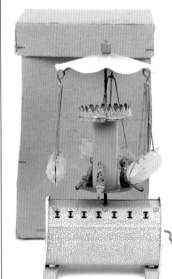

A Zeppelin tinplate carousel, probably German, crank handle operates musical roundabout, in generally excellent condition, with original plain card box.

8in (20cm) high

£120-180   VEC

A 1950s Louis Marx 'G Man Automatic' tinplate child's pistol, with rare original box and decals.

This is in excellent condition and retains its box, hence the high value. However, look for signs of age and wear as the box is being reproduced today for a collectors' market.

3.25in (8cm) high

£100-150   BB

A 1950s Czechoslovakian transfer-printed tinplate clockwork train scene, unmarked, in mint condition with original card box.

9.5in (24cm) long

£18-22   MTB

QUICK REFERENCE

- The first model trains, produced in the 1850s, were stylised, bulky and unrealistic. By the 1890s, more realistic tinplate models, with clockwork- or steam mechanisms, were being produced by German manufacturers such as Märklin (est 1759) and Gebrüder Bing (1863-1933). Many of these were exported to the US and Europe, although production and exports ceased during the two World Wars.
- Gauge sizes were introduced by Märklin in 1891. Their larger gauges (II and III) were quickly replaced by smaller gauges (I and 0) in 1910 as demand for smaller trains sets grew. By 1938, gauge I had also been discontinued, and in 1935 even gauge 0 had been replaced by the smaller 00-gauge. Märklin's HO gauge, which was even smaller, was used from 1948.

- The well-known British company Hornby began making trains in 1920 and their pre-WWII gauge 0 trains are now widely collected. Post War examples were of comparatively poor quality, and the range was discontinued in 1969. Hornby's Dublo range, designed to compete with small gauge sets by Märklin and Trix, was introduced in 1938 and is also highly collectable today. Nationalised livery trains (produced 1953-1957) are less desirable. Hornby was taken over by Tri-ang in 1964, with the name Tri-ang Hornby being used from 1965.
- As many trains were played with and have become worn or damaged, good condition examples will command the highest prices. The precise model, date and livery also affects value, with rare models being more desirable.

An early Hornby O gauge No. 2 4-4-4 clockwork Tank locomotive, LMS maroon No. 4-4-4, with nickel couplings and brass buffers, in excellent condition.

This was the only 4-4-4 gauge model made by Hornby, with the earliest models being in LMS and LNER liveries.
1923-29

£420-480 VEC

A Hornby 0 gauge EM120 0-4-0 tank loco, LNER green No.2900 20v electric, in very good condition, with reproduction box.

£150-200 VEC

A Hornby O gauge No. 2 Special 4-4-0 Loco and Tender 'COUNTY OF BEDFORD' GWR green No. 3821, 20v electric, repainted, lined and transferred.

With the crest on the tender and a black running plate used from 1930-36, this scarce 20v electric version is usually worth up to twice the value of the clockwork version.
1936-41

£700-1,000 VEC

A Hornby Dublo three-rail pre-war EDL1 4-6-2 LNER blue A4 Class Loco No. 4498 'Sir Nigel Gresley', in good condition with some wear to paint, in fair condition box, dated '9/38'.

Made from 1938-41, prewar models have full wheel valances and a push rod gear, instead of valve gear.
1938

£600-800 VEC

A Hornby Dublo three-rail EDG7 0-6-2 GWR green Tank Loco No. 6699, with gold decal to bunker rear, with horseshoe-type motor and instruction booklet dated '8/49', in excellent condition, and good condition pale blue box with 'GW' sticker to one end and dated '6/48'.
c1948

£700-1,000 VEC

A CLOSER LOOK AT A HORNBY DUBLO TRAIN

This is a rare version of this model with smoke deflectors on each side of the front of the boiler.

The deflectors indicate models that were repaired at the Binns Road factory using new 'Duchess of Montrose' bodies painted in 'Duchess of Atholl' livery.

A standard 'Duchess of Atholl' model, made from 1947-53, is usually worth under £200.

Also look out for the version with a cream nameplate, as this can fetch up to twice the price of the standard model.

A Hornby Dublo three-rail EDL2/D2 4-6-2 LMS maroon Princess Coronation class locomotive and tender No.6231 'Duchess of Atholl', in excellent condition, with repair box with end packing pieces and repair No.34064 to both ends, with tender box in good condition and dated "2/50".
1950

£700-1,000   **VEC**

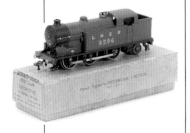

A Hornby Dublo three-rail EDL7 0-6-2 LNER green N2 Class Tank No. 9596, with horseshoe type motor and gold decal to bumper rear, in excellent condition with faded pale blue box, the lid dated '5/49'.
1949

£220-280   **VEC**

A Hornby Dublo three-rail 3232 Co-Co green Diesel Loco, complete with instruction booklet dated '8/60', in excellent condition, in excellent condition box.
1960

£180-220   **VEC**

A rare Hornby Dublo three-rail EDL7 LNER Tank Goods set, containing 0-6-2 black N2 Class Tank No. 9596, with gold decal to bunker rear and horseshoe type motor, with three NE Goods Vehicles in green/grey Open, brown Vent Van and Brake Van, and with track, controller with wires, instruction flyer, oil bottle, instruction booklet dated '9/47', purple guarantee slip, pre-war printed and tested/guarantee slip dated 30th January 1947, in excellent condition, in complete excellent condition box.

This first post-war set is very rare as most were exported when it was issued in Autumn 1947.
c1947

£1,200-1,800   **VEC**

A Hornby Dublo two-rail 2220 4-6-0 BR green Castle class locomotive No.7032 'Denbigh Castle', with instructions dated "8/59", in excellent condition with excellent condition plain red box.
1959

£200-300   **VEC**

A Hornby Dublo Suburban Electric train set, comprising SR Electric Motor Coach RN 265326, SR Electric unpowered Driving Trailer RN S77511, both in BR SR green livery, with track, in very good condition with box and instructions.

£280-320   **W&W**

TOYS AND GAMES

QUICK REFERENCE - BASSETT-LOWKE

Founded in Northampton in 1901, Bassett-Lowke was primarily a sales organisation that marketed and distributed model trains, ships and other toys made by other manufacturers. These included Wintringham of Northampton, and German companies Gebrüder Bing (from 1902), Carette, and Trix (from 1935). However, it also produced its own models, the first locomotive being made in 1903. As can be expected from such notable German makers quality was high. Many trains were designed by the company's designer Henry Greenly. It began to decline in the 1950s as children moved away from mechanical trains, and less expensive models were produced by competitors. In 1964, it sold its shops and closed a year later. The brand was acquired by a number of different people, and is owned today by Hornby, which produces new ranges under this historic name.

A Bing for Bassett-Lowke gauge I locomotive and tender 'SINGLE', GNR green No. 266, three-rail Electric, finished in green and black, with running number '266', with a modern mechanism with a Skate Pick-up, tender with 'GNR' lettering and 'Bassett-Lowke' transfer to back, in very good condition.

£800-1,200   VEC

A Bing for Bassett-Lowke gauge 1 4-4-0 clockwork locomotive and tender, LNWR black 'PRECURSOR' No. 513, finished in black, lined in red and white with 'Precursor' over front splasher and running number '513', in good condition.

£800-1,200   VEC

A Basset-Lowke Gauge 1 4-4-0 live steam locomotive and tender, Midland maroon 'COMPOUND' No. 1000, with 'LOWKE' transfer to tender, and running number '1000' sides, in fair condition.

Despite its poor condition, this is a mechanically and structurally sound model train. Some restoration will improve its visual appeal and increase its value.

£800-1,200   VEC

A Carette for Basset-Lowke gauge 1 4-4-2 three rail electric locomotive and tender, 'ATLANTIC' GNR green No. 1442, finished in green and black, lined in yellow and orange, with running number '1442', and tender with 'GNR' lettering, in good condition.

£800-1,200   VEC

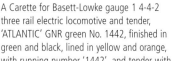

A modern Hornby for Basset-Lowke Princess class 4-6-2 three-rail electric locomotive and tender, 'Princess Victoria' No.46205, in British Railways black, numbered 85 from a limited production range, in mint condition, with guarantee slip, instructions and Basset-Lowke cloth, with box in excellent condition and with outer mailer.

£550-750   VEC

A Carette for Bassett-Lowke Gauge 1 LNWR 12-wheel Dining Saloon No. 13210, the sides in good condition, roof in fair condition.

£250-350   VEC

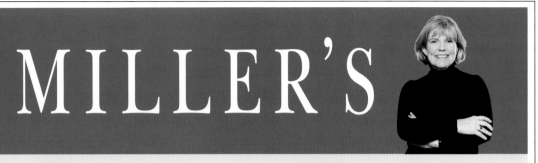

TOYS AND GAMES

Check out the brand new website at
www.millersonline.com

Miller's 20th Century Design

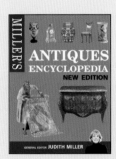

Miller's Antiques Encyclopedia

Whether you're buying or selling, take Miller's with you

A Tri-ang R56 4-6-4 maroon Baltic Tank locomotive No. 4830, with Tri-ang Railway decals, fitted with closed couplings but missing rear lamp, in excellent condition, in good condition box.

£80-120 VEC

A unique Australian Tri-ang R52 0-6-0 maroon plastic Jinty Tank locomotive, with head-lamp and no buffers, in excellent condition.

£250-350 VEC

A Tri-ang R155 Bo-Bo yellow Diesel switcher No. 5007, the early style body moulding with 'Tri-ang Railways' to sides and maroon stripe to running board, with open couplings, in excellent condition, in good condition box.

£60-90 VEC

A Tri-ang R155 Bo-Bo green Diesel switcher No. 5007, with Tri-ang Railways to sides, open couplings, fading to numbers and Tri-ang Railways transfer, in good condition with some rusting, in good condition box with lower insert.

£60-90 VEC

A rare Tri-ang TT unboxed gold-plated 4-6-2 Streamlined Merchant Navy Class Loco 'Clan Line' and three Mk. 1 Coaches, slide bar detached from connecting rod to loco left side, tender right side has glue repair to rear, in good condition, the coaches in excellent condition, but Brake Coach has rear coupling missing.

This very rare set is one of only 500 made in the mid-1960s for the Kays Mail Order Catalogue Co.

£400-600 VEC

A rare Australian Tri-ang R450A plastic New South Wales (NSWR) Suburban Overhead Electric Motor Car, in dark brown, rusting and slight damage to pantograph, in production box.

£250-350 VEC

A Tri-ang Hornby R644A Inter City passenger train set, comprising Bo-Bo BR blue class AL1 overhead electric loco No.E3001 single pantograph, two blue/grey Mk.2 second class coaches with lights and one blue/grey Mk.2 brake/first class, with instruction booklet dated "15/9/69" and instruction flyer for overhead power supply system, in excellent condition with good condition complete box with fair condition lid.

Models marked with the Tri-ang Hornby brand date from after 1964, as Tri-ang acquired the troubled Meccano Group, which owned Hornby, in that year.

1969

£80-120 VEC

MIKE DELANEY for HORNBY "O" Gauge & other VINTAGE TOY TRAINS, BUYING & SELLING

Web-site can be viewed at **www.vintagehornby.co.uk**

You can also contact us on 01993 840064 / 07979 910760

email mike@vintagehornby.co.uk or mike@vintagehornby.com

I am always interested in purchasing high quality HORNBY / BASSETT-LOWKE / MÄRKLIN / BING and other vintage O gauge items. So if you are thinking of selling single items or whole collections call me for a friendly no obligation service.

A Marklin Gauge 1 clockwork tinplate 4-4-0 locomotive and tender 'Precursor' LNWR black No. 513, finished in black red and white with 'Precursor' to front splasher and running number '513' to cab side, with a modern 3-rail four coupled mechanism fitted, the tender with the Marklin stamp under the tender, both couplings refixed, in excellent condition.

£800-1,200   **VEC**

A Wrenn W2213 4-6-2 NE Wartime black A4 Class locomotive No. 4903 'Peregrine', with larger driving wheels fitted to Mk 1 chassis, in near mint condition, in mint condition box with base stamped '91 729'.

£800-1,200   **VEC**

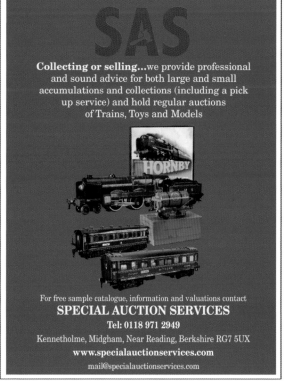

SAS

Collecting or selling...we provide professional and sound advice for both large and small accumulations and collections (including a pick up service) and hold regular auctions of Trains, Toys and Models

For free sample catalogue, information and valuations contact

SPECIAL AUCTION SERVICES

Tel: 0118 971 2949

Kennetholme, Midgham, Near Reading, Berkshire RG7 5UX

www.specialauctionservices.com

mail@specialauctionservices.com

TOYS & GAMES

QUICK REFERENCE

- Lead figures became the favourite toys of young boys in the late 18thC and early 19thC, and are now collected by grown-ups for their nostalgic value.
- Made as early as the 18th century, the first mass-produced lead figures were flat. As their popularity increased, solid figures ('rounde-bosse') were introduced. However, lead figures did not become ubiquitous until 1893, when William Britain Jr., founder of Britains (established in 1845), introduced the 'hollow-casting' method, which released the molten lead from the centre of a figure: halving the cost of a box of soldiers. This began the 'golden age' of the lead soldier, which ran until to the late 1950s, when lead was replaced by cheaper, safer plastics.
- William Britain became the largest maker of lead soldiers in the world, producing more than 100 different British Army regiments sets, and setting the standard size (2in/5.5cm) for toy soldiers. Other well-known and collectable makers include Charbens, C.B.G. Mignot, Taylor & Barrett, and John Hill Co.
- Though soldiers were the most popular form of figure, domestic and pastoral scenes, such as farms and zoos, were also produced. These were most popular after World War I, when interest in military subjects waned after the horrors of the war.
- Look for fine detailing and original paint. Completely opaque, overly bright paint or unusual colour tones may indicate a repainted figure. These should be avoided, as should figures that have had parts replaced, re-attached or customised. If you are buying a set, ensure that it is complete, and that the figures match: paintwork can vary subtly from batch to batch. Original boxes will typically add value, particularly if they are in excellent condition, as these were often thrown away or damaged, and examples are therefore scarce.

A Britains Regiments Of All Nations series Indian Army Services Corps set no. 1893, comprising officer, mule, handler and four soldiers with rifles at the trail, in mint condition, tied into box.

£100-150   W&W

A rare Britains Regiments of All Nations Australian Army Infantry set no. 2030, comprising officer and seven soldiers, all unusually in black ceremonial dress.

£150-200   W&W

A rare Britains Zoological series set no. 4Z, including rhinoceros, hippopotamus, elephant, giraffe, crocodile, camel, lion, tiger llama, penguins, three palm trees, all in good condition, in original box with good reproduction inserts, orange box with applied label, some wear.

£700-1,000   WW

A Britains Regiments Of All Nations Danish Army soldiers set no. 2018, comprising eight mounted Gardehusarregimete, a trumpeter and six Hussars and officer, in very good condition, in original box with insert, pieces not tied in, minor wear to lid.

£150-250   WW

A rare mid-1950s Britains Mammoth circus set no. 1539, comprising circus ring, ring master, four horses, lion tamer and two lions, boxing clown and kangaroo, four elephants, three additional clowns, one with long stilted legs, equestrienne and clown with hoop, both with horses, red painted wooden ring with central raised dias, two small black painted, leaf shaped metal bases, in very good condition, orange paper covered box with applied label, contents tied in.

£800-1,200   WW

An early 1950s Britains Rodeo set no. 2043, including stockade bars, posts and feet, three mounted cowboys (two with lassoos), a cowboy with lasso, a cowboy with rifle, four sitting cowboys, one additional horse, one steer and one bench, in very good condition, in original box with applied paper label andinstruction sheet to inside of lid, tied into original insert, some age wear to box.

£380-480   WW

A Britains set 178 Austro Hungarian Foot Guards, comprising eight figures, in overall good condition.

£400-600   SAS

A Britains set 225 The Kings African Rifles, with matt black face paint, in fair condition.

£15-25   SAS

A Britains Spanish Cavalry Review Order, comprising four mounted soldiers, in fair condition, two swords missing.

£150-250   SAS

A Johillco Union Confederates Set no.359, in good condition, figures lack two swords and one head, incomplete, in fair condition box with end-label.

£80-120   SAS

WANTED. Lifelong collector and international expert pays excellent prices for old military toys of all types. Especially wanted are hollow-cast lead soldiers by *"William Britain"*, solids by *"Heyde"*, *"Mignot"*, *"Lucotte"* and composition soldiers and tinplate vehicles by *"Elastolin"* and *"Lineol"*. Plastic soldiers of all make are required, in particular by *"Britains"* and *"Timpo"*. Wooden Forts and entrenchments of all types purchased. I am also interested in civilian models by the aforementioned makers. A premium is paid for items in good condition especially in original boxes. Complete collections or singles bought. Distance no object.

Contact G. M. Haley. Hippins Farm, Blackshawhead, Hebden Bridge, W. Yorks.

Telephone: +44 (0)1422 842484

Email: gedhaley@yahoo.co.uk

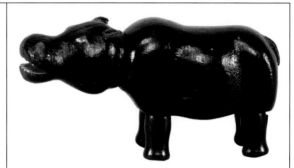

A Schoenhut reduced size jointed wood buffalo, painted in deep brown, with leather horns and rope tail.

Introduced in 1906, around six versions are known. The earliest versions had fabric manes.

6in (15cm) long

£120-180　　　　　　BER

A Schoenhut Bactrian hand-painted, jointed wood camel, two hump moulded and textured head and body, rope tail, painted eyes.

Introduced in 1908, this is the later version with a moulded, rather than carved, body and head.

£120-180　　　　　　BER

A Schoenhut reduced size hippo jointed wood figure, with painted eyes, leather ears, red painted mouth and white teeth, brown painted overall.

The reduced size hippo did not have tusks.

6.5in (16.5cm) long

£150-250　　　　　　BER

A Schoenhut jointed wood elephant, with glass eyes, leather ears, tusks, original trunk, brightly coloured woven original blanket and headdress.

Of the three versions of this popular and long-lived figure, those with howdah blankets are the most sought after.

1903-1930s　　　　　　　*9.75in (25cm) long*

£250-350　　　　　　BER

QUICK REFERENCE – SCHOENHUT FIGURES

German immigrant Albert Schoenhut founded his toy company in Philadelphia, Pennsylvania in 1872. His clown toy, introduced in 1903, became a bestseller in its day and was soon followed by the 'Humpty Dumpty' circus. Over the next few years, the range was expanded to include all manner of animals and characters and it became immensely successful. There are many variations in terms of size, shape and materials used – values vary accordingly. A smaller-sized range was introduced in the 1920s, with a very rare miniature series being sold in 1929 only. Unusually, this kangaroo was produced in one size only. Another notable variation is the type of eye. Glass eyes were used until c1918, when Schoenhut lost its supply of German-produced glass eyes due to WWI. Eyes were then painted, and many animals were also redesigned at this point. During the 1930s, handpainting proved to be too expensive and variable in terms of quality, so transfer printed (decal) eyes with black borders were used instead. Today these unique and often amusing toys are popular with folk art and toy collectors.

A Schoenhut white horse with circus platform jointed wood figure, with glass eyes, bride and platform saddle.

Introduced 1905　　　　　　*10.25in (26cm) long*

£150-250　　　　　　BER

A Schoenhut kangaroo jointed wood figure, with painted eyes, wooden tail, leather ears, open carved mouth.

Introduced 1907　　　　　*7.25in (18.5cm) highest*

£450-550　　　　　　BER

A 1920s Schoenhut reduced size lion jointed wood figure, with carved mane and rope tail.

There are over seven different types of lion. The first was produced for the circus range in 1906 and has a fabric mane. This all-wood, smaller size was sold separately in a box during the 1920s and came with either an open or closed mouth.

5.5in (14cm) long

£100-150   BER

A Schoenhut jointed wood monkey figure, with white face, two-part head, red felt outfit with yellow fringe, rope tail.

Produced from 1906-1930s, this two tone faced monkey is the earliest version. Values are reduced by over a third if the clothing is missing or damaged.

8in (20.5cm) high

£300-400   BER

A Schoenhut reduced size painted eye ostrich wood jointed figure, with closed mouth.

9.5in (24cm) long

£250-350   BER

A Schoenhut reindeer jointed wood figure in greenish-tan with white undercoat and white spots, with glass eyes, closed mouth, with leather ears, antler and tail.

This was part of the Teddy Roosvelt series – few were sold and examples are scarce today.

Introduced 1909   7in (18cm) long

£300-400   BER

A rare Schoenhut wolf wooden jointed figure, with painted eyes, brown hues, long wood tail, open mouth.

Introduced in 1908 as a farm animal as well as a circus animal, early versions of this scarce figure have fabric tails and felt tongues.

8.5in (21.5cm) long

£400-500   BER

A Schoenhut hand-painted, wooden jointed African Chief (Dude) figure, with two part face, leather ears, purple jacket, checked trousers, yellow waistcoat and tall white top hat.

The leather ears indicate that this figure was made after the Teddy Roosvelt safari sets had been discontinued. When a number of African Chief heads were discovered, leather ears were added to turn them into a different 'African Dude' character. The Arab Chief is the rarest character from the set.

c1915

£600-800   BER

QUICK REFERENCE – THE MAN FROM U.N.C.L.E.

The Man From U.N.C.L.E. was a popular American spy series comprising 105 episodes in four series originally broadcast on NBC from September 1964 to January 1968. Ian Fleming contributed to the series, which originally featured a girl teamed with Napoleon Solo: Russian agent Illya Kuryakin replaced her after a popular walk-on role in the pilot. The United Network Command for Law and Enforcement agents battled agents from Technological Hierarchy for the Removal of Undesirables and the Subjugation of Humanity (T.H.R.U.S.H.) and captured the minds of a generation. Nostalgia drives most collectors, who were young at the time the series was aired. Memorabilia is harder to find than than for most other cult TV series, particularly in good and complete condition like this action doll.

An A.C. Gilbert The Man From U.N.C.L.E. 'Napoleon Solo' doll, no.16120, with raising arm, pistol with clip, agent card, folding badge and instructions, in very good condition, in very good condition original box.
c1965   12.5in (31.5cm) high

£200-300   SAS

An A.C. Gilbert The Man from U.N.C.L.E. 'Illya Kuryakin' doll, no.16125, with raising arm, pistol with clip, agent card, folding badge and instructions, in excellent condition, in very good condition box.
c1965   12.5in (31.5cm) high

£180-220   SAS

A rare 'Made in Hong Kong' The Man From U.N.C.L.E. HC1/1718 'Illya Kuryakin' doll, in very good condition, in fair condition original box.

£280-320   SAS

An A.C. Gilbert The Man from U.N.C.L.E. 'Spy Magic Secret Agent Tricks' set, no.15330, comprising Mystery Gun, Magic Money Converter, Jewel Trick, X-Ray Scope, Lie Detector, Spy Tag, Double Agent Card Trick and Vanishing Key, in very good condition, in good condition box.

c1965

£150-250   SAS

A The Man From Uncle 'The Getaway' jigsaw puzzle, complete with box in fair condition.
c1967

£12-18   SAS

The Girl from U.N.C.L.E. was a spin-off TV series that aired on NBC for one season from September 1966 to April 1967. Although the 'girl' was first played by Mary Ann Mobley in 'The Moonglow Affair' episode of The Man from U.N.C.L.E. in February 1966, Stefanie Powers played 'April Dancer' in the spin-off series. Merchandise is unsurprisingly scarce, particularly in good condition, although it tends to be less popular than that produced for the main series.

£300-500   SAS

A Lone Star 'The Girl From U.N.C.L.E. Spy Kit', no.1337, complete and in original box in excellent condition.

A 1960s base metal ring, with 'winking' image of Illya Kuryakin and Napoleon Solo.
0.75in (2cm) high

£9-12   GCHI

A Denys Fisher 'Muhammad Ali' action figure, with punching action, complete, mint and boxed.

The yellow and white attachment fits around his waist and gives him the punch action. The clips that hold it on his body were frequently broken – if this piece is broken or missing, the value plummets to under 50% of a complete example.

1976   Box 12in (30.5cm) high

£120-180   MTB

A very rare Pedigree "Candy" soft vinyl doll, with original clothes.

A Marx black battery-operated black plastic Dalek, with flashing light, in excellent condition, in good condition original box.

This first toy Dalek, with its 'bump 'n go' movement is complete and in excellent condition. Look out for the examples made in the UK as they are more desirable than the majority of toys that were made in Hong Kong. The Daleks were created by famed Dr Who writer Terry Nation, designed by BBC designer Raymond Cusick, and first shown on screen in December 1963 in the second Dr Who serial.

c1964

£100-150   SAS

This example lacks a couple of the fingers, but a truly mint condition example could fetch over £100.

c1967   6.5in (16.5cm) high

£60-80   MTB

A PPC Mork & Mindy 'Mork' poseable action figure, with original space suit and silver plastic boots.

c1979   9.5in (24.5cm) high

£15-20   NOR

A CLOSER LOOK AT STAR TREK FIGURE

This second series of Star Trek action figures was released to coincide with the first movie in 1979 and was an attempt to cash in on the success of the Star Wars figures released in 1977.

They were produced by Mego Corp. and distributed in the UK by Pedigree – sales were not as high as expected, perhaps due to the film being slow and disappointing compared to Star Wars.

They are in mint, unopened condition which helps their value – but the discovery of a cache of mint and carded Star Trek figures in a Canadian warehouse in the late 1980s held values down.

The Kirk figure was produced for sale in Germany and bears Mego affialites Lion Rock and Airfix branding.

The Decker character only appeared in the film.

A Thermos 'Knight Rider' metal lunchbox, with K.I.T.T., Michael Knight, Devon Miles and Bonnie Barstow artwork, lacks Thermos flask, but in excellent condition.

c1983   8.5in (21.5cm) wide

£10-15   BH

Three American Mego Corp. Star Trek action figures, comprising Captain Kirk, Spock and Willard Decker, in unopened, carded condition.

c1979   Card 9in (23cm) high

£80-120   W&W

QUICK REFERENCE

- The wristwatch is a 20thC phenomenon, although examples were produced for the German navy in the late 19thC, and in 1904 Brazilian aviator Alberto Santos-Dumont ordered a wristwatch from Cartier. They became popular with the general public after WWI.
- In the last five years, vintage wristwatches have become popular as a smarter look returns to fashion. Men's magazines have promoted this look, and vintage wristwatches are now widely sought after by those wishing to own an unusual yet elegant watch. Rolex and Longines watches from the mid-20thC are sometimes more affordable than modern examples.
- Value depends on the maker, complexity of movement, style, and materials used. High-end, high quality brands such as Patek Philippe and Rolex are sought-after, with iconic models, such as Rolex's Submariner, being the most desirable. The more complex a watch is the more valuable it is likely to be. Chronographs and watches with extra features, such as moon phases, alarms or perpetual calendars are highly desirable.
- The style of a watch can help date it. Small round faces (almost like pocket watches) date from the early 20thC, with rectangular watches taking over in the 1930s. Watch cases became more stylised and innovative from the late 1940s, as well as taking on period jewellery styles. Simple, circular faces and rectangular watches were again popular during the 1950s, though this had changed by the late 1960s and 70s when many watches were made with large sculptural cases in futuristic styles. The simple, classic styles of the 1930s and 1950s are particularly popular today.

An Audemars Piguet 'Royal Oak' gentleman's brushed grey stainless steel and gilt wristwatch, no.056D34567, with a 33 jewel automatic movement adjusted to heat/cold and five positions, and original bracelet, dial and movement signed.

c1990

£2,500-3,000   **DN**

A 1950s Swiss Audemars Piguet gentleman's wristwatch, with 18ct solid gold case with two tone white and yellow gold bezel, ultra-thin 17 jewel movement with four adjustments, and signed on the dial, case and movement.

£1,500-2,000   **ML**

A 1950s-60s Ernest Borel gentleman's 'Cocktail' watch, with display skeleton back, and 17 jewel movement.

The dial on this sought-after watch is made up of moving discs with arrowheads to indicate the time. As the discs revolve, the printed 'starburst' pattern changes, creating an interesting optical effect.

£150-200   **ML**

A 1920s-30s Bulova doctor's watch, with gold-filled rectangular case, three dials, and 12-jewel movement.

This watch, used for timing in medical examinations, is rare with three dials.

£500-800   **ML**

A 1940s LeCoultre gentleman's wristwatch, triple signed on the case, dial and movement, with stainless steel case, two tone military-style 24 hour dial with luminous hands and numbers, and LeCoultre 17-jewel movement.

£250-300   **ML**

WATCHES

A Longines 'Flagship' automatic gentleman's wristwatch, with 18ct gold case, silvered dial, and date aperture.

c1970 · *1.5in (3.5cm) diam*

£300-500 · **GHOU**

An Omega Seamaster De Ville gold-plated gentleman's wristwatch, with matching bracelet, with baton numerals and date.

£150-200 · **SAS**

A CLOSER LOOK AT A WRISTWATCH

Designed in the late 1960s by André Le Marquand as a tribute to man landing on the moon, the watch was inspired by the astronauts' space helmets and visors.

It was released at the Basel Watch fair in 1972 and was followed by the rectangular and more valuable Spaceman 'Audacieuse' a few years later.

It was produced until 1977 in a range of colours, with the brighter ones being more popular. It was also produced under a variety of brands, including Fortis and Jules Jürgensen.

If the strap has been replaced with a different type, the value falls by over a third. Correct replacement straps can be found for around £20-30.

A 1970s Tressa Lux 'Spaceman' automatic wristwatch, designed by André Le Marquand, with shiny stainless steel case, copper and black face, and Corfam strap.

£80-120 · **RSS**

An Omega 'Constellation' Chronometer automatic gold plated and steel gentlemen's wristwatch, the brown dial with baton markers, with a calibrated 751 jewel movement.

1.5in (3.5cm) diam

£200-300 · **GHOU**

A 1930s Rolex Art Deco wristwatch, the square dial with Roman numerals and silver square case, marked 'Rolex' to movement.

£150-200 · **SAS**

An Edwardian Goldsmiths and Silversmiths ladies silver wristwatch, with white enamel face with Roman numerals, and plain silver case with Birmingham hallmarks.

1905

£40-60 · **SAS**

QUICK REFERENCE - SWATCH

The first Swatches were released in 1983, and were plain by comparison to the colourful, design or designer led, models the brand is known for today. With only 51 components, and plastic cases and straps, the watches could be easily mass-produced. By 1984, over one million had been made. A number of designers have produced designs for the company including Keith Haring, Vivienne Westwood and Christian Lacroix, and these are among the most valuable today. Also look out for the famed 'Jellyfish' transparent watches, commemorative Olympic watches, and limited editions. To be of interest to a collector, the watch must be in excellent condition with its original strap. Being in mint condition, with its box and paperwork makes a watch even more desirable. Although Swatch collecting has declined since the glory days of the 1990s, there is still a healthy trade over the internet, with most fetching under £200. The watch below was the first special edition produced. It is a US Special, and commemorates the First Breakdance World Championship held at the Roxy in New York City. Designed by the artists Marlyse Schmid and Bernard Muller, variations of the hands, dial and colour of the case are known and are worth roughly the same.

A Swatch 'Stormy Weather' wristwatch, GV 100, from the Dream Waves series, with multi-coloured strap.

Look for rare variation without the Swatch logo at '12 o'clock', which is worth about twice the normal version.
1989

£30-40   ML

A Swatch 'Needles' wristwatch, GB 408, from the Signal Corps series, with original perforated red strap.
1988

£30-50   ML

A Swatch 'World Record' wristwatch, GB 721, from the Sprint series, with original ribbed yellow and green straps.

1990

£30-40   ML

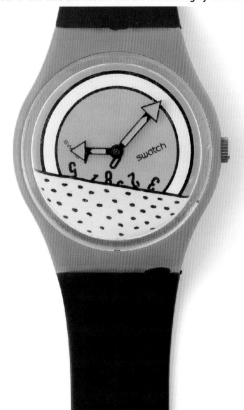

A limited edition Swatch 'Breakdance' wristwatch, GO 0001, from an edition of 9,999.

£500-600   ML

A Swatch 'Cappuccino' wristwatch, GG 121, from the Sunday Brunch series, designed by Jennifer Morla.
1992

£30-40   ML

A Swatch 'Silver Patch' wristwatch, GN 132, from the Nespolo series, with original multicoloured strap.
1993

£30-40   ML

A Hamilton gold-filled pocket watch, the dial and movement signed "Motor Barrel 952", with 19-jewel movement, adjusted to five positions.

2in (5cm) diam

£250-350   **GHOU**

A Tiffany & Co 18ct gold hunter pocket watch, the engraved scroll body with sprung cover, white enamel face with painted centre, Roman numerals and subsidiary seconds dial, the case marked 'Tiffany & Co New York No. 38676', cover marked 'T&Co 0.750'.

£450-650   **SAS**

A CLOSER LOOK AT A POCKET WATCH

The psychedelic design and 'Flower Power' wording are typical of the late 1960s when this watch was designed and made.

Loftus designed a range of watches for The Beatles' 'Apple' boutique store which opened on London's King's Road in 1967 and closed 8 months later due to financial problems. It is possible that this watch was designed for sale there.

The 'Old England' brand was used by Accurist, which made this watch. Its designer, Richard Loftus, was one of three sons of Accurist founders Asher and Rebecca Loftus.

Accurist watches were highly successful, and were worn and endorsed by celebrities including The Beatles, Twiggy and The Princess Royal.

An Old England 'Flower Power' medallion watch, probably designed for the Beatles' Apple store, by Richard Loftus, the square pendant on a gilt metal chain.

Chain 27.5in (70cm) long

£150-200   **DN**

A Waltham 10ct gold pocket watch, with Roman numerals, the engraved case marked '10ct'.

£60-90   **SAS**

A 1920s-30s Continental silver pocket watch, the gold circular face with Arabic numerals, and second subsidiary seconds dial, European control marks to interior.

£20-30   **SAS**

An unmarked silver pocket watch, with white enamel dial, Roman numerals and seconds subsidiary dial, engraved monogram to reverse.

£30-40   **SAS**

KEY TO ILLUSTRATIONS

Every item illustrated in the Miller's Collectables by Judith Miller and Mark Hill has a letter code that identifies the dealer, auction house or private collector that owns or sold it. In this way the source of the item can be identified. The list below is a key to these codes. In the list, auction houses are shown by the letter A, dealers by the letter D, and private collectors by the letter P. Inclusion in this book in no way constitutes or implies a contract or a binding offer on the part of any of our contributors to supply or sell the goods illustrated, or similar items, at the prices stated.

A&G Ⓐ
ANDERSON & GARLAND
Anderson House, Crispin Court, Newbiggin Lane, Westerhope, Newcastle upon Tyne, NE5 1BF
www.andersonandgarland.com

AAC Ⓐ
ALDERFER AUCTION COMPANY
501 Fairground Road, Hatfield, PA 19440 USA
Tel: 001 215 393 3000
www.alderferauction.com

AB Ⓟ
AUCTION BLOCKS
blockschip@aol.com

ACOG Ⓓ
THE AUTOGRAPH COLLECTORS GALLERY
7 Jessops Lane, Gedling, Nottingham, NG4 4BQ.
www.autograph-gallery.co.uk

AEM Ⓓ
ANTIQUES EMPORIUM
29 Division Street, Somerville NJ 08876, USA
Tel: 001 908 218 1234
bkr63@patmedia.net

AG Ⓓ
ANTIQUE GLASS @ FRANK DUX ANTIQUES
33 Belvedere, Lansdowne Road, Bath, BA1 5HR
Tel: 01225 312 367
www.antique-glass.co.uk

AH Ⓐ
ANDREW HARTLEY
Victoria Hall Salerooms, Little Lane, Ilkley, West Yorkshire LS29 8EA
Tel: 01943 816 363
www.andrewhartleyfinearts.co.uk

AHL Ⓓ
ANDREA HALL LEVY
PO Box 1243, Riverdale, NY 10471
Tel: 001 646 441 1726
barangrill@aol.com

AMER Ⓐ
AMERSHAM AUCTION ROOMS
125 Station Rd, Amersham, Buckinghamshire, HP7 0AH
Tel: 08700 460606
www.amershamauctionrooms.co.uk

ANT Ⓓ
THE ANTIQUE GALLERY
8523 Germantown Avenue, Philadelphia PA 19118, USA
Tel: 001 215 248 1700
www.antiquegal.com

ART Ⓓ
ARTIUS GLASS
Tel: 01458 443694
Mob: 07860 822666
www.artiusglass.co.uk

ATK Ⓐ
AUCTION TEAM KÖLN
Otto-Hahn-Str. 10
50997 Köln (Godorf), Germany
Tel: (0049) 2236 38 4340
www.breker.com

ATM Ⓓ
AT THE MOVIES
Tel: 07770 777 411
www.atthemovies.co.uk

BAD Ⓓ
BETH ADAMS
Unit GO23-25 Alfie's Antique Market, 13 Church Street, Marylebone, London NW8 8DT
Mob: 07776 136 003
www.alfiesantiques.com

BB Ⓓ
BARBARA BLAU
South Street Antiques Market 615 South 6th Street, Philadelphia, PA 19147-2128 USA
Tel: (001) 215 592 0256
bbjools@msn.com

BE Ⓐ
BEARNE'S, HAMPTON & LITTLEWOOD
St Edmund's Court, Okehampton St, Exeter, Devon, EX41LX.
Tel: 01392 413 100
info@bhandl.co.uk
www.bearnes.co.uk

BEJ Ⓓ
BÉBÉS ET JOUETS
c/o Lochend Post Office, 165 Restalrig Road, Edinburgh EH7 6HW
Tel: 0131 332 5650
bebesetjouets@tiscali.co.uk

BEL Ⓐ
BELHORN AUCTION SERVICES
PO Box 20211, Columbus, OH 43220 USA
Tel: 001 614 921 9441
www.belhorn.com

BER Ⓐ
BERTOIA AUCTIONS
2141 De Marco Drive Vineland, NJ 08360 USA
Tel: 001 856 692 1881
www.bertoiaauctions.com

BEV Ⓓ
BEVERLEY ADAMS
Stand G028-30, Alfie's Antiques Market, 13-25 Church Street, Marylebone, London NW8 8DT
Mob: 07776 136 003
www.alfiesantiques.com

BEX Ⓓ
DANIEL BEXFIELD ANTIQUES
26 Burlington Arcade, Mayfair, London. W1J 0PU
Tel: 020 7491 1720
www.bexfield.co.uk

BGL Ⓟ
BLOCK GLASS LTD
blockglss@aol.com
www.blockglass.com

BH Ⓓ
BLACK HORSE ANTIQUES SHOWCASE
2180 North Reading Road Denver, PA 17517, USA
Tel: 001 717 335 3300
www.blackhorselodge.com/Antiques.asp

BIB Ⓓ
BIBLION
1/7 Davies Mews, London W1K 5AB
Tel: 020 7629 1374
www.biblion.com

BLNY Ⓐ
BLOOMSBURY AUCTIONS
NEW YORK
6 West 48th Street, New York NY 10036-1902, USA
Tel: 001 212 719 1000
www.bloomsburyauctions.com

BLO Ⓐ
BLOOMSBURY AUCTIONS
Bloomsbury House, 24 Maddox St, London W1S 1PP
Tel: 020 7495 9494
www.bloomsburyauctions.com

BPH Ⓓ
BATTERSEA PEN HOME
PO Box 6128, Epping, CM16 4CG
Tel: 01992 578 885
www.penhome.com

C Ⓐ
COTTEES
The Market, East Street, Wareham, Dorset BH20 4NR
Tel: 01929 552 826
www.auctionsatcottees.co.uk

CANS Ⓓ
CANDY SAYS
39 Elm Road, Leigh-on-Sea, Essex, SS9 1SW
Tel: 01277 212134
www.candysays.co.uk

CARS Ⓓ
CLASSIC AUTOMOBILIA & REGALIA SPECIALISTS (C.A.R.S.)
4-4a Chapel Terrace Mews, Kemp Town, Brighton, BN2 1HU.
Tel: 01273 622 722
carsofbrighton@aol.com
www.carsofbrighton.co.uk
www.laliquemascots.co.uk

CHT Ⓐ
CHARTERHOUSE
The Long Street Salerooms, Sherborne, Dorset DT9 3BS
Tel: 01935 812 277
www.charterhouse-auctions.co.uk

COC Ⓓ
COMIC CONNECTIONS
4a Parsons Street, Banbury, Oxfordshire, OX16 5LW
Tel: 01295268989
comicman@freenetname.co.uk

CRIS Ⓓ
CRISTOBAL
26 Church Street, Marylebone, London NW8 8EP
Tel: 020 7724 7230
www.cristobal.co.uk

CW Ⓓ
CHRISTINE WILDMAN
wild123@allstream.net

CWD Ⓓ
COLLECTORS WORLD
118 Wollaton Road, Wollaton, Nottingham, NG8 1HJ.
Tel: 0115 9280347
www.collectorsworld-nottingham.com

DCP Ⓓ
THE DUNLOP COLLECTION
PO Box 6269, Statesville, NC 28687 USA
Tel: 001 871 2626
dunloppaperweights@mac.com

DODA Ⓓ
DODA ANTIQUES
434 Richards Street Vancouver, BC, Canada
Tel: 001 604 602-0559
www.dodaantiques.com

DOR Ⓓ
DOROTHEUM
Palais Dorotheum, Dorotheergasse 17, 1010 Vienna, Austria
Tel: 0043 1 515 600
www.dorotheum.com

DN Ⓐ
DREWEATTS
Donnington Priory Salerooms, Donnington, Newbury, Berkshire RG14 2JE
Tel: 01635 553 553
www.dnfa.com/donnington

DRA Ⓐ
DAVID RAGO AUCTIONS
333 North Main Street, Lambertville, NJ 08530 USA
Tel: 001 609 397 9374
www.ragoarts.com

DSC Ⓟ
DOLL SHOWCASE
squibbit@ukonline.co.uk
www.britishdollshowcase.co.uk

DUK Ⓐ
HY DUKE AND SON
The Dorchester Fine Art Salerooms, Weymouth Avenue, Dorchester, Dorset DT1 1QS
Tel: 01305 265 080
www.dukes-auctions.com

EWA Ⓓ
EAST WEST ANTIQUES
Stand SO54-56
Alfies Antiques Market,
13 Church Street, London,
NW8 8DT
Tel: 020 7723 0564
ewa_thomson@hotmail.com
www.alfiesantiques.com

FLD Ⓐ
FIELDING'S AUCTIONEERS
Mill Race Lane, Stourbridge,
West Midlands DY8 1JN
Tel: 01384 444140
www.fieldingsauctioneers.co.uk

FOF Ⓓ
FOSSACK & FURKLE
P.O. Box 733, Abington,
Cambridgeshire, CB1 6BF
Tel: 01223 894296
fossack@btopenworld.com

FRE Ⓐ
FREEMAN'S
1808 Chestnut Street,
Philadelphia, PA 19103 USA
Tel: 001 215 563 9275
www.freemansauction.com

GAZE Ⓐ
THOS. WM. GAZE & SON
Diss Auction Rooms,
Roydon Rd, Diss,
Norfolk IP22 4LN
Tel: 01379 650 306
www.twgaze.com

GOL Ⓓ
GAZELLES OF LYNDHURST
The Old Cinema, 160 Chiswick High
Road, London, W1 4PR
Tel: 02380 811610
www.gazelles.co.uk

GBA Ⓐ
GRAHAM BUDD AUCTIONS
P.O. Box 47519,
London N14 6XD
Tel: 020 8366 2525
www.grahambuddauctions.co.uk

GC Ⓟ
GRAHAM COOLEY COLLECTION
Mob: 07968 722 269
gc@itm-power.com

GCHI Ⓓ
THE GIRL CAN'T HELP IT!
Grand Central Window,
Ground Floor,
Alfie's Antiques Market,
13-25 Church Street,
London NW8 8DT
Tel: 0207 724 8984
Mob: 07958 515 614
www.thegirlcanthelpit.com

GHOU Ⓐ
GARDINER HOULGATE
Bath Auction Rooms,
9 Leafield Way, Corsham,
Nr Bath SN13 9SW
Tel: 01225 812 912
www.gardinerhoulgate.co.uk

GORL Ⓐ
GORRINGES
15 North Street, Lewes,
East Sussex BN7 2PD
Tel: 01273 472 503
www.gorringes.co.uk

GROB Ⓓ
GEOFFREY ROBINSON
Stand GO77-78 & GO91-92
Alfies Antiques Market,
13-25 Church Street,
London NW8 8DT
Tel: 07955 085 723
www.robinsonantiques.co.uk

GWRA Ⓐ
**GLOUCESTERSHIRE
WORCESTERSHIRE RAILWAY
AUCTIONS**
Tel: 01684 773 487 /
01386 760 109
www.gwra.co.uk

HALL Ⓐ
HALLS FINE ART
Welsh Bridge, Shrewsbury, SY3 8LA
Tel : 01743 284 777
www.hallsgb.com

HER Ⓐ
HERITAGE AUCTION GALLERIES
3500 Maple Avenue, 17th Floor,
Dallas, Texas 75219-3941, USA
Tel: (214) 528-3500
www.ha.com

HSR Ⓓ
HANS VINTAGE FOUNTAIN PENS
www.hanspens.com

HT Ⓐ
HARTLEY'S
Victoria Hall, Little Lane, Ilkley,
LS29 8EA
Tel: 01943 816363
www.andrewhartleyfinearts.co.uk

IVD Ⓓ
IT'S VINTAGE DARLING
Tel: 01778 344949
www.itsvintagedarling.com

JA Ⓐ
JOEL AUSTRALIA
333 Malvern Road, South Yarra,
3141, Victoria, Melbourne, Australia
www.leonardjoel.com.au

JDJ Ⓐ
JAMES D JULIA INC
PO Box 830, Fairfield,
Maine 04937 USA
Tel: 001 207 453 7125
www.juliaauctions.com

JTB Ⓓ
JIM CALL
bottles@3gsmilkbottles.com
www.3gsmilkbottles.com

KA Ⓓ
KINGSTON ANTIQUES CENTRE
29 Old London Road, Kingston-
Upon-Thames, Surrey, KT2 6ND
Tel: 020 8549 2004
johncobbold1@yahoo.co.uk
www.kingstonantiquesmarket.co.uk

KNK Ⓓ
KITSCH-N-KABOODLE
South Street Antiques Market,
615 South 6th Street, Philadelphia,
PA 19147-2128 USA
Tel: 001 215 382 1354
kitschnkaboodle@yahoo.com

KT Ⓐ
KERRY TAYLOR AUCTIONS
Unit C25,
Parkhall Road Trading Estate
40 Martell Road, London SE21 8EN
Tel: 0208 676 4600
www.kerrytaylorauctions.com

L Ⓓ
LUNA
139 Lower Parliament Street,
Nottingham, NG1 1EE
Tel: 0115 924 3267
www.luna-online.co.uk

L&T Ⓐ
LYON AND TURNBULL LTD.
33 Broughton Place,
Edinburgh EH1 3RR
Tel: 0131 557 8844
www.lyonandturnbull.com

LDY Ⓓ
LADY DOUBLE YOU
info@ladydoubleyou.com
www.ladydoubleyou.com

LHT Ⓓ
LEANDA HARWOOD
Tel: 01529 300 737
leanda.harwood@virgin.net
www.leandaharwood.co.uk

LOC Ⓐ
LOCKE & ENGLAND
18 Guy Street, Leamington Spa,
CV32 4RT
Tel: 01926 889100
www.leauction.co.uk

LT Ⓐ
LOUIS TAYLOR
Britannia House, 10 Town Road,
Hanley, Stoke on Trent ST1 2QG
Tel: 01782 214111
www.louistaylorfineart.co.uk

M&C Ⓓ
M&C CARDS
Shop 30, Antique Centre, Severn
Road, Gloucester, GL1 2LE
Tel: 01452 506 361
www.mandccards.co.uk

M20C Ⓓ
MID20THC
Tel: 07760 218 749
info@mid20c.co.uk
www.mid20c.co.uk

MA Ⓓ
MANIC ATTIC
Alfies Antiques Market, Stand
S48/49, 13-25 Church Street,
London NW8 8DT
Tel: 020 7723 6066
ianbroughton@hotmail.com

MAS Ⓐ
MASTRO AUCTIONS
Now trading as
Legendary Auctions, LLC
17542 Chicago Avenue
Lansing, IL 60438 USA
Tel: 001 708 889-9380
www.legendaryauctions.com

MCS Ⓓ
MEMORIES COLLECTORS SHOP
130/132 Brent Street, Hendon,
London, NW4 2DR
Tel: 020 8203 1500
www.memoriespostcards.co.uk

MDM Ⓓ
M&D MOIR
manddmoir@aol.com
www.manddmoir.co.uk

MHC Ⓟ
MARK HILL COLLECTION
books@markhillpublishing.com
www.markhillpublishing.com

MHT Ⓓ
MUM HAD THAT
info@mumhadthat.com
www.mumhadthat.com

ML Ⓓ
MARK LAINO
Mark of Time, 132 South 8th Street,
Philadelphia, PA 19107 USA
Tel: 001 215 922 1551
lecoultre@verizon.net
eBay ID: lecoultre

MSA Ⓓ
MANFRED SCHOTTEN ANTIQUES
109 Burford High Street, Burford,
Oxfordshire OX18 4RH
Tel: 01993 822 302
www.schotten.com

MTB Ⓓ
THE MAGIC TOYBOX
210 Havant Road, Drayton,
Portsmouth, Hampshire PO6 2EH
Tel: 02392 221 307
www.magictoybox.co.uk

MTS Ⓓ
THE MULTICOLOURED TIMESLIP
dave_a_cameron@hotmail.com
eBay ID: dave65330

NPC Ⓓ
MICHELLE GUZY
Tel: 07966 017 914
signeddandesigned@aol.com

NOR Ⓓ
NEET-O-RAMA
6 Division Street, Somerville,
NJ 08876 USA
Tel: 001 908 722 4600
koehnhome@mindspring.com
www.neetstuff.com

ON Ⓐ
ONSLOWS
The Coach House, Manor Road,
Stourpaine, Dorset DT11 8TQ
Tel: 01258 488 838
www.onslows.co.uk

OTA Ⓓ
ON THE AIR LTD
The Vintage Technology Centre,
Hawarden, Deeside, CH5 3DN
Tel: 01244 530 300
www.vintageradio.co.uk

OUT Ⓓ
OUTERNATIONAL
Tel: 0049 221 1793914
info@outernational.info
www.outernational.eu

P Ⓓ
POSTERITATI
239 Centre Street, New York, NY
10013 USA
Tel: 001 212 2226 2207
www.posteritati.com

P&I Ⓓ
PAOLA & IAIA
Unit S057-058, Alfie's Antiques Market, 13-25 Church Street, London NW8 8DT
Tel: 07751 084 135
paola_iaia_london@yahoo.co.uk
www.alfiesantiques.com

PAMW Ⓓ
PAM WEST BRITISH NOTES
PO Box 257, Sutton, Surrey, SM3 9WW.
Tel: 0208 641 3224
pamwestbritnotes@aol.com
www.britishnotes.co.uk

PC Ⓟ
PRIVATE COLLECTION

QU Ⓐ
QUITTENBAUM KUNSTAUKTIONEN
Theresienstrasse 60,
D-80333 Munich, Germany
Tel: 00 49 89 2737021-25
www.quittenbaum.de

RCC Ⓓ
ROYAL COMMEMORATIVE CHINA
Paul Wynton & Joe Spiteri
Tel: 020 8863 0625
Mob: 07930 303 358
royalcommemoratives
@hotmail.com

RET Ⓓ
RETROPOLITAN
Tel: 07772 280 565
enquiries@retropolitan.co.uk
www.retropolitan.co.uk

ROS Ⓐ
ROSEBERY'S
74-76 Knight's Hill, West Norwood, London SE27 0JD
Tel: 020 8761 2522
www.roseberys.co.uk

RSS Ⓐ
ROSSINI SVV
7 Rue Drouot, Paris 75009, France
0033 1 53 34 55 00
www.rossini.fr

RTC Ⓐ
RITCHIES
No longer trading

SAE Ⓓ
ANTIQUES EMPORIUM
29 Division Street, Somerville NJ 08876, USA
Tel: 001 908 218 1234
bkr63@patmedia.net

SAS Ⓐ
SPECIAL AUCTION SERVICES
Kennetholme, Midgham,
Nr. Reading, Berkshire RG7 5UX
Tel: 0118 971 2949
www.specialauctionservices.com

SDR Ⓐ
SOLLO:RAGO MODERN AUCTIONS
333 North Main Street, Lambertville, NJ 08530 USA
Tel: 001 609 397 9374
www.ragoarts.com

SK Ⓐ
SLOANS & KENYON
7034 Wisconsin Avenue,
Chevy Chase, Maryland 20815 USA
Tel: 001 301 634 2330
www.sloansandkenyon.com

SOR Ⓓ
SOLDIERS OF RYE
Mint Arcade, 71 The Mint, Rye, East Sussex, TN31 7EW
Tel: 01797 225952

SOTT Ⓓ
SIGN OF THE TYMES
Mill Antiques Center,
12 Morris Farm Road, Lafayette, NJ 07848 USA
Tel: 001 973 383 6028
jhap@nac.net
www.millantiques.com

SWA Ⓐ
SWANN GALLERIES IMAGE LIBRARY
104 East 25th Street, New York, NY 10010 USA
Tel: 001 212 254 4710
www.swanngalleries.com

SWO Ⓐ
SWORDERS
14 Cambridge Road, Stansted Mountfitchet, Essex CM24 8BZ
Tel: 01279 817 778
www.sworder.co.uk

TAC Ⓓ
TORONTO ANTIQUES CENTER
284 King Street West, 1st Floor, Toronto, Ontario M5V 1J2. Canada
Tel: 001 416 260-9057
askcynthia@cynthiafindlay.com
www.torontoantiquesonking.com

TBW Ⓓ
TEDDY BEARS OF WITNEY
99 High Street, Witney, Oxfordshire, OX28 6HY
Tel: 01993 706616
www.teddybears.co.uk

TCA Ⓐ
TRANSPORT CAR AUCTIONS
14 The Green, Richmond, Surrey TW9 1PX
Tel: 020 8940 2022
www.tc-auctions.com

TCM Ⓓ
TWENTIETH CENTURY MARKS
Whitegates, Rectory Road, Little Burstead, Nr Billericay, Essex, CM12 9TR
Tel: 01474 872 460
www.20thcenturymarks.co.uk

TCT Ⓓ
THE CALICO TEDDY
Tel: 001 410 433 9202
caliceteddy@aol.com
www.calicoteddy.com

TEN Ⓐ
TENNANTS
The Auction Centre, Leyburn, North Yorkshire, DL8 5SG
Tel: 01969 623 780
www.tennants.co.uk

TGM Ⓓ
THE STUDIO GLASS MERCHANT
Tel: 07775 683 961
Tel: 0208 668 2701
www.thestudioglassmerchant.co.uk

THG Ⓓ
HERITAGE
Toronto Antiques on King
284 King Street West, Toronto, Ontario M5V 1J2 Canada
Tel: 001 416 260 9057
www.torontoantiquesonking.com

TOV Ⓓ
RUPERT TOOVEY
Spring Gardens, Washington, West Sussex, RH20 3BS
Tel: 01903 891955
www.rupert-toovey.com

TSIS Ⓓ
THREE SISTERS
South Street Antiques Market,
615 South 6th Street, Philadelphia, PA 19147-2128 USA
Tel: 001 215 592 0256

TWF Ⓓ
TWICE FOUND
608 Markham Street, Mirvish Village, Toronto, Ontario M6G 2L8, Canada
Tel: 001 416 534 3904
www.twicefound.com

UCT Ⓓ
UNDERCURRENTS
28 Cowper Street, London, EC2A 4AS
Tel: 0207 251 1537
www.undercurrents.biz

VC Ⓓ
VICTOR CAPLIN
Stand G075-76, Alfie's Antiques Market, 13-25 Church Street, London NW8 8DT
Mob: 07947571592
victorcaplin@aol.com
www.alfiesantiques.com

VE Ⓓ
VINTAGE EYEWEAR OF NEW YORK CITY INC.
1A The Fantastic Umbrella Factory 4820 Old Post Road, Charlestown Rhode Island, USA
Tel: 001 917 721 6546
vintageyes60@yahoo.com

VEC Ⓐ
VECTIS AUCTIONS LTD
Fleck Way, Thornaby, Stockton on Tees TS17 9JZ
Tel: 01642 750 616
www.vectis.co.uk

VSA Ⓐ
VAN SABBEN AUCTIONS
Appelsteeg 1-B, NL-1621 BD, Hoorn, Netherlands
0031 229 268 203
www.vansabbenauctions.nl

VZ Ⓐ
VON ZEZSCHWITZ KUNST UND DESIGN GMBH & CO KG
Friedrichstrasse 1a,
80801 Munich, Germany
Tel: 00 49 89 38 98 930
www.von-zezschwitz.de

W&L Ⓓ
W&L ANTIQUES
Stand G060, Alfie's Antiques Market, 13-25 Church Street, London NW8 8DT
Tel: 0207 723 6066
Mob: 07788 486 297
teddylove@blueyonder.co.uk

W&W Ⓐ
WALLIS & WALLIS
West Steet Auction Galleries, Lewes, East Sussex BN7 2NJ
Tel: 01273 480 208
www.wallisandwallis.co.uk

WAD Ⓐ
WADDINGTON'S AUCTIONEERS
111 Bathurst Street, Toronto, Ontario, Canada M5V 2R1
Tel: 001 416 504 9100
www.waddingtons.ca

WEB Ⓐ
WEBBS
18 Manukau Road, PO Box 99 251, Newmarket, Auckland 1000, New Zealand
Tel: 09 524 6804
www.webbs.co.nz

WDL Ⓐ
KUNST-AUKTIONSHAUS MARTIN WENDL
August-Bebel-Straße 4, 07407 Rudolstadt, Germany
Tel: 0049 3672 424 350
www.auktionshaus-wendl.de

WKA Ⓐ
WIENER KUNST AUKTIONEN - PALAIS KINSKY
Freyung 4, 1010 Vienna, Austria
Tel: 00 43 15 32 42 00
www.palais-kinsky.com

WORA Ⓓ
WORCESTER ANTIQUES CENTRE
Reindeer Court, Mealcheapen Street, Worcester, WR1 4DF
Tel: 01905 610 680
worcantiques@aol.com

WW Ⓐ
WOOLLEY & WALLIS
51-61 Castle Street, Salisbury, Wiltshire SP1 3SU
Tel: 01722 424 500
www.woolleyandwallis.co.uk

ZI Ⓓ
ZEITGEIST INTERIORS
Tel: 07522 680 827
info@zeitgeist-i.com
www.zeitgeist-i.com

If you wish to have any item valued, it is advisable to contact the dealer or specialist in advance to check that they will carry out this service and whether there is a charge. While most dealers will be happy to help you with an enquiry, do remember that they are busy people with businesses to run. Telephone valuations are not possible. Please mention the Miller's Collectables by Judith Miller and Mark Hill when making an enquiry.

ADVERTISING

Dan Tinman
Lipka Arcade (Portobello Road),
Unit 13-14 Lower Ground,
282 Westbourne Grove,
London W11
Tel: 01761 462 477 or
07768 166 808
dan@dantinman.com
www.dantinman.com

Huxtins
Saturdays at: Portobello Road,
Basement Stall 11/12,
288 Westbourne Grove,
London W11
Tel: 07710 132 200
david@huxtins.com
www.huxtins.com

Junktion
The Old Railway Station,
New Bolingbroke,
Boston, Lincolnshire
Tel: 01205 480068 or
07836 345 491
junktionantiques@hotmail.com

The Tin Shop
Market Vaults, Scarborough,
North Yorkshire YO11 1EU
Tel: 01723 351 089
www.tinshop.co.uk

ANIMATION ART

Animation Art Gallery
13-14 Great Castle Street,
London W1W 8LS
Tel: 020 7255 1456
Fax: 0207 436 1256
gallery@animaart.com
www.animaart.com

ART DECO

Art Deco Etc
73 Gloucester Road, Brighton,
Sussex, BN1 3LQ
Tel: 01273 329 268
johnclark@artdecoetc.co.uk

AUTOGRAPHS

Lights, Camera Action
6 Western Gardens, Western
Boulevard, Aspley,
Nottingham, HG8 5GP
Tel: 0115 913 1116
Mob: 07970 342 363
www.lca-autographs.co.uk

Special Signings
Tel: 01438 714 728
sales@specialsignings.com
www.specialsignings.com

The Autograph Collectors Gallery
7 Jessops Lane,
Gedling, Nottingham
Tel: 0115 961 2956
graham@autograph-gallery.co.uk
www.autograph-gallery.co.uk

AUTOMOBILIA

Automobilia Planet
P.O. Box 321, Hartlepool TS24 4EL
Tel: 01429 286 146
info@automobiliaplanet.com
www.automobiliaplanet.com

C.A.R.S. of Brighton
The White Lion Garage
Clarendon Place,
Kemp Town, Brighton Sussex
Tel: 01273 622 722
Fax: 01273 622 722
whiteliongarage@fsmail.net
www.carsofbrighton.co.uk

Finesse Fine Art
Tel: 07973 886 937
tony@finesse-fine-art.com
www.finesse-fine-art.com

Junktion
The Old Railway Station,
New Bolingbroke,
Boston, Lincolnshire
Tel: 01205 480068 or
07836 345 491
junktionantiques@hotmail.com

BOOKS

Biblion
1-7 Davies Mews,
London W1K 5AB
Tel: 020 7629 1374
info@biblion.com
www.biblion.co.uk

Zardoz Books
20 Whitecroft, Dilton Marsh,
Westbury, Somerset BA13 4DJ
Tel: 01373 865 371
www.zardozbooks.co.uk

Banknotes, Bonds & Shares
Colin Narbeth & Sons Ltd
20 Cecil Court, Leicester
Square, London WC2N 4HE
Tel: 0207 379 6975
colin.narbeth@btinternet.com
www.colin-narbeth.com

Intercol
43 Templar's Crescent, Finchley,
London N3 3QR
Tel: 020 8349 2207
sales@intercol.co.uk
www.intercol.co.uk

BREWERIANA

Junktion
The Old Railway Station,
New Bolingbroke,
Boston, Lincolnshire
Tel: 01205 480068 or
07836 345 491
junktionantiques@hotmail.com

Gordon Litherland
25 Stapenhill Road,
Burton on Trent, Staffordshire
Tel: 01283 567 213 or
07952 118 987
gordon@jmp2000.com

CERAMICS

A1 Collectables
Bohemia, 46 High Street,
Hampton Wick, Surrey
Tel: 0208 977 7230
denise.woods@blueyonder.co.uk
www.a1-collectables.co.uk

Beth Adams
Stand G023-25, Alfies Antique
Market, 13-25 Church Street,
Marylebone, London NW8 8DT
Mob: 07776 136 003
www.alfiesantiques.com

The Ceramic Studio
2 Potters Hill Farm Cottages,
Langley, Witney, Oxfordshire
Tel: 01993 878 833
info@theceramicstudio.co.uk
wwww.theceramicstudio.co.uk

China Search
4 Princes Drive, Kenilworth,
Warwickshire CV8 2FD
Tel: 01926 512 402
Fax: 01926 859 311
info@chinasearch.uk.com
www.chinasearch.uk.com

Collectables
134B High Street, Honiton,
Devon EX14 1JP
Tel: 01404 470 024
chris@collectableshoniton.co.uk
www.collectableshoniton.co.uk

Cornishware.biz
Vintage-Kitsch, 1 Crown &
Anchor Cottages, Horsley,
Newcastle, Tyne & Wear
Tel: 07979 857 599
info@cornishware.biz
www.cornishware.biz

Adrian Grater
25-26 Admiral Vernon Antiques
Centre, 141-149 Portobello
Road, London W11 2DY
Tel: 0208 579 0357
adriangrater@tiscali.co.uk

Gallery 1930
18 Church St, London NW8 8EP
Tel: 020 7723 1555
Fax: 020 7735 8309
gallery1930@aol.com
www.susiecooperceramics.com

Gillian Neale Antiques
P.O. Box 247,
Aylesbury HP20 1JZ
Tel: 01296 423754
Fax: 01296-334601
gillianneale@aol.com
www.gilliannealeantiques.co.uk

Tony Horsley
P.O. Box 3127,
Brighton, East Sussex
Tel: 01273 550 770
enquiries@tonyhorsley.co.uk
www.tonyhorsley.co.uk

KCS Ceramics
Tel: 0208 384 8981
www.kcsceramics.co.uk

Louis O'Brien
Tel: 01276 32907

Past Caring
76 Essex Road, Islington,
N1 8LT

Nick Ainge
Tel: 01832 731 063
Mob: 07745 902 343
nick@ainge1930.fastnet.co.uk
decoseek.decoware.co.uk

ReMemories Antiques
74 High Street, Tenterden, Kent
Tel: 01580 763 416

Retroselect
info@retroselect.com
www.retroselect.com

Rick Hubbard Art Deco
Tel: 01794 513133
www.rickhubbard-artdeco.co.uk

Geoffrey Robinson
Stand GO77-78 & GO91-92,
Alfies Antiques Market,
13-25 Church Street,
London, NW8 8DT
Tel: 020 7723 0449
www.robinsonantiques.co.uk

Rogers de Rin
76 Royal Hospital Rd, Paradise
Walk, London SW3 4HN
Tel: 020 7352 9007
Fax: 020 7351 9407
www.rogersderin.co.uk

Sue Norman
Antiquarius, Stand L4, 135
King's Rd, London SW3 4PW
Tel: 020 7352 7217
www.sue-norman.demon.co.uk

Undercurrents
28 Cowper Street,
London, EC2A 4AS
Tel: 0207 251 1537
shop@undercurrents.biz
www.undercurrents.biz

Richard Wallis Antiks
Tel: 0208 529 1749
info@richardwallisantiks.co.uk
www.richardwallisantiks.com

CIGARETTE CARDS

Carlton Antiques
Rear No.12, Worcester Road,
Malvern,
Worcestershire WR14 4QU
Tel: 01684 573 092
www.carlton-antiques.com

COINS & MONEY

British Notes
P.O. Box 257, Sutton,
Surrey SM3 9WW
Tel: 0208 641 3224
pamwestbritnotes@aol.com
www.britishnotes.co.uk

Coincraft
44-45 Great Russell Street,
London WC1B 3LU
Tel: 0207 636 1188
info@coincraft.com
www.coincraft.com

Colin Narbeth
20 Cecil Court, Leicester
Square, London WC2N 4HE
Tel: 0207 379 6975
colin.narbeth@btinternet.com
www.colin-narbeth.com

Intercol
43 Templar's Crescent, Finchley,
London N3 3QR
Tel: 020 8349 2207
sales@intercol.co.uk
www.intercol.co.uk

COMICS

Phil's Comics
P.O. Box 3433, Brighton
Sussex BN50 9JA
Tel: 01273 673 462
phil@phil-comics.com
www.phil-comics.com

The Book Palace
Bedwardine Road, Crystal
Palace, London SE19 3AP
Tel: 020 8768 0022
www.bookpalace.com

COMMEMORATIVE WARE

Hope & Glory
131a Kensington Church Street,
London W8 7LP
Tel: 020 7727 8424

Commemorabilia
15 Haroldsleigh Avenue,
Crownhill, Plymouth
Tel: 01752 700 795
ron_smith@commemorabilia.co.uk
www.commemorabilia.co.uk

Recollections
5 Royal Arcade, Boscombe,
Bournemouth, Dorset BH1 4BT
Tel: 01202 304 441

Royal Commemorative China
Paul Wynton & Joe Spiteri
Tel: 020 8863 0625
Mob: 07930 303 358
royalcommemoratives@
hotmail.com

COSTUME & ACCESSORIES

Beyond Retro
110-112 Cheshire Street,
London E2 6EJ
Tel: 020 7613 3636
www.beyondretro.com

Cad van Swankster at The Girl Can't Help It
Alfies Antiques Market, Grand
Centre Window, Ground Floor,
13-25 Church Street,
London NW8 8DT
Tel: 020 7724 8984
Mob: 07958 515 614
sparkle@sparklemoore.com
www.thegirlcanthelpit.com

Decades
20 Lord Street West,
Blackburn BB2 1JX
Tel: 01254 693320

Echoes
650a Halifax Road, Eastwood,
Todmorden
info@echoes-vintage.co.uk
www.echoes-vintage.co.uk
Tel: 01706 817 505

Fantiques
Tel: 020 8840 4761
paula.raven@ntlworld.com

Kerry Taylor
Unit C25, Parkhall Road Trading
Estate, 40 Martell Road,
London, SE21 8EN
Tel: 0208 676 4600
www.kerrytaylorauctions.com

Linda Bee
Grays Antiques Market, 1-7 &
58 Davies Street, London W1Y
2LP
Tel/Fax: 020 7629 7034
info@graysantiques.com
www.graysantiques.com

Old Hat
66 Fulham High Street,
London SW6 3LQ
Tel: 020 7610 6558

RetroBizarre
25 St Mary's Row, Moseley,
Birmingham, B13 8HW
Tel: 0121 442 6389
info@retrobizarre.biz

Rokit
101 Brick Lane, London E1 6SE
(and other London locations)
Tel: 0207 375 3864
www.rokit.co.uk

Sparkle Moore at The Girl Can't Help It
Alfies Antiques Market, Grand
Centre Window, Ground Floor,
13-25 Church Street,
Marylebone, London NW8 8DT
Tel: 020 7724 8984 or
07958 515 614
sparkle@sparklemoore.com
www.thegirlcanthelpit.com

Steptoe's Dog Antique & Vintage Online Store
Tel: 01132 748 494
www.steptoesantiques.co.uk

Vintage Modes
Grays Antiques Market, 1-7
Davies Mews, London W1Y 5AB
Tel: 020 7409 0400
www.vintagemodes.co.uk

Vintage to Vogue
28 Milsom Street, Bath,
Avon BA1 1DG
info@vintagetovoguebath.co.uk
www.vintagetovoguebath.co.uk
Tel: 01225 337 323

Wardrobe
51 Upper North Street,
Brighton, East Sussex
Tel: 01273 202 201

COSTUME JEWELLERY

Cristobal
26 Church St, London NW8 8EP
Tel: 020 7724 7230
sminers@aol.com
www.cristobal.co.uk

Eclectica
Tel/Fax: 020 7226 5625
liz@eclectica.biz
www.eclectica.biz

Richard Gibbon
neljeweluk@aol.com

Ritzy
7 The Mall Antiques Arcade,
359 Upper Street,
London N1 0PD
Tel: 020 7704 0127

William Wain at Antiquarius
Stand J6, Antiquarius, 135
King's Road, London SW3 4PW
Tel: 020 7351 4905
w.wain@btopenworld.com

Crested China
The Crested China Company
Highfield, Windmill Hill,
Driffield, East Riding of
Yorkshire YO25 5YP
Tel: 01377 257042
dt@thecrestedchinacompany
.com
www.thecrestedchinacompany
.com

DOLLS

Bébés & Jouets
c/o Lochend Post Office, 165
Restalrig Road,
Edinburgh EH7 6HW
Tel: 0131 332 5650
bebesjouets@tiscali.co.uk

British Doll Showcase
squibbit@ukonline.co.uk
www.britishdollshowcase.co.uk

Lolli Dollies
8 Athol Terrace, Dover, Kent

Pollyanna
34 High Street, Arundel,
West Sussex
Tel: 01902 885 198 or
07499 903 457

Sandra Fellner
A18-A19 and MB026,
Grays Antique Market
Tel: 020 8946 5613
sandrafellner@blueyonder.co.uk
www.graysantiques.com

Victoriana Dolls
101 Portobello Road,
London W11 2BQ
Tel: 01737 249 525
Fax: 01737 226 254
heather.bond@homecall.co.uk

FIFTIES, SIXTIES & SEVENTIES

Twentieth Century Marks
Whitegates, Rectory Road,
Little Burstead, Near Billericay,
Essex CM12 9TR
Tel: 01474 872 460
info@20thcenturymarks.co.uk
www.20thcenturymarks.co.uk

Design20c
Tel: 01276 512329 /
0794 609 2138
sales@design20c.co.uk

Fragile Design
14-15 The Custard Factory,
Digbeth, Birmingham B9 4AA
Tel: 0121 224 7378
info@fragiledesign.com
www.fragiledesign.com

High Street Retro
39 High Street, Old Town,
Hastings, East Sussex TN34 3ER
Tel: 01424 460 068

InRetrospect
37 Upper St James Street,
Kemptown, Brighton,
East Sussex BN2 1JN
Tel: 01273 609 374

Luna
139 Lower Parliament Street,
Nottingham NG1 1EE
Tel: 0115 924 3267
info@luna-online.co.uk
www.luna-online.co.uk

Manic Attic
Alfie's Antiques Market,
Stand S48-49,
13-25 Church St,
London NW8 8DT
Tel: 020 7723 6105
ianbroughton@hotmail.com
www.alfiesantiques.com

Modern Warehouse
243b Victoria Park Road,
London E9 7HD
Tel: 0208 986 0740 or
07747 758 852
info@themodernwarehouse
.com
www.themodernwarehouse
.com

Multicoloured Timeslip
eBay Store: multicoloured
timeslip
eBay ID: dave65330
Mob: 07971 410 563
dave_a_cameron@hotmail.com

Planet Bazaar
Unit 87, The Stables Market,
Chalk Farm Road,
London NW1 8AH
Tel: 020 7485 6000
info@planetbazaar.co.uk
www.planetbazaar.co.uk

Retrocentre
Tel: 01189 507 224
al@retro-centre.co.uk
www.retro-centre.co.uk

Retropolitan
24 Wells House,
London NW10 6EE
Tel: 07772 280 565
enquiries@retropolitan.co.uk
www.retropolitan.co.uk

FILM & TV

The Prop Store of London
Great House Farm, Chenies,
Rickmansworth, Herts WD3 6EP
Tel: 01494 766 485
steve.lane@propstore.co.uk
www.propstore.co.uk

GLASS

**Andrew Lineham
Fine Glass**
Tel/Fax: 01243 576 241
Mob: 07767 702 722
andrew@antiquecoloured
glass.com
www.antiquecolouredglass.com

**Antique Glass at
Frank Dux Antiques**
33 Belvedere, Lansdown Road,
Bath, Avon BA1 5HR
Tel/Fax: 01225 312 367
m.hopkins@antique-glass.co.uk
www.antique-glass.co.uk

Artius Glass
Tel: 07860 822 666
wheeler.ron@talktalk.net
www.artiusglass.co.uk

Cloud Glass
info@cloudglass.com
www.cloudglass.com

Francesca Martire
Stand F131-137, First Floor, 13-
25 Alfies Antiques Market, 13
Church St, London NW8 0RH
Tel: 020 7724 4802
www.francescamartire.com

Glass etc
18-22 Rope Walk, Rye,
East Sussex TN31 7NA
Tel: 01797 226 600
andy@decanterman.com
www.decanterman.com

Grimes House Antiques
High Street, Moreton in Marsh,
Gloucestershire GL56 0AT
Tel: 01608 651 029
grimes_house@cix.co.uk
www.cranberryglass.co.uk

**Jeanette Hayhurst
Fine Glass**
32A Kensington Church Street,
London W8 4HA
Tel: 020 7938 1539
www.antiqueglass-london.com

Mum Had That
info@mumhadthat.com
www.mumhadthat.com

**Nigel Benson
20th Century Glass**
Mob: 07971 859 848
nigelbenson@20thcentury-
glass.com
www.20thcentury-glass.com

No Pink Carpet
Tel: 01785 249 802
www.nopinkcarpet.com

Past Caring
76 Essex Road, Islington,
N1 8LT

Pip's Trip
13 Pyne Road, Surbiton,
Surrey KT6 7BN
Tel: 08451 650 274
sales@pips-trip.co.uk
www.pips-trip.co.uk

**The Studio Glass
Merchant**
Tel: 07775 683 961
Tel: 0208 668 2701
info@thestudioglassmerchant
.co.uk
www.thestudioglassmerchant
.co.uk

KITCHENALIA

Appleby Antiques
Geoffrey Vans' Arcade,
Stand 18, 105-107 Portobello
Road, London W11
Tel/Fax: 01453 753 126
mike@applebyantiques.net
www.applebyantiques.net

**Below Stairs of
Hungerford**
103 High Street, Hungerford,
Berkshire RG17 0NB
Tel: 01488 682 317
Fax: 01488 684294
hofgartner@belowstairs.co.uk
www.belowstairs.co.uk

Jane Wicks Kitchenalia
Country Ways,
Strand Quay, Rye,
East Sussex TN31 7AY
Tel: 01424 713 635
janes_kitchen@hotmail.com

Mechanical Music
Terry & Daphne France
Tel: 01243 265 946
Fax: 01243 779 582

The Talking Machine
30 Watford Way,
London NW4 3AL
Tel: 020 8202 3473
Mob: 07774 103 139
talkingma-
chine@gramophones.ndirect.co.
uk
www.gramophones.ndirect
.co.uk

MILITARIA & MEDALS

Jim Bullock Militaria
P.O. Box 217, Romsey,
Hampshire SO51 5XL
Tel: 01794 516 455
jim@jimbullockmilitaria.com
www.jimbullockmilitaria.com

The Old Brigade
10a Harborough Road,
Kingsthorpe,
Northampton NN2 7AZ
Tel: 01604 719 389
mail@theoldbrigade.co.uk
www.theoldbrigade.co.uk

West Street Antiques
63 West Street,
Dorking, Surrey RH4 1BS
Tel: 01306 883 487
weststant@aol.com
www.antiquearmsandarmour
.com

MODERN TECHNOLOGY

Junktion
The Old Railway Station,
New Bolingbroke,
Boston, Lincolnshire
Tel: 01205 480068 or
07836 345 491
junktionantiques@hotmail.com

Pepe Tozzo
contact@tozzo.co.uk
www.tozzo.co.uk

PAPERWEIGHTS

Sweetbriar Gallery Ltd
56 Watergate Street
Chester, Cheshire, CH1 2LA
Tel: 01244 329249
sales@sweetbriar.co.uk
www.sweetbriar.co.uk

PENS & WRITING

Battersea Pen Home
PO Box 6128,
Epping CM16 4CG
Tel: 01992 578 885
Fax: 01992 578 485
orders@penhome.co.uk
www.penhome.co.uk

Hans' Vintage Pens
Tel: 01323 765 398 or
07850 771 183
hseiringer@aol.com
www.hanspens.com

Henry The Pen Man
Admiral Vernon Antiques
Market, 141-149 Portobello Rd,
London W11
Tel: 020 8530 3277
Saturdays only
www.henrysimpole.com

PLASTICS & BAKELITE

Paola & Iaia
Unit S057, Alfies Antiques
Market, 13-25 Church Street,
London NW8 8DT
Tel: 07751 084 135
paola_iaia_london@yahoo.com
www.alfiesantiques.com

POSTERS

At The Movies
info@atthemovies.co.uk
www.atthemovies.co.uk

Barclay Samson
By appointment only
Tel: 020 7731 8012
richard@barclaysamson.com
www.barclaysamson.com**DOD
O**
Alfies Antiques Market,
Stand F071,13-25 Church
Street, Marylebone, London
NW8 8DT
Tel: 020 7706 1545
www.dodoposters.com

Limelight Movie Art
135 King's Road, London
Tel: 0207 751 5584
sales@limelightmovieart.com
www.limelightmovieart.com

The Reelposter Gallery
72 Westbourne Grove,
London W2 5SH
Tel: 020 7727 4488
info@reelposter.com
www.reelposter.com

Rennies
47 The Old High Street,
Folkestone, Kent CT20 2RN
Tel: 01303 242427
info@rennart.co.uk
www.rennart.co.uk

POWDER COMPACTS

**Sara Hughes Vintage
Compacts, Antiques &
Collectables**
Mob: 0775 9697 108
sara@sneak.freeserve.co.uk

Mary & Geoff Turvil
Vintage Compacts, Small
Antiques & Collectables
Tel: 01730 260 730
mary.turvil@virgin.net
www.glitzguru.com

Wildewear
Tel: 01395 577 966

RADIOS

On the Air Ltd
The Vintage Technology Centre,
Hawarden, Deeside CH5 3DN
Tel/Fax: 01244 530 300
info@vintageradio.co.uk
www.vintageradio.co.uk

Junktion
The Old Railway Station,
New Bolingbroke,
Boston, Lincolnshire
Tel: 01205 480068 or
07836 345 491
junktionantiques@hotmail.com

Philip Knighton
1c South Street, Wellington,
Somerset TA21 8NS
Tel: 01823 661 618
philip.knighton@btconnect.com

ROCK & POP

Beanos
Middle Street, Croydon,
Surrey CR0 1RE
Tel: 0208 680 1202
shop@beanos.co.uk
www.beanos.co.uk

**Briggs Rock & Pop
Memorabilia**
Loudwater House, London
Road, Loudwater, High
Wycombe, Buckinghamshire
Tel: 01494 436 644
music@usebriggs.com
www.usebriggs.com

Collectors Corner
P.O. Box 8, Congleton, Cheshire,
CW12 4GD
Tel: 01260 270 429
dave.popcorner@ukonline.co.uk

More Than Music
PO Box 2809, Eastbourne,
East Sussex BN21 2EA
Tel: 01323 649 778
morethnmus@aol.com
www.mtmglobal.com

Spinna Disc Records
2b Union Street, Aldershot,
Hampshire GU11 1EG
Tel: 01252 327 261
www.spinnadiscrecords.com

**Sweet Memories Vinyl
Records**
101 Fratton Road, Portsmouth,
Hampshire, PO1 5AH
Tel: 02392 837730
www.vinylrecords.co.uk

Tracks
PO Box 117, Chorley,
Lancashire PR6 0UU
Tel: 01257 269726
sales@tracks.co.uk
www.tracks.co.uk

SCIENTIFIC, TECHNICAL, OPTICAL & PRECISION INSTRUMENTS

**Arthur Middleton
Antiques**
Tel: 020 7281 8445
Mob: 07887 481 102
arthur@antique-globes.com
www.antique-globes.com

Branksome Antiques
370 Poole Rd, Branksome,
Dorset BH12 1AW
Tel: 01202 763 324

Charles Tomlinson
Tel: 01244 318 395
charlestomlinson@tiscali.co.uk

SMOKING MEMORABILIA

Richard Ball
collector@lighter.co.uk
www.lighter.co.uk

Tom Clarke
Admiral Vernon Antiques
Centre, Unit 36, Portobello Rd,
London W11
Tel: 020 8802 8936

SPORTING MEMORABILIA

Manfred Schotten
109 High Street, Burford,
Oxfordshire OX18 4RH
Tel: 01993 822 302
www.schotten.com

**Old Troon Sporting
Antiques**
49 Ayr St, Troon, Ayrshire,
Scotland KA106EB
Tel: 01292 311 822
www.golf-art.co.uk

Rhod McEwan
Glengarden, Ballater,
Aberdeenshire AB35 5UB
Tel: 01339 755 429
teeoff@rhodmcewan.com
www.rhodmcewan.com

Simon Brett
Creswyke House,
Moreton-in-Marsh GL56 0LH
Tel: 01608 650 751

Warboys Antiques
St. Ives, Cambridgeshire
Tel: 01480 463891
Mob: 07831 274774
johnlambden@
sportingantiques.co.uk
www.sportingantiques.co.uk

Graham Budd
P.O. Box 47519,
London N14 6XD
Tel: 020 8366 2525
gb@grahambuddauctions.co.uk
www.grahambuddauctions.co.uk

TELEPHONES

Candlestick & Bakelite
P.O. Box 308, Orpington,
Kent BR5 1TB
Tel: 0208 467 3743
candlestick.bakelite@mac.com
www.candlestickandbakelite
.co.uk

**Retrobrick (Mobile
Phones)**
www.retrobrick.co.uk

Telephone Lines
304 High Street, Cheltenham,
Gloucestershire GL50 3JF
Tel: 01242 583 699
www.telephonelines.net

TOYS & GAMES

Automatomania
414 The Field of Dreams,
Findhorn, Forres, Moray IV36
3TA, Scotland
Tel: 01309 691 692
Mob: 07790 71 90 97
www.automatomania.com

**Collectors Old Toy Shop &
Antiques**
89 Northgate, Halifax,
West Yorkshire HX11XF
Tel: 01422 360 434
collectorsoldtoy@aol.com

Colin Baddiel
B24-B25, Grays Antique
Market, 1-7 Davies Mews,
London W1K 5AB
Tel: 020 7408 1239
toychemcol@hotmail.com

Andrew Clark Models
Unit 113, Baildon Mills,
Northgate, Baildon,
Shipley BD17 6JX
Tel: 01274 594 552
www.andrewclarkmodels.com

Dave's Classic Toys
Antiques Centre Gloucester,
1 Severn Road, The Historic
Docks, Gloucester
Tel: 01452 529 716

Donay Games
Tel: 01444 416 412
info@donaygames.co.uk
www.donaygames.com

Garrick Coleman
75 Portobello Rd,
London W11 2QB
Tel: 020 7937 5524
www.antiquechess.co.uk

Gerard Haley
Hippins Farm, Black Shawhead,
nr Hebden Bridge, Yorkshire
Tel: 01422 842 484
gedhaley@yahoo.co.uk

Hugo Lee-Jones
Tel: 01227 375 375
Mob: 07941 187 2027
electroniccollec-
tables@hotmail.com

Intercol (Playing Cards)
43 Templars Crescent,
Finchley, London N3 3QR
Tel: 020 8349 2207
Mob: 077 68 292 066
www.intercol.co.uk

John & Simon Haley
89 Northgate, North Bridge,
Halifax, Yorkshire
Tel: 01422 360 434
collectorsoldtoys@aol.com
www.collectorsoldtoyshop.com

Karl Flaherty Collectables
Tel: 02476 445 627
kfcollectables@aol.com

The Magic Toybox
210 Havant Road, Drayton,
Portsmouth
Tel: 02392 221 307
www.magictoybox.co.uk

Metropolis Toys
31 Derby Street,
Burton on Trent, Staffordshire
Tel: 01283 740 400
chris@metropolistoys.co.uk
www.metropolistoys.co.uk

Mike Delaney
Tel: 01993 840 064 or
07979 910 760
mail@vintagehornby.co.uk
www.vintagehornby.co.uk

Mimififi
27 Pembridge Road,
Notting Hill Gate,
London W11
Tel: 0207 243 3154
www.mimififi.com

**Sue Pearson Dolls & Teddy
Bears**
147 High Street, Lewes, East
Sussex BN7 1XT
Tel: 01273 472677
www.suepearson.co.uk

Teddy Bears of Witney
99 High Street, Witney,
Oxfordshire OX28 6HY
Tel: 01993 706616
www.teddybears.co.uk

Toydreams
sales@toydreams.co.uk
www.toydreams.co.uk

**The Vintage Toy &
Train Shop**
Sidmouth Antiques & Collectors'
Centre,
All Saints' Road,
Sidmouth EX10 8ES
Tel: 01395 512 588

Vintage Toy Box
contact@vintagetoybox.co.uk
www.vintagetoybox.co.uk

Wheels of Steel (Trains)
Gray's Mews Antiques Market,
B10-B11, 58 Davies Street,
London W1K 5LP
Tel: 020 7629 2813
wheelsofsteel@grays.clara.net
www.graysantiques.com

WATCHES

Kleanthous Antiques
144 Portobello Road,
London W11 2DZ
Tel: 020 7727 3649
antiques@kleanthous.com
www.kleanthous.com

70s Watches
graham@70s-watches.com
Tel: 01603 741222
www.70s-watches.com

The Watch Gallery
1129 Fulham Road,
London SW3 6RT
Tel: 020 7581 3239
www.thewatchgallery.co.uk

INDEX TO ADVERTISERS

Client	Page No	Client	Page No
Battersea Pen Home	295	KCS Ceramics	123
Briggs	303 & 327	Mike Delaney	397
British Notes	24	Miller's Online	395
CARS	17	Mullock's	345
Candlestick and Bakelite	367	On The Air	321
Charles Tomlinson	328	Onslows	303
Clarion	167	Pooks Books	11
Collectors Corner	327	Rhod McEwan	348
Connoissuer Policies	11	Sheffield Railwayana	323
Cristobal	168	Sherman & Waterman	121
Gerald Haley	399	Special Auction Services	165, 377 & 397
Gordon Litherland	347 & 368	Teddy Bears of Witney	365
GWRA	323	Telephone Lines	367
Hemswell Antiques Centre	267	Tracks	325
International Autographs	23	Vennett Smith	301 & 345
Junktion	11 & 21	Wallis & Wallis	379

CENTRES, MARKETS & SHOPS

The following list of general antiques and collectables centres, shops and markets has been organised by region. Any owner who would like to be listed in our next edition, space permitting, or who wishes to update their contact information, should email info@millers.uk.com.

LONDON

Alfie's Antiques Market
13-25 Church St, NW8 8DT
Tel: 020 7723 6066
www.alfiesantiques.com
(Closed Monday)

Antiquarius
131-141 King's Road, SW3 5EB
Tel: 020 7823 3900
www.antiquarius.co.uk

Bermondsey Market
Crossing of Long Lane &
Bermondsey St, London SE1
Tel: 020 7351 5353
Every Friday morning from 5am

Camden Passage Antiques Market
Camden Passage, Angel,
Islington N1
(Wednesday & Saturday
mornings)
www.camdenpassageislington.c
o.uk

Covent Garden Antiques Market
Jubilee Hall, Southampton
Street, Covent Garden WC2
Tel: 0207 240 7405
(Mondays from 6am)

Gray's Antiques Market
58 Davies Streets & 1-7 Davies
Mews, London W1K 5AB
Tel: 0207 629 7034
www.graysantiques.com

Kensington Antiques Centre
58-60 Kensington Church Street
W8 4DB
Tel: 0207 376 0425

Northcote Road Antiques Market
155a Northcote Road, Battersea
SW11 6QB
Tel: 0207 228 6850
www.spectrumsoft.net/nam
.htm

Palmers Green Antiques Centre
472 Green Lanes, Palmers
Green N13 5PA
Tel: 0208 350 0878
Past Caring
76 Essex Road, N1 8LT
(Opens 12pm)

Portobello Rd Market
Portobello Rd, W11
Every Saturday from 6am
www.portobelloroad.co.uk

Spitalfields Antiques Market
Lamb Street,
Commercial Street, E1
Tel: 0207 240 7405
(Thursdays from 7am)

BEDFORDSHIRE

Ampthill Antiques Emporium
6 Bedford Street, Ampthill,
Bedfordshire MK45 2NB
Tel: 01525 402131
www.ampthillantiquesemporiu
m.com

Woburn Abbey Antiques Centre
Woburn Abbey,
Woburn, WK17 9WA
Tel: 01525 292 118
www.woburnantiques.co.uk

BERKSHIRE

Great Grooms at Hungerford
Riverside House, Charnham St,
Hungerford, RG17 0EP
Tel: 01488 682 314
www.greatgrooms.co.uk

Stables Antiques Centre
1a Merchant Place (off Friar
Street), Reading, RG1 1DT
Tel: 01189 590 290

BUCKINGHAMSHIRE

Jackdaw Antiques Centre
25 West Street,
Marlow SL7 2LS
Tel: 01628 898 285

Marlow Antiques Centre
35 Station Road,
Marlow SL7 1NW
Tel: 01628 473 223

CAMBRIDGESHIRE

Cambridge Antiques Centre
206 Mill Road,
Cambridge CB1 3NF
Tel: 01223 247 324

Waterside Antiques Centre
The Wharf, Ely CB7 4AU
Tel: 01353 667 066
www.ely.org.uk/waterside.html

DERBYSHIRE

Alfreton Antique Centre
11 King Street,
Alfreton DE55 7AF
Tel: 01773 520 781
www.alfretonantiquescentre.
com

Bakewell Antiques & Works of Art
King Street, Bakewell DE45 1DZ
Tel: 01629 812 496

Heanor Antiques Centre
1-3 Ilkeston Rd, Heanor,
Derbyshire
Tel: 01773 531 181
www.heanorantiquescentre
.co.uk

Matlock Antiques & Collectables
7 Dale Road, Matlock DE4 3LT
Tel: 01629 760 808

DEVON

Quay Centre
Topsham, Nr Exeter EX3 0JA
Tel: 01392 874 006
www.quayantiques.com

ESSEX

Debden Antiques
Elder Street, Debden, Saffron
Walden CB11 3JY
Tel: 01799 543 007
www.debden-antiques.co.uk

GLOUCESTERSHIRE

Gloucester Antiques Centre
1 Severn Road, The Historic
Docks, Gloucester GL1 2LE
Tel: 01452 529 716
www.gacl.co.uk

Church Street Antiques Centre
3-4 Church Street,
Stow-on-the-Wold, GL54 1BB
Tel: 01451 870 186

Durham House Antiques
Sheep Street,
Stow-on-the-Wold GL54 1AA
Tel: 01451 870 404
www.durhamhousegb.com

Top Banana Antiques Mall
1 New Church Street,
Tetbury GL8 8DS
Tel: 0871 288 1102
www.topbananaantiques.com

HAMPSHIRE

Dolphin Quay Antique Centre
Queen Street,
Emsworth PO10 7BU
Tel: 01243 379 994

Lymington Antiques Centre
76 High Street,
Lymngton SO41 9AL
Tel: 01590 670 934

Squirrel Collectors Centre
9 New Street,
Basingstoke RG21 1DE
Tel: 01256 464 885
antiques@onmail.co.uk

HEREFORDSHIRE

Hereford Antique Centre
128 Widemarsh Street, Hereford
HR4 9HN
Tel: 01432 266242

HERTFORDSHIRE

By George Antique Centre
23 George Street,
St Albans AL3 4ES
Tel: 01727 853 032

Riverside Antiques Centre
The Maltings, Station Road,
Sawbridgeworth CM21 9JX
Tel: 01279 600 985

IRELAND

Archives Antiques Centre
88 Donegall Pass, Belfast,
County Antrim BT7 1BX
Tel: 02890 232383

Powerscourt Centre
59 South William Street
Dublin 2
Tel: (+353) (0)1 6717000

KENT

Burgate Antiques Centre
23A Palace Street,
Canterbury CT1 2DZ
Tel: 01227 456 600

Castle Antiques
1 London Road,
Westerham TN16 1BB
Tel: 01959 562 492

Copperfields Antiques & Crafts Centre
Spital Street, Dartford DA9 2DE
Tel: 01322 281 445

Nightingales
89-91 High Street, West Wickham BR4 0LS
Tel: 0208 777 0335

Otford Antiques and Collectors Centre
26-28 High St,
Otford TN15 9DF
Tel: 01959 522 025
www.otfordantiques.co.uk

Tenterden Antiques Centre
66-66A High Street,
Tenterden TN30 6AU
Tel: 01580 765 655

LANCASHIRE

The Antiques & Decorative Design Centre
56 Garstang Road,
Preston PR1 1NA
Tel: 01772 882 078

GB Antiques Centre
Leisure Park, Wyresdale Road,
Lancaster LA1 3LA
Tel: 01524 844 734
www.gbantiquescentre.com

Heskin Hall Antiques
Heskin Hall, Wood Lane, Heskin,
Chorley PR7 5PA
Tel: 01257 452 044
www.heskinhallantiques.co.uk

Kingsmill Antiques Centre
Queen Street, Harle Syke,
Burnley BB10 2HX
Tel: 01282 431 953
www.kingsmill.demon.co.uk

LINCOLNSHIRE

Hemswell Antiques Centre
Caenby Corner Estate,
Hemswell Cliff,
Gainsborough DN21 5TJ
Tel: 01427 668 389
www.hemswell-antiques.com

St Martins Antiques Centre
23a High Street, St Martins,
Stamford PE9 2LF
Tel: 01780 481 158
www.st-martins-antiques.co.uk

NORFOLK

Tombland Antiques Centre
AugustineSteward House, 14
Tombland, Norwich NR3 1HF
Tel: 01603 761 906

Old Granary Antiques Centre
King Staithe Lane,
King's Lynn PE30 1LZ
Tel: 01553 775509

NORTHAMPTONSHIRE

Brackley Antique Cellar
Drayman's Walk,
Brackley NN13 6BE
Tel: 01280 841 841

Magpies Antiques & Collectables Centre
1 East Grove,
Rushden NN10 0AP
Tel: 01933 411 404

NOTTINGHAMSHIRE

Castlegate Antiques Centre
55 Castlegate,
Newark NG24 1BE
Tel: 01933 411 404

Newark Antiques Centre
Regent House, Lombard Street,
Newark NG24 1XP
Tel: 01636 605 504

Occleshaw Antiques Centre
11 Mansfield Road, Edwinstowe
NG21 9NL
Tel: 01623 825 370

Top Hat Antiques Centre
70-72 Derby Road,
Nottingham NG1 5FD
Tel: 0115 941 9143

OXFORDSHIRE

Deddington Antiques Centre
Laurel House, Market Place,
Bull Ring, Deddington,
Nr Banbury OX15 0TT
Tel: 01869 338 968

Lamb Arcade Antique Centre
High Street,
Wallingford OX10 0BX
Tel: 01491 835 166
www.thelambarcade.co.uk

The Quiet Woman Antiques Centre
Southcombe,
Chipping Norton OX7 5QH
Tel: 01608 646 262

The Swan Antiques Centre
High Street Tetsworth, Nr Thame
OX9 7AB
Tel: 01844 281777
www.theswan.co.uk

SCOTLAND

Now and Then
9 West Crosscauseway,
Edinburgh EH8 9JW
Tel: 0131 668 2927
www.oldtoysandantiques.co.uk

Rait Village Antiques Centre
Rait, Perthshire PH2 7RT

Scottish Antiques & Arts Centre
Abernyte, Perthshire PH14 9SJ
Tel: 01828 686 401
www.scottish-antiques.com

The Peebles Antiques Centre
Innerleithen Road,
Peebles EH45 8BA
Tel: 01721 724666

SHROPSHIRE

Shrewsbury Antiques Market
Frankwell Quay Warehouse,
Shrewsbury SY3 8LG
Tel: 01743 350 916

Stretton Antiques Market
Sandford Avenue, Church
Stretton SY6 6BH
Tel: 01694 723 718

SOMERSET

Assembly Antiques
6 Saville Row, Bath BA1 2QP
Tel: 01225 448 488

Bath Antiques Market
Guinea Lane (off Landsdown
Road), Bath BA1 5NB
Tel: 07787 527 527

Bartlett St Antiques Centre
5-10 Bartlett St, Bath BA1 2QZ
Tel: 01225 466689
Monday to Saturday (excluding
Wednesday)

Old Bank Antiques Centre
14-17 & 20 Walcot Buildings,
London Rd, Bath BA1 6AD.
Tel: 01225 469282 / 338818

STAFFORDSHIRE

Compton Mill Antique Emporium
Compton Mill, Compton, Leek
Tel: 01538 373396

Curborough Hall Antiques
Watery Lane, Lichfield
Tel: 01543 417100

Lion Antiques Centre
8 Market Place, Uttoxeter (opp.
War Memorial)
Tel: 01889 567717

Potteries Antique Centre
271 Waterloo Rd, Cobridge,
Stoke-on-Trent ST6 3HR
Tel: 01782 201 455
www.potteriesantiquecentre.com

Rugeley Antique Centre
161 Main Road, Brereton,
Nr Rugeley WS15 1DX
Tel: 01889 577 166

SUFFOLK

Badgers Den Antique & Collectables Centre
6 Sun Lane, off High Street,
Newmarket
Tel: 01638 666 676

Meltord Antiques Warehouse
Hall Street, Long Melford
Tel: 01787 379 638

Snape Maltings Antiques & Collectors Centre
Saxmundham IP17 1SR
Tel: 01728 688038

SURREY

Kingston Antiques Centre
29 London Road, Kingston-
upon-Thames KT2 6ND
Tel: 0208 549 2004
www.kingstonantiquescentre
.co.uk

Pilgrims Antiques Centre
7 West Street,
Dorking, RH4 1BL
Tel: 01306 875028

Serendipity Antiques Centre
7 Petworth Road,
Haslemere GU27 2JB
Tel: 01428 642 682

SUSSEX (EAST)

The Brighton Lanes Antiques Centre
12 Meeting House Lane,
Brighton BN1 1HB
Tel: 01273 823 121

Brighton Flea Market
31a Upper St. James's Street,
Brighton BN2 1JN
Tel: 01273 624 006
www.brightonlanesantiques.co.uk

Church Hill Antiques Centre
6 Station Street,
Lewes BN7 2DA
Tel: 01273 474 842

The Emporium Antiques Centre Too
24 High Street, Lewes BN7 2LU
Tel: 01273 477 979

Lewes Antiques Centre
20 Cliffe High Street,
Lewes BN7 2AH
Tel: 01273 476 148

Snooper's Paradise
7-8 Kensington Gardens,
Brighton BN1 4AL
Tel: 01273 602558
www.northlaine.co.uk/snoopers
paradise/snoopers.html

SUSSEX (WEST)

Antique & Collectors Market
Old Orchard Building, Old House, Adversane,
Nr Billingshurst RH14 9JJ
Tel: 01403 782 186

Arundel Antiques Centre
6 High Street,
Arundel BN18 9AB
Tel: 01903 884 164
www.arundelantiques.co.uk

WALES

Afonwen Antiques
Afonwen,
nr Caerwys, nr Mold,
Flintshire CH7 5UB
Tel: 01352 720 965

Offa's Dyke Antiques Centre
4 High Street, Knighton,
Powys LD7 1AT
Tel: 01547 528 635

Second Chance Antiques & Collectables Centre
Ala Road, Pwlheli,
Gwynedd LL53 5BL
Tel: 01758 612 210

WARWICKSHIRE

Stratford-upon-Avon Antique Centre
59-60 Ely St,
Stratford-upon-Avon CV37 6LN
Tel: 01789 204180

WEST MIDLANDS

Birmingham Antiques Centre
1407 Pershore Road,
Stirchley,
Birmingham B30 2JR
Tel: 0121 459 4587

WORCESTERSHIRE

Worcester Antiques Centre
Reindeer Court, Mealcheapen Street, Worcester WR1 4DF
Tel: 01905 610 680

YORKSHIRE

The Antiques Centre York
Allenby House, 41 Stonegate,
York YO1 8AW
Tel: 01904 635 888
www.theantiquescentreyork.com

Cavendish Antique & Collectors Centre
44 Stonegate, York YO1 8AS
Tel: 01904 621 666

The Collectors' Centre
35 St Nicholas Cliff,
Scarborough YO11 2ES
Tel: 01723 365 221
www.collectors.demon.co.uk

The Ginnel Antiques Centre
Off Parliament St, Harrogate,
North Yorkshire HG1 2RB
Tel: 01423 508 857
www.theginnel.co.uk

Stonegate Antiques Centre
41 Stonegate, York YO1 8AW
Tel: 01904 613 888
www.antiquescentreyorkeshop.co.uk

DIRECTORY OF AUCTIONEERS

The following list of auctioneers who conduct regular sales by auction is organised by region. Any auctioneer who would like to be listed in the our next edition, space permitting, or to update their contact information, should email info@millers.uk.com.

LONDON

Bloomsbury Auctions
Bloomsbury House,
24 Maddox Street W1 1PP
Tel: 020 7495 9494
www.bloomsburyauctions.com

Bonhams
101 New Bond Street,
W1S 1SR
Tel: 020 7629 6602
www.bonhams.com

Christies (South Kensington)
85 Old Brompton Road,
SW7 3LD
Tel: 020 7581 7611
www.christies.com

Chiswick Auctions
1 Colville Road,
Chiswick W3 8BL
Tel: 0208 992 4442
www.chiswickauctions.co.uk

Criterion Auctioneers
53 Essex Road,
Islington N1 2SF
Tel: 0207 359 5707
41-47 Chatfield Road,
Wandsworth, SW11 3SE
Tel: 0207 228 5563
www.criterionauctions.co.uk

Graham Budd Auctions
P.O. Box 47519, N14 6XD
Tel: 0208 366 2525
www.grahambuddauctions.co.uk

Lots Road Auctions
71 Lots Road,
Chelsea SW10 0RN
Tel: 0207 376 6800
www.lotsroad.com

Rosebery's
74-76 Knights Hill,
West Norwood, SE27 0JD
Tel: 020 8761 2522
www.roseberys.co.uk

Sotheby's
34-35 New Bond Street,
W1A 2AA
Tel: 0207 293 5000
www.sothebys.com

BEDFORDSHIRE

W. & H. Peacock
The Auction Centre,
26 Newnham St,
Bedford MK40 3JR
Tel: 01234 266366
Fax: 01234 269082
www.peacockauction.co.uk

BERKSHIRE

Dreweatts
Donnington Priory, Donnington,
Nr. Newbury RG14 2JE
Tel: 01635 553553
donnington@dnfa.com
www.dnfa.com

Special Auction Services
First Floor, Kennetholme, Bath
Road, Midgham,
Nr Reading RG7 5UX
Tel: 0118 971 2949
www.specialauctionservices.com

BUCKINGHAMSHIRE
Amersham Auction Rooms
125 Station Road,
Amersham HP7 0AH
Tel: 08700 460606
www.amershamauctionrooms
.co.uk

CAMBRIDGESHIRE
Cheffins
Clifton House, 1&2 Clifton
Road, Cambridge CB1 7EA
Tel: 01223 213 343
www.cheffins.co.uk

CHANNEL ISLANDS
Martel Maides Ltd.
The Old Bank,
29 High Street GY1 2JX
Tel: 01481 713463
www.martelmaides.co.uk

CHESHIRE
Bonhams (Chester)
New House, 150 Christleton
Road, Chester CH3 5TD
Tel: 01244 313 936
www.bonhams.com

**Bob Gowland
International
Golf Auctions**
The Stables, Claim Farm, Manley
Rd Frodsham, WA6 6HT
Tel: 01928 740668
bob@internationalgolfauctions.
com

CLEVELAND
**Vectis Auctioneers
(Toys & Dolls)**
Fleck Way Thornaby,
Stockton-on-Tees TS17 9JZ
Tel: 01642 750616
www.vectis.co.uk

CORNWALL
W. H. Lane & Son
Jubilee House, Queen Street,
Penzance TR18 4DF
Tel: 01736 361447
www.whlaneauctioneers
andvaluers.co.uk

David Lay FRICS
The Penzance Auction House,
Alverton, Penzance TR18 4RE
Tel: 01736 361414
www.davidlay.co.uk

CUMBRIA
**Mitchells Fine Art
Auctioneers**
Station Road, Cockermouth
CA13 9PZ
Tel: 01900 827800
www.mitchellsfineart.com

Penrith Farmers' & Kidds
Skirsgill Saleroom, Skirsgill,
Penrith CA11 0DN
Tel: 01768 890781
www.pfandk.co.uk

DERBYSHIRE
Bamfords Ltd
The Old Picture Palace,
133 Dale Road,
Matlock DE4 3LT
Tel: 01629 574460
bamfords-www.bamfords-auc-
tions.co.uk

DEVON
Bearne's
St Edmund's Court,
Okehampton Street,
Exeter EX41LX
Tel: 01392 207000
www.bearnes.co.uk

Bonhams
Dowell St, Honiton,
Devon EX14 1LX
Tel: 01404 41872
www.bonhams.com

DORSET
Charterhouse
The Long Street Salerooms,
Sherborne, Dorset DT9 3BS
Tel: 01935 812277
www.charterhouse-auctions.co.uk

HY Duke & Sons
Weymouth Avenue, Dorchester,
Dorset DT1 1QS
Tel: 01305 265080
www.dukes-auctions.com

Onslows
The Coach House, Manor Road,
Stourpaine DT11 8TQ
Tel: 01258 488 838
www.onslows.co.uk

Semley Auctioneers
Station Rd, Semley,
Nr Shaftesbury SP7 9AN
Tel: 01747 855122
www.semleyauctioneers.com

ESSEX
Sworder & Sons
14 Cambridge Road,
Stansted Mountfitchet
CM24 8DE
Tel: 01279 817778
www.sworder.co.uk

GLOUCESTERSHIRE
Simon Chorley
Prinknash Abbey Park GL4 8EX
Tel: 01452 344499
www.simonchorley.com

Dreweatt's
St. John's Place,
Apsley Road, Clifton,
Bristol BS8 2ST
Tel: 0117 973 7201
www.dnfa.com/bristol

Cotswold Auction Co.
Chapel Walk, Cheltenham,
Gloucestershire GL50 3DS
Tel: 01242 256363
www.cotswoldauction.co.uk

**Mallams Fine Art
Auctioneers & Valuers**
26 Grosvenor Street,
Cheltenham GL52 2SG
Tel: 01242 235712
www.mallams.co.uk

Moore, Allen & Innocent
The Norcote Salerooms,
Burford Road, Norcote,
Nr Cirencester, GL7 5RH
Tel: 01285 646 050
www.mooreallen.co.uk

HAMPSHIRE
Andrew Smith & Son
The Auction Rooms,
Manor Farm, Itchen Stoke,
Nr Winchester SO24 0QT
Tel: 01962 735988
www.andrewsmithandson.com

**Jacobs & Hunt Fine Art
Auctioneers**
Lavant Street,
Petersfield GU32 3EF
Tel: 01730 233 933
www.jacobsandhunt.com

HEREFORDSHIRE
Brightwells
The Fine Art Saleroom,
Easters Court,
Leominster HR6 0DE
Tel: 01568 611122
www.brightwells.com

HERTFORDSHIRE
Tring Market Auctions
Brook Street,
Tring HP23 5EF
Tel: 01442 826 446
www.tringmarketauctions.co.uk

ISLE OF WIGHT
Shanklin Auction Rooms
79 Regent Street,
Shanklin, PO37 7AP
Tel: 01983 863441
www.shanklinauctionrooms
.co.uk

KENT
Dreweatts (Office)
10 Mount Ephraim,
Tunbridge Wells TN4 8AS
Tel: 01892 544500
www.dnfa.com/tunbridgewells

Gorringes (Office)
85 Mount Pleasant Road,
Tunbridge Wells TN2 5TD
Tel: 01892 619 670
www.gorringes.co.uk

Humberts Fine Art
The Estate Office,
Stone Street,
Cranbrook TN17 3HD
Tel: 01580 713828

Lambert & Foster
102 High Street,
Tenterden TN30 6HT
Tel: 01580 762083
www.lambertandfoster.co.uk

LANCASHIRE
Capes Dunn & Co.
38 Charles St,
Manchester M17DB
Tel: 0161 273 1911
Fax: 0161 273 3474
www.capesdunn.com

LEICESTERSHIRE
Gilding's
64 Roman Way, Market
Harborough, LE16 7PQ
Tel: 01858 410414
www.gildings.co.uk

Tennants Co.
The Auction Centre, Leyburn,
North Yorkshire, DL8 5SG
Tel: 01969 623 780
www.tennants.co.uk

LINCOLNSHIRE

Golding Young & Co.
Old Wharf Rd, Grantham,
Lincolnshire NG31 7AA
Tel: 01476 565118
www.goldingyoung.com

MERSEYSIDE

Cato, Crane & Co
6 Stanhope St, Liverpool L8 5RE
Tel: 0151 709 5559
www.cato-crane.co.uk

NORFOLK

T. W. Gaze & Son
Diss Auction Rooms, Roydon
Road, Diss IP22 4LN
Tel: 01379 650306
www.twgaze.com

**Keys Auctioneers &
Valuers**
Aylsham Salerooms, Palmers
Lane,Aylsham, NR11 6JA
Tel: 01263 733195

Knights Sporting Auctions
Cuckoo Cottage, Town Green,
Alby, Norwich NR11 7PR
Tel: 01263 768488
www.knights.co.uk

NOTTINGHAMSHIRE

Mellors & Kirk
Gregory Street,
Nottingham NG7 2NL
Tel: 0115 9790 000
www.mellorsandkirk.com

Neales of Nottingham
192 Mansfield Road,
Nottingham NG1 3HU
Tel: 0115 962 4141
www.dnfa.com/nottingham

**Vennett-Smith
Auctioneers and Valuers**
11 Nottingham Road, Gotham,
Nottingham NG11 0HE
Tel: 0115 9830541
www.vennett-smith.com

OXFORDSHIRE

Mallams
Dunmore Court, Wootton Road,
Abingdon, OX13 6BH
Tel: 01235 462840
www.mallams.co.uk

Mallams
Bocardo House,
24a St. Michaels Street,
Oxford OX1 2EB
Tel: 01865 241358
www.mallams.co.uk

Soames Country Auctions
Pinnocks Farm Estate,
Northmoor, Witney OX8 1AY
Tel: 01865 300626
www.soamesauctioneers.co.uk

SHROPSHIRE

Halls Fine Art
Welsh Bridge,
Shrewsbury SY3 8LA
Tel: 01743 284 777
www.hallsestateagents.co.uk

Walker Barnett & Hill
Cosford Auction Rooms,
Long Lane, Cosford, TF11 8PJ
Tel: 01902 375555
wbhauctions@lineone.net

Mullock Madeley
The Old Shippon,
Wall-under-Heywood,
Nr Church Stretton SY6 7DS
Tel: 01694 771771
www.mullocksauctions.co.uk

SOMERSET

Clevedon Salerooms
The Auction Centre,
Kenn Road, Kenn, Clevedon,
North Somerset BS21 6TT
Tel: 01934 830111
www.clevedon-salerooms.com

Gardiner Houlgate
9 Leafield Way, Corsham,
Bath SN13 9SW
Tel: 01225 812912
www.gardinerhoulgate.co.uk

**Lawrence's Fine Art
Auctioneers Ltd**
South Street,
Crewkerne, TA18 8AB
Tel: 01460 73041
www.lawrences.co.uk

STAFFORDSHIRE

**Potteries Specialist
Auctions**
271 Waterloo Road,
Cobridge,
Stoke-on-Trent, ST6 3HR
Tel: 01782 286622
www.potteriesauctions.com

Richard Winterton
Lichfield Auction Centre
Fradley, Lichfield, WS13 8NF
Tel: 01543 263256

Wintertons
Uttoxeter Auction Centre, Short
Street, Uttoxeter,
Staffordshire ST14 7LH
www.wintertons.co.uk

SUFFOLK

Diamond Mills
117 Hamilton Road,
Felixstowe IP11 7BL
Tel:01394 671 791
www.diamondmills.co.uk

Neal Sons & Fletcher
26 Church St,
Woodbridge IP12 1DP
Tel: 01394 382263
www.nsf.co.uk

SURREY

Barbers
The Mayford Centre,
Smarts Heath Road,
Woking GU22 0PP
Tel: 01483 728939

Clarke Gammon
4 Quarry Street,
Guildford GU1 3TY
Tel: 01483 880900
www.clarkegammon.co.uk

Ewbank Auctioneers
The Burnt Common Auction
Rooms,
London Rd, Send,
Woking GU23 7LN
Tel: 01483 223101
www.ewbankauctions.co.uk

**Dreweatt Neate
(Formerly Hamptons)**
Baverstock House,
93 High Street,
Godalming GU7 1AL
Tel: 01483 423 567
www.dnfa.com/godalming

SUSSEX (EAST)

Burstow & Hewett
Lower Lake, Battle TN33 0AT
Tel: 01424 772 374
www.burstowandhewett.co.uk

**Dreweatt Neate
(Eastbourne)**
46-50 South St,
Eastbourn BN21 4XB,
Tel: 01323 410419
www.dnfa.com

Gorringes
Terminus Road,
Bexhill-on-Sea TN39 3LR
Tel: 01424 212994
www.gorringes.co.uk

Gorringes
15 North Street,
Lewes BN7 2PD
Tel: 01273 472503
www.gorringes.co.uk

Raymond P. Inman
The Auction Galleries,
98A Coleridge Street,
Hove BN3 5AA
Tel: 01273 774777
www.invaluable.com/
raymondinman

Wallis & Wallis
West St Auction Galleries,
Lewes BN7 2NJ
Tel: 01273 480208
www.wallisandwallis.co.uk

TYNE & WEAR

Anderson and Garland
Anderson House, Crispin Court,
Newbiggin Lane, Westerhope,
Newcastle upon Tyne NE5 1BF
Tel: 0191 430 3000
www.andersonandgarland.com

Corbitts
5 Mosley St,
Newcastle-upon-Tyne NE1 1YE
Tel: 0191 232 7268
www.corbitts.com

WARWICKSHIRE

Locke & England
18 Guy Street,
Leamington Spa CV32 4RT
Tel: 01926 889100
www.leauction.co.uk

WEST MIDLANDS

Bonhams
Knowle, The Old House,
Station Road, Knowle,
Solihull B93 0HT
Tel: 01564 776151
www.bonhams.com

Fellows & Sons
Augusta House,
19 Augusta St, Hockley,
Birmingham B18 6JA
Tel: 0121 212 2131
www.fellows.co.uk

WEST SUSSEX

John Bellman
New Pound Wisborough Green,
Billingshurst RH14 0AZ
Tel: 01403 700858
www.bellmans.co.uk

Denhams
The Auction Galleries,
Dorking Road,
Warnham,
Nr Horsham RH12 3RZ
Tel: 01403 255699
www.denhams.com

Rupert Toovey
Spring Gardens,
Washington RH20 3BS,
Tel: 01903 891955
www.rupert-toovey.com

WILTSHIRE
Finan & Co
The Square, Mere,
Wiltshire BA126DJ
Tel: 01747 861411
www.finanandco.co.uk

Henry Aldridge & Sons
The Devizes Auctioneers,
Unit 1,
Bath Rd Business Centre,
Devizes SN10 1XA
Tel: 01380 729199
www.henry-aldridge.co.uk

Woolley & Wallis
51-61 Castle St,
Salisbury SP1 3SU
Tel: 01722 424500
www.woolleyandwallis.co.uk

WORCESTERSHIRE
Andrew Grant
Tel: 01905 357547
www.andrew-grant.co.uk

Gloucestershire Worcestershire Railwayana Auctions
'The Willows',
Badsey Road,
Evesham WR117PA
Tel: 01386 760109
www.gwra.co.uk

Phillip Serrell
The Malvern Saleroom,
Barnards Green Road,
Malvern WR143LW
Tel: 01684 892314
www.serrell.com

EAST YORKSHIRE
Dee, Atkinson & Harrison
The Exchange Saleroom,
Driffield YO25 6LD
Tel: 01377 253151
www.dee-atkinson-harrison.co.uk

NORTH YORKSHIRE
David Duggleby
The Vine St Salerooms,
Scarborough YO11 1XN
Tel: 01723 507111
www.davidduggleby.com

Tennants
The Auction Centre,
Leyburn DL8 5SG
Tel: 01969 623780
www.tennants.co.uk

SOUTH YORKSHIRE
A. E. Dowse & Sons
Cornwall Galleries,
Scotland Street,
Sheffield S3 7DE
Tel: 0114 2725858
www.aedowseandson.com

BBR Auctions
Elsecar Heritage Centre,
5 Ironworks Row,
Wath Rd, Elsecar,
Barnsley S74 8HJ
Tel: 01226 745156
www.onlinebbr.com

Sheffield Railwayana
4 The Glebe, Clapham,
Bedford MK41 6GA
Tel: 01234 325 341
www.sheffieldrailwayana.co.uk

WEST YORKSHIRE
Andrew Hartley Fine Arts
Victoria Hall Salerooms,
Little Lane, Ilkle LS29 8EA
Tel: 01943 816363
www.andrewhartleyfinearts.co.uk

SCOTLAND
Bonhams Edinburgh
22 Queen St,
Edinburgh EH2 1JX
Tel: 0131 225 2266
www.bonhams.com

Loves Auction Rooms
52-54 Canal St, Perth,
Perthshire PH2 8LF
Tel: 01738 633337

Lyon & Turnbull
33 Broughton Place,
Edinburgh EH1 3RR
Tel: 0131 557 8844
www.lyonandturnbull.com

Lyon & Turnbull
182 Bath St,
Glasgow G2 4HG
Tel: 0141 333 1992
Fax: 0141 332 8240
www.lyonandturnbull.com

Thomson, Roddick & Medcalf Ltd.
Coleridge House, Shaddongate,
Carlisle, Cumbria CA2 5TU
Tel: 01228 528 939
www.thomsonroddick.com

WALES
Bonhams Cardiff
7-8 Park Place, Cardiff,
Glamorgan CF10 3DP
Tel: 02920 727 980
www.bonhams.com

Peter Francis
Curiosity Salerooms,
19 King St, Carmarthen,
South Wales
Tel: 01267 233456
www.peterfrancis.co.uk

Welsh Country Auctions
2 Carmarthen Road,
Cross Hands, Llanelli,
Carmarthenshire SA14 6SP
Tel: 01269 844428
www.welshcountryauctions.co.uk

IRELAND
HOK Fine Art
4 Main St, Blackrock,
Co Dublin, Ireland
Tel: 00 353 1 2881000
fineart@hok.ie

Mealy's
The Square, Castlecomer,
County Kilkenny, Ireland
Tel: 00 353 56 41229
/41413
www.mealys.com

MAJOR FAIR & SHOW ORGANISERS

IACF (International Antique & Collectors Fair)
Newark (Nottinghamshire),
Ardingly (Sussex), Detling
(Kent), Swinderley (Nr. Lincoln)
and Shepton Mallet (Somerset)
www.iacf.co.uk

Clarion Events
Antiques for Everyone,
Birmingham
www.antiquesforeveryone.co.uk
Olympia Antiques Fairs, London
www.olympia-antiques.co.uk

Nelson Fairs
Alexandra Palace, London
www.nelsonfairs.com

Arthur Swallow Fairs
Swinderby Airfield, Lincolnshire
www.arthurswallowfairs.co.uk

The following list is organized by the type of collectable. If you would like your club, society or organisation to appear in our next edition, or would like to update details, please contact us at email info@millers.uk.com.

ADVERTISING

Antique Advertising Signs
The Street Jewellery Society, 11 Bowsden Ter, South Gosford, Newcastle-Upon-Tyne NE3 1RX

AUTOGRAPHS

A.C.O.G.B. (Autograph Club of Great Britain)
info@autographcouncil.co.uk
www.acogb.co.uk

AUTOMOBILIA

Brooklands Automobilia & Regalia Collectors' Club,
P.O. Box No 4,
Chapel Terrace Mews,
Kemp Town, Brighton,
East Sussex BN2 1HU
Tel: 01273 622 722
www.barcc.co.uk

BAXTER PRINTS

The New Baxter Society
c/o Reading Museum & Art Gallery, Blagrave Street, Reading, Berkshire RG1 1QH
www.rpsfamily.demon.co.uk

BANK NOTES

International Bank Note Society
43 Templars Crescent,
London N3 3QR
www.theibns.org

BOOKS

The Enid Blyton Society
93 Milford Hill, Salisbury,
Wiltshire SP1 2QL
Tel: 01722 331937
www.enidblytonsociety.co.uk

The Followers of Rupert
www.rupertthebear.org.uk

BOTTLES

Old Bottle Club of Great Britain
2 Strafford Avenue,
Elsecar, Nr Barnsley,
South Yorkshire S74 18AA
Tel: 01226 745 156
www.onlinebbr.com/home/

BREWERIANA

The British Beermats Collectors' Society
69 Dunnington Avenue,
Kidderminster DY10 2YT
www.britishbeermats.org.uk

CERAMICS

Beswick Collectors Club,
PO Box 310, Richmond,
Surrey TW10 7FU
www.collectingdoulton.com

Carlton Ware Collectors' International
The Carlton Factory Shop,
Copeland St, Stoke-upon-Trent,
Staffordshire ST4 1PU
Tel: 01782 410 504
www.lattimore.co.uk/deco/carlton.htm

Clarice Cliff Collectors Club
PO Box 2706, Eccleshall,
Stafford ST21 6WY
www.claricecliff.com

Fieldings Crown Devon Collectors Club
P.O. Box 462, Manvers,
Rotherham S63 7WT
Tel: 01709 874 433
www.fieldingscrowndevclub.com

Friends of Blue Ceramics Society
PO Box 122, Didcot D.O.,
Oxford OX11 0YN
www.fob.org.uk

Goss Collectors' Club
Tel: 01159 300 441
www.gosschina.com

Hornsea Pottery Collectors' & Research Society
128 Devonshire St, Keighley,
West Yorkshire BD21 2QJ
www.easyontheeye.net/hornsea/society.htm

M.I. Hummel Club (Goebel)
Porzellanfabrik, GmbH & Co.
KG, Coburger Str.7, D-96472
Rodental, Germany
Tel: +49 (0) 95 63 72 18 03
www.mihummel.com

Keith Murray Collectors' Club
Fantasque House, Tennis Drive,
The Park, Nottingham NG7 1AE

Lorna Bailey Collectors' Club
The Old Post Office, 12
Wedwood, Burslem,
Stoke-on-Trent ST6 4JH
Tel: 01782 837 341
www.lorna-bailey.co.uk

Mabel Lucie Attwell
Abbey Antiques,
63 Great Whyte, Ramsey,
Huntingdon PE26 1HL
Tel: 01487 814753
www.mabellucieattwellclub.com

Moorcroft Collectors' Club
Sandbach Rd, Burslem,
Stoke-on-Trent, ST6 2DQ
Tel: 01782 820500
www.moorcroft.com

Myott Collectors Club
P.O. Box 110, Sutton SM3 9YQ
www.myottcollectorsclub.com

Pendelfin Family Circle
Cameron Mill,
Howsin St, Burnley,
Lancashire BB10 1PP
Tel: 01282 432 301
www.pendelfin.co.uk

Poole Pottery Collectors' Club
The Quay, Poole,
Dorset BH15 1RF
Tel: 01202 666200
www.poolepottery.collectorsclub.co.uk

Potteries of Rye Collectors' Society
22 Redyear Cottages,
Kennington Rd, Ashford,
Kent TN24 0TF
www.potteries-of-rye-society.co.uk

Royal Doulton International Collectors' Club
Minton House, London Road,
Stoke-on-Trent, ST4 7QD
Tel: 01782 292292
www.royaldoulton.com/collectables

Royal Winton International Collectors' Club
Dancers End, Northall,
Bedfordshire LU6 2EU
Tel: 01525 220 272

The Shelley Group
7 Raglan Close, Frimley,
Surrey GU16 8YL
Tel: 01483 764097
www.shelley.co.uk

Susie Cooper Collectors' Group
Panorama House,
18 Oaklea Mews,
Aycliffe Village,
County Durham DL5 6JP
www.susiecooper.net

The Sylvac Collectors' Circle
174 Portsmouth Rd, Horndean,
Waterlooville, Hampshire
www.sylvacclub.com

Novelty Teapot Collectors' Club
Tel: 01257 450 366
vince@totallyteapots.com

Official International Wade Collectors' Club
Royal Works, Westport Rd,
Stoke-on-Trent, Staffs ST6 4AP
Tel: 01782 255255
www.wade.co.uk

Wade Collectors Club
PO Box 3012
Stoke-on-Trent ST3 9DD
Tel: 0845 246 2525
www.wadecollectorsclub.co.uk

Royal Worcester Collectors' Society
Severn Street,
Worcester, WR1 2NE
Tel: 01905 746 000
www.royal-worcester.co.uk

CIGARETTE CARDS

Cartopulic Society of GB
7 Alderham Avenue, Radlett,
Herts WD7 8HL

COINS, BANKNOTES & PAPER MONEY

British Numismatic Society
c/o The Warburg Institute,
Woburn Square,
London WC1H 0AB
www.fitzmuseum.cam.ac.uk/coins/britnumsoc/

Royal Numismatic Society
c/o The British Museum,
Great Russell Street,
London WC1B 3DG
Tel: 020 7636 1555
www.numismatics.org.uk

International Bank Note Society
www.theibns.or

International Bond and Share Society
www.scripophily.org

COMMEMORATIVE WARE

Commemorative Collectors Society & Commemoratives Museum
Lumless House, 77 Gainsborough Road, Winthorpe, Newark, Nottinghamshire NG24 2NR
http://commemoratives collecting.co.uk

COMICS

Association of Comic Enthusiasts
L'Hopiteau, St Martin du Fouilloux 79420, France
Tel: 00 33 549 702 114

Comic Enthusiasts Society
80 Silverdale, Sydenham, London SE26 4SJ

The Beano & Dandy Collectors' Club,
PO Box 3433, Brighton BN50 9JA
www.phil-comics.com/ collectors_club.html

COSTUME & ACCESSORIES

The British Compact Collectors' Society
P.O. BOX 64, Langford, Biggleswade SG18 9BF
www.compactcollectors.co.uk

The Costume Society
28 Eburne Road, London N7 6AU
www.costumesociety.org.uk

Hat Pin Society of GB
PO Box 089, Maidstone, ME14 9BA
www.hatpinsociety.org.uk

DISNEYANA

Walt Disney Collectors' Society
c/o Enesco, Brunthill Road, Kingstown Industrial Estate, Carlisle CA3 0EN
Tel: 01228 404 062
www.wdccduckman.com

DOLLS

Barbie Collectors' Club of GB
117 Rosemount Avenue, Acton, London W3 9LU
wdl@nipcus.co.uk'

British Doll Collectors Club
'The Anchorage', Wrotham Rd, Culverstone Green, Meopham, Kent DA13 0QW

Doll Club of Great Britain
PO Box 154, Cobham, Surrey KT11 2YE

The Fashion Doll Collectors' Club of GB
PO Box 133, Lowestoft, Suffolk NR32 1WA
Tel: 07940 248127
voden@supanet.com

EPHEMERA

The Ephemera Society
PO Box 112, Northwood, Middlesex HA6 2WT
Tel: 01923 829079
www.ephemera-society.org.uk

FILM & TV

James Bond 007 Fan Club
PO Box 007, Surrey KT15 1DY
Tel: 01483 756007

Fanderson – The Official Gerry Anderson Appreciation Society
www.fanderson.org.uk

GLASS

The Carnival Glass Society
P.O. Box 14, Hayes, Middlesex UB3 5NU
www.carnivalglasssociety.co.uk

The Glass Association
150 Braemar Road, Sutton Coldfield B73 6LZ
www.glassassociation.org.uk

Isle of Wight Studio Glass Collectors' Club
Old Park, St Lawrence, Isle of Wight, PO38 1XR
www.isleofwightstudioglass .co.uk

Jonathan Harris Studio Glass Collectors Club
Woodland House, 24 Peregrine Way, Apley Castle, Telford TF1 6TH
www.jhstudioglass.com

Pressed Glass Collectors' Club
4 Bowshot Close, Castle Bromwich B36 9UH
Tel: 0121 681 4872
www.webspawner.com/users/ pressedglass

KITCHENALIA

National Horse Brass Society
2 Blue Barn Cottage, Blue Barn Lane, Weybridge, Surrey KT13 0NH
Tel: 01932 354 193

The Old Hall Stainless Steel Tableware Collectors Club,
Sandford House, Levedale, Stafford ST18 9AH
www.oldhallclub.co.uk

The British Novelty Salt & Pepper Collectors Club
Coleshill, Clayton Road, Mold, Flintshire CH7 15X

MARBLES

Marble Collectors Unlimited
P.O. Box 206 Northborough, MA 01532-0206 USA
marblesbev@aol.com

MECHANICAL MUSIC

Musical Box Society of Great Britain
www.onbsgb.org.uk

The City of London Phonograph & Gramophone Society
www.clpgs.org.uk

METALWARE

Antique Metalware Society
PO Box 63, Honiton, Devon EX14 1HP
amsmemsec@yahoo.co.uk

MILITARIA

Military – Crown Imperial
37 Wolsey Close, Southall, Middlesex UB2 4NQ

Military Historical Society
National Army Museum, Royal Hospital Rd, London SW3 4HT
Orders & Medals Research Society
123 Turnpike Link, Croydon CR0 5NU

PAPERWEIGHTS

Paperweight Collectors Circle
P.O. Box 941, Comberton, Cambridgeshire CB3 7GQ
Tel: 02476 386 172

Caithness Glass Paperweight Collectors' Society
Caithness Glass Perth PH1 3TZ Scotland
www.caithnessglass.co.uk/ collectors

PENS & WRITING

The Writing Equipment Society
www.wesonline.org.uk

PERFUME BOTTLES

International Perfume Bottle Association
www.ipba-uk.co.uk

PLASTICS

Plastics Historical Society
31a Maylands Drive, Sidcup, Kent DA14 4SB
www.plastiquarian.com

POSTCARDS

Postcard Club of Great Britain
Drene Brennan, 34 Harper House, St.James Crescent, London SW9 7LW
Tel: 0207 771 9404
www.postcards.co.uk

POTLIDS

The Pot Lid Circle
Collins House, 32/38 Station Road, Gerrards Cross, Buckinghamshire SL9 8EL
Tel: 01753 279 001
www.thepotlidcircle.co.uk

QUILTS

The Quilters' Guild of the British Isles
St Anthony's Hall, York YO1 7PW
Tel: 01422 347 669
www.quiltersguild.org.uk

RADIOS

The British Vintage Wireless Society
59 Dunsford Close, Swindon, Wiltshire SN1 4PW
Tel: 01793 541 634
www.bvws.org.uk

RAILWAYANA

Railwayana Collectors Journal
7 Ascot Rd, Moseley, Birmingham B13 9EN

SCIENTIFIC & OPTICAL INSTRUMENTS

Scientific Instrument Society
90 The Fairway,
South Ruislip,
Middlesex HA4 0SQ
www.sis.org.uk

SEWING

International Sewing Machine Collectors' Society
www.ismacs.net

The Thimble Society
147 Portobello Road,
London W11 2DY
www.thimblesociety.com

SMOKING

Lighter Club of Great Britain
richard-ball@email.msn.com
www.lighterclub.co.uk

SPORTING

International Football Hall of Fame
info@ifhof.com,
www.ifhof.com

UK Football Programme Collectors Club,
PO Box 3236,
Norwich NR7 7BE
Tel: 01603 449 237
www.pmfc.co.uk

British Golf Collectors Society
secretary@golfcollectors.co.uk
www.britgolfcollectors.wyenet
.co.uk

Rugby Memorabilia Society
PO Box 57, Hereford HR1 9DR
www.rugby-memorabilia.co.uk

STAMPS

Postal History Society
PO Box 999, Cheltenham,
GL50 9GA
www.postalhistory.org.uk

Royal Mail Collectors' Club
Freepost, NEA1431,
Sunderland SR9 9XN

STANHOPES

The Stanhope Collectors' Club
jean@stanhopes.info
www.stanhopes.info

STAINLESS STEEEL

The Old Hall Club
Sandford House,
Levedale,
Stafford ST18 9AH
Tel: 01785 780 376
www.oldhallclub.co.uk

TEDDY BEARS & SOFT TOYS

British Teddy Bear Association
PO Box 290
Brighton, Sussex
Tel: 01273 697 974

The Dean's Collectors Club
PO Box 217,
Hereford HR1 9AB
Tel: 01981 240 966
www.deansbears.com

Merrythought International Collectors' Club
Ironbridge, Telford,
Shropshire TF8 7NJ
Tel: 01952 433 116

Steiff Club Office
Margaret Steiff GmbH,
Alleen Strasse 2,
D-89537 Giengen/Brenz,
Germany

TOYS

Action Man Club
PO Box 142,
Horsham, RH13 5FJ

The British Model Soldier Society
www.btinternet.com/~model.so
ldiers

Corgi Collectors' Club
PO Box 323, Swansea,
Wales SA1 1BJ
Hornby Collectors Club
www.hornby.co.uk

The Matchbox Toys International Collectors' Association
P.O. Box 120, Deeside,
Flintshire CH5 3HE
www.matchboxclub.com

International Society of Meccanomen
72a Old High Street,
Headington, Oxford OX3 9HW
www.meccanotec.com

The Historical Model Railway Society
Tel: 01773 745 959
www.hmrs.org.uk

The English Playing Card Society
11 Pierrepont St, Bath,
Somerset BA1 1LA
Tel: 01225 465 218
www.wopc.co.uk/epcs/

The Hornby Railway Collectors Association
PO Box 3443, Yeovil,
Somerset, BA21 4XR
www.hrca.net

Train Collectors' Society
P.O. Box 20340,
London NW11 6ZE
Tel: 020 8209 1589
www.traincollectors.org.uk

William Britain Collectors Club
P.O. Box 32,
Wokingham RG40 4XZ
Tel: 01189 737080
ales@wbritaincollectorsclub
.com

The British Smurf Collectors Club
www.kittyscavern.com

WATCHES

British Watch & Clock Collectors' Association
5 Cathedral Lane, Truro,
Cornwall TR1 2QS
Tel: 01872 264010
Fax: 01872 241953
tonybwcca@cs.com

Collectables are particularly suited to online trading. When compared with many antiques, most collectables are easily defined, described and photographed, whilst shipping is relatively easy, due to average sizes and weights. Collectables are also generally more affordable and accessible, and the internet has provided a cost effective way of buying and selling without the overheads of shops and auction rooms. A huge number of collectables are offered for sale and traded daily over the internet, with websites varying from global online marketplaces, such as eBay, to specialist dealers' sites.

• There are a number of things to be aware of when searching for collectables online. Some items being sold may not be described accurately, meaning that general category searches, and even purposefully misspelling a name, can yield results. If something looks, or sounds, too good to be true, it probably is. Using this book should give you a head start in getting to know your market, and also enable you to tell the difference between a real bargain, and something that sounds like one. Good colour photography is absolutely vital – try to find online listings that include as many images as possible, including detail shots, and check them carefully. Be aware that colours can appear differently between websites, and even between computer screens.

• Always ask the vendor questions about the object, particularly regarding condition. If no image is supplied, or you want to see another aspect of the object, ask for more information. A good seller should be happy to cooperate if approached politely and sensibly.

• As well as the 'e-hammer' price, you will very likely have to pay additional transactional fees such as packing, shipping and possibly regional or national taxes. Ask the seller for an estimate of these additional costs before leaving a bid, as this will give you a better idea of the overall amount you will end-up paying.

• In addition to large online auction sites, such as eBay, there are a host of other online resources for buying and selling. The internet can also be an invaluable research tool for collectors, with many sites devoted to providing detailed information on a number of different collectables.

INTERNET RESOURCES

Miller's Antiques & Collectables
www.millersonline.com
Miller's new website is the ultimate one-stop destination for collectors, dealers, or anyone interested in antiques and collectables. Join the Miller's Club to search through a catalogue containing many thousands of authenticated antiques and collectables, each illustrated in full colour and accompanied by a full descriptive caption and price range. Browse through practical articles written by Judith Miller, Mark Hill, and a team of experts to learn tips and tricks of the trade, as well as learning more about important companies, designs, and the designers behind them. Read Judith's daily blog, and order the full range of Millers books direct. You can also search the best fully illustrated A-Z of specialist terms on the internet; a dealer, appraiser and auctioneer database; a guide to silver hallmarks; and learn about care and repair of your antiques and collectables. The site is continually updated, so check back to see what's new.

Live Auctioneers
www.liveauctioneers.com
A free online service which allows users to search catalogues from selected auction houses in Europe, the USA and the United Kingdom. Visitors to the site can bid live via the Internet into salerooms as auctions happen. Registered users can also search through an archive of past catalogues and receive a free e-mail newsletter.

The Saleroom.com
www.the-saleroom.com
A free online service that allows users to search catalogues from selected auction houses in Europe, the USA and the United Kingdom. Visitors to the site can bid live via the internet into salerooms as auctions happen. Registered users can also search through an archive of past catalogues and receive a free e-mail newsletter.

eBay
www.ebay.com
Undoubtedly the largest and most diverse of the online auction sites, allowing users to buy and sell in an online marketplace with over 52 million registered users from across the world.

ArtFact
www.artfact.com
Provides a comprehensive database of worldwide auction listings from over 2,000 art, antiques and collectables auction houses. User can search details of both upcoming and past sales and also find information on a number of collectors' fields. Basic information is available for free, access to more in depth information requires a subscription. Online bidding live into auctions as they happen is also offered.

The Antiques Trade Gazette
www.antiquestradegazette.com
The online edition of the UK trade newspaper, including British auction and fair listings, news and events.

Maine Antique Digest
www.maineantiquedigest.com
Online version of America's trade newspaper including news, articles, fair and auction listings and more.

La Gazette du Drouot
www.drouot.com
The online home of the magazine listing all auctions to be held in France at the Hotel de Drouot in Paris. An online subscription enables you to download the magazine online.

Auction.fr
www.auction.fr
An online database of auctions at French auction houses. A subscription allows users to search past catalogues and prices realised.

Go Antiques/Antiqnet
www.goantiques.com
www.antiqnet.com
An online global aggregator for art, antiques and collectables dealers. Dealers' stock is showcased online, with users able to browse and buy.

A&M Records 327
Aalto, Axel 99
Accurist 407
Acme Pottery Co. 72
Adams, Barbara Linley 92
Adderley 166
Adie & Lovekin 329
advertising 9-12
    bookmarks 159
    calendars 12
    Disneyana 156
    dolls 159
    lead soldiers 399
    posters 312
    railwayana 323
    sports 344, 345, 347, 348
    store display 10
    telephones 367
    tins 9
    toy trains 397
aeronautica 13-14
    ashtrays 13
    models 13
    tinplate toys 388
Aetna 361
Affiches Gaillard 311
Airfix 403
Airlie, John 255
airships, toy 388
Akro Agate Company 279
Aladdin Industries 324
Aladin, Tamara 246, 247
Alaraq, Adamie 270
alarm clocks 161
Alaska Steamship Line 309
Albon, Mary 92
Aldermaston Pottery 110
Alfieri & Lacroix 312
Allen, Harry 63
Amanda Jane dolls 184
Ambleside 156
American Airlines 308
American Colourtype Co. 160
American Gum Inc 14
American Seating Co. 159
American teddy bears 361
American Tobacco Co. 340
Anchor Hocking 263, 264
Andersen, Emanuel 225
Anguhadluq, Luke 272
animals
    1950s figurine 206
    advertising tigers 10
    Beswick 40-42
    Bitossi 76
    Clermont Fine China 147
    Gallé-style cat 155
    Holmegaard decanters 227
    Italian ceramics 76
    Jema 150
    Kastrup-Holmegaard 229
    Lehmann wind-up toy 389
    Lotus Pottery 78-9
    military commemorative 163
    Murano 244
    oriental 285
    Picasso 89, 90
    Royal Copenhagen 100
    Royal Doulton 67
    Royal Worcester 104
    Scandinavian ceramics 106
    Scandinavian glass 248

Schoenhut 400-401
    silver 329, 330
    studio pottery 115
    Szeiler 117
    Wade 124-9
    Watcombe Pottery 153
    Wedgwood 266
    Weller 135
    Wemyss 138
    West German ceramic 140
AP clock/barometer 161
apothecary's scales 328
Appleby, Brigitte 43
Arequipa 146
arm rings 256
Armand Marseille 182
Arnold 384, 385
Arnold, Karl 385
Arrows 278
Art 168
Art Deco
    advertising 9, 10
    automobilia 17, 21
    Bakelite 301
    Carlton Ware 44, 45, 46
    Clarice Cliff 47, 48, 108
    costume 194
    costume jewellery 171
    Cowan 148
    cups and saucers 53, 54, 56, 59
    figures 15
    fonts 205, 352
    Fulper 68
    glass 129
    handbags 202, 203
    Lalique 230
    Myott 152
    necklaces 10
    Poole Pottery 91
    posters 307, 308, 311
    radios 318
    Robert Lallement 150
    Roseville 96
    Royal Worcester 104
    Scandinavian glass 248
    Shelley 118
    smoking memorabilia 331, 332
    Susie Cooper 116
    watches 405
    Wedgwood 130
    Weller 135
    Whitefriars 258
Art Nouveau
    advertising 9
    Czech glass 214, 215
    Doulton Lambeth 61
    Moorcroft 82
    posters 309, 310
    Royal Doulton 64
    Tiffany 237
    Whitefriars 258
Artemide 301
Arts and Crafts 140, 154
    charger 155
    vases 14
    Weller 135
Asbury, Lenore 93, 94
Ashburner, Bill 365
Ashburner, Jean 365
Ashevak, Karoo 270

Ashevak, Kenojuak 269, 272
ashtrays 13, 219, 229, 242, 243, 300, 332
Aston Martin Owner's Club 20
Atchealak, Davie 271
Atkin Brothers 330
Atkins, Elizabeth 62
Atterbury, Paul 85
Attwell, Mabel Lucie 88, 118
Aubock, Carl 300
Audemars Piguet 404
Audubon, John James 109
Augusttssen, Göte 251
Austin, Jesse 315
autographs 22-3, 346
Automobile Association 20
automobilia 16-21
avocado dishes 221
Avranches Syndicat d'Initiative 309
Axline, Ruth 133
Aynsley 53-4, 167
B&M Ceramics 14
Baccarat 286
bachelor sets 116, 350
badges
    aeronautica 14
    automobilia 14, 16, 20-21
    sporting 350
Baekeland, Dr Leo 300
Bailey, Cuthbert 67
Bailey, Ernest 55
Bainbridge, John 306
Bakelite 300-301, 318, 319, 320
    telephones 367
Baker, NJW 131
Baldwyn, Charles 103
ball gowns 193
balls
    cricket 345
    footballs 338, 351
Bally 312
Bally carvers 38, 39
Bang, Jacob 223, 224, 225, 227, 228
Bang, Michael 223-6, 229
banknotes 24-5
Barbie dolls 172, 173, 176, 178, 180
Barlow, Florence 61
Barlow, Hannah 61, 62
Barnes, A.S., & Company 343
barometers 161
Barovier, Ercole 237
Barovier & Toso 237
Barry, W.E., Ltd. 302, 303
Barstow, Bonnie 403
baseball cards 340-42, 344
basketball cards 351
basketballs 351
baskets, ceramic 45, 98, 111, 136, 155
Bass, Saul 304
Bassett-Lowke 394
Batchelder 120
Bates, Brown-Westhead, Moore & Co. 313
Bates, Elliott & Co. factory 317
Bates, Walker & Co. 316
Batkin, Maureen 132
Battaglia, Jody 365
Batterham, Richard 110
Batty, Dora 91

Baudelot 309
Bauhaus 312
Baxter, Geoffrey 234, 258-62
Bay Keramik 139, 140, 143
Baynard Press, The 311
Bazin, Frederick 19
BEA 308
beads 26-7
beadwork 10
beakers 106, 132
Beard, Geoffrey 209
Beatles, The 173, 324, 407
Beauce Pottery 146
Becker, Dorothee 301
Beech Co., H.D. 12
belt buckles 205
Benigni, Leon 307
Bennett, Avril 122, 123
Bennett, Harold 55
Bentley 16-17
Bentley, Thomas 130
Berànek glassworks 217
Bergevin, Albert 309
Bergh, Elis 249
Berry Ltd. 304
Beswick Pottery 40, 79, 149
Beyer Peacock & Co. 322
B.G.I. Co. 348
Bill, Max 300
Bing, Gebrüder 382, 384, 388, 394
birds
    Beswick 40, 41
    canes 38, 39
    car mascots 18
    Carlton Ware 46
    Carnival glass 263
    Clarice Cliff 50, 52
    commemorative vases 14
    Czech glass 218
    Inuit art 269, 271, 272
    Kastrup-Holmegaard 229
    Lotus Pottery 79
    Martin Brothers 80, 81
    Meissen 151
    Minton 152
    Murano 244
    oole Pottery 92
    Royal Doulton 63, 64
    Royal Worcester 101, 102, 103
    Scandinavian glass 249
    Stangl 109
    studio pottery 112
    Weller 135
Birtwell, Celia 194
biscuit barrels
    Carlton Ware 45
    Moorcroft 82
    Wemyss 137
biscuit boxes 137
biscuit tins 9
Bishop, Ernest 55
Bishop, Rachel 82, 84
Bishops & Stonier 14
bisque dolls 182
Bitossi 74, 75, 76, 79, 143, 150
'Bizarre Girls' 47
blouses 194
Blue Mountain Pottery 146
Bocchino, Vincent 310
Boda 249, 250

Bogelund, Gerd 100
Bohemia Glass 218
bonbon dishes 103
Bonbons Martougin 300
Bonfatti, Giovanni 310
bookmarks 159
books 28-33
    character collectables 158
    first editions 28-33
    James Bond 273-4
    pop-up 158
    sports 343, 346, 349-50
Booth 163
boots 200, 338
Borel, Ernest 404
Borské Sklo 217
bottle carriers 12
bottles
    commemorative 9
    Holmegaard 229
    Mdina Glass 232
    Murano 241
    Peter Layton 252, 253
    Surrealist designs 263
    see also ink bottles
Bouchard, Michel 307
Boucher 168
Bough 14
Bovey Tracey pottery, Devon 136
Bowden, James 346
bowls
    aeronautica 14
    Briglin 43
    Caithness Glass 208
    Carlton Ware 46
    Carnival glass 263
    Clarice Cliff 49, 50, 52
    Conrah 281
    Czech glass 214, 217, 218
    Grimwades 86
    Hornsea 71
    Kastrup-Holmegaard 229
    Moorcroft 83
    Murano 237, 239-43
    nursery ware 42, 86, 87
    Peter Layton 253
    Poole Pottery 91, 92
    Roseville 97
    Royal Copenhagen 100
    Royal Doulton 64
    Royal Winton 87
    Scandinavian glass 248, 249
    Seguso Vetri D'Arte 236
    studio glass 254, 256
    studio pottery 110, 111, 114
    Webb 257
    Wedgwood 131, 132
    Wedgwood Glass 266
    Weller 134
    WMF 268
    see also dog bowls; fruit bowls; rose bowls; sugar bowls; tea bowls
Bowman 340
boxes
    Bakelite 300
    Capo di Monte 147
    Hornsea 71
    Meissen 151
    pen 300
    see also biscuit boxes; cigarette boxes; trinket boxes

boxing 352
Boy's Own paper 346
Boz eyewear 189
Brangwyn, Sir Frank William 52, 63
Brauer, Otto 223
Bravo, David 336
Brèves Galleries 18
Briglin Pottery 43, 79
Britain 157, 398-9
British American Glass (B.A.G.) 152
British Automobile Racing Club 21
British Home Stores 207
British Railways 306, 322
Brooklands Automobile Racing Club 21
Brookmar 191
Brough, Jonathan 52, 108
Brown, S.G., Ltd 321
Brown Westhead Moore & Co. Cauldron Ware 54
Bruin 361
Buddy Box 301
Buick 16
Bulova 404
Burgess & Leigh (later Burleigh) 55
Burgess, Dorling & Leigh 55
Burleigh Ware 54, 55, 147
Burnstein Sales Organisation, A.A. 160
Bursley Ware 147
Burt, Stanley 94
Burwood Products Company 207
Bussey 345
busts, studio pottery 115
Butler, Frank 62
Butler & Wilson 168
butter dishes 46, 73
C&S Collectables 158
C. & Co. Ltd 147
Caiger-Smith, Alan 110
Caithness Glass 208-10, 287
cake stands 108, 152
calculators 328
calendars 12
Calvert Lith. Co. 12
cameras 34-7
James Bond 278
candelabra 106
candle snuffers 105
candleholders 97, 207, 220, 266, 282
candlesticks 47, 281
Candy & Co. Ltd 147
candy dishes 97
Candy Ware 147
canes 38-9
Canon 34
Cantagalli 76
Cantagalli, Ulisse 76
Capo di Monte 147
Capper, David 148
Capron, Roger 149, 153
caps
football 338
jockeys' 347
Capstan label 195
car transporters, toy 371

carafes 146, 249
Cardew, Paul 128
Cardew, Seth 111
Carette 394
Carl, Robert 182
Carlton 164
Carlton Ware 44-6, 55, 119, 132
Carmellites Shoes 197
Carn Pottery 111
Carnaby range (Holmegaard) 226
Carnival glass 263
Carpay, Frank 149
Carruthers Gould, Sir Francis 163
cars
automobilia 16-21
badges 14
James Bond 276
toy 369-70, 372-6, 377, 380, 382-3, 389
Carstens 143
Carter, Stabler & Adams pottery 91
Carter, Truda 91
Cartlidge, George 166
Carvosso 339
Cassandre (Adolphe Mouron) 307
Cassis, Cote d'Azur 201
Casson, Michael 111
Castle, Philip 302
Caswell, Shane 280
Catalin 318, 319
Cauldron 147
cauldrons 50
CBS 326
CC41 (Civilian Clothing 1941) 195
Cenedese 237, 238, 244
Cenedese, Gino 244
ceramics
aeronautica 14
Beswick 40-42
Briglin 43
Carlton Ware 44-6
Clarice Cliff 47-52
cups and saucers 53-60
Doulton animals 67
Doulton figures 65-6
Doulton Lambeth 61-2
Fulper 68-9
Hull Pottery 72-3
Italian 74-6
Lladro 77
Lotus Pottery 78-9
Mabel Lucie Attwell 88
Martin Brothers 80-81
military commemoratives 162-3
Moorcroft 82-5
Picasso 89-90
political commemoratives 164
Poole Pottery 85, 91-2
Rookwood 93-4
Roseville 95-8
royal commemoratives 165-7
Royal Copenhagen 99-100
Royal Doulton 63-7
Scandinavian 106
Shelley 53, 59, 88, 107-8
Stangl 109
studio pottery 110-15
Susie Cooper 116

Szeiler 117
teapots 118-19
tiles 120
Troika 121-3
Wade 9, 124-9
Wedgwood 130-32
Weller 133-5
Wemyss 136-8
West German 139-45
other makers 146-55
Chad Valley 183, 362, 364
champagne glasses 211-12
Champenois, F. 310
Champion Agate Company 279
Chance, W.M. 66
Chance Glass 213
Chanel, Coco 190, 202
character collectables 156-60
character jugs 64
chargers
Arts and Crafts 155
Cowan 148
Moorcroft 85
West German 144
Charles, HRH The Prince of Wales 167
Cherry Elsinore 228
Chevrolet 16
children's first editions 32-3
Chiltern Toy Works 360, 363
chintzware 57
Chlum u Trebone glassworks 216
Chopping, Richard 274
Chribskà glassworks 217
Christensen Agate Company 279
cigarette boxes 332
cigarette lighters 331
CIJ 383
Cincinnati Art Pottery 154
Clappison, John 70, 71
Clark, Ossie 194
Clarkson, Shirley 364
Clermont Fine China 147
Clews & Co. Ltd 148
Clichy 286
Cliff, Clarice 47-52, 53, 56, 108, 152
Clifford, S. 330
clips, costume jewellery 171
clocks 161
nursery ware 87
Royal Winton 87
Vitascope Bakelite 301
clockwork toys 382-91
Co-operative Wholesale Society 9, 318
coaches, toy 371
Coalport 53, 55, 164
Coates, Wells 319
coats 190, 191, 193, 194
Coca Cola 12, 308
CODEG 185
coffee cans 55, 57
coffee pots
Old Hall 283
political commemorative 164
Shelley 108
Susie Cooper 116
coffee sets 108, 116
Coibel 278
Coldrum Pottery 111
Cole, E.K., Ltd 318, 319

Cole, G.H. 101
Colledge, Glynn 149, 151
Collins, Enid 204
Collins & Cook 329
Collins London 14
Colombia 326
Combex 159
commemoratives
advertising 9
ashtrays 13
cameras 35
military 162-3
political 153, 164
royal 165-7
silver 330
vases 14
Compagnia Vetreria Muranese 240
Company of Veteran Motorists 20
condoms, Champ 344
Conrad 139
Conrah 281
Consee, Oscar 309
conserve pots 283
Continental 407
Conway Stewart pens 294
Cook, George 110
Cooper, Susie 53, 88, 116, 152
Copeland 55, 162, 166
Copeland & Garrett 165
Copeland Spode 118
Coper, Hans 110
Coral alarm clocks 161
Corde 202
Corgi 369-73
Corsina 201
costume 190-96
costume accessories 205
costume jewellery 168-71
Coty 230
Coupal, Francis 280
Courbet, S.A. 312
Courtaulds 195
Crämer, Eduard 362
cream jugs 350
creamers 228, 267
cricket 345-6, 352
Crisford & Norris 329
Crofts Candy 340
Crosby, Frederick Gordon 17, 19
Crown Devon 132, 149, 167
Crown Ducal 149
Crown Lynn 149
Crown Staffordshire 56
cruet sets 46, 71
crystal sets 321
cult, TV and film toys 402-3
Cundall, Charles 306
Cuneo, Sir Terence 306
cups
replica of FA Challenge Cup Trophy 339
studio pottery 114
cups and saucers 53-60
Aynsley 53-4
Brown Westhead Moore & Co.
Cauldron Ware 54
Burleigh Ware 54, 55
Carltonware 55
Clarice Cliff 52
Coalport 55

Copeland 55
Crown Staffordshire 56
C.T. Maling 58
Davenport 56
Fielding's Crown Devon 56
Foley 56, 57
George Jones & Sons 58
Grafton China/Royal Grafton 57
Grimwades Royal Winton 57
Hammersley 57
Haviland & Co. 58
H.M. Williamson & Sons 60
Midwinter 58
Minton Haddon Hall 58
Moorcroft 82
Noritake 58
nursery ware 87
Paragon 58, 59
R.H. & S.L. Plant 59, 60
Rosenthal 59
Royal Bayreuth 54
Royal Doulton 56
Royal Winton 87
Royal Worcester 60
Sampson Smith Ltd 60
Shelley 59, 108
Susie Cooper 116
W&B 55
Wedgwood 132
Cusick, Raymond 403
Czech glass 214-19
da Ros, Antonia 237, 244
Daguerre, Louis 34
daguerreotype 34
Daisy dolls 174-5
Daisy Manufacturing Co. 12
Dali, Salvador 263
Daly, Matthew 93
Danbarale 199
Dartington Glass 208, 220-21
Davenport 56
Davenport, Anji 84
Davidson 263
Davies, H. 103
Davies, Iestyn 254, 265, 266
De La Rue 'Onoto' pens 295
De Majo factory 238
de Rycker, O. 312
de Trey, Marianne 110
Dean's Rag Book Co. 362, 363
Debón, Salvador 77
decanters
Caithness Glass 209, 210
Dartington glass 221
Holmegaard 227, 228, 229
Lalique 231
Scandinavian glass 247, 248, 249
W. Goebel 158
Dechaux, M. 307
Dee, Henry William 330, 332
Deichmann, Eric 111
Deichmann, Kjeld 111
Deichmann Pottery 111
DeMario, Robert 168
Denby Pottery 149
Dennis, Richard 85
Dennis Chinaworks 85
Denzler, M.G. 94
desk tidies 301
D'Este, Nino 238
Devlin, Stuart 282

428   INDEX

INDEX

Dexel, Walter 268
Diana, Princess 167
Diem 363
Diers, Ed 94
Dinky 369, 374-9
dinner menus 346, 349
dinner services 116, 132
Dior, Christian 190, 193
dishes
  Anchor Hocking 263
  Cantagalli 76
  Carlton Ware 45
  Carnival glass 263
  Grimwades 86
  Honiton Pottery 150
  Hornsea 71
  Lotus Pottery 79
  Murano 243
  nursery ware 86, 88
  Pentagram 300
  Poole Pottery 92
  Roseville 96
  Royal Alma 12
  Royal Copenhagen 99
  Shelley 88
  Vallauris 153
  Wade 129
  Wedgwood 131
  West German 144
  WMF 268
  Zsolnay Pecs 155
  see also avocado dishes;
    bonbon dishes;
    butter dishes; candy dishes;
    muffin dishes
Disneyana
  ceramics 40, 124, 125-6
  character collectables 156-7
dispensers 12
Ditchfield, John 254
dog bowls 136
Dolcis Shoes 194
dolls
  advertising 159
  Amanda Jane 184
  Barbie 172, 173, 176, 178,
    180
  bisque 182
  composition 182, 183
  cult, TV and film toys 402-3
  Daisy 174-5
  fabric 183
  Linda 184
  'Marcher' 184
  miniature 185
  Miss Rosebud 184
  Pippa 176-7
  plastic 172-81, 184
  Roberta Walker 184
  rock and pop 327
  Rock Flowers 180, 181
  Shallowpool 186
  Sindy 172-3, 176, 181
  Tammy 172, 180
  'Topsy' 183
  Tressy 179
  Tudor Rose 184
  Vogue 184
DollyRockers 194
Donà, Alberto 238
Donaldson, Robert 147
Donnelly, Julia 254

doorstops 159
Dorival, George 307
Dorling family 55
Doughty, Dorothy 101
Doulton, John 61
Doulton and Company Ltd 61
Doulton Lambeth 61-2, 80, 166
drawings, Inuit art 272
Dresser, Dr Christopher 153
dresses 190, 191, 192, 193, 194
Druhle, Carin von 254
Drumlanrig Melbourne 149
Dümler & Breiden 141
Dunhill 331
Dunne Cooke, H.J. 251
Dux 301
d'Ylen, Jean 310, 312
earrings 168-71
Eastern European posters 305
Easton, Joan 365
Eatons department stores 357
Edenfalk, Bengt 251
Edinburgh & Leith 211
Editions & Publicité, Paris 311
Edward VII, King 61
Edward VIII, King (later Duke of
    Windsor) 166
Edwards, Louisa 61
Eickholdt, Robert 255
Einco 363
Eisenmann, Josef and Gabriel
    363
Eisenmann & Co. 363
EKCO 318, 319
Elbogen Pottery 106
Elfverson & Co. 251
Elisorm 331
Elizabeth, Queen, the Queen
    Mother 166, 362
Ellen, R.P. 201
Emerson 318
Emirober 324
Engmann, Kjell 249
Erector Set 277
Ericsson 367
Evan, Wendy 262
evening gowns 194
Eveson, Stanley 257
ewers 103
eyeware 187-9, 364
fabric dolls 183
FADA 318, 319
Faith, Prayer & Tract League 344
Fantoni, Marcello 74, 75, 76
Farnell 357, 359
Farnham Pottery 112
fashion dolls 172-3
Faye 363
Felten, Edith 93
fencing 352
Fenton 264, 280
Fenton, Harry 64
Fenton, W.C. 264
Ferragamo, Salvatore 197, 198
Ferrari 16
Ferrell, Frank 95, 96, 97
Ferro, Giorgio 237
Ferro, Vittorio 238
Ferro Galliano 237
Fielding's Crown Devon 56
Fiesta Glass 213
Fife Pottery 136

Fifties, Sixties and Seventies
    206-7
Figgjo Flint Turi Design 106
figures
  advertising 10
  Art Deco 15
  Fulper 69
  Inuit 269-72
  James Bond 277
  Katshutte Pottery 150
  lead 398-9
  Lladro 77
  majolica 155
  oriental 284, 285
  Royal Copenhagen 100
  Royal Doulton 65-6
  Royal Worcester 105
  sports 339, 352
  see also animals
film
  character collectables 156-60
  cult, TV and film toys 402-3
  posters 302-4
  toys and games 372-3
Findlay, A 264
fire engines, toy 379, 381, 384-5
first editions 28-33
Fischer 387, 388
Fishel, Carl 170, 400
Fisher, Denys 403
Flair Toys Ltd 174, 175
Fleming, Ian 273, 274
flower pots 73, 281
Flygsfors 250
Foale & Tuffin 172
fobs, 'Cricket' 346
Fogarty, Muriel 186
Fogelburg, Sven 257
Foley 56, 57
folk art
  canes 38-9
  pottery whistles 79
Folmer, William 34
football 333-9
  jerseys 333-4
  medals 337
  programmes 335-6
  other 338-9
footballs 338, 351
Ford & Co., John 102
Fortis 405
Franck, Kaj 106, 251
Franke & Heidecke 34
Fratelli Pagnin factory 238
Fratelli Toso 238, 239
Fray, Joseph 16, 17
Fretz & Frères 309
Friedrich 226
FROG 12
fruit bowls 51, 73, 116
Fry, Laura 133
Fuga, Aldo 238
Fuga, Mario 238
Fulper Pottery Co. 68-9
Furio, Salvador 77
Gabrhel, Jan 216
Gabriel Industries Inc. 174
Gabrielle Designs 364
Gallé, Emile 222
Gallé glass 222
galoshes 200
Gama 386, 388

Gambone, Guido 74
games, board 278
García, Fulgencia 77
Garnier, Jacques 146
Garretto, Paolo Federico 312
Gate, Simon 248
'gathering on the post'
    technique 234
GEFA A.G. 367
George III, King 101
George V, King 166
George VI, King 166, 167, 362
Gerber, Johanne 99
Gerharz, Otto, Snr 145
gfeller 368
Gibson, Philip 85
Gibson (Saddlers) 347
Gilbert, A.C. 277, 402
Gilbert, Alfred 277
Gina 201
ginger jars 84
Glasform 254
glass
  beads 26-7
  bubbly 265, 266
  Caithness 208-10
  champagne 211-12
  Chance 213
  Czech 214-19
  Dartington 220-21
  Gallé 222
  Holmegaard vases 223-9
  Isle of Wight Studio Glass 234
  Lalique 10, 18, 230-31
  Mdina Glass 232-4
  Murano 214
  Peter Layton 252-3
  Scandinavian 245-51
  studio glass 254-6
  Webb 257
  Whitefriars 234, 258-62
  other glass 263-8
glasses
  Duncan Miller 264
  reversible 267
Glasshouse 255
goblets 137, 234, 248, 250,
    267, 282
gold discs 327
Goldsmiths and Silversmiths Ltd
    405
golf 348-50
Goode, Thomas, & Co. 132, 136,
    137, 138, 162, 166
Goso 384, 386
Gothic Revival style 80
Gozo Glass 264
Graceline 189
Grafton China/Royal Grafton 57,
    119
Grant, Duncan 52
Graubaek, Yvonne 365
gravy boats 132
Gray's Pottery 116
Graystan 265
Great North Eastern Railway
    323
Gredington, Arthur 40, 41, 42
Greenly, Henry 394
Greppert & Kelch 389
Griffiths, Eric 66
Grimwades 86

Grimwades Royal Winton 57,
    86-7
Grindley 119
Grinsson, Boris 303
Griselda Pottery, Fife 136
Grisly Speilwaren 363
Grotell, Maija 110
Grueby 120, 154
Guarantee Shoe Store 199
Guatelli, Sevi 52, 108
Guci 202
Gullaskruf 250
Gulvvase bottles 223
gun memorabilia 12
Gund 361
Gunderson, Steven 112
Gunne Saxe 190
gunner's sectors 328
Güntherman 387, 388
Gustavsberg 106, 114
Hadeland 250
Hadley, James 105
hairpins 205
Hallam, Albert 40, 42
Hallam, Henry 124
Hallmark card stores 178
Halpern, Deborah 112
Hamada, Shoji 110, 113
Hamilton 407
Hamley Bros. 12
Hammersley & Co. 53, 57, 150
Hammond, David 257
Hancock, Debbie 85
Hancock, Loris 365
Hancock, S., & Sons 166
handbags 202-4
Hansen, Hans Henrik 100
Hanus, Vaclav 219
Harcuba, Jiri 214
Hardy 307
Haring, Keith 406
Harley Sport 10
Harper, William 127
Harradine, Leslie 61, 65, 66
Harris, Michael 213, 232, 233,
    234, 255, 256
Harrod's department store,
    London 52
Hartley Wood 264
Hartnell, Sir Norman 269
Hasbro 173, 327
Hasselblad 34
Hassett & Harper Ltd 332
Havas, Caen 311
Havel, Miroslav 208
Haviland & Co. 58, 150
Hawkins and Mordan 288
Haycock Press Ltd, The 306
Hayter, Sir George 165
Heal's department store, London
    112
Heavenly 326
Heck, Edna 267
Helit 300
Henderson, Lt Col Bob 354
Henk, Max 64
Henschel & Sohn 322
Herman, Sam 255, 256
Hermann 363
Hermanova glassworks 219
Hermès 202
Heron, Robert Methven 136

INDEX

Herta, Juan 77
HF Couture 194
Hill Jonathan 321
Hill, Samuel 68
Hillerich & Bradsby & Co. 343
Hine, Margaret 115
Hines Bros 165
Hires 12
Hirschberg 226
Hlava, Pavel 214, 216, 217
Hoglund, Eric 250
Holland, Roy 92
Holmegaard glass 223-9
Holmgren, Christer 229
honey pots 273
Honiton Pottery 150
Horikawa 382
Hornby 392-3, 394, 396
Hornsea Pottery 70-71
horse riding
  ceramics 41, 104
  see also racing
Hospodka, Josef 217
'Hot Lips' telephone 368
hot-water pots 116
Houghton-Butcher 37
Houston, James 272
Hovland Swanson 204
Hubley 159
Hudswell Clark & Co Ltd 322
Hughes, A. 66
Hughes, Ronald 281
Huki 387
Hull, Addis Emmett 72
Hull, A.E., Pottery 72-3
Hulme & Booth 55
Hunt, Millie 102
Huntley & Palmer 9
Hurley, E.T. 94
Hutcheson & Son Ltd 74
Ichiko 383
Ideal 172, 180, 181, 361
Illsley, Leslie 123
'incalmo' technique 239
Ingersoll 157
ink bottles 299
inkhorns 299
inkstands 350
inkwells 164, 299, 300
Innuendo 326
Inuit art 269-72
Ipeelee, Osuitok 269
Island Glass 255
Isle of Wight Studio Glass 234
Italian ceramics 74-6
Italian Royal Automobile Club 20
Jachmann, Erich 266
Jackson, Lesley 262
Jaguar 16, 19
Jankel 19
Japanese Modern Toys 383
jardinières
  Crown Devon 148
  Hornsea 70
  Roseville 97
  Troika 122

Wemyss 136
jars
  Kastrup-Holmegaard 226
  Moorcroft 82, 84
  Murano 240
  'Parker Quink Ink' 299
  Shelley 107
  studio pottery 110
  see also powder jars
Jarvis, Leonard 163
Jasba 71
Jasper ware 130
Jaytex 196
Jean Gros' French Marionettes 159
Jelinek, Vladimir 216
Jema 150
Jensen, Oluf 223
jerseys, sports 333-4, 351
Jeske, Kerstin 365
jewellery, costume 168-71
jigsaws 278
Jinks, Louise 122
Johansson, Willy 250
Johillco 399
Johnson, Stefano 337
Johnsons 166
Jones, A.B., & Sons, Ltd. 57
Jones, George, & Sons 58
Jones, Martha 61
Jordan, Charles 199
Jordison 306
Joseph, Francis 44
Joy, Bernard 336
Joy Toys 363
jug and basins 137
jug vases 142, 143, 145, 151
jugs
  A.V.E.M. 'Ansa Volante' 237
  Blue Mountain Pottery 146
  Burleigh 55, 147
  Carlton Ware 45
  Clarice Cliff 47, 48, 51
  commemorative 162, 163, 164
  Czech glass 218
  Italian 76
  Martin Brothers 81
  Moorcroft 82
  Myott 152
  royal commemoratives 165, 166
  Royal Doulton 63
  Royal Worcester 103
  Staffordshire 155
  studio pottery 111, 115
  Wade Heath 153
  Watcombe Pottery 153
  Wedgwood 132, 164
  West German 140, 145
  see also character jugs; cream jugs; milk jugs; toby jugs; water jugs
Jumbo Games 278
Jürgensen, Jules 405
Jurnikl, Rudolf 219
Kabro of Houston 193
Kacher, A. 312
Kaiser alarm clocks 161
Kastrup 223, 225, 228
Kastrup-Holmegaard 224, 226, 229
Katshutte Pottery 150

KD 385
Kedelv, Paul 250
Kellogg's 9
Kendall, June 366
Kenmac 321
Kenton Hills 150
Keto 140
King, Hamilton 12
King's Lynn Glass 266
Kirkhams 314
Kirkhill Glass 255
K.I.T.T. 403
Kittiwake 195
Klee, Paul 122
Klinger, Miroslav 218
Knickerbocker 361
Knight, Dame Laura 52, 167
Knight, Michael 403
Kodak 34, 35, 37
Kohner 157
Kosta 249, 251
Kosta Boda 249
Kralicek, Franz 352
Kralik 214
Kramer 169
Krause, George 95
Krog, Arnold 99
Krussman, Leo 400
Kummerly & Frey 312
Kyhn, Knud 99, 100
Kysela, Professor 215
La Rose 198
Laborde, Guillermo 337
Lacroix, Christian 169, 406
Lagerfeld, Karl 364
Lain, Sue 366
Lalique, René 10, 18, 230-31
Lallemant, Robert 150
Lambeth School of Art 61
lamp bases 69, 207, 209, 237
lamps
  dressing table 206
  railwayana 323
  table 207
  see also oil lamps
lampworking 218
Lancaster 34
Landberg, Nils 248
Landseer, Sir Edwin 313
Langley, Siddy 254
Langley Pottery 151
Lanvin, Jeanne 193
Larson, Lisa 106
Lascaux cave paintings 142
Laughead, Dorothy England 133
Laurentian Pottery 151
Lawley's 48, 66
Layton, Peter 252-3
Le Marquand, André 405
Leach, Bernard 110, 112, 113
Leach, David 110, 112, 113
lead figures 398-9
Learbury Clothes 10
LeCoultre 404
Leeper, Sian 84, 85
Lefèvre Utile 310
Leggat, Elizabeth 366
Lehmann 388, 389
Leica 34, 35, 36
Leigh family 55
Leitz 34, 35
Lejeune, A.E. 16

Lelée, Leopold 307
lemonade sets 108
Lengren, Zbigniew 305
Leonard, Anna B. 150
Lesney Products 327, 380, 381
letter racks 207
Lewenstein, Eileen 43
Lewis, W.O. 14, 21
Libensky, Stanislav 214
Liberty & Co. 82, 83, 112, 193
Libochovice glassworks 219
Limoges 154
Linda dolls 184
Lindeman, Clara 93
Lindner, Doris 101, 104
Lindstrand, Vicke 249
Linguard Webster & Co. 47
Linsden 300
Lion Rock 403
Liskeard Glass 287
Liskova, Vera 218
Lister, H.T. 288
Littco 159
Ljn, NY 327
Lladro 77
Lo Roco 192
locomotive name plates 322
Loetz 214, 215
Loftus, Asher 407
Loftus, Rebecca 407
Loftus, Richard 407
Londi, Aldo 74, 76, 143
London & North Eastern Railways 306
London Town 192
London Transport 306
Long, W.A. 133
Longines 405
Lonhuda Pottery 133
Lorber, Rudolph 133
Lorenzen 113
lorries, toy 378
Lotus Pottery 78-9
Lovatt & Lovatt 151
Loversal Pottery 78
loving cups
  Adderley 166
  Paragon 166, 167
  royal commemorative 166, 167
  Royal Doulton 64
  Shelley 166
  Spode 167
  Wemyss 136
Lowerdown Pottery 112
Luck & Flaw 164
Lundgren, Tyra 239
Lustre Pottery 119
Lütken, Per 223-6, 228, 229
LVMH 194
Lyttleton, D. 66
Mabie, Todd & Co. 297
Maby, Graham 327
McCarthy, Frank 275, 276
McCorquodale & Co. 308, 309, 339
McCoy 'Loy-Nel-Art' 151
Macfarlane, John 350
McGinnis, Robert 275, 276
MacIntyre & Company, James (Burslem) 82
MacIntyre of Leeds 85

MacKenzie, Jacqueline 92
McLaughlin, Sarah 133
Madoura pottery 89, 90, 149, 153
magazines, sports 343
magneto-electric machines for nervous diseases 328
Makeig-Jones, Daisy 130, 131, 132
maki-e lacquer 332
Maling, C.T. 58
Malmer, Ellen 99
Maltby, John 110, 113
Mandel 199
Manderin Jiffy Product 205
mane hair 347
Mann, Cathleen 311
Mans, Bodo 139, 140
marbles 279-80
Marcas et Bardel 231
'Marcher' dolls 184
Maresova, J. 218
Märklin 382, 384, 385
marks
  ceramic 146
  'chop' 99
  Roseville 98
Marquett 320
Marsden, Elisabeth 366
Marshall Lester 196
Martin, Charles 80
Martin, Edwin 80
Martin, Robert Wallace 80
Martin, Walter 80
Martin Brothers 80-81
Martínez, Vincente 77
Marton, Lajos 309
Marusan 387
Marx, Louis 391
Marx Fairykins 159
Marx Toys 172, 382, 388, 403
Marx TV-Tinykins 159
Marzi & Remi 139, 140
mascots, car 16-19
masks
  character 159
  costume jewellery 168
  Royal Copenhagen 100
  Troika 122
  wall 206
Maslankowski, Alan 40, 65, 67
Masutoku Toy Factory 389
Matchbox 327, 374, 380-81
Matsushita Electrical Industries 321
Mattel 172, 173, 178, 180, 181, 374, 380
Mattel Walt Disney Productions 156
Matthews, Henry 329, 330
Matura, Adolf 214, 219
Mawson, S., & Sons 328
Mayer factory 314-17
MB Games 278
Mdina Glass 232-4
Meakin, J&G 117
meat dishes 132
Meccano 12, 177, 277
medals
  cricket 346
  football 337
  golfing 350

Mego Corp. 277, 403
Meissen 151
Melbourne, Colin 40, 41, 148, 149
Melse, Danielo-Rebecca 366
Melsen, Henri 309
Melsen, Martin 309
Mende 318
menu holders 330
Merret, Christopher 211
Merry & Co. 347
Merrythought 357-8, 359
metalware 281-3
Metcalfe, Paul 113
Mettoy 369
Meunier, Henri 312
MGM 159, 160
Michelé shoes 199
Michelin 16
Michell, Roger 119
Midwinter 58, 119, 152
Miles, Devon 403
military commemoratives 162-3
milk jugs
    Carlton Ware 44
    Clarice Cliff 47
    Hammersley 150
    Old Hall 283
    Royal Worcester 103
    Shelley 88, 108
    Susie Cooper 116
    Wedgwood 132
Miller, Duncan 264
miniatures
    dolls 185
    figurines 159
    pens 292
    teddy bears 353, 355-6, 359, 365, 366
    vases 206
Minton 58, 152, 154
mirrors, wall 206
Miss Rosebud dolls 184
MJJ Productions Inc. 327
Moje, Isgard 256
Monart 265, 287
money banks/boxes
    Carlton Ware 46
    Moyer 351
    studio pottery 112
    Wade Natwest piggy banks 128
Montblanc pens 298
Moorcroft 82-5, 107
Moorcroft, Walter 82
Moorcroft, William 82, 83
Moore, Bernard 67
Mordan & Co., S. 288, 329
Moretti, Carlo 238
Moria, Jennifer 406
Morrissey, Joe 303
Morrisware 166
Moser 216
motorcycles, toy 387
Moullot 307
Mouron, Adolphe (Cassandre) 307
Moyer 351
Msistov glassworks 216
Mucha, Alphonse 310
muffin dishes 116
mugs

aeronautica 14
Carlton Ware 44
Coalport 164
commemorative 163, 164, 167
Northwood Carnival glass 263
nursery ware 86, 87, 88
Royal Winton 86, 87
Shelley 88
studio pottery 113
Wemyss 137
mules 198, 200
Muley 35
Multiple Toymakers 278
Munier, J. 307
Murano 214, 235-44
    animals 244
    marbles 280
    named 238-9
    Post-modern 240
    Seguso 235-6
    unmarked 241-3
Murphy radios 319, 320
Murray, Keith 130, 131, 265
Murray, Pat 129
murrines 238, 243, 252
music
    musical bears 360, 362
    musical tankards 167
    mustard pots 71
Myott & Sons, A. 152
Nabisco All Star Autographs 342
Namiki 332
Napuwatuk, Hank 270
Nation, Terry 403
National Westminster Bank 128
Natzler, Otto and Gertrud 110, 114
Nayytex 158, 196
necklaces 10, 26, 27, 169
Nekola, Joe 136, 138
Nekola, Karel 136, 137
NEMS Enterprises 324
Neukomm, Fred 312
New Hall Pottery 345
Newland, William 115
Newport Pottery 47
Nichols, Maria Longworth 93
Nielsen, Orla Juul 223
Nikon 34, 36
Nina Shoes 200
Nixon, Harry 61
Noke, Charles 61, 64, 65, 67
Nomura 382, 390
Nonsdale & Bartholomew 302
Noritake 58
Northern Telecom 368
Novy Bor 216
Nuilaalik, Josiah 271
nursery ware
    bowls 42
    Grimwade 86
    Shelley 88
Nutt, Terence 103
Nuutajarvi Nostjo 251
Nymolle Fajance Fabrik 106
O'Broin, Domhnall 208, 209, 210
Oi! records 326
oil bottles 71
oil lamps 267
Okalik, Annie 270
okimono 284

Okkolin, Aimo 245, 246
Okra Glass 256
Old Hall tablewares 282, 283
Olsens, J. 302
Omega 405
One Time Publications 349
Oonark, Jessie 269
oriental 284-5
Orr, Charles 208, 210
Orrefors 248, 249, 251
Orwell, Graham 42
Osborn, J.N. 317
Osswald 309
Otto Simon & B.T. Toys 181
Out Of The Blue Ceramics (Collectables Magazine) 158, 160
Owen, George 101
Paillard Bolex 37
Palet range (Holmegaard) 226
Palitoy 176, 177, 179, 181, 184
Palmqvist, Sven 248
Palshus 114
Palter de Liso 197
Pan American World Airways 308
Pangnark, John 269, 271
Pantin 287
paperweights 218, 236, 286-7
papier mâché 10
Paragon 53, 58, 59, 163, 166, 167
Parker
    51/61/65 pens 290
    Duofold pens 289, 293
    other pens 291
Parkinson, Susan 115
Pasche, John 327
Pavely, Ruth 91, 92
Paya 384
pearlware 162
Peceby, Frantisek 219
Pedigree 172, 173, 181, 403
Peltier Glass Company 279
pencil sharpeners 301
pencils see pens and pencils
Penney, JC, department store 234
pens and pencils 288-99
    Conway Stewart 294
    De La Rue 'Onoto' 295
    Montblanc 298
    Parker Duofold 289, 293
    Sheaffer 296
    Swan 297
    Waterman 292-3
    other writing equipment 299
Pentagram 300
pepperettes 330
Percy, Arthur 250
perfume atomisers 231
perfume bottles 231, 264
perfume burners 231
Perignon, Dom 211
Péron, Rene 303
Perspex 320
Peter, Dieter 143
Petersson, Stig 221
Pett, Alan 43
Philco 318, 319
Philippe, Alfred 170, 400
Philips, Ernest 101

photographs, sports 350
'Picassiettes' 115
Picasso, Pablo 89-90, 112, 115, 149
Pillsbury, Hester 134
pin trays 137
pincushions 329
Pinder, Bourne & Co. 61
pins
    Bobby Pins hairpins 205
    costume jewellery 168-71
    fishing license 352
    racing 347
pipe holders 52
pipe lighters 331
Pippa dolls 176-7
pitchers 90, 226, 228
Plant, R.H. & S.L. 59, 60
planters 52, 147
plaques
    Clarice Cliff 50
    Picasso 89
    railwayana 323
    Scandinavian 106
    Troika 121, 123
plastics 300, 301
plates
    Aynsley 167
    Carlton Ware 46
    Clarice Cliff 48, 49, 51, 52
    Cowan 148
    Haviland 150
    military commemorative 163
    Minton 152
    Moorcroft 82
    nursery ware 88
    Picasso 89, 90
    royal commemoratives 165, 167
    Royal Doulton 64
    Shelley 88
    Susie Cooper 116
    Troika 123
    Washington Pottery 324
    Wedgwood 132
Plaza 205
Pleydell-Bouverie, Katharine 115
Plichta, Jan 138
PLM Autocars 309
PLM railways 307
Plymouth Iron Windmill Co. 12
Podebrady glassworks 218
Poli, Flavio 235, 236, 241, 244
political commemoratives 164
pomades 136
Poner, Karel 215
Poole Pottery 85, 91-2, 172
pop see rock and pop
Pop Art 223, 370
Portmeirion Pottery 101
posters 302-12
    advertising 312
    Eastern European 305
    film 302-4
    James Bond 275
    rock and pop 327
    sports 37, 309, 337, 339, 352
    travel 306-9, 311
pot lids 313-17
Potter, Beatrix: ceramics 40, 42
pottery whistles 79
pounce 299

powder jars 263
Powell, Alfred 115
Powell, Barnaby 262
Powell, Julie 280
Powell, Louise 115
Powell & Sons 258
PPC 403
Prachen glassworks 217
Pratt factory 313-17
Preiss, Ferdinand 15
Price Bros. 118
prints
    cricket 346
    stencil 272
    woodcut 272
programmes, sports 335-6, 344, 349
Pryce, Peggy 186
Pucci, Emilio 194
Puché, Jose 77
Pulitzer, Lily 194
puppets, character collectables 157
Pursell, Weimer 308
Pustetto, Itamo 238
Pustetto Zanetti 238
Pye 320
quaitches 300
Quant, Mary 174, 175
Queensberry, David 149
Raban, Josef 216
racing 347
'Radio Rastus' 321
radios 318-21, 327
railwayana 322-3, 332
Raimondi & Zaccardi 310
rainmacs 196
Rame Pottery 128
Ramié, George 89
Ramié, Suzanne 89
Randle, John 287
Ravilious, Eric 130, 132
Rawson, Colin 70
Rawson, Desmond 70
RayBan 189
Raymond 320
Raymor 74, 76
Rayne 198
Read, Alfred 91, 92
record cases 206
Red Ashay 16
RE(ER) 306
Rees, Josef and Leon 363
Regal China 73
Reijmyre 251
Reilly, Robin 132
Reisser Sohne, Christoph 352
Reliable 183
Reliance Telephone Co. 367
RELR 306
Renauld 188
Renz 15
Rey, Jean François 189
Rhead, Charlotte 55, 147, 149
Rhead, Frederick 95, 107, 133
Rhythm alarm clocks 161
Rich Manufacturing Company 386
Rich Toys Inc. 386
Richard Parkinson Ltd 115
Richardson, Mike 379
Rickarby, Joan 186

Rico 387
Riddle, Gabriel 288
Ridgway factory 315
Rie, Lucie 110
Riihimäen Lasi Oy 245, 246-7
Rindskopf 214, 215
RL Toys 385
Robert 169
Robinson Brothers 346
robots, toy 391
Rock Flowers dolls 180, 181
rock and pop 324-7
Rodnoid 185
Rohman 302
Rolex 405
roll-on girdles 196
Rolls Royce 16, 19
Rookie Stars baseball cards 342
Rookwood 93-4, 95, 133
rose bowls 208, 282
Rosenthal 59, 106
Roseville Pottery 133
    Fuschia 95
    Futura 96
    marks 98
    Pine Cone 97
Rosice glassworks 219
Rosie 305
Roth Keramik 144
Rothenbusch, Fred 94
Rotolito 302
Roubícek, René 214
Rousselet 169
Rowden Barter & Co. 330
Royal Academy 52, 91
Royal Alma 12
Royal Automobile Club 20
Royal Bayreuth 54
Royal China 73
royal commemoratives 165-7
Royal Copenhagen 99-100
Royal Doulton 40, 53, 56, 58,
    61, 63-7, 118, 164
    figures 65-6
Royal Grafton see Grafton
    China/Royal Grafton
Royal Windsor Toilet Cream 314
Royal Winton 57, 86-7
Royal Worcester 53, 60, 101-5
Ruda Glasbruk 251
Rudolfova glassworks 219
rugby football 351-2
Ruscha 140, 144, 145
Ruskin Art Pottery 148
Russell, John 58, 152
Russell, R.D. 320
Sabino 16
Sadler 118, 119
Saila, Pauta 269
Saint Laurent, Yves 201
St Louis 287
salt and pepper shakers 71,
    106, 113
salt shakers 79
Salto, Axel 99, 100
salts 214
Sampson Smith Ltd 60
sandals 198
Sanderson 34, 37
Sandland, Edwin 136
Sarpaneva, Timo 239, 250
saucers

Carltonware 55
Hammersley & Co. 57
Hull Pottery 73
royal commemoratives 165
Susie Cooper 116
see also cups and saucers
Saunders & Shepherd 329
Savage, George 132
Sax, Sara 93
Saxby Farmer Ltd 323
Scandinavian ceramics 106
Scandinavian glass
    Boda 249
    Orrefors 248
    Riihimaki 245-7
    other makers 250-51
Scarpa, Carlo 239
Scatterlite 207
Scheurich 141-2
Schmid-Muller 406
Schmidt, Bruno 182
Schmidt, Carl 93
Schoenhut 400-401
Scholtis 143
Schramberg 140
Schreckengost, Viktor 148
Schreiner 169
Schreyer & Co. 382, 390
Schrötter, Rudolf 219
Schuco 12, 355-6, 382, 383, 390
Schweinberger-Gismondi, Emma
    301
scientific instruments 328
scissor snuffers 330
sculptures
    Kastrup-Holmegaard 229
    Mdina Glass 234
    studio glass 255
    studio pottery 112, 115
sea travel posters 308-9
Sears 277
Seese, Eddie 280
Seguso Vetri D'Arte 235-6, 241,
    244
Seide, A. 142
Selby Shoes 197
Selcol Ltd. 324
Selfridges 207
Serre & Cie, Lucien 307
Serrenova, Mari 330
SH 382
Shallowpool Handicrafts 186
Shaqu, Mannumi 269
Shattaline Products 207
Sheaffer pens 296
Shell 311
Shelley 53, 59, 88, 107-8, 118,
    166
Sherman, Samuel (Sambo') 194
sherry glasses 228
Sherwin & Cotton 166
Shifts International 194
Shirayamadani, Kataro 94
Shire, Peter 240
Shiroyama 332
shirts 196, 352
Shobi, Maizawa 332
shoes 197-201
Shorter, Colley 47
shot glasses 227
Shuck, Albert J. 102
Sicard, Jacques 133, 134

signs, advertising 10
silver 329-30
Simmance, Elisa 61
Simmonds, Joseph 106
Simmons, 'Schtockschnitzler' 38,
    39
Simon & Halbig 182
Simon & Schuster 350
Simon, Otto 181
Simpson, Josh 280
Simpson, W.B. 120
Simpsons Pottery 88
Sindy dolls 172-3, 176, 181
Singer Gazelle 19
Sirota, Benny 121, 123
Skeaping, John 130
Skipwith, Elizabeth 78, 79
Skipwith, Michael 78
skirts 194
Sklo Union 219
Skrdlovice glassworks 216, 217
Skruf 251
Slaney, Nicola 84
Slater, Eric 108, 118
Slater, Greg 52, 108
Slater, John 67
Slater, Walter 107
slingbacks 199
slippers 199
slips, nylon 196
Slix 195
Smith, Edward 346
Smith, John S. 306
Smith, Leslie, OBE 381
smoker's cabinets 332
smoking memorabilia 331-2
SNCF 307
snuff boxes 346
Soane & Smith 163
Soennecken 299
Soho Pottery 88
Soholm Stentoj 106
Solarstein 207
Solven, Pauline 256
Soper, Eileen 105
Sottsass, Ettore 240
Soubie, Roger 309
Souré Bag 204
Spears 278
speedboats, toy 388
Spiteri, Joe 164
Spode 101, 167
Sport Magazine 341
sports 333-52
    baseball cards 340-42
    cricket 345-6
    football 333-9
    golf 348-50
    posters 307, 309
    racing 347
    smoking memorabilia 332
    other sports 351-2
Stabler, Dr Harold 283
Stadium Products 301
Stafford & Co. 310
Staffordshire
    cricketing figurines 352
    pot lids 313-17
    water jugs 345
Standard Oil 308
Stangl Pottery 68, 109
Stanley, London 328

Starck, Philippe 368
station name boards 322
station signs 322
Staybrite 283
Steenstra, Daniel 149
Steiff 183, 353-4, 355, 364
Stein, Lea 169
steins 339
Stenberg, Vladimir and Georgii
    305
Stennett-Wilson, Ronald 266
Stern, Anthony 256
Stevens & Williams (Royal
    Brierley) 265
stiletto shoes 199, 201
Still, Nanny 246
Stinton, Harry 101, 102
Stinton, James 101, 102
Stinton, John, Jnr. 101
stockings, silk 205
stoles 205
stonecuts: Inuit art 272
store display 10
Storer, Maria 93
Stormer, Emily 62
Stowells of Chelsea 228
Strathearn 265
Stratton, Alza 150
Strauss, Ferdinand 382
Strehla 145
Strobachovà, Zdenka 216
Strömberghyttan 251
Stuart Strathearn 266
Studdy, G.E. 158
studio glass 254-6
studio pottery 110-15
Sty-Val 191
submarines, toy 388
sugar basins 116
sugar bowls
    Clarice Cliff 47
    Hammersley 150
    Holmegaard 228
    Royal Worcester 103
    Shelley 88, 108
    Susie Cooper 116
    Wedgwood 132
sugar shakers 226
sugar sifters 49, 79
sugar tongs 330
Suhajek, Jiri 216
Summersgill, J.F. 301
Sunard & Co. 330
suncatchers 229
sunglasses 187-9
Sunshine Ceramics 128
Sussex Car Club 20
Svane Apoteket 229
Svarc, Josef 218
Svoboda, Jaroslav 217
Swain & Sons, John 306
Swan pens 297
Swatch Twinphone 368
Swatch watches 406
sweaters 196
swimsuits 195
Syberg, Lars 106
Szeiler, Joseph 117
t-shirts 158, 196
table centrepieces 240
tablewares
    Holmegaard 227-8

Old Hall 282, 283
Tammy doll 172, 180
Tanfield Potter 85
tankards 47, 167, 267, 339
tankers, toy 371
tape dispensers 301
tape measures, cricketers' 345
Taplin, Millicent 130
taxis, toy 377
Taylor, H.P. & W.C. 316
tazzas 155
tea bowls 113, 165
tea services 82
tea sets 55, 88, 132
teapots 118-19
    Carlton Ware 44
    Copeland Spode 118
    'cottage ware' 118
    golfing 350
    Grindley 119
    Hull Pottery 73
    Midwinter 119
    Old Hall 283
    political commemorative 164
    Royal Doulton 118
    Royal Grafton 119
    Royal Worcester 103
    Sadler 118, 119
    Shelley 88, 108, 118
    Susie Cooper 116
    Wade Heath 157
Tebbel, Lewis 289
teddy bears 353-66
    American 361
    artists' bears 365-6
    Chad Valley 362, 364
    character bears 364
    Chiltern 360
    Farnell 359
    Merrythought 357-8
    Schuco 355-6
    Steiff 353-4
    other makers 363
telephones 367-8
television
    character collectables 156-60
    cult, TV and film toys 402-3
    toys and games 372-3
tennis 352
Terris, Colin 208, 210
Tesla Talisman 320
Thatcher, J.S. 301
Thisted Apotek 229
Thompson, Ruth Plumly 159
Thompson, Tony 321
Thomson 368
Thorsson, Nils 99
Thrower, Frank 220, 221
ties 205
Tiffany, Louis Comfort 237
Tiffany & Co. 407
tiles 120, 166
Timberlake, Mae 133
Timex 157
tinplate toys 382-91
tins 9
Tinworth, Arthur 61
Tinworth, George 61, 62
Tipp & Co. 369, 383, 387
Titanian glaze 63, 67
Tittensor, Harry 63, 65
TM Modern Toys 391

TN Toys 382, 383, 390
toast racks 45, 116
tobacco tins 9
Toby jugs
    Carlton Ware 46
    military commemorative 163
    Royal Worcester 105
toilet sets 55
Tokeo Tokei alarm clock 161
Tongue, Graham 40, 42
Toohey, Sallie 93
Tootsie Toys 374
Topps 340-42
'Topsy' dolls 183
Torben Anton 228
Toso Vetri D'Arte 240
Toulouse Lautrec, Henri de 305, 309
Townsend, Milon 280
toys and games 369-403
Character collectables 156-60
    Corgi 369-73
    cult, TV and film toys 402-3
    Dinky 374-9
    lead figures 398-9
    Matchbox 380-81
    Schoenhut 400-401
tinplate 382-91
trains 392-7
tractors, toy 371, 379, 381, 387, 388
tracts, Babe Ruth Memorial Mission 344
trailers, toy 378, 381
trains, toy 392-7
transfer sheets 160
travel posters 306-9, 311
travelling writing compendium 299
trays
    Bakelite 301
    Bursley Ware 147
    Chance Glass 213
    Clarice Cliff 51
    Coca Cola 12
    Hornsea 71
    Troika 123
    see also pin trays
'Trench Art' 13
Tressa 405
Tressy dolls 179
Triang 277, 396
Trident mark 121, 123
Trifari 170, 400
Trifari, Gustavo 170
Trifari, Krussman & Fishel (TKF) 170, 400
trinket boxes 129
trio sets 60
Trix 12, 394
Troika Pottery 121-3
trophies: aeronautica 13, 14
'tropical' cameras 37
trucks, toy 370, 371, 378, 381,

386
Tschörner, Kurt 142, 145
Tudor Rose dolls 184
Tuffin, Sally 82, 84, 85
Tuffin & Foale 85
Tugwell, Lewen 207
Tunnuq, Elizabeth 271
Tupilaks 271
Turca 241
tureens 116, 132
Turner, Helen Monroe 208
Tutankhamun 63
Tyco 380
tygs 103, 162, 166
Tyler, William Watts 93
Tynell, Helena 247
Übelacker Keramik 145
Ugyuk, Charlie 270
Ullman, Phillip 369
Ullulaq, Judas 269, 271
Ultra Electric Ltd 321
umbrella stands 301
Unis 384
unomis (tea bowls) 113
Upjohn, Charles 93
Upper Deck cards 342
urn vases 72, 73, 96, 140
urns, Fulper 68, 97, 101, 239
Usaitaijuk, Miaiji Uitangi 269
utensil holders 301
UTENS.SILO 301
utility clothing 195
Utility label 195
Val St. Lambert 255
Valentno 205
Vallauris 153
Vallien, Bertil 249
van Ruyckevelt, Ruth Esther 105
vans, toy 370, 372, 377, 378, 386
vases
    Arequipa 146
    art glass 267
    Barovier & Toso 237
    Blue Mountain Pottery 146
    Briglin 43
    bubbly glass 266
    Caithness Glass 208, 209, 210
    Candy Ware 147
    cauldron 147
    Cenedese 237, 238
    Chance Glass 213
    Clarice Cliff 47-51
    Clews & Co. Ltd 148
    commemorative 14
    Conrah 281
    Crown Devon 148, 149
    Crown Ducal 149
    Crown Lynn 149
    Czech glass 214-19
    Dartington glass 220, 221
    Davidson 263
    De Majo 238
    Denby Pottery 149

Doulton Lambeth 61, 62
Fenton 264
Fulper 68, 69
Gallé glass 222
handkerchief 213
Hartley Wood 264
Holmegaard 223-6, 229
Hornsea 70, 71
Hull Pottery 72, 73
Isle of Wight Studio Glass 234
Italian 74, 75
Kenton Hills 150
Lalique 230, 231
Langley Pottery 151
Longwy 151
Lotus Pottery 79
McCoy 'Loy-Nel-Art' 151
Martin Brothers 80, 81
Mdina Glass 232, 233
miniature 206
Moorcroft 82-5
Murano 235-9, 241, 243
Myott 152
Peter Layton 252, 253
Poole Pottery 91, 92
Pustetto Zanetti 238
Robert Lallemant 150
Rookwood 93, 94
Roseville 96, 97, 98
Royal Copenhagen 99, 100
Royal Doulton 63
Royal Worcester 101-3
Scandinavian 106
Scandinavian glass 245-51
Seguso Vetri D'Arte 236
Shelley 107, 108
Stevens & Williams (Royal Brierley) 265
Strathearn 265
Stuart 'Dark Crystal' 265
Stuart Strathearn 266
studio glass 254, 255
studio pottery 110, 111, 113, 114, 115
Troika 121, 122, 123
Vallauris 153
Vereinigte Lausitzer Glaswerke 266
Volkmar 153
Wade 129
Walley 154
Webb 257
Wedgwood 130, 131
Weller 133, 134, 135
West German 139-45
Wheatley 154
Whitefriars 258-62
WMF 268
Zsolnay Pecs 154
see also bottle vases; jug vases; urn vases
VE301 DYN radio 319
Venini & C. 239
Vercasson 310, 312

Vereinigte Lausitzer Glaswerke (VLG) 266
Vergette, Nicola 115
Versace, Gianni 190
vesta cases 331, 332
Victoria, Queen 166, 316
Villemot, Bernard 312
Villiers, Amherst 274
Viners 282
Vistosi 240
Vitascope 301
Vitra 301
Vizner, Frantisek 214, 217, 219
Vogue 184
Volkmar 153
Voltz, Charles 153
Voulkos, Peter 110
Vyletal, Josef 305
W&B 55
Waddington, John, Ltd 306, 308
Wade 9, 124-9
    character collectables 158, 160
    Disney 125-6
    Minikins 126
    Natwest piggy banks 128
    Whimsies 124, 125, 129
    other Wade 129
Wade, Sir George 124
Wade & Colcough 124
Wade Heath & Co. 117, 153, 157
Wade Potteries Ltd 124
Wadworth, John 58
Wagenfeld, Wilhelm 266
Walker, Roberta 184
Wall, Paris 311
wall plaques see plaques
wall plates 140, 148
wall pockets 97
Walley, William J. 154
Walsh Walsh 265, 266
Walt Disney Productions 156, 157
Waltham 407
Wärff, Göran 249
Warner, Jeanette 366
Washington Pottery 324
watches 404-7
    Disneyana 157
Watcombe Pottery 153
water jugs 267, 283, 345
Waterford Crystal 208
Waterlow & Sons Ltd 306
Waterman pens 292-3
Watkin, Mr (of Beswick) 41
Watson 34
Watts, John 61
Webb 256
Webb, Thomas 257
wedges 197, 198
Wedgwood 115, 130-32, 146, 165, 266
Wedgwood, Josiah 130
Wedgwood Glass 266
Weeks, Esther 136

Weidmann, Karl 268
Welch, Robert 282, 283
Weller 133-5
Weller, Samuel 133, 134
Wellings, Norah 183
Wells 384
Wells, Reginald 111
Wemyss 60, 136-8
Wescontree Ware 147
West German ceramics 139-45
Western Electric Co. 321
Western Railway 306
Westra alarm clocks 161
Westwood, Vivienne 170, 406
Wheatley, T.J. 154
White, J.K. 318
Whitefriars 234, 258-62
Whitehead & Hoag Company, The 350
Whiting & Davis 202
Whitman Publishing Company 324, 343
Whittingham, Jack 274
Wiinblad, Bjorn 106
Wileman & Co. 107
Wilkie, David, RA 315
Wilkinson, A.J. 47, 52
Wilkinson Ltd. 163
Wilkinson, Norman 306
Williamson, H.M., & Sons 60
Wilson (football manufacturer) 351
Wilson, Norman 130, 131, 308
Wilson, William 262
Wiltshaw & Robinson 44, 55
Wimmer 385
Winther, Ole 228
Wise & Greenwood 331
Wohl 199
Wood, Beatrice 110
Wood, Jon 196
woodcut prints 272
Worcester Royal Porcelain Company 101
worksplates 322
wreath pins 168
Wright, R. John 364
Württembergische Metallwarenfabrik (WMF) 266, 268
Wyton, Paul 164
Yamanaka, Yuki 366
Ysart, Paul 287
Zeischegg, Walter 300
Zeiss 34, 36, 37
Zelezny Brod 216, 218
Zemek, Frantisek 214, 216
Zeppelins, toy 388
Zetavox 318
Zsolnay Pecs 154, 155
Zuffi, Vittorio, E C. 239